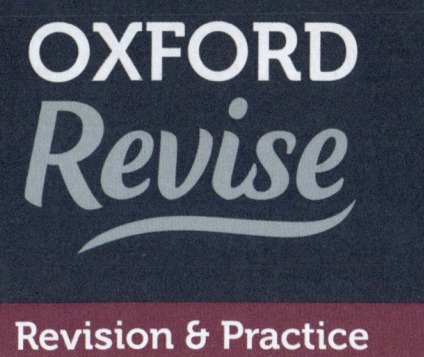

Revision & Practice

AQA GCSE 9–1 COMBINED SCIENCE: TRILOGY FOUNDATION

  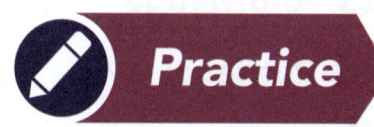

Series Editor: Primrose Kitten

Adam Boxer
Philippa Gardom Hulme
Primrose Kitten
Jo Locke

Helen Reynolds
Alom Shaha
Jessica Walmsley

Contents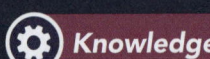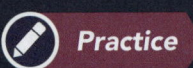

 Shade in each level of the circle as you feel more confident and ready for your exam.

How to use this book vi

B1 Cell structure	**2**
Knowledge	⊖
Retrieval	⊖
Practice	⊖

B2 Cell transport	**12**
Knowledge	⊖
Retrieval	⊖
Practice	⊖

B3 Cell division	**22**
Knowledge	⊖
Retrieval	⊖
Practice	⊖

B4 Organisation in animals	**32**
Knowledge	⊖
Retrieval	⊖
Practice	⊖

B5 Enzymes	**42**
Knowledge	⊖
Retrieval	⊖
Practice	⊖

B6 Organising plants	**52**
Knowledge	⊖
Retrieval	⊖
Practice	⊖

B7 The spread of diseases	**62**
Knowledge	⊖
Retrieval	⊖
Practice	⊖

B8 Preventing and treating disease	**72**
Knowledge	⊖
Retrieval	⊖
Practice	⊖

B9 Non-communicable diseases	**82**
Knowledge	⊖
Retrieval	⊖
Practice	⊖

B10 Photosynthesis and respiration	**92**
Knowledge	⊖
Retrieval	⊖
Practice	⊖

B11 The nervous system and homeostasis		**102**
Knowledge		
Retrieval		
Practice		
B12 Hormonal coordination		**112**
Knowledge		
Retrieval		
Practice		
B13 Variation		**122**
Knowledge		
Retrieval		
Practice		
B14 Reproduction		**132**
Knowledge		
Retrieval		
Practice		
B15 Evolution		**142**
Knowledge		
Retrieval		
Practice		
B16 Adaptation		**152**
Knowledge		
Retrieval		
Practice		

B17 Organising an ecosystem		**162**
Knowledge		
Retrieval		
Practice		
B18 Humans and biodiversity		**170**
Knowledge		
Retrieval		
Practice		
C1 The atom		**180**
Knowledge		
Retrieval		
Practice		
C2 Covalent bonding		**190**
Knowledge		
Retrieval		
Practice		
C3 Ionic bonding, metallic bonding, and structure		**200**
Knowledge		
Retrieval		
Practice		
C4 The Periodic Table		**210**
Knowledge		
Retrieval		
Practice		

For answers and more practice questions visit www.oxfordrevise.com/scienceanswers

Even more practice and interactive revision quizzes are available on kerboodle

C5 Quantitative chemistry — 220
- ⚙ Knowledge ⊝
- ⇄ Retrieval ⊝
- ✏ Practice ⊝

C6 Chemical reactions — 230
- ⚙ Knowledge ⊝
- ⇄ Retrieval ⊝
- ✏ Practice ⊝

C7 Electrolysis — 240
- ⚙ Knowledge ⊝
- ⇄ Retrieval ⊝
- ✏ Practice ⊝

C8 Energy changes — 250
- ⚙ Knowledge ⊝
- ⇄ Retrieval ⊝
- ✏ Practice ⊝

C9 Rate of reaction — 258
- ⚙ Knowledge ⊝
- ⇄ Retrieval ⊝
- ✏ Practice ⊝

C10 Equilibrium — 268
- ⚙ Knowledge ⊝
- ⇄ Retrieval ⊝
- ✏ Practice ⊝

C11 Crude oil and fuels — 276
- ⚙ Knowledge ⊝
- ⇄ Retrieval ⊝
- ✏ Practice ⊝

C12 Chemical analysis — 286
- ⚙ Knowledge ⊝
- ⇄ Retrieval ⊝
- ✏ Practice ⊝

C13 The Earth's atmosphere — 296
- ⚙ Knowledge ⊝
- ⇄ Retrieval ⊝
- ✏ Practice ⊝

C14 Using the Earth's resources — 306
- ⚙ Knowledge ⊝
- ⇄ Retrieval ⊝
- ✏ Practice ⊝

P1 Energy stores and transfers — 318
- ⚙ Knowledge ⊝
- ⇄ Retrieval ⊝
- ✏ Practice ⊝

P2 National and global energy resources — 326
- ⚙ Knowledge ⊝
- ⇄ Retrieval ⊝
- ✏ Practice ⊝

P3 Supplying electricity	336
⚙ Knowledge ⊖	
⇄ Retrieval ⊖	
✏ Practice ⊖	

P4 Electric circuits	346
⚙ Knowledge ⊖	
⇄ Retrieval ⊖	
✏ Practice ⊖	

P5 Energy of matter	356
⚙ Knowledge ⊖	
⇄ Retrieval ⊖	
✏ Practice ⊖	

P6 Atoms	366
⚙ Knowledge ⊖	
⇄ Retrieval ⊖	
✏ Practice ⊖	

P7 Nuclear radiation	376
⚙ Knowledge ⊖	
⇄ Retrieval ⊖	
✏ Practice ⊖	

P8 Forces	386
⚙ Knowledge ⊖	
⇄ Retrieval ⊖	
✏ Practice ⊖	

P9 Speed	396
⚙ Knowledge ⊖	
⇄ Retrieval ⊖	
✏ Practice ⊖	

P10 Newton's Laws of Motion	406
⚙ Knowledge ⊖	
⇄ Retrieval ⊖	
✏ Practice ⊖	

P11 Waves	416
⚙ Knowledge ⊖	
⇄ Retrieval ⊖	
✏ Practice ⊖	

P12 Magnets and electromagnets	426
⚙ Knowledge ⊖	
⇄ Retrieval ⊖	
✏ Practice ⊖	

Physics equations	436

Periodic Table	438

Notes	439

For answers and more practice questions visit www.oxfordrevise.com/scienceanswers

Even more practice and interactive revision quizzes are available on kerboodle

How to use this book

This book uses a three-step approach to revision: **Knowledge**, **Retrieval**, and **Practice**.
It is important that you do all three; they work together to make your revision effective.

1 Knowledge

Knowledge comes first. Each chapter starts with a **Knowledge Organiser**. These are clear, easy-to-understand, concise summaries of the content that you need to know for your exam. The information is organised to show how one idea flows into the next so you can learn how all the science is tied together, rather than lots of disconnected facts.

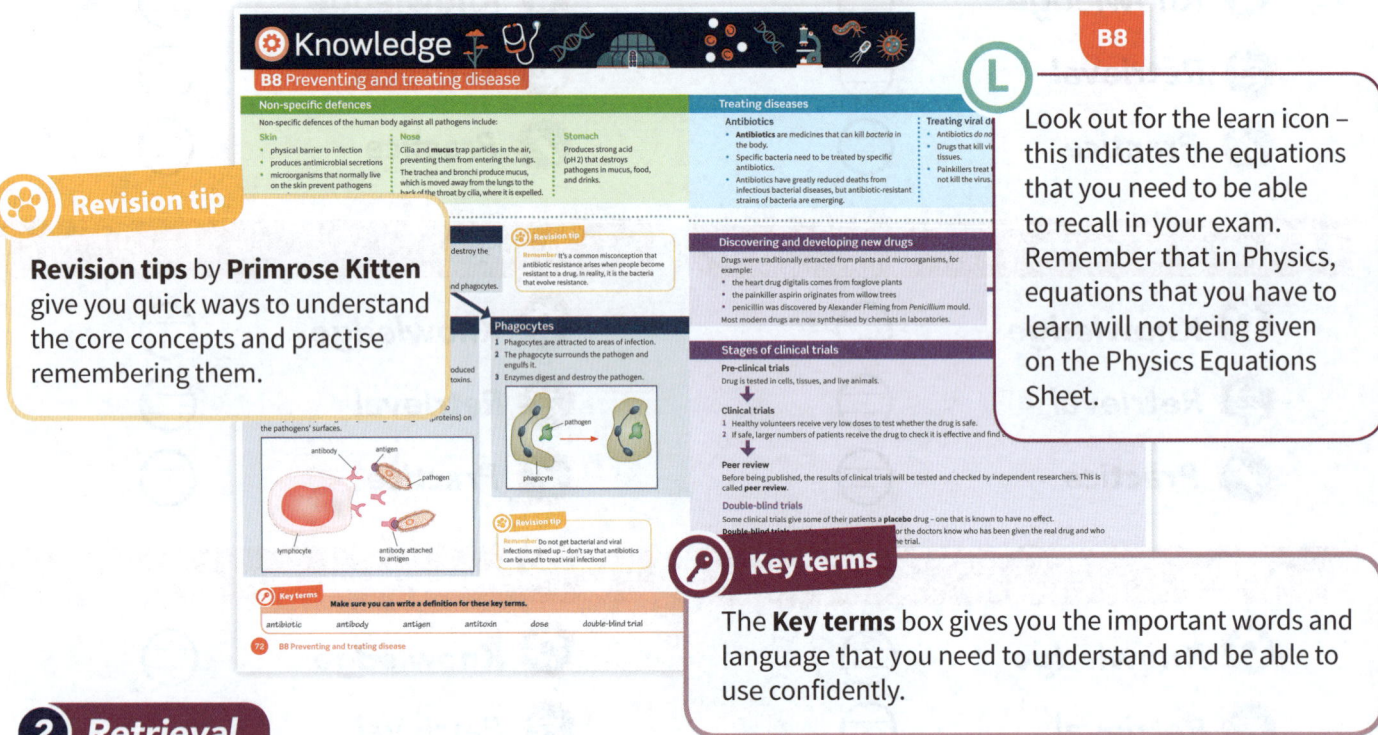

Revision tips by Primrose Kitten give you quick ways to understand the core concepts and practise remembering them.

Look out for the learn icon – this indicates the equations that you need to be able to recall in your exam. Remember that in Physics, equations that you have to learn will not being given on the Physics Equations Sheet.

The **Key terms** box gives you the important words and language that you need to understand and be able to use confidently.

2 Retrieval

The **Retrieval questions** help you learn and quickly recall the information you've acquired. These are short questions and answers about the content in the Knowledge Organiser. Cover up the answers with some paper; write down as many answers as you can from memory. Check back to the Knowledge Organiser for any you got wrong, then cover the answers and attempt *all* the questions again until you can answer all the questions correctly.

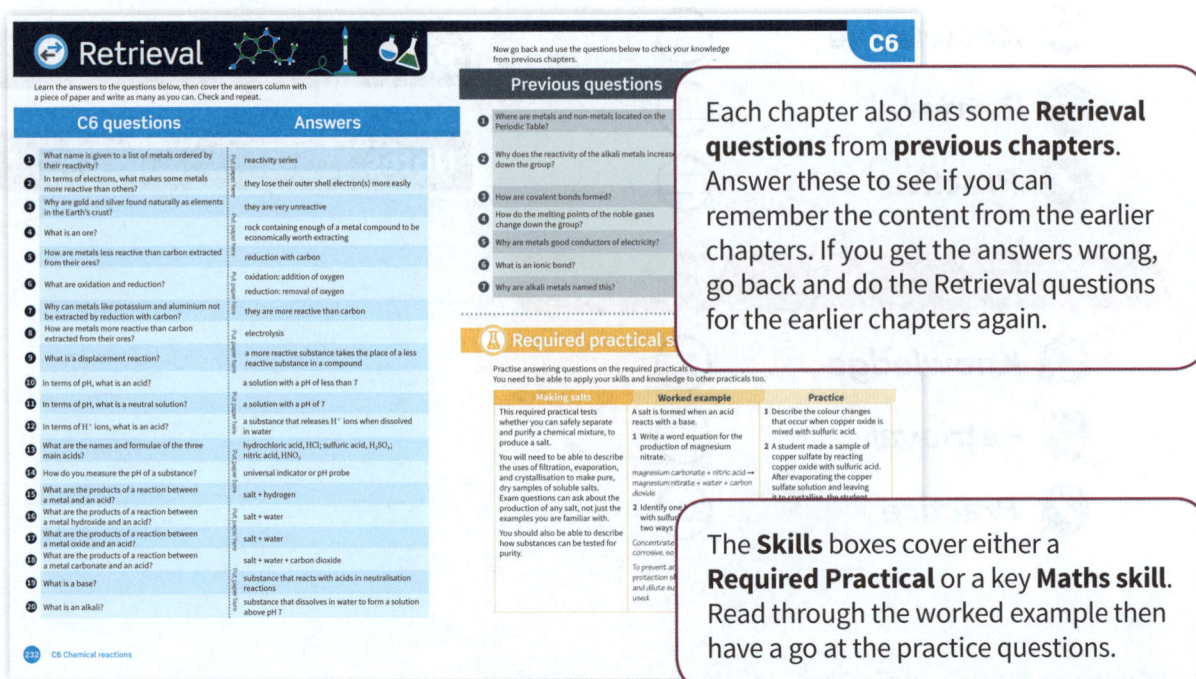

Each chapter also has some **Retrieval questions** from **previous chapters**. Answer these to see if you can remember the content from the earlier chapters. If you get the answers wrong, go back and do the Retrieval questions for the earlier chapters again.

The **Skills** boxes cover either a **Required Practical** or a key **Maths skill**. Read through the worked example then have a go at the practice questions.

Make sure you revisit the retrieval questions on different days to help them stick in your memory. You need to write down the answers each time, or say them out loud, otherwise it won't work.

3 Practice

Once you think you know the Knowledge Organiser and Retrieval answers really well you can move on to the final stage: **Practice**.

Each chapter has lots of **exam-style questions**, including some questions from previous chapters, to help you apply all the knowledge you have learnt and can retrieve.

Each question has a difficulty icon that shows the level of challenge.

 These questions build your confidence.

 These questions consolidate your knowledge.

 These questions stretch your understanding.

Make sure you attempt all of the questions no matter what grade you are aiming for.

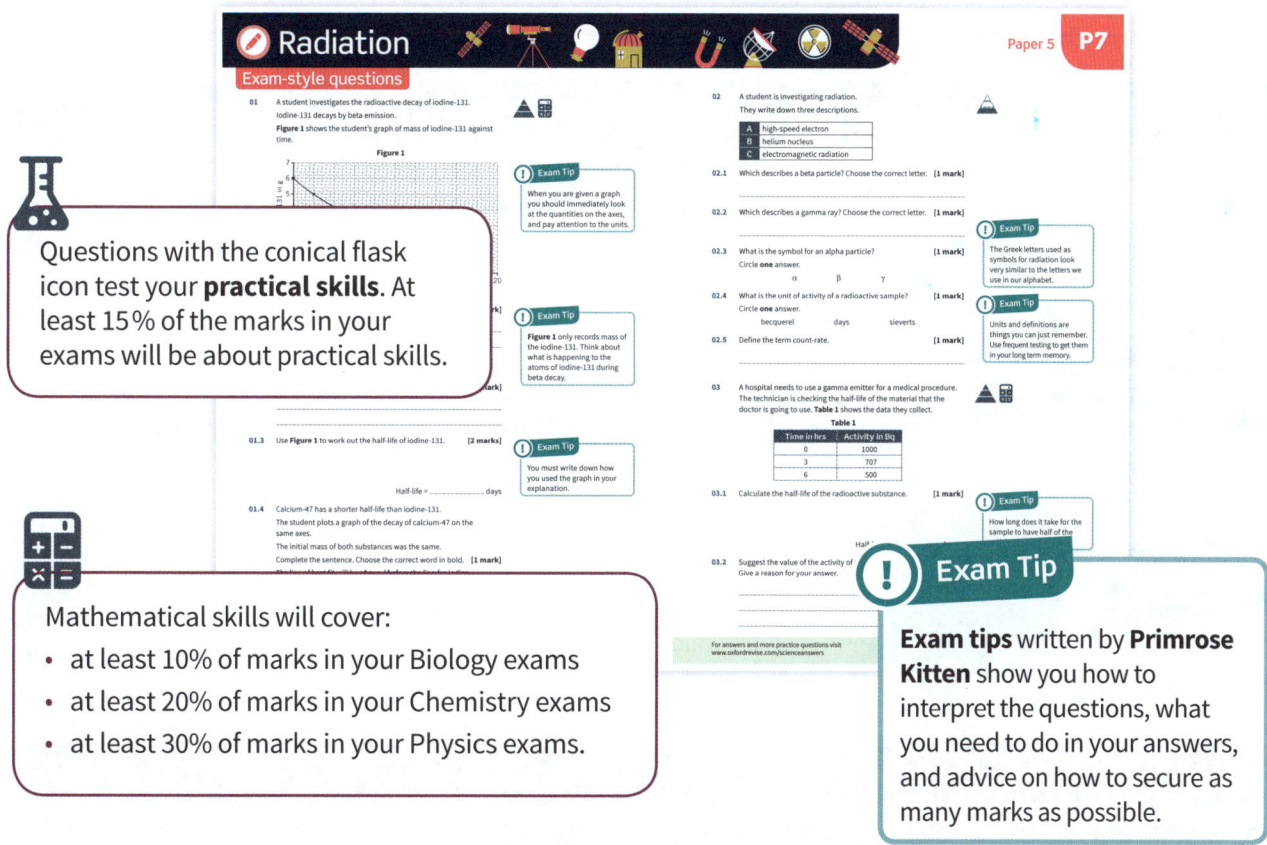

Questions with the conical flask icon test your **practical skills**. At least 15% of the marks in your exams will be about practical skills.

Mathematical skills will cover:
- at least 10% of marks in your Biology exams
- at least 20% of marks in your Chemistry exams
- at least 30% of marks in your Physics exams.

Exam tips written by **Primrose Kitten** show you how to interpret the questions, what you need to do in your answers, and advice on how to secure as many marks as possible.

kerboodle

All the **answers** are on Kerboodle and the website, along with even more exam-style questions. www.oxfordrevise.com/scienceanswers

Knowledge

B1 Cell structure

Eukaryotic cells

Animal and plant cells are **eukaryotic** cells. They have genetic material (**DNA**) that forms **chromosomes** and is contained within a **nucleus**.

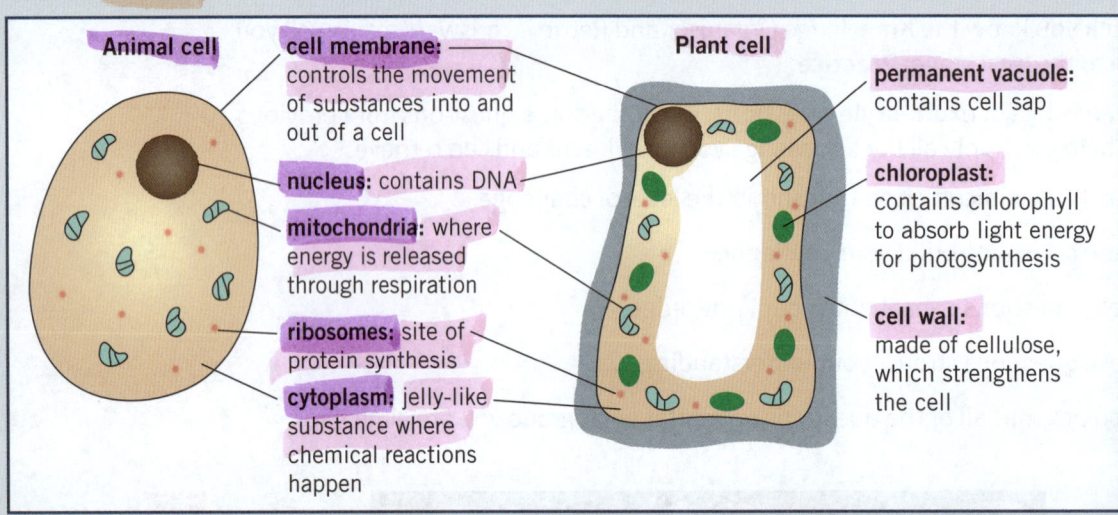

- **cell membrane:** controls the movement of substances into and out of a cell
- **nucleus:** contains DNA
- **mitochondria:** where energy is released through respiration
- **ribosomes:** site of protein synthesis
- **cytoplasm:** jelly-like substance where chemical reactions happen
- **permanent vacuole:** contains cell sap
- **chloroplast:** contains chlorophyll to absorb light energy for photosynthesis
- **cell wall:** made of cellulose, which strengthens the cell

Prokaryotic cells

Bacteria have the following characteristics:
- single-celled
- no nucleus – have a single loop of DNA
- have small rings of DNA called **plasmids**
- smaller than eukaryotic cells

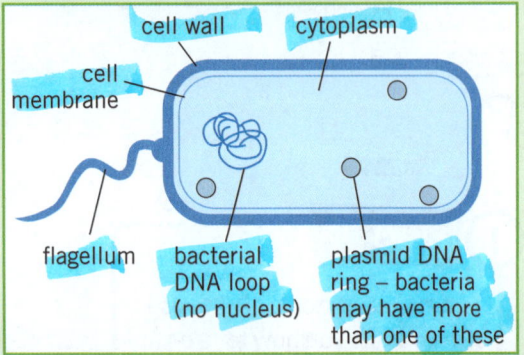

flagellum, cell membrane, cell wall, cytoplasm, bacterial DNA loop (no nucleus), plasmid DNA ring – bacteria may have more than one of these

Comparing sub-cellular structures

Structure	Animal cell	Plant cell	Prokaryotic cell
cell membrane	✓	✓	✓
cytoplasm	✓	✓	✓
nucleus	✓	✓	—
cell wall	—	✓	✓
chloroplasts	—	✓	—
permanent vacuole	—	✓	—
DNA free in cytoplasm	—	—	✓
plasmids	—	—	✓

Microscopes

Light microscope	Electron microscope
uses light to form images	uses a beam of electrons to form images
living samples can be viewed	samples cannot be living
relatively cheap	expensive
low magnification	high magnification
low **resolution**	high resolution

To calculate the **magnification** of an image:

$$\text{magnification} = \frac{\text{image size}}{\text{actual size}}$$

Electron microscopes allow you to see sub-cellular structures, such as ribosomes, that are too small to be seen with a light microscope.

B1

Specialised cells

Cells in animals and plants differentiate to form different types of cells. Most animal cells differentiate at an early stage of development, whereas a plant's cells differentiate throughout its lifetime.

Specialised cell	Function	Adaptations
sperm cell	fertilise an ovum (egg)	• tail to swim to the ovum and fertilise it • lots of mitochondria to release energy from respiration, enabling the sperm to swim to the ovum
red blood cell	transport oxygen around the body	• no nucleus so more room to carry oxygen • contains a red pigment called haemoglobin that binds to oxygen molecules • flat bi-concave disc shape to increase surface area-to-volume ratio
muscle cell	contract and relax to allow movement	• contains protein fibres, which can contract to make the cells shorter • contains lots of mitochondria to release energy from respiration, allowing the muscles to contract
nerve cell	carry electrical impulses around the body	• branched endings, called dendrites, to make connections with other neurones or effectors • myelin sheath insulates the axon to increase the transmission speed of the electrical impulses
root hair cell	absorb mineral ions and water from the soil	• long projection speeds up the absorption of water and mineral ions by increasing the surface area of the cell • lots of mitochondria to release energy for the active transport of mineral ions from the soil
palisade cell	enable photosynthesis in the leaf	• lots of chloroplasts containing chlorophyll to absorb light energy • located at the top surface of the leaf where it can absorb the most light energy

Key terms

Make sure you can write a definition for these key terms.

cell membrane cell wall chloroplast chromosome cytoplasm DNA
eukaryotic magnification mitochondria nucleus permanent vacuole
plasmid prokaryotic resolution ribosome

B1 Knowledge 3

Retrieval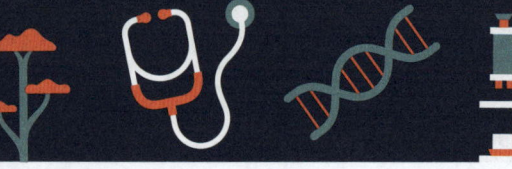

Learn the answers to the questions below, then cover the answers column with a piece of paper and write as many as you can. Check and repeat.

B1 questions | Answers

#	Question	Answer
1	What are two types of eukaryotic cell?	animal and plant
2	What type of cell are bacteria?	prokaryotic
3	Where is DNA found in animal and plant cells?	in the nucleus
4	What is the function of the cell membrane?	controls movement of substances into and out of the cell
5	What is the function of mitochondria?	site of respiration to transfer energy for the cell
6	What is the function of chloroplasts?	contain chlorophyll to absorb light energy for photosynthesis
7	What is the function of ribosomes?	enable production of proteins (protein synthesis)
8	What is the function of the cell wall?	strengthens and supports the cell
9	What is the structure of the main genetic material in a prokaryotic cell?	single loop of DNA
10	How are electron microscopes different to light microscopes?	electron microscopes use beams of electrons instead of light, cannot be used to view living samples, are much more expensive, and have a much higher magnification and resolution
11	What is the function of a red blood cell?	carries oxygen around the body
12	Give three adaptations of a red blood cell.	no nucleus, contains a red pigment called haemoglobin, and has a bi-concave disc shape
13	What is the function of a nerve cell?	carries electrical impulses around the body
14	Give two adaptations of a nerve cell.	branched endings, myelin sheath insulates the axon
15	What is the function of a sperm cell?	fertilises an ovum (egg)
16	Give two adaptations of a sperm cell.	tail, contains lots of mitochondria
17	What is the function of a palisade cell?	carries out photosynthesis in a leaf
18	Give two adaptations of a palisade cell.	lots of chloroplasts, located at the top surface of the leaf
19	What is the function of a root hair cell?	absorbs minerals and water from the soil
20	Give two adaptations of a root hair cell.	long projection, lots of mitochondria

B1 Cell structure

Maths skills B1

Practise your maths skills using the worked example and practice questions below.

Resolution	Worked example	Practice
The resolution of a device is the smallest change that the device can measure. Selecting equipment with the appropriate resolution is important in scientific investigations. If the resolution of a digital watch is one second, one second is the smallest amount of time it can measure. Some stopclocks have smaller resolutions, for example a resolution of 0.01 seconds. This means that they can measure times of 0.01, 1.29, or 9.62 seconds, whereas a digital watch could not.	What is the resolution of the following equipment? The resolution of this thermometer is 1 °C, as this is the smallest change that it can detect. 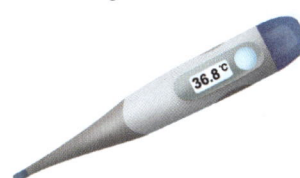 The resolution of this digital thermometer is 0.1 °C, as it can measure readings such as 1.1 °C, 8.9 °C, and 36.7 °C.	What are the resolutions of the following pieces of equipment? 1 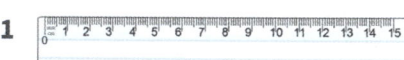 2 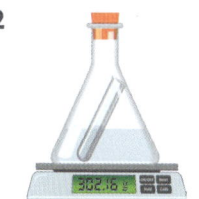 3 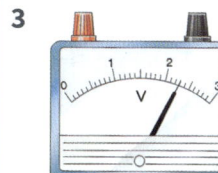

Required practical skills

Practise answering questions on the required practicals using the example below. You need to be able to apply your skills and knowledge to other practicals too.

Looking at cells	Worked example	Practice
In this practical you need to be able to use a light microscope to view plant and animal cells. You should be able to • describe how to set up a microscope • label parts of a microscope • describe how to focus on a slide containing a specimen • make a labelled scientific drawing of what you observe. You also need to be able to determine the magnification of an object under a microscope, and use this to calculate the real size of the object.	A student wanted to determine the actual size of the cell they observed under a microscope. They measured the size of the cell image as 15 mm, the objective lens magnification was 40×, and the eyepiece magnification was 10×. Determine the actual size of the cell. Give your answer in standard form. **Step 1:** determine the magnification $$\frac{\text{total}}{\text{magnification}} = \frac{\text{objective lens}}{\text{magnification}} \times \frac{\text{eyepiece lens}}{\text{magnification}}$$ total magnification = 40 × 10 = 400 **Step 2:** put the numbers in the equation $$\text{magnification} = \frac{\text{size of image}}{\text{actual size of object}}$$ $$400 = \frac{15}{\text{actual size of object}}$$ **Step 3:** rearrange the equation and find the answer $$\text{actual size of object} = \frac{15}{400} = 0.0375 \text{ mm}$$ **Step 4:** convert your answer to standard form $0.0375 = 3.75 \times 10^{-2}$ mm	1 Describe how you could identify a cell as an animal or plant cell by looking at it using a light microscope. Include the names and visual descriptions of any important organelles. 2 A student wrote a method for focusing a microscope image of a cell. *'Set the microscope at the highest objective lens, then look down the eyepiece while you use the fine focus to find the cell.'* Suggest improvements to this method. 3 Draw a labelled image of an animal cell.

B1 Retrieval 5

Exam-style questions

01 **Figure 1** shows a plant cell.

Figure 1

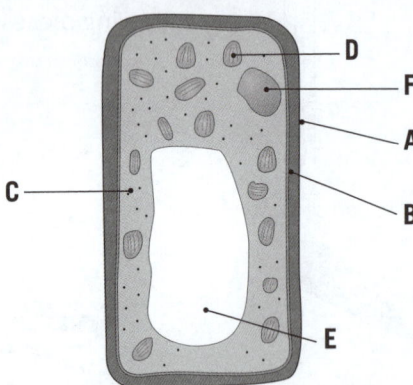

01.1 Identify the letter on **Figure 1** that is pointing to the following parts of the cell. [6 marks]

cell wall _____A_____
cell membrane _____B_____
chloroplast _____D_____
nucleus _____F_____
vacuole _____E_____
cytoplasm _____C_____

> **Exam Tip**
> Labelling cells is a frequent exam question. Start with the labels that you know, this will leave fewer options to choose from for the ones you're less sure about.

01.2 Name the part of the cell where photosynthesis takes place. [1 mark]

chloroplast

01.3 Describe the function of the nucleus. [1 mark]

controls the DNA of the cell

01.4 Identify **one** feature shown in **Figure 1** that allows you to conclude that this is a plant cell and not an animal cell. [1 mark]
Tick **one** box.

cell wall   [✓]
cytoplasm   [ ]
nucleus   [ ]
cell membrane [ ]

> **Exam Tip**
> Which of these is not in an animal cell?

B1 Cell structure

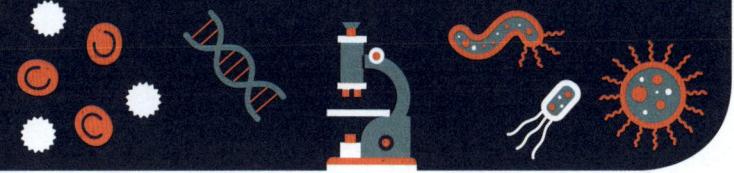

Paper 1 B1

02 Plant and animal cells contain a number of components.

02.1 Complete **Table 1** by ticking to show whether each cell component is found in plant cells only, animal cells only, or both. **[4 marks]**

Table 1

Cell component	Plant cell only	Animal cell only	Both
nucleus			✓
cell wall	✓		
cytoplasm			✓
permanent vacuole	✓		

Exam Tip
Only put one tick in each row – the question is worth four marks, so you need four ticks.

02.2 Draw **one** line from each cell component to its function. **[4 marks]**

Cell component — Function

- nucleus — contains sap to keep the cell firm
- mitochondrion — controls what comes in and out of a cell
- chloroplast — where respiration occurs
- vacuole — contains genetic material and controls the cell
- cell membrane — where photosynthesis occurs

Exam Tip
You need to get all five correct to get full marks, so don't leave any out.

02.3 Name the piece of equipment that should be used to view cell components. **[1 mark]**

microscope ✓

03 Muscle cells are an example of a specialised cell.

03.1 Define the term specialised cell. **[1 mark]**
a cell that has adaption

03.2 The biceps contain muscle cells.
Describe the function of a muscle cell. **[1 mark]**
brings movement to body through movement

03.3 Describe **one** other example of where muscles are found in the body. **[2 marks]**
bicep

03.4 Explain why muscle cells have lots of mitochondria. **[2 marks]**
to generate energy need for movement

Exam Tip
Think about the function of mitochondria.

03.5 Explain **one** other feature of a muscle cell. **[2 marks]**
to help respiration

04 A student collected a sample of cells by taking a saliva swab from the inside of their cheek.

04.1 Suggest **one** safety measure that the student should take during this procedure. [1 mark]

wher googles

04.2 **Figure 2** shows a cheek cell viewed under a light microscope magnified at ×1350.

Identify structure **X** in **Figure 2**. [1 mark]

> **Exam Tip**
> The safety measure must be linked to the practical in the question – there is no point talking about hot Bunsen burners as they are not used in this experiment.

Figure 2

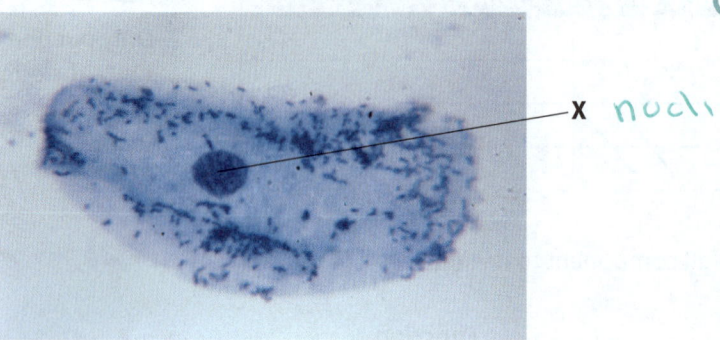

X *nuclias*

04.3 Before viewing the cheek cells, the student added methylene blue to the cell sample.

Explain why methylene blue dye was added. [1 mark]

to see the stuler of cell more clearly

> **Exam Tip**
> Look at what structures have been dyed in **Figure 2**.

04.4 Identify **one** way the student could observe structures within the cell in greater detail.

Choose **one** answer. [1 mark]

use a magnifying glass
~~use a higher-powered objective lens~~ ✓
use a larger sample of cells

10

05 This question is about specialised animal cells.

05.1 Choose the correct words from the box to complete the sentences on specialised animal cells. Each word may be used once, more than once, or not at all. [6 marks]

| sperm | functions | nerve | muscle |
| movement | egg | impulses |

Specialised cells have a number of special features that enable them to perform their ___functions___.

___nerve___ cells carry electrical ___impulses___ around the body.

___Sperm___ cells contain male genetic material.

___muscle___ cells contract to cause ___movement___.

> **Exam Tip**
> Even if you're not sure about one of the answers, try to fill in as many as you can.

B1 Cell structure

05.2 Identify **one** process by which cells develop into specialised cells.
Choose **one** answer. [1 mark]

diffusion
(differentiation)
digestion
decay

05.3 Give **one** example of a specialised plant cell. [1 mark]

root hair cell

06 **Figure 3** shows an image of a bacterial cell and a plant cell.

Figure 3

plant cell

bacterial cell

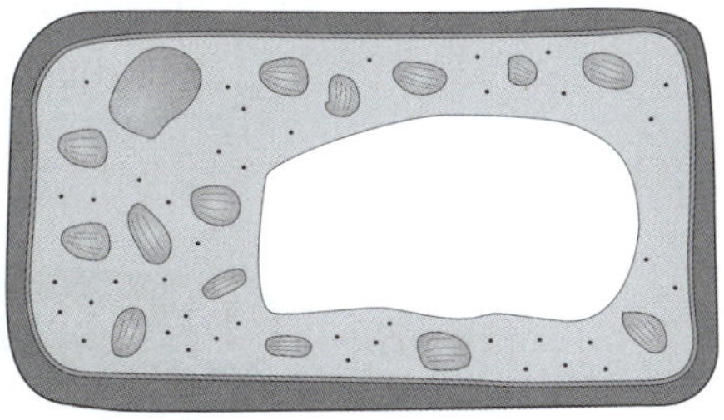

06.1 Identify which **two** components are found in both the plant and bacterial cell.

Choose **two** answers. [1 mark]

~~plasmid~~
~~nucleus~~
(cell wall)
~~vacuole~~
(cytoplasm)

> **Exam Tip**
> Use the images to help you cross out any answers you are sure are wrong, and then see which options you're left with.

06.2 Only the bacterial cell has a flagellum.
Describe the function of the flagellum. [1 mark]

06.3 Describe **one** other difference between plant and bacterial cells. vacuole [1 mark]

06.4 Identify which **one** of the following cells is a prokaryotic cell.
Give a reason for your answer. [1 mark]

(bacterial cell)
plant cell

It dosent have a nucleus like plant and animals cells

07 Figure 4 represents a root hair cell.

Figure 4

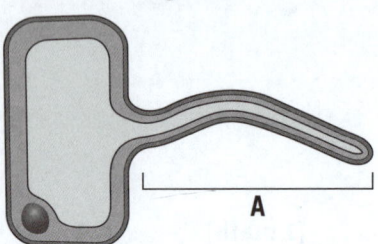

07.1 Choose **one** type of organism that contains root hair cells. **[1 mark]**

(plant) ← circled
~~animal~~
bacterium
amoeba

Exam Tip

Use the name to give you a clue to the location of *root* hair cells.

07.2 Identify **one** function of part **A** in **Figure 4**.
Choose **one** answer. **[1 mark]**

to absorb oxygen
to remove carbon dioxide
(to absorb water) ← circled
to remove nutrients

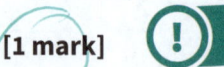

Exam Tip

Part **A** of the root hair cell increases the surface area of the cell.

07.3 Circle the appropriate bold words to complete the following sentences about root hair cells. **[4 marks]**

Root hair cells have a **large** / **small** surface area to **minimise** / **maximise** the rate of osmosis.
They contain no **chloroplasts** / **mitochondria**, meaning that they are **able** / **unable** to carry out photosynthesis.

08 A scientist took an image of human cheek cells. It was produced using a light microscope.

08.1 Describe how to prepare a slide of cheek cells to view under a light microscope. **[6 marks]**

08.2 Sketch a diagram of the cell you would expect to see.
Label the organelles that are visible in the cell. **[3 marks]**

Exam Tip

In **08.2** the command word is 'sketch'. You only need to draw a rough diagram of a cell. This is not fine art so shading or too much detail won't get you any marks and will take up valuable time.

08.3 Write down which additional piece of information you should include with a microscope drawing. **[1 mark]**

08.4 Some organelles will not be visible because a light microscope does not have a high enough resolution.
Define the term resolution. **[1 mark]**

08.5 Suggest how the scientist could produce an image showing the missing organelles. **[1 mark]**

B1 Cell structure

B1

09 A student was asked to measure the width of a strand of human hair.

09.1 Select the most appropriate piece of apparatus for the student to use.

Choose **one** answer. [1 mark]

metre rule

30 cm rule

(microscope with scale)

telescope with scale

> **Exam Tip**
> Try to imagine doing the experiment and see if that helps you work out which piece of equipment you would use.

09.2 The width of a human hair is about the same width as an animal cell.

Which of the following sizes is closest to the width of a human hair?

Choose **one** answer. [1 mark]

1 nm   (1 mm)   1 m   1 km

09.3 The student measured the width of the hair five times.

Choose **one** anomaly in their results from the box. [1 mark]

| 80 μm | 78 μm | 85 μm | (125 μm) | 74 μm |

> **Exam Tip**
> Which result is very different to the others?

09.4 Suggest what the student should do with this anomalous result.
remeser and try it agciy [1 mark]

10 **Figure 5** shows some plant cells as viewed under a light microscope.

Figure 5

A
B
C

10.1 Identify the cell membrane in **Figure 5**. [1 mark]

10.2 Ribosomes are present in plant cells but cannot be seen using a light microscope.

Describe the function of ribosomes. [1 mark]

10.3 Name **one** other subcellular structure that is present in plant cells but cannot be seen in **Figure 5**. [1 mark]

10.4 Describe how to prepare a sample of plant cells and view them under a light microscope. [6 marks]

> **Exam Tip**
> When you're writing a method, the key thing to remember is that it has to be complete. Don't skip any steps, even if they seem obvious.

For answers and more practice questions visit www.oxfordrevise.com/scienceanswers

Even more practice and interactive revision quizzes are available on kerboodle

B1 Practice 11

Knowledge

B2 Cell transport

Comparing diffusion, osmosis, and active transport

	Diffusion	Osmosis	Active transport
Definition	The spreading out of particles, resulting in a net movement from an area of higher **concentration** to an area of lower concentration.	The diffusion of water from a **dilute** solution to a concentrated solution through a **partially permeable membrane**.	The movement of particles from a more dilute solution to a more concentrated solution using energy from respiration.
Movement of particles	Particles move down the concentration **gradient** – from an area of *high* concentration to an area of *low* concentration.	Water moves from an area of *lower* solute concentration to an area of *higher* solute concentration.	Particles move against the concentration gradient – from an area of *low* concentration to an area of *high* concentration.
Energy required?	no – **passive process**	no – passive process	yes – using energy released during respiration
Examples	**Humans** • Nutrients in the small intestine diffuse into the blood in the **capillaries** through the **villi**. • Oxygen diffuses from the air in the **alveoli** into the blood in the capillaries. Carbon dioxide diffuses from the blood in the capillaries into the air in the alveoli. • **Urea** diffuses from cells into the blood for excretion by the kidneys. **Fish** • Oxygen from water passing over the gills diffuses into the blood in the **gill filaments**. • Carbon dioxide diffuses from the blood in the gill filaments into the water. **Plants** • Carbon dioxide used for photosynthesis diffuses into leaves through the **stomata**. • Oxygen produced during photosynthesis diffuses out of the leaves through the stomata.	**Plants** Water moves by osmosis from a dilute solution in the soil to a concentrated solution in the **root hair cell**.	**Humans** Active transport allows sugar molecules to be absorbed from the small intestine when the sugar concentration is higher in the blood than in the small intestine. **Plants** Active transport is used to absorb mineral ions into the root hair cells from more dilute solutions in the soil.

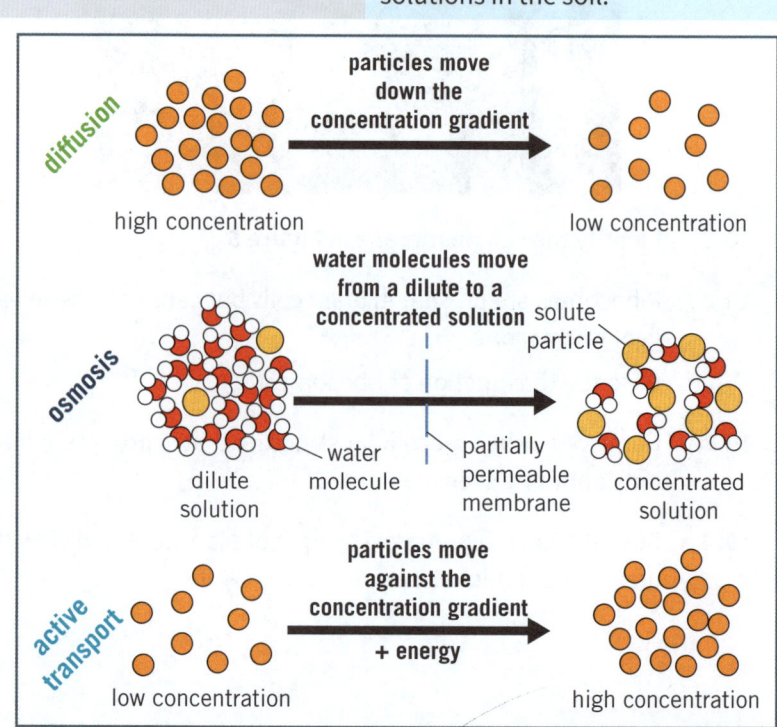

12 B2 Cell transport

B2

Factors that affect the rate of diffusion

① Difference in concentration
The steeper the concentration gradient, the faster the rate of diffusion.

② Temperature
The higher the temperature, the faster the rate of diffusion.

③ Surface area of the membrane
The larger the membrane surface area, the faster the rate of diffusion.

Adaptations for exchanging substances

Single-celled organisms have a large surface area-to-volume ratio. This allows enough molecules to be transported across their cell membranes to meet their needs.

Multicellular organisms have a small surface area-to-volume ratio. This means they need specialised organ systems and cells to allow enough molecules to be transported into and out of their cells.

Exchange surfaces work most efficiently when they have a large surface area, a thin membrane, and a good blood supply.

Villi in the small intestine
for absorbing nutrients

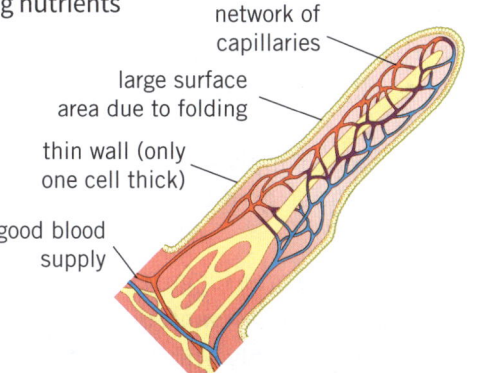

- network of capillaries
- large surface area due to folding
- thin wall (only one cell thick)
- good blood supply

Alveoli in the lungs
for gas exchange

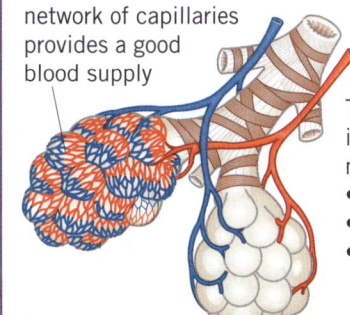

network of capillaries provides a good blood supply

The rate of diffusion is increased because the membrane of the alveoli
- has a large surface area
- is moist
- is only one cell thick (short diffusion pathway).

Fish gills
for gas exchange

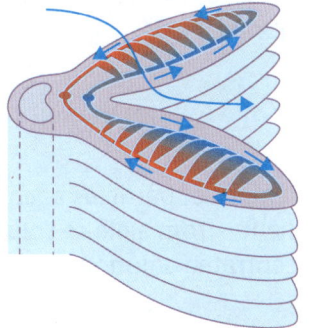

Fish gills are made up of stacks of thin filaments with
- a large surface area to increase diffusion
- a network of capillaries (good blood supply).

Root hair cells
for uptake of water and minerals

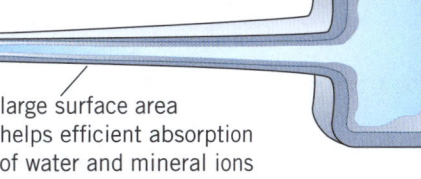

- lots of mitochondria to take in mineral ions by active transport
- large surface area helps efficient absorption of water and mineral ions

Key terms
Make sure you can write a definition for these key terms.

active transport   alveoli   capillaries   concentration   diffusion   dilute
gill filament   gradient   osmosis   partially permeable membrane
passive process   root hair cell   stomata   urea   villi

B2 Knowledge

Retrieval

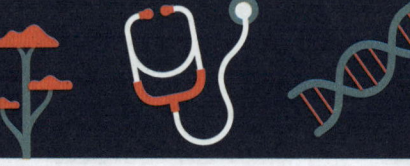

Learn the answers to the questions below, then cover the answers column with a piece of paper and write as many as you can. Check and repeat.

B2 questions | Answers

#	Question	Answer
1	What is diffusion?	net movement of particles from an area of high concentration to an area of low concentration along a concentration gradient – this is a passive process (does not require energy from respiration)
2	Name three factors that affect the rate of diffusion.	concentration gradient, temperature, membrane surface area
3	How are villi adapted for exchanging substances?	• long and thin – increases surface area • one-cell-thick membrane – short diffusion distance • good blood supply – maintains a steep concentration gradient
4	How are the lungs adapted for efficient gas exchange?	• alveoli – large surface area • moist membranes – increases rate of diffusion • one-cell-thick membranes – short diffusion distance • good blood supply – maintains a steep concentration gradient
5	How are fish gills adapted for efficient gas exchange?	• large surface area for gases to diffuse across • thin layer of cells – short diffusion distance • good blood supply – maintains a steep concentration gradient
6	What is osmosis?	diffusion of water from a dilute solution to a concentrated solution through a partially permeable membrane
7	Give one example of osmosis in a plant.	water moves from the soil into the root hair cell
8	What is active transport?	movement of particles against a concentration gradient – from a dilute solution to a more concentrated solution – using energy from respiration
9	Why is active transport needed in plant roots?	concentration of mineral ions in the soil is lower than inside the root hair cells – the mineral ions must move against the concentration gradient to enter the root hair cells
10	What is the purpose of active transport in the small intestine?	sugars can be absorbed into the blood when the concentration of sugar in the small intestine is lower than the concentration of sugar in the blood

B2 Cell transport

B2

Now go back and use the questions below to check your knowledge from previous chapters.

Previous questions | Answers

#	Question	Answer
1	Give two adaptations of a root hair cell.	long projection, lots of mitochondria
2	What is the function of a red blood cell?	carries oxygen around the body
3	What type of cell are bacteria?	prokaryotic
4	What is the function of ribosomes?	enable production of proteins (protein synthesis)
5	Give two adaptations of a nerve cell.	branched endings, myelin sheath insulates the axon
6	What is the function of a sperm cell?	fertilises an ovum (egg)
7	Give two adaptations of a sperm cell.	tail, contains lots of mitochondria
8	How are electron microscopes different to light microscopes?	electron microscopes use beams of electrons instead of light, cannot be used to view living samples, are much more expensive, and have a much higher magnification and resolution

Required practical skills

Practise answering questions on the required practicals using the example below. You need to be able to apply your skills and knowledge to other practicals too.

Osmosis in cells

Different concentrations of sugar and salt solutions both affect the movement of water by osmosis, causing cells to lose or gain water, and changing the mass of a tissue sample.

For this practical you need to be able to accurately measure length, mass, and volume to measure osmosis in cells.

You will need to be comfortable applying this knowledge to a range of samples, not just to the typical example of potato tissue, as osmosis happens in all cells.

Worked example

A sample of carrot was placed into a 0.75 mol/dm³ sugar solution for 30 minutes. The mass of the carrot was recorded before and after this.

Initial mass = 6.02 g

Final mass = 3.91 g

1. Determine the percentage change in mass of the sample.

Change in mass = 3.91 − 6.02 = −2.11 g

Percentage change in mass = $\left(\frac{-2.11}{6.02}\right) \times 100 = -35\%$

(a minus sign is used because the sample has lost mass)

2. Explain why this experiment should be repeated, and give one other variable that should be controlled.

The experiment should be repeated to give a more reliable result, and to allow calculation of a mean loss in mass for the sample. The dimensions of the carrot samples need to be controlled between repeats.

Practice

1. Give one reason why it is important to dry the samples of carrot cores before they are weighed.

2. When repeating this experiment using different concentrations of sugar solution, a student found that one sample did not change mass. Suggest what this tells you about the concentration of the solution. Assume no error in the experiment.

3. Two students set up this experiment. Student A said that each sample of carrot must have the same starting mass. Student B argued that each sample must have the same length and width. Explain which student is correct.

B2 Retrieval 15

Practice

Exam-style questions

01 A group of students investigated how the mass of a potato sample changed over time, when placed into sugar solutions of varying concentrations.

They set up their equipment as shown in **Figure 1**.

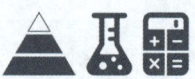

Figure 1

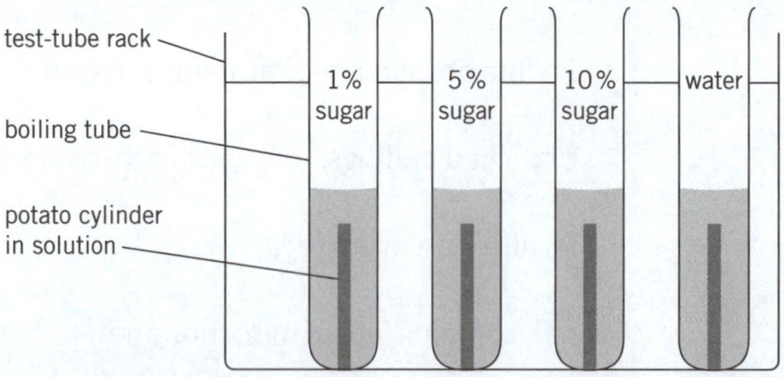

test-tube rack, boiling tube, potato cylinder in solution — 1% sugar, 5% sugar, 10% sugar, water

01.1 Identify the independent variable in their investigation. **[1 mark]**

Tick **one** box.

- mass of potato sample ☐
- concentration of sugar solution ✓
- time potato placed in sugar solution ☐

01.2 Use **Figure 1** to identify **two** variables that the students controlled. **[2 marks]**

Tick **two** boxes.

- mass of potato sample at start ✓
- volume of sugar solution ✓
- change in mass of potato sample ☐
- light intensity ☐

16 B2 Cell transport

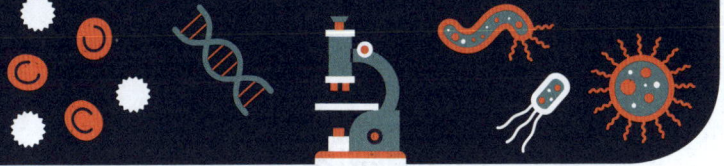

Paper 1 B2

01.3 The students' results are shown in **Table 1**.

Table 1

Solution	0% sugar solution	1% sugar solution	5% sugar solution	10% sugar solution
Starting mass in g	3.1	3.3	3.1	3.4
Final mass in g	3.4	3.5	2.9	2.7
Change in mass in g	+0.3	+0.2	−0.2	−0.7

Complete the results table by calculating the change in mass for the 10% sugar solution. **[1 mark]**

 **Exam Tip**

If you're not sure how to calculate the change in mass, use the 1% or 5% as practice calculations where you've already been given the answer.

Change in mass = −0.7 g

01.4 Plot the students' results of sugar concentration against change in mass on **Figure 2**. Draw a line of best fit. **[2 marks]**

Figure 2

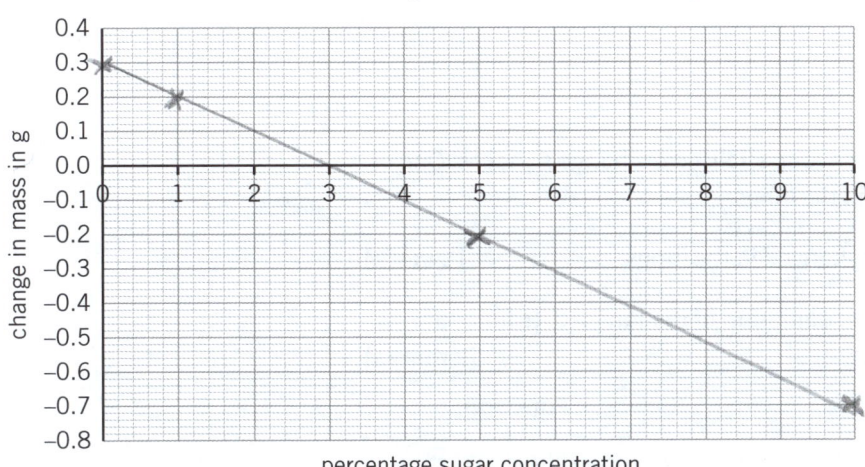

percentage sugar concentration

Exam Tip

Always plot points on graphs using crosses, dots are not clear enough and can get hidden under lines of best fit, and dots within circles are not specific enough.

01.5 Use the graph to determine the concentration of sugar present in the potato. **[1 mark]**

more sugar concentrate the change mass decreases

02 Many substances move into and out of cells by diffusion.

02.1 Choose the appropriate bold words to complete this description of diffusion. **[4 marks]**

Diffusion is the **spreading out** / **clumping together** of particles in a gas or **solid** / **liquid**.

Particles move from an area of **low** / **high** concentration to an area of **low** / **high** concentration.

02.2 Which part of the cell do substances diffuse through? [1 mark]
Tick **one** box.

cell membrane [✓]

cytoplasm [ ]

vacuole [ ]

02.3 Identify **two** factors that can speed up the rate of diffusion. [2 marks]
Tick **two** boxes.

higher temperature [✓]

lower temperature [ ]

larger surface area [ ]

smaller concentration gradient [✓]

02.4 Osmosis is a type of diffusion.
Name the substance that moves during osmosis. [1 mark]

dilute substance

03 Multicellular organisms have specialised exchange surfaces. One of these surfaces is found in the lungs.

03.1 Name **one** substance exchanged in the lungs. [1 mark]

03.2 Draw **one** line from each adaptation of the lungs to its function. [2 marks]

Adaptation	Function
lots of alveoli (air sacs)	short diffusion distance
air sacs have thin walls	increase surface area
good blood supply	maintain concentration gradient

(lots of alveoli → increase surface area; air sacs have thin walls → short diffusion distance; good blood supply → maintain concentration gradient)

03.3 Name **one** other exchange surface in animals. [1 mark]

> **Exam Tip**
> Always read the questions carefully: **02.2** says to tick *one* box, but **02.3** says to tick *two*.

> **Exam Tip**
> The digestive system has lots of exchange surfaces.

B2 Cell transport

B2

04 Substances can move into and out of cells by the processes of diffusion and active transport.

04.1 Complete **Table 2** by ticking **two** boxes. **[2 marks]**

Table 2

Statement	Active transport	Diffusion
requires energy	✓	
moves substances against the concentration gradient	✓	

04.2 Identify **one** situation where active transport is used.
Choose **one** answer. **[1 mark]**

~~movement of mineral ions into plant roots~~
movement of food through the oesophagus
movement of carbon dioxide into a leaf

04.3 Identify **one** situation where diffusion is used.
Choose **one** answer. **[1 mark]**

movement of mineral ions into plant roots
movement of food through the oesophagus
~~movement of carbon dioxide into a leaf~~

05 A chef took an uncooked chip, measured its mass, and placed the chip into a bowl of water.
The chef left the chip for 20 minutes and then took its mass again. The results are shown in **Table 3**.

Table 3

Original mass in g	3.0
Final mass in g	3.5

05.1 Calculate the percentage change in the mass of the potato chip using the following formula. **[2 marks]**

$$\text{percentage change in mass} = \frac{\text{final mass} - \text{original mass}}{\text{original mass}} \times 100$$

> **Exam Tip**
> This question is similar to the required practical on osmosis with potato cores. This is a new context but the idea is exactly the same.

05.2 The chef concluded that the potato chip increased in mass because water moved out of the potato chip. Is the chef correct?
Give a reason for your answer. **[2 marks]**

> **Exam Tip**
> Don't be scared if you've never seen an equation like this before – all you need to do it plug in your answers into the right parts of the equation.

05.3 Predict what would happen to the mass if the chef placed the potato chip into a bowl of salt water.
Explain your answer. **[2 marks]**

06 Active transport requires energy. This is released by respiration.

06.1 Identify the part of the cell where respiration takes place.
Choose **one** answer. **[1 mark]**

chloroplast   cytoplasm   mitochondrion   nucleus

06.2 **Figure 3** shows the relationship between the rates of respiration and active transport.

Describe the trend shown in the graph. **[1 mark]**

06.3 Explain why a root hair cell uses active transport. **[2 marks]**

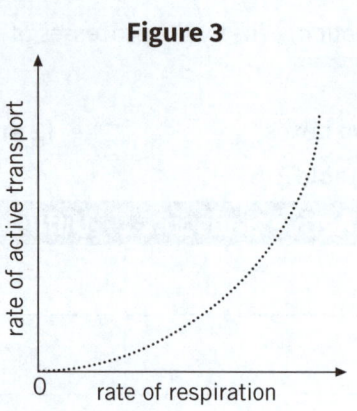

Figure 3

> **Exam Tip**
>
> **06.2** is a one-mark question so only a simple description is needed.

07 This question is about the transport of substances into and out of cells.

07.1 Select the type of transport used in each situation in **Table 4** by ticking the most appropriate box. **[3 marks]**

Table 4

The movement of:	Diffusion	Osmosis	Active transport
carbon dioxide from the blood to the lungs			
mineral ions in the soil into root hair cells			
water across a cell membrane			

> **Exam Tip**
>
> You don't have to start with the top row – if you know how mineral ions move then start with that one.

07.2 **Figure 4** shows two regions separated by a partially permeable membrane.

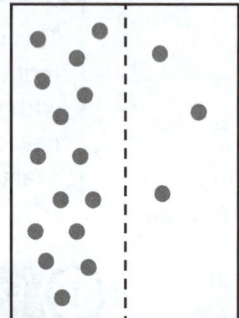

Figure 4

Identify the direction of diffusion by adding an arrow on **Figure 4**. **[1 mark]**

07.3 Choose the correct diagram to show the distribution of the particles when the diffusion in **Figure 4** is no longer occurring. **[1 mark]**

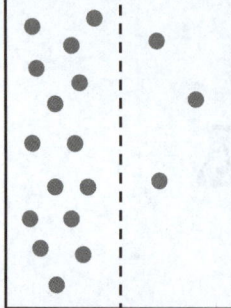 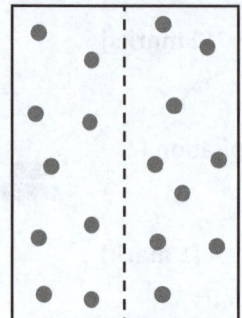 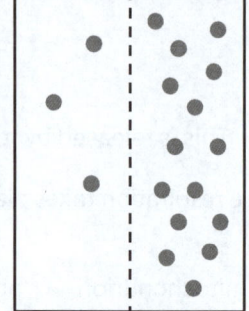

20 B2 Cell transport

B2

08 A scientist planned to carry out an investigation to determine which variety of apple was the sweetest. The scientist had access to the following equipment:

- range of different apples
- cork borer
- scalpel
- balance
- distilled water
- test tubes
- test-tube rack
- measuring cylinder
- sucrose solutions at six different concentrations.

Plan an investigation the scientist could carry out to determine the sugar concentration of each variety of apple. **[6 marks]**

> **! Exam Tip**
> Planning an experiment is an important skill to practise. Make sure you clearly plan out what you're going to do and think about safety.

09 Plant roots absorb water from the soil by osmosis.

09.1 Define the term osmosis. **[1 mark]**

09.2 Once inside the root, water continues to move from cell to cell as it moves towards the xylem vessel. **Figure 5** shows three cells within the root. Each cell contains a different concentration of salt. Water can move from cell to cell in any direction.

Identify which cell will gain water the fastest.
Give a reason for your answer. **[2 marks]**

09.3 Xylem vessels transport water throughout the plant.
Describe the structure of the xylem vessels. **[2 marks]**

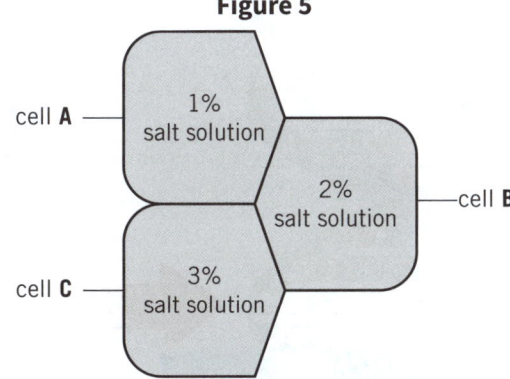

Figure 5

10 Substances such as water and ions need to move in and out of cells.

10.1 Draw **one** line between each process and the correct method of transport. **[2 marks]**

Process	Transport method
movement of oxygen from the lungs into the bloodstream	active transport
movement of mineral ions from the soil into plant roots	osmosis
movement of water into a plant cell	diffusion

> **! Exam Tip**
> It is important to learn examples for each mechanism that moves water or ions in and out of cells.

10.2 Complete the sentence using the correct bolded words. **[2 marks]**

Cells that carry out active transport contain **many / few** mitochondria so that there will be sufficient **chemicals / energy**.

10.3 Explain why active transport is usually required to move glucose from the small intestine into the bloodstream. **[3 marks]**

Knowledge

B3 Cell division

Chromosomes

The **nucleus** of a cell contains **chromosomes**. Each chromosome carries a large number of **genes** made of DNA molecules.

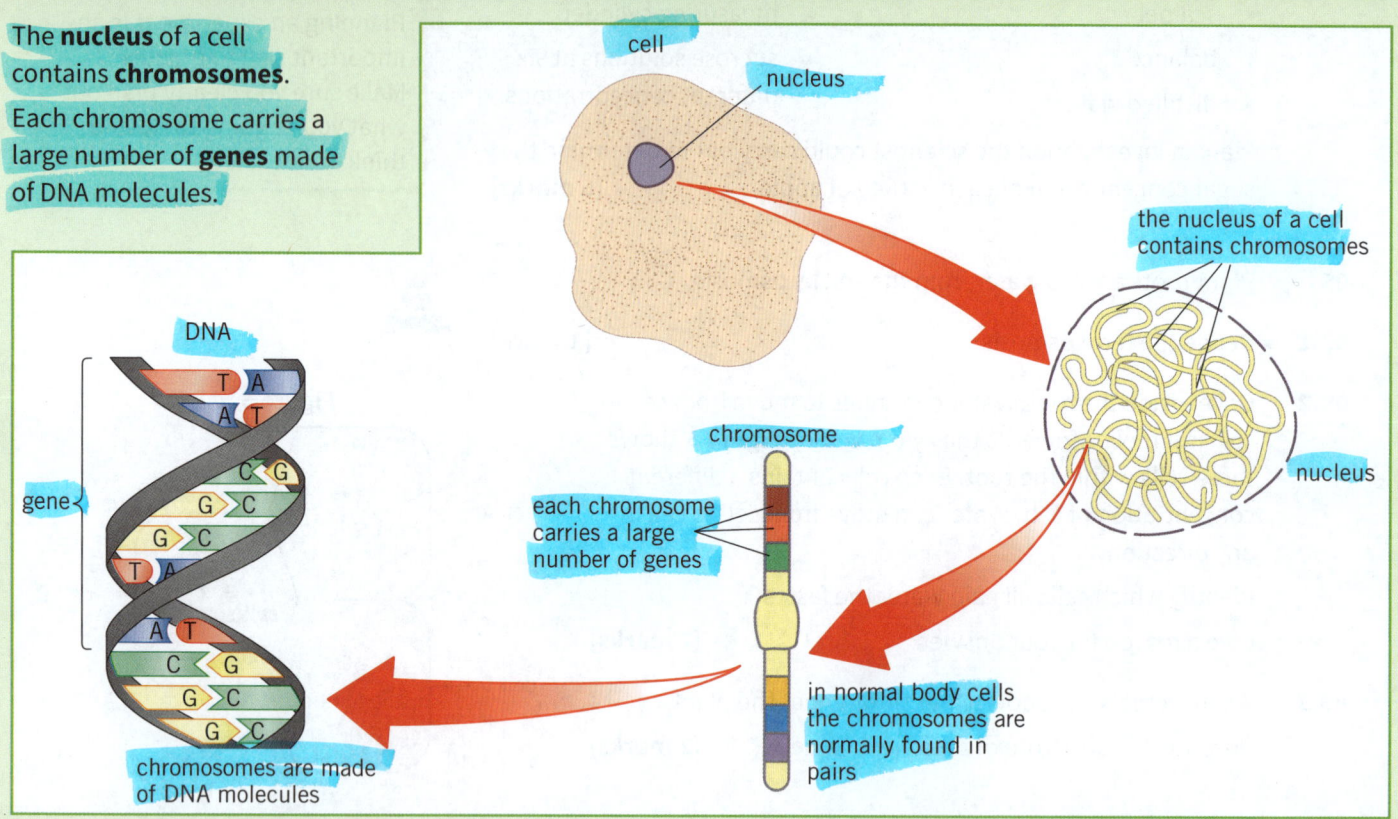

The cell cycle

Body cells divide to form two identical **daughter cells** by going through a series of stages known as the **cell cycle**.

Cell division by **mitosis** is important for the growth and repair of cells, for example, the replacement of skin cells. Mitosis is also used for asexual reproduction.

There are three main stages in the cell cycle:

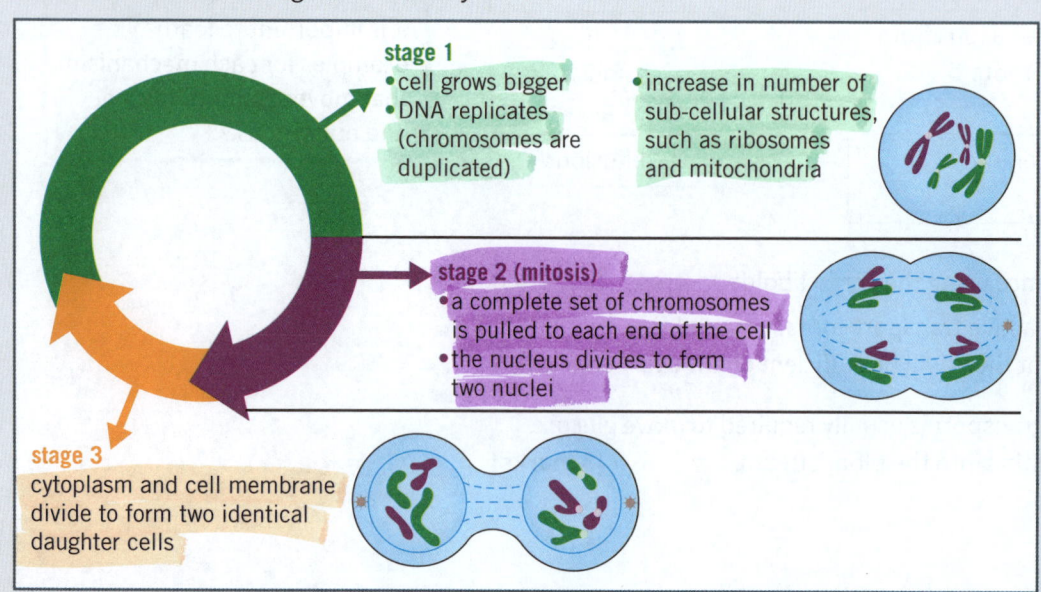

> **Revision tip**
>
> **Remember** Mitosis has a *t* in it, so that should help you remember that it makes *two* daughter cells.

B3 Cell division

B3

Stem cells in medicine

A stem cell is an undifferentiated cell that can develop into one or more types of specialised cell.

There are two types of stem cell in mammals: **adult stem cells** and **embryonic stem cells**.

Stem cells can be **cloned** to produce large numbers of identical cells.

Type of stem cell	Where are they found?	What can they differentiate into?	Advantages	Disadvantages
adult stem cells	specific parts of the body in adults and children – for example, bone marrow	can only differentiate to form certain types of cells – for example, stem cells in bone marrow can only differentiate into types of blood cell	• fewer ethical issues – adults can consent to have their stem cells removed and used • an already established technique for treating diseases such as leukaemia • relatively safe to use as a treatment and donors recover quickly	• requires a donor, potentially meaning a long wait time to find someone suitable • can only differentiate into certain types of specialised cells, so can be used to treat fewer diseases
embryonic stem cells	early human embryos (often taken from spare embryos from fertility clinics)	can differentiate into any type of specialised cell in the body – for example, a nerve cell or a muscle cell	• can treat a wide range of diseases as can form any specialised cell • may be possible to grow whole replacement organs • usually no donor needed as they are obtained from spare embryos from fertility clinics	• ethical issues as the embryo is destroyed and each embryo is a potential human life • risk of transferring viral infections to the patient • newer treatment so relatively under-researched – not yet clear if they can cure as many diseases as thought
plant meristem	meristem regions in the roots and shoots of plants	can differentiate into all plant cell types – they can be used to create clones of whole plants	• rare species of plants can be cloned to prevent extinction • plants with desirable traits, such as disease resistance, can be cloned to produce large numbers of identical plants • fast and low-cost production of large numbers of plants	• cloned plants are genetically identical, so a whole crop is at risk of being destroyed by a single disease or genetic defect

Therapeutic cloning

In **therapeutic cloning**
- cells from a patient's own body are used to create a cloned early embryo of themselves
- stem cells from this embryo can be used for medical treatments and growing new organs
- these stem cells have the same genes as the patient, so are less likely to be rejected when transplanted.

 **Key terms**

Make sure you can write a definition for these key terms.

adult stem cell   cell cycle
chromosome   clone   daughter cells
embryonic stem cell   gene
meristem   mitosis
nucleus   therapeutic cloning

B3 Knowledge

Retrieval

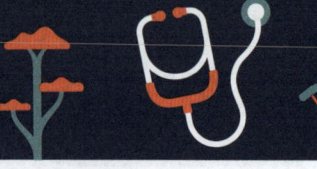
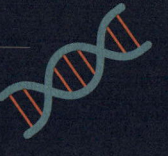

Learn the answers to the questions below, then cover the answers column with a piece of paper and write as many as you can. Check and repeat.

	B3 questions	Answers
1	What is a stem cell?	undifferentiated cell that can differentiate into one or more specialised cell types
2	What are adult stem cells?	stem cells from adults that can only differentiate into certain specialised cells
3	Where can adult stem cells be found?	bone marrow
4	What are embryonic stem cells?	stem cells from embryos that can differentiate into any specialised cell
5	Where are embryonic stem cells found?	early human embryos (usually from spare embryos from fertility clinics)
6	What is therapeutic cloning?	patient's cells are used to create an early embryo clone of themselves – stem cells from the 'embryo' can then be used to treat the patient's medical conditions
7	Give one advantage of using therapeutic cloning.	stem cells from the 'embryo' are not rejected when transplanted because they have the same genes as the patient
8	Give one advantage of using adult stem cells.	fewer ethical issues as obtained from adults who can consent to their use
9	Give two disadvantages of using adult stem cells.	• can take a long time for a suitable donor to be found • can only differentiate into some specialised cell types, so treat fewer diseases
10	Give two advantages of using embryonic stem cells.	• can differentiate into any specialised cell, so can be used to treat many diseases • easier to obtain as they can be taken from spare embryos from fertility clinics
11	Give two disadvantages of using embryonic stem cells.	• ethical issues surrounding their use, as every embryo is a potential life • potential risks involved with treatments, such as transfer of viral infections
12	What are plant meristems?	area where rapid cell division occurs in the tips of roots and shoots
13	Give two advantages of using plant meristems to clone plants.	• rare species can be cloned to protect them from extinction • plants with special features (e.g., disease resistance) can be cloned to produce many copies
14	Give one disadvantage of using plant meristems to clone plants.	no genetic variation, so, for example, an entire cloned crop could be destroyed by a disease
15	What is cell division by mitosis?	body cells divide to form two identical daughter cells
16	What is the purpose of mitosis?	growth and repair of cells, asexual reproduction
17	What happens during the first stage of the cell cycle?	cell grows bigger, chromosomes duplicate, number of sub-cellular structures (e.g., ribosomes and mitochondria) increases
18	What happens during mitosis?	one set of chromosomes is pulled to each end of the cell and the nucleus divides
19	What happens during the third stage of the cell cycle?	the cytoplasm and cell membrane divide, forming two identical daughter cells

Now go back and use the questions below to check your knowledge from previous chapters.

B3

Previous questions | Answers

#	Question	Answer
1	Where is DNA found in animal and plant cells?	in the nucleus
2	What are two types of eukaryotic cell?	animal and plant
3	What is the function of the cell membrane?	controls movement of substances into and out of the cell
4	What is the function of mitochondria?	site of respiration to release energy for the cell
5	What is the function of chloroplasts?	contain chlorophyll to absorb light energy for photosynthesis
6	What is the function of the cell wall?	strengthens and supports the cell
7	What is diffusion?	net movement of particles from an area of high concentration to an area of low concentration along a concentration gradient – this is a passive process (does not require energy from respiration)
8	What is osmosis?	diffusion of water from a dilute solution to a concentrated solution through a partially permeable membrane

Maths skills

Practise your maths skills using the worked example and practice questions below.

Converting units

The size of a cell or organelle is most often shown in millimetres (mm), micrometres (μm), or nanometres (nm). You may be asked to convert between mm, μm, and nm. If you are converting from a smaller unit to a larger unit, your number should get smaller. If you are converting a larger unit to a smaller unit, the number should get bigger.

Worked example

- to convert mm to μm: multiply the mm reading by 1000
- to convert μm to nm: multiply the μm reading by 1000
- to convert nm into μm: divide the reading by 1000
- to convert μm into mm: divide the reading by 1000

Cell	Size in mm	Size in μm	Size in nm
red blood cell	7 ÷ 1000 = 0.007	7	7 × 1000 = 7000
leaf cell	0.06	0.06 × 1000 = 60	60 × 1000 = 60 000
egg cell	100 ÷ 1000 = 0.1	100 000 ÷ 1000 = 100	100 000

Practice

Convert the following sizes to complete the table.

Structure	Size in mm	Size in μm	Size in nm
ant	3		
human hair		100	
palisade leaf cell		70	
plant cell ribosome			20
HIV virus			100
egg cell mitochondrion	0.002		

B3 Retrieval 25

Practice

Exam-style questions

01 **Figure 1** shows some plant cells undergoing mitosis.

Figure 1

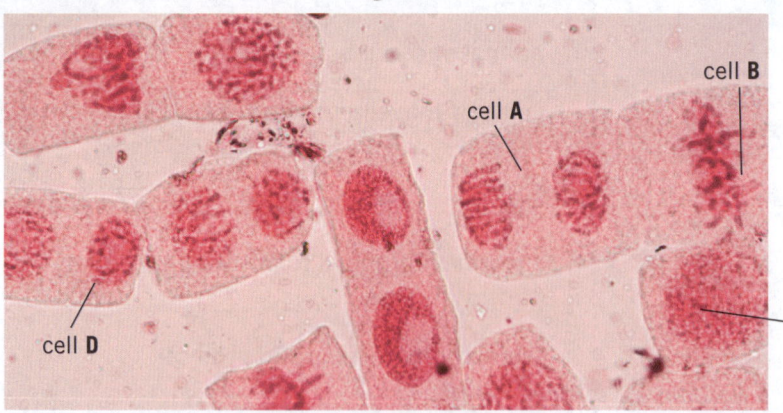

01.1 Identify the statement that best describes mitosis. **[1 mark]**

Tick **one** box.

process by which cells divide to produce two different cells ☐

process by which cells divide to produce two identical cells ☐

process by which cells divide to produce four different cells ☐

process by which cells divide to produce four identical cells ☐

> **Exam Tip**
> The way that I remember this is:
> mi**T**osis
> **W**
> **O**

01.2 **Table 1** shows four main steps in cell division.

Complete **Table 1** to identify the cell from **Figure 1** that is undergoing each step. **[3 marks]**

Table 1

Step	Description	Cell in Figure 1
1	cell is growing and the DNA is replicating	
2	chromosomes line up in the middle of the cell	
3	one set of chromosomes is pulled to each end of the cell	
4	two nuclei are formed	

> **Exam Tip**
> In **Figure 1** the DNA and chromosomes are stained in dark pink.

01.3 The final step in cell division is not shown in **Figure 1**.
Describe what takes place in this final step. **[2 marks]**

_____

_____

_____

26 B3 Cell division

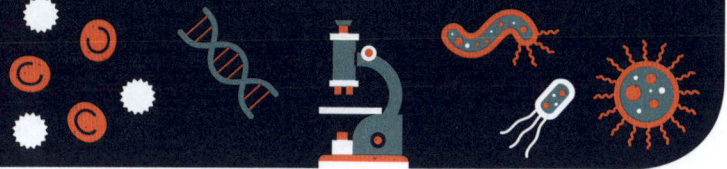

Paper 1 **B3**

02 Stem cells have the potential to treat many diseases such as diabetes.

Patients with Type 1 diabetes have to inject themselves regularly with insulin as their cells cannot make this hormone. Scientists are hopeful that stem cells could one day be used to treat Type 1 diabetes.

02.1 Circle the appropriate bold words to complete this description of a stem cell. **[2 marks]**

Stem cells are **differentiated / undifferentiated** cells. They have the potential to form other types of cell by the process of **differentiation / mitosis**.

! **Exam Tip**

Even if you're not sure of the first answer, you can try and do the second one.

02.2 Suggest the role that stem cells could play in a diabetic person's body. **[1 mark]**

_____

02.3 In 2008, a small scientific study was carried out where patients with Type 1 diabetes were treated using adult stem cells harvested from their own body.

Draw **two** lines from each type of stem cell to the correct features. **[4 marks]**

Type of stem cell	Feature
adult stem cells	found in embryos
embryonic stem cells	found in bone marrow
	can produce certain cell types in the body
	can produce all cell types in the body

! **Exam Tip**

You need four lines in total for this question:
1 Where are adult stem cells found?
2 Where are embryonic stem cells found?
3 What do adult stem cells produce?
4 What do embryonic stem cells produce?

02.4 Suggest **one** advantage of using stem cells from the actual patient instead of using stem cells from a donor. **[1 mark]**

_____
_____

02.5 Suggest **one** disadvantage of using stem cells to treat diabetes. **[1 mark]**

_____
_____

03 The nucleus of a cell contains genetic material.

03.1 Draw **one** line from each genetic term to its definition. **[2 marks]**

Genetic term	Definition
gene	the chemical that makes up genetic material
DNA	a section of DNA that codes for a characteristic
chromosome	a long strand of DNA

> **! Exam Tip**
>
> It might help to start by finding that largest one first and work down to smallest – but make sure your answer starts with the smallest on the left, as the question asks for the structures to be ordered from smallest to largest.

03.2 Order the structures in the box from smallest to largest. **[3 marks]**

| chromosome | nucleus | gene | cell |

03.3 Complete the following sentence. **[1 mark]**

In body cells, _____ are normally found in pairs.

04 **Figure 2** represents the stages of the cell cycle in a human.

Figure 2

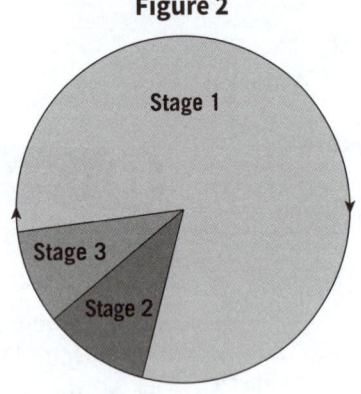

04.1 Identify the stage in the cycle representing mitosis. **[1 mark]**

04.2 Identify the stage in the cycle representing when cells are growing. **[1 mark]**

> **! Exam Tip**
>
> During the cell cycle, growing takes the longest amount of time. This is followed by mitosis.

04.3 Identify **two** subcellular structures from the list below that would be replicated during stage 1.

Choose **two** answers. **[2 marks]**

ribosomes   chloroplasts   muscle   mitochondria

> **! Exam Tip**
>
> The key to answering **04.3** is in the main body of the question: '...cell cycle in a *human*'.

28 B3 Cell division

B3

05 **Figure 3** shows how genetic material is arranged inside a cell.

05.1 Identify parts **A–C** in **Figure 3** using the words from the box.
[3 marks]

| gene | chromosome | nucleus | cytoplasm |

Figure 3

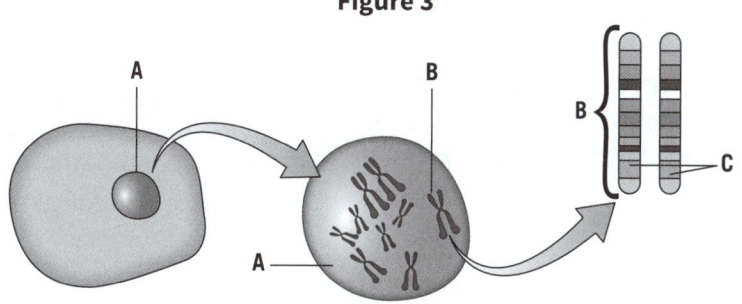

> **Exam Tip**
>
> As the images move from left to right they are getting magnified, so **A** in the middle image is a larger version of **A** in the left image.

05.2 Choose the correct term from the box to complete each sentence. Each word may be used once, more than once, or not at all. **[5 marks]**

| genes | chromosomes | ribosomes | DNA |
| nucleus | nuclear | characteristic |

Genetic material is stored in a sub-cellular structure called the

_____ .

The chemical that contains instructions for the organism is called

_____ .

Long strands of this chemical are called _____ .

_____ are sections of DNA. They hold information that codes for a particular _____ .

05.3 Write down how many copies of each chromosome a human body cell contains. **[1 mark]**

06 Cells in many areas of the human body undergo cell division.

06.1 Give **one** reason why cells need to divide. **[1 mark]**

06.2 The main steps in cell division are given in **Table 2**, but they are in the wrong order.

Number each sentence in **Table 2** to place the sentences into the correct order. The first step has been done for you. **[4 marks]**

Table 2

Step of cell division	Order
chromosomes line up in the middle of the cell	
two identical cells are formed	
DNA replicates	1
cell membrane divides	
one set of chromosomes is pulled to each end of the cell	
two nuclei are formed	

> **Exam Tip**
>
> For your revision you can write these steps out on pieces of paper and move them around until you're happy you've got the correct order.

06.3 Name the process by which body cells divide. **[1 mark]**

07 *Daphnia* are single celled organisms that live in water.

A scientist looks at some *Daphnia* through a microscope by placing some live *Daphnia* onto a slide.

07.1 Name the part of a microscope used to hold a microscope slide.

Choose **one** answer. **[1 mark]**

eyepiece lens   stage   focusing knob   objective lens

> **! Exam Tip**
>
> It doesn't matter if you don't know what *Daphnia* are, they are just the context for this question. Expect to come across some new names in biology as the exams will introduce new contexts to test you on.

07.2 The microscope is set to 20× magnification. The *Daphnia* measure 2 mm in diameter.

Calculate the observed size of the *Daphnia*. Use the equation:

$$\text{magnification} = \frac{\text{size of image}}{\text{size of real object}}$$

Choose **one** answer. **[1 mark]**

2 mm   0.1 mm   0.2 mm   40 mm

07.3 Draw **two** lines from each type of microscope to the correct characteristics. **[4 marks]**

Type of microscope	Characteristic
light microscope	greater magnification
electron microscope	lower magnification
	can observe living organisms
	can only observe dead organisms

> **! Exam Tip**
>
> You need to draw four lines in total – start by selecting which type of microscope has which magnification, then select which are used to observe dead or living organisms.

07.4 Give **one** reason why the scientist should not use an electron microscope to observe *Daphnia*. **[1 mark]**

08 All cells in the human body contain genetic information.

08.1 Complete the sentences.

The nucleus of a cell contains _____. It is arranged into long strands called _____.

These long strands contain a large number of _____ that code for specific characteristics.

08.2 Why is cell differentiation important in the development of an embryo into a baby? Choose **one** answer. **[1 mark]**

increase the number of cells

provide genetic variation from the parents

specialised cells make different parts of the body

08.3 Describe the main steps in mitosis. **[4 marks]**

09 Stem cells are found in both plants and animals.

09.1 Name the area in a plant where stem cells are located. **[1 mark]**

30   **B3 Cell division**

09.2 **Figure 4** shows a diagram of a root tip of a plant.
Identify the letter (**A–D**) in **Figure 4** indicating where stem cells are located in the root tip. **[1 mark]**

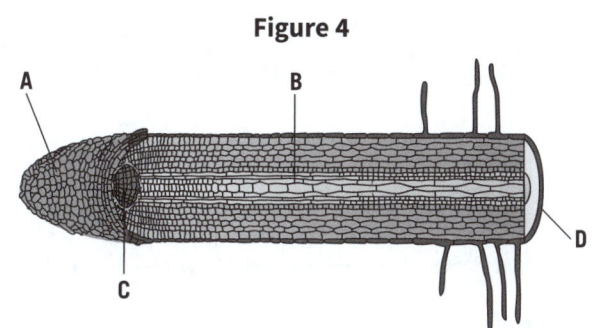

Figure 4

> **Exam Tip**
> Think about the function that stem cells perform in root tips.

09.3 Identify the sequence that correctly describes the steps plant stem cells go through to produce a root hair cell.
Choose **one** answer. **[1 mark]**

differentiation → DNA replication → elongation → mitosis
elongation → differentiation → DNA replication → mitosis
DNA replication → elongation → mitosis → differentiation
DNA replication → mitosis → elongation → differentiation

> **Exam Tip**
> Work through these slowly, crossing off any you know are incorrect, and hopefully that will only leave one answer.

09.4 Tick **one** box in each row of **Table 3** to identify the differences between plant and animal stem cell differentiation. **[2 marks]**

Table 3

Statement	Animal stem cells	Plant stem cells
differentiation occurs at a very early stage		
differentiation occurs throughout life		
differentiated cells produced are permanent		
differentiation can be reversed or changed		

10 A scientist takes a cutting from a plant.

10.1 Select the statement that best describes why the meristem in the cutting allows a new plant to grow.
Choose **one** answer. **[1 mark]**

meristems contain differentiated cells
meristems contain undifferentiated cells
meristems are where new roots form
meristems respond to light

10.2 Explain why this technique is a form of cloning. **[1 mark]**

10.3 Suggest **two** advantages of using this technique to produce new plants of this species, as opposed to letting the plant reproduce naturally. **[2 marks]**

> **Exam Tip**
> Remember to read the question fully – 10.3 is only asking about the advantages not the disadvantages.

Knowledge

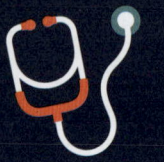

B4 Organisation in animals

There are five **levels of organisation** in living organisms:

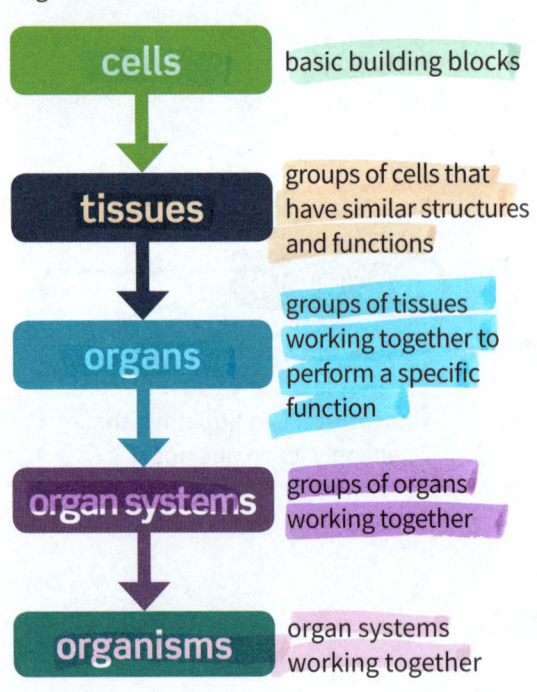

- **cells** — basic building blocks
- **tissues** — groups of cells that have similar structures and functions
- **organs** — groups of tissues working together to perform a specific function
- **organ systems** — groups of organs working together
- **organisms** — organ systems working together

Digestive system

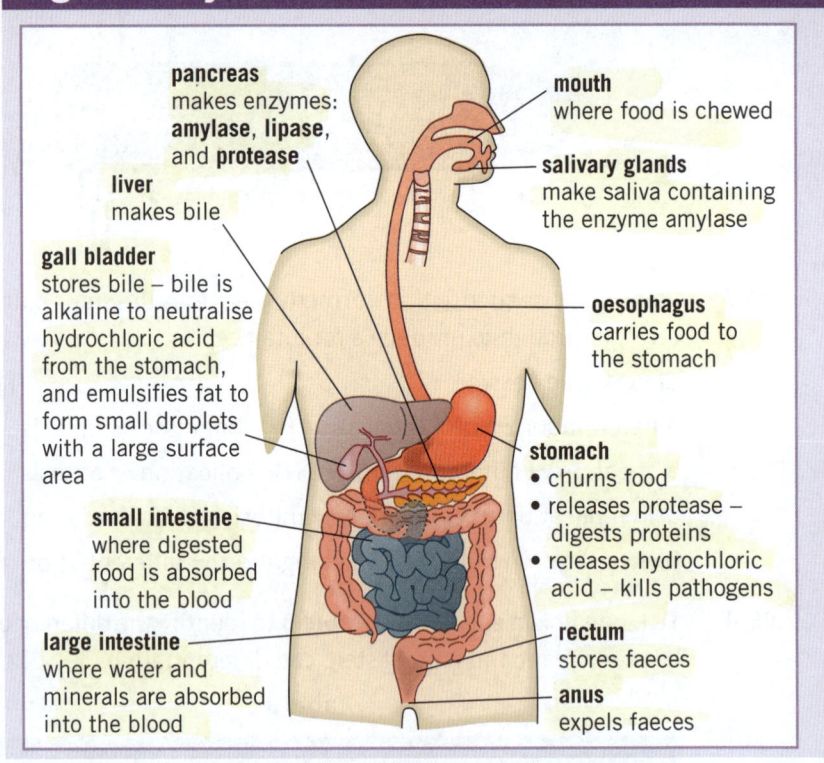

- **pancreas** makes enzymes: **amylase, lipase,** and **protease**
- **liver** makes bile
- **gall bladder** stores bile – bile is alkaline to neutralise hydrochloric acid from the stomach, and emulsifies fat to form small droplets with a large surface area
- **small intestine** where digested food is absorbed into the blood
- **large intestine** where water and minerals are absorbed into the blood
- **mouth** where food is chewed
- **salivary glands** make saliva containing the enzyme amylase
- **oesophagus** carries food to the stomach
- **stomach**
  - churns food
  - releases protease – digests proteins
  - releases hydrochloric acid – kills pathogens
- **rectum** stores faeces
- **anus** expels faeces

Lungs

When breathing in, air moves
1. into the body through the mouth and nose
2. down the trachea
3. into the **bronchi**
4. through the **bronchioles**
5. into the **alveoli** (air sacs).

Oxygen then diffuses into the blood in the network of **capillaries** over the surface of the alveoli.

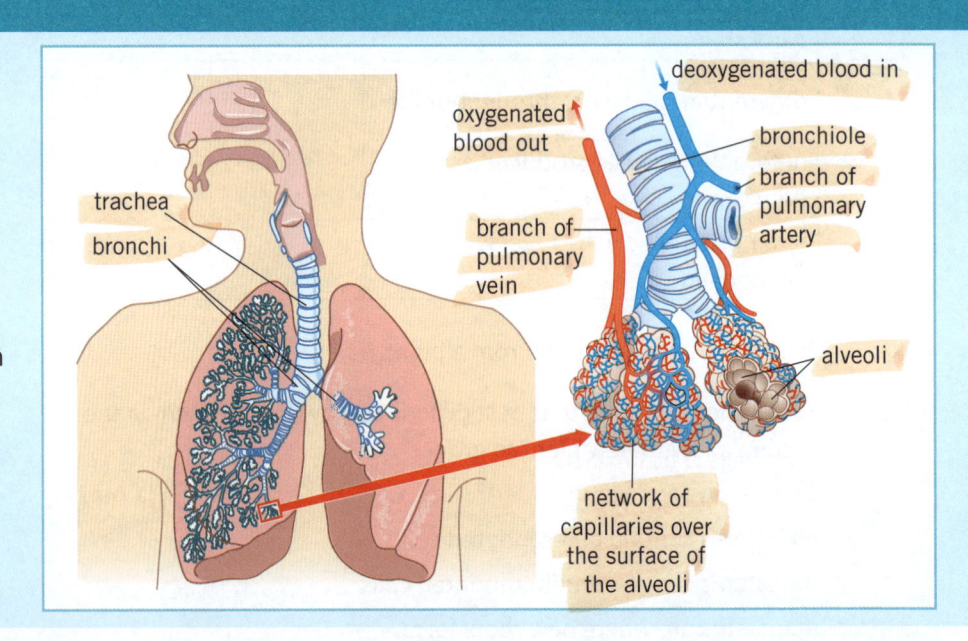

Labels: trachea, bronchi, oxygenated blood out, deoxygenated blood in, bronchiole, branch of pulmonary artery, branch of pulmonary vein, alveoli, network of capillaries over the surface of the alveoli

The circulatory system

Blood is a tissue made up of four main components

- **red blood cells** – bind to oxygen and transport it around the body
- **plasma** – transports substances and blood cells around the body
- **platelets** – form blood clots to create barriers to infections
- **white blood cells** – part of the immune system to defend the body against pathogens

32 B4 Organisation in animals

B4

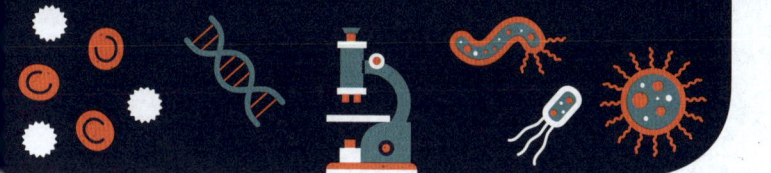

Blood vessels

The structure of each blood vessel relates to its function.

Vessel	Function	Structure	Diagram
artery	• carries blood *away from* the heart • under high pressure	• thick, muscular, and elastic walls • the walls can stretch and withstand high pressure • small lumen	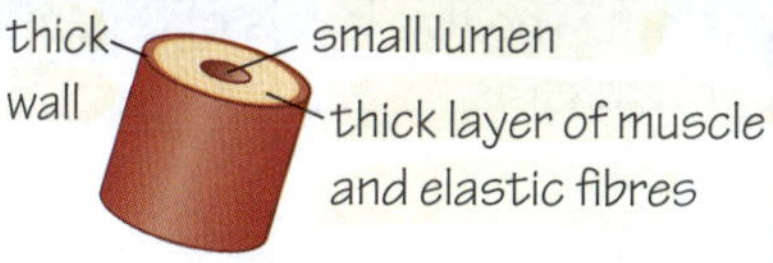 thick wall, small lumen, thick layer of muscle and elastic fibres
vein	• carries blood *to* the heart • under low pressure	• have valves to stop blood flowing the wrong way • thin walls • large lumen	 relatively thin wall, large lumen, often has valves
capillary	• carries blood to tissues and cells • connects arteries and veins	• one-cell-thick – short diffusion distance for substances to move between the blood and tissues (e.g., oxygen into cells and carbon dioxide out) • very narrow lumen	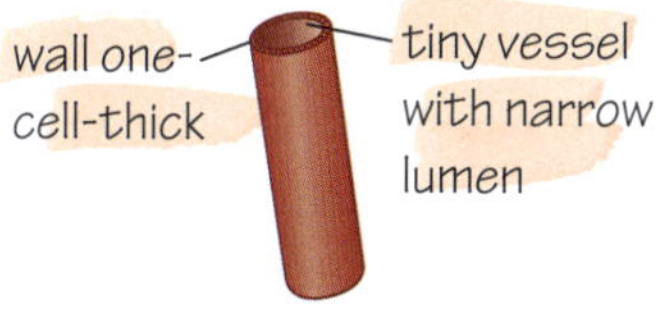 wall one-cell-thick, tiny vessel with narrow lumen

The heart

The heart is the organ that pumps blood around your body. It is made from **cardiac muscle** tissue, which is supplied with oxygen by the **coronary artery**.

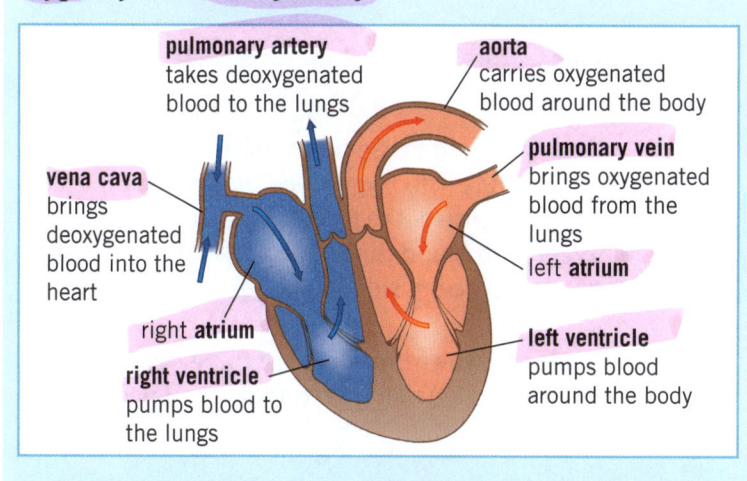

pulmonary artery takes deoxygenated blood to the lungs

aorta carries oxygenated blood around the body

pulmonary vein brings oxygenated blood from the lungs

vena cava brings deoxygenated blood into the heart

left **atrium**

right **atrium**

left ventricle pumps blood around the body

right ventricle pumps blood to the lungs

Heart rate is controlled by a group of cells in the right atrium that generate electrical impulses, acting as a pacemaker. Artificial pacemakers can be used to control irregular heartbeats.

Double circulatory system

The human circulatory system is described as a **double circulatory system** because blood passes through the heart twice for every circuit around the body:

- the right ventricle pumps blood to the lungs where gas exchange takes place
- the left ventricle pumps blood around the rest of the body.

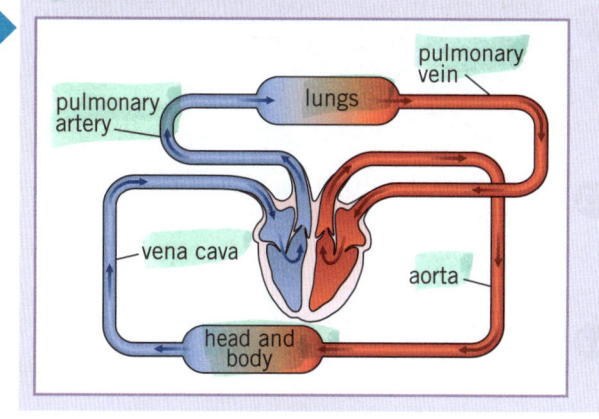

pulmonary artery, lungs, pulmonary vein, vena cava, aorta, head and body

Key terms

Make sure you can write a definition for these key terms.

alveoli   amylase   aorta   artery   atrium   bronchi   bronchiole   capillary   cardiac muscle
coronary artery   double circulatory system   lipase   organ   organ system   plasma   platelet
protease   pulmonary artery   pulmonary vein   tissue   vein   vena cava   ventricle

B4 Knowledge

Retrieval

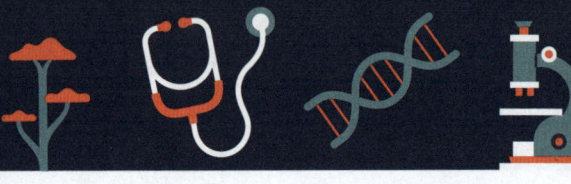

Learn the answers to the questions below, then cover the answers column with a piece of paper and write as many as you can. Check and repeat.

	B4 questions		Answers
1	Name the five levels of organisation in living organisms.	Put paper here	cells → tissues → organs → organ systems → organisms
2	What is a tissue?	Put paper here	a group of cells with similar structures and functions
3	What is an organ?	Put paper here	a group of tissues working together to perform a specific function
4	What is the function of bile in digestion?	Put paper here	neutralise hydrochloric acid from the stomach and emulsify fat to form small droplets with a large surface area
5	What is the function of saliva in digestion?	Put paper here	lubrication to help swallowing – contains amylase to break down starch
6	Name three enzymes produced in the pancreas.	Put paper here	amylase, protease, lipase
7	Name the four main components of blood.	Put paper here	red blood cells, white blood cells, plasma, platelets
8	What is the function of platelets?	Put paper here	form blood clots – prevent the loss of blood and stop wounds becoming infected
9	Name the substances transported in the blood plasma.	Put paper here	hormones, proteins, urea, carbon dioxide, glucose
10	Why is the human circulatory system described as a double circulatory system?	Put paper here	blood passes through the heart twice for every circuit around the body – deoxygenated blood is pumped from the right side of the heart to the lungs, and the oxygenated blood that returns from the lungs is pumped from the left side of the heart to the body
11	How does the structure of an artery relate to its function?	Put paper here	carries blood away from the heart under high pressure – has a small lumen and thick, elasticated walls that can stretch
12	How does the structure of a vein relate to its function?	Put paper here	carries blood back to the heart at low pressure – doesn't need thick, elasticated walls, but has valves to prevent blood flowing the wrong way
13	How does the structure of a capillary relate to its function?	Put paper here	carries blood to cells and tissues – has a one-cell-thick wall to provide a short diffusion distance
14	List the structures air passes through when breathing in.	Put paper here	mouth/nose → trachea → bronchi → bronchioles → alveoli

B4 Organisation in animals

Now go back and use the questions below to check your knowledge from previous chapters.

B4

Previous questions | Answers

	Previous questions	Answers
1	What is the purpose of active transport in the small intestine?	sugars can be absorbed when the concentration of the sugar in the small intestine is lower than the concentration of the sugar in the blood
2	What is therapeutic cloning?	patient's cells are used to create an early embryo clone of themselves – stem cells from the embryo can then be used to treat the patient's medical conditions
3	What is a stem cell?	undifferentiated cell that can differentiate into one or more specialised cell types
4	Give one disadvantage of using plant meristems to clone plants.	no genetic variation, so, for example, an entire cloned crop could be destroyed by a disease
5	What is active transport?	movement of particles against a concentration gradient – from a dilute solution to a more concentrated solution – using energy from respiration

Required practical skills

Practise answering questions on the required practicals using the example below. You need to be able to apply your skills and knowledge to other practicals too.

Food tests

There are different ways to test for different compounds found in food:

- ethanol test for lipids (fats) – colour change from colourless to cloudy white if present
- Benedict's test for sugars – colour change from blue to red if present
- iodine test for starch (carbohydrates) – colour change from brown to blue-black if present
- Biuret reagent test for protein – colour change from blue to purple if present.

You need to be able to identify and describe the correct method, and results, for each test.

Worked example

A student wanted to test a sample for the presence of protein using Biuret reagent. Write a risk assessment for this activity.

1 Write down general safety practices in labs:
- wear goggles to protect your eyes
- wash hands at the end of the practical
- clear up any spills quickly
- do not eat any of the food.

2 Write down what things could hurt you in the practical, and how they could hurt you:
- Biuret reagent – irritant
- glass – can break
- pipette – can poke you in the eyes.

3 Write down how you can prevent these hurting you:
- wash hands after touching Biuret reagent, and if it is ingested or it gets into the eyes inform a teacher immediately
- if glass is broken inform a teacher immediately
- point pipettes downwards.

Practice

1 A student picked up solution A and added it to a sample of food. Solution A was blue and turned purple after adding it to the food.

Name solution A and identify the food type present in the sample.

2 Benedict's test for sugar requires the solution to be heated. One way to do this is by heating the test tube in a beaker of water using a Bunsen burner.

Give an alternative method of heating the solution.

3 When testing a sample for protein in a test tube, a student found that the top of the sample tested positive whereas the bottom did not.

Give a reason for this result.

B4 Retrieval 35

Practice

Exam-style questions

01 An athlete's lung volume was measured over a period of time. The data for one respiratory cycle is shown in **Figure 1**.

Figure 1

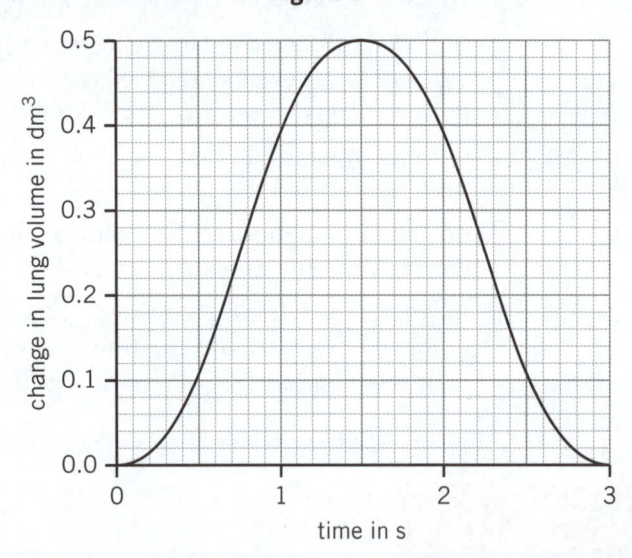

01.1 Describe how the athlete's lung volume changes over the three-second period shown. **[2 marks]**

_____
_____
_____

> **Exam Tip**
>
> For this question you need to use the data and describe the shape of the line and how it changes.

01.2 Use **Figure 1** to determine the volume of air taken in when the athlete inhales. **[1 mark]**

_____ dm^3

01.3 The athlete's total lung volume before inhalation was 5.00 dm^3. Calculate their total lung volume after inhalation. **[2 marks]**

_____ dm^3

01.4 Calculate how many respiratory cycles will take place in 60 s. **[3 marks]**

_____ cycles

36   B4 Organisation in animals

Paper 1 — B4

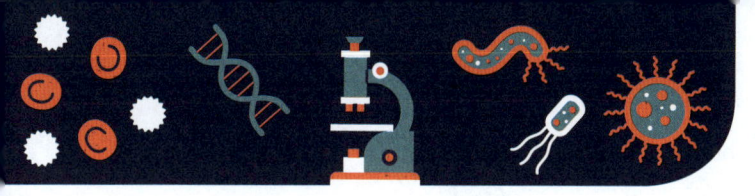

01.5 Select which of the following changes take place in the athlete's chest cavity between 0 and 1.5 s. **[2 marks]**

Tick **two** boxes.

rib cage moves in and down ☐

rib cage moves up and out ☐

diaphragm contracts and moves down ☐

diaphragm relaxes and moves up ☐

> **Exam Tip**
> Read the question carefully, 01.5 only refers to the first part of the graph not all of it.

02 A student carried out a number of food tests on an unknown sample. Their results are shown in **Table 1**.

Table 1

Nutrient tested for	Reagent used	Result
starch	Y	yellow–orange
sugar	Benedict's solution	blue
protein	Biuret reagent	purple
X	ethanol	cloudy white layer formed

> **Exam Tip**
> A reagent is a chemical or solution that is used in a practical.

02.1 Identify nutrient **X** that is detected by adding ethanol to the food sample. **[1 mark]**

_____

02.2 Identify reagent **Y** that is used to test a food sample for starch. **[1 mark]**

_____

02.3 Biuret reagent is corrosive.

Suggest **one** safety precaution that the student should have taken when using Biuret reagent. **[1 mark]**

_____

> **Exam Tip**
> Make sure your suggestion is related to the practical.

02.4 The student thought that the food sample contained starch, sugar and protein. Is the student correct?

Circle **one** answer for each of the statements below. **[3 marks]**

The food sample contains starch.   yes   no

The food sample contains sugar.   yes   no

The food sample contains protein.   yes   no

03 **Figure 2** represents cross-sectional areas through the three main types of blood vessel.

Figure 2

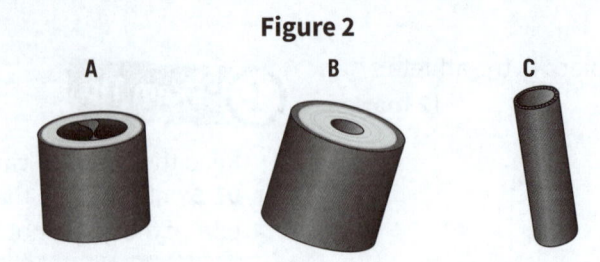

A B C

03.1 Identify which blood vessel in **Figure 2** represents an artery. **[1 mark]**

03.2 Explain **one** way arteries are adapted for their function. **[2 marks]**

03.3 Blood in the arteries is usually bright red because it is full of oxygen.

Identify the artery where this is **not** true.

Choose **one** answer. **[1 mark]**

aorta   vena cava   pulmonary artery   coronary artery

03.4 Give a reason for your answer to **03.3**. **[1 mark]**

03.5 Describe **two** reasons why it is important that blood is transported to every cell in the body. **[2 marks]**

> **Exam Tip**
> Think about the function of the artery and link it to the width of the walls – that should help you identify the correct vessel.

04 **Figure 3** shows the main structures in the human gas exchange system.

04.1 Use words from the following box to label the structures in **Figure 3**. **[4 marks]**

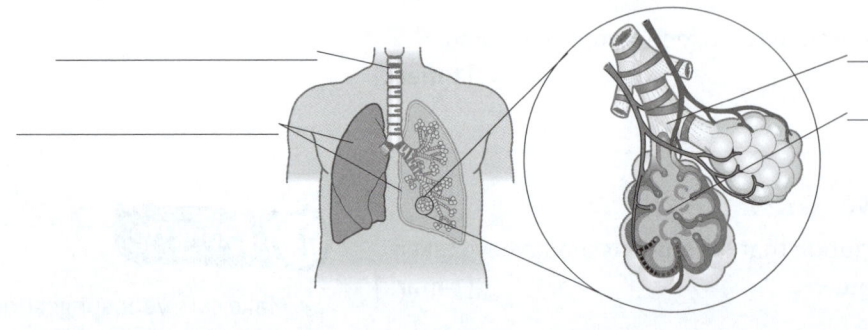

| diaphragm | lung | heart | alveolus |
| trachea | oesophagus | bronchiole | |

Figure 3

04.2 Name the structure that protects the lungs from damage. **[1 mark]**

04.3 The alveoli are adapted to allow as much oxygen to enter the body as possible.

Describe **two** ways the alveoli are adapted for gas exchange. **[2 marks]**

04.4 Describe the changes that take place in the chest cavity when a person breathes in. **[3 marks]**

> **Exam Tip**
> Use **Figure 3** to see the adaptations of this surface.

38 B4 Organisation in animals

05 The digestive system is made up of a number of organs that work together.

05.1 Circle the correct term to complete the sentence. **[1 mark]**

The digestive system is an example of **a tissue / an organism / an organ system**.

05.2 **Figure 4** shows some organs from the digestive system.

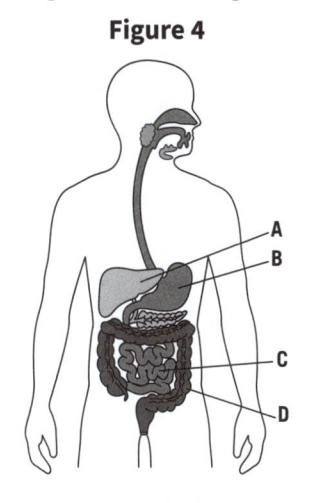

Figure 4

> **Exam Tip**
>
> To help you revise the digestive system, annotate **Figure 4** with the names of each organ, the function of each organ, and what digestive enzymes are produced or act there.

Choose the correct organs from the box to identify organs **A** and **C** from **Figure 4**. **[2 marks]**

| small intestine | stomach | liver | large intestine |

05.3 Identify **one** organ from **Figure 4** that is responsible for absorbing water from undigested food. **[1 mark]**

05.4 The stomach is made up of a number of tissues.

Draw **one** line from each type of stomach tissue to its function. **[2 marks]**

Stomach tissue	Function
muscular tissue	churns the food and digestive juices of the stomach together
glandular tissue	covers the inside and outside of the stomach
epithelial tissue	produces the digestive juices

06 A student was provided with an unknown food sample and the following apparatus:
- test tubes (in a test-tube rack)
- Benedict's solution
- water bath
- Biuret reagent
- iodine
- ethanol.

The food sample had been ground into a powder using a pestle and mortar.

Explain how the student could test the food sample for the presence of starch, sugar, fats, and protein. **[6 marks]**

07 Multicellular organisms have five levels of organisation.

07.1 Draw **one** line from each level of organisation to its definition. **[4 marks]**

Level of organisation	Definition
cell	group of organs working together to perform a function
organism	group of similar cells working together
tissue	group of tissues working together to perform a function
organ	building blocks of life
organ system	group of organ systems working together

> **Exam Tip**
> Make sure your lines are clear, and be careful when rubbing out wrong answers.

07.2 Identify **one** function of the circulatory system in the human body. Choose **one** answer. **[1 mark]**

to transport materials around the body in the blood

to take in carbon dioxide and remove oxygen

to produce new organisms

07.3 The digestive system is responsible for breaking down and absorbing food.
Identify the **two** organs found in this system. **[2 marks]**

lungs   liver   brain   stomach

08 **Figure 5** shows a photograph of a blood smear taken using a light microscope.

Figure 5

[Figure 5: blood smear with labels A, B, C]

> **Exam Tip**
> When blood smears are stained, red blood cells stay red but white blood cells often look pink or purple.

08.1 Identify the label pointing to a white blood cell in **Figure 5**. **[1 mark]**

08.2 Draw **one** line from each component of blood to its function. **[3 marks]**

Blood component	Function
red blood cells	fight disease
white blood cells	transport oxygen
plasma	transports blood cells
platelets	clot the blood

B4 Organisation in animals

08.3 Blood is an example of a tissue. Suggest why. [1 mark]

08.4 Describe **one** way red blood cells are adapted to perform their function. [1 mark]

09 Below is a list of structures found in the human body.

| brain | nervous system | sperm | egg |
| blood | circulatory system | uterus | heart |

09.1 Choose a correct structure from the box to identify **one** example for each of the following statements. Each term may be used once, more than once, or not at all. [4 marks]

an example of a cell

an example of an organ

an example of a tissue

the organ system that transfers impulses

> **Exam Tip**
>
> There are a few different correct options here, so don't fret if you're trying to decide between two answers as they might both be right.

09.2 The human body has five levels of organisation.

Identify the correct order of these levels of organisation in order of size, from smallest to biggest. Two have been done for you. [2 marks]

| organ | ~~cell~~ | tissue | ~~organism~~ | organ system |

cell < _____ < _____ < _____ < organism

09.3 Describe what is meant by a tissue. [1 mark]

10 **Figure 6** shows a cross-section through the human heart.

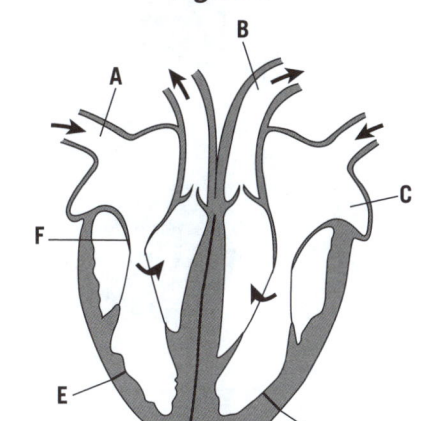

Figure 6

magnification: × 0.75

> **Exam Tip**
>
> The first thing you need to do when you see an image of a heart is to write which side of the heart is the right side and which is the left – remember that this is the opposite way around to how it looks on the page.

10.1 Identify which label in **Figure 6** is pointing to the left atrium. [1 mark]

10.2 Name the blood vessels labelled **A** and **B**. [2 marks]

10.3 Identify and describe the function of part **F**. [2 marks]

10.4 Humans have a double circulatory system.

Describe what this means. [2 marks]

Knowledge

B5 Enzymes

Enzymes

Enzymes are large proteins that **catalyse** (speed up) reactions. Enzymes are not changed in the reactions they catalyse.

Lock and key theory

This is a simple model of how enzymes work:

1. The enzyme's **active site** (where the reaction occurs) is a specific shape.
2. The enzyme (the lock) will only catalyse a specific reaction because the **substrate** (the key) fits into its active site.
3. At the active site, enzymes can break molecules down into smaller ones or bind small molecules together to form larger ones.
4. When the products have been released, the enzyme's active site can accept another substrate molecule.

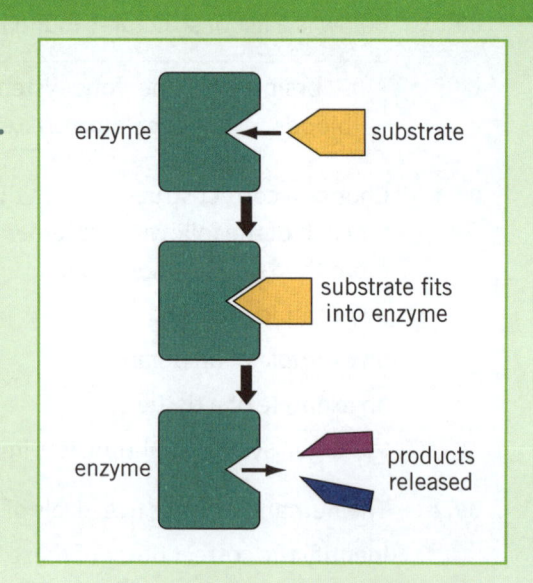

The effect of temperature on enzymes

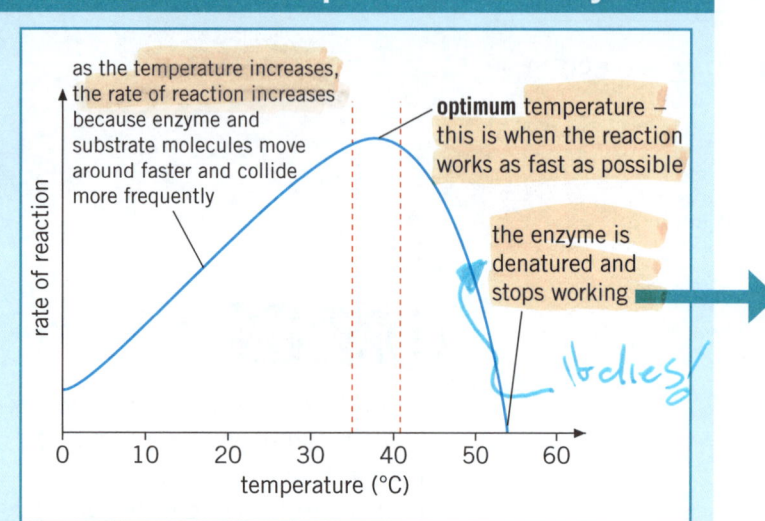

- as the temperature increases, the rate of reaction increases because enzyme and substrate molecules move around faster and collide more frequently
- **optimum** temperature – this is when the reaction works as fast as possible
- the enzyme is denatured and stops working

(graph: rate of reaction vs temperature (°C), 0–60)

Denaturation

At extremes of pH or at very high temperatures the shape of an enzyme's active site can change.

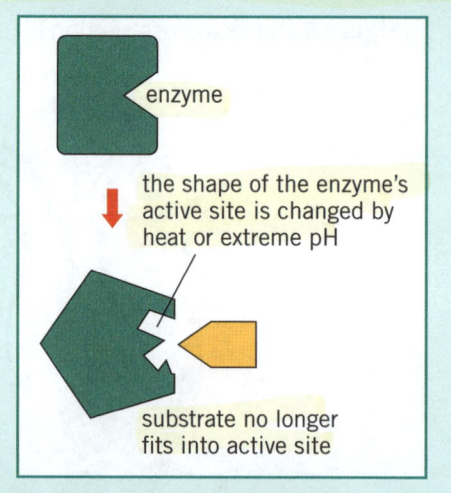

- the shape of the enzyme's active site is changed by heat or extreme pH
- substrate no longer fits into active site

The substrate can no longer bind to the active site, so the enzyme cannot catalyse the reaction – the enzyme has been **denatured**.

> **Revision tip**
>
> **Remember** This is one area where biology and chemistry overlap. The first part of the graph can be explained by the collision theory you have learnt in your chemistry lessons.

Key terms

Make sure you can write a definition for these key terms.

active site   amylase   catalyse   denatured   enzyme

B5

Digestive enzymes

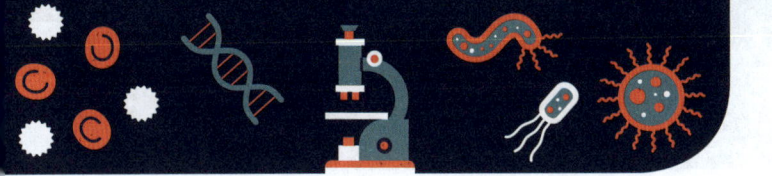

Digestive enzymes convert food into small, soluble molecules that can then be absorbed into the bloodstream. These are summarised in the table below.

These products of digestion can be used to build new carbohydrates, lipids, and proteins.

Some of the glucose produced is used in respiration.

Enzyme	Sites of production	Reaction catalysed
amylase	• salivary glands • pancreas • small intestine	starch → simple sugars
proteases	• stomach • pancreas • small intestine	proteins → amino acids
lipases	• pancreas • small intestine	lipids → fatty acids and glycerol

The effect of pH on enzymes

Different enzymes have different optimum pH values.

This allows enzymes to be adapted to work well in environments with different pH values. Since parts of the digestive system differ greatly in pH, the enzymes that work there have different optimum pH values.

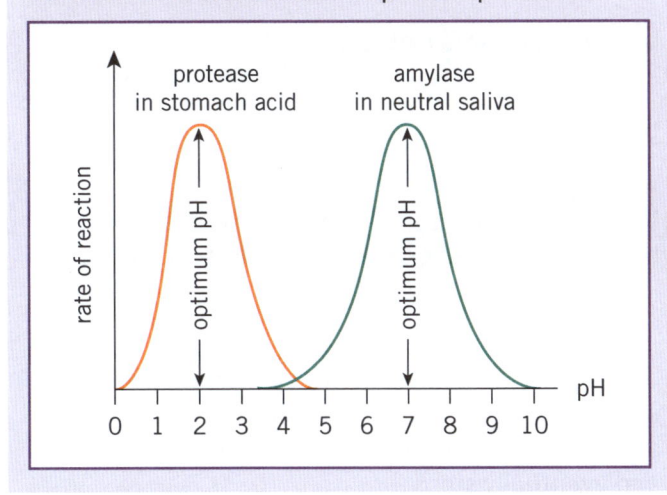

[Graph showing rate of reaction vs pH: protease in stomach acid peaks at optimum pH around 2; amylase in neutral saliva peaks at optimum pH around 7]

Revision tip

Practice Enzyme activity graphs are common in exam questions. Make sure you can draw them, recognise their shapes, and explain fully what is going on in each part of the graph.

Remember When you're talking about enzymes, it is very important that you use the correct terms. When the active site breaks down, an enzyme becomes denatured – lots of students write that the enzyme has died, or has been killed. This is incorrect and will lose you marks in the exam.

Practice The lock and key mechanism also applies when joining two substrates together. The mechanism is very similar to what you have already covered and this could be a good opportunity to show your knowledge in a new context.

lipase   F a G   lock and key   spesil reatcn   optimum   reches apex   protease   Protins   substrate

B5 Knowledge   43

Retrieval

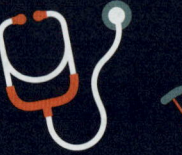

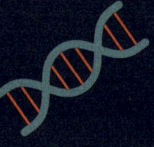

Learn the answers to the questions below, then cover the answers column with a piece of paper and write as many as you can. Check and repeat.

B5 questions | Answers

#	Question	Answer
1	What are enzymes? *Proteins*	protein molecules that catalyse specific reactions in organisms
2	What does catalyse mean? *Speed up*	speed up a reaction
3	Why are enzymes described as specific?	each enzyme only catalyses a specific reaction, because the active site only fits together with certain substrates (like a lock and key)
4	Describe the function of amylase.	to break down starch into simple sugars
5	Where is amylase produced?	salivary glands, pancreas, and small intestine
6	Describe the function of proteases.	to break down proteins into amino acids
7	Where are proteases produced?	stomach, pancreas, and small intestine
8	Describe the function of lipases.	to break down lipids into fatty acids and glycerol
9	Where are lipases produced?	pancreas and small intestine
10	What are two factors that affect the rate of activity of an enzyme?	temperature and pH
11	What does denatured mean?	the shape of an enzyme's active site is changed by high temperatures or an extreme pH, so it can no longer bind with the substrate
12	Describe the effect of temperature on enzyme activity.	as temperature increases, rate of reaction increases until it reaches the optimum for enzyme activity – above this temperature, enzyme activity decreases and eventually stops
13	Describe the effect of pH on enzyme activity.	different enzymes each have a different optimum pH at which their activity is greatest – at a pH much lower or higher than this, enzyme activity decreases and stops
14	Why do different digestive enzymes have different optimum pHs?	different parts of the digestive system have very different pHs – the stomach is strongly acidic and the pH in the small intestine is close to neutral

B5 Enzymes

Now go back and use the questions below to check your knowledge from previous chapters.

B5

Previous questions | Answers

#	Previous questions	Answers
1	What is the function of saliva in digestion?	lubrication to help swallowing, contains amylase to break down starch
2	Why is active transport needed in plant roots?	concentration of mineral ions in the soil is lower than inside the root hair cells – the mineral ions must move against the concentration gradient to enter the root hair cells
3	What happens during mitosis?	one set of chromosomes is pulled to each end of the cell and the nucleus divides
4	Where are embryonic stem cells found?	early human embryos (usually from spare embryos from fertility clinics)
5	How does the structure of an artery relate to its function?	carries blood away from the heart under high pressure – has a small lumen and thick, elasticated walls that can stretch
6	What is the function of a nerve cell?	carries electrical impulses around the body
7	What are plant meristems?	area where rapid cell division occurs in the tips of roots and shoots
8	Name the five levels of organisation in living organisms.	cells → tissues → organs → organ systems → organisms

Required practical skills

Practise answering questions on the required practicals using the example below. You need to be able to apply your skills and knowledge to other practicals too.

Rate of enzyme reaction | Worked example | Practice

Rate of enzyme reaction

This practical tests your ability to accurately measure and record time, temperature, volume, and pH.

You will need to know how to find the rate of a reaction by using a continuous sampling technique to measure the time taken for an indicator to change colour.

You will be familiar with measuring the effect of pH on the rate of reaction of amylase digesting starch, using iodine as an indicator. However, you need to be able to apply the methods of this practical to different enzymes and substrates.

Worked example

A class carried out an investigation into the effect that pH has on the ability of amylase to break down carbohydrates. They timed how long it took for the amylase to break down starch at different pH values between 5 and 11.

Suggest the results the class would observe.

The optimal pH of amylase is around 7, so the time taken to break down starch will be shortest at pH 7. At pH values lower than 7 it will take longer to break down the starch – it will take the longest time at pH 5, decreasing in time taken until pH 7. Above pH 7 it will take a longer time to break down the starch, and the amylase may stop breaking down the starch entirely at pH 11.

Practice

1 A student wanted to repeat the experiment on the following day to compare their results.

Suggest why using the same enzyme solution on two different days would not give comparable results.

2 Suggest how the class might have timed how long it took for the amylase to break down the starch.

3 Give one variable the class must control for this experiment to be valid.

B5 Retrieval   45

Practice

Exam-style questions

01 Enzymes play an important role in digestion.

01.1 Draw **one** line from each type of enzyme to the nutrient it breaks down. **[2 marks]**

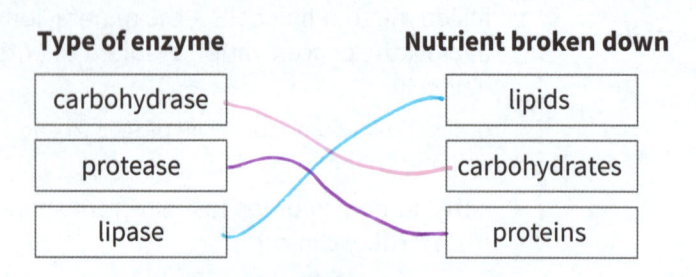

Type of enzyme	Nutrient broken down
carbohydrase	lipids
protease	carbohydrates
lipase	proteins

carbohydrase — carbohydrates; protease — proteins (lines drawn to lipids and crossed)

> **Exam Tip**
> The names of the enzyme are very similar to the names of the nutrients they break down.

01.2 Amylase is an enzyme that breaks down starch.

Identify **one** product that is produced when starch is broken down. **[1 mark]**

Tick **one** box.

- amino acids ☐
- glycerol ☐
- fatty acids ☐
- glucose ✓

01.3 Enzymes are described as catalysts.

Describe **one** feature of a catalyst. **[1 mark]**

a catalyst speeds reactions up

02 Many of the human body's enzymes are involved in digestion.

02.1 Choose words from the box below to complete the sentences on digestive enzymes. **[4 marks]**

| reaction | active | increase | decrease |
| specific | catalysts | substance | |

Enzymes are biological ___catalysts___ .

They ___increase___ the rate of a reaction without being used up.

Enzymes are ___substance___ to one type of reaction.

The substrate is a particular shape that fits into the enzyme's ___active___ site.

> **Exam Tip**
> This question starts with the definition of an enzyme – this is a very important definition to learn.

B5 Enzymes

Paper 1 B5

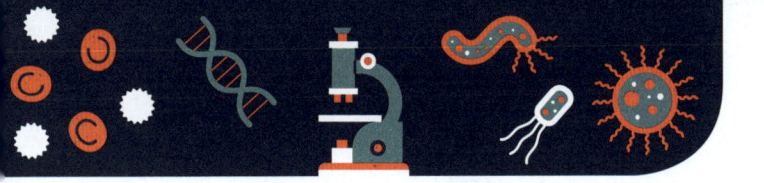

02.2 Identify which substrate (**A**, **B**, **C**, or **D**) the enzyme would break down in **Figure 1**. [1 mark]

_____

Figure 1

enzyme

substrates   A   B   C   D

> **Exam Tip**
> Look at the shape of the active site of the enzyme (in black) and see if any of the substrates (in white) have a corresponding shape that would fit in the gap.

02.3 Temperature affects the rate of enzyme-controlled reactions.

Name **one** other factor that affects the rate of an enzyme controlled reaction. [1 mark]

different ph scales

03 Lipase is an enzyme that breaks down lipids.

03.1 Name the products when a lipid is broken down. [1 mark]

03.2 Name **one** organ in the body where lipase is made. [1 mark]

03.1 - evapration (gas)

03.2 - small intestins

03.3 -

03.3 A group of students investigated the effect of temperature on the action of the enzyme lipase.

They used the following method in their investigation:

1 Add 10 cm³ of lipid solution to a test tube.
2 Add 2 cm³ of lipase solution to a second test tube.
3 Place both test tubes into a water bath set at 20 °C.
4 Leave in the water bath for five minutes.
5 Add the lipid solution to the lipase solution and mix.
6 Remove a sample of the mixture every five minutes and test for the presence of lipids. Continue until no lipid is detected.
7 Repeat the experiment every 5 °C between temperatures of 20 °C and 50 °C.

Name the independent variable in the investigation. [1 mark]

03.4 - to caues a reaction or to make it a fair test

03.4 Suggest why the lipase solution and lipid solution were left in the water bath for five minutes before mixing. [1 mark]

03.5 The students' results are shown in **Table 1**.

Table 1

Temperature in °C	Mean time taken until no lipid remained in min
20	20
25	15
30	10
35	5
40	10
45	20
50	lipid still present after 30 minutes of testing

Describe the effect on the breakdown of the lipid when the temperature was increased between 20 °C and 35 °C. **[1 mark]**

03.6 Explain the result that was observed at 50 °C. **[2 marks]**

> **Exam Tip**
> Read the question carefully: it is only asking about a small section of the results. Try highlighting those results before you look at the pattern.

04 **Figure 2** shows the rate of an enzyme controlled reaction.

Figure 2

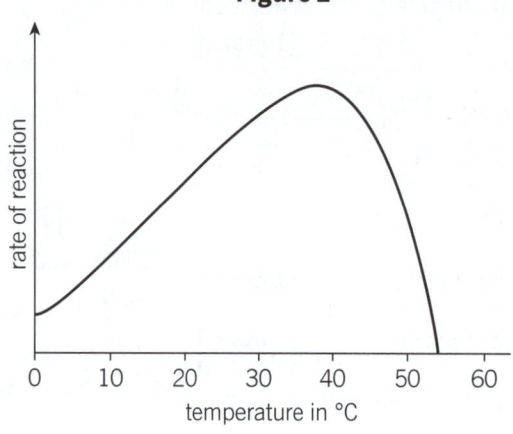

04.1 Look at **Figure 2**.

Identify which of the following **two** statements are true. **[2 marks]**

Between 10 °C and 30 °C, as temperature increases the rate of reaction increases.

Between 30 °C and 50 °C, as temperature increases the rate of reaction decreases.

The enzyme does not catalyse the reaction at 0 °C.

The enzyme does not catalyse the reaction at 60 °C.

> **Exam Tip**
> One from each pair of statements is true – look at them together and decide which descriptions best fit the graph.

04.2 Identify the optimum temperature the enzyme works at.

Choose **one** answer. **[1 mark]**

0 °C   28 °C   37 °C   54 °C

04.3 Circle the correct bold words to complete the sentences. **[3 marks]**

At very high temperatures enzymes **start / stop** working. They are said to be **natural / denatured**. This means that the shape of the **active / inactive** site has changed.

48 B5 Enzymes

05 **Figure 3** shows how pH affects the activity of a protease enzyme.

Figure 3

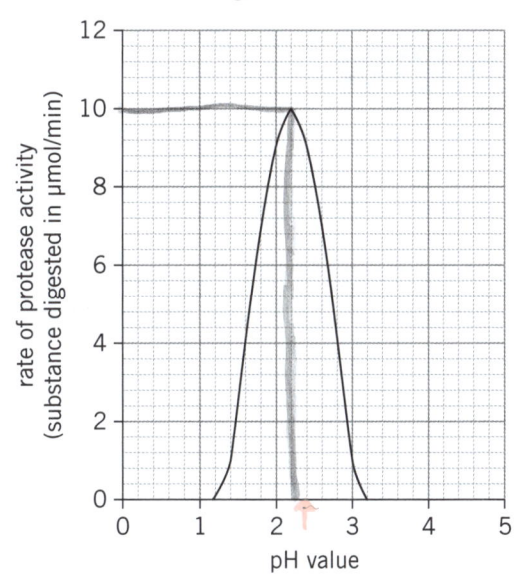

[Graph: rate of protease activity (substance digested in μmol/min) on y-axis (0–12) vs pH value on x-axis (0–5), showing a peak at pH ~2 reaching 10 μmol/min]

05.1 Name the substance that proteases break down into amino acids. **[1 mark]**

05.2 Describe **one** use of amino acids in the human body. **[1 mark]**
to brake down food

05.3 Use **Figure 3** to identify the optimum pH of the enzyme. **[1 mark]**
2.1

> **Exam Tip**
> Look for the peak of the graph – this is where the activity is highest.

05.4 Suggest where the enzyme in **Figure 3** is found in the body. Choose **one** answer. **[1 mark]**

mouth   large intestine   stomach   (small intestine)

05.5 Give **one** reason for your answer to **05.4**. **[1 mark]**
bese most enzym ar loced int small intesting

06 A student was studying the effect of pH on the enzyme activity of an unknown carbohydrase. They were provided with the following apparatus:

- test tubes and rack
- spotting tiles
- 10 cm³ measuring cylinder
- 3 cm³ pipettes
- glass stirring rod
- stopwatch
- safety goggles
- starch solution
- carbohydrase solution
- iodine solution
- thermometer
- pH buffer solutions.

Explain how the student could investigate the effect of pH on the rate of reaction of the enzyme. **[6 marks]**

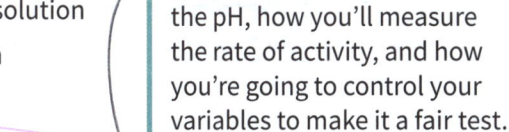

> **Exam Tip**
> Clearly state how to change the pH, how you'll measure the rate of activity, and how you're going to control your variables to make it a fair test.

07 A student was studying the effect of pH on amylase. Amylase breaks down starch into simple sugars.

The student collected starch solution at pH 4, and added amylase. A sample of the solution was taken every 30 s, and iodine was added. When no colour change was detected, the student knew that the starch had been digested.

The experiment was repeated at pH values of 5, 6, 7, and 8. The student's results are shown in **Table 2**.

Table 2

pH	Time to digest starch in s
4	600
5	360
6	210
7	120
8	180

07.1 Choose the word that best describes amylase.

Choose **one** answer. **[1 mark]**

enzyme   acid   buffer   **carbohydrate**

07.2 Write down the colour change the student would have seen when iodine was added to the starch solution. **[1 mark]**

black or light yellow

07.3 Using the results in **Table 2**, plot a graph of pH against time taken to digest starch on **Figure 4**. Include a line of best fit. **[3 marks]**

Figure 4

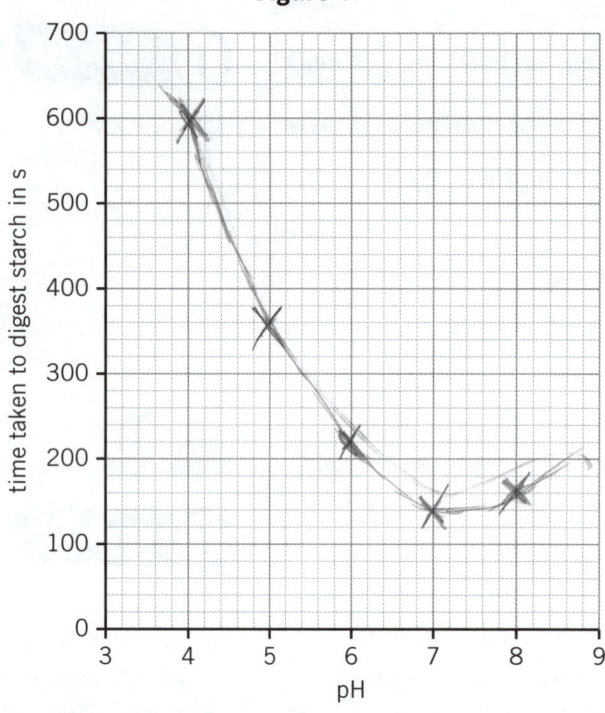

07.4 Write down the optimum pH value for amylase digestion. **[1 mark]**

fat   optimum pH = 7

08 Lipases are used to break down lipids.

08.1 Identify the products that are produced when lipids are broken down.

Choose **one** answer. **[1 mark]**

fatty acids and glycerol   simple sugars   amino acids

08.2 Lipases are made in the small intestine.

Identify **one** other place where lipases are produced in the human body. **[1 mark]**

mouth   stomach   **pancreas**

08.3 Lipases cannot break down proteins.
Complete the following sentences using the most appropriate words from the box to explain why. **[5 marks]**

| lipid | lock | protein | active | inactive | specific |

The ___lock___ and key theory is used to explain why lipases are unable to break down protein molecules. Each enzyme is ___specific___ to a particular substrate. Lipases have a certain shaped ___active___ site, which ___protein___ molecules are unable to fit into. Only ___lipid___ molecules have the correct shape and so are able to interact with lipase.

Exam Tip
This is a great paragraph to help you revise this section.

09 Biological washing powders have digestive enzymes added to them.

09.1 Fat stains are often difficult to get out of clothes.
Name the type of enzyme that is able to break down fats. **[1 mark]**

amylase

09.2 A scientist measured the time it took a biological washing powder to remove a fat stain at different temperatures.
The results are shown in **Table 3**.

Table 3

Temperature in °C	Time to remove stain in min	Rate per min
30	25	_____
40	10	0.10
50	50	0.02
60	stain not removed	–

The rate of a chemical reaction can be calculated using the formula:

$$\text{rate} = \frac{1}{\text{time}}$$ — key!

Complete **Table 3** by calculating the rate of stain removal at 30 °C. **[1 mark]**

09.3 Suggest why the biological washing powder was unable to remove the fat stain at 60 °C. **[1 mark]**

10 Large multicellular organisms require systems to exchange gases efficiently.

10.1 Select the statement that best explains why single-celled organisms do not require gas exchange organs.
Choose **one** answer. **[1 mark]**
Single-celled organisms have a small surface area-to-volume ratio.
Single-celled organisms have a large surface area-to-volume ratio.
Single-celled organisms have a small surface area.
Single-celled organisms have a large surface area.

Exam Tip
You can start by finding the ones that you know are wrong so that you narrow down the options.

10.2 Explain the changes that occur in the body causing air to be drawn into the lungs. **[4 marks]**

10.3 Explain how the alveoli are adapted for gas exchange. **[3 marks]**

Knowledge

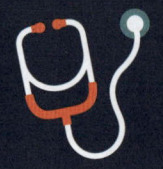

B6 Organising plants

Tissues in leaves

Leaves are organs because they contain many tissues that work together to perform photosynthesis.

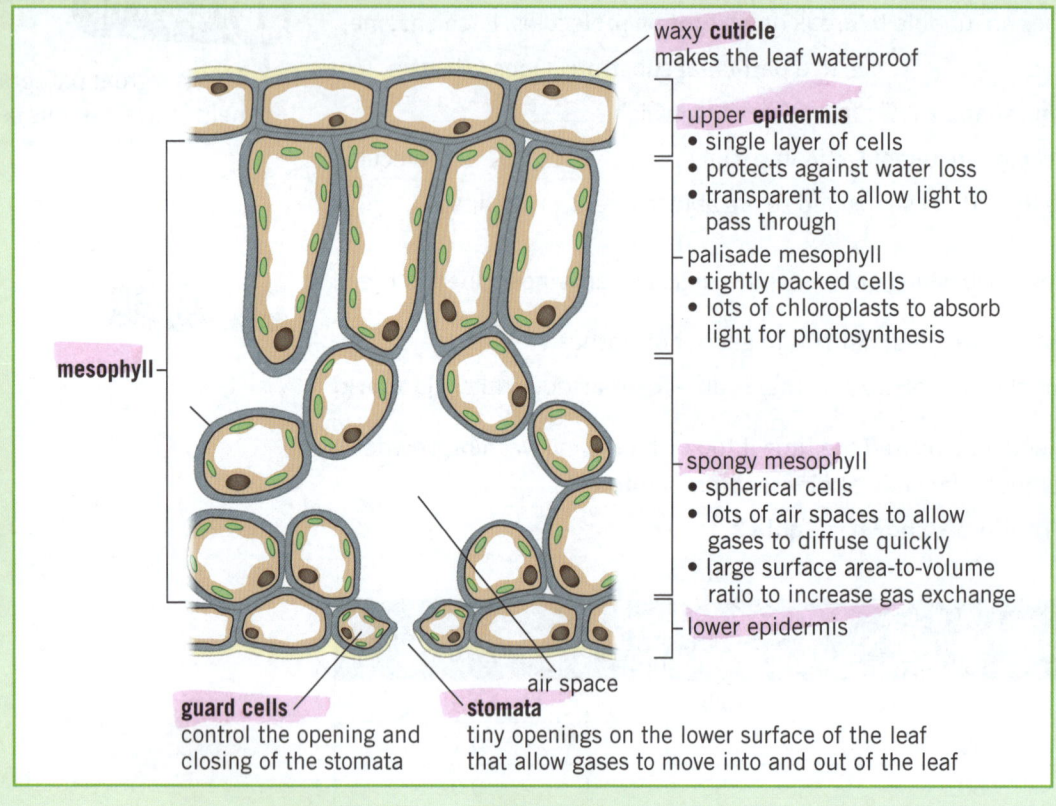

waxy cuticle
makes the leaf waterproof

upper epidermis
- single layer of cells
- protects against water loss
- transparent to allow light to pass through

palisade mesophyll
- tightly packed cells
- lots of chloroplasts to absorb light for photosynthesis

spongy mesophyll
- spherical cells
- lots of air spaces to allow gases to diffuse quickly
- large surface area-to-volume ratio to increase gas exchange

lower epidermis

air space

guard cells
control the opening and closing of the stomata

stomata
tiny openings on the lower surface of the leaf that allow gases to move into and out of the leaf

Stomata

Stomata are tiny openings in the undersides of leaves – this placement reduces water loss through evaporation.

They control gas exchange and water loss from leaves by
- allowing diffusion of carbon dioxide into the plant for photosynthesis
- allowing diffusion of oxygen out of the plant.

Guard cells are used to open and close the stomata.

When a plant has plenty of water, the guard cells become **turgid**. The cell wall on the inner surface is very thick, so it cannot stretch as much as the outer surface. So as the guard cells swell up, they curve away from each other, opening the stoma.

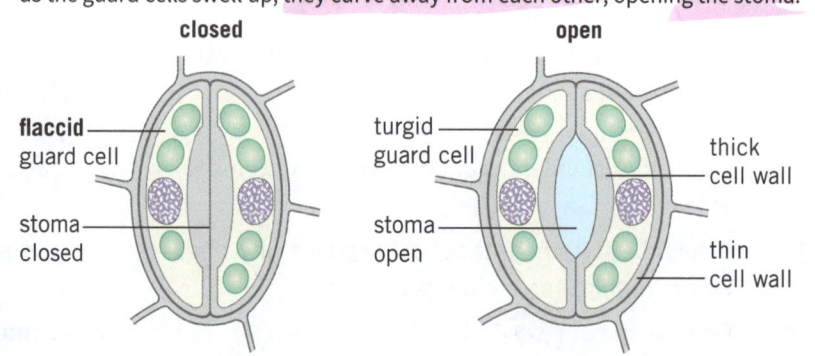

closed
- **flaccid** guard cell
- stoma closed

open
- turgid guard cell
- thick cell wall
- stoma open
- thin cell wall

Key terms

Make sure you can write a definition for these key terms.

| cuticle | epidermis | flaccid | guard cell | mesophyll | phloem | stomata |
| translocation | transpiration | transpiration stream | turgid | xylem |

B6

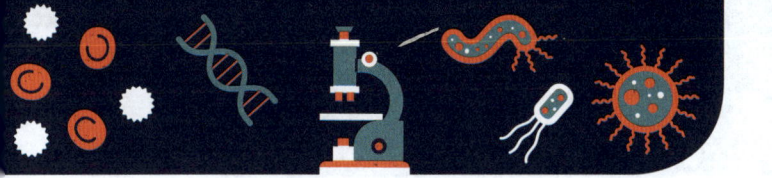

Transpiration

Description: Water is lost through the stomata by evaporation. This pulls water up from the roots through the **xylem** and is called **transpiration**. The constant movement of water up the plant is called the **transpiration stream**.

Importance:
- provides water to cells to keep them turgid
- provides water to cells for photosynthesis
- transports mineral ions to leaves

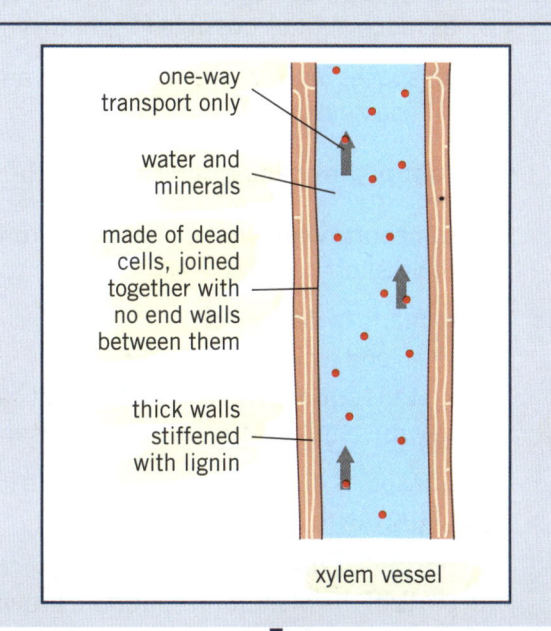

Specialised tissues:
- one-way transport only
- water and minerals
- made of dead cells, joined together with no end walls between them
- thick walls stiffened with lignin

xylem vessel

Translocation

The movement of dissolved sugars from the leaves to the rest of the plant through the **phloem**.

- moves dissolved sugars made in the leaves during photosynthesis to other parts of the plant
- this allows the sugars to be used in respiration, growth, and glucose storage

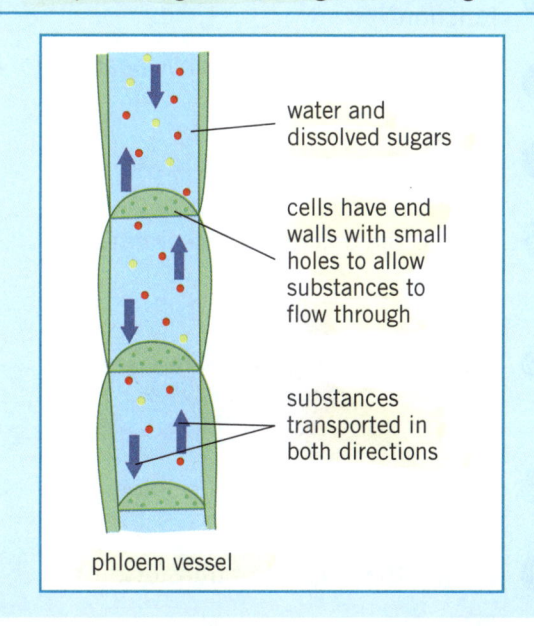

Specialised tissues:
- water and dissolved sugars
- cells have end walls with small holes to allow substances to flow through
- substances transported in both directions

phloem vessel

Factors affecting the rate of transpiration

Factor	Effect on transpiration	Because...
temperature	higher temperatures *increase* the rate of transpiration	water evaporates faster in higher temperatures
humidity	lower humidity *increases* the rate of transpiration	the drier the air, the steeper the concentration gradient of water molecules between the air and leaf
wind speed	more wind *increases* the rate of transpiration	wind removes the water vapour quickly, maintaining a steep concentration gradient
light intensity	higher light intensity *increases* the rate of transpiration	stomata open wider to let more carbon dioxide into the leaf for photosynthesis

Root hair cells

- increase absorption of water and mineral ions into the root by increasing the root surface area
- contain lots of mitochondria to transfer energy, which is used to take in mineral ions by active transport

B6 Knowledge

Retrieval

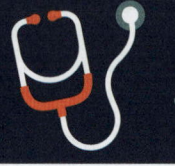

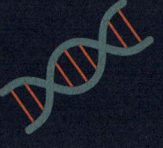

Learn the answers to the questions below, then cover the answers column with a piece of paper and write as many as you can. Check and repeat.

	B6 questions	Answers
1	Why is a leaf an organ?	there are many tissues inside the leaf that work together to perform photosynthesis
2	How is the upper epidermis adapted for its function?	• single layer of transparent cells allow light to pass through • cells secrete a waxy substance that makes leaves waterproof
3	How is the palisade mesophyll adapted for its function?	tightly packed cells with lots of chloroplasts to absorb as much light as possible for photosynthesis
4	How is the spongy mesophyll adapted for its function?	air spaces increase the surface area and allow gases to diffuse quickly
5	What is the function of the guard cells?	control the opening and closing of the stomata
6	What is the function of the xylem?	transports water and mineral ions from the roots to the rest of the plant
7	Give three adaptations of the xylem.	• made of dead cells • no end wall between cells • walls strengthened by a chemical called lignin to withstand the pressure of the water
8	What is the function of the phloem?	transports dissolved sugars from the leaves to the rest of the plant
9	What is the purpose of translocation?	transports dissolved sugars from the leaves to other parts of the plant for respiration, growth, and storage
10	Define the term transpiration.	movement of water from the roots to the leaves through the xylem
11	What is the purpose of transpiration?	• provides water to keep cells turgid • provides water to cells for photosynthesis • transports mineral ions to leaves
12	Name four factors that affect the rate of transpiration.	temperature, light intensity, humidity, wind speed
13	What effect does temperature have on the rate of transpiration?	higher temperatures increase the rate of transpiration
14	What effect does humidity have on the rate of transpiration?	higher levels of humidity decrease the rate of transpiration
15	Why does increased light intensity increase the rate of transpiration?	stomata open wider to let more carbon dioxide into the leaf for photosynthesis
16	What is the function of the stomata?	allow diffusion of gases into and out of the plant
17	Where are most stomata found?	underside of leaves
18	What is the advantage to the plant of having a high number of stomata at this location?	reduces the amount of water loss through evaporation

B6 Organising plants

B6

Now go back and use the questions below to check your knowledge from previous chapters.

Previous questions | Answers

#	Question	Answer
1	List the structures air passes through when breathing in.	mouth/nose → trachea → bronchi → bronchioles → alveoli
2	Give one advantage of using therapeutic cloning.	stem cells are not rejected when transplanted because they have the same genes as the patient
3	How does the structure of a vein relate to its function?	carries blood back to the heart at low pressure – doesn't need thick, elasticated walls, but has valves to prevent blood flowing the wrong way
4	What does denatured mean?	shape of an enzyme's active site is changed by high temperatures or an extreme pH, so it can no longer bind with the substrate
5	How are villi adapted for exchanging substances?	• long and thin – increases surface area • one-cell-thick membrane – short diffusion pathway • good blood supply – maintains a steep concentration gradient

Put paper here

Maths skills

Practise your maths skills using the worked example and practice questions below.

Calculating rate of transpiration

Transpiration cannot be measured directly. Instead it is determined by measuring the decrease in mass of a plant due to water loss, or by measuring the volume of water absorbed by the plant.

A potometer can be used to determine the rate of transpiration by measuring the volume of water absorbed by a plant.

The volume of water absorbed can be calculated by measuring the distance travelled by an air bubble in a given time in the potometer. The faster the bubble moves, the greater the rate of water uptake, and the greater the assumed rate of transpiration.

Worked example

A group of students used a potometer to measure the volume of water absorbed by a plant under three different conditions over 25 minutes. Their results were

- normal conditions: 2.4 ml water absorbed
- high temperature: 3.1 ml water absorbed
- low humidity: 3.5 ml water absorbed.

Work out the transpiration rate of the plant under each condition.

$$\text{transpiration rate (ml/min)} = \frac{\text{volume of water absorbed (ml)}}{\text{time (min)}}$$

normal conditions: $\frac{2.4}{25} = 0.096$ ml/min

high temperature: $\frac{3.1}{25} = 0.124$ ml/min

low humidity: $\frac{3.5}{25} = 0.140$ ml/min

Practice

1. The table below shows the volume of water absorbed by a plant under three different conditions in ten minutes.

   Calculate the transpiration rate for the plant under each condition.

Conditions	Volume of water in ml	Time in min	Transpiration rate in ml/min
normal	1.1	10	
high temperature	1.3	10	
low humidity	1.5	10	

2. Which condition produced the highest transpiration rate? Explain this result.

3. How would you expect the volume of water absorbed to differ to normal conditions if a fan was set up to blow air over the plant?

B6 Retrieval 55

Practice

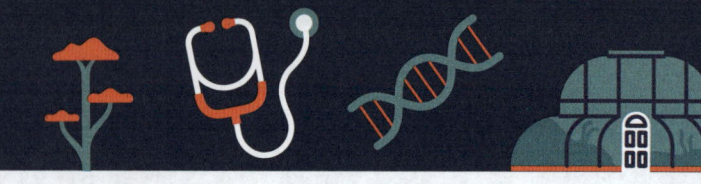

Exam-style questions

01 A student removed four leaves (**A**, **B**, **C**, and **D**) of approximately the same size from an oak tree.

Petroleum jelly was spread over the surface of leaves **A**–**C**. Petroleum jelly is waterproof and prevents water being lost from the leaves.

All four leaves were then hung from a piece of string as shown in **Figure 1**.

Figure 1

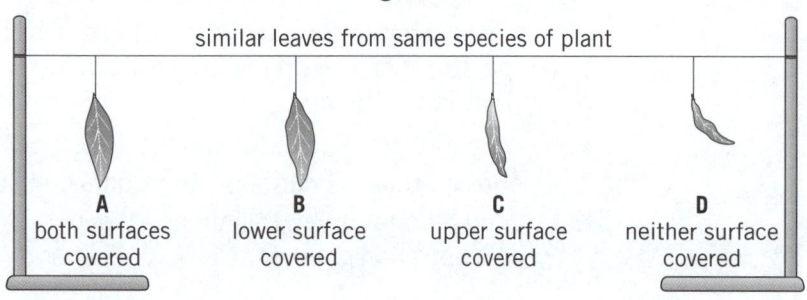

similar leaves from same species of plant

A	B	C	D
both surfaces covered	lower surface covered	upper surface covered	neither surface covered

01.1 Identify **one** reason why no petroleum jelly was spread over the surface of leaf **D**. **[1 mark]**

Tick **one** box.

increase the reliability of the investigation ☐

compare with no petroleum jelly ☐

provide repeat measurements ☐

01.2 Name the apparatus used to measure the mass of each leaf at regular intervals. **[1 mark]**

_____

01.3 The results of the investigation are shown in **Table 1**.

Table 1

Leaf	A	B	C	D
starting mass in g	3.3	3.4	2.8	2.9
end mass in g	1.6	1.1	0.7	0.3
loss in mass in g	1.7	2.3		2.6

Calculate the loss in mass of leaf **C**. **[1 mark]**

> **! Exam Tip**
>
> To calculate mass lost you need to do: starting mass in g minus end mass in g.

Loss in mass = _____ g

56 B6 Organising plants

Paper 1 — B6

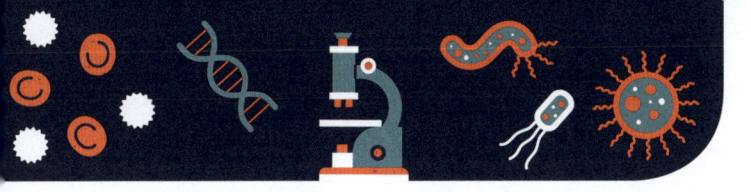

01.4 Use the information in **Table 1** to select which of the following conclusions are true. **[2 marks]**

Tick **two** boxes

- more water is lost from the lower surface than the upper surface ☐
- more water is lost from the upper surface than the lower surface ☐
- water is lost from both surfaces ☐
- no water is lost from the leaf surfaces ☐

> **Exam Tip**
> On **Figure 1**, write the mass lost next to each leaf. This should help you quickly identify which one lost more water, and which surface it came from.

01.5 Suggest **one** reason for the student's findings. **[1 mark]**

_____
_____

02 Multicellular organisms have five levels of organisation.

02.1 Choose the correct terms from the box to identify an example of an organism, an organ, and a tissue. **[3 marks]**

| leaf   plant   flower   spongy mesophyll   stomata |

An organism: _____

An organ: _____

A tissue: _____

> **Exam Tip**
> There are two organs on the list, you can pick either of them.

02.2 Draw **one** line to match each plant tissue type to its function. **[2 marks]**

Plant tissue	Function
meristem	transports water around the plant
xylem	contains rapidly dividing cells for growth
phloem	carries dissolved food around the plant

B6 Practice 57

02.3 The palisade mesophyll carries out photosynthesis.

Identify the structure that would be present in high numbers. **[1 mark]**

Tick **one** box.

root hairs ☐

chloroplasts ☐

mitochondria ☐

ribosomes ☐

> **Exam Tip**
> This structure needs to be present in plant cells, and need light for photosynthesis.

02.4 Suggest why the stem of a plant is an example of a plant organ. **[1 mark]**

_____

_____

03 **Figure 2** shows a plant cell.

Figure 2

03.1 Identify which part of a plant the cell has been taken from.

Choose **one** answer. **[1 mark]**

root   xylem tissue   phloem tissue   palisade mesophyll

> **Exam Tip**
> Look at the structres within the cell and think about their function – which part of the plant performs these functions?

03.2 Give a reason for your answer to **03.1**. **[1 mark]**

03.3 Describe how water moves between cells in a leaf. **[2 marks]**

03.4 The main function of a leaf is to perform photosynthesis to provide food for the plant.

Describe how the tissues inside a leaf are organised to maximise photosynthesis. **[6 marks]**

> **Exam Tip**
> To get full marks in **03.4**, you need to include information about the different parts of the leaf: the top, the middle, and the bottom.

04 A student carried out an investigation on beech leaves to compare the number of stomata present on the upper and lower surfaces of the leaf.

04.1 Describe how the student could take samples from the leaf to count the number of stomata present. **[3 marks]**

04.2 The student's results are shown in **Table 2**.

Table 2

Surface	Number of stomata present					Mean
	Sample 1	Sample 2	Sample 3	Sample 4	Sample 5	
Upper	1	2	2	3	2	2
Lower	36	42	35	41	37	

Calculate the mean result for the lower surface of the leaf.
Give your answer to **two** significant figures. **[2 marks]**

> **Exam Tip**
> The first two significant figures are before the decimal place, so your answer will be a whole number.

04.3 The student concluded that most stomata are found on the lower surface of a beech leaf.
Explain why this is an advantage for a beech tree. **[2 marks]**

05 The xylem and phloem transport substances around the plant.

05.1 Identify the substance transported by the phloem.
Choose **one** answer. **[1 mark]**

water   chlorophyll   mineral ions   sugars

05.2 Complete **Table 3** to show the differences between the xylem and phloem. Tick **one** box in each row. **[4 marks]**

Table 3

Feature	Found in xylem	Found in phloem
made up of living cells		
contain sieve plates		
walls containing lignin		
supported by companion cells		

> **Exam Tip**
> Don't assume that there is an equal number of ticks for the xylem and the phloem.

05.3 Name the process that allows dissolved sugars to be transported around a plant. **[1 mark]**

06 **Figure 3** is a diagram of the cross-section of a leaf.

Figure 3

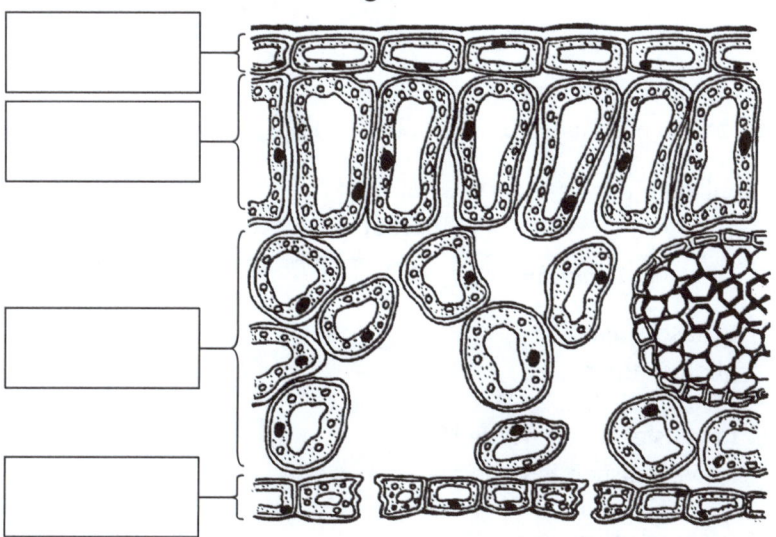

> **Exam Tip**
> Recognising the different cells within a leaf is important. You should also be able to name them and give their specific functions.

06.1 Label the layers of the leaf in **Figure 3**, using the correct terms from the box. **[4 marks]**

| spongy mesophyll | palisade mesophyll | upper epidermis |
| lower epidermis | xylem | phloem |

06.2 Identify the layer of the leaf that: **[3 marks]**

carries out most photosynthesis in the leaf

contains the stomata

contains air spaces.

06.3 Name the part of the leaf that allows oxygen and water vapour to diffuse out of the leaf. **[1 mark]**

07 A group of students investigated how different factors affected the rate of transpiration in a basil plant.

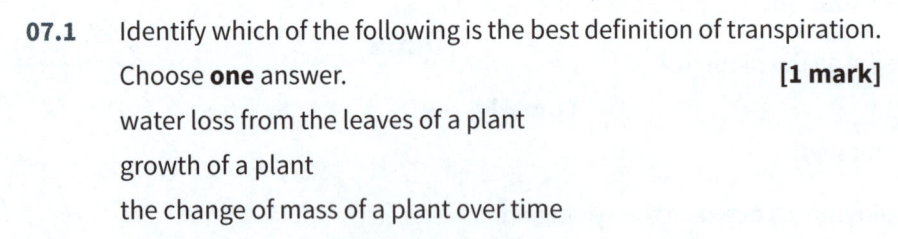

07.1 Identify which of the following is the best definition of transpiration. Choose **one** answer. **[1 mark]**

water loss from the leaves of a plant

growth of a plant

the change of mass of a plant over time

Exam Tip

Transpiration in basil works in the same way as other examples you've studied in class.

07.2 Identify **one** piece of apparatus used to measure the rate of transpiration in the laboratory.
Choose **one** answer. **[1 mark]**

barometer   potometer   hygrometer   thermometer

07.3 For each of the factors in **Table 4**, tick the appropriate column to show if the change causes an increase or a decrease in the rate of transpiration. **[4 marks]**

Table 4

Factor change	Increase	Decrease
increase in temperature		
increase in humidity		
increase in air speed		
greater light intensity		

Exam Tip

Don't tick both increase and decrease for the same factor, you won't get any marks for that row.

08 As well as anchoring a plant into the ground, roots are also responsible for the uptake of water and mineral ions from the soil.

08.1 Draw **one** line from each root hair cell adaptation to how this helps the cell perform its function. **[2 marks]**

Cell adaptation   **Function**

to absorb light for photosynthesis

large surface area available

to transfer energy needed for active transport into the cell

many mitochondria

to speed up movement of water into the cell by osmosis

B6 Organising plants

08.2 **Figure 4** represents the movement of water and mineral ions into the root hair cell.

Figure 4

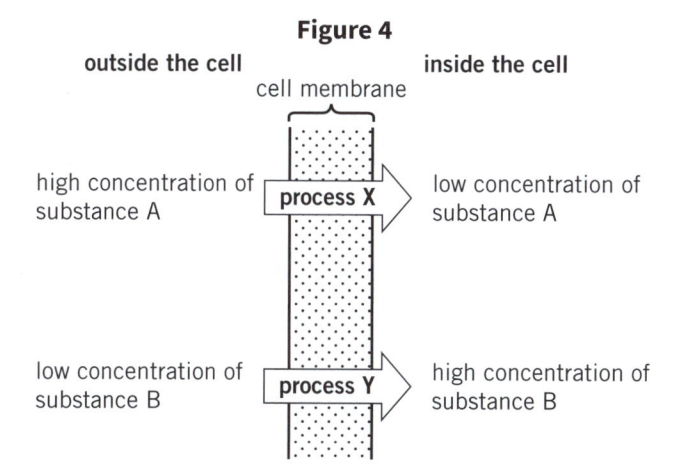

outside the cell | inside the cell
cell membrane

high concentration of substance A → process X → low concentration of substance A

low concentration of substance B → process Y → high concentration of substance B

Identify which process (**X** or **Y**) in **Figure 4** represents the uptake of mineral ions. Explain your answer. **[2 marks]**

Exam Tip

To help your revision, try to name the two processes.

08.3 Name the type of vessel that transports mineral ions around the plant. **[1 mark]**

08.4 Describe **one** use of mineral ions in a plant. **[1 mark]**

09 **Figure 5** shows a cross-section through a leaf as seen through a microscope.

Figure 5

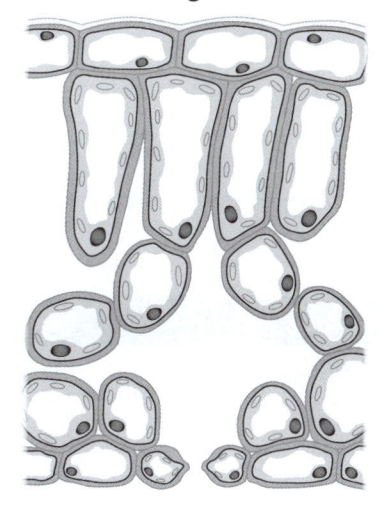

09.1 Identify and label a stoma on **Figure 5**. **[1 mark]**

09.2 Describe the role of guard cells in controlling water loss from a leaf. **[2 marks]**

Exam Tip

Remember that stomata are the gaps in the epidermis.

09.3 A scientist calculated that the width of the cross-section they were viewing through the microscope was 250 μm. Estimate the width of the guard cell. **[1 mark]**

Knowledge

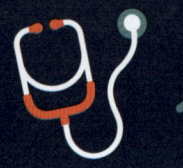

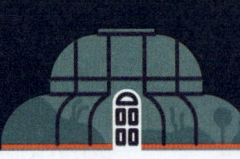

B7 The spread of diseases

Pathogens

Microorganisms that cause disease are called **pathogens**.

There are four types of pathogen:
- bacteria
- fungi
- protists
- viruses.

Pathogens can be spread:
- in the air
- in water
- through direct contact.

Viruses live and reproduce rapidly inside an organism's cells. This can damage or destroy the cells.

Viruses

	Spread by	Symptoms	Prevention and treatment
measles	inhalation of droplets that are produced by infected people sneezing and coughing	• fever • red skin rash • complications can be fatal	• painkillers to treat the symptoms • young children are vaccinated to immunise them against measles
HIV (human immunodeficiency virus)	exchange of body fluids such as: • sexual contact • blood when drug users share needles	• flu-like symptoms at first • virus attacks the body's immune cells, which can lead to AIDS – this is when the immune system is so damaged that it cannot fight off infections or cancers	• antiretroviral drugs – but these can cause serious side effects • barrier methods of contraception, such as condoms • using clean needles
TMV (tobacco mosaic virus – plants)	• direct contact of plants with infected plant material • animal and plant vectors • soil – the pathogen can remain in soil for decades	• mosaic pattern of discolouration on the leaves – where chlorophyll is destroyed • reduces a plant's ability to photosynthesise, affecting growth	• removing infected plants

Bacteria reproduce rapidly inside organisms and may produce **toxins** that damage tissues and cause illness.

Bacteria

	Spread by	Symptoms	Prevention and treatment
Salmonella	bacteria in or on food being ingested	Salmonella bacteria and the toxins they produce cause • fever • abdominal cramps • vomiting • diarrhoea	• poultry are vaccinated against Salmonella bacteria to control spread
gonorrhoea	direct sexual contact – gonorrhoea is a **sexually transmitted disease (STD)**	• thick yellow or green discharge from the vagina or penis • pain when urinating	• treatment with antibiotics (many antibiotic-resistant strains have appeared) • barrier methods of contraception

Key terms

Make sure you can write a definition for these key terms.

bacterium   communicable disease   fungicide   fungus   herd immunity   pathogen

B7

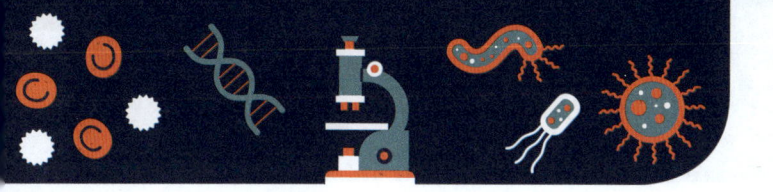

Fungi	Spread by	Symptoms	Prevention and treatment
rose black spot	water and wind	• purple or black spots on leaves, which turn yellow and drop early • reduces a plant's ability to photosynthesise, affecting growth	• fungicides • affected leaves removed and destroyed

Protists	Spread by	Symptoms	Prevention and treatment
malaria	mosquitos feed on the blood of infected people and spread the protist when they feed on another person – organisms that spread disease by carrying pathogens between people are called **vectors**	• recurrent episodes of fever • can be fatal	• prevent mosquito vectors breeding • mosquito nets to prevent bites • anti-malarial medicine

Controlling the spread of communicable disease

There are a number of ways to help prevent the spread of **communicable diseases** from one organism to another.

Hygiene
Hand washing, disinfecting surfaces and machinery, keeping raw meat separate, covering mouth when coughing/sneezing, etc.

Isolation
Isolation of infected individuals – people, animals, and plants can be isolated to stop the spread of disease.

Controlling vectors
If a vector spreads a disease, destroying or controlling the population of the vector can limit the spread of disease.

Vaccination
Vaccination can protect large numbers of individuals against diseases.

Revision tip
Remember Communicable diseases is another way of saying infectious diseases.

Vaccination

Vaccination involves injecting small quantities of dead or inactive forms of a pathogen into the body.

↓

This stimulates white blood cells to produce the correct antibodies for that pathogen.

↓

If the same pathogen re-enters the body, the correct antibodies can be produced quickly to prevent infection.

Herd immunity

If a large proportion of a population is vaccinated against a disease, the disease is less likely to spread, even if there are some unvaccinated individuals.

---

protist • sexually transmitted disease (STD) • toxin • vaccination • vector • virus

B7 Knowledge 63

Retrieval

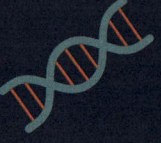

Learn the answers to the questions below, then cover the answers column with a piece of paper and write as many as you can. Check and repeat.

	B7 questions	Answers
1	What is a communicable disease?	a disease that can be transmitted from one organism to another
2	What is a pathogen?	a microorganism that causes disease
3	Name four types of pathogen.	bacteria, fungi, protists, viruses
4	How can pathogens spread?	air, water, direct contact
5	How do bacteria make you ill?	produce toxins that damage tissues
6	How do viruses make you ill?	reproduce rapidly inside cells, damaging or destroying them
7	Name three viral diseases.	measles, HIV, tobacco mosaic virus
8	Name two bacterial diseases.	*Salmonella*, gonorrhoea
9	Name one fungal disease.	rose black spot
10	Describe an example of a protist disease.	malaria – caused by a protist pathogen that is spread from person to person by mosquito bites, and causes recurrent fevers
11	Name four methods of controlling the spread of communicable disease.	good hygiene, isolating infected individuals, controlling vectors, vaccination
12	What does a vaccine contain?	small quantities of a dead or inactive form of a pathogen
13	How does vaccination protect against a specific pathogen?	vaccination stimulates the body to produce antibodies against a specific pathogen – if the same pathogen re-enters the body, white blood cells rapidly produce the correct antibodies
14	What is herd immunity?	when most of a population is vaccinated against a disease, meaning it is less likely to spread

64   B7 The spread of diseases

B7

Now go back and use the questions below to check your knowledge from previous chapters.

Previous questions | Answers

#	Question	Answer
1	Why are enzymes described as specific?	each enzyme only catalyses a specific reaction, because the active site only fits together with certain substrates (like a lock and key)
2	How is the palisade mesophyll adapted for its function?	tightly packed cells with lots of chloroplasts to absorb as much light as possible for photosynthesis
3	What is the function of a root hair cell?	absorbs minerals and water from the soil
4	What is cell division by mitosis?	body cells divide to form two identical daughter cells
5	What is the function of the phloem?	transport dissolved sugars from the leaves to the rest of the plant
6	Where are adult stem cells found?	bone marrow
7	What is the purpose of plant transpiration?	• provide water to keep cells turgid • provide water to cells for photosynthesis • transport mineral ions to leaves
8	Describe the effect of pH on enzyme activity.	different enzymes each have a different optimum pH at which their activity is greatest – at a pH much lower or higher than this, enzyme activity decreases and stops

Maths skills

Practise your maths skills using the worked example and practice questions below.

Calculating percentage change

To calculate percentage change you need to work out the difference between the two numbers you are comparing.

Then, you divide the difference by the original number and multiply the answer by 100.

If your answer is a negative number, this equals a percentage decrease.

$$\text{percentage change} = \frac{\text{difference}}{\text{original number}} \times 100$$

Worked example

In 2009, the number of deaths in England caused by MRSA was 800. In 2010, the number of deaths had fallen to 500.

Calculate the percentage change in the number of deaths caused by MRSA between 2009 and 2010.

Work out the difference in the two numbers you are comparing:

500 − 800 = − 300

Divide the difference (300) by the original number:

$$\frac{-300}{800} = -0.375$$

Multiply by 100:

−0.375 × 100 = − 37.5

Percentage change in deaths caused by MRSA = − 37.5 %

Practice

The table below gives information about the number of deaths per year in England from MRSA and *Clostridium difficile* over four years.

Year	MRSA	C. difficile
2007	1800	8100
2008	1730	5300
2009	800	3890
2010	500	4570

1. Calculate the percentage change in deaths caused by MRSA from 2007 to 2008.

2. Calculate the percentage change in deaths caused by *C. difficile* from 2007 to 2008.

3. Calculate the percentage change in deaths caused by *C. difficile* from 2009 to 2010.

Practice

Exam-style questions

01 Diseases can be communicable (infectious) or non-communicable.

01.1 Identify **two** communicable diseases. **[2 marks]**
Tick **two** boxes.

cancer ☐

measles ☐

heart disease ☐

gonorrhoea ☐

> **Exam Tip**
> Read all instructions carefully – often students lose marks because they don't tick the correct number of boxes.

01.2 Identify **two** features of a communicable disease. **[2 marks]**
Tick **two** boxes.

caused by a pathogen ☐

caused by a mutation ☐

can be spread between organisms ☐

cannot be spread between organisms ☐

01.3 Communicable diseases affect plants as well as animals.
Name **one** example of a communicable disease in plants. **[1 mark]**

_____

02 Communicable diseases are often caused by bacteria and viruses.

02.1 Complete **Table 1** to identify the characteristics of a bacterial or a viral pathogen.
Tick **one** box in each row. **[3 marks]**

Table 1

Feature	Bacteria	Viruses
cause disease by producing toxins		
use host organism's cells to reproduce		
divide by binary fission		

66   **B7 The spread of diseases**

Paper 1 — B7

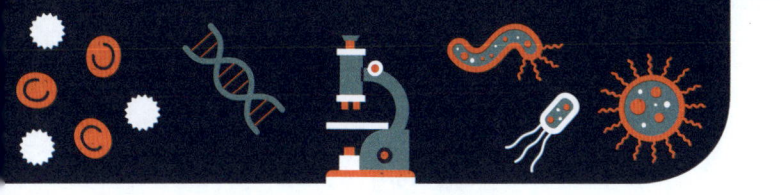

02.2 Identify **two** diseases that are caused by viruses. **[2 marks]**
Tick **two** boxes.

measles ☐

HIV ☐

Salmonella food poisoning ☐

gonorrhoea ☐

02.3 Malaria is not caused by a bacteria or a virus.
Name the type of microorganism that causes malaria. **[1 mark]**

_____

02.4 Name the vector for this disease. **[1 mark]**

> **! Exam Tip**
> The vector is how the disease is carried.

_____

03 The spread of communicable diseases can often be prevented.

03.1 Draw **one** line from each method of disease transmission to the correct method used to prevent the spread of disease. **[3 marks]**

Method of disease transmission	Method used to prevent spread
	cover with a dressing
raw meat	cook thoroughly
sneezing	
	wear mask to cover nose and mouth
contaminated water	
open wounds	use sterilising tablets before consuming

03.2 Identify **two** pathogens from the list.
Choose **two** answers. **[2 marks]**

bacteria   mosquitoes   viruses   dogs

03.3 Suggest why communicable diseases often spread rapidly between students attending the same school. **[1 mark]**

04 Communicable diseases are caused by different types of pathogen.

04.1 Draw **one** line from each disease to the correct pathogen type that causes the disease. **[3 marks]**

Disease	Pathogen type
Salmonella	virus
rose black spot	bacterium
malaria	fungus
measles	protist

Exam Tip

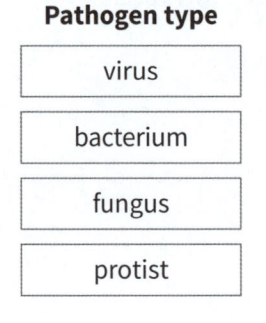

If you only know one or two, match those boxes straight away. That will leave you with fewer options to help you work out the remainders.

04.2 Give **one** symptom caused by measles. **[1 mark]**

04.3 Describe how measles is spread. **[1 mark]**

04.4 In 2018, there were 14.4 reported cases of measles per million people in the United Kingdom. The UK population in 2018 was 66 million.
Calculate the number of cases of measles in the UK in 2018. **[1 mark]**

04.5 In Ukraine in 2018, the number of cases of measles was 1204 per million people.
Calculate how many more cases of measles there were per million people in the Ukraine compared to the UK in 2018. **[1 mark]**

Exam Tip

The wording of these two questions is very similar but they are asking for different things using different calculations – don't do the same thing for each answer.

05 Malaria is responsible for millions of deaths each year.

05.1 Choose words from the box to complete the following sentences about malaria. **[4 marks]**

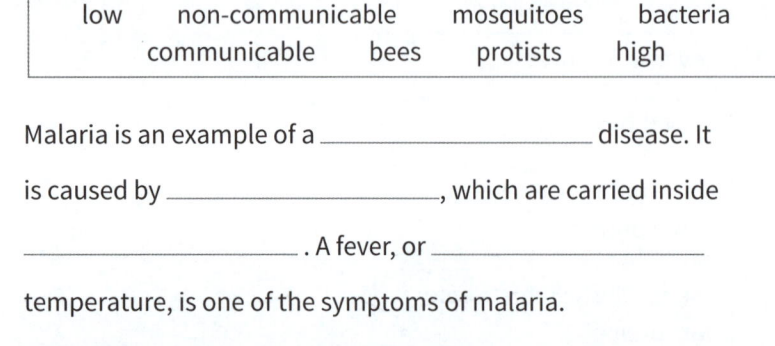

| low | non-communicable | mosquitoes | bacteria |
| communicable | bees | protists | high |

Malaria is an example of a _____ disease. It is caused by _____, which are carried inside _____. A fever, or _____ temperature, is one of the symptoms of malaria.

Exam Tip

There are two words that fit in each space in the sentence, for example high or low – work out the pairs for each gap, then choose the one that you think is correct.

05.2 Describe how each of the following techniques can be used to prevent the spread of malaria. **[3 marks]**
nets placed over beds
spraying buildings with insecticides
anti-malarial drugs

05.3 Suggest why malaria is more common in rural regions. **[1 mark]**

B7 The spread of diseases

B7

06 *Salmonella* food poisoning is an example of a communicable disease.

06.1 Name the type of pathogen that causes *Salmonella* food poisoning. **[1 mark]**

06.2 Other than being caused by a pathogen, describe **one** characteristic of a communicable disease. **[1 mark]**

06.3 *Salmonella* is often spread by contaminated meat.

Describe **two** ways to control the spread of *Salmonella* food poisoning through contaminated meat. **[2 marks]**

06.4 Name **two** symptoms of *Salmonella* food poisoning. **[2 marks]**

> **Exam Tip**
>
> The key here is knowing the definition of a communicable disease and how it is different from a non-communicable disease.

07 Rose black spot is a serious disease that affects rose plants.

07.1 Name the type of pathogen that causes rose black spot disease. **[1 mark]**

07.2 Give **two** symptoms of rose black spot disease. **[2 marks]**

07.3 Explain why a plant infected with rose black spot disease does not grow properly. **[2 marks]**

07.4 A commercial flower grower notices that several of their plants are infected with rose black spot disease.

Give **two** possible treatment options available to the grower to prevent further spread of the infection. **[2 marks]**

> **Exam Tip**
>
> The name gives you a clue to one of the symptoms.

08 Tobacco mosaic virus (TMV) is a plant disease.

08.1 Give **two** reasons why TMV is an example of a communicable disease. **[2 marks]**

08.2 Choose the most appropriate bold words to complete the following sentences about TMV. **[4 marks]**

Tobacco mosaic virus infects many plant species, including tomato plants. It causes leaves to become **brighter / discoloured**. Less **chlorophyll / cytoplasm** is present in the leaves, so the rate of **respiration / photosynthesis** decreases. This affects the rate of **growth / absorption** of the plant.

08.3 The tobacco mosaic virus is able to survive in soil for around 50 years. TMV is most commonly spread between plants by mechanical transmission – through workers' hands and tools. Some species of insects also act as vectors for TMV.

Use this information to suggest **two** ways gardeners and farmers could try to prevent the spread of TMV. **[2 marks]**

> **Exam Tip**
>
> Take each sentence one at a time, if you're not sure which word fits the first sentence then you can still try the rest of the paragraph.

For answers and more practice questions visit www.oxfordrevise.com/scienceanswers

Even more practice and interactive revision quizzes are available on kerboodle

B7 Practice 69

09 Diseases can often be recognised by the symptoms they cause.

09.1 Draw **one** line from each disease to the correct symptom. **[3 marks]**

Disease	Symptom
Salmonella	purple or black spots on leaves
rose black spot	discolouration of leaves
gonorrhoea	fever, vomiting, diarrhoea
tobacco mosaic virus	yellow or green discharge from sexual organs

09.2 Complete the following sentences about sexually transmitted diseases. **[4 marks]**

_____ and _____ are two examples of sexually transmitted diseases. They are spread through sexual intercourse. Some forms of contraception, such as _____, are effective at preventing the spread of these types of diseases. This is because they provide a _____, preventing the pathogens being passed from one person to another.

Exam Tip

Not all forms of contraception will work for this, read the whole paragraph first and check the type of contraception you selected is one that will work in this context.

09.3 A school suffers from an outbreak of whooping cough, an infectious disease spread by droplet infections or direct contact with an infected person or contaminated surface.

Choose **three** steps that would help the school to control the spread of the infection. **[3 marks]**

Send infected children home.
Prevent visitors from coming into the school.
Employ a new school nurse.
Wash surfaces with disinfectant.
Teach students about the benefits of vaccination.

10 Rose black spot is a disease that affects roses. It leads to yellow and black patterns on the leaves.

10.1 Identify the type of pathogen that causes rose black spot. **[1 mark]**

fungus   virus   bacterium   protist

10.2 Identify the correct chemical that can be used to treat rose black spot. **[1 mark]**

insecticide   herbicide   fungicide   pesticide

10.3 Explain why antibiotics cannot be used to treat rose black spot. **[2 marks]**

70 B7 The spread of diseases

11 **Figure 1** shows some of the organs in the human digestive system.

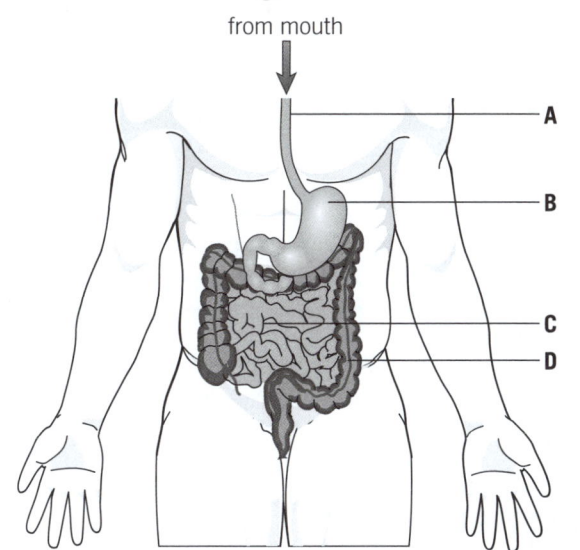

Figure 1

11.1 Match the letter (**A–D**) to the correct organ from the box. **[4 marks]**

| small intestine | large intestine | oesophagus | stomach |

11.2 Identify the organ from the box in **11.1** where nutrients are absorbed into the body from digested food. **[1 mark]**

11.3 The pancreas is not shown in **Figure 1**.

Which description below best describes the function of the pancreas in digestion?

Choose **one** answer. **[1 mark]**

adds acid to partly digested food

produces enzymes

kills microorganisms

Exam Tip

Not every diagram you see of the body will look the same as the ones you've used in class so you need to be able to identify organs by shape and position.

12 Bacteria are an example of prokaryotes.

12.1 Which of the following is the approximate size of a prokaryote?

Choose **one** answer. **[1 mark]**

100 nm   1 μm   10 μm   0.1 mm

12.2 Both plant cells and prokaryotic cells have cell walls.

Describe **one** difference between the cell wall of a plant cell, and the cell wall of a bacterial cell. **[1 mark]**

12.3 Suggest which feature needs to be present on a bacterial cell if it needs to move in water. **[1 mark]**

Exam Tip

Very large and very small units can seem more complicated than they really are. Make sure you know the order from largest to smallest:

km > m > cm > mm > μm > nm

Knowledge

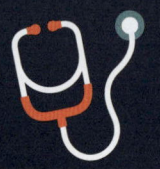

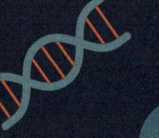

B8 Preventing and treating disease

Non-specific defences

Non-specific defences of the human body against all pathogens include:

Skin
- physical barrier to infection
- produces antimicrobial secretions
- microorganisms that normally live on the skin prevent pathogens growing

Nose
Cilia and **mucus** trap particles in the air, preventing them from entering the lungs.

The trachea and bronchi produce mucus, which is moved away from the lungs to the back of the throat by cilia, where it is expelled.

Stomach
Produces strong acid (pH 2) that destroys pathogens in mucus, food, and drinks.

White blood cells

If a pathogen enters the body, the immune system tries to destroy the pathogen.

The function of **white blood cells** is to fight pathogens.

There are two main types of white blood cell – lymphocytes and phagocytes.

> **Revision tip**
>
> **Remember** It's a common misconception that antibiotic resistance arises when people become resistant to a drug. In reality, it is the bacteria that evolve resistance.

Lymphocytes

Lymphocytes fight pathogens in two ways:

Antitoxins

Lymphocytes produce **antitoxins** that bind to the toxins produced by some pathogens (usually bacteria). This neutralises the toxins.

Antibodies

Lymphocytes produce **antibodies** that target and help to destroy specific pathogens by binding to **antigens** (proteins) on the pathogens' surfaces.

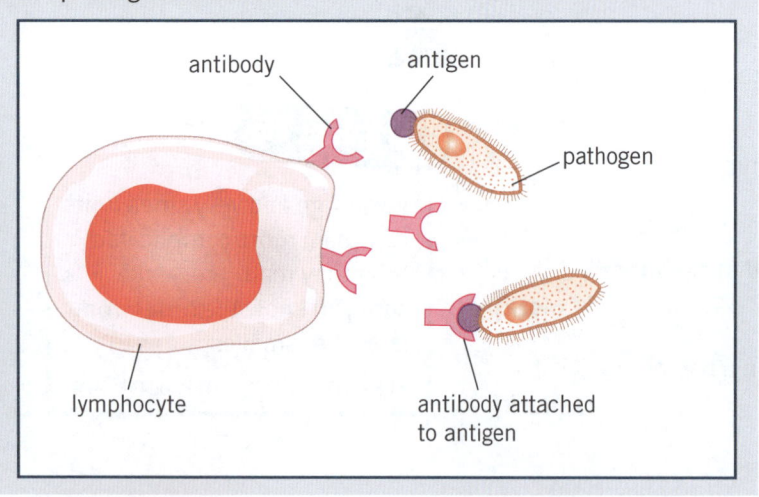

Phagocytes

1. Phagocytes are attracted to areas of infection.
2. The phagocyte surrounds the pathogen and engulfs it.
3. Enzymes digest and destroy the pathogen.

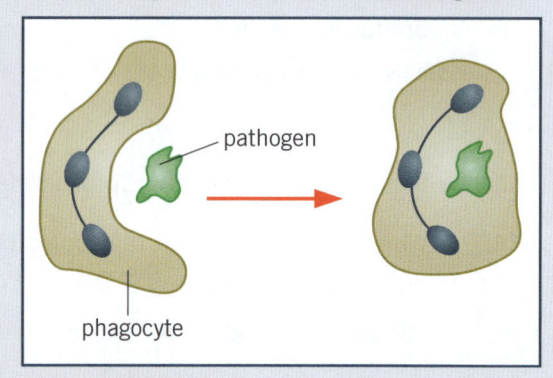

> **Revision tip**
>
> **Remember** Do not get bacterial and viral infections mixed up – don't say that antibiotics can be used to treat viral infections!

Key terms

Make sure you can write a definition for these key terms.

| antibiotic | antibody | antigen | antitoxin | dose | double-blind trial |

B8

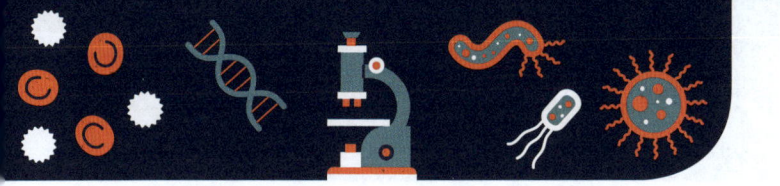

Treating diseases

Antibiotics
- **Antibiotics** are medicines that can kill *bacteria* in the body.
- Specific bacteria need to be treated by specific antibiotics.
- Antibiotics have greatly reduced deaths from infectious bacterial diseases, but antibiotic-resistant strains of bacteria are emerging.

Treating viral diseases
- Antibiotics *do not* affect viruses.
- Drugs that kill viruses often damage the body's tissues.
- Painkillers treat the symptoms of viral diseases but do not kill the virus.

Discovering and developing new drugs

Drugs were traditionally extracted from plants and microorganisms, for example:
- the heart drug digitalis comes from foxglove plants
- the painkiller aspirin originates from willow trees
- penicillin was discovered by Alexander Fleming from *Penicillium* mould.

Most modern drugs are now synthesised by chemists in laboratories.

New drugs are extensively tested and trialled for:
- **toxicity** – is it harmful?
- **efficacy** – does it work?
- **dose** – what amount is safe and effective to give?

Stages of clinical trials

Pre-clinical trials
Drug is tested in cells, tissues, and live animals.

Clinical trials
1. Healthy volunteers receive very low doses to test whether the drug is safe.
2. If safe, larger numbers of patients receive the drug to check it is effective and find the optimum dose.

Peer review
Before being published, the results of clinical trials will be tested and checked by independent researchers. This is called **peer review**.

Double-blind trials
Some clinical trials give some of their patients a **placebo** drug – one that is known to have no effect.

Double-blind trials are when neither the patients nor the doctors know who has been given the real drug and who has been given the placebo. This reduces biases in the trial.

---

efficacy   mucus   peer review   placebo   toxicity   white blood cell

B8 Knowledge 73

Retrieval

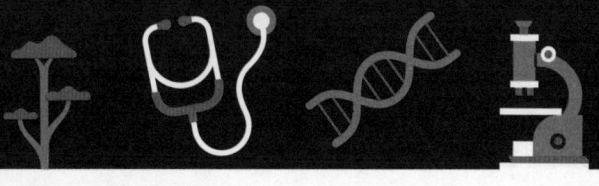

Learn the answers to the questions below, then cover the answers column with a piece of paper and write as many as you can. Check and repeat.

B8 questions | Answers

#	Question	Answer
1	What non-specific systems does the body use to prevent pathogens getting into it?	• skin • cilia and mucus in the nose, trachea, and bronchi • stomach acid
2	What three functions do white blood cells have?	• phagocytosis • producing antibodies • producing antitoxins
3	What happens during phagocytosis?	phagocyte is attracted to the area of infection, engulfs a pathogen, and releases enzymes to digest the pathogen
4	What are antigens?	proteins on the surface of a pathogen
5	Why are antibodies a specific defence?	antibodies have to be the right shape for a pathogen's unique antigens, so they target a specific pathogen
6	What is the function of an antitoxin?	neutralise toxins produced by pathogens by binding to them
7	What is an antibiotic?	a drug that kills bacteria but not viruses
8	What do painkillers do?	treat some symptoms of diseases and relieve pain
9	What properties of new drugs are clinical trials designed to test?	toxicity, efficacy, and optimum dose
10	What happens in the pre-clinical stage of a drug trial?	drug is tested on cells, tissues, and live animals
11	What is a placebo?	medicine with no effect that is given to patients instead of the real drug in a trial
12	What is a double-blind trial?	a trial where neither patients nor doctors know who receives the real drug and who receives the placebo

B8 Preventing and treating disease

B8

Now go back and use the questions below to check your knowledge from previous chapters.

Previous questions | Answers

#	Question	Answer
1	What is an organ?	group of tissues working together to perform a specific function
2	Why is a leaf an organ?	there are many tissues inside the leaf that work together to perform photosynthesis
3	What is herd immunity?	when most of a population is vaccinated against a disease, meaning it is less likely to spread
4	Describe an example of a protist disease.	malaria – caused by a protist pathogen that is spread from person to person by mosquito bites, and causes recurrent fevers
5	Name four factors that affect the rate of transpiration.	temperature, light intensity, humidity, wind speed
6	Where is amylase produced?	salivary glands, pancreas, small intestine
7	What happens during the third stage of the cell cycle?	the cytoplasm and cell membrane divide, forming two identical daughter cells

Maths skills

Practise your maths skills using the worked example and practice questions below.

Standard form

Standard form is a way of writing very large or very small numbers. For example, in biology we can use standard form when working with the size of cells and organelles as they are so small.

When writing a number in standard form, you first write a digit between 1 and 10, then you write $\times 10^n$, where the power of ten represents how big or small the number is.

For large numbers, positive powers of ten shift the digit to the left of the decimal point:

$23\,000\,000 = 2.3 \times 10^7$

For small numbers, negative powers of ten shift the digit to the right of the decimal point:

$0.000\,000\,23 = 2.3 \times 10^{-7}$

Worked example

Examples of powers of 10:

10^1	10
10^3	1000
10^7	10 000 000
10^{-3}	0.001
10^{-7}	0.000 000 1

What is 700 000 written in standard form?

700 000 can be written as $7 \times 100\,000$

$100\,000 = 10 \times 10 \times 10 \times 10 \times 10 = 10^5$

so $700\,000 = 7 \times 10^5$

What is 0.000 4 written in standard form?

0.000 4 can be written as 4×0.0001

$0.0001 = 10^{-4}$

so $0.0004 = 4 \times 10^{-4}$

Practice

1. The World Health Organization estimates that 3×10^8 people are infected with malaria every year. Convert this number to an expanded figure.

2. Scientists estimate that malaria kills 2×10^6 people every year. Convert this number to an expanded figure.

3. The table below gives data relating to diabetes in the UK. Write the figures in the table in standard form.

Data	Figure	Standard form
population of UK in 2015	65 000 000	
number of people diagnosed with diabetes	3 450 000	
estimated number of people with undiagnosed diabetes	549 000	

B8 Retrieval 75

Practice

Exam-style questions

01 **Figure 1** shows the number of cases of measles in the United States between 1962 and 1974.

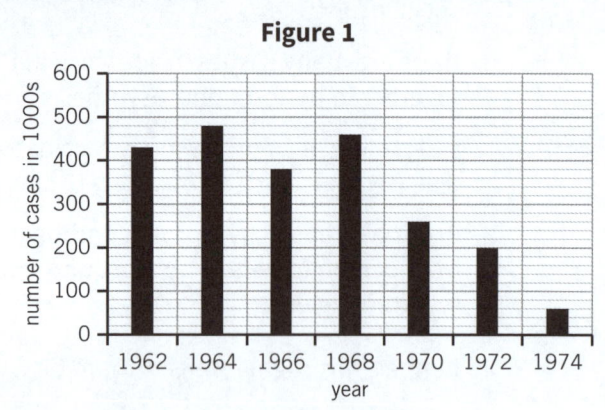

Figure 1

[Bar chart showing number of cases in 1000s on y-axis (0-600) against year on x-axis (1962-1974). Values approximately: 1962: 430, 1964: 480, 1966: 380, 1968: 460, 1970: 260, 1972: 200, 1974: 60]

01.1 Write the year where most cases of measles were recorded. **[1 mark]**

_____

01.2 Write the number of cases of measles recorded in 1966. **[1 mark]**

_____

> **Exam Tip**
> Use a ruler to help you read the number of cases off the y-axis.

01.3 The US government introduced a vaccination programme to protect the population against measles.

Identify the type of microorganism that causes the measles infection. **[1 mark]**

Tick **one** box.

bacterium ☐

virus ☐

fungus ☐

protist ☐

01.4 Identify the most likely year that a measles vaccination programme was introduced. **[1 mark]**

Tick **one** box.

1962 ☐

1968 ☐

1974 ☐

> **Exam Tip**
> Mark each year mentioned here on the graph and then look to see if any coincide with a decrease in measles cases.

76 B8 Preventing and treating disease

Paper 1 **B8**

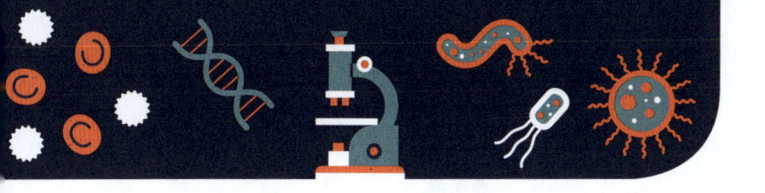

02 **Figure 2** shows a section of nasal epithelium. This is a type of tissue found in the nose. It provides a non-specific defence against disease.

Figure 2

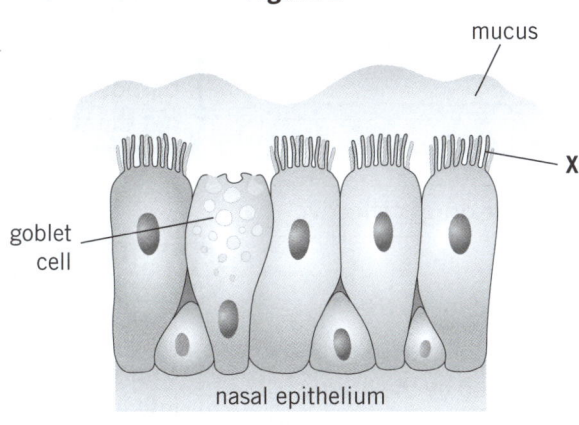

02.1 Describe why **Figure 2** is an example of a tissue. **[1 mark]**

_____
_____

02.2 Suggest the function of the goblet cells. **[1 mark]**

_____

> **Exam Tip**
> Look at how the structure of the goblet cell is different to the other cells.

02.3 Identify structure **X** on **Figure 2** and explain its role in defending against disease. **[3 marks]**

Tick **one** box.

cilium ☐

flagellum ☐

villus ☐

> **Exam Tip**
> All three of these structures are long and wavy, but they have different functions.

Explanation: _____
_____
_____

02.4 The skin is another example of a non-specific defence against disease. It acts as a barrier to microorganism entry.

Describe how the skin protects itself after its surface is punctured. **[2 marks]**

_____
_____
_____

For answers and more practice questions visit www.oxfordrevise.com/scienceanswers

Even more practice and interactive revision quizzes are available on kerboodle

B8 Practice 77

03 Before a medical drug can be licensed to be prescribed by a doctor, it has to undergo a number of stages of testing.

03.1 Draw **one** line from each stage of drug testing to its purpose.
[3 marks]

Stage of drug testing	Purpose of test
small dose on healthy volunteers	to find out if the drug is toxic
testing on cells	to determine the optimum dose
large numbers of patients	to check for side effects
small number of patients	to prove the drug is effective

> **Exam Tip**
> It might help to start with the purpose of the test to work out the stage of drug testing.

03.2 Drug trials are very expensive. They are often paid for by the company that wants to sell the drug.

Suggest **one** reason why people who are employed by the drug company should not take part in the trial. [1 mark]

> **Exam Tip**
> Think about why drug companies might want to influence the results.

03.3 Describe what is meant by a double blind trial. [3 marks]

03.4 Suggest why instead of using a placebo, trials often use an existing treatment for the condition being targeted. [1 mark]

04 Vaccinations are used to prevent a person from catching communicable diseases.

04.1 Complete the sentences to explain how a vaccine works. Use words from the box. [4 marks]

| cell | pathogen | create | antibodies |
| open | destroy | bodies | immune |

An inactive _____ is injected into the body.

This causes white blood cells to produce _____ .

If a live version of the pathogen enters the body later, the antibodies will be able to _____ it before it causes disease.

The person is now _____ to the disease.

04.2 Choose the best explanation for why pathogens in a vaccine cannot cause disease. Choose **one** answer. [1 mark]

They are dead or weakened forms of the pathogen.

They are present in too small a number to cause disease.

They have already been destroyed by white blood cells.

04.3 Some vaccines can cause side effects. However, most are not severe or long-lasting.

Name **one** common side effect of a vaccine. [1 mark]

> **Exam Tip**
> If you have had a vaccine recently, try to remember how you felt after it happened.

B8 Preventing and treating disease

05 Penicillin was first discovered in 1928.

05.1 Identify the scientist who discovered penicillin.
Choose **one** answer. [1 mark]
Charles Darwin
Alexander Fleming
Joseph Lister
Edward Jenner

05.2 Identify the source penicillin was discovered from.
Choose **one** answer. [1 mark]
foxglove   willow   mould   bacteria

05.3 Explain why a doctor would not prescribe antibiotics to treat a measles infection. [2 marks]

05.4 Penicillin and erythromycin are two examples of the many antibiotic drugs available.
Suggest why doctors have a range of antibiotic drugs available to prescribe. [2 marks]

> **Exam Tip**
> You need to be able to name the drugs that were found from each of these sources.

> **Exam Tip**
> For **05.3**, think about the type of pathogen that causes measles.

06 The human body uses a number of defence mechanisms to protect itself against disease.

06.1 Identify which of the following is a non-specific defence mechanism.
Choose **one** answer. [1 mark]
antibody production
antitoxin production
mucus production in trachea
production of bile

06.2 Draw **one** line from each body part to the non-specific defence mechanism used by that body part. [3 marks]

Body part	Non-specific defence mechanism
	produce tears that contain enzymes to kill bacteria
cut skin	contains acid to kill pathogens
nose	forms a scab to prevent pathogen entry
stomach	internal hairs act as a barrier to pathogen entry

06.3 Name the body system that is responsible for fighting disease. [1 mark]

07 Some strains of bacteria are becoming resistant to the drugs used to treat them.

07.1 Name the type of drug that can be used to treat bacterial diseases. **[1 mark]**

07.2 Scientists are developing new drugs to treat diseases caused by new strains of bacteria.

Reorder the steps (**1–7**) to show the process scientists follow to develop a new medical drug. The first and last steps have been done for you. **[4 marks]**

1   Laboratory testing on cells and tissue cultures
2   Testing on small group of patients with the bacterial infection
3   ~~Drug is approved for use~~
4   Testing on large group of patients with bacterial infection
5   Laboratory testing on live animals
6   ~~Identification of potential new compounds that kill bacteria~~
7   Testing on small group of healthy volunteers

6						3

Exam Tip

Make sure to cross off the steps you've used, as it is easy to get mixed up and add steps twice.

07.3 Suggest **one** potential source of a bacteria-killing drug. **[1 mark]**

07.4 When new drugs are tested, a double-blind trial is often used. Explain what this means. **[2 marks]**

08 Measles used to be a very common disease in children. It spreads quickly through droplet infection.

08.1 Describe why measles cannot be treated using antibiotics. **[1 mark]**

08.2 People who have been infected with measles may be advised to take aspirin.

Identify the plant that aspirin originates from. **[1 mark]**

foxglove   willow tree   mould   tomatoes

Exam Tip

It is important that you know what antibiotics are used for and the consequences of misuse.

08.3 Explain why aspirin may be beneficial for a person with measles, even though it does not cure the disease. **[2 marks]**

08.4 The best way to prevent the spread of measles is through a national vaccination programme.

Describe how the measles vaccine works. **[4 marks]**

08.5 In 2017–2018, 91.2% of children in the UK were vaccinated against measles. This was the lowest recorded vaccination level since 2010–2011.

Suggest how this will affect the number of people who are infected with measles. **[2 marks]**

09 A range of medical drugs are available to treat illnesses and disease. Some common medical drugs are shown here.

aspirin	penicillin	paracetamol	digitalis
amoxicillin	statins	insulin	

09.1 Write down the name of **one** medical drug from the box that is used as a painkiller. **[1 mark]**

09.2 Write down the name of **one** medical drug from the box that kills bacteria. **[1 mark]**

09.3 Choose the medical drug from the box that is used to treat heart rhythm problems. **[1 mark]**

09.4 Complete the following sentences about medical drugs by choosing the most appropriate bold words. **[4 marks]**

Some drugs are designed to treat the **symptoms / properties** of a disease. This makes the patient feel **worse / better**, but does not treat the source of the infection.

Other drugs are designed to kill **pathogens / antibodies**. These drugs provide a **cure / cause** for a particular disease or condition.

> **Exam Tip**
>
> Groups of similar drugs have similar sounding names – for example both drugs ending in –cillin are used for the same thing.

10 Most children in the UK are vaccinated against tetanus. Tetanus is a serious disease caused by a bacterial toxin that affects the nervous system.

10.1 Name the component in the vaccine that will make a child immune to tetanus. **[1 mark]**

10.2 There is also a vaccine to treat a disease called mumps.

Give **two** advantages of vaccinating a large proportion of the population against mumps. **[2 marks]**

10.3 Another vaccination offers protection against some of the bacteria that cause meningitis.

Explain why a person who has only received vaccinations against tetanus and mumps would not have protection against meningitis. **[3 marks]**

Knowledge

B9 Non-communicable diseases

Coronary heart disease

Coronary heart disease (CHD) occurs when the coronary arteries become narrowed by the build-up of layers of fatty material within them.

This reduces the flow of blood, resulting in less oxygen for the heart muscle, which can lead to heart attacks.

Health issues

Health is the state of physical and mental well-being.

The following factors can affect health:

- communicable and non-communicable diseases
- diet
- stress
- exercise
- life situations

Different types of disease may interact, for example

- defects in the immune system make an individual more likely to suffer from infectious diseases
- viral infections can trigger cancers
- immune reactions initially caused by a pathogen can trigger allergies, such as skin rashes and asthma
- severe physical ill health can lead to depression and other mental illnesses.

Treating cardiovascular diseases

Treatment	Description	Advantages	Disadvantages
stent	inserted into blocked coronary arteries to keep them open	• widens the artery – allows more blood to flow, so more oxygen is supplied to the heart • less serious surgery	• can involve major surgery – risk of infection, blood loss, blood clots, and damage to blood vessels • risks from anaesthetic used during surgery
statins	drugs that reduce blood **cholesterol** levels, slowing down the deposit of fatty material in the arteries	• effective • no need for surgery • can prevent CHD from developing	• possible side effects such as muscle pain, headaches, and sickness • cannot cure CHD, so patient will have to take tablets for many years
replace faulty heart valves	heart valves that leak or do not open fully, preventing control of blood flow through the heart, can be replaced with biological or mechanical valves	• allows control of blood flow through the heart • long-term cure for faulty heart valves	• can involve major surgery – risk of infection, blood loss, blood clots, and damage to blood vessels • risks from anaesthetic used during surgery
transplants	if the heart fails a donor heart, or heart and lungs, can be transplanted **artificial hearts** can be used to keep patients alive while waiting for a heart transplant, or to allow the heart to rest during recovery	• long-term cure for the most serious heart conditions • treats problems that cannot be treated in other ways	• transplant may be rejected if there is not a match between donor and patient • lengthy process • major surgery – risk of infection, blood loss, blood clots, and damage to blood vessels • risks from anaesthetic used during surgery

B9

Risk factors and non-communicable diseases

A **risk factor** is any aspect of your lifestyle or substance in your body that can increase the risk of a disease developing.

Some risk factors cause specific diseases. Other diseases are caused by multiple factors interacting.

Risk factor	Disease	Effects of risk factor
diet (obesity) and amount of exercise	Type 2 diabetes	body does not respond properly to the production of insulin, so blood glucose levels cannot be controlled
	cardiovascular diseases	increased blood cholesterol can lead to CHD
alcohol	impaired liver function	long-term alcohol use causes liver cirrhosis (scarring), meaning the liver cannot remove toxins from the body or produce sufficient bile
	impaired brain function	damages the brain and can cause anxiety and depression
	altered development of unborn babies	alcohol can pass through the placenta, risking miscarriages, premature births, and birth defects
smoking	lung disease and cancers	cigarettes contain carcinogens, which can cause cancers
	altered development of unborn babies	chemicals can pass through the placenta, risking premature births and birth defects
carcinogens, such as ionising radiation, and genetic risk factors	cancers	for example, tar in cigarettes and ultraviolet rays from the Sun can cause cancers
		some genetic factors make an individual more likely to develop certain cancers

Cancer

Cancer is the result of changes in cells that lead to uncontrolled growth and division by mitosis.

Rapid division of abnormal cells can form a **tumour**.

Malignant tumours are cancerous tumours that invade neighbouring tissues and spread to other parts of the body in the blood, forming secondary tumours.

Benign tumours are non-cancerous tumours that do not spread in the body.

Treatment of non-communicable diseases linked to lifestyle risk factors – such as poor diet, drinking alcohol, and smoking – can be very costly, both to individuals and to the Government.

A high incidence of these lifestyle risk factors can cause high rates of non-communicable diseases in a population.

Key terms

Make sure you can write a definition for these key terms.

artificial heart   benign   carcinogen   cholesterol   coronary heart disease   health
malignant   risk factor   statin   stent   transplant   tumour

B9 Knowledge   83

Retrieval

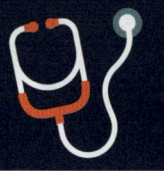

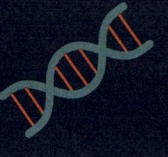

Learn the answers to the questions below, then cover the answers column with a piece of paper and write as many as you can. Check and repeat.

B9 questions | Answers

#	Question	Answer
1	What is coronary heart disease?	layers of fatty material build up inside the coronary arteries, narrowing them – resulting in a lack of oxygen for the heart
2	What is a stent?	a device inserted into a blocked artery to keep it open, allowing more blood and oxygen to the heart
3	What are statins?	drugs that reduce blood cholesterol levels, slowing the rate of fatty material deposit
4	What is a faulty heart valve?	heart valve that doesn't open properly or leaks
5	How can a faulty heart valve be treated?	replace with a biological or mechanical valve
6	When do heart transplants take place?	in cases of heart failure
7	What are artificial hearts used for?	keep patients alive while waiting for a transplant, or allow the heart to rest for recovery
8	Define health.	state of physical and mental well-being
9	What factors can affect health?	disease, diet, stress, exercise, life situations
10	What is a risk factor?	aspect of lifestyle or substance in the body that can increase the risk of a disease developing
11	Give five risk factors.	poor diet, smoking, lack of exercise, alcohol, carcinogens
12	What is cancer?	a result of changes in cells that lead to uncontrolled growth and cell division by mitosis
13	What are malignant tumours?	cancerous tumours that can spread to neighbouring tissues and other parts of the body in the blood, forming secondary tumours
14	What are benign tumours?	non-cancerous tumours that do not spread in the body
15	What two types of risk factor affect the development of cancers?	lifestyle and genetic risk factors
16	What is a carcinogen?	a substance that can cause cancers to develop

84 B9 Non-communicable diseases

B9

Now go back and use the questions below to check your knowledge from previous chapters.

Previous questions | Answers

#	Question	Answer
1	What is a communicable disease?	disease that can be transmitted from one organism to another
2	What is a pathogen?	microorganism that causes disease
3	What is a double-blind trial?	a trial where neither patients nor doctors know who receives the real drug and who receives the placebo
4	Describe the function of lipases.	to break down lipids into fatty acids and glycerol
5	What are antibiotics?	drugs that kill bacteria but not viruses
6	What do painkillers do?	treat some symptoms of diseases and relieve pain
7	Give one example of osmosis in a plant.	water moves from the soil into the root hair cell
8	Where are most stomata found?	underside of leaves
9	Why is the human circulatory system a double circulatory system?	blood passes through the heart twice – deoxygenated blood is pumped from the right side of the heart to the lungs, and the oxygenated blood that returns is pumped from the left side of the heart to the body

Maths skills

Practise your maths skills using the worked example and practice questions below.

Calculating rate of blood flow

The rate of blood flow in the body changes in response to things like exercise and illnesses.

Blood flow increases during exercise to deliver oxygen to working muscles and to remove waste products.

The rate of blood flow can be reduced by non-communicable diseases such as coronary heart disease.

To calculate rate of blood flow:

rate of blood flow (ml/min)

$$= \frac{\text{volume of blood (ml)}}{\text{time (min)}}$$

Remember to add units to your answer. Rate of blood flow can be measured in ml/min or l/hr – check the question to see which units you need to use.

Worked example

1660 ml of blood is pumped through a vein in four minutes.

Calculate the rate of blood flow through the vein in ml/min.

volume of blood = 1660 ml

time = 4 min

rate of blood flow = $\frac{1660}{4}$

= 415 ml/min

You may have to convert millilitres to litres if given a large volume. To do this, divide the volume in ml by 1000.

Practice

1. 3540 ml of blood is pumped through an artery in 3.5 min.

   Calculate the rate of blood flow through the artery in ml/min.

2. 11 540 ml of blood is pumped through an artery in 12.5 minutes.

   Calculate the rate of blood flow through the artery in ml/min.

3. 670 l of blood is pumped through the heart in 1 hr.

   Calculate the rate of blood flow through the heart in ml/min.

Practice

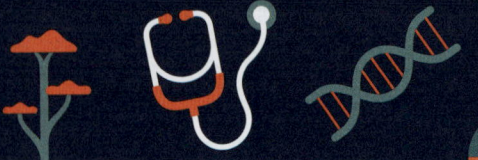

Exam-style questions

01 Both communicable and non-communicable diseases are major causes of ill health.

01.1 Identify **two** features of a non-communicable disease. **[2 marks]**
Tick **two** boxes.

caused by a microorganism ☐

not caused by a pathogen ☐

spreads easily between organisms ☐

cannot be spread between organisms ☐

> **! Exam Tip**
>
> The options here are two pairs of statements that are opposite to each other – this means you should only tick one *or* two and then three *or* four.

01.2 A number of lifestyle factors can affect the risk of a person developing a non-communicable disease.

Draw **one** line from each lifestyle factor to an example of a disease it can cause. **[2 marks]**

Lifestyle factor	Non-communicable disease
alcohol	liver disease
smoking	lung cancer
UV radiation	skin cancer

> **! Exam Tip**
>
> Think about the organ that these lifestyle factors will affect the most. Then try and link the non-communicable disease to it. Smoking is a good one to start with.

01.3 Although communicable and non-communicable diseases have separate causes, some conditions are linked.

Draw **one** line from each of the following diseases to the condition it may cause. **[2 marks]**

Disease	Condition
human papilloma virus (HPV)	further infections
immune system defects	depression
severe physical ill health	cervical cancer

86   B9 Non-communicable diseases

Paper 1 — B9

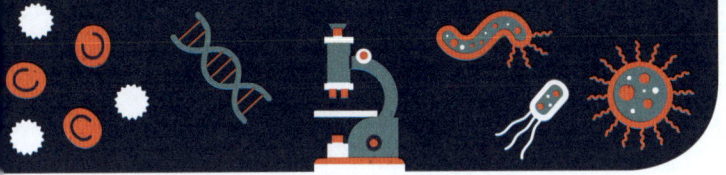

02 Stents can be used to treat blocked blood vessels.

02.1 Choose the best definition of a stent and its use. **[1 mark]**
Tick **one** box.

An operation where a blocked piece of blood vessel is replaced with a new piece of vessel. ☐

A small mesh tube that is inserted into the blood vessel to keep it open. ☐

A drug that thins the blood so it flows more easily through a blood vessel. ☐

A drug that reduces the build-up of cholesterol. ☐

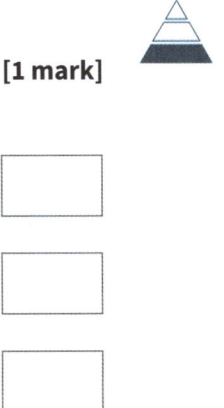

02.2 There are a number of risks and benefits associated with having a stent.

Draw **one** line from each statement to show whether it is a benefit or a risk of having a stent. **[2 marks]**

- can result in an irregular heartbeat
- long-term success rate is high
- patient needs to take blood-thinning drugs
- lowers the risk of the patient having a heart attack

benefit

risk

> **Exam Tip**
> Take each statement one at a time. Assess it carefully to see if it would be a benefit (a good thing) or a risk (a bad thing).

02.3 Give **one** risk factor that increases the likelihood of a person having a blocked blood vessel. **[1 mark]**

_____

03 **Figure 1** shows the main causes of death in the UK in 2012 for people under the age of 75. The total number of deaths recorded in this period was 150 000.

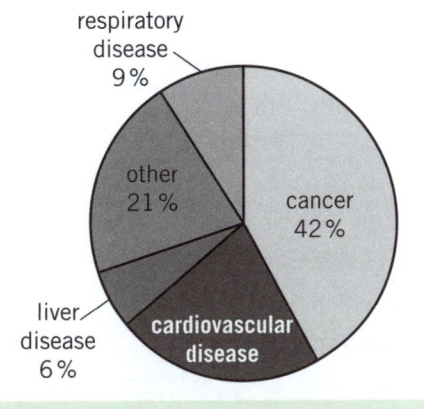

Figure 1

- respiratory disease 9%
- other 21%
- cancer 42%
- liver disease 6%
- cardiovascular disease

> **Exam Tip**
> The whole way around a pie chart is 100%. This means all the pieces of the pie chart need to add up to 100%.

B9 Practice

03.1 Describe what is meant by cardiovascular disease (CVD). **[1 mark]**

03.2 Determine the percentage of people under the age of 75 who died in 2012 due to CVD. **[1 mark]**

03.3 Calculate the number of people under the age of 75 who died in 2012 due to CVD. **[2 marks]**

03.4 Explain **three** ways a person could reduce their risk of CVD. **[6 marks]**

> **Exam Tip**
>
> **03.4** is a six-mark question asking for three things – this means you will get one mark for saying how a person could reduce the risk and the second mark for explaining why that would be effective for each of your three suggestions.

04 Drinking alcohol has a number of effects on the human body.

04.1 Identify the organs that alcohol can damage.

Choose **two** answers. **[2 marks]**

liver ears brain pancreas

04.2 **Figure 2** shows how the amount of alcohol a person drinks affects their risk of death.

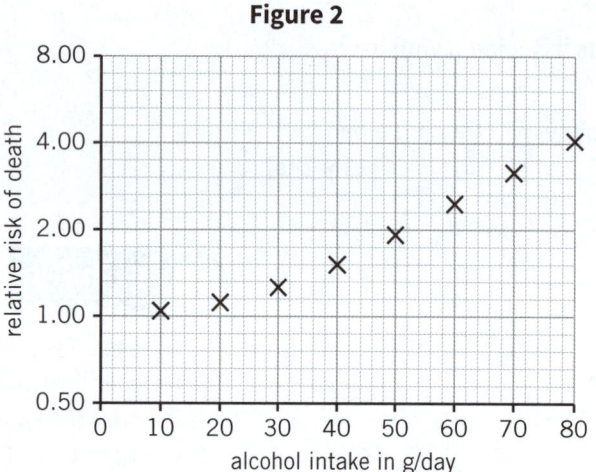

Figure 2

[Scatter graph: x-axis "alcohol intake in g/day" from 0 to 80; y-axis "relative risk of death" from 0.50 to 8.00. Points plotted approximately at (10, 1.05), (20, 1.1), (30, 1.2), (40, 1.5), (50, 1.9), (60, 2.5), (70, 3.2), (80, 4.0).]

Identify the type of correlation shown in **Figure 2**. **[1 mark]**

> **Exam Tip**
>
> Draw a curved line of best fit on to the graph to help you answer the questions.

04.3 Use **Figure 2** to predict a person's relative risk of death if they drink 60 g of alcohol each day. **[1 mark]**

> **Exam Tip**
>
> Use a ruler to draw a line from the cross at 60 g to the y-axis to help you read the value.

04.4 Regularly drinking large amounts of alcohol increases the risk of a person developing mouth cancer.

Explain whether mouth cancer is an example of a communicable or non-communicable disease. **[2 marks]**

05 In order to improve health, scientists collect information about people's lifestyle choices and the likelihood of suffering from a disease. For example, data have been collected about people who smoke, and their risk of developing lung cancer.

05.1 Choose the correct bold words to complete the following sentences about smoking. **[4 marks]**

Scientists have collected data that shows that smokers are **more / less** likely to develop lung cancer than people who do not smoke. This is an example of a **causal mechanism / correlation**.

Cigarette smoke contains **carbon monoxide / tar**, which has been proved to cause cancer. This is an example of a **causal mechanism / correlation**.

B9 Non-communicable diseases

05.2 Identify the name given to chemicals that cause cancer.
Choose **one** answer. **[1 mark]**

radiation   carcinogen   buffer   antigen

05.3 Smoking has been linked to a number of health problems other than lung cancer. Draw **one** line from each chemical in cigarettes to the effect it may have. **[2 marks]**

Chemical   **Effect**

nicotine

carbon monoxide

paralyses cilia causing 'smoker's cough'

less oxygen transported

increases heart rate

06 Every year many patients need to have heart valve replacements.

06.1 Describe the function of the heart valve labelled **X** in **Figure 3**. **[2 marks]**

Figure 3

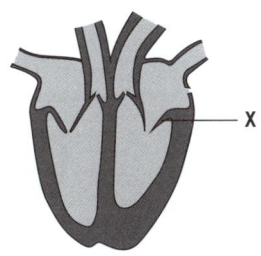

> **Exam Tip**
> Look at the shape of the valve – it may give you a clue to its function.

06.2 Over time heart valves can become leaky.

Identify which of the following are problems associated with a leaky valve. Choose **two** answers. **[2 marks]**

more blood leaves the heart than normal

less blood leaves the heart than normal

blood coming into the heart chamber mixes with blood that has not left, making the heart less efficient

blood contains more red blood cells than normal

06.3 **Table 1** contains information about two types of heart valve.

Table 1

	Mechanical heart valve	Biological heart valve
Material	titanium	usually cow or pig tissue, but can be from a human donor
Timescale	20 years	10–15 years
Medication	anti-coagulation medication to prevent blood clotting around the valve	not required

A 20-year-old patient requires a heart valve replacement. Use the information in **Table 1** to give **one** advantage and **one** disadvantage of the patient having a mechanical heart valve over a biological valve replacement. **[2 marks]**

> **Exam Tip**
> All of the information you need to answer this question can be found in the table – use two different coloured pens to identify the advantages and disadvantages.

07 To reduce the number of deaths from non-communicable diseases, scientists study large volumes of data to search for possible links between risk factors and disease.

07.1 Describe the difference between a risk factor that shows a correlation with the incidence of a disease and a risk factor that shows causation of a disease. **[2 marks]**

07.2 Give **one** risk factor for a disease that you cannot control. **[1 mark]**

07.3 Unprotected exposure to sunlight is a risk factor for developing skin cancer.

Explain what is meant by the term cancer. **[2 marks]**

07.4 Explain how sun exposure increases a person's risk of developing skin cancer. **[2 marks]**

07.5 Smoking is a risk factor for the development of tumours. Most tumours caused by smoking are malignant.

Explain the difference between a benign and a malignant tumour. **[3 marks]**

08 One measure of a person's health is their body mass index (BMI). BMI is calculated using the following formula:

$$BMI\ (kg/m^2) = \frac{mass}{height^2}$$

08.1 A student has a mass of 48 kg and a height of 1.5 m.

Calculate the student's BMI. **[2 marks]**

08.2 Using **Table 2**, identify which weight category the student belongs to. **[1 mark]**

Table 2

Weight categories	BMI in kg/m²
underweight	<18.5
healthy weight	18.5–24.9
overweight	25–29.9
obese	30+

! Exam Tip

Make sure you do the division and the square in the correct order.

08.3 In 2016, 26% of adults in the UK were classified as obese.

Describe **two** disease risks associated with obesity. **[2 marks]**

08.4 A public health campaign aims to increase levels of exercise amongst the population by encouraging people to walk or cycle to work, rather than take public transport or drive.

Explain how this campaign could help to reduce obesity levels in the population. **[2 marks]**

! Exam Tip

What effect will people walking more have on obesity?

B9 Non-communicable diseases

09 If a person has a high level of cholesterol in their blood, it increases their risk of having a heart attack or a stroke.

09.1 Using words in the box, complete the following sentences to explain how the build-up of cholesterol can cause a heart attack. **[4 marks]**

| carbohydrate | narrow | fatty | reduces |
| more | widen | increases | less |

_____ material builds up inside the coronary arteries and causes them to _____ .

This _____ blood flow so _____ oxygen gets to the heart muscle.

09.2 Give **one** factor that can affect the level of cholesterol in a person's blood. **[1 mark]**

09.3 Name the drug that is commonly prescribed to reduce blood cholesterol levels. **[1 mark]**

> **Exam Tip**
> Cholesterol and carbohydrates are both biological molecules that sound similar, but it is important not to get them confused as they are very different. During your revision, make a list of all the new words you've learnt to help you remember them.

10 Fresh cow's milk is a mixture containing water, lipids, protein, and lactose sugar. It also contains some vitamins and minerals.

10.1 Describe the chemical test that could be used to show that there is protein present in milk. **[2 marks]**

> **Exam Tip**
> Give the name of the test, how the test is carried out, and the positive result.

10.2 Lactose cannot be absorbed into the body. It must be digested by the enzyme lactase into the sugars glucose and galactose, which can then be absorbed.

Suggest why lactose cannot be absorbed into the blood. **[1 mark]**

10.3 Lactase can be added to fresh milk to pre-digest the lactose. This makes 'lactose-free' milk, which is suitable for people who do not produce enough lactase of their own. A company that produces lactose-free milk investigated the effect of temperature on lactase. Their results are shown in **Table 3**.

> **Exam Tip**
> Lact**a**se is an enzyme that breaks down lact**o**se.

Table 3

Temperature in °C	Time taken to digest lactose in min
25	20
30	14
35	11
40	11
45	29
50	no digestion

Explain why no digestion occurred at 50 °C. **[3 marks]**

Knowledge

B10 Photosynthesis and respiration

Photosynthetic reaction

Photosynthesis is a chemical reaction where energy is transferred from the environment as light from the Sun to the leaves of a plant. This is an **endothermic** reaction.

Chlorophyll, the green pigment in **chloroplasts** in the leaves, absorbs the light energy. Leaves are well-adapted to increase the rate of photosynthesis when needed.

Rate of photosynthesis

A **limiting factor** is anything that limits the rate of a reaction when it is in short supply.

The limiting factors for photosynthesis are:
- temperature
- carbon dioxide concentration
- light intensity
- amount of chlorophyll.

Less chlorophyll in the leaves reduces the rate of photosynthesis. More chlorophyll may be produced by plants in well-lit areas to increase the photosynthesis rate.

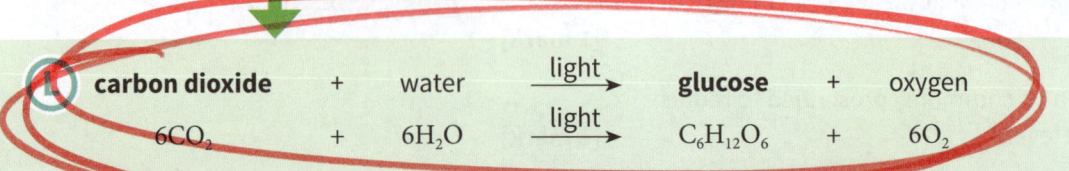

carbon dioxide + water $\xrightarrow{\text{light}}$ **glucose** + oxygen

$6CO_2$ + $6H_2O$ $\xrightarrow{\text{light}}$ $C_6H_{12}O_6$ + $6O_2$

Uses of glucose from photosynthesis

- Converted into insoluble starch for storage.
- For respiration to release energy.
- Produce cellulose to strengthen cell walls.
- Produce fat or oil (lipids) for storage.
- Produce amino acids for protein synthesis – nitrate from the soil is also needed for this.

Limiting factors and photosynthesis rate

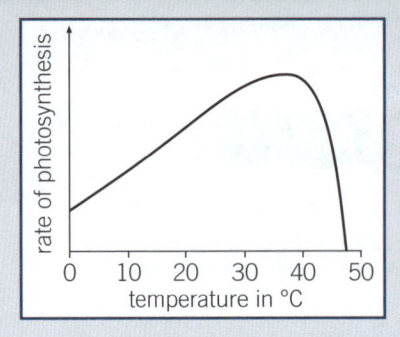

- At low temperatures the rate of photosynthesis is low because the reactant molecules have less kinetic energy.
- Photosynthesis is an enzyme-controlled reaction, so at high temperatures the enzymes are denatured and the rate quickly decreases.

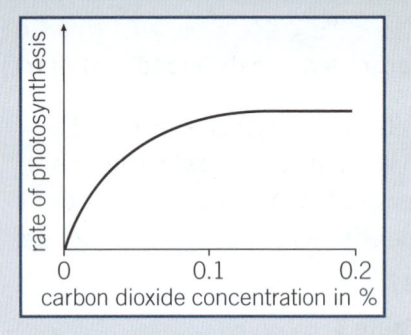

- Carbon dioxide is used up in photosynthesis, so increasing carbon dioxide concentration increases the rate of photosynthesis.
- At a certain point, another factor becomes limiting.
- Carbon dioxide is often the limiting factor for photosynthesis.

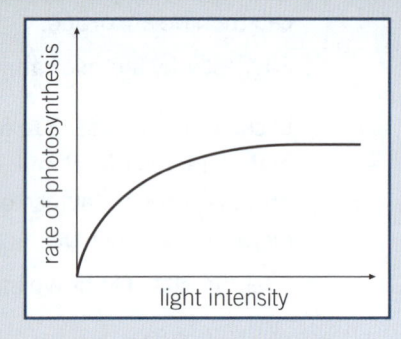

- Light energy is needed for photosynthesis, so increasing light intensity increases the rate of photosynthesis.
- At a certain point, another factor becomes limiting.
- Photosynthesis will stop if there is little or no light.

Key terms

Make sure you can write a definition for these key terms.

aerobic anaerobic carbon dioxide chlorophyll chloroplast endothermic exothermic fermentation glucose lactic acid limiting factor metabolism mitochondria oxidation photosynthesis respiration

B10

Cellular respiration

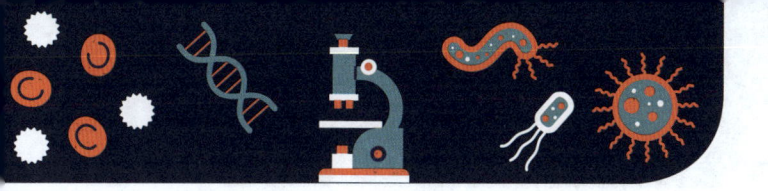

Cellular **respiration** is an **exothermic** reaction that occurs continuously in the **mitochondria** of living cells to supply the cells with energy.

The energy released during respiration is needed for all living processes, including

- chemical reactions to build larger molecules, for example, making proteins from amino acids
- muscle contraction for movement
- keeping warm.

Respiration in cells can take place aerobically (using oxygen) or anaerobically (without oxygen).

Aerobic respiration uses the complete **oxidation** of glucose to release a large amount of energy.

Anaerobic respiration uses the incomplete oxidation of glucose and releases much less energy per glucose molecule than aerobic respiration.

Aerobic respiration

glucose + oxygen → carbon dioxide + water

$C_6H_{12}O_6 + 6O_2 \rightarrow 6CO_2 + 6H_2O$

Anaerobic respiration in muscles

glucose → **lactic acid**

$C_6H_{12}O_6 \rightarrow 2C_3H_6O_3$

Metabolism

Metabolism is the sum of all the reactions in a cell or the body.

The energy released by respiration in cells is used for the continual enzyme-controlled processes of metabolism that produce new molecules.

Metabolic processes include the synthesis and breakdown of:

Carbohydrates
- synthesis of larger carbohydrates (starch, glycogen, and cellulose) from simple sugars
- breakdown of glucose in respiration to release energy

Proteins
- synthesis of amino acids from glucose and nitrate ions
- amino acids used to form proteins
- excess proteins broken down to form urea for excretion

Lipids
- synthesis of lipids from one molecule of glycerol and three molecules of fatty acid

Fermentation

Anaerobic respiration in plant and yeast cells is represented by the equation:

glucose → ethanol + carbon dioxide

Anaerobic respiration in yeast cells is called **fermentation**.

The products of fermentation are important in the manufacturing of bread and alcoholic drinks.

Response to exercise

During exercise the human body reacts to the increased demand for energy.

If insufficient oxygen is supplied, anaerobic respiration takes place instead, leading to the build-up of lactic acid.

During long periods of vigorous exercise, muscles become fatigued and stop contracting efficiently.

Removal of lactic acid

lactic acid in the muscles
↓
transported to the liver in the blood
↓
lactic acid is converted back to glucose

B10 Knowledge

Retrieval

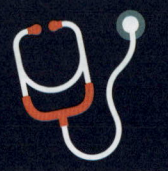

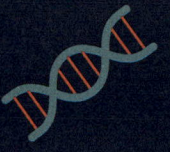

Learn the answers to the questions below, then cover the answers column with a piece of paper and write as many as you can. Check and repeat.

B10 questions | Answers

#	Question	Answer
1	Where does photosynthesis occur?	chloroplasts in the leaves of a plant
2	What is the name of the green pigment in leaves?	chlorophyll
3	Write the balanced symbol equation for aerobic respiration.	$C_6H_{12}O_6 + 6O_2 \rightarrow 6CO_2 + 6H_2O$
4	What type of energy is used in photosynthesis?	light energy
5	Give the word equation for photosynthesis.	carbon dioxide + water → glucose + oxygen
6	Why does aerobic respiration release more energy per glucose molecule than anaerobic respiration?	oxidation of glucose is complete in aerobic respiration and incomplete in anaerobic respiration
7	Define the term limiting factor.	anything that limits the rate of a reaction when it is in short supply
8	Give the limiting factors of photosynthesis.	• temperature • carbon dioxide concentration • light intensity • amount of chlorophyll
9	Write the word equation for anaerobic respiration in plant and yeast cells.	glucose → ethanol + carbon dioxide
10	Define the term cellular respiration.	an exothermic reaction that occurs continuously in the mitochondria of living cells to release energy from glucose
11	Describe how temperature affects the rate of photosynthesis.	increasing temperature increases the rate of photosynthesis as the reaction rate increases – at high temperatures enzymes are denatured so the rate of photosynthesis quickly decreases
12	What do organisms need energy for?	• chemical reactions to build larger molecules • muscle contraction for movement • keeping warm
13	What is the difference between aerobic and anaerobic respiration?	aerobic respiration uses oxygen, anaerobic respiration does not
14	How do plants use the glucose produced in photosynthesis?	• respiration • convert it into insoluble starch for storage • produce fat or oil for storage • produce cellulose to strengthen cell walls • produce amino acids for protein synthesis

B10 Photosynthesis and respiration

Now go back and use the questions below to check your knowledge from previous chapters.

B10

Previous questions | Answers

#	Previous questions	Answers
1	What is a stent?	a device inserted into a blocked artery to keep it open, allowing more blood and oxygen to the heart
2	How is the upper epidermis adapted for its function?	• single layer of transparent cells allows light to pass through • cells secrete a waxy substance that makes leaves waterproof
3	Why do different digestive enzymes have different optimum pHs?	different parts of the digestive system have very different pHs – the stomach is strongly acidic, and the pH in the small intestine is close to neutral
4	Name the substances transported in the blood plasma.	hormones, proteins, urea, carbon dioxide, glucose
5	How do viruses make you ill?	reproduce rapidly inside cells, damaging or destroying them
6	What factors can affect health?	disease, diet, stress, exercise, life situations
7	What are benign tumours?	non-cancerous tumours that do not spread in the body
8	Why are antibodies a specific defence?	antibodies have to be the right shape for a pathogen's unique antigens, so they target a specific pathogen

Required practical skills

Practise answering questions on the required practicals using the example below. You need to be able to apply your skills and knowledge to other practicals too.

Rate of photosynthesis

You should be able to accurately measure changes in the rate of photosynthesis of a plant, and how the rate changes in response to changes in the environment.

This requires being able to describe how to measure the rate of a reaction or biological process by collecting a gas produced. For example, collecting bubbles of oxygen produced by pondweed to compare the volume of gas produced at different light intensities.

It is important to understand how different factors affect rates of photosynthesis, including light intensity, temperature, and carbon dioxide concentration.

Worked example

A student used an inverted test tube to investigate the number of bubbles released from a piece of pondweed in a beaker of water in a ten-minute period. They repeated each measurement five times.

1 Identify the dependent variable in this experiment.

Number of bubbles released.

2 Explain how the student could use this set up to investigate how light intensity affects the rate of photosynthesis.

Carry out the experiment described above with a switched on lamp placed exactly 10 cm from the pondweed. Record the number of bubbles produced over 10 mins, repeating the experiment five times. Move the lamp 10 cm further away from the pondweed, and repeat the same experiment. Calculate the mean number of bubbles produced for each light intensity, and compare the results.

Practice

1 Suggest how the student could change the experiment to give a more accurate measurement of the gas released.

2 Explain how temperature affects the rate of plant photosynthesis.

3 Name a piece of equipment that could be used to investigate how temperature affects the amount of gas released by the pondweed.

B10 Retrieval

Practice

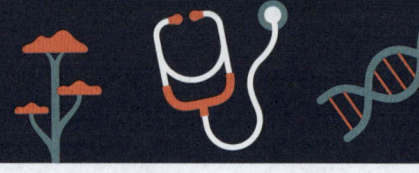

Exam-style questions

01 **Figure 1** shows a cross-section through a leaf.

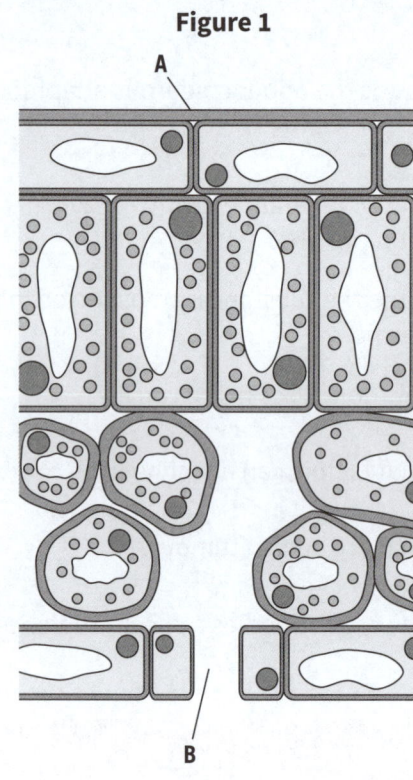

01.1 Identify structure **B**. **[1 mark]**
Tick **one** box.

- palisade cell ☐
- chloroplast ✓
- stoma ☐
- cuticle ☐

Figure 1

01.2 Identify the function of structure **A** in photosynthesis. **[1 mark]**
Tick **one** box.

- take in nutrients ☐
- prevent water loss ☐
- absorb light ✓
- gas exchange ☐

01.3 Explain **one** way a leaf is adapted to absorb light fo photosynthesis. **[2 marks]**

chloroplast help to absorb the light energy

01.4 Explain **one** way a leaf is adapted to take in carbon dioxide for photosynthesis. **[2 marks]**

_____

_____

02 **Figure 2** shows the main components in an animal cell as seen under a light microscope.

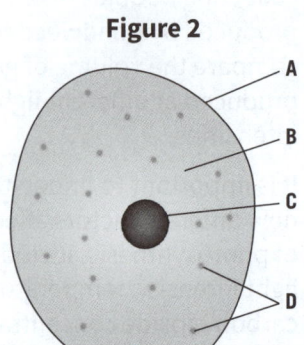

02.1 Identify the part of the cell (**A**–**D**) where respiration occurs. **[1 mark]**

_____

Figure 2

96   B10 Photosynthesis and respiration

Paper 1 **B10**

02.2 Identify the correct products of respiration. **[1 mark]**
Tick **one** box.

glucose + oxygen ☐

glucose + carbon dioxide ☐

carbon dioxide + water ☐

water + oxygen ☐

> **! Exam Tip**
> Light is not a product or a reactant of photosynthesis – it should be placed above the arrow, not before or after it.

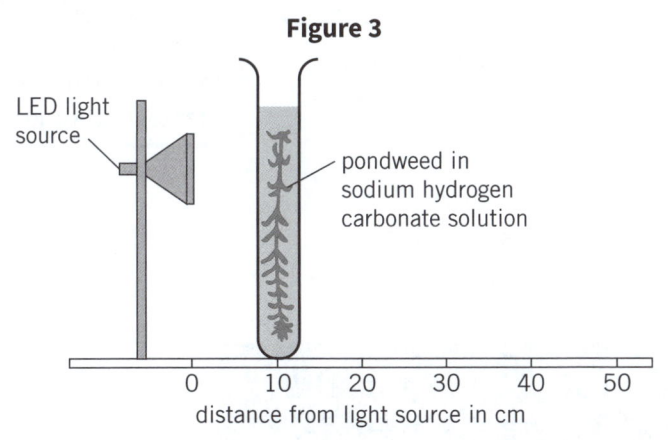

02.3 Give **one** use of energy by the body. **[1 mark]**

_____

02.4 When a person is exercising vigorously, muscle cells can switch to a form of respiration that occurs without the use of oxygen.
Name this type of respiration. **[1 mark]**

_____

02.5 Give **one** reason why animal cells normally respire with oxygen.
[1 mark]

_____

03 A student set up the apparatus in **Figure 3** to investigate the effect of light intensity on photosynthesis in pondweed.

Figure 3

LED light source — pondweed in sodium hydrogen carbonate solution

0 10 20 30 40 50
distance from light source in cm

03.1 Identify the independent variable in this investigation. **[1 mark]**

03.2 Give the reason the pondweed was placed in a solution of sodium hydrogen carbonate. **[1 mark]**

03.3 The student measured the rate of photosynthesis of the pondweed by counting the number of oxygen bubbles produced in one minute.
Describe how you could test the bubbles to show they contained oxygen. **[2 marks]**

> **! Exam Tip**
> Try to predict which gases are going to be released from sodium hydrogen carbonate, and what effect they might have on photosynthesis.

B10 Practice 97

03.4 The student's results are shown in **Table 1**.
Plot the data on **Figure 4**. [3 marks]

Table 1

Distance from light source in cm	Number of bubbles produced per minute
10	15
20	8
30	4
40	2
50	0

Figure 4

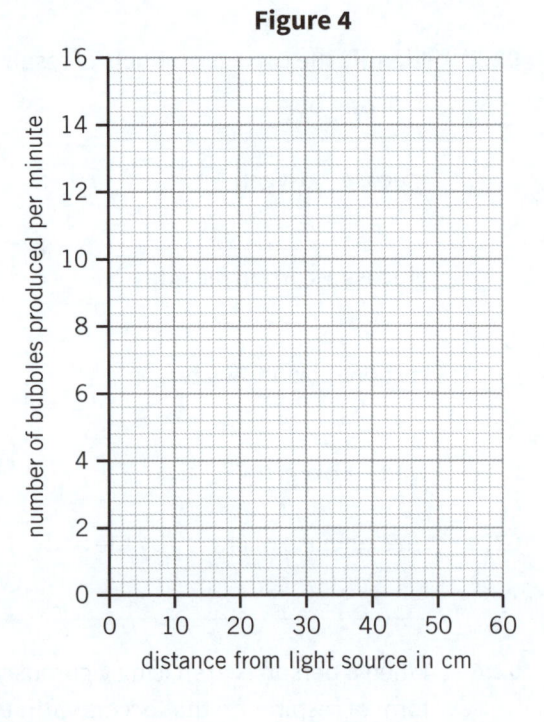

03.5 Describe the trend shown by your graph in **Figure 4**. [1 mark]

03.6 Use **Figure 4** to estimate the number of bubbles that would be produced per minute at 25 cm. [1 mark]

03.7 The student stated that counting bubbles was not an accurate way of measuring the volume of oxygen produced. Write down **one** reason why the student is correct. [1 mark]

03.8 Suggest **one** improvement the student could make to improve the accuracy of this investigation. [1 mark]

04 When a person exercises, a number of changes take place in their body.

04.1 Choose the appropriate bold words to complete the following sentences. [5 marks]

When you exercise, your muscles contract **more rapidly / more slowly**. This means your cells need to respire **slower / faster** to transfer the energy needed.

At the same time, your breathing rate **decreases / increases** and you breathe more **deeply / shallowly**. This increases the amount of **carbon dioxide / oxygen** in the blood, which is needed for respiration.

> **Exam Tip**
> The two paragraphs can be completed independently – if you're not sure about the first section, imagine doing some exercise and then try to apply that to the second section.

04.2 Exercise causes a person's heart rate to fluctuate. A group of students (**A–E**) measured their heart rates at rest, and after ten minutes of jogging. The results are shown in **Table 2**.

Table 2

Student	Heart rate at rest in beats per min	Heart rate after exercise in beats per min	Time taken for heart rate to return to resting rate in min
A	80	107	8
B	77	125	9
C	89	128	10
D	78	115	7
E	75	104	6

Describe the results of the students' investigation. [2 marks]

B10 Photosynthesis and respiration

04.3 Identify which student (**A–E**) had the biggest change in pulse rate. **[1 mark]**

04.4 Suggest which student (**A–E**) was the fittest.
Give **one** reason for your answer. **[2 marks]**

> **Exam Tip**
> The reason you give must include data from **Table 2**.

05 Respiration takes place in all living plant and animal cells.

05.1 Describe the purpose of respiration. **[2 marks]**

05.2 Organisms can respire both aerobically and anaerobically. **Table 3** summarises the similarities and differences between these processes.
Complete **Table 3**. **[4 marks]**

> **Exam Tip**
> There are three key equations you need to know here: aerobic respiration, anaerobic respiration in plants, and anaerobic respiration in animals.

Table 3

Type of respiration	aerobic	anaerobic	
Organism it occurs in	plants and animals	plants	animals
Oxygen required?	yes	no	
Glucose required?	yes		yes
Carbon dioxide produced?	yes	yes	
Other products produced	water		lactic acid

05.3 Describe **two** ways yeast is used to produce food products using anaerobic respiration. **[4 marks]**

> **Exam Tip**
> There are two products from fermentation – each one can be used in a different way by the food industry.

06 Plants and algae make their own food by photosynthesis.

06.1 Choose the correct words from the box to complete the word equation for photosynthesis. **[2 marks]**

| water | nitrogen | sugar | starch | oxygen |

carbon dioxide + _____ $\xrightarrow{\text{light}}$ glucose + _____

06.2 Identify where photosynthesis takes place in a cell.
Choose **one** answer. **[1 mark]**

chloroplast   cytoplasm   nucleus   mitochondrion

06.3 During the process of photosynthesis, energy is transferred to the plant cells by light.
Identify which type of reaction best describes photosynthesis.
Choose **one** answer. **[1 mark]**

oxidation   reduction   endothermic   exothermic

> **Exam Tip**
> Remember that exothermic reactions release energy and endothermic reactions absorb energy.

06.4 As well as light, plants need to take in carbon dioxide to photosynthesise.
Name the structure that allows carbon dioxide to enter the leaf. **[1 mark]**

07 The rate of photosynthesis is affected by a number of factors.

07.1 Complete **Table 4** by adding ticks to show whether the following factors increase, decrease, or cause no change to the rate of photosynthesis. **[4 marks]**

Table 4

Factor	Increase rate of photosynthesis	Decrease rate of photosynthesis	No change to the rate of photosynthesis
increasing light intensity			
increasing nutrient availability			
decreasing carbon dioxide concentration			
increasing chlorophyll present in leaf			

07.2 Identify the graph (**A**, **B**, or **C**) in **Figure 5** that correctly shows the effect of increasing temperature on the rate of photosynthesis. **[1 mark]**

Figure 5

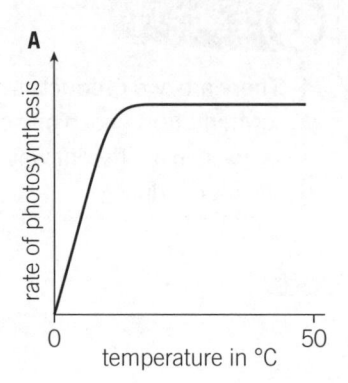

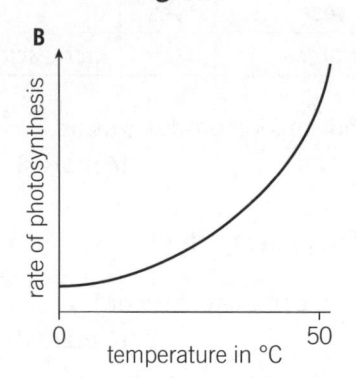

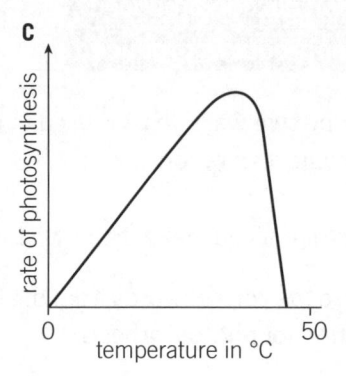

07.3 The greater the rate of photosynthesis, the greater the rate of glucose production in a plant.

Give **two** uses of glucose in plants. **[2 marks]**

08 Respiration supplies all the energy needed for living processes.

08.1 Complete the word equation for respiration using some of the words in the box. **[2 marks]**

| water | fat | methane | oxygen |

glucose + _____ → carbon dioxide + _____ (+ energy)

08.2 Identify which of the following statements are correct about aerobic respiration.

Choose **two** answers. **[2 marks]**

aerobic respiration is an exothermic reaction

aerobic respiration produces lactic acid

aerobic respiration transfers more energy per glucose molecule than anaerobic respiration

aerobic respiration can take place without oxygen

08.3 Identify where respiration takes place in a cell. **[1 mark]**

B10 Photosynthesis and respiration

09 All living organisms metabolise chemical compounds.

09.1 Define the term metabolism. [1 mark]

09.2 Explain how respiration maintains the rate of metabolism in an organism. [3 marks]

09.3 Two examples of metabolic reactions are:
- the formation of lipids
- the conversion of glucose into starch (in plants) or glycogen (in animals).

Name the molecules required to form a lipid. [2 marks]

09.4 Plants convert glucose to starch, and animals convert glucose to glycogen.
Explain why this is necessary. [2 marks]

10 Organisms are made up of a number of organ systems. One example is the digestive system.

10.1 Give another example of an organ system and describe its function. [2 marks]

10.2 The main organs in the digestive system are labelled in **Figure 6**.

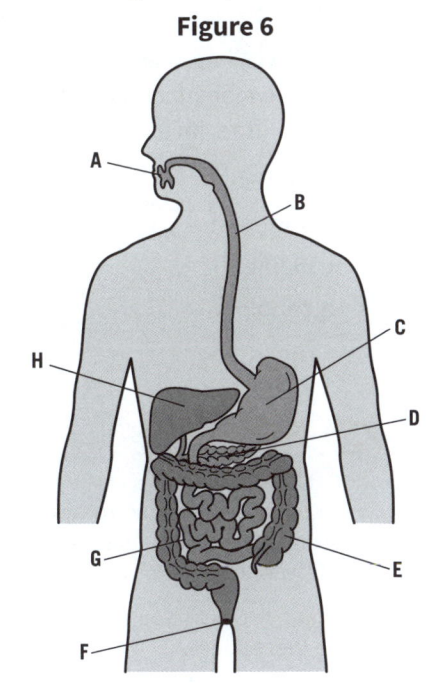

Figure 6

Identify the label that shows the liver. [1 mark]

10.3 Describe the function of organ **G**. [1 mark]

10.4 Give **one** reason why organ **C** contains hydrochloric acid. [1 mark]

> **Exam Tip**
>
> For your revision, try to label all of the organs.

Knowledge

B11 The nervous system and homeostasis

The nervous system

Function

The nervous system enables humans to react to their surroundings and to coordinate their behaviour – this includes both voluntary and **involuntary** actions.

Structure

The nervous system is made up of the **central nervous system** (CNS) and a network of nerves.

The CNS comprises the **brain** and **spinal cord**.

Nervous system responses

Stimulus	Receptor	Coordinator	Effector	Response
a change in the environment (**stimulus**) is detected by **receptors**	information from receptors passes along cells (**neurones**) to the CNS as electrical impulses	the CNS coordinates the body's response to the stimulus	**effectors** bring about a response, such as glands secreting hormones or muscles contracting	the body responds to the stimulus

Homeostasis

Homeostasis is the regulation of internal conditions (of a cell or whole organism) in response to internal and external changes, to maintain optimum conditions for functioning.

This maintains optimum conditions for all cell functions and enzyme action.

In the human body, this includes control of:

- blood glucose concentration
- body temperature
- water levels.

The automatic control systems of homeostasis may involve nervous responses or chemical responses.

All control systems involve:

- receptor cells, which detect stimuli (changes in the environment)
- **coordination centres** (such as the brain, spinal cord, or pancreas), which receive and process information from receptors
- effectors (muscles or glands), which produce responses to restore optimum conditions.

Factors affecting reaction time

There are many factors that can affect human reaction time, including:

- tiredness
- distractions
- caffeine
- alcohol.

Revision tips

Practice The way control systems work makes a good six-mark question – practise writing long answers on these topics.

Practice Ensure you can sketch and label all the diagrams on these pages.

Key terms

Make sure you can write a definition for these key terms.

brain   central nervous system   coordination centre   effectors   homeostasis

102   B11 The nervous system and homeostasis

B11

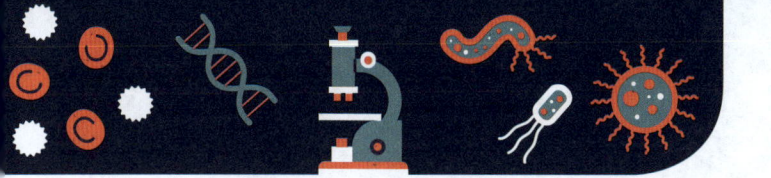

Reflex arcs

Reflex actions of the nervous system are automatic and rapid – they do not involve the conscious part of the brain.

Reflex actions are important for survival because they help prevent damage to the body.

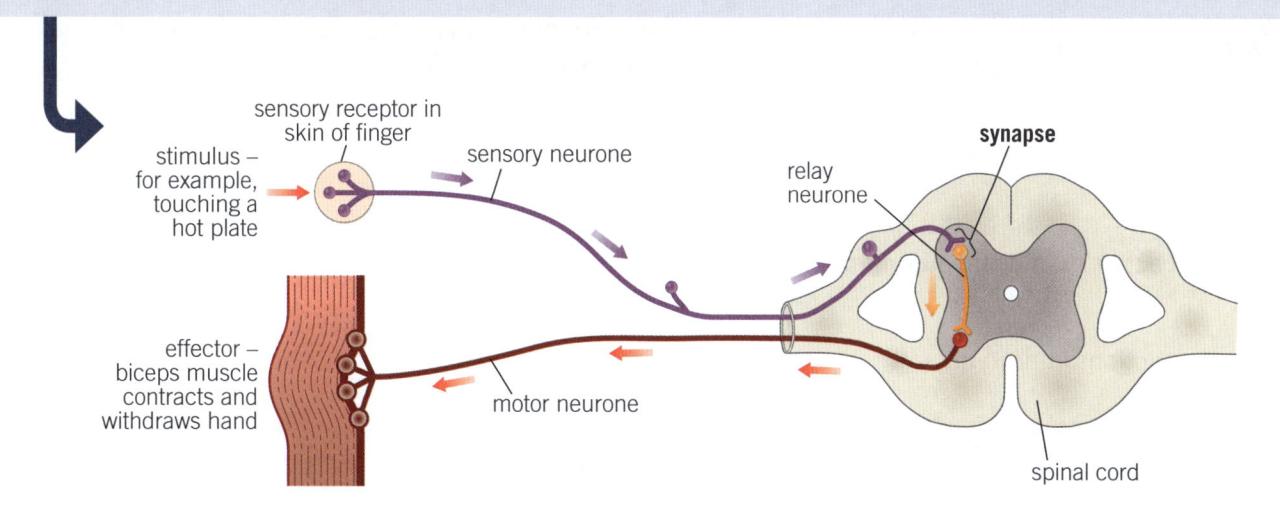

Diagram labels: stimulus – for example, touching a hot plate; sensory receptor in skin of finger; sensory neurone; relay neurone; **synapse**; spinal cord; motor neurone; effector – biceps muscle contracts and withdraws hand

Reflex arc structures

Neurones
carry electrical impulses around the body – relay neurones connect sensory neurones to motor neurones

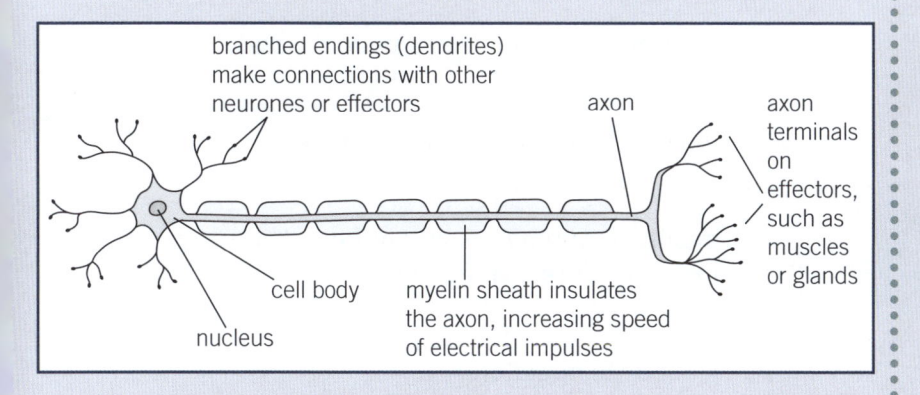

Diagram labels: branched endings (dendrites) make connections with other neurones or effectors; axon; axon terminals on effectors, such as muscles or glands; cell body; nucleus; myelin sheath insulates the axon, increasing speed of electrical impulses

Synapses
gaps between neurones, which allow electrical impulses in the nervous system to cross between neurones

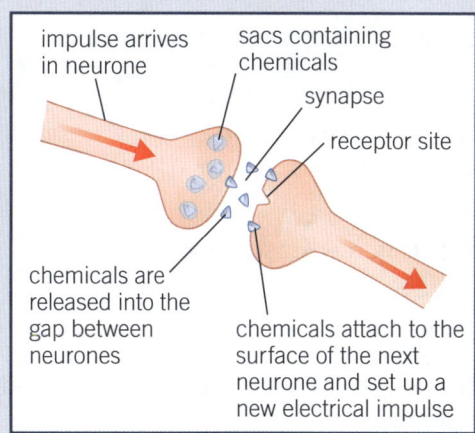

Diagram labels: impulse arrives in neurone; sacs containing chemicals; synapse; receptor site; chemicals are released into the gap between neurones; chemicals attach to the surface of the next neurone and set up a new electrical impulse

---

involuntary   neurones   receptors   reflex action   spinal cord   stimulus   synapse

B11 Knowledge 103

Retrieval

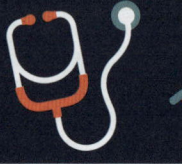

Learn the answers to the questions below, then cover the answers column with a piece of paper and write as many as you can. Check and repeat.

	B11 questions	Answers
1	What is the function of the nervous system?	enables organisms to react to their surroundings and coordinates behaviour
2	What are the two parts of the central nervous system?	brain and spinal cord
3	Why are reflex actions rapid and automatic?	they do not involve the conscious part of the brain
4	Why are reflex actions important?	for survival and to prevent damage to the body
5	Give the pathway of a nervous response.	stimulus → receptor → coordinator → effector → response
6	What is a stimulus?	a change in the internal or external environment
7	What is a synapse?	junction between two neurones where chemicals are released, allowing impulses to cross
8	What is the function of neurones?	carry electrical impulses around the body
9	What is homeostasis?	maintenance of a constant internal environment
10	Why is homeostasis important?	maintains optimal conditions for cell and organ function, and enzyme activity
11	Give three internal conditions controlled in homeostasis.	• body temperature • blood glucose concentration • water levels
12	Give three things all control systems include.	receptors, coordination centres, and effectors
13	Name three coordination centres.	• brain • spinal cord • pancreas
14	Name two types of effectors.	muscles and glands

104 B11 The nervous system and homeostasis

B11

Now go back and use the questions below to check your knowledge from previous chapters.

Previous questions & Answers

#	Previous questions	Answers
1	Define the term cellular respiration.	an exothermic reaction that occurs continuously in the mitochondria of living cells to release energy from glucose
2	How is lactic acid removed from the body?	lactic acid in muscles → blood transports to the liver → lactic acid converted back to glucose
3	How does the body supply the muscles with more oxygenated blood during exercise?	heart rate, breathing rate, and breath volume increase
4	Describe how light intensity affects the rate of photosynthesis.	increasing light intensity increases the rate of photosynthesis until another factor becomes limiting
5	What effect does humidity have on the rate of transpiration?	higher levels of humidity decrease the rate of transpiration
6	What is coronary heart disease?	layer of fatty material builds up inside the coronary arteries, narrowing them – results in a lack of oxygen for the heart
7	What is a stent?	a device inserted into a blocked artery to keep it open, allowing more blood and oxygen to the heart

Put paper here

Required practical skills

Practise answering questions on the required practicals using the example below. You need to be able to apply your skills and knowledge to other practicals too.

Reaction times	Worked example	Practice
You need to be able to describe how to plan an experiment and choose suitable variables to change, to explore how different variables affect reaction times. You should be able to: • write hypotheses predicting the effects of changing single variables • identify independent and dependent variables • evaluate results in terms of accuracy and precision • understand how different factors affect human reaction times.	Write a method to test the effect of caffeine consumption on human reaction time. Working in pairs, have one person hold a ruler vertically with zero at the bottom. The second person should steady their arm on the edge of a bench underneath the ruler. The first person should drop the ruler, and the second person should catch the ruler between thumb and forefinger without moving their arm. Record the number on the ruler above the catcher's thumb. Repeat this at least three more times. The second person should then consume a caffeinated drink, and the entire experiment should be repeated.	Using the method in the worked example, answer the following questions: 1 Give two things that must be controlled for the investigation to be a fair test. 2 Explain why it would not be appropriate for the same person to drop *and* catch the ruler in an experiment on reaction times. 3 Why should the test of reaction time be repeated multiple times before and after consumption of the caffeinated drink?

B11 Retrieval 105

Practice

Exam-style questions

01 A student carried out an investigation to determine whether a person's reaction time was quicker with their dominant hand.

The student used the following steps:

1. The student investigator (Student **A**) held a ruler just above a second student's hand (Student **B**).
2. Student **A** let go of the ruler. Student **B** caught it as soon as possible.
3. Student **A** measured the distance that the ruler fell before it was caught by Student **B**.
4. Student **A** used a conversion table to convert the distance measured into the reaction time of Student **B**.
5. The experiment was then repeated with Student **B**'s other hand.

01.1 Identify the dependent variable in this investigation. **[1 mark]**

Tick **one** answer.

height the ruler was dropped from ☐

distance the ruler fell ☐

time it took to catch the ruler ☐

> **Exam Tip**
> The dependant variable is the one we measure.

01.2 Identify **one** variable that should be controlled in this investigation. **[1 mark]**

_____

_____

01.3 Student **A** carried out the test on five left-handed students. The results are shown in **Table 1**.

Table 1

	Student	1	2	3	4	5	Mean
Reaction time in s	Left hand	0.25	0.23	0.39	0.25	0.27	
	Right hand	0.28	0.24	0.25	0.27	0.26	0.26

Identify the anomalous result from the experiment. **[1 mark]**

_____

01.4 Calculate the mean reaction time for the left hand results. **[1 mark]**

> **Exam Tip**
> Make sure you don't include the anomalous result in your calculation.

Mean = _____ s

106 B11 The nervous system and homeostasis

Paper 2 **B11**

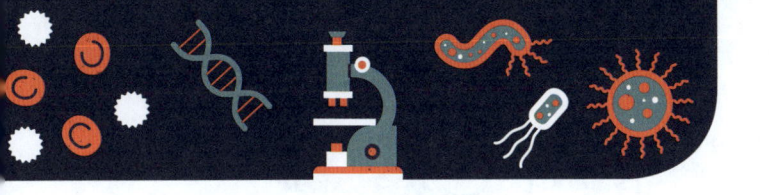

01.5 Student **A** reached the following conclusion:

'Left-handed people's reaction times are faster when using their dominant (left) hand.'

Give **one** reason why you might agree with this statement. **[1 mark]**

_____
_____

> **! Exam Tip**
> Use data from the experiment and **Table 1**.

01.6 Give **one** reason why you might disagree with this statement. **[1 mark]**

_____
_____

02 Homeostasis is a process that occurs in the human body.

02.1 Identify **one** statement that best describes the process of homeostasis. **[1 mark]**

Tick **one** box.

the increase in blood glucose level ☐

the regulation of internal conditions in response to external or internal changes ☐

the reduction in pH of partially digested food ☐

the automatic impulse produced from a stimulus to protect a person from harm ☐

> **! Exam Tip**
> This is a very important definition to learn.

02.2 Identify **two** systems that are controlled by homeostasis. **[2 marks]**

Tick **two** boxes.

blood oxygen concentration ☐

nerve impulses ☐

body water concentration ☐

digestive enzyme activity ☐

B11 Practice 107

02.3 Choose the most appropriate bold words to complete the sentences about an automatic control system. **[5 marks]**

Homeostasis may involve **nervous / stress-based** or chemical responses. These responses are **automatic / manual**, which means there does not need to be conscious thought to bring about the response.

Control systems are made up of **effectors / receptors**, which detect stimuli, **coordination centres / brains**, that process the information, and **effectors / receptors**, which bring about a response.

> **Exam Tip**
> This may seem like a tricky question, but if you take each sentence one at a time it will seem less daunting.

03 A student wanted to find out if a person's reaction time can be improved by learning a response to a stimulus.

The student used a computer program to measure the reaction time. This worked by displaying a symbol on the computer screen. The software then measured the time it took for a person to press a key on the keyboard when the symbol appeared.

03.1 Draw **one** line from each variable in the experiment to the type of variable it is. **[2 marks]**

Variable in experiment	Type of variable
use the same computer key	independent variable
number of times stimulus was repeated	dependent variable
reaction time	control variable

> **Exam Tip**
> This is very similar to the required practical you will have done, the difference is the person is pushing a button instead of catching a ruler, but the same knowledge can still be applied to this new context.

03.2 The student collected and recorded their data in **Table 2**.

Table 2

Repeat number	Reaction time in s
1	0.34
2	0.32
3	0.34
4	0.30
5	0.29
6	0.29
7	0.45
8	0.26
9	0.27
10	0.25

The student collected an anomalous result.
Circle the anomaly in **Table 2**. **[1 mark]**

03.3 Suggest **one** reason why this anomaly occurred. **[1 mark]**

03.4 Describe the trend shown in this investigation. **[1 mark]**

> **Exam Tip**
> Go though the data and see if any results are not similar to the others.

B11 The nervous system and homeostasis

04 To keep an organism healthy both the nervous system and the hormonal system need to work together.

04.1 Define the term homeostasis. **[1 mark]**

04.2 One purpose of homeostasis is to provide optimal conditions for enzymes to work in.
Name **two** factors that can affect the rate of enzyme action. **[2 marks]**

04.3 Homeostasis involves a number of automatic control systems. Describe why they are described as automatic systems. **[1 mark]**

04.4 Using examples, describe the main components of a control system. **[6 marks]**

> **Exam Tip**
>
> You only need to write down two factors, not all of them – writing more than is required in the question won't get you more marks it will just waste time in the exam.

05 Your body reacts to changes in its surroundings using the nervous system.

05.1 Complete the following sentences using appropriate words from the box. **[5 marks]**

| a receptor | an effector | the brain |
| an impulse | a hormone | a stimulus |

A change in our external environment is known as _____. This change is detected by _____ cell and _____ is sent along a neurone to the central nervous system (CNS). _____ decides how to respond and sends an impulse to _____ .

05.2 Identify the effectors from the following.
Choose **two** answers. **[2 marks]**

eye   muscle   gland   ear

05.3 The human body contains three different types of neurone.
Draw **one** line from each type of neurone to its function. **[2 marks]**

Type of neurone	Function
relay neurone	transmits impulses between receptors and the CNS
motor neurone	transmits impulses within the CNS
sensory neurone	transmits impulses between the CNS and effectors

05.4 For neurones to communicate effectively, information has to pass from one neurone to another via chemicals.
Name the gap that these chemicals diffuse across. **[1 mark]**

> **Exam Tip**
>
> Make sure you understand how this 'gap' functions and the difference between it and the transmission of a signal along a neurone.

06 The body reacts to some external stimuli using reflex actions.

06.1 Identify **two** reflex actions from the following list.
Choose **two** answers. **[2 marks]**

blinking   running   talking   coughing

06.2 Identify **two** features of a reflex action from the following list.
Choose **two** answers. **[2 marks]**

rapid   slow   requires thought   automatic

06.3 Statements **A**–**D** describe the main steps involved in a reflex action when a person touches a hot surface.
- **A** muscle contracts to move arm away
- **B** receptor detects hot surface
- **C** impulse travels to an effector along the motor neurone
- **D** impulse travels along the sensory neurone to the central nervous system

Write statements **A**–**D** in the correct order to describe the reflex action. **[3 marks]**

> **Exam Tip**
> A reflex action could be in response to touching something that causes pain. Use this as an example to think about when answering this question.

07 Homeostasis is the maintenance of a constant internal environment.

07.1 Identify which of the following conditions are controlled by homeostasis.
Choose **two** answers. **[2 marks]**

rate of digestion

body temperature

blood glucose concentration

blood oxygen concentration

07.2 Homeostasis involves automatic control systems.
Draw **one** line to match each part of the control system to its function. **[2 marks]**

Part of control system	Function
receptors	receive and process information
effectors	detect changes in the environment
coordination centres	bring about responses

07.3 Give **one** example of a coordination centre. **[1 mark]**

110   B11 The nervous system and homeostasis

08 A scientist studied the effect of caffeine on human reaction time. The scientist first measured five students' reaction times by dropping a ruler from a specific height and measuring the time taken for the ruler to be caught by each student (**A–E**).

The five students then had a caffeinated drink and the test was repeated.

The results are shown in **Table 4**.

Table 4

Student	Reaction time before caffeine drink in s	Reaction time after caffeine drink in s
A	0.80	0.68
B	0.70	0.60
C	0.85	0.78
D	0.65	0.60
E	0.90	0.82

> **Exam Tip**
>
> Read through the body of the text carefully and pick out what has been changed (independent variable), what has been measured (dependant variable), and what has been kept the same (controls). This will help with answering the questions and is great practice for the exams.

08.1 Identify the independent variable in this investigation.
Choose **one** answer. [1 mark]

height ruler was dropped from

volume of caffeine drunk

time taken to catch ruler

whether caffeine has been drunk or not

08.2 Give **one** variable the scientist should have controlled. [1 mark]

08.3 Complete the sentence to explain the trend shown in the results by choosing the most appropriate bold words. [2 marks]

Caffeine **speeds up / slows down** body reactions because after a person drinks caffeine their reaction time **increases / decreases**.

08.4 Suggest **one** improvement the students could make to their investigation. [1 mark]

09 As a car driver approached a set of traffic lights, the lights turned red. This caused the driver to press the brake pedal with their foot, slowing the car down.

09.1 In this response, what is the changing traffic light?
Choose **one** answer. [1 mark]

the coordinator   the effector   the receptor   the stimulus

> **Exam Tip**
>
> This is not a reflex arc.

09.2 In this response, what is the coordination centre?
Choose **one** answer. [1 mark]

the eye   the brain   a synapse   the spinal cord

09.3 Whilst the driver is waiting at the traffic lights, an insect flies close to the driver's eye. The driver's eye closes in response.

Explain how the driver's response to the insect is different to the response to the changing traffic lights. [3 marks]

Knowledge

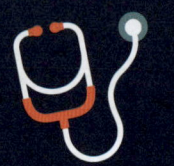

B12 Hormonal coordination

Human endocrine system

The **endocrine system** is composed of glands that secrete chemicals called **hormones** into the bloodstream.

The blood carries hormones to a target organ, where an effect is produced.

Compared to the nervous system, the effects caused by the endocrine system are slower but act for longer.

The **pituitary gland**, located in the brain, is known as a 'master gland', because it secretes several hormones into the blood.

These hormones then act on other glands to stimulate the release of other hormones, and bring about effects.

The table below describes the roles of the main hormones secreted from the different endocrine glands.

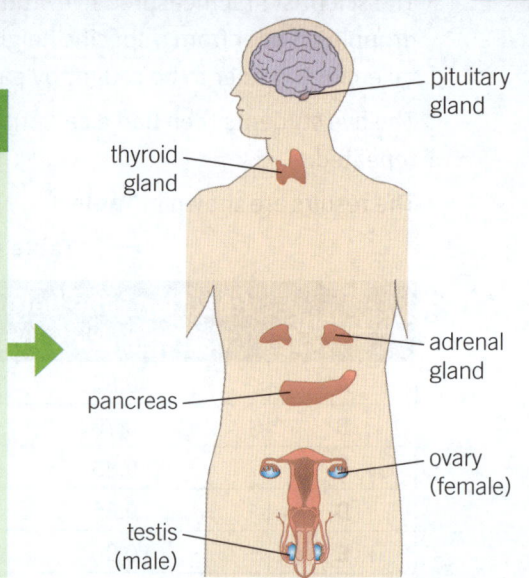

Endocrine gland	Role of the hormones
Pituitary	• controls growth in children • stimulates the thyroid gland to make thyroxine to control the metabolic rate • in females – stimulates the ovaries to produce and release eggs, and make oestrogen • in males – stimulates the testes to make sperm and testosterone
Thyroid	• controls the rate of metabolism in the body
Pancreas	• controls blood glucose levels
Adrenal	• **adrenaline** prepares the body for stress • involved in the 'fight or flight' response
Ovaries	• control the development of female secondary sexual characteristics • control the menstrual cycle
Testes	• control the development of male secondary sexual characteristics • involved in the production of sperm

Control of blood glucose levels

Blood glucose (sugar) concentration is monitored and controlled by the pancreas.

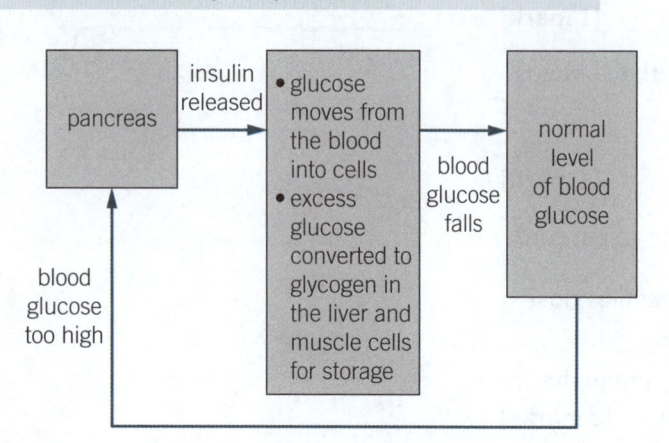

pancreas → insulin released → • glucose moves from the blood into cells • excess glucose converted to glycogen in the liver and muscle cells for storage → blood glucose falls → normal level of blood glucose

blood glucose too high

Diabetes

Diabetes is a non-communicable disease where the body either cannot produce or cannot respond to insulin, leading to uncontrolled blood glucose concentrations.

Type 1 diabetes is caused by the pancreas no longer producing insulin. It is early-onset, and is commonly treated through insulin injections, and also diet control and exercise.

Type 2 diabetes arises when the body doesn't respond to the insulin produced. It tends to be late-onset, and is commonly treated through a carbohydrate-controlled diet and exercise.

B12

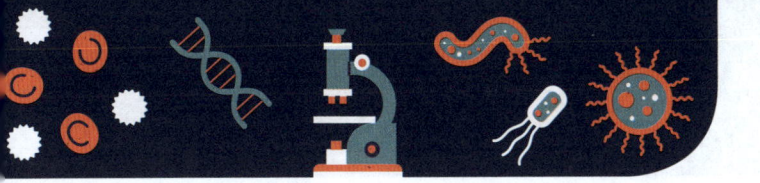

Hormones in human reproduction

During puberty, reproductive hormones cause the secondary sex characteristics to develop:

Oestrogen
- main female reproductive hormone
- produced in the ovary
- at puberty, eggs begin to mature and one is released every ~28 days

Testosterone
- main male reproductive hormone
- produced by the testes
- stimulates sperm production

Several hormones are involved in the **menstrual cycle**. Their functions are given in the table.

Hormone	Released by	Function
follicle stimulating hormone (FSH)	pituitary gland	• causes eggs to mature in the ovaries • stimulates ovaries to produce oestrogen
luteinising hormone (LH)	pituitary gland	• stimulates the release of mature eggs from the ovaries (**ovulation**)
oestrogen	ovaries	• causes lining of **uterus** wall to thicken • inhibits release of FSH • stimulates release of LH
progesterone	ovaries	• maintains thick uterus lining • inhibits release of FSH and LH

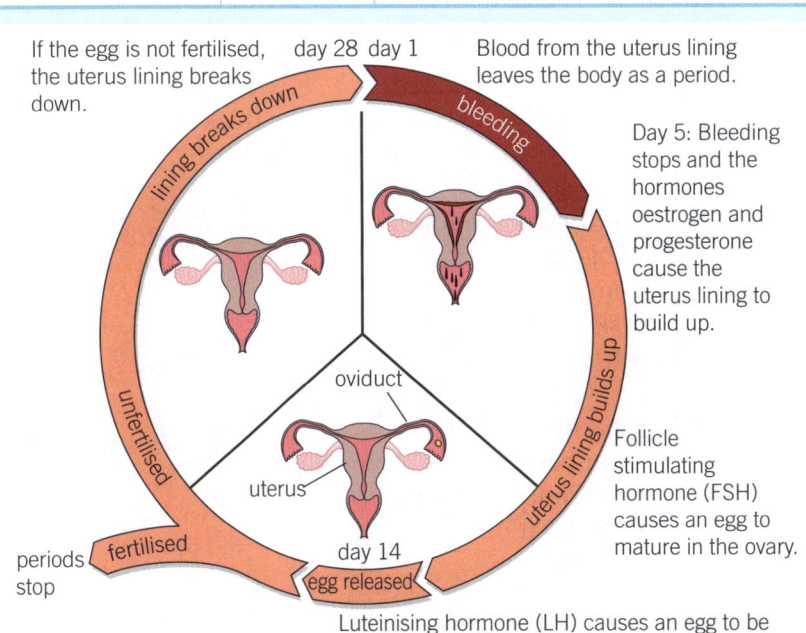

If the egg is not fertilised, the uterus lining breaks down.

day 28 day 1 — Blood from the uterus lining leaves the body as a period.

Day 5: Bleeding stops and the hormones oestrogen and progesterone cause the uterus lining to build up.

Follicle stimulating hormone (FSH) causes an egg to mature in the ovary.

day 14 egg released

Luteinising hormone (LH) causes an egg to be released. The egg travels down the oviduct towards the uterus.

periods stop — fertilised — unfertilised — lining breaks down — bleeding — uterus lining builds up

Contraception

Fertility can be controlled by a variety of hormonal and non-hormonal methods of **contraception**.

Hormonal contraception
- oral contraceptives – contain hormones to inhibit FSH production so no eggs mature
- injection, implant, skin patch, or intrauterine devices (IUD) – slowly release progesterone to inhibit maturation and release of eggs; can last months or years

Non-hormonal contraception
- barrier methods, for example, condoms and diaphragms – prevent sperm reaching the egg
- copper IUD – prevents the implantation of an embryo
- surgical methods of male and female sterilisation
- spermicidal agents – kill or disable sperm
- abstaining from intercourse when an egg may be in the oviduct

Key terms
Make sure you can write a definition for these key terms.

adrenal   adrenaline   contraception   endocrine   follicle stimulating hormone   insulin   luteinising hormone   menstrual cycle   oestrogen   ovulation   pancreas   pituitary   progesterone   thyroid

B12 Knowledge   113

Retrieval

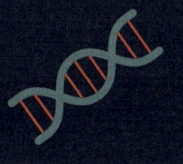

Learn the answers to the questions below, then cover the answers column with a piece of paper and write as many as you can. Check and repeat.

B12 questions | Answers

#	Question	Answer
1	What is the endocrine system?	system of glands that secrete hormones into the bloodstream
2	How do the effects of the endocrine system compare to those of the nervous system?	endocrine system effects are slower but act for longer
3	Where is the pituitary gland located?	brain
4	Which organ monitors and controls blood glucose concentration?	pancreas
5	Which hormone regulates blood glucose levels?	insulin
6	What is the cause of Type 1 diabetes?	pancreas produces insufficient insulin
7	What is the cause of Type 2 diabetes?	body cells no longer respond to insulin
8	What is the function of FSH?	• causes eggs to mature in the ovaries • stimulates ovaries to produce oestrogen
9	What is the function of LH?	stimulates the release of an egg
10	What is the function of oestrogen?	• causes lining of uterus wall to thicken • control the levels of FSH and LH
11	What are the methods of hormonal contraception?	• oral contraceptives • injection • implant • skin patch • IUD
12	What are the methods of non-hormonal contraception?	• barrier methods • copper IUD • spermicidal agents • sterilisation • abstinence
13	Which endocrine glands control secondary sexual characteristics?	ovaries in females, testes in males

B12 Hormonal coordination

B12

Now go back and use the questions below to check your knowledge from previous chapters.

Previous questions / Answers

	Previous questions	Answers
1	Why are reflex actions described as rapid and automatic?	they do not involve the conscious part of the brain
2	What are the two parts of the central nervous system?	brain and spinal cord
3	Write the balanced symbol equation for aerobic respiration.	$C_6H_{12}O_6 + 6O_2 \rightarrow 6CO_2 + 6H_2O$
4	Give the pathway of a nervous response.	stimulus → receptor → coordinator → effector → response

Put paper here

Maths skills

Practise your maths skills using the worked example and practice questions below.

Trends in graphs

You need to be able to look at a graph and interpret what the graph tells us about the variables that have been tested.

You will often be asked to 'describe the trend' that the graph shows, or to 'describe the effect of X on Y'.

In order to do this, you will need to mention how the variable on one axis affects the variable on the other axis.

If you want to gain marks for this type of question, you have to mention the variables and also use the data from the graph, such as key dates or significant rises and falls.

Worked example

[Bar chart: percentage of children under 5 years old that died from infectious diseases vs year. 1750: ~68, 1850: ~12, 1950: ~2, 2015: ~1]

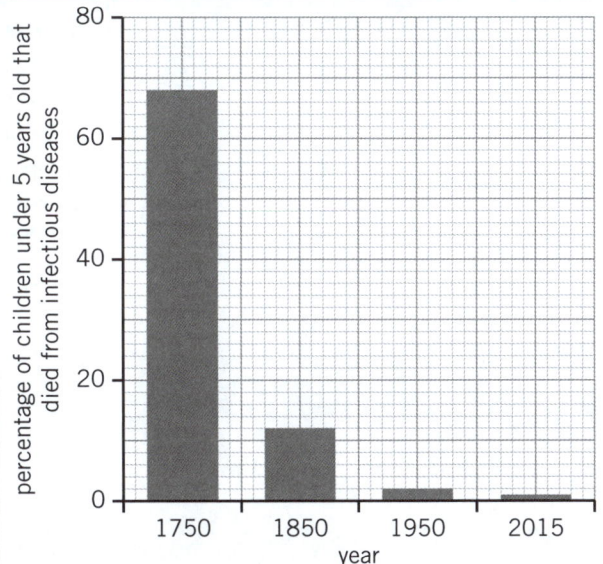

The graph shows the percentage of children under five years old who died from infectious diseases in the UK, in four different years.

Describe how the percentage of children who died from infectious diseases changed from 1750 to 1850.

To gain full marks you should include data from the graph above.

There was a significant decrease in the percentage of children under five years old who died from infectious diseases, going from 68% of children in 1750 to 12% in 1850.

An answer stating only that the percentage of children who died decreased would not get full marks.

Practice

The graph shows the number of deaths per million in England linked to methicillin-resistant *Staphylococcus aureus* (MRSA) between 1994 and 2010.

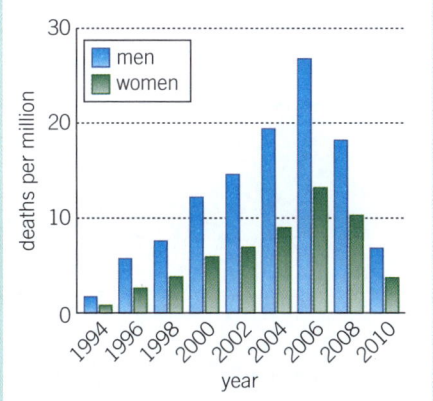

[Bar chart: deaths per million vs year (1994–2010), showing men and women]

Describe the trend for deaths in women linked to MRSA.

B12 Retrieval 115

Practice

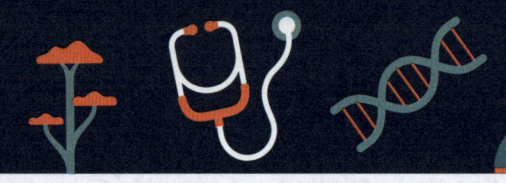

Exam-style questions

01 The endocrine system contains many glands.

01.1 Identify the glands (**A–E**) in **Figure 1** using words from the box. **[5 marks]**

> pituitary gland   pancreas   thyroid
> adrenal gland   ovary   testis

Figure 1

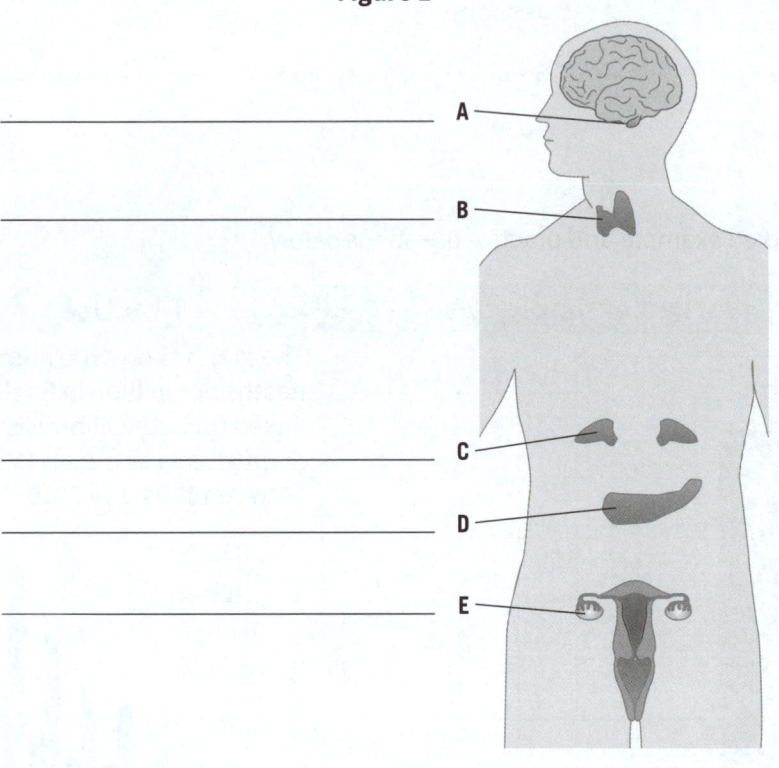

A _____

B _____

C _____

D _____

E _____

Exam Tip

Ovaries are part of the female reproductive system and testes are part of the male reproductive system – this means that if this figure has ovaries, it won't also have testes.

01.2 Name the gland in **Figure 1** that releases adrenaline. **[1 mark]**

01.3 Name the hormone released by the thyroid gland. **[1 mark]**

01.4 Explain why the pituitary gland is often referred to as a master gland. **[3 marks]**

116   **B12 Hormonal coordination**

Paper 2 **B12**

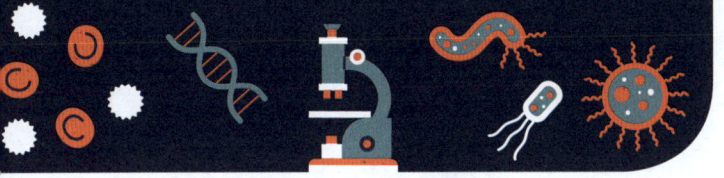

02 Contraception can be used to prevent pregnancy.

02.1 Identify the types of contraception that contain hormones. **[2 marks]**

Tick **two** boxes.

contraceptive pill ☐

condom ☐

progesterone implant ☐

surgical sterilisation ☐

02.2 Draw **one** line from each method of contraception to the way it prevents pregnancy. **[3 marks]**

Contraception	Method
spermicidal agents	prevents eggs being released from the ovary
surgical sterilisation	physical barrier that prevents sperm meeting an egg
condom	prevents sperm entering the semen
coordination centres	kills sperm

02.3 Condoms are over 98% effective at preventing pregnancy if used correctly.

Give **one** other advantage of using a condom during sexual intercourse. **[1 mark]**

> **Exam Tip**
> Condoms are a barrier form of contraception.

03 Many women used contraceptives that contain hormones.

03.1 Give the name of **one** form of contraception that does **not** contain hormones. **[1 mark]**

03.2 Contraceptive pills contain oestrogen.
Name the endocrine gland that releases oestrogen. **[1 mark]**

03.3 Describe how oestrogen in the contraceptive pill prevents a person getting pregnant. **[2 marks]**

B12 Practice 117

04 Blood glucose concentration is monitored and controlled by the pancreas.

04.1 Name the chemical reaction that glucose is used for to release energy to body cells. **[1 mark]**

04.2 Complete **Figure 2** to show how the pancreas controls blood glucose levels. **[4 marks]**

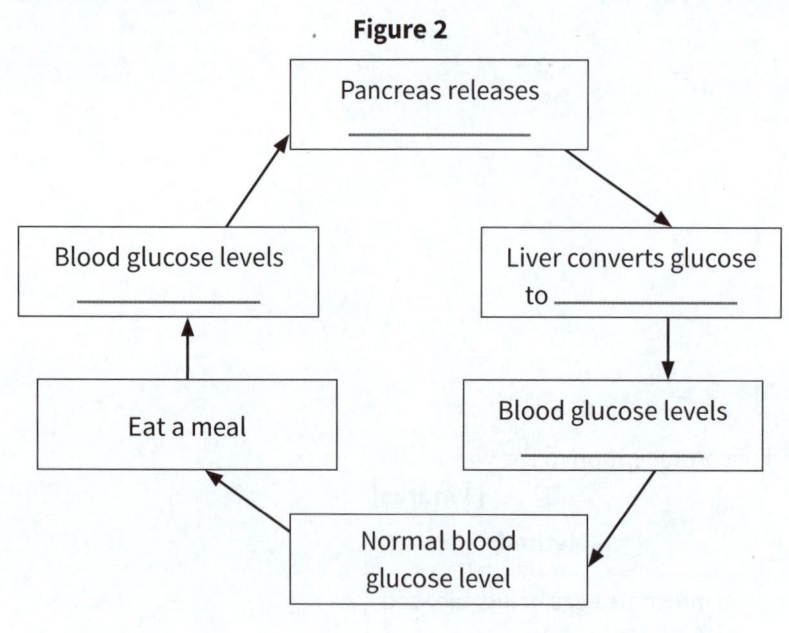

Figure 2

Pancreas releases _____

Blood glucose levels _____

Eat a meal

Liver converts glucose to _____

Blood glucose levels _____

Normal blood glucose level

> **! Exam Tip**
> Lots of the words in this topic have similar spellings and sounds. Practise writing these words to make sure you don't get confused in your exam.

04.3 Name the disorder a person will suffer from if their pancreas does not produce insulin. **[1 mark]**

> **! Exam Tip**
> Be specific when you name the type of disease.

05 The endocrine system is made up of glands and hormones.

05.1 Draw **one** line between each part of the endocrine system and its function. **[2 marks]**

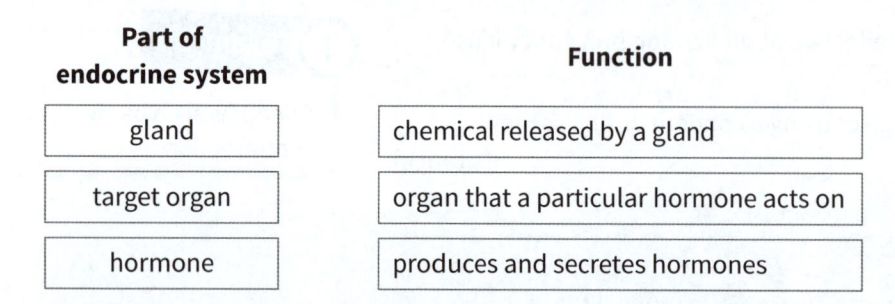

Part of endocrine system	Function
gland	chemical released by a gland
target organ	organ that a particular hormone acts on
hormone	produces and secretes hormones

05.2 Name the tissue that transports hormones around the body. **[1 mark]**

05.3 Choose the correct bold words to complete the following sentences comparing the actions of the nervous system and the endocrine system. **[2 marks]**

The effects of the endocrine system are **slower / faster** than those of the nervous system.

The effects of the endocrine system last for a **longer / shorter** time than those of the nervous system.

> **! Exam Tip**
> The key to **05.3** is to think about how the messages are sent via the two different systems.

B12 Hormonal coordination

06 Hormones play an important role in homeostasis.

06.1 Identify the hormone that is most likely to increase after consuming a chocolate bar.

Choose **one** answer. [1 mark]

adrenaline   insulin   glucagon   thyroxine

06.2 Explain your answer to **06.1**. [4 marks]

06.3 Explain why blood glucose levels need to be maintained at a constant level. [3 marks]

07 During puberty, hormones cause secondary sexual characteristics to develop.

07.1 In **Table 1**, identify the secondary sexual characteristics that occur in males, females, or both, by adding a tick in the correct boxes. [4 marks]

Table 1

Characteristic	Male	Female	Both
fat deposited on hips			
growth of underarm hair			
sperm production starts			
growth spurt			

> **Exam Tip**
> You only need one tick in each row, but one column will have two ticks in it.

07.2 Identify the hormone responsible for causing the male secondary sexual characteristics.

Choose **one** answer. [1 mark]

thyroxine   testosterone   oestrogen   insulin

> **Exam Tip**
> Often, the name of the hormone and the organ that produces it are very similar.

07.3 Name the organ that produces this hormone. [1 mark]

08 The body responds to changes in its internal and external environment using the endocrine and nervous systems.

08.1 Write down the name given to a change that occurs in a person's environment. [1 mark]

08.2 Name the hormone that is released in response to a stressful situation. [1 mark]

08.3 Compare the way that hormones in the endocrine system act, to the way a reflex arc works in the nervous system. [6 marks]

> **Exam Tip**
> For a compare question you need to discuss similarities and differences – it can help to draw a table with some notes in first before you start to write the answer out in full.

09 Oestrogen is responsible for causing secondary sexual characteristics to develop in females.

09.1 Identify the organ that produces oestrogen.
Choose **one** answer. **[1 mark]**

uterus   vagina   ovary   fallopian tube

09.2 One change that occurs during puberty is the start of periods (menstruation).
Describe **one** other change at this time that only occurs in females. **[1 mark]**

09.3 The menstrual cycle is controlled by a number of hormones.
Draw **one** line from each hormone to its function. **[2 marks]**

Hormone	Function
Follicle stimulating hormone (FSH)	causes an egg to mature in the ovary
Luteinising hormone (LH)	maintains the lining of the uterus
Progesterone	causes egg to be released from the ovary

Once a female has started her periods she may need to use contraception to prevent pregnancy if she is sexually active.

Figure 3 shows the effectiveness of a number of forms of contraception.

Figure 3

Bar chart showing contraception type (y-axis) vs proportion of women with unexpected pregnancy in first year of use (x-axis, 0% to 90%):
- IUD
- patch
- pill
- diaphragm
- condom
- rhythm method
- spermicides
- no method

> **Exam Tip**
> Spelling these hormones can be confusing, but it is important to try and learn how to spell them correctly – this will help avoid confusion over your meaning in an exam.

> **Exam Tip**
> This graph may come as a bit of a surprise but there is not a method of contraception that is 100 % effective.

> **Exam Tip**
> Remember, contraception is designed to stop pregnancy – look carefully at the label on the x-axis.

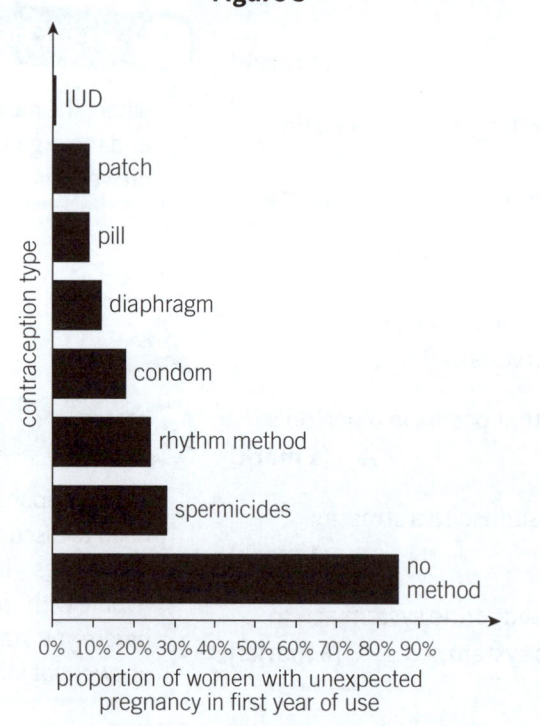

09.4 Name the most effective form of contraception. **[1 mark]**

09.5 Suggest **two** reasons why a couple may choose to use a different form of contraception to the most effective method named in **09.4**. **[2 marks]**

120 B12 Hormonal coordination

10 There are two types of diabetes – Type 1 and Type 2 diabetes.

10.1 Identify the correct statements about Type 1 diabetes.
Choose **two** answers. [2 marks]

pancreas does not produce enough insulin
body cells no longer respond to insulin
condition usually identified during childhood
condition usually identified during adulthood

10.2 Identify the factor that increases a person's risk of developing Type 2 diabetes.
Choose **one** answer. [1 mark]

UV radiation   smoking   obesity

10.3 Diabetes cannot be cured, but the condition can be managed through treatment.

Choose the appropriate bold words to complete the following sentences about Type 1 and Type 2 diabetes. [4 marks]

Type 1 diabetes can be controlled by regular injections of **insulin / glucagon**. This causes blood glucose levels to **rise / fall** to normal levels.

Type 2 diabetes can often be managed by controlling the amount of **protein / carbohydrate** in the diet and by exercising **more / less**.

> **Exam Tip**
> Type 1 and Type 2 diabetes have a different time of onset, and occur due to different reasons.

11 The human menstrual cycle is controlled by the interaction of four hormones.

11.1 Select the hormone that triggers ovulation.
Choose **one** answer. [1 mark]

FSH   LH   oestrogen   progesterone

11.2 Name the hormone that stimulates the release of LH. [1 mark]

11.3 Describe how progesterone and oestrogen control the lining of the uterus throughout the menstrual cycle. [3 marks]

11.4 Suggest and explain what would happen to the level of progesterone if a woman became pregnant. [2 marks]

11.5 Name **one** example of a type of contraception that contains progesterone. [1 mark]

Knowledge

B13 Variation

Variation in populations

Differences in the characteristics of individuals in a population is called **variation**.

Variation may be due to differences in
- the genes they have inherited, for example, eye colour (genetic causes)
- the environment in which they have developed, for example, language (environmental causes)
- a combination of genes and the environment.

Mutation

There is usually a lot of genetic variation within a population of a species – this variation arises from **mutations**.

A mutation is a change in a DNA sequence:
- mutations occur continuously
- very rarely a mutation will lead to a new phenotype
- most mutations have no or little effect
- if a new phenotype is suited to an environmental change, it can lead to a relatively rapid change in the species – this is the theory of evolution by natural selection

Selective breeding

Selective breeding (artificial selection) is the process by which humans breed plants and animals for particular genetic characteristics.

Humans have been using selective breeding for thousands of years, since first breeding crops from wild plants and domesticating animals.

Process of selective breeding:
1. choose parents with the desired characteristic from a mixed population
2. breed them together
3. choose offspring with the desired characteristic and breed them together
4. continue over many generations until all offspring show the desired characteristic

The characteristic targeted in selective breeding can be chosen for usefulness or appearance, for example
- disease resistance in food crops
- animals that produce more meat or milk
- domestic dogs with a gentle nature
- larger or unusual flowers.

Disadvantages of selective breeding:
- can lead to **inbreeding**, where some breeds are particularly prone to inherited defects or diseases
- reduces variation, meaning all members of a species could be susceptible to certain diseases

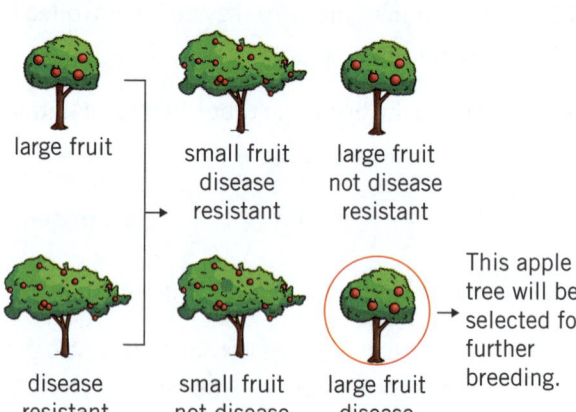

large fruit → small fruit disease resistant | large fruit not disease resistant

disease resistant → small fruit not disease resistant | large fruit disease resistant

This apple tree will be selected for further breeding.

Key terms

Make sure you can write a definition for these key terms.

genetically modified   genetic engineering   inbreeding

122 B13 Variation

B13

Genetic engineering

Genetic engineering is a process that involves changing the genome of an organism by introducing a gene from another organism to produce a desired characteristic.

Genetic engineering involves cutting out the genes from the chromosomes of humans and other organisms, and then transferring these into the cells of different organisms.

For example:
- Bacterial cells have been genetically engineered to produce useful substances, such as human insulin to treat diabetes.
- Plant crops have been genetically engineered to be resistant to diseases, insects, or herbicides, or to produce bigger and better fruits and higher crop yields. Crops that have undergone genetic engineering are called **genetically modified** (GM).

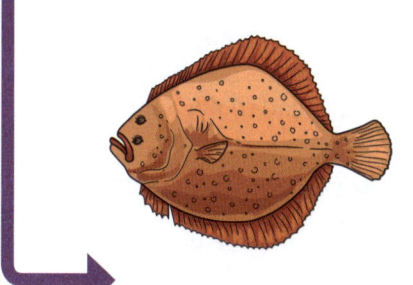

Flounder fish produce a chemical that stops their blood from freezing in the very cold water they live in.

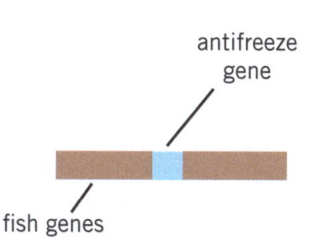

Scientists take the antifreeze gene from the flounder fish...

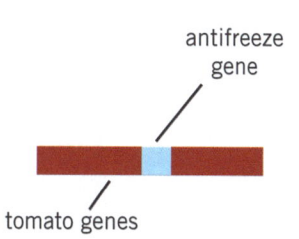

...and insert it into the DNA of tomato cells.

These cells then grow into tomato plants that can survive frost.

There are many benefits to genetic engineering in agriculture and medicine, but also some risks and moral objections.

Benefits	Risks
• potential to overcome some inherited human diseases • can lead to higher value of crops as GM crops have bigger yields than normal • crops can be engineered to be resistant to herbicides, make their own pesticides, or be better adapted to environmental conditions	• genes from GM plants and animals may spread to other wildlife, which could have devastating effects on ecosystems • potential negative impacts on populations of wild flowers and insects • ethical concerns, for example, in the future people could manipulate the genes of fetuses to ensure certain characteristics • some people believe the long-term effects on health of eating GM crops have not been fully explored

mutation   selective breeding   tissue culture   variation

B13 Knowledge

Retrieval

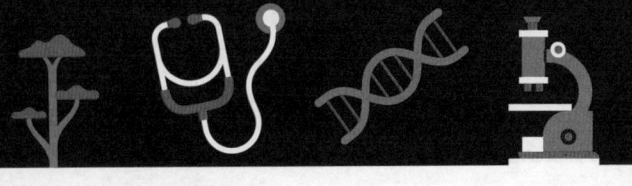

Learn the answers to the questions below, then cover the answers column with a piece of paper and write as many as you can. Check and repeat.

B13 questions | Answers

#	Question	Answer
1	What is variation?	differences in the characteristics of individuals in a population
2	What can cause variation?	genetic causes, environmental causes, and a combination of genes and the environment
3	How do new phenotype variants occur?	mutations
4	What are the effects of mutations?	most have no effect on phenotype, some influence existing phenotype, very few lead to new phenotypes
5	What is selective breeding?	breeding plants and animals for particular characteristics
6	Describe the process of selective breeding.	1 choose parents with the desired characteristic 2 breed them together 3 choose offspring with the desired characteristic and breed again 4 continue over many generations until all offspring show the desired characteristic
7	What are the consequences of inbreeding?	inherited defects and diseases
8	What is genetic engineering?	modifying the genome of an organism by introducing a gene from another organism to give a desired characteristic
9	How have plant crops been genetically engineered?	• to be resistant to diseases/herbicides/pesticides • to produce bigger fruits • to give higher yields
10	What concerns are there about genetically engineered crops?	• possible detrimental effects on wild flowers and insects • the effects on human health may not be fully understood
11	How have bacteria been genetically engineered?	to produce useful substances, such as human insulin to treat diabetes

B13

Now go back and use the questions below to check your knowledge from previous chapters.

Previous questions | Answers

#	Question	Answer
1	What is the cause of Type 1 diabetes?	pancreas produces insufficient insulin
2	What are the methods of hormonal contraception?	oral contraceptives, injection, implant, IUD, or skin patch
3	Give three things all control systems include.	receptors, coordination centres, and effectors
4	What do organisms need energy for?	• chemical reactions to build larger molecules • muscle contraction for movement • keeping warm
5	Give three internal conditions controlled in homeostasis.	body temperature, blood glucose concentration, and water levels
6	What is the endocrine system?	system of glands that secrete hormones into the bloodstream

Maths skills

Practise your maths skills using the worked example and practice questions below.

Mean, median, mode, and range

When interpreting data, scientists often need to calculate the average or range of a set of data.

You need to be able to calculate the range, and different types of averages (mean, median, and mode).

Mean: the calculated average of the numbers.

Median: the number in the middle.

Mode: the number that occurs most often.

Range: the difference between the largest and the smallest values.

Worked example

For the following list of numbers, we can calculate the mean, median, mode, and range.

13, 18, 13, 14, 13, 16, 14, 21, 13

Mean

Add all the values together, and divide by the total number of values.

13 + 18 + 13 + 14 + 13 + 16 + 14 + 21 + 13 = 135

$\frac{135}{9} = 15$

Median

Write the values in order and determine which one is in the middle. If there is an even number of values, take the mean of the two values in the middle.

~~13, 13, 13, 13,~~ $\boxed{14}$ ~~14, 16, 18, 21~~

14 is the middle value so the median = 14

Mode

13 appears the most times in the data.

Range

The largest value (21) minus the smallest value (13).

21 − 13 = 8

Practice

Stomata on a leaf can be seen using a light microscope. The number of stomata differs depending on the location on the plant.

The table below gives the number of stomata a student counted from different areas on one leaf.

Leaf area	Number of stomata	
	Upper surface	Lower surface
1	4	42
2	1	43
3	0	45
4	4	43
5	1	39

Calculate the following:

1. The mean number of stomata on the lower surface of the leaf.
2. The median number of stomata on the upper surface of the leaf.
3. The mode number of stomata on the lower surface of the leaf.
4. The range in the number of stomata on the upper surface of the leaf.

B13 Retrieval

Practice

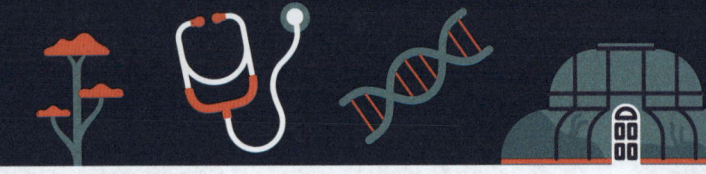

Exam-style questions

01 A gardener grows and sells tomatoes. The gardener wishes to selectively breed tomato plants, so that the crops have a high yield and produce sweet tomatoes.

01.1 Statements **A**–**E** show steps the gardener should follow to achieve optimum results.

- **A** use the seeds from the fruits of the plants produced to grow new plants
- **B** cross-pollinate the plants
- **C** continue over many generations
- **D** select plants producing a high yield of tomatoes, and plants producing sweet tomato fruits
- **E** from the offspring, select the plants produced for high yielding plants with sweet tasting tomatoes

Write the letters of the statements (**A**–**E**) in the correct order in the boxes to show how the gardener could selectively breed the tomato plants. **[4 marks]**

first					last

> **! Exam Tip**
>
> Read over the statements a couple of times before you decide which order they should go in, then use a pencil to number them so you can rub them out if you change your mind.

01.2 Draw **one** line from each characteristic of the selectively bred tomato plants to its benefit to the gardener. **[2 marks]**

Characteristic	Benefit
greater mass of tomatoes produced	higher price can be charged per tomato
more fruit produced per plant	less land required to produce same number of tomatoes
sweeter tomatoes more in demand	more profit produced

01.3 Suggest and explain **one** other characteristic the gardener could selectively breed for, to ensure a high yield of tomatoes. **[2 marks]**

_____

_____

_____

126   B13 Variation

Paper 2   **B13**

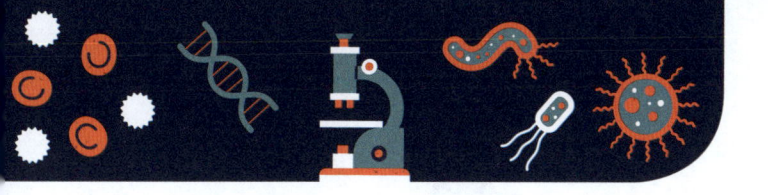

02 A group of students investigated the variation in height amongst students in their school. Their results are recorded in **Table 1**.

Table 1

Height in cm	100 ≤ h < 120	120 ≤ h < 140	140 ≤ h < 160	160 ≤ h < 180	180 ≤ h < 200
Number of students	12	18	36	22	6

02.1 Complete the graph of this data in **Figure 1**. [2 marks]

Figure 1

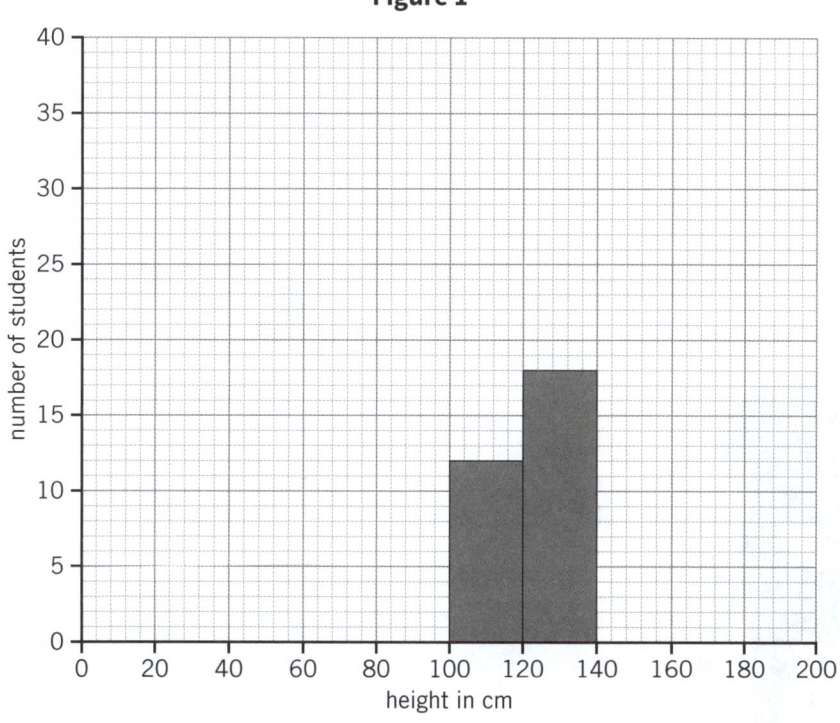

> **Exam Tip**
>
> Use a ruler when drawing the bars on the graph paper.

02.2 Name which height class is the mode. [1 mark]

_____

02.3 Identify what causes this variation. [1 mark]
Tick **one** box.

genes ☐

environment ☐

both ☐

> **Exam Tip**
>
> Make sure that you know the difference between mean, median, and mode.

> **Exam Tip**
>
> Are identical twins *exactly* the same height?

02.4 Give a reason for your answer to question **02.3**. [1 mark]

_____

_____

03 Some plant crops have been genetically modified to improve their characteristics.

03.1 Explain what is meant by the term genetically modified. **[2 marks]**

03.2 Plant crops can also be influenced by the environment.

Identify which of the characteristics are influenced by genes, or the environment, or both, by matching them to the correct box. **[4 marks]**

Characteristic

large leaves

how tall it grows

resistance to frost

size of fruit

Variable

genetic

environmental

both

03.3 Give **one** advantage of the genetic modification of plant crops compared to selective breeding. **[1 mark]**

04 Figure 2 shows two of puppies born from the same parents.

Figure 2

04.1 The puppies show variation.
Define the term variation. **[1 mark]**

04.2 Name **one** characteristic that is inherited by the puppies. **[1 mark]**

04.3 Give **one** characteristic that is affected by the puppies' genes and the environment. **[2 marks]**
Explain your answer.

04.4 Most breeds of dog have been selectively bred for certain characteristics.
Give **one** disadvantage of selective breeding. **[1 mark]**

B13 Variation

05 Differences exist between members of the same species.

05.1 Complete the following sentences using the most appropriate words from the box. **[5 marks]**

blood	genes	environment	variation
	species	offspring	parents

Organisms in a _____ share many of the same characteristics. This allows them to reproduce to produce fertile _____ .

Differences within a species are known as _____.

This can occur as a result of the _____ the organism inherits, the _____ in which the organism lives or a combination of both.

> **Exam Tip**
> Not every word will be used – don't let that worry you.

05.2 Tick the correct column in **Table 2** to show whether each human characteristic is caused by genetic variation, environmental variation, or both. **[4 marks]**

Table 2

Human characteristic	Genetic variation	Environmental variation	Both
body mass			
tattoo			
blood group			
intelligence			

> **Exam Tip**
> Each row will only have one tick.

05.3 Describe why a child may look similar to their parents, but will not be identical to either their mother or father. **[1 mark]**

06 Scientists are able to alter the genetic material in an organism to create offspring with a desired characteristic. This process is known as genetic engineering.

06.1 Complete the sentences to explain how genetic engineering occurs by choosing the most appropriate bold words. **[4 marks]**

Scientists can insert **body fluids / genes** into an organism that have been taken from an organism of **the same / a different** species to produce desired characteristics. When the organism **reproduces / dies**, the genes are passed on to the **partner / offspring**.

06.2 Genetic engineering has a number of advantages over selective breeding.

Identify **two** advantages of genetic engineering from the statements below. Choose **two** answers. **[2 marks]**

can occur in one generation

requires special equipment

targets single genes

creates more variation in a species

06.3 Give **one** example of genetic engineering. **[1 mark]**

06.4 Suggest **one** risk associated with genetic engineering. **[1 mark]**

07 This question is about selective breeding.

07.1 Identify the best description of selective breeding.
Choose **one** answer. **[1 mark]**

introducing a gene from another organism to give a desired characteristic

breeding plants and animals for particular genetic characteristics

using the differences in individuals within a population

only breeding organisms at certain times of the year

07.2 Identify the effect of selective breeding on the variation within a population.
Choose **one** answer. **[1 mark]**

selective breeding increases variation in a population

selective breeding has no effect on variation in a population

selective breeding decreases variation in a population

07.3 Food crops such as wheat have been selectively bred over many years to make the plant more useful to humans.
Using **Figure 3**, give **one** difference between wild wheat and domesticated wheat. **[1 mark]**

07.4 Explain how wheat has been selectively bred for the characteristic named in **07.3**. **[4 marks]**

> **Exam Tip**
>
> **07.1** is asking for the *best* description – some answers maybe close to correct but not the best.

Figure 3

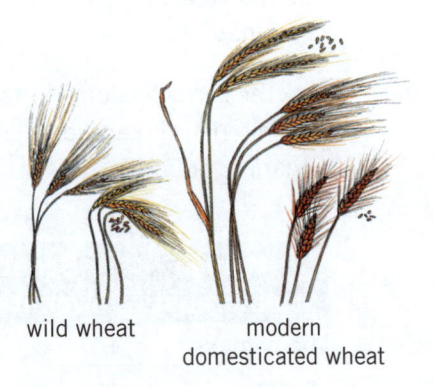

wild wheat   modern domesticated wheat

08 A group of students investigated the variation in the growth of ivy leaves on the sunny side of a fence, compared to those growing in the shade. The group studied the size of ten leaves. Five leaves grew in full sun and five grew in the shade.

The group measured the width of each leaf at its widest point. Their results are shown in **Table 3**.

Table 3

Conditions	Leaf 1	Leaf 2	Leaf 3	Leaf 4	Leaf 5	Mean
sun	4.6	5.2	4.1	4.8	3.8	4.5
shade	4.5	6.1	6.2	5.8	4.9	

Width in cm

08.1 Write down the range of widths for leaves grown in the sun. **[1 mark]**

08.2 Complete **Table 3** by calculating the mean width of leaves grown in the shade. **[1 mark]**

08.3 Using the correct bold words, complete the students' conclusion. **[3 marks]**

Leaves growing in the shade are **smaller / larger** to help them absorb **less / more** sunlight for **photosynthesis / respiration**.

08.4 Identify what causes this variation in the leaves.
Choose **one** answer. **[1 mark]**

genes   environment   both

130   **B13 Variation**

09 Both farmers and animal breeders have been selectively breeding organisms for thousands of years.

09.1 Draw **one** line to match each organism to the characteristic it is often bred for. **[3 marks]**

Organism	Characteristic
cows	thick coats
domestic dogs	high milk production
sheep	sweet smelling
roses	gentle nature

Exam Tip
Think about the things people like about each plant or animal.

09.2 Identify which of the following are features of a selective breeding programme.
Choose **two** answers. **[2 marks]**
identifying parents with desired characteristics
identifying genes from a foreign organism
repeating the breeding process for many generations
significantly altering the characteristics in one generation

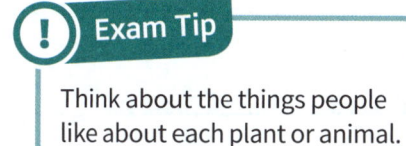

Exam Tip
Breeding for characteristics humans find desirable isn't always good for the animal being bred.

09.3 Give **one** disadvantage of selectively breeding dogs. **[1 mark]**

10 Bacteria are genetically engineered to produce useful substances such as insulin.

10.1 Name the condition insulin can be used to treat. **[1 mark]**

10.2 Choose the most appropriate bold words to complete the paragraph describing how insulin can be produced from bacteria. **[4 marks]**

Genes / **proteins** that code for the production of insulin are identified and removed from a **human** / **bacterial** cell. They are inserted into bacteria. Bacteria reproduce **many** / **few** times producing **small** / **large** quantities of insulin. The insulin is taken to treat patients.

10.3 Insulin can also be harvested from pigs for use in human medical treatment.
Suggest **one** benefit of obtaining insulin from bacteria as opposed to animals. **[1 mark]**

10.4 Name **one** other organism that is genetically modified by humans. **[1 mark]**

Knowledge

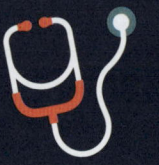

B14 Reproduction

Types of reproduction

Sexual reproduction	Asexual reproduction
two parents	one parent
cell division through **meiosis**	cell division through **mitosis**
joining (fusion) of male and female sex cells (**gametes**) – sperm and egg in animals, pollen and ovule in plants	no fusion of gametes
produces non-identical offspring that are genetically different to parents	produces offspring that are genetically identical to parent (**clones**)
results in wide variation within offspring and species	no mixing of genetic information

Meiosis

Meiosis is a type of cell division that makes gametes in the reproductive organs.

Meiosis halves the number of chromosomes in gametes, and **fertilisation** (joining of two gametes) restores the full number of chromosomes.

The fertilised cell divides by mitosis, producing more cells. As the embryo develops, the cells differentiate.

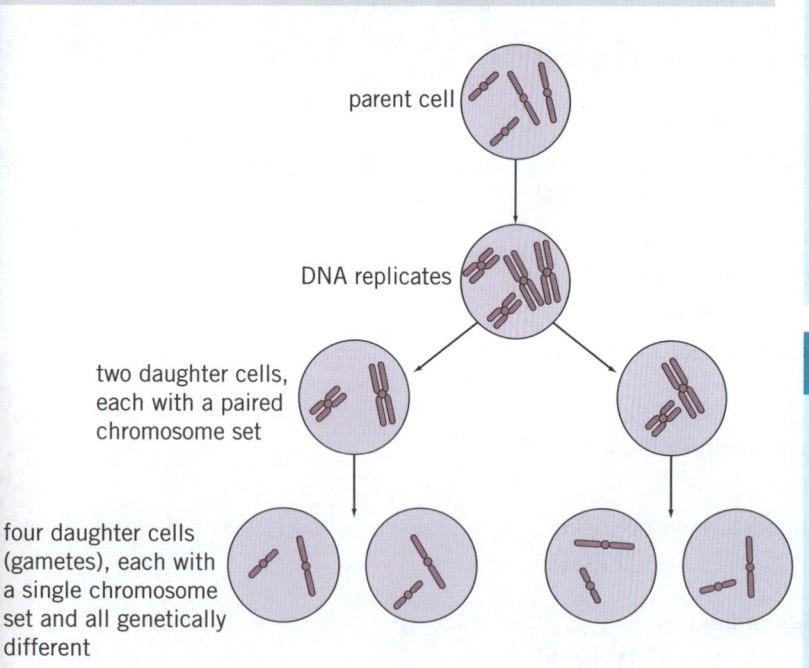

parent cell

DNA replicates

two daughter cells, each with a paired chromosome set

four daughter cells (gametes), each with a single chromosome set and all genetically different

DNA and the genome

Genetic material in the nucleus of a cell is composed of **DNA**.

DNA is made up of two strands forming a **double helix**.

DNA is contained in structures called **chromosomes**.

A **gene** is a small section of DNA on a chromosome that codes for a specific sequence of amino acids, to produce a specific protein.

The **genome** of an organism is the entire genetic material of that organism.

The whole human genome has been studied, and this has allowed scientists to:

- search for genes linked to different diseases
- understand and treat inherited disorders
- trace human migration patterns from the past.

Inherited disorders

Some disorders are due to the inheritance of certain **alleles**:

- Polydactyly (extra fingers or toes) is caused by a **dominant** allele.
- Cystic fibrosis (a disorder of cell membranes) is caused by a **recessive** allele.

Embryo screening and gene therapy may ease suffering from these disorders, but there are ethical issues surrounding their use.

Key terms

Make sure you can write a definition for these key terms.

allele	chromosome	clone	DNA	dominant
genome	genotype	heterozygous	homozygous	meiosis

B14

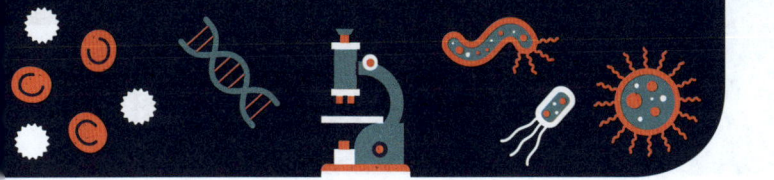

Genetic inheritance

You need to be able to explain these terms about genetic inheritance:

gamete	specialised sex cell formed by meiosis
chromosome	long molecule made from DNA, found in the nucleus of cells
gene	sequence of DNA that codes for a protein – some characteristics are controlled by a single gene (e.g., fur colour in mice and red-green colour-blindness in humans), but most are controlled by multiple genes interacting
allele	different forms of the same gene
dominant	allele that only needs one copy to be expressed (it is always expressed)
recessive	allele that needs two copies present to be expressed
homozygous	when an individual carries two copies of the same allele for a trait
heterozygous	when an individual carries two different alleles for a trait
genotype	combination of alleles an individual has
phenotype	physical expression of the genotype – the characteristic shown

Genetic crosses

A **genetic cross** is when you consider the offspring that might result from two known parents. **Punnett squares** can be used to predict the outcome of a genetic cross, allowing us to see the genotypes the offspring might have and their phenotypes.

For example, the cross bb (brown fur) × BB (black fur) in mice:

		mother	mother
		B	B
father	b	Bb	Bb
father	b	Bb	Bb

- offspring genotype: 100 % Bb
- offspring phenotype: all black fur (B is dominant)

Sex determination

Normal human body cells contain 23 pairs of chromosomes – one of these pairs determines the sex of the offspring.

In human females the sex chromosomes are the same (XX, homozygous), and in males they are different (XY, heterozygous).

A Punnett square can be used to determine the probability of offspring being male or female. The probability is always 50 % in humans as there are two XX outcomes and two XY outcomes.

		mother	mother
		X	X
father	X	XX	XX
father	Y	XY	XY

---

double helix	fertilisation	gamete	gene	genetic cross
mitosis	phenotype	Punnett square	recessive

B14 Knowledge	133

Retrieval

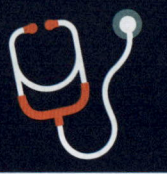

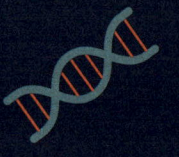

Learn the answers to the questions below, then cover the answers column with a piece of paper and write as many as you can. Check and repeat.

B14 questions | Answers

#	Question	Answer
1	What is sexual reproduction?	joining (fusion) of male and female gametes
2	What type of cell division is involved in sexual reproduction?	meiosis
3	What type of cell division is involved in asexual reproduction?	mitosis
4	What is meiosis?	cell division that produces four daughter cells (gametes), each with a single set of chromosomes
5	What are the male and female sex chromosomes in humans?	• XX – female • XY – male
6	What are the male and female gametes in flowering plants?	• pollen – male gamete • ovule – female gamete
7	What is the genetic material in cells called?	DNA
8	What is the structure of DNA?	two complementary strands forming a double helix
9	What is a gene?	small section of DNA that codes for a particular amino acid sequence, to make a specific protein
10	What are alleles?	different forms of the same gene
11	What is a recessive allele?	allele that needs both copies to be present to be expressed
12	What is a dominant allele?	allele that is expressed even if only one copy is present
13	What is a genome?	the entire genetic material of an organism
14	Define the term homozygous.	two of the same alleles present in an organism
15	Define the term heterozygous.	two different alleles present in an organism
16	What type of allele causes polydactyly?	dominant allele
17	What type of allele causes cystic fibrosis?	recessive allele
18	How many chromosomes do normal human body cells have?	23 pairs (46)
19	Why is studying the human genome important?	• search for genes linked to certain diseases • understanding and treatment of inherited disorders • tracing past human migration

B14 Reproduction

B14

Now go back and use the questions below to check your knowledge from previous chapters.

Previous questions | Answers

#	Previous questions	Answers
1	What happens to muscles during long periods of activity?	muscles become fatigued and stop contracting efficiently
2	Describe the process of selective breeding.	1 choose parents with the desired characteristic 2 breed them together 3 choose offspring with the desired characteristic and breed again 4 continue over many generations until all offspring show the desired characteristic
3	What is the function of follicle stimulating hormone?	causes eggs to mature in the ovaries, and stimulates ovaries to produce oestrogen
4	What can cause variation?	genetic causes, environmental causes, and a combination of genes and the environment
5	What is the difference between aerobic and anaerobic respiration?	aerobic respiration uses oxygen, anaerobic respiration does not
6	How have bacteria been genetically engineered?	to produce useful substances, such as human insulin to treat diabetes

Maths skills

Practise your maths skills using the worked example and practice questions below.

Probability

Probability is a number that tells you how likely something is to happen.

It is important that you understand probability as this is key to genetic inheritance.

For example, you could be asked to work out the probability of a child inheriting a genetic disease from its parents using a Punnett square.

A value for probability can be expressed in the form of a fraction, decimal, or percentage.

Probability can be calculated using the formula:

$$\text{probability} = \frac{\text{number of ways the outcome can happen}}{\text{total number of outcomes}}$$

Worked example

The Punnett square shows the inheritance of sex chromosomes in a genetic cross between two parents.

	X	Y
X	XX	XY
X	XX	XY

male = XY
female = XX

What is the probability that the offspring from the genetic cross will be female?

- number of ways the outcome can happen = 2
- total number of outcomes = 4
- probability = $\frac{2}{4}$ = 0.5

This probability can also be expressed as a fraction $\left(\frac{1}{2}\right)$ or a percentage (50%).

Practice

1 The Punnett square shows the inheritance of eye colour in a genetic cross. BB and Bb represent brown eyes; bb represents blue eyes.

What is the probability that the offspring of the cross would have blue eyes?

	B	b
B	BB	Bb
b	Bb	bb

2 The Punnett square shows whether the offspring of a genetic cross between plants will be tall or short. TT and Tt represent tall plants, and tt represents short plants.

What is the probability that the offspring of the cross would be tall?

	T	t
T	TT	Tt
t	Tt	tt

Practice

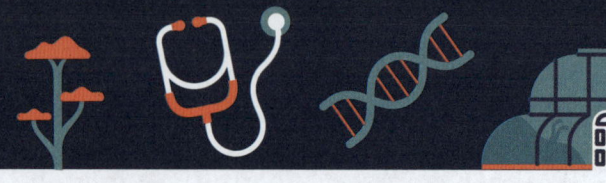

Exam-style questions

01 **Figure 1** shows the sex chromosomes from two people, **A** and **B**.

Figure 1

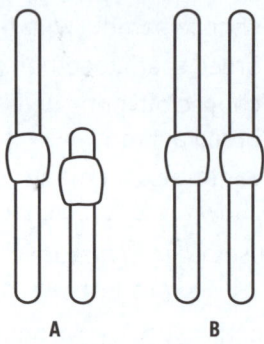

A   B

> **Exam Tip**
>
> People who are genetically female have two X chromosomes (XX), and people who are genetically male have an X chromosome and a Y chromosome (XY).

01.1 Identify which image (**A** or **B**) in **Figure 1** represents the chromosomes from a female. Explain your answer. **[2 marks]**

_____

_____

01.2 Name the part of the cell that contains the chromosomes. **[1 mark]**

_____

> **Exam Tip**
>
> Chromosomes hold the DNA, so think about where in a cell would you find the DNA.

01.3 Carry out a genetic cross using the Punnett square below to show how sex chromosomes are inherited. **[1 mark]**

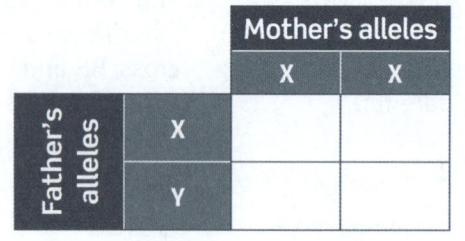

		Mother's alleles	
		X	X
Father's alleles	X		
	Y		

> **Exam Tip**
>
> Either go down or across first – mixing up the order can lead to confusion.

01.4 Use your Punnett square to calculate the probability of a couple having a baby girl. **[1 mark]**

Probability = _____

01.5 A couple has a second child.

Identify the probability that both children are girls. **[1 mark]**

Tick **one** box.

$\frac{1}{2}$ ☐ $\frac{1}{4}$ ☐

$\frac{1}{8}$ ☐ $\frac{1}{16}$ ☐

> **Exam Tip**
>
> These are two independent events – use your maths skills here.

136   B14 Reproduction

Paper 2 **B14**

02 Sea anemones are animals that live in the ocean. They are closely related to coral.

Sea anemones can reproduce sexually and asexually.

02.1 Name the type of cell division used in asexual reproduction. **[1 mark]**

_____

02.2 Order the following statements (**A**–**E**) in the boxes below to outline the main stages in asexual reproduction. **[4 marks]**
- **A** one set of chromosomes is pulled to each end of the cell
- **B** cytoplasm and cell membrane divide
- **C** two copies of the chromosomes are formed
- **D** two identical cells are formed
- **E** the nucleus divides

start					

02.3 Sea anemones also reproduce sexually.

Give **two** differences between the processes of sexual and asexual reproduction. **[2 marks]**

1 _____

2 _____

> **Exam Tip**
> Make sure you read the question – you only need to list differences not similarities.

03 There are two types of cell division that occur in humans: meiosis and mitosis.

03.1 Identify where meiosis occurs in a female body.

Choose **one** answer. **[1 mark]**

uterus   ovaries   vagina   cervix

03.2 Identify where meiosis occurs in a male body.

Choose **one** answer. **[1 mark]**

penis   sperm duct   testes   prostate

> **Exam Tip**
> 03.2 is asking where sperm is made.

03.3 Compare the processes of mitosis and meiosis in **Table 1** by adding ticks to show which type of cell division is being described. **[4 marks]**

Table 1

Feature	Meiosis	Mitosis
produces clones		
produces four gametes		
halves the number of chromosomes in a cell		
cell divides once		

04 Children inherit their genetic make-up from their parents.

04.1 Complete the following sentences about genetic inheritance by circling the correct bold words. **[5 marks]**

Each human gamete contains **23 / 46 / 92** chromosomes. When a sperm and an egg fuse, a new cell called a zygote is formed. This new cell contains **23 / 46 / 92** chromosomes.

Two forms of each gene are inherited – these are called **alleles / dominant / recessive**. If one form of the gene is **allele / dominant / recessive** – this form is always expressed if present. The other form of the gene is **allele / dominant / recessive** – a person must inherit this form of the gene from both parents if it is to be expressed.

04.2 Eye colour is controlled by a gene. Two forms of the gene exist:
- brown eyes – dominant – B
- blue eyes – recessive – b

Classify each of the possible genotypes by drawing **one** line to match each allele combination to its correct description. **[2 marks]**

Allele combination	Description
BB	homozygous recessive
Bb	homozygous dominant
bb	heterozygous

04.3 Write down the phenotype for each of the allele combinations: BB, Bb, and bb. **[3 marks]**

04.4 A couple is expecting a baby. The father has blue eyes and the mother has brown eyes.

Select the correct statement about their new baby's eye colour.

Choose **one** answer. **[1 mark]**

The baby will definitely have brown eyes.

The baby could have brown eyes or blue eyes.

The baby will definitely have blue eyes.

04.5 Give a reason for your answer to **04.4**. **[1 mark]**

05 All living organisms contain genetic information.

05.1 Identify **two** features of DNA from the following list. **[2 marks]**

DNA is a monomer

DNA is a polymer

DNA is made up of four strands

DNA is twisted into a helix

> **Exam Tip**
>
> Make sure you select two answers from the list.

B14 Reproduction

05.2 Draw **one** line from each genetic term to its definition. **[3 marks]**

Genetic term	Definition
gene	part of a cell containing DNA
chromosome	entire genetic material found in an organism
genome	section of DNA coding for a characteristic
nucleus	long strand of DNA

Exam Tip
There are lots of new words to learn in this topic – it is important that you know all of your definitions.

05.3 Suggest **one** benefit of studying the human genome. **[1 mark]**

06 Most species of tomato have 24 chromosomes present in the nuclei of their cells.

06.1 Write down how many chromosomes would be present in an adult tomato cell. **[1 mark]**

06.2 Write down how many chromosomes would be present in a tomato pollen cell. **[1 mark]**

Exam Tip
A pollen cell is a plant gamete.

06.3 Tomato plants reproduce sexually.
Identify from the list below the **two** features of sexual reproduction. **[2 marks]**

there is no mixing of genetic information
two parents are required
gametes fuse together
clones are produced

06.4 Describe the main steps needed to create a tomato pollen cell. **[4 marks]**

07 Some disorders are inherited.

07.1 Identify a dominant inherited disorder from the following list.
Choose **one** answer. **[1 mark]**

heart attack   measles   headache   polydactyly

Exam Tip
People with polydactyly have extra fingers or toes.

07.2 Cystic fibrosis is another example of an inherited disorder.
Identify **two** correct statements about the disorder. **[2 marks]**

caused by a dominant allele
caused by a recessive allele
causes a person to have extra fingers or toes
affects cell membranes resulting in thick mucus being produced

07.3 If a couple is at high risk of having a child with cystic fibrosis they may consider having their embryos screened for the disorder.

Draw **one** line from each statement to show whether it is a social, economic, or ethical consideration of screening embryos. **[4 marks]**

| enables parents to evaluate potential impact on their lives |
| cost of procedure small compared with cost of lifetime care |
| belief that an unborn fetus has a 'right to life' |
| allows a couple to consider whether they are able to financially support the child |

ethical

social

economic

> **Exam Tip**
> One of the boxes on the right will have two lines going into it.

08 To create a new organism, two gamete cells need to join together.

08.1 Complete **Figure 2** using words from the box to show what happens in human reproduction. Each term may be used once, more than once, or not at all. **[5 marks]**

| 23 | 46 | mitosis | meiosis | fertilisation | screening |

Figure 2

sperm contains _____ chromosomes

egg contains _____ chromosomes

cell divides by _____

during _____ the genetic material joins together.

each nucleus in an embryo contains _____ chromosomes.

> **Exam Tip**
> To help you revise, use a pencil to write the words in the spaces until you're sure of the correct answer.

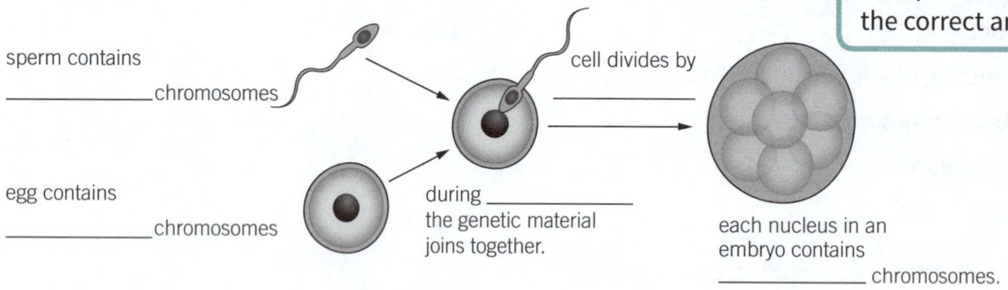

08.2 Humans reproduce by sexual reproduction.

Identify **two** features of this type of reproduction from the statements below. **[2 marks]**

it involves one parent

it involves two parents

genetically different offspring are produced

genetically identical offspring are produced

08.3 Many plants also reproduce sexually.

Name the gametes found in plants. **[2 marks]**

09 The genetic material found in the nuclei of human cells is made from the chemical DNA.

09.1 Describe the main features of the structure of DNA. **[3 marks]**

09.2 Genes are small sections of DNA. Each gene contains a code.

Describe what a gene codes for. **[2 marks]**

B14 Reproduction

09.3 In 2003, scientists announced that they had sequenced the entire human genome.

Define the term genome. **[1 mark]**

09.4 Outline some of the important benefits of sequencing the human genome. **[3 marks]**

10 A student investigated the anaerobic respiration of yeast.

The student used the equipment in **Figure 3**. They used a gas syringe to measure the volume of gas produced and repeated the investigation at a number of different temperatures.

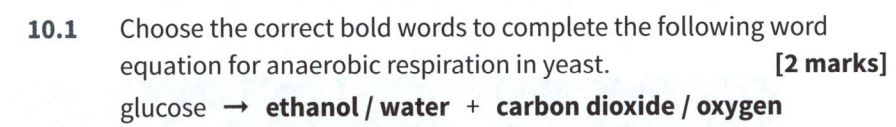

10.1 Choose the correct bold words to complete the following word equation for anaerobic respiration in yeast. **[2 marks]**

glucose → **ethanol / water** + **carbon dioxide / oxygen**

10.2 Draw **one** line from each variable in the experiment to its description. **[2 marks]**

Variable	Description
control variable	temperature
independent variable	volume of gas produced
dependent variable	time over which gas is collected

Figure 3

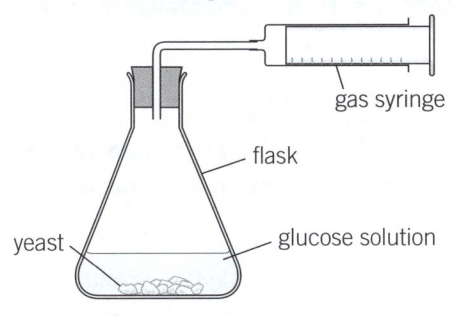

gas syringe, flask, yeast, glucose solution

Exam Tip

CID and SAM can help you remember the variables:
- **C**ontrolled — **S**ame
- **I**ndependent — **A**lter
- **D**ependant — **M**easure

10.3 The student's results are shown in **Table 2**.

Plot this data on **Figure 4**. **[3 marks]**

Table 2

Temperature in °C	10	20	30	40	50
Volume of gas collected in cm^3	20	35	42	50	10

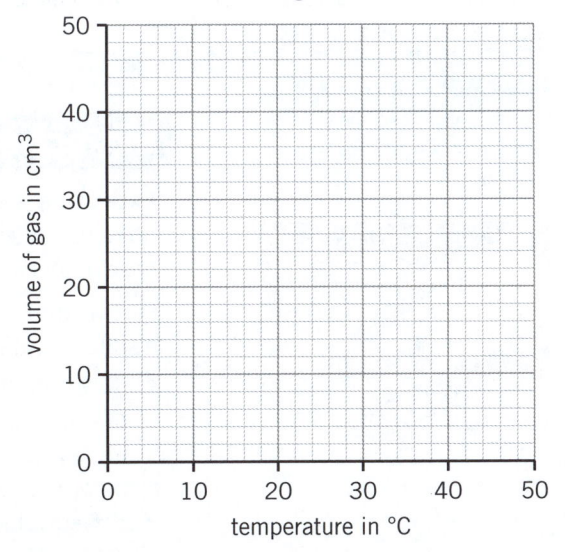

Figure 4

[Graph: volume of gas in cm^3 (y-axis, 0–50) vs temperature in °C (x-axis, 0–50)]

10.4 Describe the trend shown in your graph. **[2 marks]**

Knowledge

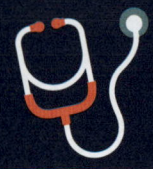

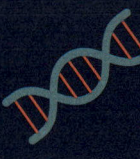

B15 Evolution

Theory of evolution

Evolution is the gradual change in the inherited characteristics of a population over time.

Evolution occurs through the process of **natural selection** and may result in the formation of new species.

Key terms
Make sure you can write a definition for these key terms.

antibiotic resistance
binomial system   evolution
evolutionary tree   extinction
fossil record   natural selection
three-domain system

Process of natural selection

The theory of evolution by natural selection states that
- organisms within species show a wide range of variation in phenotype
- individuals with characteristics most suited to the environment are more likely to survive and breed successfully
- these characteristics are then passed on to their offspring.

Evidence for evolution

The theory of evolution by natural selection is now widely accepted because there are lots of data to support it, such as
- it has been shown that characteristics are passed on to offspring in genes
- evidence from the **fossil record**
- the evolution of **antibiotic resistance** in bacteria.

Fossils

Fossils are the remains of organisms from millions of years ago, which are found in rocks.

Fossils can be formed from
- parts of an organism that do not decay because one or more of the conditions needed for decay are absent
- hard parts of an organism (e.g., bones) when replaced by minerals
- preservation of the traces of organisms (e.g., burrows, footprints, and rootlet traces).

Benefits of the fossil record	Problems with the fossil record
• can tell scientists how individual species have changed over time • fossils allow us to understand how life developed over the Earth's history • fossils can be used to track the movement of a species or its ancestors across the world	• many early organisms were soft-bodied, so most decayed before producing fossils • there are gaps in the fossil record as not all fossils have been found and others have been destroyed by geological or human activity – this means scientists cannot be certain about how life began on Earth

1 The reptile dies and falls to the ground

2 The flesh decays, leaving the skeleton to be covered in sand or soil and clay before it is damaged

3 Protected, over millions of years, the skeleton becomes mineralised and turns to rock. The rocks shift in the earth with the fossil trapped inside

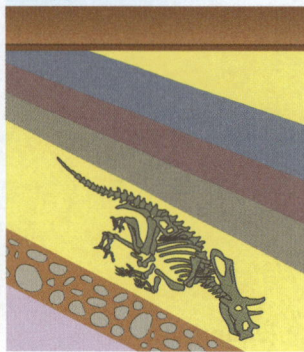

4 Eventually, the fossil emerges as the rocks move and erosion takes place

Extinction

Extinction is when there are no remaining individuals of a species still alive.

Factors that may contribute to a species' extinction include
- new predators
- new diseases or pathogens
- increased competition for resources or mates
- catastrophic events (e.g., asteroid impacts, volcanic eruptions, earthquakes)
- changes to the environment (e.g., climate change, destruction of habitats).

B15

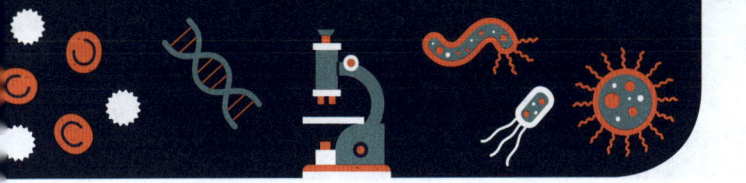

Resistant bacteria

Bacteria can evolve rapidly because they reproduce very quickly.

This has led to many strains of bacteria developing antibiotic resistance, such as MRSA. The development of antibiotic resistance in bacteria is evidence for the theory of evolution by natural selection.

Emergence of antibiotic resistance

The development of new antibiotics is expensive and slow, so it cannot keep up with the emergence of new strains of antibiotic-resistant bacteria.

To reduce the rise of antibiotic-resistant strains
- doctors should only prescribe antibiotics for serious bacterial infections
- patients should complete their courses of antibiotics so all bacteria are killed and none survive to form resistant strains
- the use of antibiotics in farming and agriculture should be restricted.

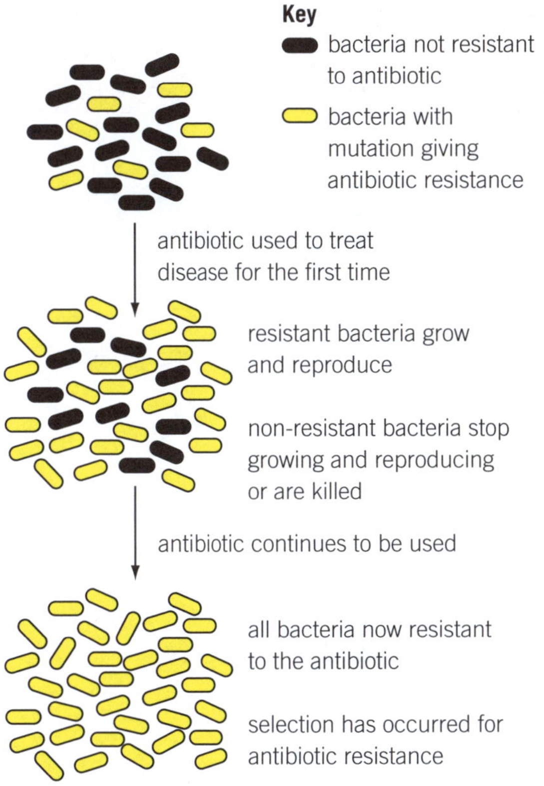

Key
- ● bacteria not resistant to antibiotic
- ● bacteria with mutation giving antibiotic resistance

antibiotic used to treat disease for the first time

resistant bacteria grow and reproduce

non-resistant bacteria stop growing and reproducing or are killed

antibiotic continues to be used

all bacteria now resistant to the antibiotic

selection has occurred for antibiotic resistance

Classification of living organisms

Carl Linnaeus developed a system to classify living things into groups, based on their structure and characteristics.

New models of classification were proposed as the understanding of biochemical processes developed and improvements in microscopes led to discoveries of internal structures.

There is now a **three-domain system** developed by Carl Woese, dividing organisms into:
- Archaea (primitive bacteria usually living in extreme environments)
- Bacteria (true bacteria)
- Eukaryota (including protists, fungi, plants, and animals).

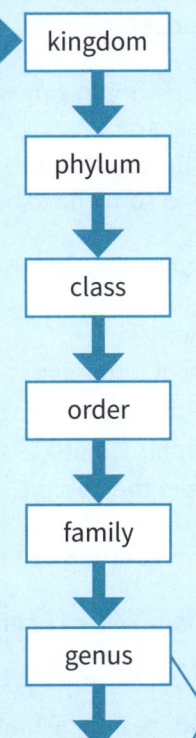

kingdom → phylum → class → order → family → genus → species

organisms are named by the **binomial system** of genus and species

Evolutionary trees

Evolutionary trees use current classification data for living organisms and fossil data for extinct organisms to show how scientists believe organisms are related.

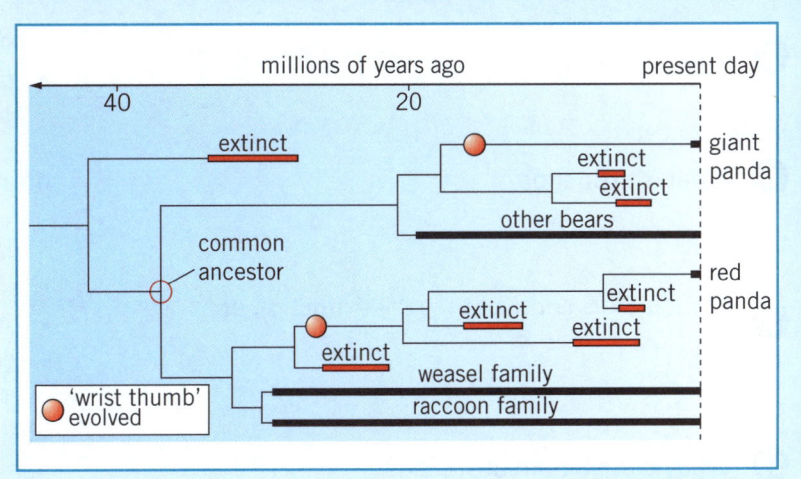

millions of years ago — present day
40 — 20

giant panda
other bears
red panda
weasel family
raccoon family

common ancestor
'wrist thumb' evolved

Revision tip

Remember Lots of students get the key words in this topic mixed up – evolution and natural selection are linked but are not the same so learn the differences carefully.

B15 Knowledge 143

Retrieval

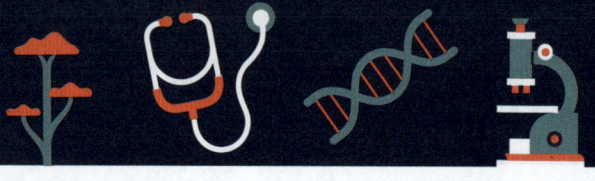

Learn the answers to the questions below, then cover the answers column with a piece of paper and write as many as you can. Check and repeat.

B15 questions | Answers

#	Question	Answer
1	What is evolution?	change in the inherited characteristics of a population over time through natural selection, which may result in a new species
2	What is the theory of evolution by natural selection?	the organisms that are best adapted to their environment are most likely to survive and pass on these characteristics to their offspring
3	What evidence supports the theory of evolution?	• parents pass on their characteristics to offspring in genes • fossil record evidence • evolution of antibiotic-resistant bacteria
4	What are fossils?	remains of organisms from millions of years ago, found in rocks
5	How might fossils be formed?	• parts of an organism do not decay because the conditions needed for decay are absent • traces of organisms are preserved • parts of an organism are replaced by minerals
6	What are the benefits of the fossil record?	can learn how species changed and how life developed on Earth, and can track the movement of species across the world
7	What are the problems with the fossil record?	• many early organisms were soft-bodied so did not form fossils • gaps in the fossil record as not all fossils have been found and some have been destroyed
8	What is extinction?	no individuals of a species are still alive
9	What factors contribute to the extinction of a species?	• predators • diseases or pathogens • competition for resources or mates • catastrophic events • changes in the habitat
10	What is the binomial system?	naming of organisms by their genus and species
11	What classification system did Carl Woese introduce?	three-domain system of Archaea, Bacteria, and Eukaryota
12	Why can bacteria evolve rapidly?	they reproduce at a fast rate
13	How do antibiotic-resistant strains of bacteria develop?	mutations that allow the strain to survive and reproduce in the presence of the antibiotic

B15 Evolution

B15

Now go back and use the questions below to check your knowledge from previous chapters.

Previous questions / Answers

	Previous questions	Answers
1	How do new phenotype variants occur?	mutations
2	What is cancer?	a result of changes in cells that lead to uncontrolled growth and cell division by mitosis
3	Name the four main components of blood.	red blood cells, white blood cells, plasma, platelets
4	What are artificial hearts used for?	keep patients alive while waiting for a transplant, or allow the heart to rest for recovery
5	What is a genome?	the entire genetic material of an organism
6	What are the male and female sex chromosomes in humans?	XX – female, XY – male
7	How many chromosomes do normal human body cells have?	23 pairs (46)

Maths skills

Practise your maths skills using the worked example and practice questions below.

Significant figures

In science you are often asked to give numbers expressed to two or three significant figures (s.f.).

This is to avoid giving irrelevant or unnecessary figures in a very small or large number, or to avoid introducing error in a result.

Significant figures can also be used to make large or complicated calculations simpler.

A key point to remember is that leading zeros (before a decimal point) are *never* significant.

Worked example

Zeros within a number count as significant figures. For example, 3.28034 has six significant figures.

Leading zeros are never significant, so 0.00760 has 3 significant figures.

Example 1:

Round 2.837076 to 3 s.f.

First count the significant figures from left to right, giving 2.83 to 3 s.f.

As the 4th digit is a 7, the answer is rounded up, giving 2.84.

Example 2:

Round 0.03601 to 3 s.f.

Number the significant figures, remembering that leading zeros are never significant.

As the 4th digit is a 1, the answer is not rounded up, giving 0.0360.

Practice

1. Round 0.009909 to 3 s.f.
2. Round 53879 to 2 s.f.
3. Round 0.005089 to 1 s.f.
4. Round 98347 to 2 s.f.
5. Round 3.5175 to 3 s.f.

Practice

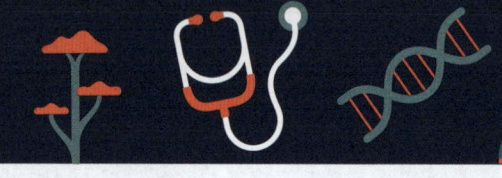

Exam-style questions

01 Scientists believe that species evolve through the process of natural selection.

01.1 Circle the most appropriate bold word to complete the sentence. **[1 mark]**

The theory of evolution by natural selection states that all organisms have evolved from simple life forms that existed **tens / hundreds / thousands / millions** of years ago.

01.2 Rearrange statements **A**–**F** to explain how natural selection occurs. The first statement has been done for you. **[4 marks]**

- **A** More organisms within the species have the advantageous characteristic.
- **B** Process is repeated over many generations.
- **C** Genes that code for advantageous characteristics are passed on to offspring.
- **D** The organisms with the characteristics that are best suited to the environment survive and reproduce, and less well-adapted organisms die.
- **E** New species can evolve where all organisms have the adaptations.
- **F** Organisms in a species show variation.

F					

> **Exam Tip**
> The layout of the answer shows you that **F** is the first statement so you don't need to use that one.

01.3 Over time, evolution can result in the development of a new species.

Define the term species. **[1 mark]**

_____

02 Scientists have developed the theory of evolution.

02.1 Choose the most appropriate words from the box to complete the sentences about evolution. **[5 marks]**

| millions | genes | selection | evolved | reproduced |
| | thousands | survive | differentiated | |

All organisms living today have _____ from a common ancestor.

This process has taken _____ of years and has occurred as a result of natural _____ .

The organisms that are best adapted to their environment _____ and reproduce, passing on the _____ that code for these characteristics to their offspring.

> **Exam Tip**
> There are more words than there are spaces, this means some words will not be used. When you are filling in the answer lines, it can help to put a small cross next to the ones you have used – don't completely cross them out as you may change your mind and use them elsewhere.

146 B15 Evolution

Paper 2 **B15**

02.2 Identify the scientist who developed the theory of evolution by natural selection. **[1 mark]**

Tick **one** box.

Lamarck ☐   Lister ☐

Darwin ☐   Fleming ☐

02.3 Fossils provide evidence for evolution.

Describe what is meant by the term fossil. **[2 marks]**

_____
_____
_____

02.4 Give **one** other piece of evidence for evolution. **[1 mark]**

_____

> **! Exam Tip**
>
> Make sure this is different evidence to fossil evidence – you won't get any marks for repeating other parts of the question.

03 Species that cannot adapt sometimes go extinct.

03.1 Identify the most accurate description of extinction.

Choose **one** answer. **[1 mark]**

The range of organisms living in an area.

Only a small population of a species present in the world.

No individuals of a species found anywhere in the world.

Organisms of a species are only found living in captivity.

03.2 Draw **one** line from each factor to how it could lead to extinction of a species. **[3 marks]**

Factor	Reason for extinction
outbreak of a new disease	lack of food causing starvation
prolonged drought	organisms of a species are all killed by microorganisms
introduction of new competitors	loss of habitat leads to death of organisms
deforestation	lack of water leads to death of organisms

03.3 Suggest **one** technique scientists may use to try to prevent extinction. **[1 mark]**

04 Fossils provide evidence of organisms that existed millions of years ago.

04.1 Describe **three** ways fossils can be made. **[3 marks]**

04.2 Explain why there are gaps in the fossil record. **[3 marks]**

04.3 Fossils provide evidence for Darwin's theory of evolution by natural selection.

Give **one** reason why people did not believe Darwin's theory when he first proposed it. **[1 mark]**

04.4 Give **one** other piece of evidence for Darwin's theory. **[1 mark]**

05 Some bacteria have evolved to become resistant to antibiotics.

05.1 Order the statements **A**–**E** to correctly describe the main steps for a population of bacteria to become resistant. **[4 marks]**

   A when exposed to the antibiotic, bacteria without the mutation die and resistant bacteria reproduce

   B genes that code for resistance are passed on

   C random mutations occur in the genes of individual bacterial cells

   D more bacteria in the population have antibiotic resistance

   E some mutations protect the bacterial cell from an antibiotic

05.2 Some *Staphylococcus aureus* bacteria are resistant to the antibiotic methicillin. These bacteria are known as MRSA. In some cases, infection with MRSA can lead to death.

Figure 1 shows the number of UK deaths due to MRSA, per million people between the years 1994 and 2011.

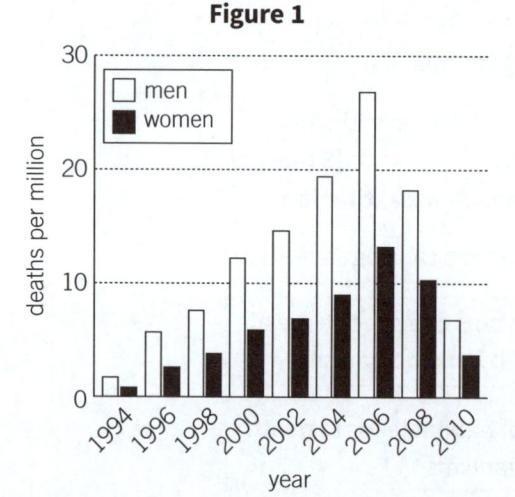

Figure 1

Identify the year when there was the most female deaths from MRSA. **[1 mark]**

05.3 Identify **two** trends shown in the data. **[2 marks]**

05.4 Describe **one** way that the spread of antibiotic resistant bacteria can be reduced or prevented. **[1 mark]**

> **Exam Tip**
>
> The command word at the start of a question tells you what the examiner is looking for in the answer. *Describe* questions are what a thing looks or acts like, whereas *explain* questions are the why something looks or acts the way it does.

> **Exam Tip**
>
> **05.3** is asking for *two* trends so you need to clearly identify *two* different patterns in the data – look at the peaks in the graph and at the difference between the genders.

B15 Evolution

B15

06 New species develop as a result of natural selection.

06.1 Define the term species. **[1 mark]**

06.2 **Figure 2** shows part of the evolutionary tree of primates.

Figure 2

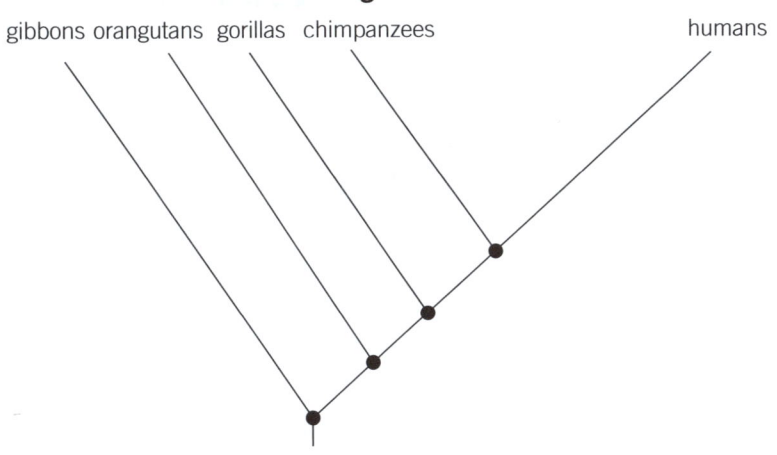

gibbons orangutans gorillas chimpanzees   humans

Identify the organism in **Figure 2** that most recently shared a common ancestor with humans. **[1 mark]**

06.3 In 1858, Darwin proposed his theory of evolution by natural selection.

Use the words from the box to complete the passage that describes how organisms evolve by natural selection. **[4 marks]**

| genes | die | DNA | genotype | phenotype |
| similarities | | survive | variation | |

Individual organisms within a species show _____ as a result of differences in their DNA. Individuals who have characteristics that are most suited to their environment are more likely to _____ and reproduce. The individuals pass on these favourable _____ to their offspring. This results in more individuals displaying these favourable characteristics in their _____ .

> **! Exam Tip**
>
> During your revision, reading the sentences out loud with the different words in the spaces can help you work out which word fits best in each gap.

07 Organisms are classified into groups based on their structure and characteristics. This system was devised by Carl Linnaeus in the 18th century.

07.1 In the Linnaean system the largest group is known as a kingdom. Identify the kingdoms in the following list.

Choose **two** answers. **[2 marks]**

animals   vegetables   fungi   insects

For answers and more practice questions visit www.oxfordrevise.com/scienceanswers

Even more practice and interactive revision quizzes are available on kerboodle

B15 Practice

07.2 The organisms are further classified into smaller and smaller groups.

Use the terms in the box to complete the different levels in the Linnaean classification system. The first and last terms have been completed for you. **[4 marks]**

| class | order | genus | ~~kingdom~~ |
| family | phylum | ~~species~~ |

| kingdom | | | | | | species |

07.3 Species is the smallest group in the classification system.

Describe what is meant by the term species. **[1 mark]**

08 Charles Darwin developed the theory for evolution by natural selection.

08.1 Identify the most accurate description of evolution from the following statements.

Choose **one** answer. **[1 mark]**

differences in characteristics within a species

when no more individuals of a species are left anywhere in the world

changes in a species over time

production of clones

08.2 Fossils provide evidence to support evolution.

Draw **one** line to link each fossil type to the method they are formed by. **[2 marks]**

Fossil type	Method
footprint	parts of the organism were replaced by minerals as they decayed
ammonite	preserved trace of an organism
insect in amber	parts of the organism did not decay as conditions for decay were absent

08.3 The fossil record is incomplete.

Give **one** reason why we do not have fossils of every organism that has ever existed. **[1 mark]**

09 Organisms are traditionally classified into groups based on structure and characteristics.

09.1 Identify the scientist who originally created this form of classification.

Choose **one** answer. **[1 mark]**

Linnaeus   Woese   Darwin   Wallace

B15 Evolution

09.2 Tigers have the scientific name *Panthera tigris*.

Draw **one** line to match each classification level to the name of the classification tigers belong to. [2 marks]

Classification level	Tiger classification
species	animal
genus	tigris
kingdom	Panthera

09.3 A 'three domain system' of classification is now used in biology.

Describe **one** development that has helped provide evidence for this classification system. [1 mark]

09.4 Draw **one** line to match each type of organism to the domain that they are classified in. [2 marks]

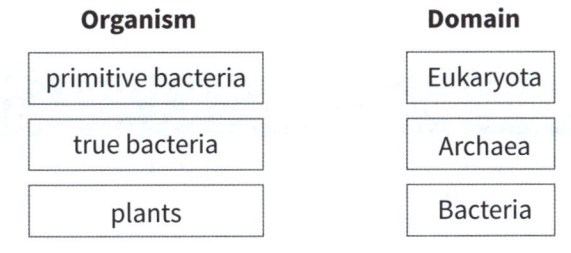

Organism	Domain
primitive bacteria	Eukaryota
true bacteria	Archaea
plants	Bacteria

10 Figure 3 shows an evolutionary tree for some dinosaurs.

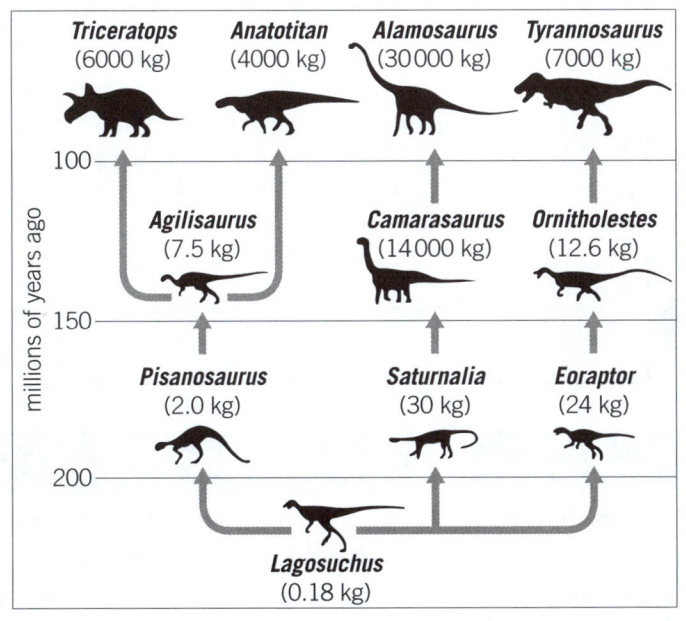

Figure 3

Triceratops (6000 kg) *Anatotitan* (4000 kg) *Alamosaurus* (30 000 kg) *Tyrannosaurus* (7000 kg)

Agilisaurus (7.5 kg) *Camarasaurus* (14 000 kg) *Ornitholestes* (12.6 kg)

Pisanosaurus (2.0 kg) *Saturnalia* (30 kg) *Eoraptor* (24 kg)

Lagosuchus (0.18 kg)

(y-axis: millions of years ago; 100, 150, 200)

10.1 Define the term extinct. [1 mark]

10.2 Write down the name of the common ancestor of *Triceratops* and *Anatotitan*. [1 mark]

10.3 Describe the trend in the mass of the dinosaurs over time. [1 mark]

10.4 Estimate the time taken for *Saturnalia* to evolve into *Camarasaurus*. [1 mark]

Exam Tip

You can make an estimate based on the axis on the left hand side (millions of years).

Knowledge

B16 Adaptation

Ecosystem organisation

Individual organisms
↓
Population
the total number of organisms of the same species that live in one specific geographical area
↓
Community
group of two or more populations of different species living in one specific geographical area
↓
Ecosystem
the interaction of a community of living organisms with the non-living parts of their environment

A stable community is one where all the species and environmental factors are in balance so that population sizes remain fairly constant.

An example of this is the interaction between predator and prey populations, which rise and fall in a constant cycle so that each remains within a stable range.

Competition

To survive and reproduce, organisms require a supply of resources from their surroundings and from the other living organisms there.

This can create competition, where organisms within a community compete for resources.

There are two types of competition – **interspecific competition** is between organisms of *different* species, and **intraspecific competition** is between organisms of the *same* species.

Animals often compete for
- food
- mates
- territory.

Plants often compete for
- light
- space
- water and mineral ions from the soil.

Interdependence

Within a community each species **interacts** with many others and may depend on other species for things like food, shelter, pollination, and seed dispersal.

If one species is removed it can affect the whole community – this is called **interdependence**.

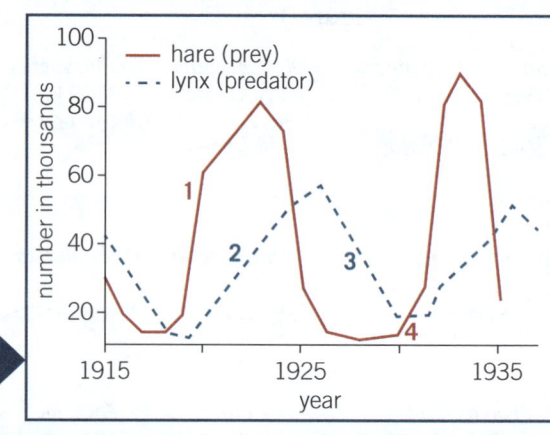

[Graph: number in thousands vs year (1915–1935), showing hare (prey) solid line and lynx (predator) dashed line, with labels 1, 2, 3, 4]

1 If the population of hares increases there is a larger food supply for the lynx.

2 This can therefore support more lynx, so more offspring survive.

3 The growing numbers of lynx kill more hares and eventually reduce the food supply. The number of lynx starts to decrease.

4 The hare population starts to increase once more due to the lack of predators – the cycle then begins again.

Abiotic factors

Abiotic factors are non-living factors in the ecosystem that can affect a community.

Too much or too little of the following abiotic factors can negatively affect the community in an ecosystem:
- carbon dioxide levels for plants
- light intensity
- moisture levels
- oxygen levels for animals that live in water
- soil pH and mineral content
- temperature
- wind intensity and direction

Biotic factors

Biotic factors are living factors in the ecosystem that can affect a community.

For example, the following biotic factors would all negatively affect populations in a community:
- decreased availability of food
- new predators arriving
- new pathogens
- competition between species, for example, one species outcompeting another for food or shelter, causing a decline in the other species' population

B16

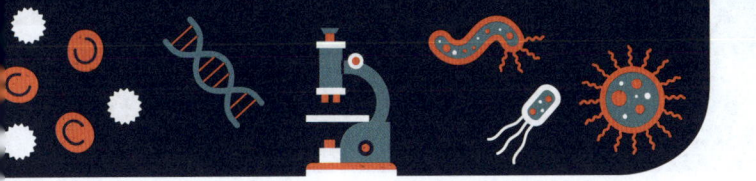

Adaptations of organisms

Organisms have features – **adaptations** – that enable them to survive in the conditions in which they live. The adaptations of an organism may allow it to outcompete others, and provide it with an evolutionary advantage.

Structural adaptations
The physical features that allow an organism to successfully compete:
- sharp teeth to hunt prey
- colouring that may provide camouflage to hide from predators or to hunt prey
- a large or small body-surface-area-to-volume ratio

Behavioural adaptations
The behaviour of an organism that gives it an advantage:
- making nests to shelter offspring or attract a mate
- courtship dances to attract a mate
- use of tools to obtain food
- working together in packs

Functional adaptations
Adaptations related to processes that allow an organism to survive:
- photosynthesis in plants
- production of poisons or venom to deter predators or kill prey
- changes in reproduction timings

You can work out how an organism is adapted to where it lives when given information on its environment and what it looks like.

For example, without the following adaptations the organisms below would be at a disadvantage in their environment.

Organism	Example adaptations
	• white fur for camouflage when hunting prey • feet with large surface area to distribute weight on snow • small ears to reduce heat loss • thick fur for insulation
	• feet with large surface area to distribute weight on sand • hump stores fat to provide energy when food is scarce • tough mouth and tongue to allow camel to eat cacti • long eyelashes to keep sand out of eyes
	• spines instead of leaves to reduce surface area and therefore water loss, and to deter consumers • long roots to reach water underground • large, fleshy stem to store water

Some organisms are **extremophiles**, which means they live in environments that are very extreme where most other organisms could not survive. For example, areas with
- very high or low temperatures
- extreme pressures
- high salt concentrations
- highly acidic or alkaline conditions
- low levels of oxygen or water.

Bacteria that live in deep sea vents are extremophiles.

Deep sea vents are formed when seawater circulates through hot volcanic rocks on the seafloor. These environments have very high pressures and temperatures, no sunlight, and are strongly acidic.

Key terms
Make sure you can write a definition for these key terms.

abiotic factor   adaptation   biotic factor   community   ecosystem   extremophile
interaction   interdependence   interspecific competition   intraspecific competition   population

B16 Knowledge   153

Retrieval

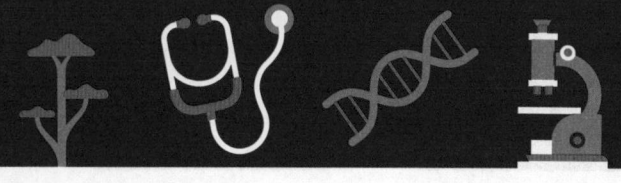

Learn the answers to the questions below, then cover the answers column with a piece of paper and write as many as you can. Check and repeat.

B16 questions / Answers

#	Question	Answer
1	What is a population?	total number of organisms of the same species that live in a specific geographical area
2	What is a community?	group of two or more populations of different species living in a specific geographical area
3	What is an ecosystem?	the interaction of a community of living organisms with the non-living parts of their environment
4	What is competition?	contest between organisms within a community for resources
5	What is interdependence?	when species in a community depend on others for resources and shelter
6	What do animals often compete for?	food, mates, and territory
7	What do plants often compete for?	light, space, water, and mineral ions
8	What is an abiotic factor?	non-living factor that can affect a community
9	List the abiotic factors that can affect a community.	• carbon dioxide levels for plants • light intensity • moisture levels • oxygen levels for animals that live in water • soil pH and mineral content • temperature • wind intensity and direction
10	What is a biotic factor?	living factor that can affect a community
11	List the biotic factors that can affect a community.	• availability of food • new predators • new pathogens • competition between species
12	What is a stable community?	when all species and environmental factors are in balance, so population sizes remain fairly constant
13	How do adaptations help an organism?	enable the organism to survive in the conditions in which it lives
14	What are the three types of adaptations?	structural, behavioural, and functional
15	What is an extremophile?	an organism that lives in a very extreme environment
16	What makes an environment extreme?	• very high or low temperatures • extreme pressures • high salt concentrations • highly acidic or alkaline conditions • lack of oxygen or water

154 B16 Adaptation

B16

Now go back and use the questions below to check your knowledge from previous chapters.

Previous questions | Answers

#	Question	Answer
1	What classification system did Carl Woese introduce?	three-domain system of Archaea, Bacteria, and Eukaryota
2	How might fossils be formed?	• parts of an organism do not decay because the conditions needed for decay are absent • traces of organisms are preserved • parts of an organism are replaced by minerals
3	Where is the pituitary gland located?	brain
4	Describe how temperature affects the rate of photosynthesis.	increasing temperature increases the rate of photosynthesis as the reaction rate increases – at high temperatures enzymes are denatured so the rate of photosynthesis quickly decreases
5	What is the function of an antitoxin?	neutralise toxins produced by pathogens by binding to them
6	What is the function of the nervous system?	it enables organisms to react to their surroundings and coordinates behaviour

Put paper here

Maths skills

Practise your maths skills using the worked example and practice questions below.

Estimations

Estimates are often used in science before an exact calculation is done, or when exact calculations are not practical, such as when dealing with large numbers like population sizes.

For example, if you count how many snails live in 1 m² of a habitat, you can use this value to estimate how many snails live in an area of 10 m².

You can also make estimates from sets of data.

To make an estimate based on a graph, try drawing a line or curve of best fit through the data points. This will enable you to draw a straight line tangent between two points, from which you can make an estimate.

Worked example

A grassy field on a farm measured 120 metres by 90 metres.

A student wanted to estimate the number of daisies growing in the field.

The student placed a 1 m × 1 m quadrat in one position in the field.

To estimate the number of daisy plants in the field:

Number of daisies in 1 × 1 m quadrat = 7

Area of the field (120 × 90) = 10 800 m²

7 × 10 800 = 75 600 daisies estimated in the field

Practice

1. The average number of dandelions in a 1 metre by 1 metre square of a park is 6. The park measures 230 metres by 350 metres.

   Estimate the number of dandelions in the park.

2. The average number of daisies in a 1 metre by 1 metre square of a field is 28. The field measures 180 metres by 80 metres.

   Estimate the number of daisies in the field.

B16 Retrieval

Practice

Exam-style questions

01 Common seals are found in the waters surrounding the UK.

01.1 Draw **one** line to match each physical adaptation of a seal to its importance for survival. **[2 marks]**

Adaptation	Importance
blubber	to swim
claws	to walk on ice
flippers	to stay warm

> **Exam Tip**
> Blubber is another name for fat.

01.2 Identify why seals have closable ears and nostrils. **[1 mark]**
Tick **one** box.

protect them from loud noises ☐

prevent pathogens from entering ☐

prevent water entering when diving ☐

01.3 Arctic seals are another species of seal adapted to live in cold regions of the world.

Suggest **one** way Arctic seals may differ from the common seal. **[1 mark]**

_____

01.4 Give **one** reason for your answer to **01.3**. **[1 mark]**

_____

02 Desert foxes and Arctic foxes have similarities and differences in their appearance. These are summarised in **Table 1**.

Table 1

Type of fox	Desert fox	Arctic fox
Habitat	desert	ice sheets
Fur colour	pale yellow	white
Ear size	large	small
Foot hairiness	covered in hairs on both surfaces	covered in hairs on both surfaces
Body features	specialised kidneys that reduce water loss from body	have a thick layer of fat underneath skin

B16 Adaptation

Paper 2   **B16**

02.1 Using **Table 1**, give **one** way Arctic foxes are adapted to living in the cold. **[1 mark]**

_____

> **Exam Tip**
>
> **02.1** is specifically asking about the adaptations to the cold so make sure that your answer is about that.

02.2 Suggest why the two species of fox are different colours. **[1 mark]**

_____

02.3 Suggest **one** reason why the feet of the desert fox are covered in hairs. **[1 mark]**

_____

03 Organisms compete with each other for resources.

03.1 Identify the resources that animals often compete for.
Choose **three** answers. **[3 marks]**

food   space to hunt   water   light   space to grow

> **Exam Tip**
>
> **03.1** is asking about animals – be careful, as some of the options are for plants only.

03.2 Plants also compete with each other for resources.
Draw **one** line to match each resource to the reason the plant needs it to survive. **[3 marks]**

Resource	Reason
light	for healthy growth
water	to produce glucose by photosynthesis
space	to allow roots to absorb enough water and leaves to absorb enough light
minerals	for photosynthesis and to keep their cells rigid

03.3 Species within a community may depend on each other.
Identify what this dependency is called.
Choose **one** answer. **[1 mark]**

competition   adaptation   ecology   interdependence

03.4 Bees and plants depend on each other.
Circle the correct bold words to complete the sentences. **[2 marks]**
Bees depend on plants for **pollen / nectar / water** as a source of food.
Plants depend on bees to transfer **pollen / nectar / water** between plants to allow plants to reproduce.

04 The type and number of organisms present in an ecosystem depends on the abiotic and biotic factors present.

04.1 Write the words from the box into **Table 2** to show the abiotic and biotic factors in a pond ecosystem. **[2 marks]**

temperature   predators   soil pH   presence of pathogens

Table 2

Abiotic factor	Biotic factor

> **Exam Tip**
> Abiotic factors are not living, biotic factors are ones that are living.

04.2 Write down whether the following factors are likely to increase or decrease the population of an animal living in a pond ecosystem. **[3 marks]**

increase in the availability of food

increase in the number of predators

increase in the number of pathogens

04.3 The pond has a number of plants growing in it. A tree grows and shades an area of the pond.

Describe how the change in light intensity will affect the growth of the plants in the pond. **[1 mark]**

> **Exam Tip**
> Think about what process plants use light for, and what the products of that reaction are used for.

05 Blackberry bushes are commonly found in UK hedgerows. They are often referred to as brambles as they have long, thorny, and arching stems. They can grow up to several metres tall.

05.1 Suggest **two** ways a blackberry bush is adapted to its environment. **[2 marks]**

05.2 Blackberry seeds are found within the blackberry fruit.

Suggest how blackberry seeds are dispersed. **[2 marks]**

> **Exam Tip**
> Think about what happens to blackberry fruits.

05.3 Explain the advantages to the blackberry bush of dispersing its seeds far from the parent bush. **[2 marks]**

06 There are a number of levels of organisation within an ecosystem.

06.1 Draw **one** line from each level of organisation to its definition. **[3 marks]**

Level of organisation   **Definition**

habitat — living organisms and physical conditions present in an area

community — total number of organisms of one species present in an area

ecosystem — place where an organism lives

population — group of different species that interact within an ecosystem

158   **B16 Adaptation**

06.2 The animals within an ecosystem compete with each other for a number of factors.

Describe how each of these factors is important in the survival of a species. **[2 marks]**

availability of mates

sufficient food and water

> **Exam Tip**
>
> This is only a two-mark question so you don't need to write a lot, but make sure it is clear which part of your answer relates to which factor.

06.3 Plants also compete for a number of factors.

Give **one** factor plants compete for. **[1 mark]**

07 Plants reproduce using seeds.

07.1 Circle the appropriate bold words to complete the sentences explaining why plants spread their seeds. **[5 marks]**

Plants spread their seeds as **far away from / close to** the parent and other seedlings as possible. This is called **seed dispersal / pollination**. This **decreases / increases** the seedlings' chance of survival as it **decreases / increases** competition between the plants for resources such as **food / light**.

07.2 Plants have a number of adaptations to enable them to spread their seeds.

Identify the dispersal method used by each seed.

Tick **one** column for each row. **[4 marks]**

Seeds	Spread by wind	Spread by animals
dandelion		
chestnut		
tomato		
sycamore		

07.3 Suggest and explain **one** way the tomato fruit is adapted to disperse its seeds effectively. **[2 marks]**

08 An ecosystem is made up of a community interacting with the environment. The size and make-up of the community are affected by the abiotic and biotic factors present in the ecosystem. One example of an ecosystem is a woodland.

08.1 Describe what is meant by a community. **[1 mark]**

08.2 Give **one** example of an abiotic factor in a woodland. **[1 mark]**

08.3 Give **one** example of a biotic factor in a woodland. **[1 mark]**

08.4 Beech trees and ivy compete in a woodland ecosystem.

Name **two** resources these species compete for. **[2 marks]**

08.5 Describe **one** way beech trees support the presence of animals in a woodland. **[1 mark]**

> **Exam Tip**
>
> There are lots you of options for **08.2** and **08.3** but writing more than one example for each won't get you any more marks.

09 Plants and animals have adapted over time to enable them to survive.

09.1 Draw **one** line to match each physical adaptation of an animal to its importance for survival. **[2 marks]**

Adaptation	Importance
thick fur	to stay warm
large ears	to catch prey
sharp claws	to detect predators

09.2 Cacti have adapted over time in order to survive. Some of the adaptations of cacti are given below (**A–E**).

A covered in spines
B waxy layer that covers the plant
C thin spines instead of large leaves
D swollen stems
E widespread shallow roots

Choose the adaptation (**A–E**) that enables a cactus to: **[3 marks]**

avoid being eaten

store water

collect available moisture

09.3 Moisture levels affect the rate cacti grow at.

Name **one** other abiotic factor that affects the rate that plants grow at. **[1 mark]**

10 Deer can be found living in the wild in large areas of woodland in the UK.

10.1 Which of the following describes a woodland in which deer live? Choose **one** answer. **[1 mark]**

a community   a population   a climate   a habitat

10.2 Identify which of the following are examples of biotic factors that affect deer populations.

Choose **two** answers. **[2 marks]**

hunting   light intensity   rainfall   mass of grass present

10.3 Intraspecific competition is competition within a species.

Identify and explain **two** resources that deer compete with each other for. **[4 marks]**

10.4 Some factors can affect a population indirectly. For example, temperature can indirectly affect a population of starfish. This is because rising temperatures kill coral, which is the food source of the starfish.

Explain how light intensity indirectly affects the size of a deer population. **[3 marks]**

> **! Exam Tip**
>
> **10.4** is a great question as it is testing your ability to link different topics together in a new context – you know all the science, this is giving you the chance to practice applying it to get you ready for the exam.

160   B16 Adaptation

11 A group of people became ill after eating out in a restaurant. Health and safety inspectors suspect that the customers got food poisoning caused by bacteria on the rice. **Table 3** gives details of how four different restaurants stored their rice.

Table 3

Name of restaurant	Storage method	Time in storage in hours	Storage temperature in °C
Tom's Diner	rice in an open container	8	30
George's Hot Dinners	rice left on a hot plate	1	50
Amira's Kitchen	rice frozen in a freezer compartment	24	−5
Betty's Home Cooking	rice in a sealed container	5	20

11.1 Suggest which restaurant the diners are most likely to have eaten in. **[1 mark]**

11.2 Explain your answer to **11.1**. **[2 marks]**

11.3 Name **one** way to treat food poisoning. **[1 mark]**

11.4 Suggest why uncooked rice can be stored for many months in a packet or jar without spoiling. **[1 mark]**

11.5 Some diseases are contagious.

Suggest and explain **two** ways you could prevent a contagious disease being spread between individuals living in the same house. **[4 marks]**

12 Some people keep mice as pets. Mice can have brown fur or white fur. Brown fur (B) is dominant over white fur (b).

12.1 Define the term genotype. **[1 mark]**

12.2 A pet shop owner crosses a male mouse with brown fur with a female mouse with white fur.

Complete the Punnett square. **[1 mark]**

	Female alleles	
Male alleles	b	b
B		
B		

12.3 Calculate the percentage of offspring that will have white fur. **[1 mark]**

12.4 The female mouse is crossed with another male mouse. This male mouse also has brown fur.

Give the **two** genotypes for fur colour the male mouse could have. **[2 marks]**

12.5 The pet shop owner wants to breed more mice with white fur.

Give the genotype of the male mouse **and** the female mouse the shop owner should cross to guarantee all offspring have white fur. **[2 marks]**

Knowledge

B17 Organising an ecosystem

Levels of organisation

Feeding relationships within a community can be represented by **food chains**.

Photosynthetic organisms that synthesise molecules are the **producers** of all **biomass** for life on Earth, and so are the first step in all food chains.

A range of experimental methods using transects and quadrats are used by ecologists to determine the distributions and abundances of different species in an ecosystem.

Consumers that kill and eat other animals are **predators**, and those that are eaten are **prey**.

Apex predators are carnivores with no predators.

Organisms usually have more complex feeding relationships, with more than one predator and more than one food source. These can be shown in a food web.

- all food chains begin with a producer, for example, a green plant or alga producing glucose through photosynthesis
- slugs are primary consumers – they are **herbivores** that eat producers
- sparrows are secondary consumers – they are **carnivores** that eat primary consumers
- hawks are tertiary consumers – they are carnivores that eat secondary consumers

How materials are cycled

All materials in the living world are recycled, providing the building materials for future organisms.

The carbon cycle
- organic compounds in green plants
- death → organic compounds in dead organisms
- feeding → organic compounds in consumers
- death
- carbon compounds in fossil fuels
- decay and decomposition – CO₂ released as microorganisms respire
- respiration returns CO₂ to the atmosphere
- respiration
- CO₂ in the air and dissolved in water, particularly oceans
- burning (combustion)
- photosynthesis removes CO₂ from the environment

The water cycle
- condensation – as moist air rises it cools, water vapour condenses back into liquid water droplets producing clouds
- cooling
- precipitation – as water droplets in clouds get heavier they fall as rain, snow, or hail
- water vapour
- evaporation – the Sun heats the Earth's surface and water is turned from a liquid into water vapour, forming warm, moist air
- transpiration and respiration – loss of water vapour from plants and animals directly to the atmosphere
- surface run-off
- percolation – water trickles through gaps in soils and rocks
- ocean

Key terms

Make sure you can write a definition for these key terms.

- biomass
- carbon cycle
- carnivore
- consumer
- evaporation
- food chain
- herbivore
- precipitation
- predator
- prey
- producer
- water cycle

Retrieval

Learn the answers to the questions below, then cover the answers column with a piece of paper and write as many as you can. Check and repeat.

B17 questions / Answers

B17 questions	Answers
What is a producer?	organism that makes its own food, usually by photosynthesis
What is a food chain?	representation of the feeding relationships within a community
What is a consumer?	organism that eats other organisms for food
What is a herbivore?	organism that only eats producers (plants/algae)
What is a predator?	organism that kills and eats other organisms
What is a prey organism?	organism that is killed and eaten by another organism
What is an apex predator?	carnivore with no predators

Required practical skills

Practise answering questions on the required practicals using the example below. You need to be able to apply your skills and knowledge to other practicals too.

Field investigations

For this investigation, you will practise applying appropriate sampling techniques in the field to look at plant population sizes. Two methods of sampling with quadrats are covered:

1. Transect lines – stretching a tape measure along the ground, placing a quadrat at even points along it, and recording the number of plants within each quadrat.

2. Random sampling – using tape measures to form a square area, generating random numbers corresponding to where in that area you should place the quadrat, and recording the number of plants within each quadrat.

You should be able to describe and explain the purpose of each sampling method.

Worked example

A student used a quadrat measuring 25 cm by 25 cm to sample the number of daisies in a field. The average number of daisies within a quadrat was found to be 17. The total area of the field was 320 m².

1. Estimate the number of daisies in the field.

$$25 \text{ cm} = 0.25 \text{ m}$$
$$\text{area of quadrat} = 0.25 \times 0.25$$
$$= 0.0625 \text{ m}^2$$
$$\frac{320}{0.0625} = 5120$$
$$\text{population estimate} = 5120 \times 17$$
$$= 87040 \text{ daisies}$$

2. Give a reason why the student should use random sampling in this investigation.

Random sampling reduces any bias in the results, meaning they are more reliable.

Practice

1. A student wanted to measure how the distance from a water source affected the size of a plant.

   Write a method to carry out this investigation.

2. A quadrat measures 15 cm by 15 cm.

   Give the area of the quadrat in m².

3. An ecologist wanted to estimate the quantity of plastic floating in an ocean.

   Write a method for this investigation.

B17 Retrieval 163

Practice

Exam-style questions

01 A group of students surveyed the daisies growing on their school field. They took a series of eight samples using a 1 m × 1 m quadrat and recorded their results in **Table 1**.

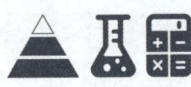

Table 1

Sample site number	1	2	3	4	5	6	7	8
Number of daisies	11	14	14	5	14	15	8	15

01.1 Write down the median number of daisies from the students' samples. **[1 mark]**

Median = _____ daisies

> **Exam Tip**
> You need to know the difference between the mean, the median, and the mode, and be able to use them in an exam.

01.2 Calculate the mean number of daisies from the students' samples. **[1 mark]**

Mean = _____ daisies

> **Exam Tip**
> The number of daisies are from different sites, not repeated measurements from the same site, so you can't have any anomalous results.

01.3 Sample site **4** had the lowest number of daisies.

Suggest and explain **one** possible reason for the lower number of daisies measured in this sample. **[2 marks]**

_____

_____

_____

02 A group of students wanted to estimate the number of thistle plants growing on a large lawn.

02.1 Identify which of the following is a biotic factor that could affect the population of thistles. **[1 mark]**

Tick **one** box.

water availability ☐

presence of other plant species ☐

light intensity ☐

soil pH ☐

164   B17 Organising an ecosystem

Paper 2 **B17**

02.2 Identify the piece of equipment that should be used to estimate the number of thistle plants. **[1 mark]**

Tick **one** box.

potometer ☐

tape measure ☐

stopwatch ☐

quadrat ☐

> **Exam Tip**
> You should be able to give the function of each of these pieces of equipment.

02.3 Rearrange steps **A–E** to describe the procedure the students should follow to estimate the number of thistle plants present on the lawn. **[4 marks]**

A Count the number of thistles present in the sample area

B Multiply the mean number of thistles (per m²) by the area of the lawn

C Repeat measurement at a number of different sites

D Use a grid and random number generator to decide where to carry out a sample

E Calculate the mean number of thistles present

start					

> **Exam Tip**
> For your revision, you can write each step out on separate pieces of paper and move them around until they are in the correct order.

03 The carbon cycle is essential for life on Earth.

03.1 Describe the main processes in the carbon cycle. **[6 marks]**

03.2 Explain how **two** human activities are causing changes to the natural balance of the carbon cycle. **[4 marks]**

> **Exam Tip**
> For **03.1** you could draw a diagram.

04 The food chain in **Figure 1** contains sparrows, slugs, hawks, and grass.

Figure 1

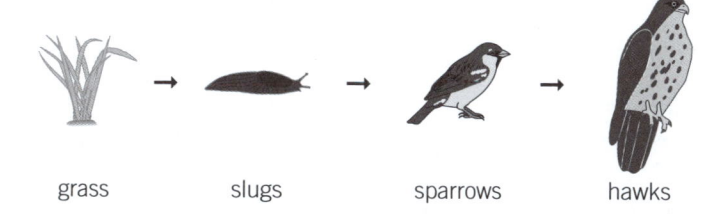

grass → slugs → sparrows → hawks

04.1 Give the name of the producer in the food chain. **[1 mark]**

04.2 Give the name of a predator in the food chain. **[1 mark]**

04.3 Give the name of a prey organism in the food chain. **[1 mark]**

04.4 Give the name of the tertiary consumer in the food chain. **[1 mark]**

05 Materials are constantly being recycled in the environment.

05.1 Use appropriate words from the box to complete the sentences explaining how recycling occurs. **[5 marks]**

| dies | roots | droppings | nutrients |
| oxygen | leaves | decomposers |

When an organism _____, or a tree loses its _____, or an animal produces _____, the waste is broken down by _____. This returns _____ to the environment where they can be used again.

05.2 Identify which of the following organisms are decomposers. Choose **one** answer. **[1 mark]**

microorganisms   insects   viruses   plants

05.3 Identify **two** reasons why decomposers are important for the environment.
Choose **two** answers. **[2 marks]**

provide habitats for organisms
make nutrients available for other organisms
produce oxygen
prevent build-up of dead organisms

05.4 Name **one** element that decomposers recycle. **[1 mark]**

06 **Figure 2** shows a food chain of some organisms found in an ocean.

Figure 2

aquatic plant → crab → octopus → seal

06.1 Identify the producer in this food chain. **[1 mark]**

06.2 Identify the tertiary consumer in this food chain. **[1 mark]**

06.3 Give the source of energy for this food chain. **[1 mark]**

06.4 Identify **one** prey organism from this food chain. **[1 mark]**

06.5 Suggest and explain **one** adaptation of the prey organism named in **06.4**. **[2 marks]**

06.6 Suggest and explain what would happen to the number of crabs if the seal population was infected with a fatal virus. **[3 marks]**

> **Exam Tip**
>
> Remember that in a food chain the arrow represents the direction of energy flow. It can also be use to show which animals eat which – so here, crab → octopus means that the crab is eaten by the octopus.

166 B17 Organising an ecosystem

07 Water is constantly cycled around the environment.

07.1 Draw **one** line from each stage in the water cycle to its definition. **[3 marks]**

Stage in water cycle	Definition
evaporation	loss of water vapour from plants
condensation	water falling from the atmosphere to the Earth
precipitation	water changes from a gas into a liquid
transpiration	water changes from a liquid into a gas

Exam Tip

This topic has lots of key words that we don't often use in our day-to-day life, meaning that learning all of them can be tricky. Try making flashcards to help you learn them.

07.2 Name the source of energy for the water cycle. **[1 mark]**

07.3 The water cycle provides fresh water for animals to drink. Give **one** other use of water for either plants or animals. **[1 mark]**

Exam Tip

There is one main source of energy for life on Earth.

08 **Figure 3** shows the relationship between the populations of lynx (predators) and hares (prey) living in the same area.

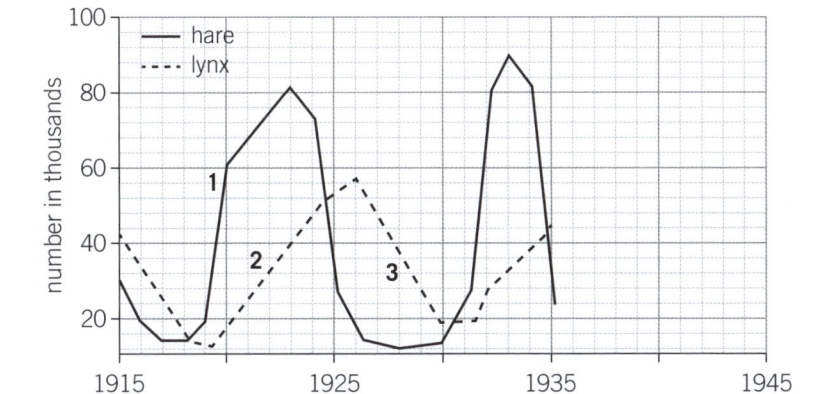

Figure 3

[Graph showing hare (solid line) and lynx (dashed line) populations in thousands from 1915 to 1945, with points labelled 1, 2, and 3 on the hare curve]

Exam Tip

Use a ruler to draw a line from the point on the graph to the axis – this will help you avoid making mistakes when reading the graph.

08.1 Write down the year when the population of hares was highest. **[1 mark]**

08.2 Write down how many lynx were present in 1926. **[1 mark]**

08.3 Match the following statements to the steps (**1–3**) in **Figure 3**. **[2 marks]**

population of lynx is decreasing as their food supply has become scarce

population of lynx is increasing as there is plenty of food available

population of hares is increasing as there are few predators

08.4 Suggest how the populations of hares and lynx would have changed between 1935 and 1940. **[2 marks]**

09 Figure 4 shows the main steps in the carbon cycle.

Figure 4

09.1 Name the processes represented by the arrows **A**, **B**, and **C** in Figure 3. [3 marks]

09.2 Arrow **D** represents photosynthesis.
Identify the correct word equation for photosynthesis.
Choose **one** answer. [1 mark]

carbon dioxide + oxygen → glucose + water

carbon dioxide + water → glucose + oxygen

glucose + oxygen → carbon dioxide + water

oxygen + water → carbon dioxide + glucose

> **Exam Tip**
> The equation for photosynthesis is the opposite of the equation for respiration – you need to know the word and symbol equations for both.

09.3 Only a small amount of the total carbon found on Earth is being cycled. The rest is stored in carbon sinks.
Name **one** carbon sink. [1 mark]

09.4 Describe the role of microorganisms in recycling carbon. [2 marks]

10 Water is constantly recycled in the ecosystem through the water cycle.

10.1 Describe the importance of the water cycle for animals. [1 mark]

10.2 The water cycle provides fresh water to plants. Plants need water to grow.
Identify the process that plants use to produce food.
Choose **one** answer. [1 mark]

Decomposition   Respiration   Photosynthesis

168 B17 Organising an ecosystem

10.3 Water is an abiotic factor that is important for plant communities.

Give **two** other abiotic factors that can affect plants and explain why they are important. **[4 marks]**

10.4 Complete the **Figure 5** with the correct stages of the water cycle. **[4 marks]**

Figure 5

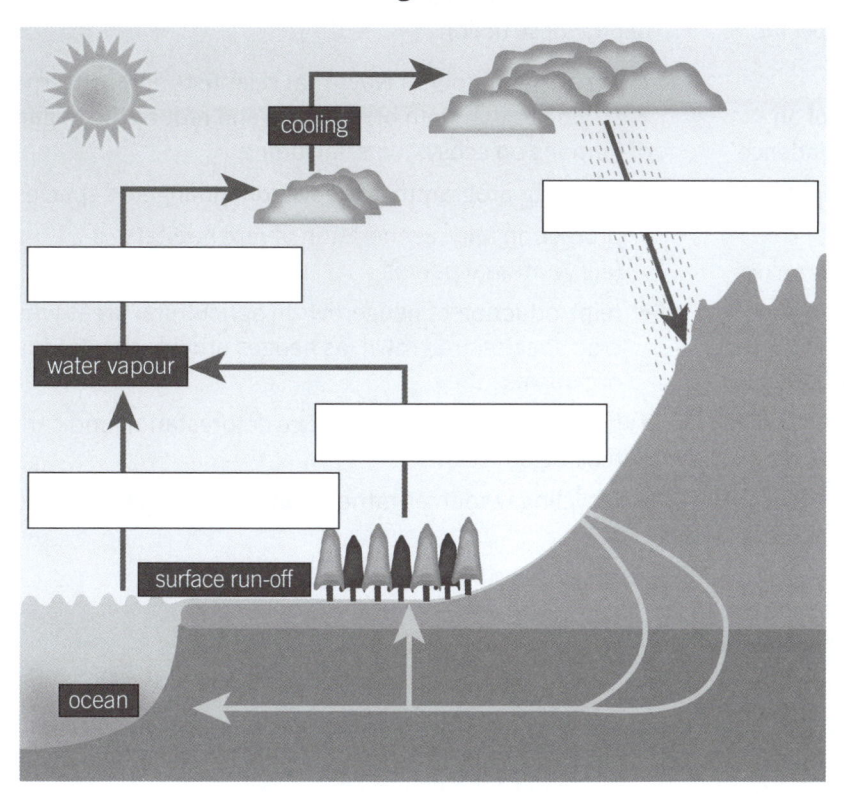

11 Genetic information is passed on to an organism's offspring through its DNA.

11.1 Tick **one** box in each row of **Table 2** to show whether the characteristics are inherited from an organism's parents or not. **[3 marks]**

Table 2

Characteristic	Inherited from parents	Not inherited from parents
eye colour		
tattoo		
measles infection		

11.2 Explain why children of the same parents often look similar but not identical. **[4 marks]**

11.3 Write down what is meant by a genetic mutation. **[1 mark]**

11.4 Give **one** possible advantage and **one** possible disadvantage of a genetic mutation. **[2 marks]**

> **Exam Tip**
> Make sure you read the question, giving two advantages for **11.4** won't get full marks.

Knowledge

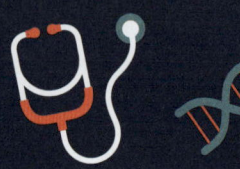

B18 Humans and biodiversity

Biodiversity

Biodiversity is the variety of all the different species of organisms (plant, animal, and microorganism) on Earth, or within a specific ecosystem.

High biodiversity ensures the stability of an ecosystem because it reduces the dependence of one species on another for food or habitat maintenance.

The future of the human species depends on us maintaining a good level of biodiversity. Many human activities, such as **deforestation**, are reducing biodiversity, but only recently have measures been taken to try to prevent this.

High biodiversity is important for maintaining healthy ecosystems, such as sustaining complex **food webs**:

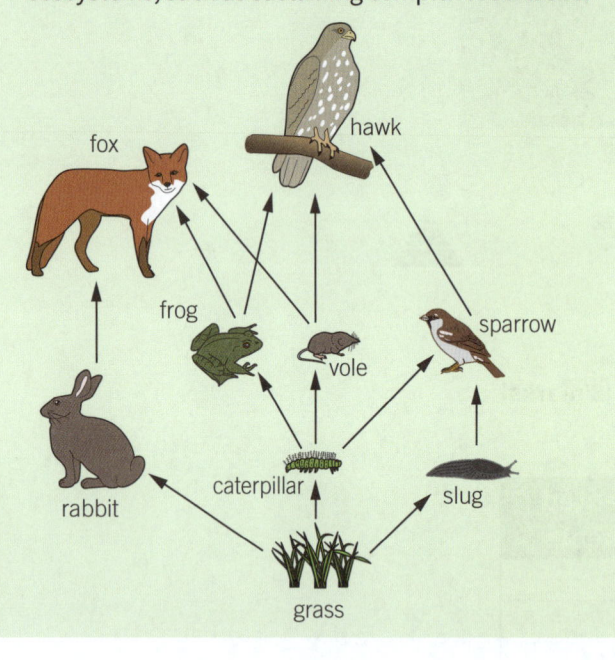

Maintaining biodiversity

Many habitats are currently under threat due to changes caused by human activities, such as deforestation, climate change, and habitat destruction.

There are a number of ways that scientists and concerned citizens are trying to maintain biodiversity and reduce the negative impact of humans on ecosystems, including

- breeding programmes in zoos for endangered species
- protection and regeneration of rare habitats (e.g., national parks)
- reintroduction of hedgerows in agricultural areas where single crop species are grown, as hedges provide habitat for many organisms
- government policies to reduce deforestation and carbon dioxide emissions
- recycling resources rather than dumping waste in landfill.

Revision tip

Remember Food webs are made up of many food chains, all you need to do is follow the arrows from the producer (grass) to the final consumer.

For example, from the food web on the left you can find this food chain:

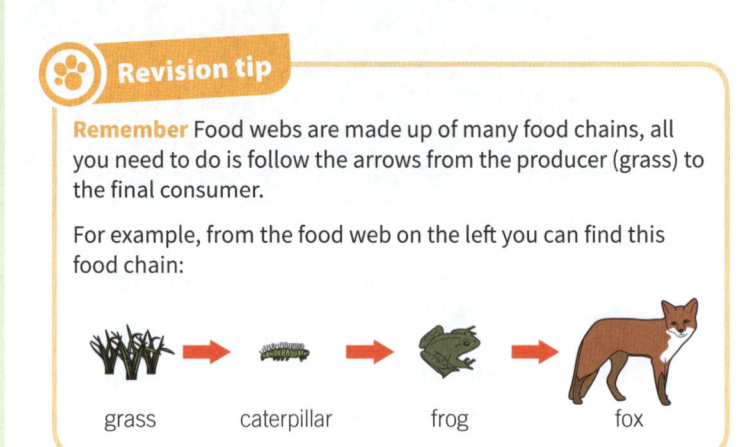

grass → caterpillar → frog → fox

Key terms

Make sure you can write a definition for these key terms.

biodiversity   biofuel   deforestation   food web

B18

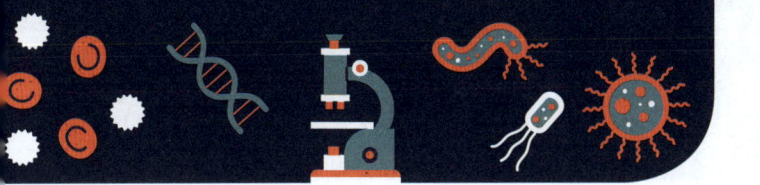

Global warming

Levels of carbon dioxide and methane in the atmosphere are increasing due to human activity, contributing to **global warming** and climate change.

Global warming is the gradual increase in the average temperature of the Earth.

This scientific consensus is based on systematic reviews of thousands of peer-reviewed publications.

Global warming has resulted in
- large-scale habitat change and reduction, causing a decrease in biodiversity
- extreme weather and sea level changes
- migration of species to different parts of the world, affecting ecosystems
- threats to the security and availability of food.

Waste management

Rapid growth of the human population and increases in the standard of living mean that humans are using more resources and producing more waste.

Waste and chemical materials need to be properly handled in order to reduce the amount of **pollution** they cause. Pollution kills plants and animals, and can accumulate in food chains, reducing biodiversity.

Pollution can occur
- in water, from sewage, fertiliser run-off, or toxic chemicals (e.g., from factories)
- in air, from smoke and acidic gases
- on land, from landfill and toxic chemicals.

Land use and deforestation

Rapid population growth has led to humans using much more land for building, quarrying, farming, and dumping waste. This reduces the area in which animals can live and can further destroy habitats through pollution.

For example, the destruction of **peat bogs** (areas of partially decayed vegetation) to produce garden compost has decreased the amount of this important habitat, and the biodiversity it supports. The decay or burning of peat for energy also releases carbon dioxide into the atmosphere, contributing to global warming.

Large-scale deforestation in tropical areas has been carried out to provide land for cattle and rice fields, and to grow crops for **biofuels**.

This has resulted in
- large amounts of carbon dioxide being released into the atmosphere due to burning of trees
- extinctions and reductions in biodiversity as habitats are destroyed
- climate change, as trees absorb carbon dioxide and release water vapour.

> **Revision tip**
>
> **Remember** Global warming is a major *cause* of climate change – you will cover this concept in chemistry.

global warming   peat bog   pollution

B18 Knowledge   171

Retrieval

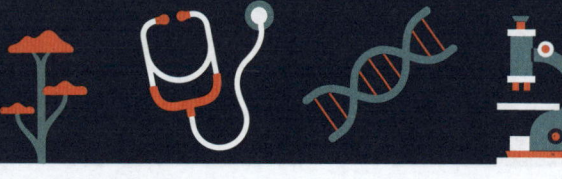

Learn the answers to the questions below, then cover the answers column with a piece of paper and write as many as you can. Check and repeat.

B18 questions | Answers

#	Question	Answer
1	What is biodiversity?	the variety of all the different species of organisms on Earth, or within an ecosystem
2	What is the advantage of high biodiversity?	ensures stability of ecosystems by reducing the dependence of one species on another
3	How are humans trying to maintain biodiversity?	• breeding programmes • protection of rare habitats • reintroduction of hedgerows • reduction of deforestation and carbon dioxide emissions • recycling resources
4	Why are more resources being used, and more waste produced, by humans?	rapid growth in human population and increase in the standard of living
5	How are humans reducing the land available for other organisms?	• building • quarrying • farming • dumping waste
6	What are the negative impacts of the destruction of peat bogs?	• reduces amount of available habitat, causing decreases in biodiversity • burning or decay of peat releases carbon dioxide into the atmosphere
7	Why have humans carried out large-scale deforestation in tropical areas?	• to provide land for cattle and rice fields • to grow crops for biofuels
8	What gases are increasing in atmospheric levels and contributing to global warming?	carbon dioxide and methane
9	How does pollution occur in water?	• sewage disposal • fertiliser run-off • toxic chemical run-off
10	How does pollution occur on land and in air?	• smoke and acidic gases in air • landfill and toxic chemicals on land

B18 Humans and biodiversity

B18

Now go back and use the questions below to check your knowledge from previous chapters.

Previous questions | Answers

#	Question	Answer
1	What is a food chain?	representation of the feeding relationships within a community
2	What is a biotic factor?	a living factor that can affect a community
3	What is a herbivore?	organism that only eats producers (plants/algae)
4	What is an ecosystem?	the interaction of a community of living organisms with the non-living parts of their environment
5	What evidence supports the theory of evolution?	• parents pass on their characteristics to offspring in genes • fossil record evidence • evolution of antibiotic-resistant bacteria
6	What is a producer?	organism that makes its own food, usually by photosynthesis
7	How do antibiotic-resistant strains of bacteria develop?	mutations that allow the strain to survive and reproduce

Maths skills

Practise your maths skills using the worked example and practice questions below.

Surface area-to-volume ratio

Knowledge of surface area-to-volume ratio is important in biology, for example, it explains the body size adaptations of organisms, and is important for the rate at which transportation processes such as diffusion occur.

To calculate it, you first need to calculate the surface area and volume of the object.

For the surface area of a cube, find the area of one face and multiply by six (a cube has six faces).

To find the volume of a cube, use the formula:
length × width × height

To calculate surface area to volume ratio:

surface area-to-volume ratio $= \dfrac{\text{surface area}}{\text{volume}}$

Worked example

What is the surface area-to-volume ratio of the cube below?

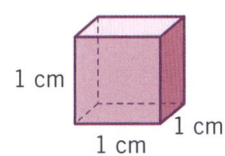

1 cm × 1 cm × 1 cm

To calculate surface area (cm^2):

Area of one side of the cube = 1 × 1 = 1 cm^2

The cube has six sides, so:

surface area = 1 × 6 = 6 cm^2

To calculate volume (cm^3):

1 × 1 × 1 = 1 cm^3

Surface area-to-volume ratio:

$\dfrac{6}{1}$ = 6:1 ratio

Practice

Work out the surface area (cm^2), volume (cm^3), and surface area-to-volume ratio for cubes with the following dimensions:

1 2 cm × 2 cm × 2 cm
2 5 cm × 5 cm × 5 cm
3 12 cm × 12 cm × 12 cm

B18 Retrieval   173

Practice

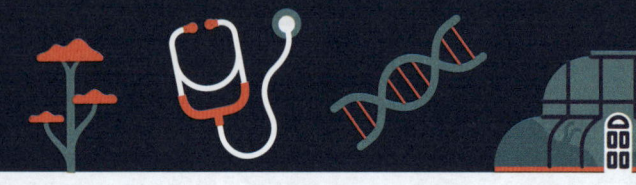

Exam-style questions

01 Large areas of the Amazon rainforest have been cleared for buildings and roads.

01.1 Identify the word that best describes this change in land use. **[1 mark]**

Tick **one** box.

afforestation ☐

leaching ☐

deforestation ☐

eutrophication ☐

01.2 Suggest **one** other reason why the land may have been cleared. **[1 mark]**

_____

> **! Exam Tip**
> Think of any use, apart from buildings, that requires larges open areas of land.

01.3 Removing trees can lead to increased carbon dioxide levels in the Earth's atmosphere.

Describe **one** way that the removal of trees increases atmospheric carbon dioxide. **[1 mark]**

_____
_____

> **! Exam Tip**
> This is linked to an equation for a process that all plants use.

01.4 Explain **one** way that the biodiversity of animals living in an area could be affected by the removal of trees. **[2 marks]**

_____
_____
_____

01.5 The removal of peat also affects the biodiversity of organisms living in peat bog habitats. Peat is removed from peat bogs to be used as cheap compost and as a fuel.

Evaluate the consequences of the removal of peat from peat bogs by humans. **[4 marks]**

_____
_____
_____
_____
_____

B18 Humans and biodiversity

Paper 2 — B18

02 Air pollution is a significant problem in many UK cities.

02.1 Give **one** reason why air pollution is a concern to humans. **[1 mark]**

_____

02.2 Nitrogen oxides (NO$_x$) are one of the many air pollutants present in busy cities. Identify the main source of nitrogen oxides. **[1 mark]**

Tick **one** box.

car exhausts ☐

factories ☐

burning coal ☐

burning wood ☐

> **Exam Tip**
>
> Don't worry about the x in NO$_x$, it simply means that it can be any number – NO, NO$_2$, or NO$_3$, the exact number is not important to answer the question.

02.3 **Table 1** shows how the concentration of nitrogen oxides varied over a one-week period in a UK city.

Table 1

Day of the week	Monday	Tuesday	Wednesday	Thursday	Friday	Saturday	Sunday
NO$_x$ concentration in µg/m^3	125	110	120	123	130	85	70

Calculate the mean atmospheric concentration of NO$_x$. **[1 mark]**

Mean = _____ µg/m^3

> **Exam Tip**
>
> Even though some of the results are different from each other, there are no anomalous results in this data set as there is only one measurement for each day.

02.4 Suggest **one** conclusion from this data. **[1 mark]**

_____
_____

02.5 Give a reason for your answer to **02.4**. **[1 mark]**

_____
_____

02.6 Suggest and explain **one** way to reduce the mean NO$_x$ concentration. **[2 marks]**

Suggestion: _____

Explanation: _____

_____

B18 Practice

03 Biodiversity is important in maintaining a stable ecosystem.

03.1 Define what is meant by the term biodiversity. **[1 mark]**

03.2 Identify the **two** factors that can increase biodiversity.
Choose **two** answers. **[2 marks]**
breeding programmes
deforestation
monoculture farming
reintroduction of hedgerows

03.3 Describe why an area of woodland with multiple species of tree is more stable than an area containing only one tree species. **[3 marks]**

> **Exam Tip**
> 03.3 is a three-mark question so you need to give reasons with your answer.

04 **Table 2** shows the UK's recycling rate over a period of five years.

Table 2

Year	Recycling rate in %
2010	40.4
2011	42.9
2012	43.9
2013	44.1
2014	44.9

04.1 Name **one** material that can be recycled. **[1 mark]**

04.2 Describe the trend shown in **Table 2**. **[1 mark]**

04.3 Give **two** environmental benefits of recycling. **[2 marks]**

04.4 Based on the figures in **Table 2**, suggest a value for the recycling rate in 2015. **[1 mark]**

> **Exam Tip**
> 04.2 is only a one-mark question. This mean that you only need to give the basic trend that can be seen from the data.

05 The total area of peat bogs and peatlands in the UK is decreasing.

05.1 Choose the appropriate bold words to complete the sentences describing how peat is formed. **[4 marks]**
Peat forms over **hundreds / thousands** of years in peat bogs.
Peat is formed from **animal / plant** material that did not decay properly due to **acidic / alkaline** conditions **with / without** oxygen.

05.2 Identify **two** uses of peat from the following list.
Choose **two** answers. **[2 marks]**
to improve soil nutrient content
as a fuel
as animal feed
as a pesticide

B18 Humans and biodiversity

05.3 The large-scale removal of peat from peat bogs has had a number of negative effects on the environment.

Draw **one** line from each statement to its effect on the environment.
[2 marks]

Statement	Effect
	decreases biodiversity
removal of peat destroys habitats	increases biodiversity
burning peat releases carbon dioxide	contributes to global warming
	causes depletion of ozone layer

06 It is important to ensure that healthy populations of animals and plants are maintained in the wild.

06.1 Choose appropriate words from the box to complete the sentences.
[3 marks]

| shelter | greater | lower | biodiversity |

The variety of organisms present within an ecosystem is known as _____.

The _____ the variety of species present, the more stable an ecosystem is.

This is because the organisms depend on each other for factors such as food and _____ .

> **Exam Tip**
> You don't have to start at the beginning, you might find it easier to start with the last sentence.

06.2 Agriculture often leads to a decrease in biodiversity in an area.

Draw **one** line to match each farming technique to the way it reduces biodiversity.
[2 marks]

Farming technique	Effect on biodiversity
removing hedgerows	kills insects such as bees that are needed to pollinate plants
using pesticides	kills unwanted plants that provide food for animals
using herbicides	removes plants and reduces habitats

06.3 Describe **one** way farmers can help to increase biodiversity on their farms.
[1 mark]

07 Changes in the concentration of some gases in the atmosphere have led to global warming. Most scientists believe this is a result of human activities.

07.1 Identify **two** gases that contribute to global warming.
Choose **two** answers. **[2 marks]**

nitrogen oxide   sulfur dioxide   carbon dioxide   methane

07.2 Name **one** human activity that can cause an increase in the level of **one** of the gases in **07.1**. **[1 mark]**

07.3 Global warming is leading to a number of environmental changes.
Draw **one** line to match each environmental change to its potential impact. **[3 marks]**

Biological change   **Impact**

rising sea levels	low-lying areas flood resulting in loss of habitat
hotter or colder seasons	loss of plant species
less rainfall in areas	loss of habitats for polar bears
melting ice sheets	change in migration patterns

08 The world's population is increasing. This increasing population has led to an increase in pollution.

08.1 Give **one** reason why an increasing human population creates more pollution. **[1 mark]**

08.2 There are many types of pollution.
For each of the following types of pollution, write down if it is a form of air pollution, water pollution, or land pollution. **[4 marks]**

rubbish disposal in landfill sites
fertilisers
sewage
smoke from burning fuels

> **Exam Tip**
> One type of pollution will be used twice.

08.3 Circle the correct bold words to complete the sentences on a form of air pollution. **[4 marks]**

When fossil fuels are burnt, **magnesium / sulfur dioxide** is released into the atmosphere.

This **dissolves / diffuses** in the rainwater in clouds, making the water **acidic / alkaline**.

The rainwater falls as an **acid / alkali**, which damages plants and trees.

> **Exam Tip**
> Make sure your answers make sense together in the whole paragraph, for example don't say something is acidic and then later say the same thing is alkaline.

B18 Humans and biodiversity

B18

09 The human population has increased rapidly over the last few hundred years.

09.1 Give **two** reasons why the human population has increased. **[2 marks]**

09.2 Describe how the increase in human population is reducing the land available to other animals. **[2 marks]**

09.3 Increasing human population also increases pollution. Name **two** ways that causes water to become polluted. **[2 marks]**

09.4 Describe **two** ways car exhaust gases cause negative environmental effects. **[2 marks]**

10 Gorse plants have a number of adaptations to help them survive.

10.1 Draw **one** line from each adaptation to its function. **[3 marks]**

Adaptation	Function
flowers	reduce water loss
sharp spines	so herbivores do not eat the plant
small leaves	to attract insects to pollinate them

10.2 Gorse plants grow in sunny regions, usually in dry, sandy soils. Suggest and explain how the roots of gorse plants may appear. **[2 marks]**

> **! Exam Tip**
> In dry areas, the roots will have adapted to try and reach as much water as possible.

10.3 Other than water, give **two** factors that plants compete for. **[2 marks]**

10.4 Apart from competition with other gorse plants, a number of biotic factors can affect the population of gorse plants present in an area.

Describe how **one** other biotic factor could reduce the population of gorse bushes in an area. **[2 marks]**

For answers and more practice questions visit www.oxfordrevise.com/scienceanswers

Even more practice and interactive revision quizzes are available on kerboodle

B18 Practice 179

Knowledge

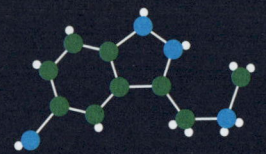

C1 The atom

Development of the model of the atom

Dalton's model
John Dalton thought of the **atom** as a solid sphere that could not be divided into smaller parts. His model did not include **protons**, **neutrons**, or **electrons**.

The plum pudding model
Scientists' experiments resulted in the discovery of sub-atomic charged particles. The first to be discovered were electrons – tiny, negatively charged particles.

The discovery of electrons led to the plum pudding model of the atom – a cloud of positive charge, with negative electrons embedded in it. Protons and neutrons had not yet been discovered.

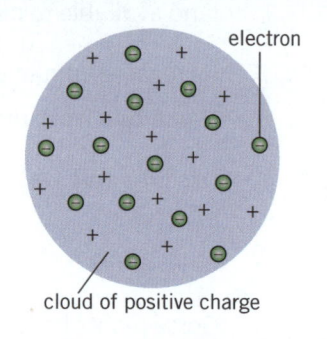

Alpha scattering experiment
1. Scientists fired small, positively charged particles (called alpha particles) at a piece of gold foil only a few atoms thick.
2. They expected the alpha particles to travel straight through the gold.
3. They were surprised that some of the alpha particles bounced back and many were deflected (alpha scattering).
4. To explain why the alpha particles were repelled the scientists suggested that the positive charge and mass of an atom must be concentrated in a small space at its centre. They called this space the **nucleus**.

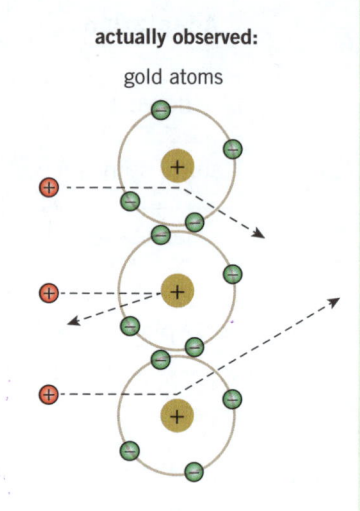

Nuclear model
Scientists replaced the plum pudding model with the nuclear model and suggested that the electrons **orbit** (go around) the nucleus, but not at set distances.

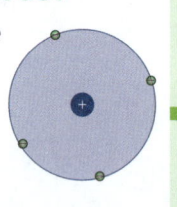

Electron shell (Bohr) model
Niels Bohr calculated that electrons must orbit the nucleus at fixed distances. These orbits are called **shells** or **energy levels**.

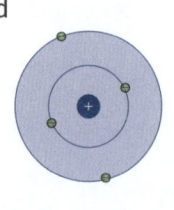

The proton
Further experiments provided evidence that the nucleus contained smaller particles called protons. A proton has an opposite charge to an electron.

Size
The atom has a radius of 1×10^{-10} m. Nuclei (plural of nucleus) are around 10 000 times smaller than atoms and have a radius of around 1×10^{-14} m.

Relative mass
One property of protons, neutrons, and electrons is **relative mass** – their masses compared to each other. Protons and neutrons have the same mass, so are given a relative mass of 1. It takes almost 2000 electrons to equal the mass of a single proton – their relative mass is so small that we can consider it as 0.

The neutron
James Chadwick carried out experiments that gave evidence for a particle with no charge. Scientists called this the neutron and concluded that the protons and neutrons are in the nucleus, and the electrons orbit the nucleus in shells.

180 C1 The atom

C1

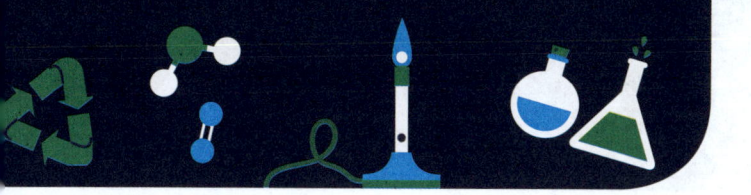

Atoms and particles

The Periodic Table lists over 100 types of atoms that differ in the number of protons, neutrons, and electrons they each have.

	Relative charge	Relative mass	
proton	+1	1	= atomic number
neutron	0	1	= mass number – atomic number
electron	–1	0 (very small)	= same as the number of protons

All atoms have equal numbers of protons and electrons, meaning they have no overall charge:

total negative charge from electrons = total positive charge from protons

Drawing atoms

Electrons in an atom are placed in fixed shells. You can put
- up to two electrons in the first shell
- eight electrons each in the second and third shells.

You must fill up a shell before moving on to the next one.

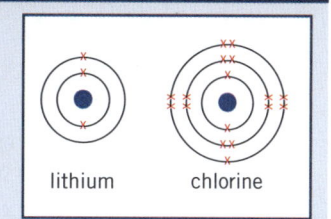

lithium   chlorine

Elements and compounds

Elements are substances made of one type of atom. Each atom of an element will have the same number of protons.

Compounds are made of different types of atoms chemically bonded together. The atoms in a compound have different numbers of protons.

Isotopes

Atoms of the same element can have a different number of neutrons, giving them a different overall mass number. Atoms of the same element with different numbers of neutrons are called **isotopes**.

The **relative atomic mass** is the average mass of all the atoms of an element (note that **abundance** means the percentage of atoms with a certain mass):

$$\text{relative atomic mass} = \frac{(\text{abundance of isotope 1} \times \text{mass of isotope 1}) + (\text{abundance of isotope 2} \times \text{mass of isotope 2})...}{100}$$

Mixtures

A mixture consists of two or more elements or compounds that are not chemically combined together.

The substances in a mixture can be separated using physical processes.

These processes do not use chemical reactions.

Separating mixtures

- filtration – insoluble solids from a liquid
- crystallisation – soluble solid from a solution
- simple distillation – solvent from a solution
- fractional distillation – two liquids with similar boiling points
- paper chromatography – identify substances from a mixture in solution

Key terms

Make sure you can write a definition for these key terms.

abundance	atom	atomic number	compound	electron	element
energy level	isotope	neutron	nucleus	orbit	proton
relative atomic mass	relative charge	relative mass	shell

C1 Knowledge   181

Retrieval

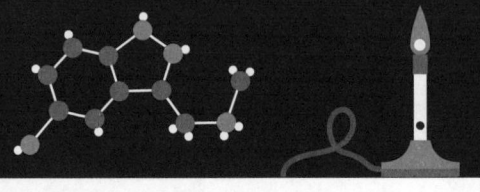

Learn the answers to the questions below, then cover the answers column with a piece of paper and write as many as you can. Check and repeat.

C1 questions / Answers

#	C1 questions	Answers
1	What is an atom?	smallest part of an element that can exist
2	What is Dalton's model of the atom?	atoms as solid spheres that could not be divided into smaller parts
3	What is the plum pudding model of the atom?	sphere of positive charge with negative electrons embedded in it
4	What did scientists discover in the alpha scattering experiment?	some alpha particles were deflected by the gold foil – this showed that an atom's mass and positive charge must be concentrated in one small space (the nucleus)
5	Describe the nuclear model of the atom.	dense nucleus with electrons orbiting it
6	What did Niels Bohr discover?	electrons orbit in fixed energy levels (shells)
7	What did James Chadwick discover?	uncharged particle called the neutron
8	Where are protons and neutrons?	in the nucleus
9	What is the relative mass of each sub-atomic particle?	proton: 1, neutron: 1, electron: 0 (very small)
10	What is the relative charge of each sub-atomic particle?	proton: +1, neutron: 0, electron: −1
11	How can you find out the number of protons in an atom?	the atomic number on the Periodic Table
12	How can you calculate the number of neutrons in an atom?	mass number − atomic number
13	Why do atoms have no overall charge?	they have equal numbers of positive protons and negative electrons
14	How many electrons would you place in the first, second, and third shells?	up to 2 in the first shell and up to 8 in the second and third shells
15	What is an element?	substance made of one type of atom
16	What is a compound?	substance made of more than one type of atom chemically joined together
17	What is a mixture?	two or more substances not chemically combined
18	What are isotopes?	atoms of the same element (same number of protons) with different numbers of neutrons
19	What are the four physical processes that can be used to separate mixtures?	filtration, crystallisation, distillation, fractional distillation, chromatography
20	What is relative mass?	the average mass of all the atoms of an element

C1 The atom

Required practical skills

Practise answering questions on the required practicals using the example below.
You need to be able to apply your skills and knowledge to other practicals too.

Chromatography	Worked example	Practice
This practical shows the separation of coloured substances by making paper chromatograms. You need to be able to describe the method of chromatography, including the solutes and solvents involved, and define the stationary and mobile phases. Food colourings are often used for this practical, but remember any coloured mixture could be used in an exam question.	A student carried out a paper chromatography experiment to determine what inks make up a sample. They observed the following results. solution A B C D inks **1** Determine which of the inks (B, C, and D) are present in solution A. *Compare the spots on the chromatogram to determine which inks make up solution A – the spots for inks B and C all align with spots for solution A, so these are all present in solution A.* **2** Give a reason why an original line is drawn in pencil. *Pencil does not interact with the mobile phase, and therefore will not interfere with the chromatogram.*	**1** Two students were setting up a chromatography experiment. Student A wanted to leave the experiment until the solvent front had moved three-quarters of the way up the paper, and student B wanted to leave it for 15 minutes. Which method do you agree with? Give an explanation for your answer. **2** A student carried out a chromatography experiment on an ink. Their chromatogram showed that the ink was made up of three dyes. Sketch the student's chromatogram.

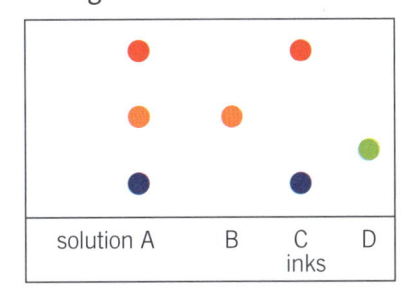

C1 Retrieval 183

Practice

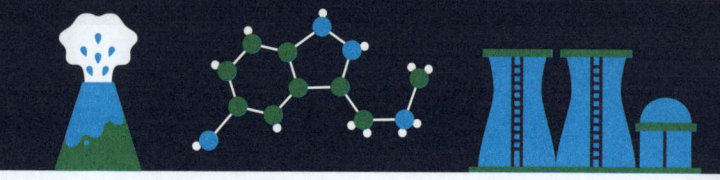

Exam-style questions

01.1 Draw **one** line from each sub-atomic particle to the relative charge. **[2 marks]**

Sub-atomic particle		Relative charge
neutron	—	+1
proton	—	0
electron	—	−1

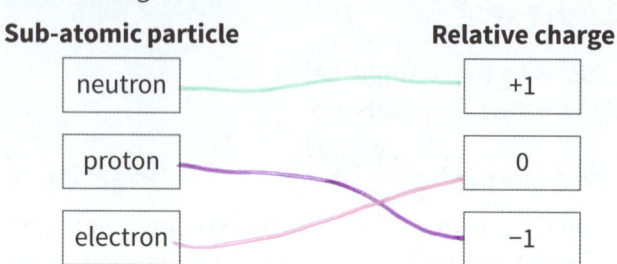

(neutron → 0; proton → +1; electron → −1)

01.2 A particle has 4 protons and 4 electrons.
Give the charge on the particle. **[1 mark]**

4

01.3 A particle has 5 protons and 4 electrons.
Determine whether the particle is an atom or an ion. **[1 mark]**

Is a Ion

> **Exam Tip**
> An ion is an atom that has lost or gained electrons.

01.4 An atom has 6 protons in its nucleus.
Complete the dot and cross diagram to show the number of electrons in the atom. **[2 marks]**

> **Exam Tip**
> Start from the innermost shell.

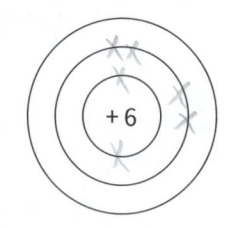

01.5 Determine the identity of the atom in **01.4**. **[1 mark]**

_____

> **Exam Tip**
> Remember it is the atomic number – the number of protons – that determines the identity of an atom.

01.6 Complete the following sentence.
Isotopes are atoms of an element that have the same number of __*protons*__ but different number of __*nutrons*__. **[1 mark]**

01.7 The chemical symbol of silicon is $^{28}_{14}Si$.
Describe an atom of silicon in terms of the number of protons, neutrons, and electrons, and their charges. **[2 marks]**

_____

_____

02 A student has a mixture of copper powder and water. The copper powder is a solid. It does not dissolve in the water.

The student uses the equipment in **Figure 1** to separate the copper from the water.

184 C1 The atom

Paper 3 | **C1**

Figure 1

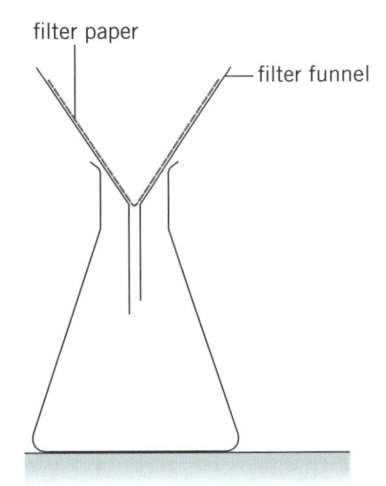

filter paper
filter funnel

02.1 Name the process that the student uses to separate the copper from the water. **[1 mark]**

Tick **one** box.

crystallisation ☐

distillation ☐

filtration ☐

heating ☐

02.2 Draw a cross on **Figure 1** where the copper powder will be collected. **[1 mark]**

02.3 The student also has a mixture of salt in water. The salt is dissolved in the water.

Name the process that the student uses to separate the salt from the water. **[1 mark]**

Tick **one** box.

crystallisation ☐

distillation ☐

filtration ☐

evaporation ☐

> **! Exam Tip**
>
> This is a required practical, so hopefully you remember doing it in class. The copper powder will be a black solid, can you recall where that was?

C1 Practice | 185

03 Different scientists made different contributions to the development of the model of the atom.

03.1 Draw **one** line from each scientist to the contribution they made. **[2 marks]**

Scientists	Contribution
	the nucleus contains neutrons
Niels Bohr	atoms contain electrons
James Chadwick	electrons orbit the nucleus at certain distances
	atoms are tiny spheres

> **Exam Tip**
> There will be two boxes left out at the end, don't let this worry you.

03.2 Describe the alpha particle scattering experiment, and how it showed that the mass of an atom was concentrated in a positively-charged nucleus. **[6 marks]**

03.3 The electron was discovered when a beam containing electrons was deflected towards a positive charge. Neutrons were not shown to be in the nucleus until 20 years after the nuclear model of the atom was accepted. Suggest a reason why it took so long to prove that neutrons existed. **[1 mark]**

> **Exam Tip**
> Is there any way the neutrons could be deflected?

03.4 **Figure 2** shows the plum pudding model and the nuclear model of an atom. Use **Figure 2** and your knowledge to compare the two models of the atom. **[6 marks]**

Figure 2

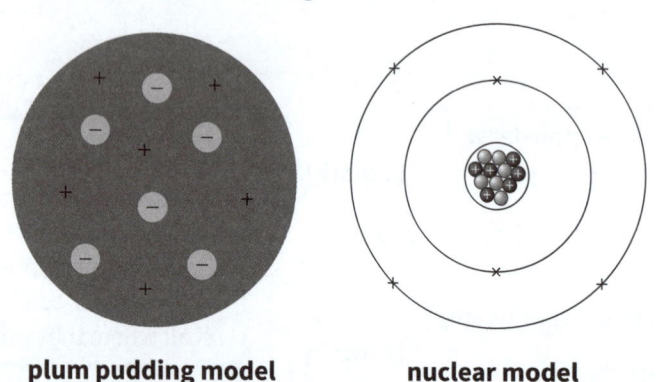

plum pudding model   nuclear model

04.1 Carbon dioxide is made of one carbon atom and two oxygen atoms. Identify the correct chemical formula for carbon dioxide. Choose **one** answer. **[1 mark]**

Co_2 cO^2 CO^2 CO_2

04.2 Identify the three elements in H_2SO_4. Use the Periodic Table to help you. **[3 marks]**

> **Exam Tip**
> Capital letters are very important in chemical formulae. A capital letter is the difference between carbon dioxide gas and a lump of metal cobalt.

C1 The atom

C1

04.3 How many atoms are in one molecule of NaOH?
Choose **one** answer. **[1 mark]**

1   2   3   4

> **Exam Tip**
> Look for the capital letters!

05 A student has the compound CuXO$_4$. The student does not know the identity of the element X. The relative formula mass of the compound is 159.5.

05.1 Calculate the relative atomic mass of X. Relative atomic masses A_r: Cu = 63.5   O = 16. **[3 marks]**

> **Exam Tip**
> There are 4 oxygens so you need to include 4 × 16 =

05.2 Use your answer to **05.1** to identify X. **[1 mark]**

05.3 The atomic number of oxygen is 8. Calculate how many neutrons are in a nucleus of oxygen. **[1 mark]**

05.4 Explain why the relative atomic mass of copper, Cu, is not a whole number. **[2 marks]**

06 A scientist uses the following symbols to represent some substances.

- potassium atom: ●
- chlorine atom: ■
- sodium atom: ◆ 
- water: ▲

06.1 Which symbol represents a compound? **[1 mark]**

06.2 The scientist uses the symbols to draw a representation of four samples they have (**Figure 3**).

Figure 3

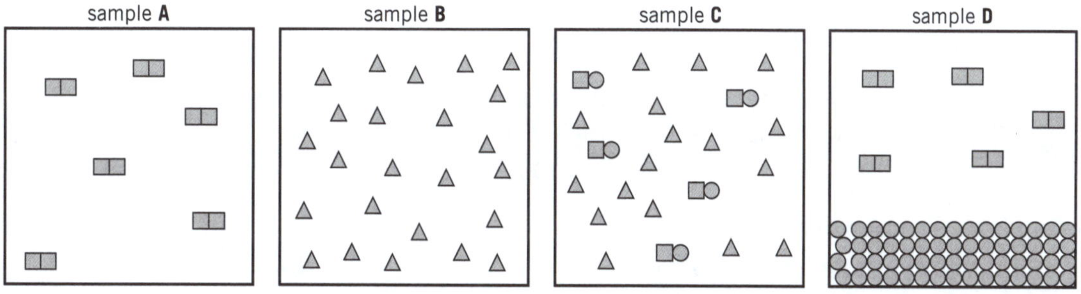

sample **A**   sample **B**   sample **C**   sample **D**

Which sample contains a pure element? **[1 mark]**

06.3 Which sample contains a mixture of two compounds? **[1 mark]**

06.4 Which sample contains a mixture of two elements? **[1 mark]**

06.5 The scientists uses their symbols to draw the following representation of the compound sodium chloride.

◆■

Write the chemical formula for this substance. **[1 mark]**

> **Exam Tip**
> Use the key carefully when answering this question.

07.1 Complete the sentences. Choose the answers from the box. **[3 marks]**

| innermost | highest | lowest | outermost | 2 | 8 |

Electrons fill the _____ energy level first. The lowest energy levels are the _____ shells. The shell closest to the nucleus can hold up to _____ electrons.

07.2 An atom has the electronic structure 2,8,1. Is this atom boron or sodium? Use the Periodic Table to help you. **[1 mark]**

07.3 Oxygen has 8 electrons. Complete the dot and cross diagram to show the electronic structure of oxygen. **[2 marks]**

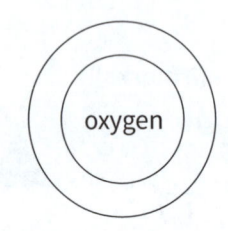

> **! Exam Tip**
> Start from the innermost shell and then count until you get 8 electrons.

08 This question is about isotopes.

08.1 Define the term isotope. **[1 mark]**

08.2 Boron has two isotopes: boron-10 and boron-11. Compare atoms of boron-10 and boron-11. **[3 marks]**

08.3 The percentage abundance of boron-11 is 80%. Calculate the relative atomic mass of boron. **[3 marks]**

$$\text{relative atomic mass} = \frac{(\text{percentage abundance isotope 1} \times \text{mass of isotope 1}) + (\text{percentage abundance isotope 2} \times \text{mass of isotope 2})}{100}$$

09 A student has a selection of mixtures:
- sodium chloride salt dissolved in water
- sand and water
- green ink.

09.1 Name the physical process that can be used to separate the sand and water mixture. **[1 mark]**

09.2 Describe a method that the student could use to obtain the sodium chloride from the mixture. In your method include any equipment you would use. **[6 marks]**

> **! Exam Tip**
> A physical process is one that doesn't change the chemicals involved.

09.3 The student thinks that the green ink is made up of a mixture two dyes. Name the physical process the student could use to identify

C1 The atom

whether they are correct. [1 mark]

10.1 Define the term compound. [1 mark]

10.2 Draw **one** line from each term to the correct particle diagram. [2 marks]

Key term | Particle diagram

compound

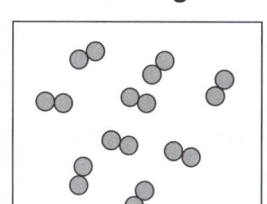

element

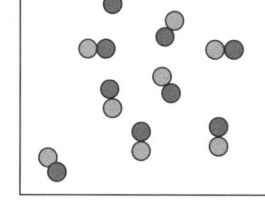

mixture

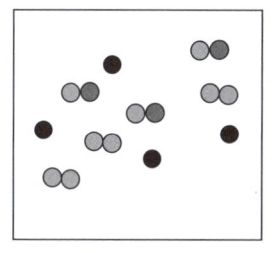

Exam Tip

Only draw one line to and from each box. Too many lines will mean you won't gain the mark, even if you give a correct answer.

10.3 A student has a mixture that contains sand, water, and ethanol. Ethanol is a liquid. The student wants to separate out the mixture into three parts: sand, ethanol, and water.

Name the **two** processes used to separate the parts of the mixture. [2 marks]

10.4 **Figure 4** shows the equipment used by the student to separate the sand from the mixture. Label the equipment **A–D**.

Figure 4

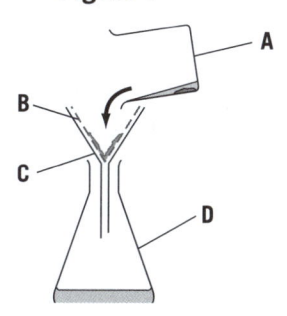

Knowledge

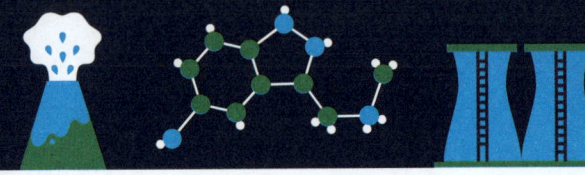

C2 Covalent bonding

Particle model

The three states of matter can be represented in the particle model.

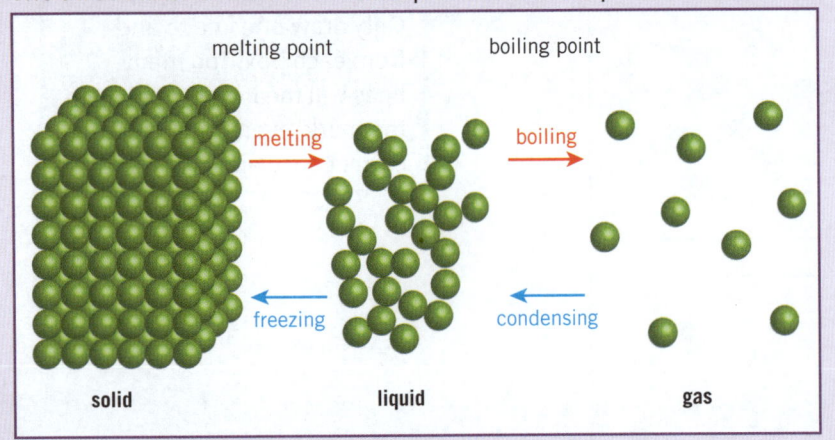

This model assumes that:
- There are no forces between the particles.
- All particles in a substrate are spherical.
- The spheres are solid.

The amount of energy needed to change the state of a substance depends on the forces between the particles. The stronger the forces between the particles, the higher the melting or boiling point of the substance.

Covalent bonding

Atoms can share or transfer electrons to form strong chemical bonds.

A **covalent bond** is when electrons are *shared* between **non-metal** atoms.

The number of electrons shared depends on how many extra electrons an atom needs to make a full outer shell.

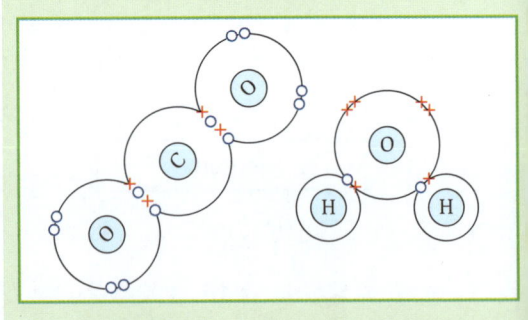

If you include electrons that are shared between atoms, each atom has a full outer shell.

Single bond = each atom shares one pair of electrons.
Double bond = each atom shares two pairs of electrons.

Covalent structures

When atoms form covalent bonds different types of structures can be formed. The structure depends on how many atoms there are and how they are bonded. There are three main types of covalent structure:

Giant covalent

Many billions of atoms, each one with a strong covalent bond to a number of others.

An example of a giant covalent structure is diamond.

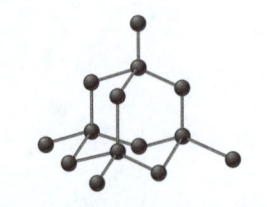

Small molecules

Each molecule contains only a few atoms with strong covalent bonds between these atoms. Different molecules are held together by weak **intermolecular forces**.

For example, water is made of small molecules.

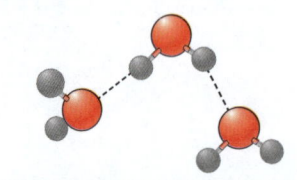

Large molecules

Many repeating units joined by covalent bonds to form a chain.

The small section is bonded to many identical sections to the left and right. The 'n' represents a large number.

Separate chains are held together by intermolecular forces that are stronger than in small molecules.

Polymers are examples of long molecules.

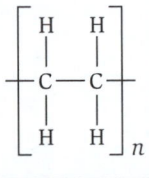

Key terms

Make sure you can write a definition for these key terms.

boiling point   covalent bond   delocalised electrons   double bond
large molecules   melting point   nanotube   non-metal

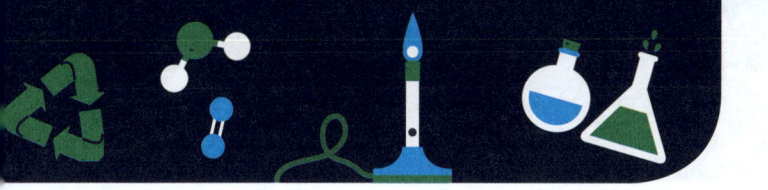

C2

Properties	High melting and boiling points because the strong covalent bonds between the atoms must be broken to melt or boil the substances. This requires a lot of energy. Solid at room temperature.	Low melting and boiling points because only the intermolecular forces need to be overcome to melt or boil the substances, not the bonds between the atoms. This does not require a lot of energy as the intermolecular forces are weak. Normally gaseous or liquid at room temperature.	Melting and boiling points are low compared to giant covalent substances but higher than for small molecules. Large molecules have stronger intermolecular forces than small molecules, which require more energy to overcome. Normally solid at room temperature.

Most covalent structures do not conduct electricity because they do not have **delocalised electrons** or ions that are free to move to carry charge.

Graphite

Graphite is a giant covalent structure, but is different from other giant covalent substances.

Structure
Made only of carbon – each carbon atom bonds to three others, and forms hexagonal rings in layers. Each carbon atom has one spare electron, which is delocalised and therefore free to move around the structure.

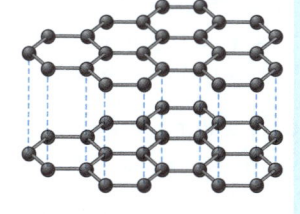

Hardness
The layers can slide over each other because they are not covalently bonded. Graphite is therefore softer than diamond, even though both are made only of carbon, as each atom in diamond has four strong covalent bonds.

Conductivity
The delocalised electrons are free to move through graphite, so can carry charges and allow an electrical current to flow. Graphite is therefore a conductor of electricity.

Graphene

Graphene consists of only a single layer of graphite. Its strong covalent bonds make it a strong material that can also conduct electricity. It is also used in composites and high-tech electronics.

Fullerenes

- hollow cages of carbon atoms bonded together in one molecule
- can be arranged as a sphere or a tube (called a **nanotube**)
- molecules held together by weak intermolecular forces, so can slide over each other
- conduct electricity

Spheres
Buckminsterfullerene was the first fullerene to be discovered, and has 60 carbon atoms.

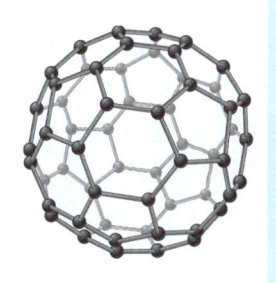

Other fullerenes exist with different numbers of carbon atoms arranged in rings that form hollow shapes.

Fullerenes like this can be used as lubricants and in drug delivery.

Nanotubes

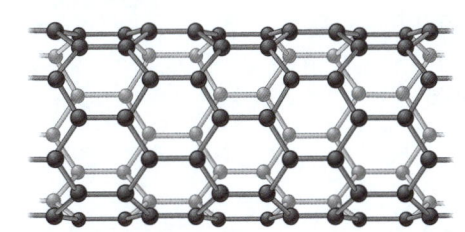

The carbon atoms in nanotubes are arranged in cylindrical tubes.
Their high **tensile strength** (they are difficult to break when pulled) makes them useful in electronics.

---

fullerene   giant covalent   graphene   graphite   intermolecular forces   polymers   single bond   small molecules   tensile strength

Retrieval

Learn the answers to the questions below, then cover the answers column with a piece of paper and write as many as you can. Check and repeat.

C2 questions / Answers

#	C2 questions	Answers
1	How are covalent bonds formed?	by atoms sharing electrons
2	Which type of atoms form covalent bonds between them?	non-metals
3	Describe the structure and bonding of a giant covalent substance.	billions of atoms bonded together by strong covalent bonds
4	Describe the structure and bonding of small molecules.	small numbers of atoms group together into molecules with strong covalent bonds between the atoms and weak intermolecular forces between the molecules
5	Describe the structure and bonding of polymers.	many identical molecules joined together by strong covalent bonds in a long chain, with weak intermolecular forces between the chains
6	Why do giant covalent substances have high melting points?	it takes a lot of energy to break the strong covalent bonds between the atoms
7	Why do small molecules have low melting points?	only a small amount of energy is needed to break the weak intermolecular forces
8	Why do large molecules have higher melting and boiling points than small molecules?	the intermolecular forces are stronger in large molecules
9	Why do most covalent substances not conduct electricity?	they do not have delocalised electrons or ions
10	Describe the structure and bonding in graphite.	each carbon atom is bonded to three others in hexagonal rings arranged in layers – it has delocalised electrons and weak forces between the layers
11	Why can graphite conduct electricity?	the delocalised electrons can move through the graphite
12	Explain why graphite is soft.	layers are not bonded so can slide over each other
13	What is graphene?	one layer of graphite
14	Give two properties of graphene.	strong, conducts electricity
15	What is a fullerene?	hollow cage of carbon atoms arranged as a sphere or a tube
16	What is a nanotube?	hollow cylinder of carbon atoms
17	Give two properties of nanotubes.	high tensile strength, conduct electricity
18	Give three uses of fullerenes.	lubricants, drug delivery (spheres), high-tech electronics

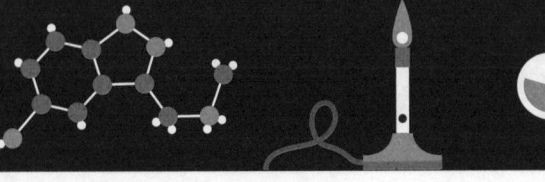

Now go back and use the questions below to check your knowledge from previous chapters.

C2

Previous questions / Answers

	Previous questions	Answers
1	What is an atom?	smallest part of an element that can exist
2	Describe the nuclear model of the atom.	dense nucleus with electrons orbiting it
3	Where are protons and neutrons?	in the nucleus
4	What is the relative mass of each sub-atomic particle?	proton: 1, neutron: 1, electron: 0 (very small)
5	What is the relative charge of each sub-atomic particle?	proton: +1, neutron: 0, electron: −1
6	How can you find out the number of protons in an atom?	the atomic number on the Periodic Table
7	How can you calculate the number of neutrons in an atom?	mass number − atomic number
8	Why do atoms have no overall charge?	they have equal numbers of positive protons and negative electrons
9	What is an element?	substance made of one type of atom
10	What is a compound?	substance made of more than one type of atom chemically joined together

Maths skills

Practise your maths skills using the worked example and practice questions below.

Unit conversion

Scientists use different units depending on what is most useful to them. For example, when talking about the size of molecules it doesn't make sense to talk about them in kilometres, so we can use nanometres instead.

Whenever we do a calculation we need to make sure the units are the same, so have to do a unit conversion.

The table below shows you how some units can be compared to each other.

Unit	Standard form in m
1 metre (m)	1×10^{0} m
1 centimetre (cm)	1×10^{-2} m
1 millimetre (mm)	1×10^{-3} m
1 micrometre (μm)	1×10^{-6} m
1 nanometre (nm)	1×10^{-9} m
1 picometre (pm)	1×10^{-12} m

Worked example

Express 120 cm in metres.

When converting to a larger unit, multiply the original value by the value in metres in standard form.

$120 \times 1 \times 10^{-2} = 1.2$ m

Express 120 m in centimetres.

When converting to a smaller unit, divide the original value by the value in metres in standard form.

$= \dfrac{120}{1 \times 10^{-2}} = 12\,000$ cm

Practice

1. Express 400 cm in metres.
2. Express 20 m in millimetres.
3. Express 0.8 m in nanometres.

C2 Retrieval 193

Practice

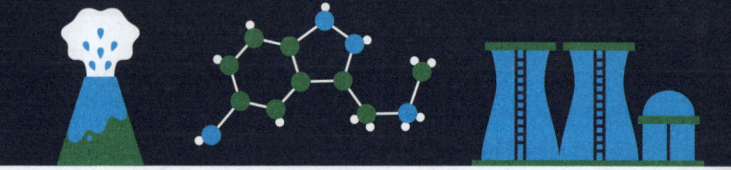

Exam-style questions

01 Ammonia is a compound with the formula NH₃.

01.1 Ammonia is made up of hydrogen and what other element? **[1 mark]**

Tick **one** box.

ammonium ☐   nitrogen ☐

neon ☐   sodium ☐

> **Exam Tip**
> Ammonia is one of the compounds mentioned on the specification. However, you should be able to apply your knowledge to any compound given in an exam.

01.2 Name the type of bonding in ammonia. **[1 mark]**

_____

01.3 Draw **three** dots and **three** crosses to complete the dot and cross diagram of ammonia. **[1 mark]**

01.4 What is one property of ammonia? **[1 mark]**

Tick **one** box.

conducts electricity ☐   high boiling point ☐

hard ☐   low melting point ☐

02 Compare the physical properties of diamond and graphite.

In your answer, use ideas about bonding to explain the differences in properties. **[6 marks]**

_____
_____
_____
_____
_____
_____
_____

> **Exam Tip**
> Both of these are made from pure carbon but have different bonding and properties.

194   C2 Covalent bonding

Paper 3 C2

03 This question is about polymers.

03.1 Choose the correct words to complete the sentence. **[3 marks]**

Polymers are very **long / short** molecules that are made up from **a few / lots of** small repeating units joined together by **weak / strong** covalent bonds.

03.2 Poly(propene) is a polymer.
Name the monomer that forms poly(propene). **[1 mark]**

> **! Exam Tip**
> To name a polymer you add "poly" in front of the name.

03.3 **Figure 1** shows the structure of poly(ethene) and the monomer that forms it. **Figure 2** shows the structure of chloroethene.

Figure 1

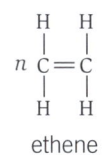

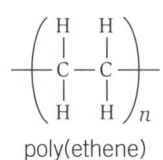

n C=C (ethene, with H atoms)

(—C—C—)$_n$ poly(ethene)

Figure 2

C=C (chloroethene, with H, H, H, Cl)

Chloroethene forms the polymer poly(chloroethene).
Draw the structure of poly(chloroethene). **[2 marks]**

03.4 The formula of poly(ethene) can be written as $(C_2H_4)_n$.
Write the formula for poly(chloroethene). **[1 mark]**

04 Covalent bonding occurs between non-metal atoms.

04.1 Which of the following describes covalent bonding best?
Choose **one** answer. **[1 mark]**

electrons are lost   electrons are swapped
electrons are gained   electrons are shared

> **! Exam Tip**
> Think about how you draw covalent bonding. That should help you answer this question.

04.2 Draw **one** line from each compound to the correct covalent structure. **[3 marks]**

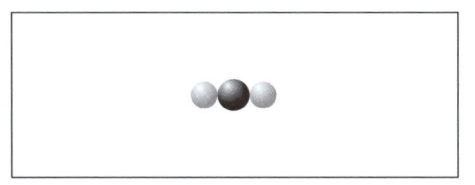

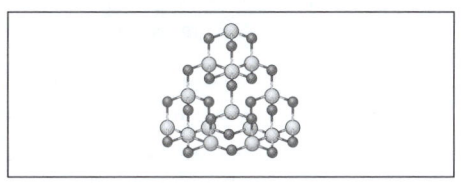

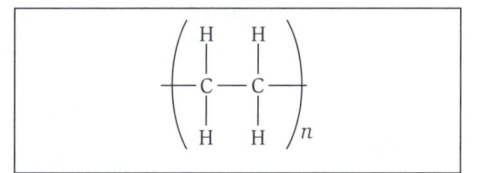

Compound	Covalent structure
(diatomic molecule image)	giant covalent structure
(lattice structure image)	polymer
(polymer structure image)	simple molecule

04.3 **Figure 3** shows two compounds. All of the atoms in each compound are joined by covalent bonding.

Figure 3

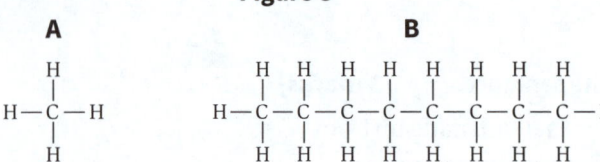

A

```
    H
    |
H — C — H
    |
    H
```

B

```
    H   H   H   H   H   H   H   H
    |   |   |   |   |   |   |   |
H — C — C — C — C — C — C — C — C — H
    |   |   |   |   |   |   |   |
    H   H   H   H   H   H   H   H
```

Compound **A** has a boiling point of −161.5 °C. Compound **B** has a boiling point of 125.6 °C.

Complete the following sentence. Use the words from the box. **[2 marks]**

| covalent bonds | higher | intermolecular forces | lower |

Compound **A** has a _____ boiling point than compound **B** because it is a smaller molecule. Therefore, it has weaker _____.

> **! Exam Tip**
> The boiling point of compound **A** is a negative number, this confuses a lot of people so read the question carefully.

05.1 Explain why most compounds with covalent bonding do not conduct electricity. **[2 marks]**

05.2 Name the compound with covalent bonding that can conduct electricity. Explain why. **[2 marks]**

05.3 **Table 1** shows the structure and boiling points of three covalent molecules.

Table 1

Compound	Structure	Boiling point in °C
silicon dioxide		2230.0
octane		125.6
hydrogen fluoride		19.5

Explain the difference in the boiling points of the three compounds in **Table 1**. In your answer, refer to the size of the compounds, the intermolecular forces, and covalent bonds. **[6 marks]**

> **! Exam Tip**
> Question **05.3** tells you what the examiners are looking for. Make sure you write about each of the points in your answer.

05.4 Predict the boiling point of buckminsterfullerene. Explain your answer. **[3 marks]**

05.5 The structure of the compounds in **Table 1** are represented by ball and stick diagrams.
Give **one** limitation of representing silicon dioxide using a ball and stick model. **[1 mark]**

C2 Covalent bonding

06 This question is about compounds made of carbon.

06.1 A carbon atom has 4 electrons in its outermost shell. How many electrons does a carbon atom need to gain a full outer shell?
Choose **one** answer. **[1 mark]**

1   4   6   8

06.2 Carbon burns in oxygen to form carbon dioxide.
Complete the word equation for this reaction. **[1 mark]**

_____ + oxygen → _____

Exam Tip
The answer is written in the question, just be careful pulling out the information you need.

06.3 Identify the type of structure that carbon dioxide has.
Choose **one** answer. **[1 mark]**

fullerene   giant covalent   polymer   simple molecule

06.4 Diamond is also made of carbon. What is the structure of diamond?
Choose **one** answer. **[1 mark]**

A   B 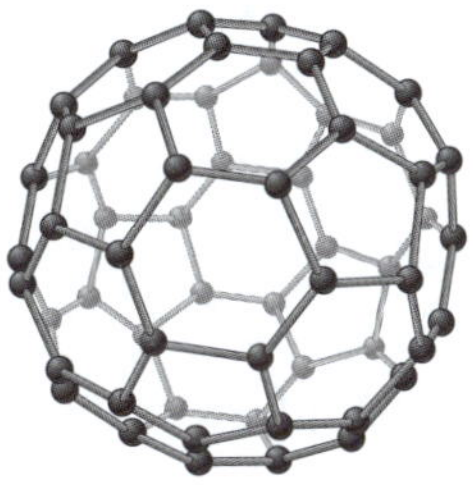   C

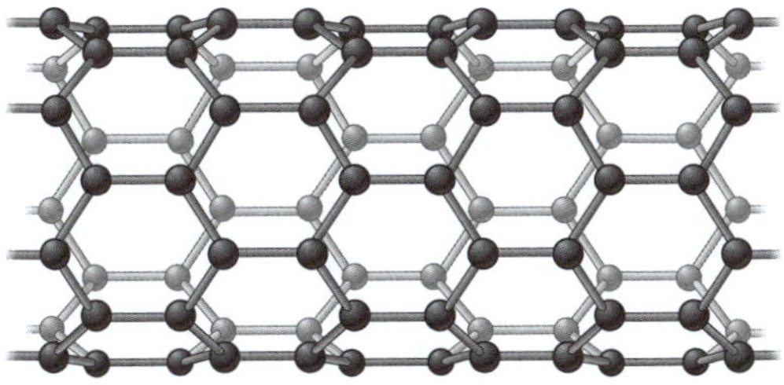

06.5 Describe **one** way in which the properties of diamond are different to the properties of carbon dioxide. **[1 mark]**

06.6 Methane is a compound made of carbon and hydrogen. A hydrogen atom has 1 electron in its outermost shell. Complete the chemical formula of methane. **[1 mark]**

CH_____

07 Carbon forms many different structures.

07.1 Complete the sentences. **[3 marks]**

The carbon in diamond makes _____ carbon–carbon bonds.

Diamond is very large and has a very _____ melting point. Diamond is very _____.

07.2 Explain why graphite has similar properties to metals. **[2 marks]**

Exam Tip
This is a two mark explain question. This means that your answer should include a why.

08 Water, H_2O, is a small covalent molecule.
Figure 4 shows a molecule of water.

Figure 4

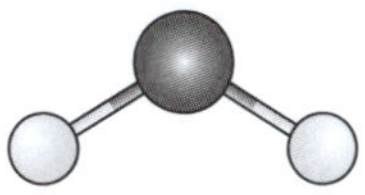

08.1 Complete the sentences.
Choose the correct words from the box.

| covalent | white | ionic | black | water |

The _____ sphere represents oxygen atoms. The _____ sphere represents hydrogen atoms. The bars between the spheres represent _____ bonds. **[3 marks]**

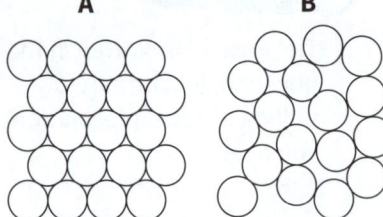

08.2 The boiling point of water is 100 °C and the melting point is 0 °C. What state of matter is water at 25 °C?
Choose **one** answer. [1 mark]

gas   liquid   solid

08.3 Which particle diagram shows water at 25 °C?
Choose **one** answer. [1 mark]

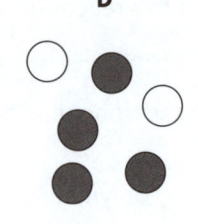

A   B   C   D

> **Exam Tip**
> You can assume each clear circle is one molecule of water.

08.4 Oxygen has 6 electrons in its outer shell. Complete the dot and cross diagram of water. [1 mark]

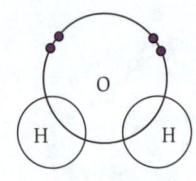

09 Graphene and fullerenes are made of only one element.

09.1 Name the element that graphene and fullerenes are made from. [1 mark]

09.2 Draw **one** line from each structure to the name of the structure. [3 marks]

> **Exam Tip**
> Sometimes the name gives the shape away.

Structure	Name
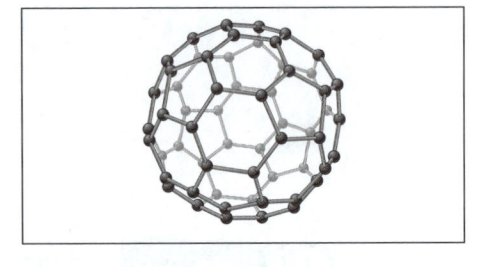	buckminsterfullerene
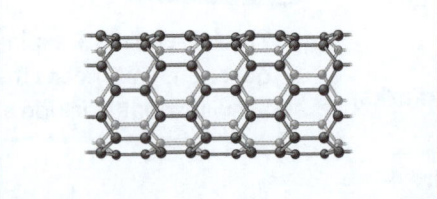	carbon nanotubes
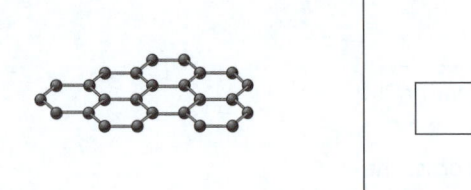	graphene
	graphite

> **Exam Tip**
> Ensure you know the difference between graphite and graphene.

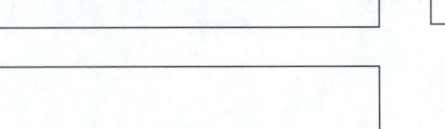

C2 Covalent bonding

09.3 Complete the sentence. **[2 marks]**

Graphene is a good _____ of electricity, so it is used in _____.

09.4 Give **one** use of fullerenes. **[1 mark]**

10 A student had samples of three substances, **X**, **Y**, and **Z**.

The student tested which of the substances conduct electricity.

Table 2

Substance	Does it conduct electricity?
X	no
Y	no
Z	yes

10.1 Give the letter of the substance in **Table 2** that could consist of nanotubes. **[1 mark]**

10.2 Give **one** other property of nanotubes. **[1 mark]**

10.3 Give **two** uses of nanotubes.

For each use, explain how the properties of nanotubes make them suitable for this use. **[2 marks]**

> **Exam Tip**
> There is only one piece of information given in the table so use this to find the odd one out!

Knowledge

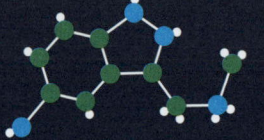

C3 Ionic bonding, metallic bonding, and structure

Ions

As well as sharing electrons, atoms can gain or lose electrons to give them a full outer shell. The number of protons is then different from the number of electrons. The resulting particle has a charge and is called an **ion**.

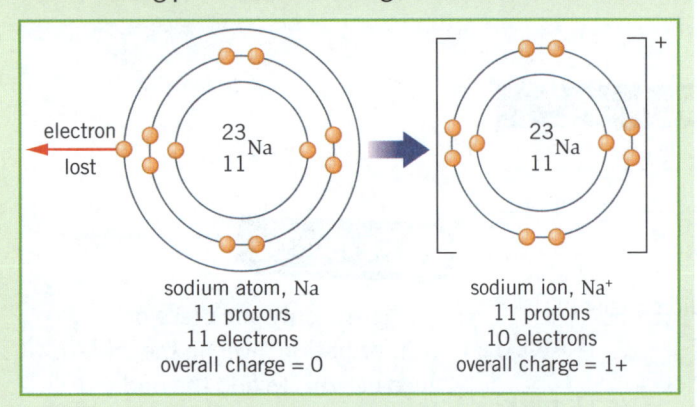

electron lost

sodium atom, Na
$^{23}_{11}$Na
11 protons
11 electrons
overall charge = 0

sodium ion, Na$^+$
$^{23}_{11}$Na
11 protons
10 electrons
overall charge = 1+

Ionic bonding

When metal atoms react with non-metal atoms they **transfer** electrons to the non-metal atom (instead of sharing them).

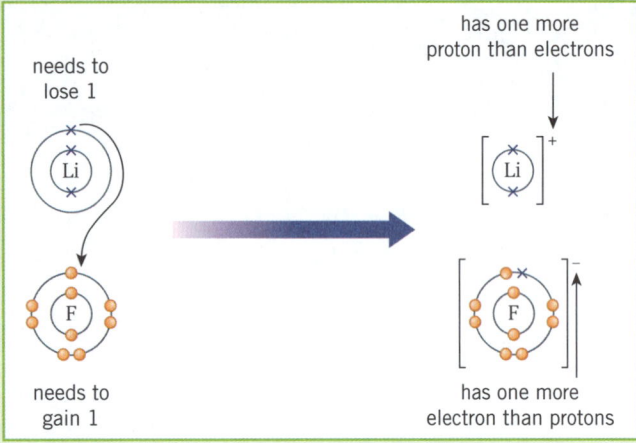

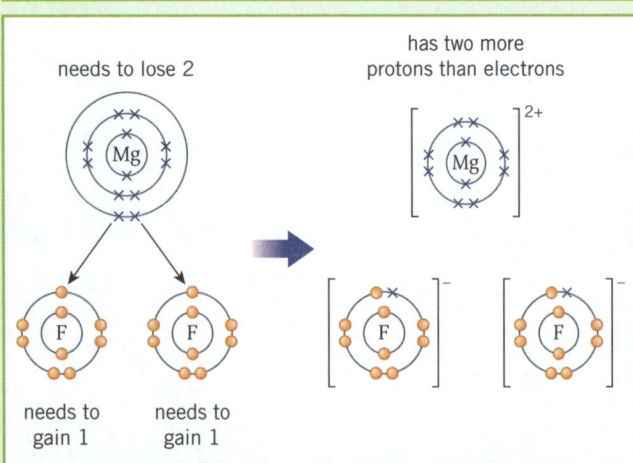

needs to lose 1 — Li
needs to gain 1 — F

has one more proton than electrons — [Li]$^+$
has one more electron than protons — [F]$^-$

needs to lose 2 — Mg
needs to gain 1 — F, F

has two more protons than electrons — [Mg]$^{2+}$
[F]$^-$ [F]$^-$

Metal atoms lose electrons to become positive ions. Non-metal atoms gain electrons to become negative ions.

Giant ionic lattice

When metal atoms transfer electrons to non-metal atoms you end up with positive and negative ions. These are attracted to each other by the strong **electrostatic force of attraction**. This is called **ionic bonding**.

The electrostatic force of attraction works in all directions, so many billions of ions can be bonded together in a 3D structure.

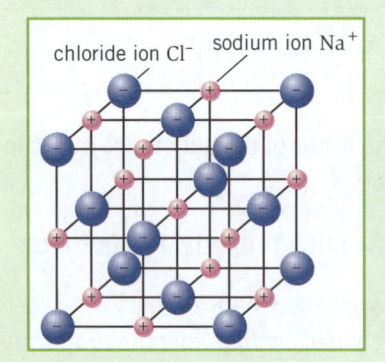

chloride ion Cl$^-$ sodium ion Na$^+$

Ionic structure

Formulae

The formula of an ionic substance can be worked out
1. from its bonding diagram:
   for every one magnesium ion there are two fluoride ions – so the formula for magnesium fluoride is MgF$_2$
2. from a lattice diagram:
   there are nine Fe^{2+} ions and 18 S$^-$ ions – simplifying this ratio gives a formula of FeS$_2$

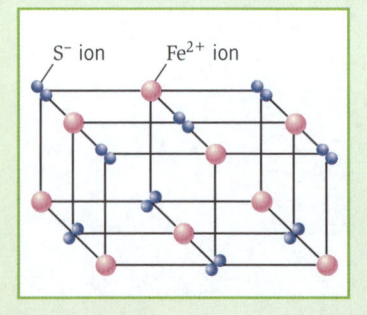

S$^-$ ion   Fe^{2+} ion

> **Revision tip**
>
> **Practice** Students often get the drawings for ionic and covalent bonds confused. Make sure you get them the correct way round – electrons are *transferred* in ionic bonds but *shared* in covalent bonds.

C3 Ionic bonding, metallic bonding, and structure

C3

Ionic properties

Melting and boiling points
Ionic substances have high melting and boiling points because the electrostatic force of attraction between oppositely charged ions is strong and so requires lots of energy to break.

Conductivity
Solid ionic substances do not conduct electricity because the ions are fixed in position and not free to carry charge.

When melted or dissolved in water, ionic substances do conduct electricity because the ions are free to move and carry charge.

Metallic structure

Metals
The atoms that make up metals form layers. The electrons in the outer shells of the atoms are **delocalised** – this means they are free to move through the whole structure.

The positive metal ions are then attracted to these delocalised electrons by the electrostatic force of attraction.

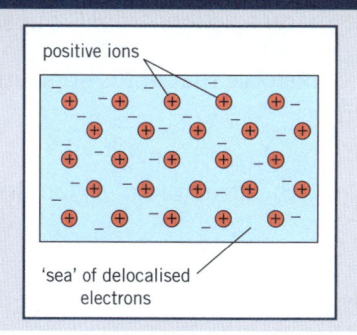

positive ions

'sea' of delocalised electrons

Metallic properties

Hardness
Pure metals are **malleable** (soft) because the layers can slide over each other.

Conductivity
Metals are good **conductors** of electricity and of thermal energy because delocalised electrons are free to move through the whole structure.

Melting and boiling point
Metals have high melting and boiling points because the electrostatic force of attraction between metal ions and delocalised electrons is strong so lots of energy is needed to break it.

Alloys
Pure metals are often too soft to use as they are. Adding atoms of a different element can make the resulting mixture harder because the new atoms will be a different size to the pure metal's atoms. This will disturb the regular arrangement of the layers, preventing them from sliding over each other.

The harder mixture is called an **alloy**.

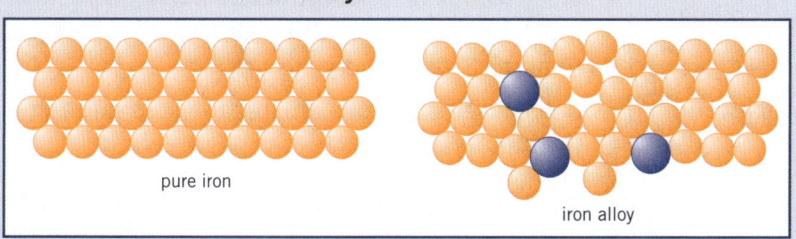

pure iron

iron alloy

Key terms
Make sure you can write a definition for these key terms.

| alloy | conductivity | conductor | delocalised electron | electrostatic force of attraction |
| ion | ionic bond | lattice | layer | malleable | transfer |

C3 Knowledge   201

Retrieval

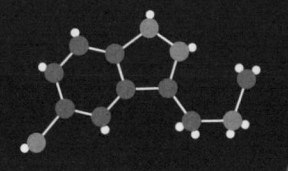

Learn the answers to the questions below, then cover the answers column with a piece of paper and write as many as you can. Check and repeat.

	C3 questions	Answers
1	What is an ion?	atom that has lost or gained electrons
2	Which kinds of elements form ionic bonds?	metals and non-metals
3	What charges do ions from Groups 1 and 2 form?	Group 1 forms 1+, Group 2 forms 2+
4	What charges do ions from Groups 6 and 7 form?	Group 6 forms 2−, Group 7 forms 1−
5	Name the force that holds oppositely charged ions together.	electrostatic force of attraction
6	Describe the structure of a giant ionic lattice.	regular structure of alternating positive and negative ions, held together by the electrostatic force of attraction
7	Why do ionic substances have high melting points?	electrostatic force of attraction between positive and negative ions is strong and requires lots of energy to break
8	Why don't ionic substances conduct electricity when solid?	ions are fixed in position so cannot move, and there are no delocalised electrons
9	When can ionic substances conduct electricity?	when melted or dissolved
10	Why do ionic substances conduct electricity when melted or dissolved?	ions are free to move and carry charge
11	Describe the structure of a pure metal.	layers of positive metal ions surrounded by delocalised electrons
12	Describe the bonding in a pure metal.	strong electrostatic forces of attraction between metal ions and delocalised electrons
13	What are four properties of pure metals?	malleable, high melting/boiling points, good conductors of electricity, good conductors of thermal energy
14	Explain why pure metals are malleable.	layers can slide over each other easily
15	Explain why metals have high melting and boiling points.	electrostatic force of attraction between positive metal ions and delocalised electrons is strong and requires a lot of energy to break
16	Why are metals good conductors of electricity and of thermal energy?	delocalised electrons are free to move through the metal
17	What is an alloy?	mixture of a metal with atoms of another element
18	Explain why alloys are harder than pure metals.	different sized atoms disturb the layers, preventing them from sliding over each other

C3 Ionic bonding, metallic bonding, and structure

C3

Now go back and use the questions below to check your knowledge from previous chapters.

Previous questions / Answers

#	Previous questions	Answers
1	Describe the structure and bonding of a giant covalent substance.	billions of atoms bonded together by strong covalent bonds
2	Why do atoms have no overall charge?	the have equal numbers of positive protons and negative electrons
3	Why can graphite conduct electricity?	the delocalised electrons can move through the graphite
4	Why do large molecules have higher melting and boiling points than small molecules?	the intermolecular forces are stronger in large molecules
5	What did James Chadwick discover?	uncharged particle called the neutron
6	Give three uses of fullerenes.	lubricants, drug delivery (spheres), high-tech electronics
7	Give two properties of nanotubes.	high tensile strength, conduct electricity
8	How many electrons would you place in the first, second, and third shells?	up to 2 in the first shell and up to 8 in the second and third shells

Put paper here

Maths skills

Practise your maths skills using the worked example and practice questions below.

2D and 3D models

Scientists often use models to describe what things look like and how they act.

These models can be 2D or 3D but they are always just approximations – they are there to help you understand but have strengths and weaknesses.

Worked example

The model shows how the layers in a metal alloy are disturbed. What are the strengths and weaknesses of this model?

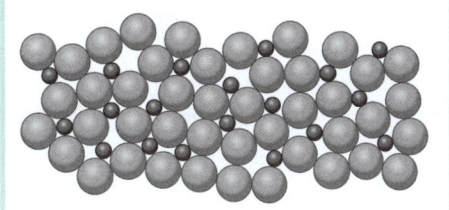

The model is in two dimensions, which helps you to see how the layers are disturbed by atoms of different sizes.

However, the metal is normally three dimensional, which this model does not show, so it is not an accurate representation of the metal's structure.

Practice

Compare and contrast the two models below showing the structure of methane.

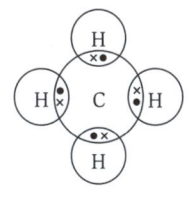

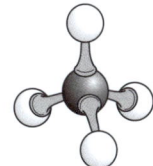

C3 Retrieval 203

Practice

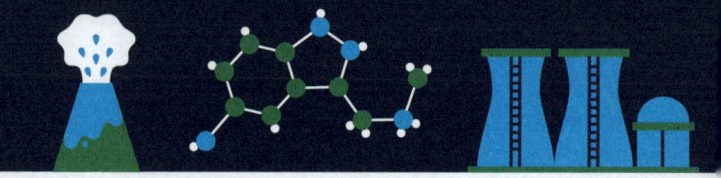

Exam-style questions

01 This question is about ionic bonding.

01.1 Complete the sentence. Choose the correct word from the box. **[1 mark]**

| delocalised | shared | transferred |

In an ionic bond, the electrons are _____.

01.2 Draw **one** line from each atom to the correct description of what happens to the electrons in that atom in an ionic bond. **[2 marks]**

Atom: metal atom, non-metal atom

Description: gains electrons, loses electrons, shares an electron

01.3 Identify how atoms are held together in an ionic bond. **[1 mark]**
Tick **one** box.

- electrostatic attraction ☐
- free moving delocalised electrons ☐
- intermolecular forces ☐

> **Exam Tip**
> Remember that an electron has a negative charge. Think about how the electrons move in an ionic bond, and how that will affect the charge on the atoms involved.

02 Sodium and chlorine react to form sodium chloride. Sodium chloride is an ionic compound.

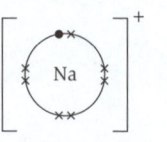

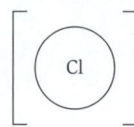

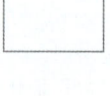

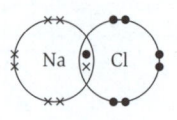

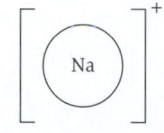

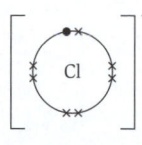

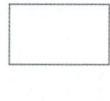

02.1 Identify the dot and cross diagram of sodium chloride. **[1 mark]**
Tick **one** box.

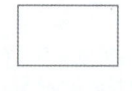

> **Exam Tip**
> We draw ionic bonding with square brackets and not overlapping circles.

---

204 C3 Ionic bonding, metallic bonding, and structure

Paper 3 — C3

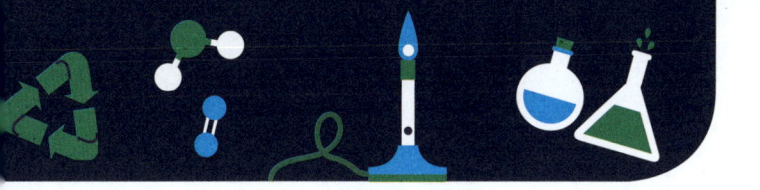

02.2 **Figure 1** shows the structure of sodium chloride.

Figure 1

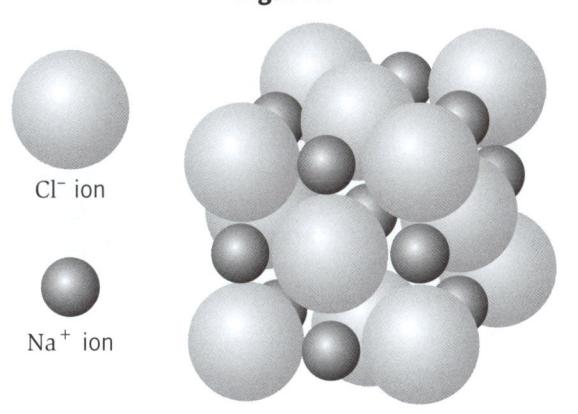

Cl⁻ ion

Na⁺ ion

Give the empirical formula of sodium chloride. **[1 mark]**

_____

> **Exam Tip**
> There are lots of scientific terms, like empirical formula, that you need to know. The empirical formula is the simplest ratio of the atoms or ions in a giant structure. Look at **Figure 1** – for every chlorine ion, how many sodium ions are there?

02.3 Give **one** property of sodium chloride. **[1 mark]**

_____

02.4 Sodium is a metal. Compare the bonding in sodium with the bonding in sodium chloride. **[6 marks]**

_____
_____
_____
_____
_____
_____
_____
_____

> **Exam Tip**
> Start by describing the bonding in sodium, then describe the bonding in sodium chloride. Finally, give at least one way in which the bonding in sodium and sodium chloride is similar, and one in which it is different

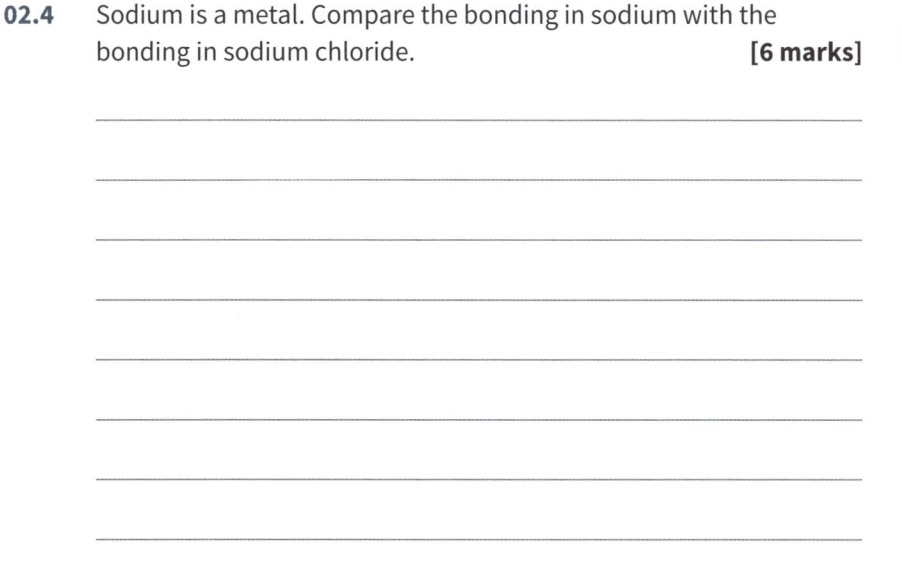

03.1 Which property is typical of metals?
Choose **one** answer. **[1 mark]**

They are poor conductors of heat.
They conduct electricity in the solid state but not in the liquid state.
They conduct electricity in the liquid state but not in the solid state.
They conduct electricity in the solid and liquid states.

03.2 Describe the bonding in a pure metal. **[3 marks]**

03.3 Explain why the bonding in a pure metal means that metals can be shaped. **[2 marks]**

03.4 Mercury is a metal. It is a liquid at room temperature.
Suggest why mercury is an unusual metal. **[1 mark]**

> **Exam Tip**
> While **03.2** and **03.3** may seem like very similar questions the answers are very different to each other.

For answers and more practice questions visit www.oxfordrevise.com/scienceanswers

Even more practice and interactive revision quizzes are available on kerboodle

C3 Practice 205

04 This question is about ionic bonding.

04.1 Complete the sentences on ionic bonding. **[3 marks]**

Ionic compounds have a _____ structure made up of lots of ions. The ions are held together by an _____ attraction between oppositely charged ions. The force of attraction acts in _____ directions.

04.2 Explain why ionic compounds have high melting and boiling points. **[2 marks]**

04.3 Lithium chloride is an ionic compound. Draw a dot and cross diagram to show the bonding in lithium chloride. **[2 marks]**

04.4 A student uses the set up in **Figure 2** to test the conductivity of lithium and solid lithium chloride.

Describe what the student will observe when lithium and when solid lithium chloride are tested. **[2 marks]**

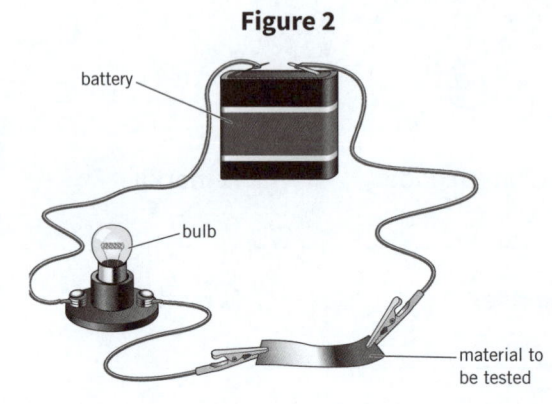

Figure 2 (battery, bulb, material to be tested)

> **Exam Tip**
> Use the Periodic Table to work out how many electrons are on the outer shell of both lithium and chlorine before you start drawing.

04.5 The student repeats the experiment using lithium chloride dissolved in water.
Explain what the student would observe. **[2 marks]**

05.1 Which substance shows metallic bonding?
Choose **one** answer. **[1 mark]**

hydrogen fluoride   oxygen
magnesium   sodium chloride

05.2 Draw **one** line from each property in metals to the correct explanation for that property. **[3 marks]**

Property	Explanation
	ions/atoms are arranged in layers
good conductors of thermal energy	
	lots of energy needed to overcome strong bonds
pure metals are soft	
	delocalised electrons
high melting point	
	large molecules with strong intermolecular forces

> **Exam Tip**
> You can use the Periodic Table to help identify metals and non-metals. Non-metals can be found on the right and metals are on the left.

> **Exam Tip**
> One of these explanations is for a property of structures with covalent bonding. Try to work out which one is wrong.

206 C3 Ionic bonding, metallic bonding, and structure

05.3 Bronze is a mixture of copper metal and tin metal.
Name this type of mixture. [1 mark]

05.4 Complete the sentence. [2 marks]

Bronze is _____ than pure copper because the tin atoms _____ the layers of copper atoms.

06 **Figure 3** shows the boiling points of three substances:
- the metal element mercury, Hg
- ethanol, C_2H_5OH
- hexanol, $C_6H_{13}OH$

Each substance is represented by a letter.

Figure 3

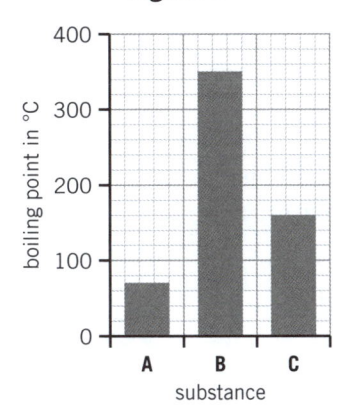

06.1 Give the boiling point of substance **B**. [1 mark]

06.2 Which substance has a boiling point of 78 °C? [1 mark]

06.3 Suggest which letter represents each substance. Explain your answer. [6 marks]

> **! Exam Tip**
>
> This is a 6 mark question, so you need to say *why* each letter represents each substance. Think about the structure of each of the compounds and how it will affect their boiling points.

07 Lithium and fluorine react to form lithium fluoride.

07.1 Draw **one** line from each substance to its correct bonding. [2 marks]

Substance	Bonding
fluorine	covalent
lithium	ionic
lithium fluoride	metallic

07.2 Figure 4 shows a model of metallic bonding.

Figure 4

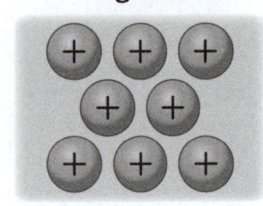

Use **Figure 4** and your knowledge to describe metallic bonding. **[3 marks]**

07.3 Complete the dot and cross diagram of lithium fluoride. **[1 mark]**

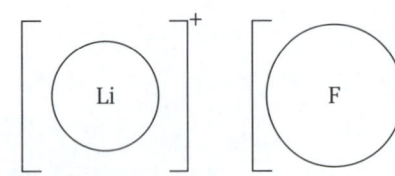

$[Li]^+$ $[F]^-$

Exam Tip

Your dot and cross diagram should make it clear how the electrons have moved. It is a dot *and* cross diagram, so you should use dots and crosses.

07.4 Complete the sentences. **[2 marks]**

Molten lithium fluoride **does / does not** conduct electricity. This is because the ions are **free to move / fixed in place**, so charge can flow.

08 Magnesium and chlorine react to form magnesium chloride. **Figure 5** shows the structure of magnesium chloride.

Figure 5

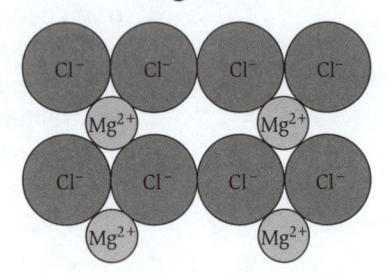

08.1 Determine the empirical formula of magnesium chloride. **[1 mark]**

08.2 Calculate the relative formula mass of magnesium chloride. Relative atomic masses A_r: Cl = 35.5   Mg = 24. **[1 mark]**

08.3 Name the type of bonding found in chlorine. **[1 mark]**

08.4 Explain how the structure and properties of pure magnesium are similar to the structure and properties of graphite. **[6 marks]**

08.5 Explain why alloying a metal can make it more useful. **[6 marks]**

Exam Tip

Question **08.5** is asking you to link a change in property to how useful a metal can be. Don't forget to refer to that in your answer.

09 Calcium is a metal in Group 2 of the Periodic Table. Sulfur is a non-metal in Group 6 of the Periodic Table.

09.1 Give the charges of the ions formed by calcium and by sulfur. **[1 mark]**

C3 Ionic bonding, metallic bonding, and structure

09.2 Add the electrons in the outermost shells to complete the dot and cross diagram showing how calcium and sulfur react. **[3 marks]**

$$Ca \;+\; S \;\rightarrow\; [\;Ca\;]\;[\;S\;]$$

09.3 **Figure 6** shows a ball and stick model of calcium sulfide.

Figure 6

Give **one** advantage and **one** limitation of using the ball and stick model to represent an ionic compound. **[2 marks]**

> ! **Exam Tip**
>
> Compare this to other models of ionic compounds you have seen.

10 **Table 1** shows some data about four substances.

Table 1

Substance	State at 25°C	Melting point in °C	Boiling point in °C	Conducts electricity when solid	Conducts electricity when liquid
A		−219	−183	no	no
B	solid	1538	2862	yes	yes
C	solid	801	1465	no	yes
D		−7	59	no	no

10.1 Complete **Table 1** to show the states of substance **A** and substance **D**. **[2 marks]**

10.2 Explain how you can tell that substance **B** is a metal. **[2 marks]**

10.3 Identify which substance is sodium chloride. Explain your answer. **[4 marks]**

10.4 Identify which substance in **Table 1** represents oxygen. **[1 mark]**

10.5 Describe the structure and bonding in substance **D**. **[2 marks]**

> ! **Exam Tip**
>
> Think about the properties that each type of compound has.

Knowledge

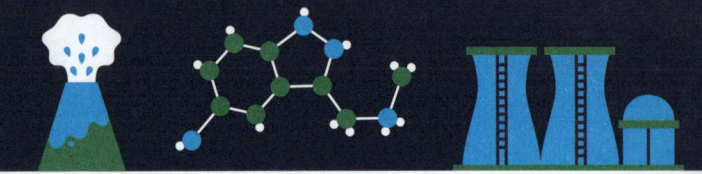

C4 The Periodic Table

Development of the Periodic Table

The modern Periodic Table lists approximately 100 elements. It has changed a lot over time as scientists have organised the elements differently.

The first lists of elements, Mendeleev's Periodic Table, and the modern Periodic Table have a number of differences in how they list the discovered elements.

> **Revision tip**
>
> **Practice** This topic makes a great six mark question, or an interpretation and evaluate question.
>
> This is an area the exam board could ask you to apply your knowledge in a new context and introduce unfamiliar examples.

	First lists of elements	Mendeleev's Periodic Table	Modern Periodic Table
How are elements ordered?	by atomic mass	normally by atomic mass but some elements were swapped around	by atomic number
Are there gaps?	no gaps	gaps left for undiscovered elements	no gaps – all elements up to a certain atomic number have been discovered
How are elements grouped?	not grouped	grouped by chemical properties	grouped by the number of electrons in the outer shell
Metals and non-metals	no clear distinction	no clear distinction	metals to the left, non-metals to the right
Problems	some elements grouped inappropriately	incomplete, with little explanation for why some elements had to be swapped to fit in the appropriate groups	—

Mendeleev was able to accurately predict the properties of undiscovered elements based on the positions of the gaps in his table.

Sub-atomic discoveries

The discovery of electrons allowed scientists to work out that elements with the same number of electrons in their outer shell had similar chemical properties.

The discovery of protons allowed scientists to order the elements in the Periodic Table by their atomic number.

The discovery of neutrons led to scientists discovering **isotopes**. The discovery of neutrons also helped to explain why some elements didn't seem to fit when the Periodic Table was organised by atomic mass (like iodine and tellurium).

Group 0

Elements in **Group 0** are called the **noble gases**. Noble gases have the following properties:

- full outer shells, so do not need to lose or gain electrons
- very unreactive (**inert**) so exist as single atoms as they do not bond to form molecules
- boiling points that increase down the group.

Key terms

Make sure you can write a definition for these key terms.

alkali metal   chemical properties   displacement   Group   halogen   inert   isotope
noble gas   Periodic Table   reactivity   undiscovered   unreactive

C4

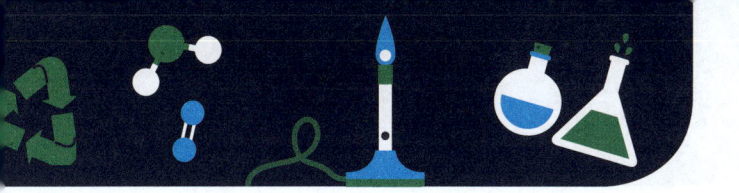

Group 1 elements

Group 1 elements react with oxygen, chlorine, and water, for example:

lithium + oxygen → lithium oxide
lithium + chlorine → lithium chloride
lithium + water → lithium hydroxide + hydrogen

Group 1 elements are called **alkali metals** because they react with water to form an alkali (a solution of their metal hydroxide).

> **Revision tip**
>
> **Remember** The reaction of Group 1 metals with water is rather spectacular. You may remember seeing a demonstration of this in class – some of the tiny lumps of metal burst into flames when they hit the water and whizz around, fizzing as the hydrogen is released.

Group 1 properties

Group 1 elements all have one electron in their outer shell. They are very reactive because they only need to lose one electron to react.

Reactivity increases down Group 1 because as you move down the group:
- the atoms increase in size
- the outer electron is further away from the nucleus, and there are more shells shielding the outer electron from the nucleus
- the electrostatic attraction between the nucleus and the outer electron is weaker
- so it is easier to lose the one outer electron.

The melting point and boiling point decreases down Group 1.

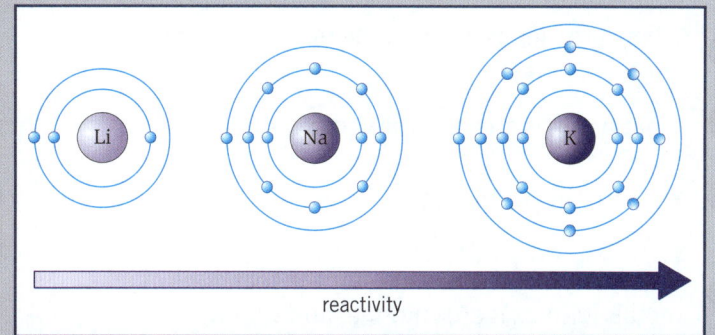

Group 7 elements

Group 7 elements are called the **halogens**. They are non-metals that exist as molecules made up of pairs of atoms.

Name	Formula	State at room temperature	Melting point and boiling point	Reactivity
fluorine	F_2	gas		
chlorine	Cl_2	gas	increases down the group	decreases down the group
bromine	Br_2	liquid		
iodine	I_2	solid		

Group 7 reactivity

Reactivity decreases down Group 7 because as you move down the group:
- the atoms increase in size
- the outer shell is further away from the nucleus, and there are more shells between the nucleus and the outer shell
- the electrostatic attraction from the nucleus to the outer shell is weaker
- so it is harder to gain the one electron to fill the outer shell.

Group 7 displacement

More reactive Group 7 elements can take the place of less reactive ones in a compound. This is called **displacement**.

For example, fluorine displaces chlorine as it is more reactive:

fluorine + potassium chloride → potassium fluoride + chlorine

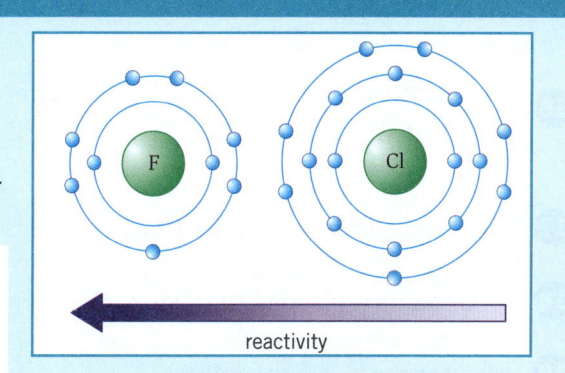

C4 Knowledge 211

Retrieval

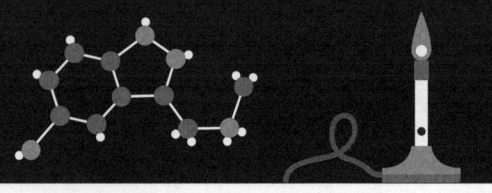

Learn the answers to the questions below, then cover the answers column with a piece of paper and write as many as you can. Check and repeat.

C4 questions | Answers

#	Question	Answer
1	How is the modern Periodic Table ordered?	by atomic number
2	How were the early lists of elements ordered?	by atomic mass
3	Why did Mendeleev swap the order of some elements?	to group them by their chemical properties
4	Why did Mendeleev leave gaps in his Periodic Table?	to leave room for elements that had not yet been discovered
5	Why do elements in a group have similar chemical properties?	have the same number of electrons in their outer shell
6	Where are metals and non-metals located on the Periodic Table?	metals to the left, non-metals to the right
7	What name is given to the Group 1 elements?	alkali metals
8	Why are the alkali metals named this?	they are metals that react with water to form an alkali
9	Give the general equations for the reactions of alkali metals with oxygen, chlorine, and water.	metal + oxygen → metal oxide metal + chlorine → metal chloride metal + water → metal hydroxide + hydrogen
10	How does the reactivity of the alkali metals change down the group?	increases (more reactive)
11	Why does the reactivity of the alkali metals increase down the group?	they are larger atoms, so the outermost electron is further from the nucleus, meaning there are weaker electrostatic forces of attraction and more shielding between the nucleus and outer electron, and it is easier to lose the electron
12	What name is given to the Group 7 elements?	halogens
13	Give the formulae of the first four halogens.	F_2, Cl_2, Br_2, I_2
14	How do the melting points of the halogens change down the group?	increase (higher melting point)
15	How does the reactivity of the halogens change down the group?	decrease (less reactive)
16	Why does the reactivity of the halogens decrease down the group?	they are larger atoms, so the outermost shell is further from the nucleus, meaning there are weaker electrostatic forces of attraction and more shielding between the nucleus and outer shell, and it is harder to gain an electron
17	What is a displacement reaction?	when a more reactive element takes the place of a less reactive one in a compound
18	What name is given to the Group 0 elements?	noble gases
19	Why are the noble gases inert?	they have full outer shells so do not need to lose or gain electrons
20	How do the melting points of the noble gases change down the group?	increase (higher melting point)

C4 The Periodic Table

C4

Now go back and use the questions below to check your knowledge from previous chapters.

Previous questions | Answers

#	Question	Answer
1	Describe the nuclear model of the atom.	dense nucleus with electrons orbiting it
2	Which type of atoms form covalent bonds between them?	non-metals
3	What charge do ions from Group 7 form?	1−
4	Describe the structure of a giant ionic lattice.	regular structure of alternating positive and negative ions, held together by the electrostatic force of attraction
5	What is a mixture?	two or more substances not chemically combined
6	What are four properties of pure metals?	malleable, high melting/boiling points, good conductors of electricity, good conductors of thermal energy
7	Give three uses of fullerenes.	lubricants, drug delivery (spheres), high-tech electronics

Maths skills

Practise your maths skills using the worked example and practice questions below.

Plotting straight lines

When numerical data is plotted onto a graph you usually need to draw a line of best fit.

Sometimes this will be a straight line, but other times it will be a curve. You should draw whichever type of line fits the data.

Worked example

A scientist burnt different elements in oxygen to see how the elements' masses change depending on the mass of oxygen used.

Mass of oxygen in g	Mass increase of element in g
5.0	2.1
10.0	4.0
15.0	6.2
20.0	8.1
25.0	9.8

This produces a graph with a **positive correlation** – as the value on the x-axis increases, so does the value on the y-axis.

With a **negative correlation**, as the value on the x-axis increases, the value on the y-axis decreases.

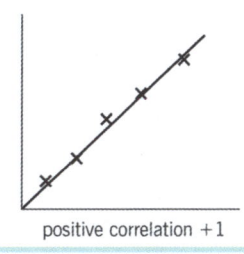

positive correlation +1

Practice

In another experiment, scientists obtained the data below.

Mass of oxygen in g	Mass increase of element in g
0.0	0.0
4.0	5.2
8.0	10.1
12.0	14.7
16.0	19.8
20.0	25.1

1 Using graph paper, draw a graph for these data and include a straight line of best fit.

2 Does your graph show a positive or negative correlation?

3 In another experiment, scientists looked at how the mass of a 5.0 g element increased as it was heated.

Where does the line of best fit start on this graph, compared to on your graph?

C4 Retrieval

Practice

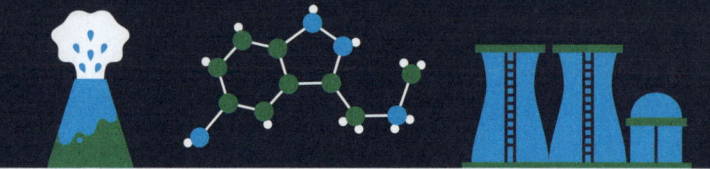

Exam-style questions

01 An early Periodic Table organised the elements by atomic mass.

01.1 Complete the sentence. **[1 mark]**

The atomic mass of an atom of an element is the number of _____ plus _____.

01.2 What **two** errors did Periodic Tables that were organised by atomic mass have? **[2 marks]**
Tick **two** boxes.

Elements were not organised by their state at room temperature. ☐

Elements were missing. ☐

Elements were placed in the wrong groups. ☐

Metal elements were separated from non-metal elements. ☐

01.3 Mendeleev developed a Periodic Table that overcame these problems. What two things did Mendeleev do in his Periodic Table? Tick **two** boxes. **[2 marks]**

Left gaps for elements he predicted were still to be discovered. ☐

Listed the different isotopes of the elements. ☐

Organised the elements by atomic number. ☐

Swapped the order of some elements to group the elements by their chemical properties. ☐

> **Exam Tip**
>
> Mendeleev is one of the few scientists named in the specification. However, don't let the name put you off. Focus on the chemistry knowledge you know.

01.4 Complete the sentence.

The elements in the modern Periodic Table are organised by _____ number. This is the number of _____ in an atom of the element. **[2 marks]**

02 **Figure 1** shows the electronic structures of four atoms. Each atom is labelled with a letter. The letters are not the chemical symbols of the elements.

Figure 1

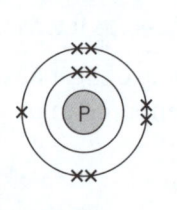

P   Q   R   S

214   C4 The Periodic Table

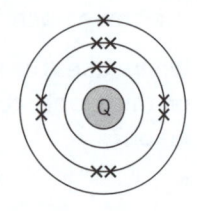

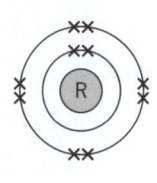

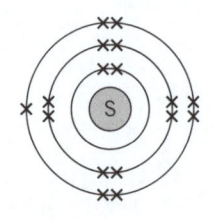

Paper 3 **C4**

02.1 Give the letter of the atom of a Group 1 element. **[1 mark]**

_____

> **Exam Tip**
> Look at the number of electrons in the outer most shell.

02.2 Give the letter of the atom of an unreactive element and explain why this element is unreactive. **[2 marks]**

_____

_____

02.3 Give the letters of **two** atoms of elements that are in the same group on the Periodic Table. **[1 mark]**

_____

03.1 Draw **one** line from each group of the Periodic Table to the correct name for that group. **[2 marks]**

Group	Name
Group 0	alkali metals
Group 1	halogens
Group 7	noble gases

03.2 Draw the full electronic structure of the Group 0 element argon. **[2 marks]**

> **Exam Tip**
> Start by working out how many electrons argon has.

03.3 Give the reason why Group 0 elements are unreactive. **[1 mark]**

03.4 Write the electronic structure of the Group 1 element sodium. **[1 mark]**

03.5 Sodium reacts with oxygen.
Name the product of this reaction. **[1 mark]**

03.6 Potassium also reacts with oxygen.
Identify whether the reaction of potassium with oxygen is more vigorous or less vigorous than the reaction of sodium and oxygen. **[1 mark]**

03.7 The early Periodic Table ordered the elements by atomic weight. Using argon and potassium as an example, explain why ordering the elements by atomic mass led to some elements being in the wrong order. **[2 marks]**

> **Exam Tip**
> Look at the mass numbers on the Periodic Table.

04 This question is about the elements of Group 7.

04.1 Give the number of electrons in the outer shell of a Group 7 element. **[1 mark]**

For answers and more practice questions visit www.oxfordrevise.com/scienceanswers

Even more practice and interactive revision quizzes are available on kerboodle

C4 Practice

04.2 Which is the most reactive element in Group 7?
Choose **one** answer. **[1 mark]**

bromine   chlorine   fluorine   iodine

04.3 Draw **one** line from the Group 7 ionic compound to the correct dot and cross diagram. **[2 marks]**

Group 7 compound	Dot and cross diagram 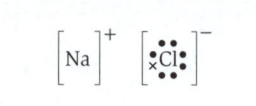
hydrogen bromide	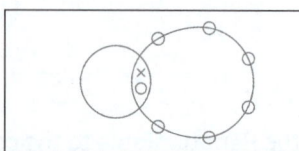 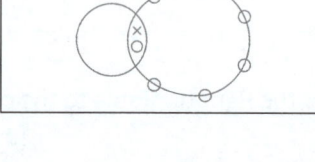 $[Na]^+ \; [Cl]^-$
sodium chloride	(two overlapping circles with dots and crosses)
	(two overlapping circles with dots and crosses)

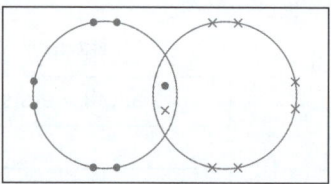

> **! Exam Tip**
>
> Start by identifying which compound is an ionic compound and which is covalent.

04.4 More reactive elements displace less reactive elements from their compounds. For each of the pairs of substances in **Table 1**, identify whether a displacement reaction will occur. **[3 marks]**

Table 1

Substances	Displacement reaction	No displacement reaction
chlorine and potassium iodide		
bromine and sodium chloride		
iodine and lithium bromide		

> **! Exam Tip**
>
> Where are the different elements in **Table 1** found on the reactivity series? This will help you work out whether a displacement reaction would occur.

05 This question is about Group 1 elements.

05.1 Complete the sentence. **[1 mark]**

The elements in Group 1 are all **metals / non-metals**.

05.2 The reactivity of the Group 1 elements changes as you move down the group. Put these elements in order from least reactive to most reactive. **[3 marks]**

caesium   sodium   rubidium   lithium   potassium

least reactive   most reactive

_____ < _____ < _____ < _____ < _____

05.3 The elements in Group 1 undergo a number of reactions. Draw **one** line from each pair of reactants to the correct products. **[3 marks]**

Reactants | Products

- sodium + chlorine
- sodium + water
- sodium + oxygen

- sodium oxide
- sodium chloride + hydrogen
- sodium chloride
- sodium hydroxide + hydrogen
- sodium oxide + hydrogen

05.4 Suggest why Group 1 elements are kept in oil. **[1 mark]**

05.5 A student has a sample of sodium. It is a dull grey colour. Sodium is soft enough to cut. Upon cutting the inside is shiny. Explain these observations. **[5 marks]**

05.6 The student adds a lump of potassium to a large bowl of water that contains universal indicator. Describe and explain any observations the student would make. **[6 marks]**

> **! Exam Tip**
>
> You don't get given any information you don't need. There are three bits of information in **05.5**. Try underlining each piece of information and then tick them off once you're referred to them in your answer.

06 Neon and argon are elements of Group 0 in the Periodic Table.

06.1 Identify whether neon and argon are metal or non-metal elements. Using the Periodic Table, give a reason for your answer. **[1 mark]**

06.2 How many electrons are in the outer shell of neon and argon? Choose **one** answer. **[1 mark]**

0   1   2   8

06.3 The boiling points of Group 0 elements change as you move down the group. Put the boiling points of the following Group 0 elements in order from lowest to highest. **[2 marks]**

| neon | helium | radon | argon |

lowest boiling point   highest boiling point

_____ < _____ < _____ < _____

07 Rubidium is in Group 1 of the Periodic Table.

07.1 Identify whether rubidium is a metal or a non-metal. **[1 mark]**

07.2 Give the products when rubidium reacts with liquid water.
Choose **one** answer. [1 mark]

rubidium oxide and oxygen

rubidium hydroxide and oxygen

rubidium oxide and hydrogen

rubidium hydroxide and hydrogen

07.3 Rubidium also reacts with oxygen.
Write the word equation for this reaction. [1 mark]

07.4 Sodium is another element in Group 1 of the Periodic Table.
Sodium reacts with bromine.

Complete the balanced symbol equation for the reaction between sodium and bromine. Include state symbols. [2 marks]

_____ Na (_____) + Br$_2$ (_____) → _____ NaBr(s)

> **Exam Tip**
> Put state symbols after the reactants and a number in front of the product.

07.5 Rubidium also reacts with bromine. Explain the difference in the reactivity of sodium and rubidium with bromine. [4 marks]

08 Magnesium is a Group 2 metal.

08.1 Identify the charge of the ion that magnesium forms. [1 mark]

08.2 Magnesium reacts with chlorine to form magnesium chloride. Draw a dot and cross diagram for magnesium chloride. [3 marks]

08.3 Strontium is another Group 2 metal. Predict how the reactivity of strontium will compare to the reactivity of magnesium.
Explain your answer. [3 marks]

08.4 Predict whether sodium will be more or less reactive than magnesium when reacting with chlorine.
Explain your answer. [2 marks]

09 Group 1 and Group 7 elements react together.

09.1 Draw a dot and cross diagram to show the bonding in potassium bromide. [3 marks]

09.2 A student mixed some potassium bromide with three other Group 7 elements. Identify which mixture will lead to a displacement reaction. Give the products of the reaction. [2 marks]

   A astatine and potassium bromide

   B chlorine and potassium bromide

   C iodine and potassium bromide

> **Exam Tip**
> The dot and cross diagram of sodium chloride is mentioned on the specification. Potassium and bromine are in the same groups as sodium and chlorine, so use what you know about the bonding of sodium chloride to work out the answer.

09.3 Explain the difference in the trend in reactivity of the Group 1 and Group 7 elements. [6 marks]

09.4 Group 1 elements also react with water. Write the word equation for the reaction of sodium and water. [2 marks]

> **Exam Tip**
> Question **09.4** asks for a word equation, so writing a symbol equation won't get any marks.

218   C4 The Periodic Table

10 The columns of the Periodic Table are called Groups. The elements in a Group have similar properties.

10.1 Draw **one** line from each Group to a property of the elements in that Group. **[3 marks]**

Group	Property
	react with water to make alkaline solutions
Group 0	react with metals to make covalent compounds
	are inert
Group 1	displace more reactive elements from their compounds
Group 7	react with metals to make ionic compounds

10.2 Explain the difference in the trend in reactivity down Group 1 and Group 7. **[6 marks]**

10.3 Explain the reactivity of Group 0. **[2 marks]**

11.1 Give the name of Group 1 in the Periodic Table. **[1 mark]**

11.2 Why do elements in the same group of the Periodic Table have similar chemical properties? Choose **one** answer. **[1 mark]**

They have the same number of electrons in the shell nearest the nucleus.

They have the same number of electron shells.

They have the same number of electrons in the shell furthest from the nucleus.

They have the same number of electrons.

11.3 Caesium is a Group 1 element. Bromine is a Group 7 element. Name the product when caesium reacts with bromine. **[1 mark]**

12 Steel is an alloy of iron and carbon.

12.1 Identify which element in steel is a metal. **[1 mark]**

12.2 Complete the sentences.
Choose the correct words from the box. **[3 marks]**

harder   softer   distorted   longer   slide over   squash into

Alloys are _____ than pure metals because the layers of atoms are _____. As such, the layers cannot _____ each other.

12.3 Explain why metals have high melting points. **[2 marks]**

> **Exam Tip**
> These explain questions mean you need to make reference to the number of electrons and shells.

> **Exam Tip**
> Use the location on the Periodic Table to help work out if they are metals or non metals.

Knowledge

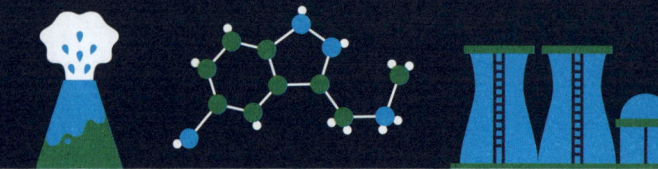

C5 Quantitative chemistry

Conservation of mass

The **conservation of mass** states that atoms cannot be created or destroyed in a chemical reaction. Atoms are rearranged into new substances. All the atoms you had in the reactants must be present in the products.

When it comes to measuring the mass of a reaction, you would expect the mass at the start to be the same as the mass at the end. However, sometimes the mass can appear to change.

Decrease in mass

In some reactions the mass appears to decrease. This is normally because a gas is produced in the reaction and lost to the surroundings. For example:

sodium + water → sodium hydroxide + hydrogen
$2Na(s) + 2H_2O(l) \rightarrow 2NaOH(aq) + H_2(g)$

The mass of the sodium and the water at the start of the reaction will be more than the mass of the sodium hydroxide at the end of the reaction, because hydrogen atoms have been lost as a gas.

Increase in mass

In some reactions the mass appears to increase. This is normally because one of the reactants is a gas. For example:

sodium + chlorine → sodium chloride
$2Na(s) + Cl_2(g) \rightarrow 2NaCl(s)$

The mass of the sodium at the start of the reaction will be lower than the mass of sodium chloride at the end of the reaction. This is because atoms from the gaseous chlorine have been added to the sodium, increasing the mass.

Balancing symbol equations

When writing symbol equations you need to ensure that the number of each atom on each side is equal.

$H_2 + O_2 \rightarrow H_2O$

unbalanced

there are 2 hydrogen atoms on each side, but 2 oxygen atoms in the reactants and 1 in the product

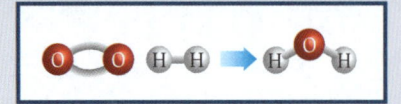

$2H_2 + O_2 \rightarrow 2H_2O$

balanced

there are 4 hydrogen atoms on each side, and 2 oxygen atoms on each side

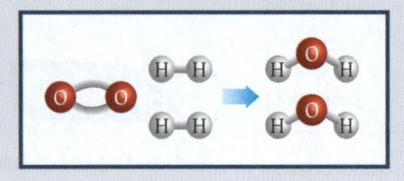

State symbols

A balanced symbol equation should also include state symbols.

State	Symbol
solid	(s)
liquid	(l)
gas	(g)
aqueous or dissolved in water	(aq)

Key terms

Make sure you can write a definition for these key terms.

balanced　　calculation　　cm³　　dilute
formula mass　　mass　　ratio　　solution　　solute

C5

Ratios

Look back at the reaction. In the reaction between hydrogen and oxygen, the ratio of hydrogen to oxygen molecules is 2:1. This means that for every *one* molecule of oxygen, you would need *two* molecules of hydrogen, for example:

- If you had 10 molecules of oxygen you would need 20 molecules of hydrogen.
- If you had 2 molecules of oxygen you would need 4 molecules of hydrogen.
- If you had 1.75 molecules of oxygen you would need 3.5 molecules of hydrogen.

A balanced symbol equation shows the ratios of the reactants and products in a chemical reaction.

Revision tip

Sometimes you may get concentration in mol/dm³ and need to convert it into g/dm³.

concentration in g/dm³ = concentration in mol/dm³ × M_r

Formula mass

Every substance has a **formula mass**, M_r.

formula mass M_r = sum of the relative atomic masses of all the atoms in the formula

Concentration

Concentration is the amount of **solute** in a volume of **solvent**. The unit of concentration is g/dm³. Concentration can be calculated using:

$$\text{concentration (g/dm}^3\text{)} = \frac{\text{mass (g)}}{\text{volume (dm}^3\text{)}}$$

Sometimes volume is measured in cm³:

$$\text{volume (dm}^3\text{)} = \frac{\text{volume (cm}^3\text{)}}{1000}$$

- lots of solute in little solution = high concentration
- little solute in lots of solution = low concentration

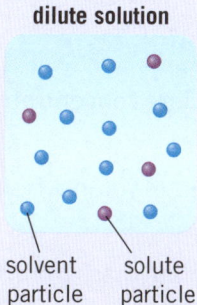

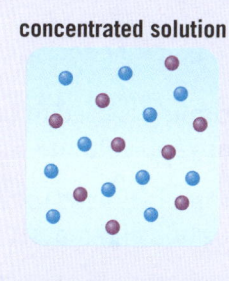

dilute solution · concentrated solution

solvent particle · solute particle

---

concentration · conservation · dm³ · equation
solvent · state · surroundings · volume

C5 Knowledge 221

Retrieval

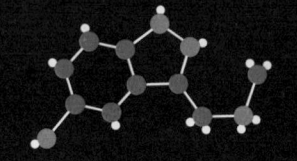

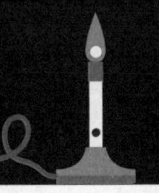

Learn the answers to the questions below, then cover the answers column with a piece of paper and write as many as you can. Check and repeat.

C5 questions | Answers

#	Question	Answer
1	What is the conservation of mass?	in a chemical reaction, atoms are not created or destroyed, just rearranged, so total mass before = total mass after the reaction
2	When a metal forms a metal oxide, why does the mass increase?	atoms from gaseous oxygen have been added
3	When an acid reacts with a metal, why does the mass decrease?	a gas is produced and escapes
4	What is relative formula mass?	the sum of the relative atomic masses of each atom in a substance
5	What are the four state symbols and what do they stand for?	(s) solid, (l) liquid, (g) gas, (aq) aqueous or dissolved in water
6	How can you tell when a symbol equation is balanced?	the number of atoms of each element is the same on both sides
7	What is a unit for concentration?	g/dm^3
8	Which formula is used to calculate concentration from mass and volume?	concentration $(g/dm^3) = \dfrac{mass\ (g)}{volume\ (dm^3)}$
9	Which formula is used to calculate volume from concentration and mass?	volume $(dm^3) = \dfrac{mass\ (g)}{concentration\ (g/dm^3)}$
10	Which formula is used to calculate mass from concentration in g/dm^3 and volume?	mass (g) = concentration (g/dm^3) × volume (dm^3)
11	How can you convert a volume reading in cm^3 to dm^3?	divide by 1000
12	If the amount of solute in a solution is increased, what happens to its concentration?	increases
13	If the volume of water in a solution is increased, what happens to its concentration?	decreases

C5 Quantitative chemistry

C5

Now go back and use the questions below to check your knowledge from previous chapters.

Previous questions | Answers

#	Question	Answer
1	Why did Mendeleev leave gaps in his Periodic Table?	leave room for elements that had not yet been discovered
2	What is a mixture?	two or more substances not chemically combined
3	How are covalent bonds formed?	by atoms sharing electrons
4	Why does the reactivity of the halogens decrease down the group?	they are larger atoms, so the outermost shell is further from the nucleus, meaning there are weaker electrostatic forces of attraction and more shielding between the nucleus and outer shell, and it is harder to gain an electron
5	Why do most covalent substances not conduct electricity?	they do not have delocalised electrons or ions
6	Give the formulae of the first four halogens	F_2, Cl_2, Br_2, I_2
7	Give two properties of nanotubes.	high tensile strength, conduct electricity
8	Why are metals good conductors of electricity and of thermal energy?	delocalised electrons are free to move through the metal

Maths skills

Practise your maths skills using the worked example and practice questions below.

Plotting curves

Remember that you need to draw a line of best fit when numerical data are plotted on a graph.

Some data will need a curved line of best fit, rather than a straight one.

It is important to remember that you draw the line that best fits the data.

Worked example

The alkanes have the boiling points given below.

Plot the data on a graph, and draw an appropriate line of best fit.

Number of carbon atoms	Boiling point in °C
1	−162.0
2	−89.0
3	−42.0
4	0.0
5	36.0
6	69.0

A graph displaying this data will have a curved line of best fit.

The graph shows a positive correlation – as the number of carbon atoms increases, so does the boiling point.

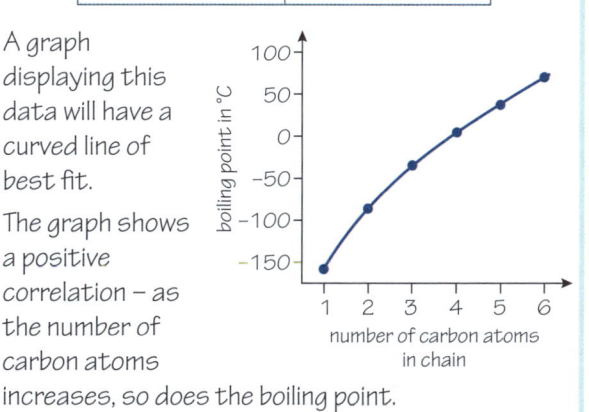

Practice

A different group of hydrocarbons have the boiling points given below.

Number of carbon atoms	Boiling point in °C
4	5.1
5	44.7
6	72.8
8	106.0
9	112.4
10	115.6

1. Plot a graph of these results. Draw an appropriate line of best fit.
2. Use your graph from **1** to predict the boiling point of a hydrocarbon in this group with seven carbon atoms.
3. Does your graph show a positive or negative correlation?

C5 Retrieval 223

Practice

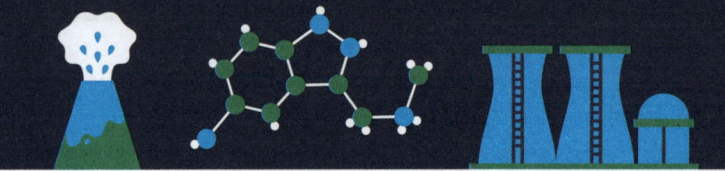

Exam-style questions

01 The balanced symbol equation for the reaction between water and carbon dioxide is:

$6H_2O + 6CO_2 \rightarrow C_6H_{12}O_6 + 6O_2$

01.1 Which statement is correct? **[1 mark]**

Tick **one** box.

6 water molecules react with 6 carbon dioxide molecules. ☐

There are 6 hydrogen atoms in a water molecule. ☐

There are more carbon atoms in the products than in the reactants. ☐

> **Exam Tip**
>
> Be sure you're clear on the difference between the large and the small numbers within a chemical formula.

01.2 In the reaction, water is a liquid and carbon dioxide is a gas.

Give the state symbols for water and carbon dioxide. **[2 marks]**

water _____

carbon dioxide _____

01.3 Give the total number of oxygen atoms in the products. **[1 mark]**

Circle **one** answer.

2   6   12   18

01.4 Complete the sentences. **[3 marks]**

There are **the same / a different** number of oxygen atoms on both sides of the equation. This is because **lots of / no** atoms are lost or made during a chemical reaction. This is the law of the **conservation / dissipation** of mass.

02 A student burnt magnesium to form magnesium oxide.

Figure 1

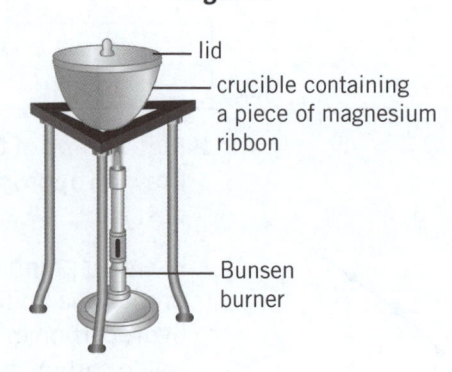

- lid
- crucible containing a piece of magnesium ribbon
- Bunsen burner

224   C5 Quantitative chemistry

Paper 3 **C5**

02.1 Complete the symbol equation for the reaction. Balance the equation. **[3 marks]**

_____ Mg(s) + _____ (_____) → _____ MgO(s)

02.2 The mass of the crucible and magnesium ribbon at the start of the experiment was 106 g. At the end of the experiment, the mass of the crucible and product was 110 g.
Explain why the mass has increased. **[2 marks]**

02.3 Magnesium is a Group 2 element.
Draw a dot and cross diagram to show the bonding in magnesium oxide. **[3 marks]**

> **Exam Tip**
> In the brackets, you're expected to put the state symbols, and the chemical element goes before the brackets.

03 The symbol equation shows the reaction between lithium and hydrochloric acid.

$Li(s) + HCl(aq) \rightarrow LiCl(aq) + H_2(g)$

03.1 Balance the symbol equation. **[2 marks]**

03.2 Identify the product that is an aqueous solution. **[1 mark]**

03.3 The hydrochloric acid solution was produced by dissolving 7.3 g of hydrogen chloride in 500 cm³ of water.
Identify the substance that is the solute. **[1 mark]**

03.4 Calculate the concentration of the hydrochloric acid in g/dm³. **[3 marks]**

03.5 A student carried out the reaction in a conical flask on a top-pan balance. Explain what the student would observe. **[2 marks]**

> **Exam Tip**
> Use the state symbols in the equation to help you answer **03.5**.

04 Zinc reacts with hydrochloric acid to form zinc chloride and hydrogen.

04.1 Identify the balanced symbol equation for the reaction between zinc and hydrochloric acid. **[1 mark]**

A $Zn + HCl \rightarrow ZnCl + H_2$
B $Zn + 2HCl \rightarrow ZnCl_2 + H_2$
C $Zn + 2HCl \rightarrow ZnCl_2 + H$
D $Zn + 2HCl \rightarrow ZnCl + H_2$

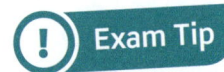

> **Exam Tip**
> Count up the number of each element on each side of the arrow.

C5 Practice

04.2 3.25 g of zinc reacts with 3.65 g of hydrochloric acid.
Calculate the total mass of both hydrogen and
zinc chloride formed. **[1 mark]**

04.3 Zinc also reacts with sulfuric acid, H_2SO_4.
Calculate the relative formula mass of sulfuric acid. Relative
atomic mass A_r: H = 1   S = 32   O = 16   **[2 marks]**

05 Some students investigated the reaction of calcium carbonate with hydrochloric acid:

$CaCO_3(s) + 2HCl(aq) \rightarrow CaCl_2(aq) + CO_2(g) + H_2O(l)$

The students measured the volume of carbon dioxide gas made in 60 seconds. The students repeated the experiment five times. **Table 1** shows their results.

Table 1

Experiment number	Volume of carbon dioxide gas produced in 60 seconds in cm³
1	52
2	49
3	48
4	56
5	51

05.1 Calculate the mean volume of carbon dioxide gas. **[1 mark]**

05.2 Give the range of the values obtained in **Table 1**. **[1 mark]**

05.3 What is the best estimate of the volume of gas obtained?
Choose **one** answer. **[1 mark]**

mean ± 3   mean ± 4   mean ± 6   mean ± 8

> **Exam Tip**
> Range means different things in maths and science. In science we need the lowest number to the highest number. Give this as two values not just one.

06 Sulfur dioxide reacts with oxygen to make sulfur trioxide.
$2SO_2(g) + O_2(g) \rightarrow 2SO_3(g)$

06.1 Write down what the number 3 means in the formula SO_3. **[1 mark]**

06.2 Calculate the relative formula mass M_r of sulfur dioxide.
Relative atomic masses A_r: S = 32   O = 16   **[1 mark]**

06.3 In an experiment, 1.28 g of sulfur dioxide produced 1.62 g of sulfur trioxide.
Calculate the mass of oxygen that reacted. **[1 mark]**

> **Exam Tip**
> Remember there are two oxygen atoms in sulfur dioxide.

C5 Quantitative chemistry

07.1 Draw **one** line from each state symbol to the correct state it represents, and to the correct particle diagram for that state. **[3 marks]**

(aq)   gas

(g)   solid

(l)   liquid

(s)   aqueous

07.2 A student added solid magnesium to hydrochloric acid. The reaction produced hydrogen gas and magnesium chloride. The magnesium chloride is dissolved in water.

Complete the symbol equation for the reaction by adding state symbols. **[2 marks]**

Mg(____) + 2HCl(____) → H$_2$(____) + MgCl$_2$(____)

07.3 What is the relative formula mass of magnesium chloride? Choose **one** answer. **[1 mark]**

29   46   59.5   95

Exam Tip
Make sure you're using the correct numbers from the Periodic Table. You need to use the mass number, not the atomic number.

07.4 The concentration of hydrochloric acid used in the reaction was 19 g/dm^3.

Calculate the mass of hydrochloric acid in 0.5 dm^3. **[1 mark]**

07.5 The student carried out the reaction in a conical flask placed on a top-pan balance.

Exam Tip
One of the products will escape from the conical flask.

Complete the sentences. Choose the correct words from the box. **[2 marks]**

| decreased | increased | gas | liquid | solution |

The student observed that as the reaction proceeded the mass _____. This is because a _____ was produced.

08 Figure 2 shows an element from the Periodic Table.

Figure 2

| 55 |
| Mn |
| manganese |
| 25 |

08.1 Use **Figure 2** to identify the number of protons and neutrons in manganese.
Choose **one** answer. [1 mark]

- **A** 55 protons   25 neutrons
- **B** 25 protons   55 neutrons
- **C** 25 protons   30 neutrons
- **D** 30 protons   25 neutrons

08.2 Manganese forms the compound manganese dioxide, MnO_2.
Calculate the relative formula mass of MnO_2.
Relative atomic mass A_r: O = 16 [2 marks]

> **Exam Tip**
> You can find the mass of manganese in part one of the question.

08.3 Manganese is a metal.
Identify the type of bonding in manganese dioxide.
Choose **one** answer. [1 mark]

covalent   intermolecular   ionic   metallic

09 A student has a potassium sulfate solution with a concentration of $10 g/dm^3$. They pour some of the solution into the measuring cylinder shown in **Figure 3**.

Figure 3

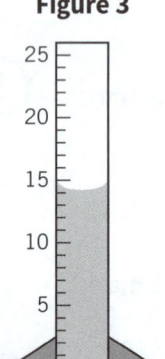

09.1 Give the reading on the measuring cylinder shown in **Figure 3**. [1 mark]

09.2 Calculate the mass of potassium sulfate in the solution in the measuring cylinder. Use your reading from **09.1**. [3 marks]

> **Exam Tip**
> Remember to read from the bottom of the meniscus.

09.3 The student wanted to measure out $5 cm^3$ of the solution.
Which size of measuring cylinder would be the most appropriate?
Choose **one** answer.

$10 cm^3$ $25 cm^3$ $50 cm^3$ $100 cm^3$

C5 Quantitative chemistry

Explain your answer. **[3 marks]**

10 This question is about sodium chloride, NaCl. A teacher makes sodium chloride by adding burning sodium to a container of chlorine gas.

10.1 Suggest **one** safety precaution the teacher should take. **[1 mark]**

10.2 Write the balanced symbol equation for the overall reaction. **[2 marks]**

! **Exam Tip**

Chlorine is a diatomic gas.

10.3 Sodium chloride is soluble in water.
Define the term soluble. **[1 mark]**

10.4 The teacher wants to make 450 cm³ of a solution of sodium chloride with a concentration of 29.2 g/dm³.
Calculate the mass of sodium chloride the teacher needs. **[3 marks]**

! **Exam Tip**

The first thing you need to do is to write down the equation for concentration.

10.5 **Figure 4** shows the top-pan balance the teacher uses to measure the mass of sodium chloride.

Figure 4

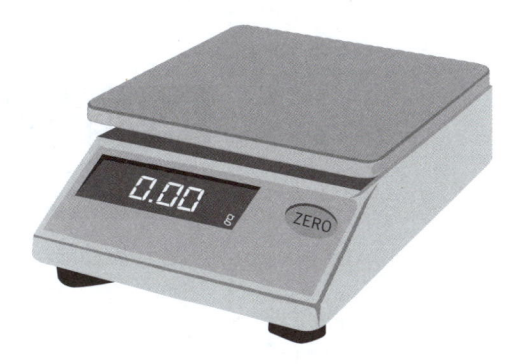

Give the error range of the top-pan balance. **[1 mark]**

10.6 Describe the structure and bonding in solid sodium chloride.
In your answer, outline how the ions are made and give their charges. **[6 marks]**

Knowledge

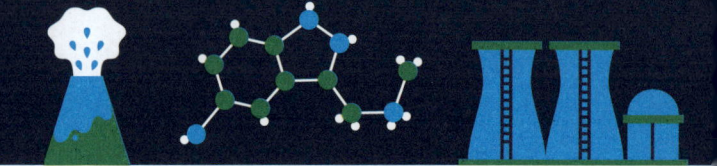

C6 Chemical reactions

Reactions of metals

The **reactivity** of a metal is how chemically reactive it is. When added to water, some metals react very vigorously – these metals have *high* reactivity. Other metals will barely react with water or acid, or won't react at all – these metals have *low* reactivity.

Reactivity series

The reactivity series places metals in order of their reactivity.

Sometimes, for example in the table below, hydrogen and carbon are included in the series, even though they are non-metals.

Reaction with water	Reaction with acid	Metal	Reactivity	Extraction method
fizzes, gives off hydrogen gas	explodes	potassium	high reactivity	electrolysis
		sodium		
		lithium		
reacts very slowly	fizzes, gives off hydrogen gas	calcium	decreasing reactivity	
		magnesium		
		aluminium (carbon)		
		zinc		
		iron		
no reaction	reacts slowly with warm acid	tin		reduction with carbon
		lead (hydrogen)		
		copper		
	no reaction	silver	low reactivity	mined from the Earth's crust
		gold		

Metal extraction

Some metals, like gold, are so unreactive that they are found as pure metals in the Earth's crust and can be mined.

Most metals exist as compounds in rock and have to be extracted from the rock. If there is enough metal compound in the rock to be worth extracting it is called an **ore**.

Metals that are less reactive than carbon can be extracted by reduction with carbon. For example:

iron oxide + carbon → iron + carbon dioxide

Metals that are more reactive than carbon can be extracted using a process called **electrolysis**.

Reduction and oxidation

If a substance gains oxygen in a reaction, it has been **oxidised**.

If a substance loses oxygen in a reaction, it has been **reduced**.

For example:

iron + oxygen → iron oxide

iron has been oxidised

iron oxide + carbon → iron + carbon dioxide

iron oxide has been reduced

Displacement reactions

In a **displacement** reaction a *more* reactive element takes the place of a *less* reactive element in a compound.

For example, iron is more reactive than copper, so iron displaces the copper in copper sulfate.

copper sulfate + iron → iron sulfate + copper

$CuSO_4(aq) + Fe(s) \rightarrow FeSO_4(aq) + Cu(s)$

Reactivity and ions

A metal's reactivity depends on how readily it forms an **ion** by losing electrons.

In the displacement reaction of copper sulfate and iron, iron forms an ion more easily than copper.

At the end of the reaction you are left with iron ions, not copper ions.

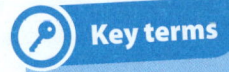

Key terms

Make sure you can write a definition for these key terms.

acid   alkali   base   crystallisation   displacement
metal   neutralisation   ore   oxidation   pH   reactivity

C6

Acids and alkalis

Acids are compounds that, when dissolved in water, release H^+ ions. There are three main acids: sulfuric acid, H_2SO_4, nitric acid, HNO_3, and hydrochloric acid, HCl.

Alkalis are compounds that, when dissolved in water, release OH^- ions. The **pH** scale is a measure of acidity and alkalinity. It runs from 1 to 14.
- Aqueous solutions with pH < 7 are acidic.
- Aqueous solutions with pH > 7 are alkaline.
- Aqueous solutions with pH = 7 are neutral.

Reactions of acids

Reactions of acids with metals
Acids react with some metals to form salts and hydrogen gas.

magnesium + hydrochloric acid → magnesium chloride + hydrogen

Reactions of acids with metal hydroxides
Acids react with metal hydroxides to form salts and water.

hydrochloric acid + sodium hydroxide → sodium chloride + water

The ionic equation for this reaction is always

$$H^+(aq) + OH^-(aq) \rightarrow H_2O(l)$$

Reactions of acids with metal oxides
Acids react with metal oxides to form salts and water.

hydrochloric acid + sodium oxide → sodium chloride + water

Reactions of acids with metal carbonates
Acids react with metal carbonates to form a salt, water, and carbon dioxide.

hydrochloric acid + sodium carbonate → sodium chloride + water + carbon dioxide

neutralisation reactions

Naming salts

Acid	hydrochloric acid	sulfuric acid	nitric acid
Formula	HCl	H_2SO_4	HNO_3
Ions formed in solution	H^+ and Cl^-	$2H^+$ and SO_4^{2-}	H^+ and NO_3^-
Type of salt formed	metal chloride	metal sulfate	metal nitrate
Sodium salt example	sodium chloride, NaCl	sodium sulfate, Na_2SO_4	sodium nitrate, $NaNO_3$

Indicators

Indicators can show if something is an acid or an alkali.

- **Universal indicator** gives an approximate pH of a solution.

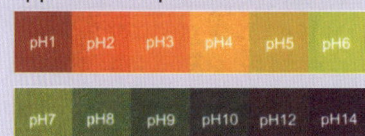

| pH1 | pH2 | pH3 | pH4 | pH5 | pH6 |
| pH7 | pH8 | pH9 | pH10 | pH12 | pH14 |

- Electronic pH probes give the exact pH of a solution.

Alkalis and bases

Bases neutralise acids to form water in **neutralisation** reactions.

Some metal hydroxides dissolve in water to form alkaline solutions – these are alkalis.

Some metal oxides and metal hydroxides do *not* dissolve in water. They are bases, but are not alkalis.

Revision tip

Practice Spend time practising the equations for the different reactions of acids, and make sure you know the products they form.

You need to be able to apply these equations to new situations.

---

electrolysis   extraction   indicator   ion
reactivity series   reduction   salt   universal indicator

Retrieval

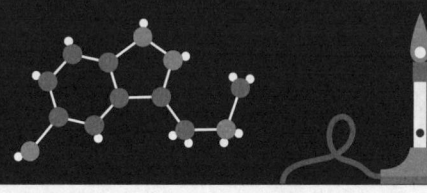

Learn the answers to the questions below, then cover the answers column with a piece of paper and write as many as you can. Check and repeat.

C6 questions | Answers

#	Question	Answer
1	What name is given to a list of metals ordered by their reactivity?	reactivity series
2	In terms of electrons, what makes some metals more reactive than others?	they lose their outer shell electron(s) more easily
3	Why are gold and silver found naturally as elements in the Earth's crust?	they are very unreactive
4	What is an ore?	rock containing enough of a metal compound to be economically worth extracting
5	How are metals less reactive than carbon extracted from their ores?	reduction with carbon
6	What are oxidation and reduction?	oxidation: addition of oxygen; reduction: removal of oxygen
7	Why can metals like potassium and aluminium not be extracted by reduction with carbon?	they are more reactive than carbon
8	How are metals more reactive than carbon extracted from their ores?	electrolysis
9	What is a displacement reaction?	a more reactive substance takes the place of a less reactive substance in a compound
10	In terms of pH, what is an acid?	a solution with a pH of less than 7
11	In terms of pH, what is a neutral solution?	a solution with a pH of 7
12	In terms of H^+ ions, what is an acid?	a substance that releases H^+ ions when dissolved in water
13	What are the names and formulae of the three main acids?	hydrochloric acid, HCl; sulfuric acid, H_2SO_4; nitric acid, HNO_3
14	How do you measure the pH of a substance?	universal indicator or pH probe
15	What are the products of a reaction between a metal and an acid?	salt + hydrogen
16	What are the products of a reaction between a metal hydroxide and an acid?	salt + water
17	What are the products of a reaction between a metal oxide and an acid?	salt + water
18	What are the products of a reaction between a metal carbonate and an acid?	salt + water + carbon dioxide
19	What is a base?	substance that reacts with acids in neutralisation reactions
20	What is an alkali?	substance that dissolves in water to form a solution above pH 7

C6 Chemical reactions

C6

Now go back and use the questions below to check your knowledge from previous chapters.

Previous questions | Answers

#	Previous questions	Answers
1	Where are metals and non-metals located on the Periodic Table?	metals to the left, non-metals to the right
2	Why does the reactivity of the alkali metals increase down the group?	they are larger atoms, so the outermost electron is further from the nucleus, meaning there are weaker electrostatic forces of attraction and more shielding between the nucleus and outer electron, and it is easier to lose the electron
3	How are covalent bonds formed?	by atoms sharing electrons
4	How do the melting points of the noble gases change down the group?	increase (higher melting point)
5	Why are metals good conductors of electricity?	they contain delocalised electrons that are free to move through the whole structure
6	What is an ionic bond?	bond formed by the transfer of electrons from a metal atom to a non-metal atom
7	Why are alkali metals named this?	they are metals that react with water to form an alkali

Required practical skills

Practise answering questions on the required practicals using the example below. You need to be able to apply your skills and knowledge to other practicals too.

Making salts	Worked example	Practice
This required practical tests whether you can safely separate and purify a chemical mixture, to produce a salt. You will need to be able to describe the uses of filtration, evaporation, and crystallisation to make pure, dry samples of soluble salts. Exam questions can ask about the production of any salt, not just the examples you are familiar with. You should also be able to describe how substances can be tested for purity.	A salt is formed when an acid reacts with a base. **1** Write a word equation for the production of magnesium nitrate. magnesium carbonate + nitric acid → magnesium nitrate + water + carbon dioxide **2** Identify one hazard of working with sulfuric acid, and describe two ways to prevent this hazard. Concentrated sulfuric acid is corrosive, so can cause burns. To prevent any hazards, eye protection should be worn at all times and dilute sulfuric acid should be used.	**1** Describe the colour changes that occur when copper oxide is mixed with sulfuric acid. **2** A student made a sample of copper sulfate by reacting copper oxide with sulfuric acid. After evaporating the copper sulfate solution and leaving it to crystallise, the student found two different crystals in the basin. Small white crystals formed around the edges and larger blue crystals formed in the middle. Name the two types of crystal. **3** The student used filter paper in the production of their copper sulfate sample. Describe the function of the filter paper.

C6 Retrieval

Practice

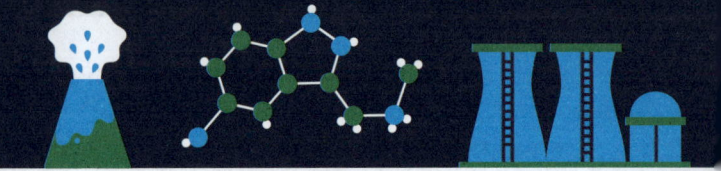

Exam-style questions

01 A student investigated the reaction between an acid and an alkali.

The student put 25 cm³ of sodium hydroxide into a beaker. Sodium hydroxide is an alkali. They added hydrochloric acid to the sodium hydroxide in the beaker, 1 cm³ at a time.

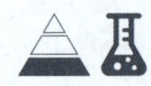

After each addition of hydrochloric acid the student measured the pH of the solution.

01.1 Suggest how the student measured the pH of the solution. **[1 mark]**

_____

> **Exam Tip**
> There are several correct answers here – think about methods you might have used during class practicals.

01.2 Draw **one** line from each solution to its correct pH. **[2 marks]**

Solution	pH
	1
hydrochloric acid	
	7
sodium hydroxide	
	14

01.3 After 25 cm³ of hydrochloric acid was added to the sodium hydroxide, the pH of the solution was 7.

What type of reaction has occurred between the sodium hydroxide and hydrochloric acid? **[1 mark]**

Tick **one** box.

- combustion ☐
- oxidation ☐
- neutralisation ☐
- reduction ☐

01.4 Choose the correct words from the box to complete the sentences. **[2 marks]**

| hydroxide ions | hydrogen ions | water |

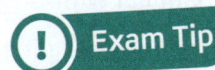

> **Exam Tip**
> Each word is only used once – cross each off after you've used it.

Acidic solutions contain lots of _____ that have the symbol H^+.

Alkaline solutions have lots of _____ that have the formula OH^-.

When an acid and an alkali react together they produce

_____.

C6 Chemical reactions

Paper 3 — C6

01.5 Draw **one** line from each acid to the salt it produces. **[3 marks]**

Acid — **Salt**

Acids: hydrochloric acid, nitric acid, sulfuric acid

Salts: hydrochloride, nitrate, sulfide, chloride, nitride, sulfate

> **Exam Tip**
> The names of the salts only change a little from the name of the acid.

02 Iron is found naturally as iron(III) oxide. To obtain pure iron, iron(III) oxide is reacted with carbon.

02.1 Identify whether the iron is oxidised or reduced. Give **one** reason for your answer. **[2 marks]**

_____
_____
_____

02.2 Balance the symbol equation for the extraction of iron from iron(III) oxide. **[1 mark]**

_____ Fe_2O_3 + _____ C → _____ Fe + _____ CO_2

02.3 Explain why you do not need to react gold with carbon to obtain pure gold. **[2 marks]**

_____
_____
_____

03 A student made pure crystals of copper sulfate by reacting copper oxide powder with sulfuric acid.

03.1 Copper oxide comes with the safety warnings shown in **Figure 1**. Identify the hazard that each sign represents. **[3 marks]**

Figure 1

C6 Practice 235

03.2 **Figure 2** shows the measuring cylinder the student used to measure out the sulfuric acid.

Give the volume of sulfuric acid the student used. **[1 mark]**

Figure 2

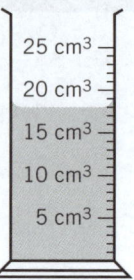

25 cm³
20 cm³
15 cm³
10 cm³
5 cm³

Exam Tip

The surface of the liquid is curved – this is called the meniscus. Remember what part of the meniscus you need to read from.

03.3 Both copper oxide and copper sulfate can cause serious eye damage. Give **two** precautions the student should follow when reacting copper oxide and sulfuric acid. **[2 marks]**

03.4 The student poured the reaction mixture into an evaporating dish and heated it using a blue flame from a Bunsen burner. Suggest a safer method to evaporate the reaction mixture. **[1 mark]**

04 This question is about the reactivity series.

04.1 Draw **one** line from each metal to the correct method of obtaining the pure metal. **[1 mark]**

Metal	Method to obtain pure metal
aluminium	electrolysis
gold	reduction with carbon
iron	found as pure metal

Exam Tip

You have to learn the reactivity series for your exam. There are many fun phrases to help you with this. Pick one that you'll remember, or make up your own.

04.2 Copper is often found as a compound called copper oxide.
Name the element bonded to copper in copper oxide. **[1 mark]**

04.3 Pure copper is produced by reacting copper oxide with carbon.
Choose the correct words from the box to complete the word equation for the reaction. **[2 marks]**

| carbon | carbon dioxide | oxygen |

copper oxide + _____ → copper + _____

Exam Tip

You can still gain marks in **04.4** by identifying whether copper is oxidised or reduced, even if you can't explain why. Always try to answer the parts of questions that you know, even if you can't answer them fully.

04.4 Identify whether the copper is oxidised or reduced.
Circle **one** answer.

        oxidised   reduced

Give a reason for your answer. **[2 marks]**

05 This question is about the reactivity series.

05.1 Which of these pairs of substances react together in a displacement reaction? Choose **one** answer. **[1 mark]**

zinc and magnesium chloride solution

zinc and copper chloride solution

iron and zinc sulfate solution

iron and magnesium sulfate solution

Exam Tip

Identify which metal from each pair is the most reactive.

236   C6 Chemical reactions

05.2 Name the gas formed when sodium reacts with water. **[1 mark]**

05.3 Lithium also reacts with water. Does lithium react more vigorously or less vigorously with water than sodium?
Circle **one** answer. **[1 mark]**

more vigorously   less vigorously

05.4 Lithium is added to a solution of copper chloride.
Name the substances formed. **[1 mark]**

05.5 Use your answers to **05.1** through **05.4** to put copper, lithium, sodium, and zinc in order of reactivity. **[3 marks]**

most reactive   least reactive

_____ > _____ > _____ > _____

06 This question is about the formation of salts.

06.1 Complete the following word equations to show the formations of different salts. **[3 marks]**

sulfuric acid + magnesium hydroxide → _____ + _____

calcium + _____ → calcium chloride + _____

_____ + nitric acid → potassium _____ + hydrogen

06.2 Calcium carbonate, $CaCO_3$, reacts with sulfuric acid, H_2SO_4, to produce calcium sulfate, $CaSO_4$, and two other products. Complete the balanced symbol equation for this reaction. **[2 marks]**

$CaCO_3$ + _____ → $CaSO_4$ + _____ + _____

06.3 Name the salt produced when sodium hydroxide reacts with sulfuric acid. **[1 mark]**

06.4 A student added sodium hydroxide to sulfuric acid 1 cm³ at a time. After each addition, they recorded the pH of the solution. **Figure 3** shows their results.

Figure 3

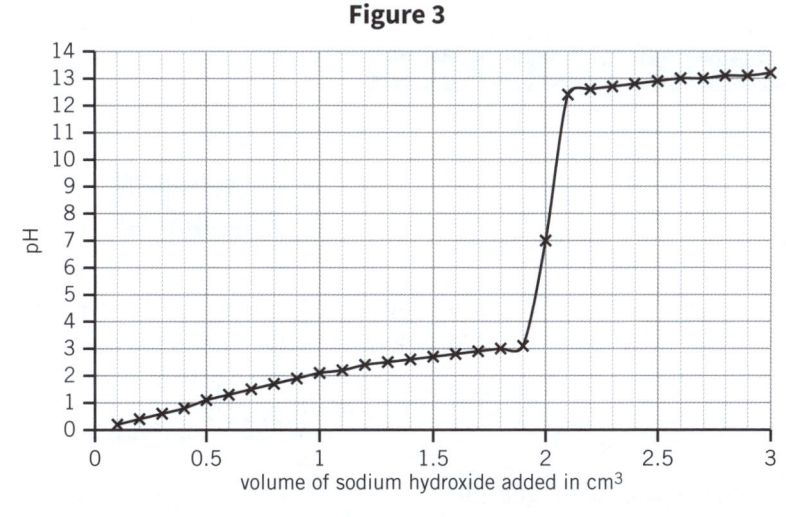

Determine the volume of sodium hydroxide that produced a neutral pH. **[1 mark]**

> **Exam Tip**
>
> Look back at the general equations for the formation of different salts to help you work out the product and reactants.

> **Exam Tip**
>
> Start by adding in the formula for sulfuric acid, then work out the rest of the products from the relevant salt equation.

> **Exam Tip**
>
> Draw lines on the graph to show you working, this will help prevent mistakes and show the examiner you know what you're doing!

07 A student wants to make pure crystals of a soluble salt by reacting zinc oxide with hydrochloric acid.

07.1 Complete the sentence. [1 mark]

A soluble salt _____ in water.

07.2 Name a piece of equipment the student can use to measure 10 g of zinc oxide. [1 mark]

07.3 Which piece of equipment in **Figure 4** is most appropriate to measure 50 cm³ of hydrochloric acid? Choose **one** answer. [1 mark]

Figure 4

A   B   C   D

> **Exam Tip**
>
> Preparing a pure salt is one of your required practicals. You should remember doing a practical similar to this. Try to remember what equipment you used and the method you carried out.

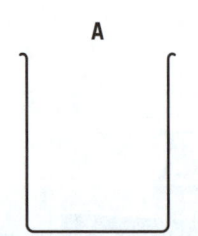

07.4 After mixing the zinc oxide and hydrochloric acid together, the student passed the mixture through filter paper within a funnel. Describe why the student did this. [1 mark]

07.5 Name the salt produced in this reaction. Choose **one** answer. [1 mark]

zinc chloride   zinc hydrochloride
zinc chlorine   zinc hydrochloric

07.6 Complete the word equation for the reaction between zinc oxide and hydrochloric acid. [1 mark]

zinc oxide + hydrochloric acid → _____ + _____

08 A student carried out a series of reactions to determine the order of reactivity of four metals. **Table 1** shows their results.

Table 1

Metal	Reaction with water	Reaction with acid
A	no reaction	slow reaction
B	no reaction	rapid reaction
C	rapid reaction	rapid reaction
D	rusts slowly	slow reaction

> **Exam Tip**
>
> You will need to consider the reactions of each metal with water and the reactions of each with acid to work this out.

08.1 Use the data in **Table 1** to put the metals in order of reactivity. One has been done for you. [2 marks]

most reactive   least reactive

C > _____ > _____ > _____

08.2 One of the metals is magnesium. When a piece of magnesium ribbon is added to acid, bubbles form slowly on the surface of the metal. Magnesium does not react with water.

Identify which metal from **Table 1** is magnesium. [1 mark]

238 C6 Chemical reactions

08.3 One of the metals is sodium. Sodium reacts violently with water, and the reaction between sodium and acid is too violent to carry out in a school. Identify which metal in **Table 1** is sodium. [1 mark]

08.4 When sodium reacts with water it loses an electron. Draw the dot and cross diagram of the ion formed when sodium reacts with water. [1 mark]

08.5 Write a balanced symbol equation for the reaction between sodium and water. [2 marks]

Exam Tip
Write out the complete symbol equation first, then balance it after.

08.6 Calcium reacts slowly with cold water. Explain the difference in reactivity between sodium and calcium. [2 marks]

09 This question is about reactions of magnesium.

09.1 Which of these metals has the greatest tendency to form positive ions? Choose **one** answer. [1 mark]

iron   lithium   magnesium   zinc

09.2 Name the product formed in the reaction between magnesium and oxygen. [1 mark]

09.3 Identify whether magnesium is oxidised or reduced in the reaction in **09.2**. Give a reason for your answer. [2 marks]

09.4 Magnesium cannot be extracted from the compound formed in **09.2** by reaction with carbon. Explain why. [2 marks]

10 This question is about the pH scale. A student measured the pH of some solutions. **Table 2** shows the results the student obtained.

Table 2

Solution	pH
A	7
B	2
C	10
D	5
E	12

10.1 Name **two** ways of measuring the pH of a solution. [2 marks]

10.2 Give the letter of the neutral solution. [1 mark]

10.3 Give the letter of the most alkaline solution. [1 mark]

10.4 Give the letter of the solution that has the highest concentration of hydrogen ions, H^+. [1 mark]

Exam Tip
Remember, pH is a measure of the number of H^+ ions in a solution.

10.5 Some alkali is added to solution **A**. Write whether the pH increases, decreases, or stays the same. [1 mark]

Knowledge

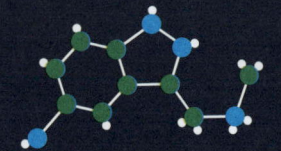

C7 Electrolysis

Electrolysis

In the process of **electrolysis**, an electric current is passed through an **electrolyte**. An electrolyte is a liquid or solution that contains ions and so can conduct electricity. This causes the ions to move to the **electrodes**, where they form pure elements.

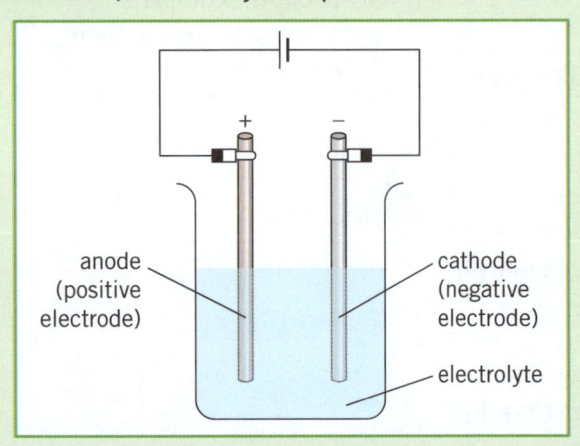

- anode (positive electrode)
- cathode (negative electrode)
- electrolyte

Electrolysis of molten compounds

Solid ionic compounds do not conduct electricity as the ions cannot move.

To undergo electrolysis they must be molten or dissolved, so the ions are free to move.

When an ionic compound is molten:

- The positive metal ions are *attracted* to the **cathode**, where they will *gain* electrons to form the pure metal.
- The negative non-metal ions are *attracted* to the **anode**, where they will *lose* electrons and become the pure non-metal.

For example, molten sodium chloride, NaCl, can undergo electrolysis to form

- sodium at the cathode
- chlorine at the anode.

Electrolysis of aqueous solutions

Solid ionic compounds can also undergo electrolysis when dissolved in water.

- It requires less energy to dissolve ionic compounds in water than it does to melt them.
- However, in the electrolysis of solutions, the pure elements are not always produced. This is because the water can also undergo ionisation:

$$H_2O(l) \rightarrow H^+(aq) + OH^-(aq)$$

Revision tip

Remember In an exam, don't PANIC.

Here is an easy way to remember which electrode is which:

Positive
Anode
Negative
Is
Cathode

Reactivity series (most reactive to least reactive):
potassium, sodium, calcium, magnesium, aluminium, **(carbon)**, zinc, iron, tin, lead, **(hydrogen)**, copper, silver, gold, platinum

Products at the anode

In the electrolysis of a solution:

- If the non-metal contains oxygen, then oxygen gas is formed at the anode.
- If the non-metal ion is a halogen, then the halogen gas is formed at the anode.

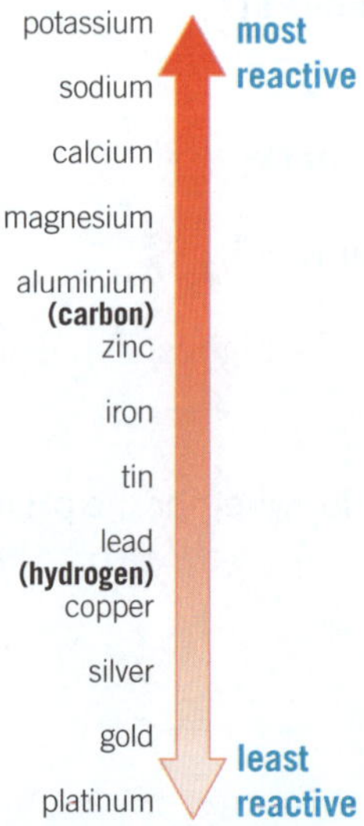

Products at the cathode

In the electrolysis of a solution, if the metal is *more* **reactive** than hydrogen then hydrogen gas is formed at the cathode. The metal ions remain in solution.

Key terms

Make sure you can write a definition for these key terms.

| anode | cathode | cryolite | electrode |

240   C7 Electrolysis

Electrolysis of aluminium oxide

Electrolysis can be used to extract metals from their ionic compounds.

Electrolysis is used if the metal is *more* reactive than carbon.

Aluminium is extracted from aluminium oxide by electrolysis.
1. The aluminium oxide is mixed with a substance called **cryolite**, which lowers the melting point.
2. The mixture is then heated until it is molten.
3. The resulting molten mixture undergoes electrolysis.

   aluminium oxide → aluminium + oxygen

   $2Al_2O_3(l)$ → $4Al(l)$ + $3O_2(g)$

   cathode: pure aluminium is formed

   anode: oxygen is formed

In the electrolysis of aluminium, the anode is made of graphite (carbon).

The graphite reacts with the oxygen to form carbon dioxide and so slowly wears away. It therefore needs to be replaced frequently.

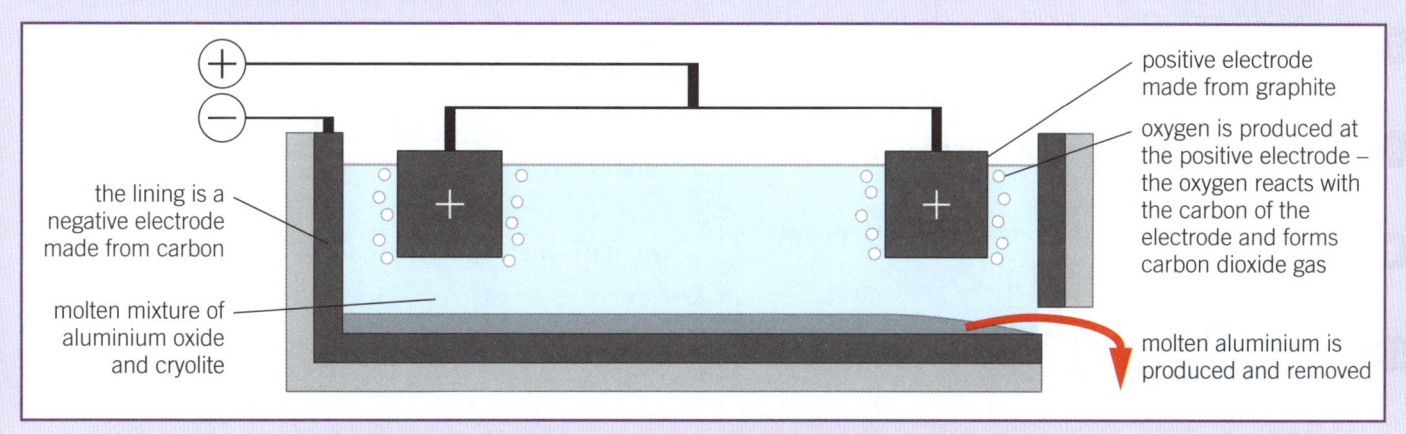

Revision tip

Practice The electrolysis of aluminium oxide is a great six mark question, but you may also be asked about the electrolysis of different molten compounds or aqueous solutions.

Make sure you understand the process of electrolysis, the relevant key words, and the products formed at the negative and positive electrodes.

electrolysis   electrolyte   reactivity

Retrieval

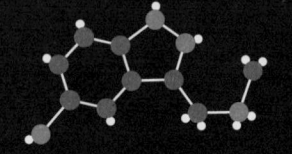

Learn the answers to the questions below, then cover the answers column with a piece of paper and write as many as you can. Check and repeat.

C7 questions | Answers

#	Question	Answer
1	What is electrolysis?	the process of using electricity to extract elements from a compound
2	What is the name of the positive electrode?	anode
3	What is the name of the negative electrode?	cathode
4	What is an electrolyte?	a liquid or solution that contains ions and so can conduct electricity
5	Where are metals formed?	cathode
6	Where are non-metals formed?	anode
7	How can ionic substances be electrolysed?	by melting or dissolving them, and then passing a direct current through them
8	Why can solid ionic substances not be electrolysed?	they do not conduct electricity, or the ions cannot move
9	In the electrolysis of solutions, when is the metal *not* produced at the cathode?	when the metal is more reactive than hydrogen
10	In the electrolysis of a metal halide solution, what is produced at the anode?	halogen gas
11	In the electrolysis of a metal sulfate solution, what is produced at the anode?	oxygen
12	What is the equation for the ionisation of water?	$H_2O(l) \rightarrow H^+(aq) + OH^-(aq)$
13	What metals are extracted from ionic compounds by using electrolysis?	metals that are more reactive than carbon
14	In the electrolysis of aluminium oxide, why is the aluminium oxide mixed with cryolite?	to lower the melting point
15	In the electrolysis of aluminium oxide, what are the anodes made of?	graphite
16	In the electrolysis of aluminium oxide, why do the anodes need to be replaced?	they react with the oxygen being formed

C7 Electrolysis

C7

Now go back and use the questions below to check your knowledge from previous chapters.

Previous questions / Answers

#	Previous questions	Answers
1	What are the names and formulae of the three main acids?	hydrochloric acid, HCl; sulfuric acid, H_2SO_4; nitric acid, HNO_3
2	How are metals less reactive than carbon extracted from their oxides?	reduction with carbon
3	In terms of pH, what is an acid?	a solution with a pH of less than 7
4	In terms of oxygen, what is reduction?	loss of oxygen
5	How do you measure the pH of a substance?	universal indicator or pH probe
6	What is the equation for a neutralisation reaction between an acid and an alkali?	$H^+(aq) + OH^-(aq) \rightarrow H_2O(l)$
7	How can you obtain a solid salt from a solution?	crystallisation
8	Why is gold found naturally as an element in the Earth's crust?	gold is very unreactive
9	In terms of pH, what is a neutral solution?	a solution with a pH of 7

Required practical skills

Practise answering questions on the required practicals using the example below. You need to be able to apply your skills and knowledge to other practicals too.

Electrolysis	Worked example	Practice
You need to be able to describe the method of electrolysis, and label the experimental set-up for electrolysis. Electrolysis uses electricity to break ionic compounds down into simpler compounds or elements. Metals or hydrogen are made at the negative electrode, and non-metal molecules are made at the positive electrode. You will need to be able to apply the principles of electrolysis to any example, as many solutions can undergo electrolysis. This includes predicting the products of electrolysis for different solutions, identifying which ions move to each electrode, and writing equations for the reactions at the two electrodes.	The electrolysis of aqueous sodium chloride gives three products. Identify these products and state how we can test for them. The three products are chlorine gas, Cl_2, hydrogen gas, H_2, and sodium hydroxide solution, NaOH. To test for hydrogen gas, collect the gas in a test tube and insert a glowing splint – it should burn with a squeaky pop noise. To test for chlorine gas, collect the gas in a test tube and insert damp litmus paper – the litmus paper will bleach white. Sodium hydroxide can be tested for using universal indicator – the solution will turn purple as sodium hydroxide is an alkali.	1 State what you would observe at each electrode during the electrolysis of copper(II) chloride. 2 Give the products of the electrolysis of sodium sulfate. 3 Explain why the electrodes must not touch each other during electrolysis.

C7 Retrieval 243

Practice

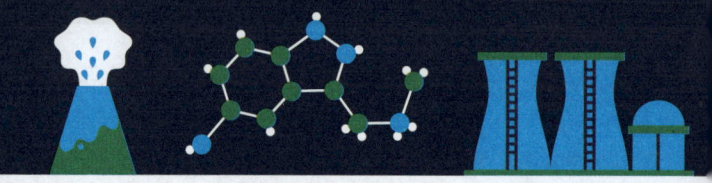

Exam-style questions

01 **Figure 1** shows the electrolysis of molten sodium chloride.

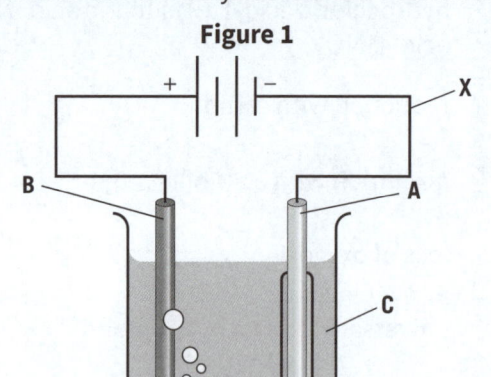

Figure 1

01.1 Identify parts **A–C**. Choose the correct words from the box.

[3 marks]

| anode | cathode | cryolite | electrolyte |

A _____

B _____

C _____

01.2 Identify the substance made at each electrode in **Figure 1**.

Draw **one** line from each electrode to the correct substance. [2 marks]

Electrode   **Substance formed**

A   chlorine

B   sodium

                          water

> **Exam Tip**
> Think about the charge of the ions produced – they will be attracted to the electrode with the opposite charge.

01.3 Why was molten sodium chloride used and not solid sodium chloride? [1 mark]

Tick **one** box.

It requires less energy to electrolyse molten sodium chloride compared to solid sodium chloride. ☐

Ions are not free to move in solid sodium chloride. ☐

Sodium chloride is a liquid at room temperature. ☐

244 C7 Electrolysis

Paper 3 C7

01.4 A student adds a bulb to the circuit at the place labelled **X**. Describe what the student would observe. **[1 mark]**

_____

_____

02 A student investigated how the potential difference in a circuit influenced the rate of bubbles given off at the positive electrode. They used copper chloride as the electrolyte and chlorine gas was released.

02.1 Identify the independent variable and the dependent variable. **[2 marks]**

Independent variable: _____

Dependent variable: _____

02.2 The student's results are given in **Table 1**.

Table 1

Potential difference in V	Number of bubbles produced in 2 minutes
1	43
2	59
3	94
4	136
5	

Give the range for the potential difference in **Table 1**. **[1 mark]**

_____

> **Exam Tip**
> This is one area where there is a difference in what is required in maths and science. In maths, the range is a single value; in science, it is given as the lowest value to the highest value.

02.3 The teacher said that the student could not carry out the experiment at 5 V as the experiment was too dangerous. Suggest why. **[2 marks]**

_____

_____

_____

02.4 The student counted the number of bubbles released in 2 minutes. Suggest an improvement to the method that would increase the accuracy of the experiment. **[1 mark]**

_____

_____

> **Exam Tip**
> This is similar to the photosynthesis experiment in biology. Think about the equipment you might use in that experiment.

03 Aluminium oxide, Al_2O_3, is an ionic compound that undergoes electrolysis to extract pure aluminium. **Figure 2** shows the set-up for the electrolysis of aluminium oxide.

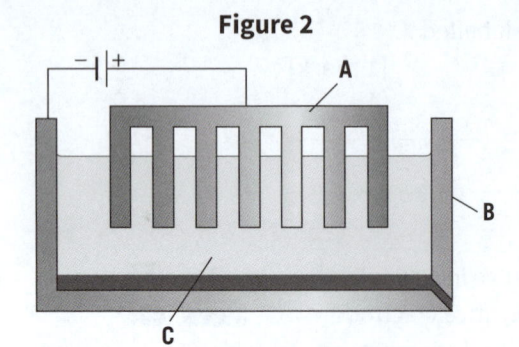

Figure 2

03.1 Identify the **two** elements in aluminium oxide. [1 mark]

03.2 On **Figure 2** draw an arrow where the pure aluminium is removed from. [1 mark]

03.3 Name the element that the electrodes are made of. [1 mark]

03.4 Explain why the electrodes have to be continually replaced. [3 marks]

03.5 Give the letter of the negative electrode. [1 mark]

03.6 Cryolite is added to the aluminium oxide mixture before electrolysis. Explain why. [3 marks]

> **Exam Tip**
> This doesn't look like the traditional set-up for electrolysis, nor does it look like the diagram from the knowledge organiser. The diagrams in your exam will not be the same as those you've come across in your studies, so you need to be confident identifying the different parts.

04 A student carries out the electrolysis of aqueous copper chloride and sodium chloride.

04.1 Identify the type of bonding in copper chloride and sodium chloride. [1 mark]

04.2 Both copper chloride and sodium chloride produce bubbles when undergoing electrolysis.
Identify the electrode that the bubbles will appear at.
Circle **one** answer. [1 mark]

anode   cathode

04.3 Name the gas produced in the electrolysis of aqueous copper chloride. [1 mark]

> **Exam Tip**
> Chloride ions are negatively charged. They will be attracted to the positively charged electrode.

05 Aluminium is manufactured by electrolysis.

05.1 Suggest why reduction with carbon is not an appropriate method to manufacture aluminium. [1 mark]

05.2 Name the element the cathode is made of in the electrolysis of aluminium. [1 mark]

C7 Electrolysis

05.3 A mixture of aluminium oxide and cryolite forms the electrolyte. Explain the purpose of the cryolite. **[3 marks]**

05.4 Explain why aluminium is produced at the cathode, and not the anode. **[2 marks]**

05.5 In the electrolysis of aluminium oxide, explain why the anode has to be replaced regularly. **[2 marks]**

> **Exam Tip**
>
> The electrolysis of aluminium oxide is a common topic for exams so make sure you know the method well.

06 Lead bromide is an ionic compound that can undergo electrolysis. Molten lead bromide can form the ions Pb^{2+} and Br^-.

06.1 Complete the sentences. **[2 marks]**

When an electric current passes through molten lead bromide:

The Pb^{2+} ions move to the _____.

The Br^- ions move to the _____.

06.2 Name the two substances formed in the electrolysis of molten lead bromide.

Choose **one** pair of answers. **[1 mark]**

anode	cathode
oxygen	hydrogen
oxygen	lead
bromine	hydrogen
bromine	lead

06.3 Give **one** observation you would see during the electrolysis of molten lead bromide. **[1 mark]**

> **Exam Tip**
>
> An observation is what you would see. This is a one mark 'give' question, so your answer only needs to be brief.

07 A student wanted to carry out an electrolysis experiment on potassium sulfate.

07.1 Describe the method the student should use to carry out the electrolysis of potassium sulfate.

Include a labelled diagram of the apparatus you would use. **[6 marks]**

07.2 Explain what the student would observe at the anode. **[2 marks]**

07.3 Another student carried out an electrolysis experiment on copper sulfate.

Describe what the student would observe at the cathode in the electrolysis of copper sulfate solution.

Explain why this is different from what the student would observe at the cathode in the electrolysis of potassium sulfate. **[4 marks]**

> **Exam Tip**
>
> Remember to clearly label anything you include in your diagram.

08 A chemist has three magnesium salts (**Table 2**).

Table 2

Magnesium salt	Chemical formula	Melting point in °C
magnesium chloride		714.0
magnesium nitrate	$Mg(NO_3)_2$	88.9
magnesium phosphate	$Mg_3(PO_4)_2$	1184.0

08.1 Complete **Table 2** by writing the chemical formula for magnesium chloride. **[1 mark]**

08.2 The chemist wants to extract magnesium metal from one of the salts using electrolysis.

Identify which salt is the most suitable. Explain your answer. **[6 marks]**

08.3 Name the electrode at which the magnesium metal is produced. **[1 mark]**

> **Exam Tip**
> **Table 2** includes the salt melting points, suggesting this is important to consider in your answer.

09 Molten zinc chloride is electrolysed using inert electrodes.

09.1 Name the electrode that positively-charged ions move towards during electrolysis. **[1 mark]**

09.2 Give the products at the anode and cathode in the electrolysis of molten zinc chloride.

Choose **one** pair of answers. **[1 mark]**

anode	cathode
zinc	chlorine
chlorine	zinc
zinc	hydrogen
chlorine	hydrogen

09.3 Explain why solid zinc chloride cannot be used for electrolysis. **[3 marks]**

09.4 The symbol equation for the electrolysis of molten zinc chloride is

$ZnCl_2(\_\_\_\_) \rightarrow Zn(\_\_\_\_) + Cl_2(\_\_\_\_)$

Complete the symbol equation by adding state symbols. **[1 mark]**

> **Exam Tip**
> Remember, in this question the zinc chloride is molten.

10 Potash is an ore that contains potassium. Anglesite is an ore containing lead. Both potash and anglesite are mined as rocks from the ground.

10.1 Define the term ore. **[1 mark]**

10.2 Suggest which metal ore should be extracted using electrolysis. **[1 mark]**

10.3 Potassium was not discovered until 1807, whereas lead has been used since ancient times. Suggest why. **[1 mark]**

11 This question is about chromatography experiments.

11.1 Give **two** uses of chromatography. **[2 marks]**

11.2 A student has a mixture of coloured liquids. The student thinks that the mixture contains three different substances dissolved in water.

Sketch the chromatogram the student would see if there are three substances dissolved in water.

Label the sample and the solvent front. **[2 marks]**

11.3 The student carried out a chromatography experiment to identify whether the mixture contains three substances. They used water as the solvent. The student's chromatogram showed that the mixture contained only one substance dissolved in water.

Name **one** method the student could use to separate the substance from the water. **[1 mark]**

11.4 Explain how to distinguish a pure substance from an impure substance, other than using chromatography. **[2 marks]**

> **Exam Tip**
>
> Students sometimes panic when they see something they don't recognise from the specification. Question **10** is a good example. Potash and anglesite are not in the specification, but metal ores are. Don't let the unfamiliar names put you off – you are expected to apply what you know.

> **Exam Tip**
>
> Don't forget to label everything in your diagram.

Knowledge

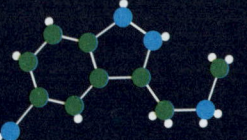

C8 Energy changes

Energy changes

During a chemical reaction, energy transfers occur. Energy can be transferred:
- to the surroundings – **exothermic**
- from the surroundings – **endothermic**

This energy transfer can cause a temperature change.

Energy is always conserved in chemical reactions. This means that there is the same amount of energy in the Universe at the start of a chemical reaction as at the end of the chemical reaction.

The surroundings

When chemists say energy is transferred from or to "the surroundings" they mean "everything that isn't the reaction".

For example, imagine you have a reaction mixture in a test tube. If you measure the temperature around the test tube using a thermometer, the thermometer is then part of the surroundings.
- If the thermometer records an increase in temperature, the reaction in the test tube is exothermic.
- If the thermometer records a decrease in temperature, the reaction in the test tube is endothermic.

Reaction profiles

A **reaction profile** shows whether a reaction is exothermic or endothermic.

The **activation energy** is the minimum amount of energy that particles must have to react when they collide.

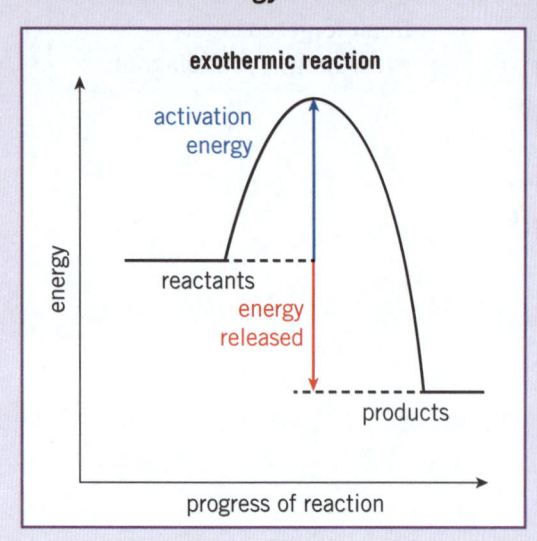

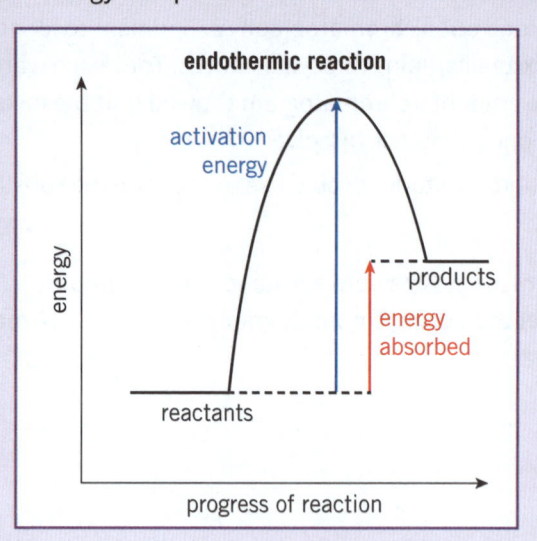

Exothermic and endothermic reactions

Reaction	Energy transfer	Temperature change	Example	Everyday use
exothermic	to the surroundings	temperature of the surroundings increases	• oxidation • combustion • neutralisation	• self-heating cans • hand warmers
endothermic	from the surroundings	temperature of the surroundings decreases	• thermal decomposition • citric acid and sodium hydrogen carbonate	• sports injury packs

Key terms

Make sure you can write a definition for these key terms.

activation energy   combustion   endothermic   exothermic
neutralisation   oxidation   reaction profile   thermal decomposition

Retrieval

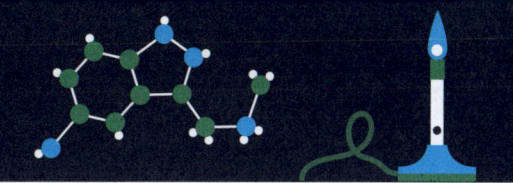

Learn the answers to the questions below, then cover the answers column with a piece of paper and write as many as you can. Check and repeat.

C8 questions | Answers

#	C8 questions	Answers
1	What is an exothermic energy transfer?	energy transfer to the surroundings
2	What is an endothermic energy transfer?	energy transfer from the surroundings
3	What is a reaction profile?	diagram showing how the energy changes in a reaction
4	What is the activation energy?	minimum amount of energy required before a collision will result in a reaction

Put paper here

Required practical skills

Practise answering questions on the required practicals using the example below. You need to be able to apply your skills and knowledge to other practicals too.

Temperature changes	Worked example	Practice
This practical tests your ability to accurately measure mass, temperature, and volume to investigate changes during chemical reactions. You should be able to describe how to measure temperature change after mixing a strong acid with a strong alkali. You also need to know • general equations for reactions of acids • how to determine the formula of ionic compounds from the charges of their ions • formulae of ions involved in neutralisation reactions.	Write a method to investigate how the volume of sodium hydroxide added to hydrochloric acid affects the temperature change of the reaction. Place a polystyrene cup inside a beaker. Pour 30 cm³ of dilute hydrochloric acid into the cup, place the lid on the cup and insert a thermometer through a hole in the cup. Record the temperature of the acid. Pour 5 cm³ sodium hydroxide solution into the cup and stir the solution. Record the highest temperature the reaction reaches on the thermometer. Repeat the experiment, increasing the amount of sodium hydroxide each time by 5 cm³, up to 40 cm³. Repeat the entire experiment two times to get repeat measurements.	1 Describe the function of the beaker in the experiment. 2 Is the reaction in this experiment exothermic or endothermic? Explain your answer. 3 Give a balanced equation for the reaction between sodium hydroxide and hydrochloric acid.

C8 Retrieval

Practice

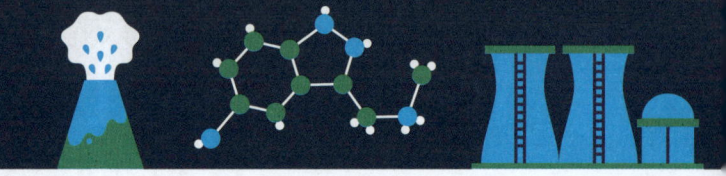

Exam-style questions

01 During a chemical reaction, energy is transferred.

01.1 Choose the correct words from the box to complete the sentences. You can use each word once, more than once, or not at all. **[4 marks]**

| conserved | exothermic | decrease | endothermic | increase |

A reaction that transfers energy to the surroundings is called an _____ reaction. The temperature of the surroundings will _____.

A reaction where energy is taken in from the surroundings is called an _____ reaction. The temperature of the surroundings will _____.

The total amount of energy is always _____ in a chemical reaction.

Exam Tip

These two sentences are opposites – the words missing from them will also be opposite to each other.

01.2 A neutralisation reaction transfers energy to the surroundings. Give one other reaction that transfers energy to the surroundings. **[1 mark]**

Tick **one** box.

citric acid and sodium hydrogencarbonate ☐

combustion ☐

thermal decomposition ☐

Exam Tip

Make sure you know the key examples of both exothermic and endothermic reactions.

01.3 Name **one** everyday use of reactions that transfer energy to the surroundings. **[1 mark]**

_____

02 A student investigated the energy transfers in the neutralisation of hydrochloric acid.

The student used the following method:
1. Add 25 cm³ of 36.5 g/dm³ hydrochloric acid to a beaker.
2. Measure the temperature of the acid.
3. Measure 25 cm³ of 40 g/dm³ sodium hydroxide and add to beaker.
4. Start the timer.
5. Measure the temperature of the solution every 15 seconds for 2 minutes.

252 C8 Energy changes

Paper 3 — C8

Table 1 shows their results.

Table 1

Time in s	Temperature in °C
0	25.0
15	25.3
30	25.7
45	26.0
60	26.2
75	26.4
90	26.5
105	26.5
120	26.5

02.1 Suggest a piece of equipment to measure the temperature change of the reaction. **[1 mark]**

_____

> **Exam Tip**
> There are a few different answers you could give, but you only need to suggest **one** piece of equipment.

02.2 Identify **one** safety precaution the student should take. **[1 mark]**

_____

02.3 Calculate the temperature change in the reaction. Give the unit of temperature. **[2 marks]**

Temperature change = _____

02.4 The student plotted their results on **Figure 1**.

Figure 1

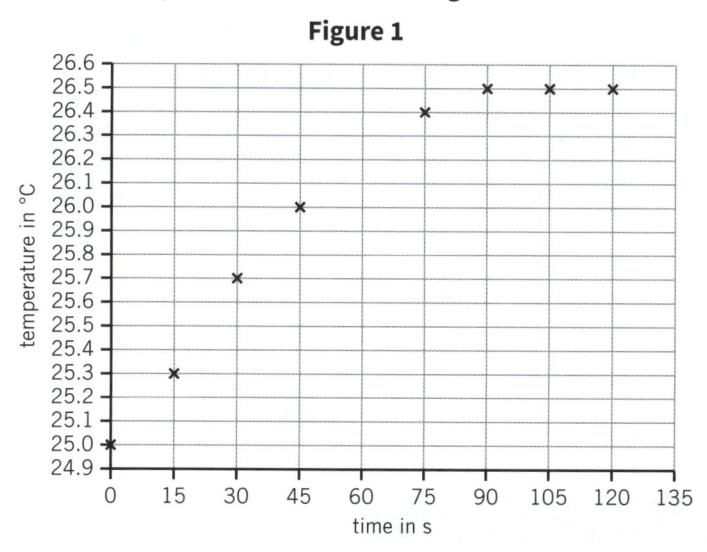

> **Exam Tip**
> When plotting the point on **Figure 1**, check that it fits with all the other data – it shouldn't be an outlier.

Complete **Figure 1** by plotting the point for 60 seconds. **[1 mark]**

02.5 Is the reaction exothermic or endothermic? Circle **one** answer.

            endothermic   exothermic

Give a reason for your answer.   **[2 marks]**

_____

03 Sport injuries are treated by putting a hot or cold pack onto the site of injury. A company is launching two new instant temperature packs – one hot and one cold. For each pack, you push a button and the temperature changes:
- The hot pack goes from room temperature (25 °C) to above 60 °C.
- The cold pack goes from room temperature (25 °C) to below 10 °C.

Each pack can only be used once and cannot be recycled.

03.1 Table 2 shows some data about each pack.

Identify which pack is the hot pack and which is the cold pack. **[1 mark]**

03.2 Determine how long pack **A** stayed at the desired temperature. **[1 mark]**

03.3 Which pack can be used at the desired temperature for the longest? **[1 mark]**

03.4 What type of reaction is used in pack **B** to produce the temperature change? Circle **one** answer. **[1 mark]**

Table 2

Time in minutes	Temperature in °C Pack A	Temperature in °C Pack B
0	25	25
5	66	4
10	66	3
15	66	4
20	66	3
25	65	4
30	64	9
35	66	12
40	65	15
45	59	18
50	55	21
55	51	25

           endothermic   exothermic

03.5 A sports club currently uses hot water bottles for injuries. When a player is injured, they boil some water in a kettle and pour it into the hot water bottle. The club also has some hot water bottles that they have filled with water and put in a freezer. The hot water bottles can be used many times.

Evaluate whether the club should switch to the new instant temperature packs or continue to use hot water bottles. **[6 marks]**

> **Exam Tip**
>
> Question **03** is testing your ability to interpret the data given in the table, your ability to apply what you know to an unfamiliar situation, and your working scientifically skills.

04 This question is about endothermic and exothermic reactions.

04.1 Tick **one** cell in the table to identify whether each reaction is endothermic or exothermic. **[4 marks]**

Reaction	Endothermic	Exothermic
citric acid and sodium hydrogencarbonate		
combustion		
neutralisation		
thermal decomposition		

254   C8 Energy changes

04.2 Which statement is true for an exothermic reaction? Choose **one** answer. [1 mark]

It transfers energy to the surroundings.

It transfers energy from the surroundings.

The energy of the products is higher than the energy of the reactants.

The temperature of the surroundings decreases.

> **Exam Tip**
> It can help if you replace the word energy with the word heat.

04.3 Iron oxide reacts with aluminium to produce aluminium oxide and iron. The reaction occurs at a high enough temperature that the iron produced is molten. Identify whether the reaction is exothermic or endothermic. [1 mark]

05 Some students dissolved four substances in water.

This is the method they used:

1 Transfer 100 cm^3 of water to a beaker.
2 Measure the temperature of the water.
3 Add 1 spatula measure of the substance, in powder form, to the water.
4 Measure the new temperature of the water.

Table 3 shows their results.

> **Exam Tip**
> This is one of the required practicals. Try to remember what you did in class when answering this question.

Table 3

Substance	Temperature of water at the start in °C	Temperature of solution immediately after dissolved in °C
A	20	25
B	21	17
C	21	31
D	22	6

05.1 Suggest the apparatus that could be used instead of a beaker to improve the validity of this experiment. Give a reason for your suggestion. [2 marks]

05.2 Suggest what the students should do between steps **3** and **4**. Give a reason for your suggestion. [2 marks]

> **Exam Tip**
> How could the results for the change in temperature be improved?

05.3 Give the letter of the substance that dissolves in the most endothermic process. [1 mark]

05.4 Predict how the temperature changes would alter if the students repeated the experiment using 200 cm^3 of water in step **1**. [1 mark]

06 A student wanted to compare the temperature changes when different metals reacted with hydrochloric acid. The student set up the apparatus shown in **Figure 2**.

Figure 2

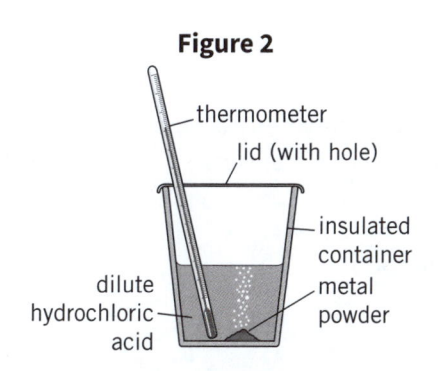

thermometer
lid (with hole)
insulated container
metal powder
dilute hydrochloric acid

For answers and more practice questions visit www.oxfordrevise.com/scienceanswers

Even more practice and interactive revision quizzes are available on kerboodle

06.1 Give the dependent variable in the investigation. [1 mark]

06.2 Give **two** control variables in the investigation. [2 marks]

06.3 **Table 4** shows the student's results.

Table 4

Metal	Temperature of acid at the start in °C	Temperature of the mixture immediately after reaction in °C	Temperature change in °C
magnesium	19.0	36.7	
zinc	19.5	25.6	
copper	20.4	20.4	0.0

Suggest a reason for the results for copper. [1 mark]

06.4 Complete the missing values in **Table 4**. [1 mark]

06.5 Identify which metal has the most exothermic reaction with hydrochloric acid. Give a reason for your answer. [2 marks]

> **Exam Tip**
> Compare the changes in temperature for the different metals in **Table 4**.

07 **Figure 3** shows the reaction profile of four reactions: **A**, **B**, **C**, and **D**. The reaction profiles are drawn to scale.

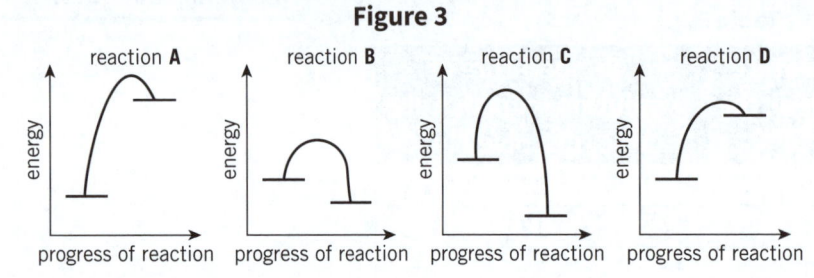

Figure 3

reaction **A**   reaction **B**   reaction **C**   reaction **D**

(energy vs progress of reaction graphs for each)

07.1 Give the letters of **two** reaction profiles that could show combustion reactions. [1 mark]

07.2 Give the letter of the reaction with the smallest activation energy. [1 mark]

07.3 Give the letter of the reaction that is most exothermic. [1 mark]

> **Exam Tip**
> Write endothermic or exothermic underneath each reaction profile in **Figure 3** to help you answer these questions.

08 This question is about the reaction between iron and oxygen.

08.1 Complete the word equation for the reaction. Choose the correct answer from the box. [1 mark]

| iron oxygen   iron oxide   oxygen ironide   oxygen iron |

iron + oxygen → _____

08.2 Identify what type of reaction occurs between iron and oxygen. Choose **one** answer. Give a reason for your answer. [2 marks]

combustion   oxidation
electrolysis   neutralisation

256 C8 Energy changes

08.3 Complete the following sentences. **[2 marks]**

A chemical reaction can only occur when the reacting particles _____ with sufficient energy.

The minimum amount of energy the particles must have is called the _____.

08.4 The temperature of the surroundings increases during the reaction between iron and oxygen. Identify whether this reaction is exothermic or endothermic. **[1 mark]**

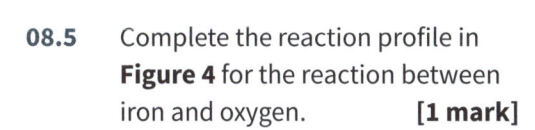

Figure 4

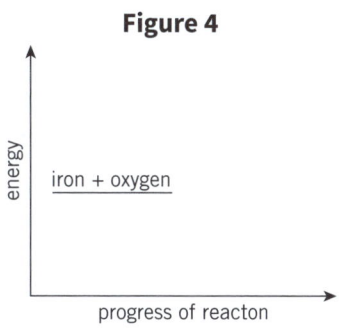

(graph: energy vs progress of reaction, with "iron + oxygen" labelled)

08.5 Complete the reaction profile in **Figure 4** for the reaction between iron and oxygen. **[1 mark]**

09 Two students mixed solutions of sulfuric acid and potassium hydroxide together and measured the resulting temperature change. Student **A** used a thermometer and student **B** used a data logger.

09.1 Suggest whether the thermometer or data logger gave the most accurate set of data. **[1 mark]**

09.2 Student **B** recorded the data shown in **Table 5**.

Table 5

	First test	Second test	Third test	Mean temperature change
Temperature change in °C	32.6	32.9	32.5	

Calculate the mean temperature change. Give your answer to one decimal place. **[2 marks]**

> **Exam Tip**
> The answer involves a recurring digit after the decimal point. Make sure you round this number correctly.

09.3 Student **A** says:

"We need to record the temperature as soon as we mix the solutions."

Student **B** thinks this is wrong and says:

"We need to wait until the temperature has reached its highest value before recording it."

Determine which student is correct. Give a reason for your answer. **[2 marks]**

09.4 The higher the temperature of a particle, the more energy the particle has. A third student carried out the experiment between sulfuric acid and potassium hydroxide at 5 °C. The student found that there was only a very small increase in the temperature. Suggest why the third student found this result. **[3 marks]**

> **Exam Tip**
> To answer this question you need to use ideas about rates of reaction.

Knowledge

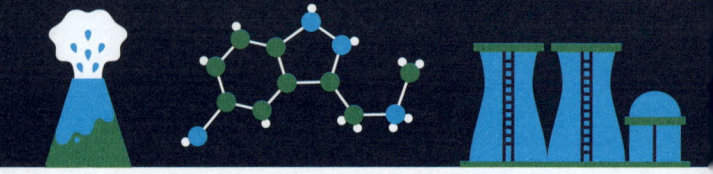

C9 Rate of reaction

Rates of reaction

The **rate of a reaction** is how quickly the reactants turn into the products.

To calculate the rate of a reaction, you can measure:

- how quickly a reactant is used up

  (L) mean rate of reaction = $\dfrac{\text{quantity of reactant used}}{\text{time taken}}$

- how quickly a product is produced.

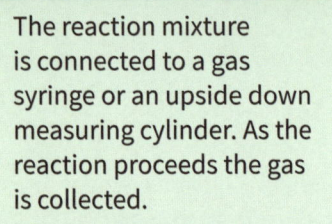

  (L) mean rate of reaction = $\dfrac{\text{quantity of product formed}}{\text{time taken}}$

For reactions that involve a gas, this can be done by measuring how the mass of the reaction changes or the volume of gas given off by the reaction.

Volume of gas produced

The reaction mixture is connected to a gas syringe or an upside down measuring cylinder. As the reaction proceeds the gas is collected.

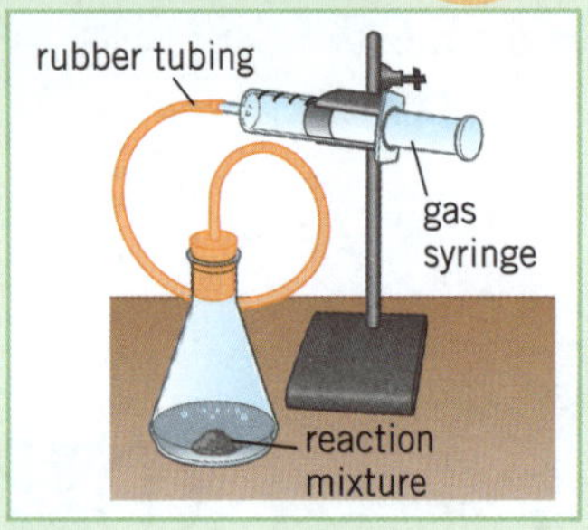

The rate for the reaction is then:

$$\text{rate} = \dfrac{\text{volume of gas produced}}{\text{time taken}}$$

Volume is measured in cm³ and time in seconds, so the unit for rate is cm³/s.

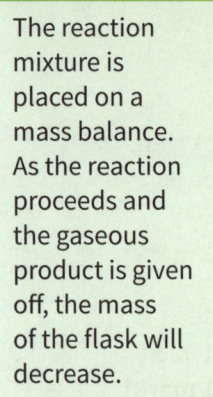

Change in turbidity or colour

Some reactions in solution produce an insoluble solid called a **precipitate**. The precipitate makes the solution go cloudy.

The reaction mixture is placed on a piece of white paper with a solid black cross drawn on.

You then time how long it takes from the addition of a reactant for the cross to no longer be visible.

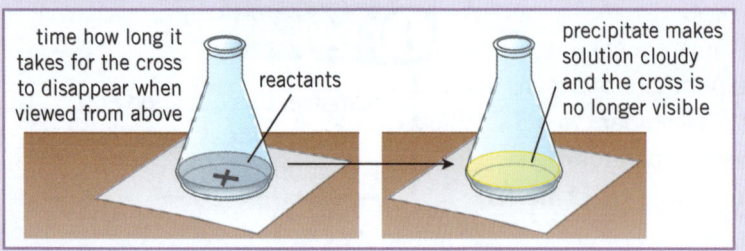

The shorter the time it takes for the cross to 'disappear', the faster the rate of the reaction.

Change in mass

The reaction mixture is placed on a mass balance. As the reaction proceeds and the gaseous product is given off, the mass of the flask will decrease.

The rate for the reaction is then:

$$\text{rate} = \dfrac{\text{change in the mass}}{\text{time taken}}$$

The mass is measured in grams and time is measured in seconds. Therefore, the unit of rate is g/s.

Calculating rate from graphs

The results from an experiment can be plotted on a graph.

- A steep gradient means a high rate of reaction – the reaction happens quickly.
- A shallow gradient means a low rate of reaction – the reaction happens slowly.

Mean rate between two points in time

To get the mean rate of reaction between two points in time:

mass at 100 seconds: 0.80 g
mass at 50 seconds: 0.56 g
change in mass: 0.80 − 0.56 = 0.24 g
change in time: 100 s − 50 s = 50 s

mean rate of reaction between 50 and 100 seconds = $\dfrac{0.24\,\text{g}}{50\,\text{s}} = 4.8 \times 10^{-3}$ g/s

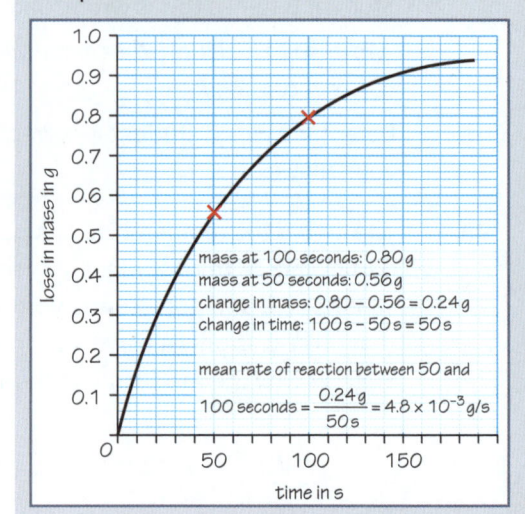

C9

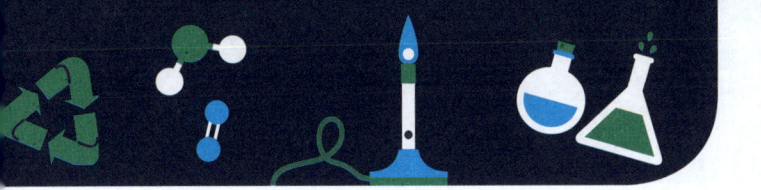

Collision theory

For a reaction to occur, the reactant particles need to collide. When the particles collide, they need to have enough energy to react or they will just bounce apart. This amount of energy is called the **activation energy**.

You can increase the rate of a reaction by:
- increasing the **frequency of collisions**
- increasing the energy of the particles when they collide.

Factors affecting rate of reaction

Condition that increases rate	How is this condition caused?	Why it has that effect
increasing the temperature	Heat the container in which the reaction is taking place.	1. Particles move faster, leading to more frequent collisions. 2. Particles have more energy, so more collisions result in a reaction. Note that these are two separate effects.
increasing the concentration of solutions	Use a solution with more solute in the same volume of solvent.	There are more reactant particles in the reaction mixture, so collisions become more frequent.
increasing the pressure of gases	Increase the number of gas particles you have in the container or make the container smaller.	Less space between particles means more frequent collisions.
increasing the surface area of solids	Cut the solid into smaller pieces, or grind it to create a powder, increasing the surface area. Larger pieces decrease the surface area.	Only reactant particles on the surface of a solid are able to collide and react. The greater the surface area the more reactant particles are exposed, leading to more frequent collisions.

Catalysts

Some reactions have specific substances called **catalysts** that can be added to increase the rate. These substances are not used up in the reaction.

A catalyst provides a different reaction pathway that has a lower activation energy. As such, more particles will collide with enough energy to react, so more collisions result in a reaction.

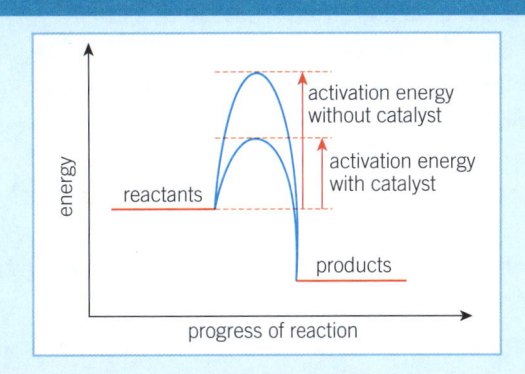

Key terms

Make sure you can write a definition for these key terms.

activation energy	catalyst	collision	collision theory
frequency of collision	gradient	precipitate	rate of reaction

C9 Knowledge 259

Retrieval

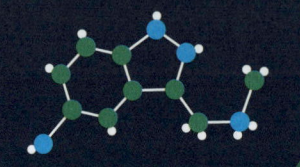

Learn the answers to the questions below, then cover the answers column with a piece of paper and write as many as you can. Check and repeat.

C9 questions / Answers

#	Question	Answer
1	What is the rate of a reaction?	how quickly reactants are used up or products are produced
2	What is the equation for calculating the mean rate of reaction?	mean rate = $\dfrac{\text{change in quantity of product or reactant}}{\text{time taken}}$
3	What is the unit for rate of reaction in a reaction involving a change in mass?	g/s
4	What is the unit for rate of reaction in a reaction involving a change in volume?	cm^3/s
5	How can you measure the rate of a reaction that produces a gas?	measure change in mass using a balance; measure volume of gas produced using a syringe or upside down measuring cylinder
6	What is a precipitate?	an insoluble solid in a solution
7	How can you measure the rate of a reaction that produces a precipitate?	measure how long it takes for a cross to disappear
8	What is the activation energy?	the minimum amount of energy colliding particles need to have before a reaction will take place
9	What effect does increasing concentration have on the rate of reaction?	increases
10	Why does increasing concentration have this effect?	more reactant particles in the same volume lead to more frequent collisions
11	What effect does increasing pressure have on the rate of reaction?	increases
12	Why does increasing pressure have this effect?	less space between particles means more frequent collisions
13	What effect does increasing surface area have on the rate of reaction?	increases
14	Why does increasing surface area have this effect?	more reactant particles are exposed and able to collide, leading to more frequent collisions
15	What effect does increasing temperature have on the rate of reaction?	increases
16	Why does increasing temperature have this effect?	particles move faster, leading to more frequent collisions – particles have the same activation energy, so more collisions result in a reaction
17	What is a catalyst?	a substance that increases the rate of a reaction but is not used up in the reaction
18	How do catalysts increase the rate of a reaction?	lower the activation energy of the reaction, so more collisions result in a reaction

C9 Rate of reaction

C9

Now go back and use the questions below to check your knowledge from previous chapters.

Previous questions / Answers

#	Previous questions	Answers
1	What is an exothermic energy transfer?	energy transfer to the surroundings
2	What is electrolysis?	the process of using electricity to extract elements from a compound
3	In terms of H^+ ions, what is an acid?	a substance that releases H^+ ions when dissolved in water
4	What is an electrolyte?	a liquid or solution that contains ions and so can conduct electricity
5	What are the products of a reaction between a metal hydroxide and an acid?	salt + water
6	What name is given to a list of metals ordered by their reactivity?	reactivity series
7	In the electrolysis of aluminium oxide, what are the anodes made of?	graphite
8	What force holds ionic compounds together?	strong electrostatic forces of attraction between oppositely-charged ions

Put paper here

Required practical skills

Practise answering questions on the required practicals using the example below. You need to be able to apply your skills and knowledge to other practicals too.

Rates of reaction

From this practical, you should be able to describe two ways in which the rate of a reaction can be measured. These are:

1. measuring the production of a gas
2. measuring changes in the colour or turbidity of a solution

You need to be able to describe the method for collecting gas with an inverted measuring cylinder, and for measuring the colour or turbidity change in a reaction.

There are different methods of measuring rates of reaction, but remember that these principles are applicable to all of them.

Worked example

Silver chloride is an insoluble salt that can be made in the following reaction. Suggest how the rate of this reaction could be measured.

$AgNO_3(aq) + NaCl(aq) \rightarrow NaNO_3(aq) + AgCl(s)$

The reactants are both colourless solutions. Solid silver chloride will form as a precipitate and make the solution appear cloudy.

One way of measuring the rate of the reaction is to look at the rate of production of silver chloride precipitate. This could be measured by placing the beaker with the reacting solution on a piece of white paper with a black cross printed on it, and measuring the time taken for the cross to disappear.

Practice

1. Give three factors that can affect the rate of a reaction.
2. Give two methods that can be used to determine the rate of a reaction where a gas is produced.
3. Suggest another method to measure the rate of the production of silver chloride precipitate.

C9 Retrieval 261

Practice

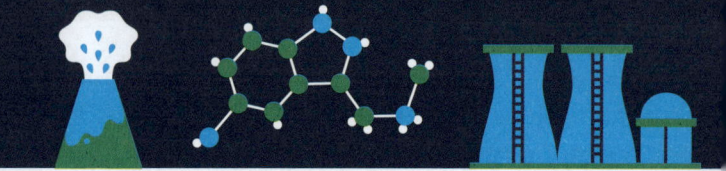

Exam-style questions

01 A student investigates the reaction between magnesium and hydrochloric acid. **Figure 1** shows their experimental set-up.

Figure 1

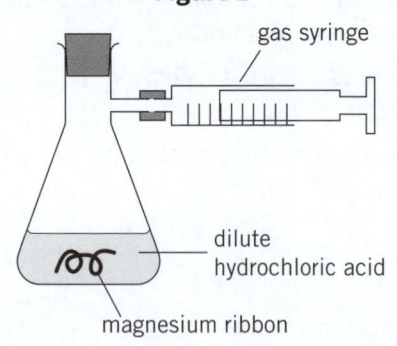

gas syringe
dilute hydrochloric acid
magnesium ribbon

01.1 Complete the balanced symbol equation by adding the correct state symbols. **[2 marks]**

Mg(_____) + 2HCl(_____) → MgCl$_2$(aq) + H$_2$(_____)

01.2 Which condition can affect the rate of the reaction between magnesium and hydrochloric acid? **[1 mark]**

Tick **one** answer.

mass of magnesium ribbon ☐

pressure of gas ☐

temperature ☐

volume of hydrochloric acid ☐

> **Exam Tip**
> A gas syringe is another way of collecting gas. As gas is produced the syringe gets fuller and the plunger is pushed out, showing how much gas has been collected. It is similar to using an inverted measuring cylinder in a water bath to collect gas.

> **Exam Tip**
> **Figure 1** gives you a lot of information to answer this question.

01.3 The student repeated the experiment using powdered magnesium. Their results are shown in **Table 1**.

Table 1

	Volume of gas produced in 1 minute in cm^3
magnesium ribbon	45
powdered magnesium	79

Write down the rate of reaction for magnesium ribbon in cm^3/s. **[1 mark]**

_____ cm^3/s

262 C9 Rate of reaction

Paper 4 **C9**

01.4 Use **Table 1** to determine whether the rate of reaction for the powdered magnesium was faster or slower than magnesium ribbon. Circle **one** answer.

faster   slower

Give a reason for your answer. **[2 marks]**

_____

_____

01.5 Another student investigated the reaction between magnesium and hydrochloric acid by measuring the decrease in mass.

Name the piece of equipment the student can use to measure the decrease in mass. **[1 mark]**

_____

02 Sulfuric acid reacts with sodium carbonate to form carbon dioxide, water, and a salt.

02.1 Write a word equation for the reaction between sulfuric acid and sodium carbonate. **[2 marks]**

_____

02.2 The student carried out the experiment twice – once each with 49 g/dm³ and 98 g/dm³ concentrations of sulfuric acid.

Which concentration of sulfuric acid will give the highest rate of reaction? **[1 mark]**

Circle **one** answer.

49 g/dm³   98 g/dm³

02.3 To determine the rate of reaction, the student measured the volume of carbon dioxide gas produced every minute for 10 minutes. Their results are shown on **Figure 2**.

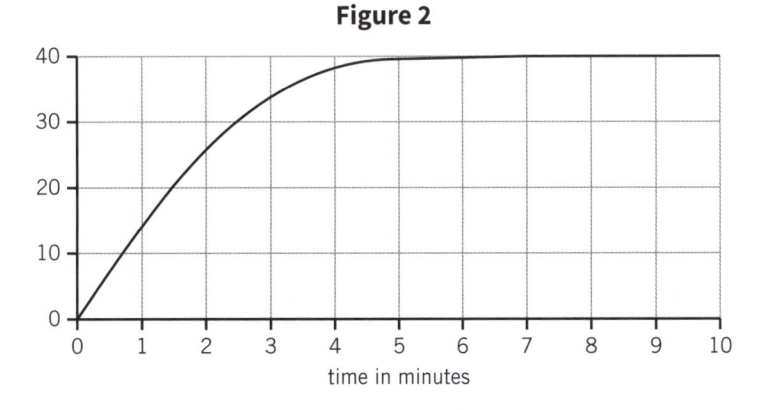

Figure 2

[Graph showing a curve rising steeply from 0 and levelling off at 40, with x-axis "time in minutes" from 0 to 10]

Suggest a suitable label for the *y*-axis in **Figure 2**. **[1 mark]**

02.4 **Figure 2** was produced using 49 g/dm³ sulfuric acid. Draw the line expected for 98 g/dm³ sulfuric acid. **[2 marks]**

> **Exam Tip**
> This is one of the general salt equations. It's really important that you are able to recall and apply these in an exam.

> **Exam Tip**
> Remember, the concentration of the acid affects the rate of the reaction, not how much of the carbon dioxide is produced.

For answers and more practice questions visit www.oxfordrevise.com/scienceanswers

Even more practice and interactive revision quizzes are available on kerboodle

C9 Practice

03 A student wanted to look at the rate of reaction between calcium carbonate and nitric acid. Their results are shown in **Table 2**.

Table 2

Time in s	Volume of gas released in cm³						
	Lumps of calcium carbonate				Powdered calcium carbonate			
	Test 1	Test 2	Test 3	Mean	Test 1	Test 2	Test 3	Mean
30	18	19	23	20	43	44	48	45
60	42	37	41	40	96	98	91	95
105	82	42	88		146	151	153	150
150	133	137	135	135	207	213	242	210

03.1 Give the independent variable and dependent variable of the investigation. **[2 marks]**

03.2 Suggest **one** improvement to the way the student has collected the data in **Table 2**. **[1 mark]**

03.3 Calculate the missing mean result. **[1 mark]**

03.4 The student plotted the mean results from powdered calcium carbonate (**Figure 3**). Plot the mean results for the lumps of calcium carbonate onto **Figure 3**. **[1 mark]**

Figure 3

> **Exam Tip**
>
> You can use **Table 2** to work out the variables.

> **Exam Tip**
>
> Whenever you are asked to calculate a mean, look out for any outliers. If you include an outlier in your calculation, you won't get any marks.

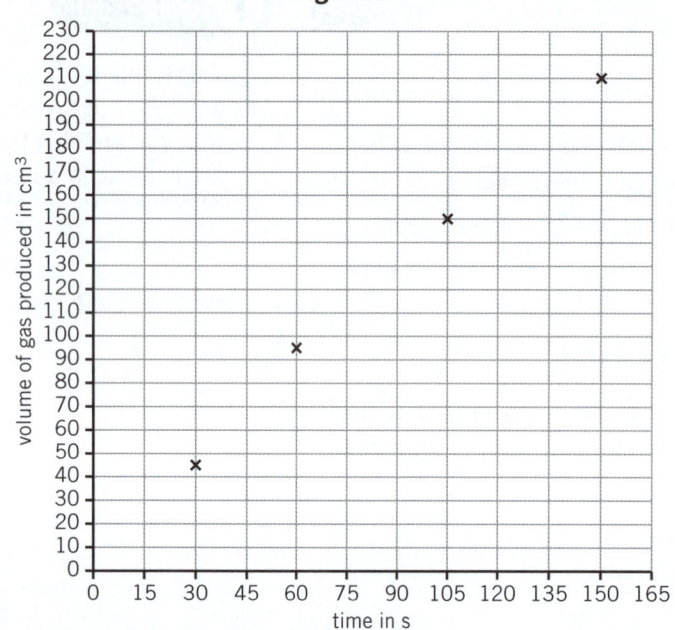

03.5 Explain why the powdered calcium carbonate has a faster rate of reaction than lumps of calcium carbonate. **[2 marks]**

04 A student investigated the reaction between sodium thiosulfate and hydrochloric acid.

sodium thiosulfate + hydrochloric acid →
_____ + sulfur dioxide + _____ + water

$Na_2S_2O_3(aq) + 2HCl(aq) \rightarrow 2NaCl(aq) + SO_2(g) + S(s) + H_2O(l)$

04.1 Complete the word equation. **[1 mark]**

C9 Rate of reaction

04.2 The student used the experimental set-up shown in **Figure 4**.

Describe how the student measured the rate of the reaction. **[1 mark]**

04.3 Suggest **one** improvement to the experimental set-up. **[1 mark]**

04.4 The student carried out the experiment at five different temperatures. **Table 3** shows their results.

Figure 4

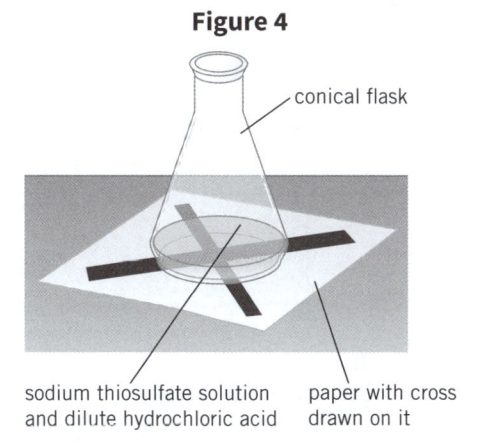

conical flask
sodium thiosulfate solution and dilute hydrochloric acid
paper with cross drawn on it

Table 3

Temperature in °C	Time taken for completion of reaction in s
5	reaction did not reach completion
15	427
25	312
35	184
45	65

Describe the trend shown by the data. **[1 mark]**

04.5 Explain the result for 5 °C. **[2 marks]**

04.6 Give **one** other condition that would affect the rate of the reaction between sodium thiosulfate and hydrochloric acid. **[1 mark]**

05 Lithium reacts with water to form lithium hydroxide and hydrogen gas.

$2Li(s) + 2H_2O(l) \rightarrow 2LiOH(aq) + H_2(g)$

One way to determine the rate of reaction is to measure the volume of hydrogen gas produced.

05.1 Write another method that can be used to measure the rate of reaction between lithium and water. **[4 marks]**

05.2 Write the equation used to calculate the rate of reaction for the method you described in **05.1**. **[1 mark]**

05.3 Give the correct unit for the rate of reaction for the method you described in **05.1**. Choose **one** answer. **[1 mark]**

cm^3/s g/s s/cm^3 s/g

05.4 A student wrote:

"As hydrogen gas is produced, increasing the pressure will increase the rate of reaction."

Is the student correct? **[1 mark]**

> **Exam Tip**
>
> When you are asked to suggest an improvement to a method, think about whether you can use any equipment that could reduce human error and so improve the accuracy of the readings.

> **Exam Tip**
>
> You should always try to use scientific terminology when you answer a question. In **04.5** you need to use the terms activation energy and collision to gain full marks.

> **Exam Tip**
>
> Remember, mean rate of reaction = change in quantity/time. What quantity is changing in your method?

> **Exam Tip**
>
> The '/' in a unit means 'per', so g/s means grams per second.

06 Zinc is a metal. It reacts with dilute nitric acid. The products of the reaction are zinc nitrate and a gas.

06.1 Name the gas formed in the reaction. [1 mark]

06.2 Which one of these changes will make the reaction rate slower? Choose **one** answer. [1 mark]

decreasing the acid concentration

increasing the temperature

decreasing the size of the pieces of zinc

increasing the pressure

06.3 Predict and explain the effect of decreasing the temperature on the rate of reaction. [3 marks]

07 **Figure 5** shows the reaction profile for an uncatalysed reaction.

Figure 5

07.1 Onto **Figure 5** sketch a second line to show the reaction profile of a catalysed reaction. [1 mark]

07.2 On **Figure 5** label the activation energy for the catalysed reaction. [1 mark]

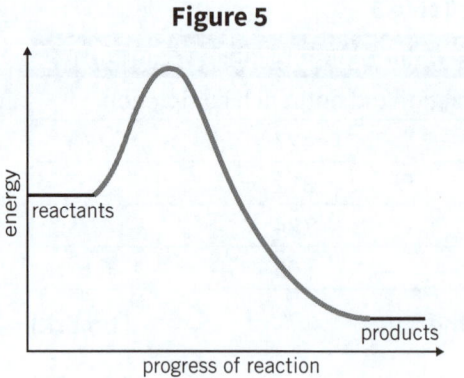

> **Exam Tip**
>
> The energy levels of the reactants and products don't change, so the line still starts and ends in the same place.

07.3 Give the general name of catalysts in biological systems. [1 mark]

07.4 Explain the effect that a catalyst has on the activation energy of a reaction. [2 marks]

08 **Table 4** shows some data for a chemical reaction.

Table 4

Time in s	Mass in g
0	198
30	188
60	180
90	174
120	172
150	170

08.1 Identify the dependent variable in the experiment. [1 mark]

08.2 Calculate the mean rate of the reaction. [3 marks]

08.3 Identify which chemical reaction the experiment investigated. Choose **one** answer. [1 mark]

$HCl(aq) + NaOH(aq) \rightarrow NaCl(aq) + H_2O(l)$

$3O_2(g) + C_2H_6O(l) \rightarrow 2CO_2(g) + 3H_2O(l)$

$MgO(s) + H_2SO_4(aq) \rightarrow MgSO_4(aq) + H_2O(l)$

$Ca(s) + 2HCl(aq) \rightarrow CaCl_2(aq) + H_2(g)$

> **Exam Tip**
>
> Look at the state symbols of the products *and* the reactants to help you work out the answer.

C9 Rate of reaction

08.4 Plot the data from **Table 4** on **Figure 6**. Draw a line of best fit. **[3 marks]**

Figure 6

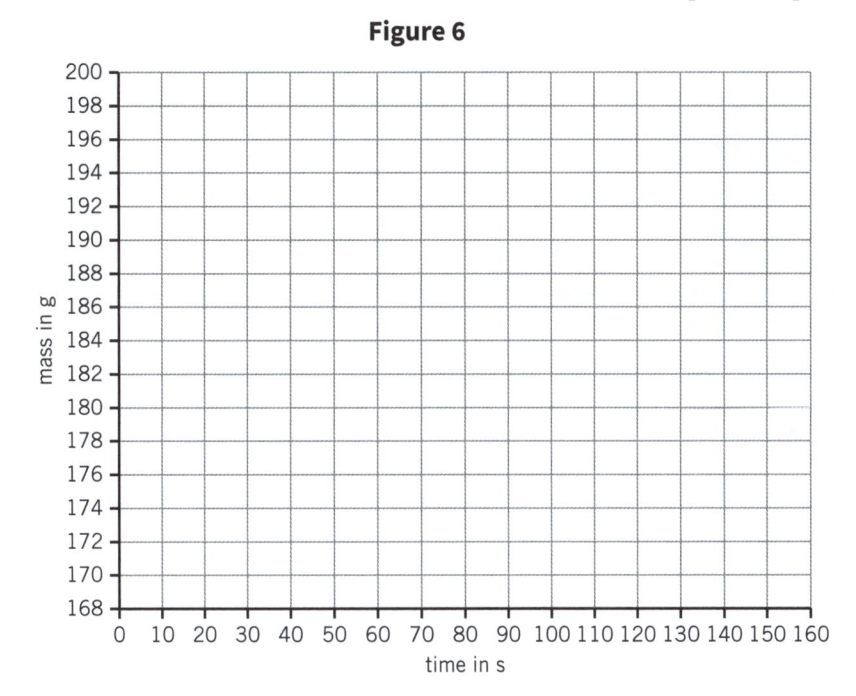

(graph with y-axis "mass in g" from 168 to 200, x-axis "time in s" from 0 to 160)

08.5 Draw a tangent onto the data line in **Figure 6** at 20 seconds and another tangent at 100 seconds. **[2 marks]**

08.6 Explain the difference in the rate of reaction at 20 seconds and at 100 seconds. **[4 marks]**

> **Exam Tip**
> A tangent is a straight line that touches the line of best fit at only one point.

09 Potassium iodide acts as a catalyst for the decomposition of hydrogen peroxide.

09.1 What does a catalyst do? Choose **one** answer. **[1 mark]**

decreases reaction rate by providing a pathway with a lower activation energy

increases reaction rate by providing a pathway with a higher activation energy

decreases reaction rate by providing a pathway with a higher activation energy

increases reaction rate by providing a pathway with a lower activation energy

09.2 **Figure 7** shows the reaction profile for the catalysed reaction.

Which arrow shows the activation energy for the catalysed reaction? **[1 mark]**

Figure 7

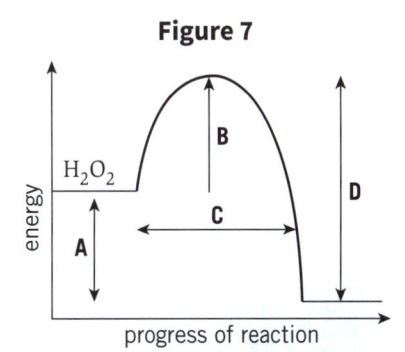

(reaction profile diagram with arrows A, B, C, D; H$_2$O$_2$ labelled on reactant level; axes "energy" vs "progress of reaction")

09.3 Balance the symbol equation for the decomposition of hydrogen peroxide, and give the missing state symbol. **[2 marks]**

____H$_2$O$_2$(aq) → (____H$_2$O____) + O$_2$(g)

09.4 Give the reason why potassium iodide is not given in the balanced symbol equation in **09.3**. **[1 mark]**

> **Exam Tip**
> Start by balancing the oxygen atoms, then check the hydrogen atoms.

Knowledge

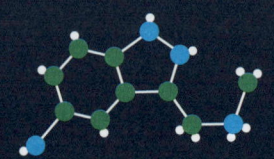

C10 Equilibrium

Reversible reactions

In some reactions, the products can react to produce the original reactants. This is called a **reversible reaction**. When writing chemical equations for reversible reactions, use the ⇌ symbol.

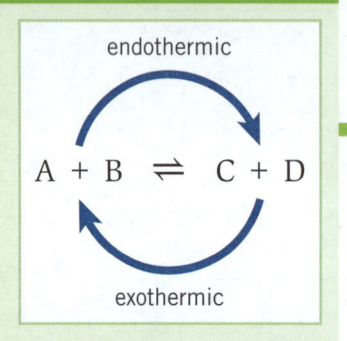

$$A + B \rightleftharpoons C + D$$

(endothermic / exothermic)

In this reaction:

- A and B can react to form C and D – the forward reaction
- C and D can react to form A and B – the reverse reaction.

The different directions of the reaction have opposite energy changes.

If the forward reaction is *endothermic*, the reverse reaction will be *exothermic*.

The same amount of energy is transferred in each direction.

Equilibrium

In a **closed system** no reactants or products can escape. If a reversible reaction is carried out in a closed system, it will eventually reach **dynamic equilibrium** – a point in time when the forward and reverse reactions have the same rate.

At dynamic equilibrium:

- The reactants are still turning into the products.
- The products are still turning back into the reactants.
- The rates of these two processes are *equal*, so overall the amount of reactants and products are constant.

Dynamic equilibrium

At dynamic equilibrium the amounts of reactant and product are constant, but not necessarily equal.

You could have a mixture of reactants and products in a 50:50 ratio, in a 75:25 ratio, or in any ratio at all.

How dynamic equilibrium is reached

Progress of reaction	start of reaction	middle of reaction	at dynamic equilibrium
Amount of A + B	high	decreasing	constant
Frequency of collisions A + B	high	decreasing	constant
Rate of forward reaction	high	decreasing	same as rate of reverse reaction
Amount of C + D	zero	increasing	constant
Frequency of collisions C + D	no collisions	increasing	constant
Rate of reverse reaction	zero	increasing	same as rate of forward reaction

Graph: rate of reaction vs time — forward reaction curve decreases, reverse reaction curve increases, equilibrium is reached at this point.

Key terms

Make sure you can write a definition for these key terms.

closed system   dynamic equilibrium   reversible reaction

Retrieval

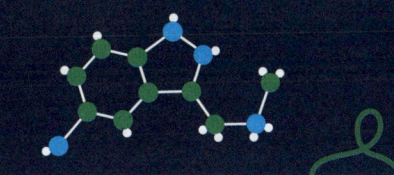

Learn the answers to the questions below, then cover the answers column with a piece of paper and write as many as you can. Check and repeat.

C10 questions | Answers

Question	Answer
What is a reversible reaction?	the reactants turn into products and the products turn into reactants
Which symbol shows a reversible reaction?	⇌
What is dynamic equilibrium?	the point in a reversible reaction when the rate of the forward and reverse reactions are the same

Previous questions | Answers

Question	Answer
How do catalysts increase the rate of a reaction?	lower the activation energy of the reaction, so more collisions result in a reaction
What effect does increasing temperature have on the rate of reaction?	increases
What is endothermic energy transfer?	energy transfer from the surroundings
How can unreactive metals be extracted?	reduction of their oxides using carbon

Maths skills

Practise your maths skills using the worked example and practice questions below.

Ratios, fractions, and percentages

In chemistry we often use ratios, fractions, and percentages to describe mixtures. These are different mathematical forms of numbers that represent the same thing.

A **ratio** compares the size of two or more quantities.

A **fraction** can express a part of a whole number, or shows one number divided by another in an equation.

A **percentage** is a number expressed as a fraction of 100.

Worked example

A stoppered flask contains a gas that is a mixture of 70 atoms of neon and 50 atoms of helium.

The **ratio** of neon atoms to helium atoms in the mixture is 70:50, which simplifies to 7:5 by dividing each side by the highest common factor (in this case, 10).

The **fraction** of atoms that are neon is:

$$\frac{70}{(70+50)} = \frac{70}{120} = \frac{7}{12}$$

The **percentage** of atoms that are helium is:

$$\left(\frac{50}{(70+50)}\right) \times 100 = 41.67\%$$

Practice

1. An equilibrium mixture contains 45 cm³ of H_2 and 22.5 cm³ of O_2. What is the ratio of H_2 to O_2?

2. What fraction of the total volume in this mixture is O_2?

3. A different equilibrium mixture contains 92 cm³ of H_2, 154 cm³ of N_2, and 23 cm³ of NH_3. What is the ratio of the three different substances?

4. What is the percentage of NH_3 and N_2 combined out of the whole mixture?

Practice

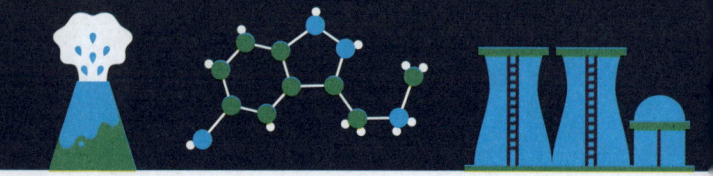

Exam-style questions

01 This question is about reversible reactions.

01.1 Choose the correct words or symbols from the box to complete the sentences. Each word or symbol can be used once, more than once, or not at all. **[3 marks]**

| reactants | products | ⇌ | ⇔ |

In a chemical reaction, the _____ react together to form the _____.

When the equation for a chemical reaction contains the _____ symbol, this means that the _____ can also react to reform the _____.

01.2 Which of the following is **not** a reversible process? **[1 mark]**
Tick **one** answer.

combustion of paper ☐

ice melting ☐

thermal decomposition of ammonium chloride ☐

water condensing on a mirror ☐

> **Exam Tip**
> Reversible means being able to undo something. Which of these reactions cannot be undone?

01.3 Name the state that is reached when a reversible reaction is carried out within a sealed apparatus where the reactants and products cannot escape. **[1 mark]**

_____

01.4 The forwards reaction of a reversible reaction is exothermic.
Is the backwards reaction exothermic or endothermic? **[1 mark]**
Circle **one** answer.

exothermic   endothermic

270   C10 Equilibrium

Paper 4 C10

02 A student heats a sample of ammonium chloride in a test tube. The ammonium chloride breaks down into ammonia gas and hydrogen chloride gas.

solid ammonium chloride ⇌ ammonia gas + hydrogen chloride gas

As the student heats the ammonium chloride, a white solid forms at the top of the test tube (**Figure 1**).

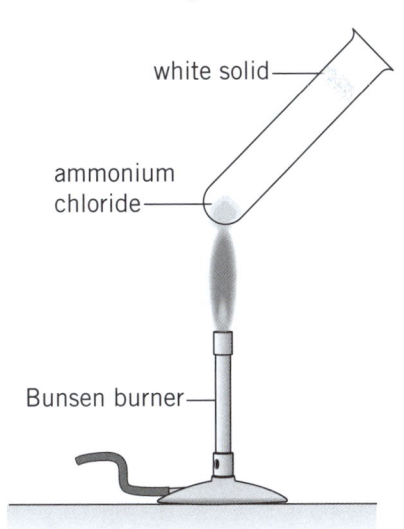

Figure 1

02.1 Predict what the white solid is. **[1 mark]**

_____
_____
_____

02.2 Explain your prediction in **02.1**. **[3 marks]**

_____
_____
_____
_____
_____

02.3 Another student heats hydrated blue copper(II) sulfate crystals in a test tube. Water is given off to form white anhydrous copper(II) sulfate crystals. This process is reversible.

Predict what the student would observe if water was added to the

Exam Tip

Think about the different colours of the two compounds – this colour change is reversible.

C10 Practice 271

02.4 The student holds the test tube whilst they add the water.
Predict what they would feel as water is added. **[1 mark]**

_____
_____
_____

03 A chemical reaction can be represented as:
$$A + B \rightleftharpoons C + D$$

03.1 Define the $\rightleftharpoons$ symbol. **[1 mark]**

03.2 Identify what letters represent the reactants. **[1 mark]**

03.3 Ammonia is produced from the chemical reaction between nitrogen and hydrogen.
Balance the symbol equation for the formation of ammonia. **[1 mark]**

$N_2(g) + $ _____ $H_2(g) \rightleftharpoons$ _____ $NH_3(g)$

> **Exam Tip**
> Start by balancing the number of nitrogen atoms, then balance the hydrogen atoms.

03.4 The formation of ammonia is exothermic.
Identify the energy change involved in the reaction of ammonia to form nitrogen and hydrogen. **[1 mark]**

03.5 A student says:
"*More energy is transferred when ammonia forms nitrogen and hydrogen, than when nitrogen and hydrogen react to form ammonia.*"
State whether the student is correct. **[1 mark]**

04 When heated, blue hydrated copper sulfate crystals form white anhydrous copper sulfate.

04.1 Identify whether this change is endothermic or exothermic. **[1 mark]**

04.2 Give **two** observations you would observe if you added water to anhydrous copper sulfate crystals. **[2 marks]**

04.3 Identify the type of bonding between the copper and sulfate ions in copper sulfate. **[1 mark]**

04.4 Suggest **one** safety precaution that should be taken when heating hydrated copper sulfate crystals. **[1 mark]**

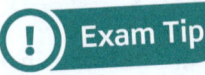

> **Exam Tip**
> You are asked for two observations in **04.2**. For one observation, you need to use the information from the introduction.
> For the other observation, you need to use the information from **04.1**.

05 Hydrogen reacts with iodine to form hydrogen iodide.
$$H_2(g) + I_2(g) \rightleftharpoons 2HI(g)$$

05.1 Identify what the $\rightleftharpoons$ symbol tells you about the reaction. **[1 mark]**

C10 Equilibrium

05.2 The reaction reaches equilibrium in apparatus that prevents the escape of reactants and products.

Describe what happens to the particles of H_2, I_2, and HI at equilibrium. **[1 mark]**

05.3 The forward reaction is endothermic.

Describe the energy transfers involved in the forward reaction. **[1 mark]**

05.4 Explain how the rate of the reaction between hydrogen and iodine could be increased. **[2 marks]**

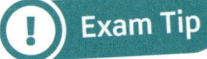

> **Exam Tip**
> How could you change the temperature to increase the rate of reaction, given your answer to **05.3**?

06 Solid ammonium chloride can be made by reacting two gases.

hydrogen chloride + ammonia ⇌ ammonium chloride

HCl(_____) + NH_3(_____) ⇌ NH_4Cl(_____)

06.1 Complete the balanced symbol equation by adding state symbols. **[1 mark]**

06.2 The reaction is reversible. What is a reversible reaction? Choose **one** answer. **[1 mark]**

The rate of the reaction is very slow.

The products and reactants can react together.

The products of the reaction can react to produce the original reactants.

> **Exam Tip**
> Think about what the word reversible means outside of your science lessons.

06.3 Complete the sentence. **[1 mark]**

When the reaction is carried out in a sealed container, the reaction reaches _____.

07 A student carries out a reaction and finds that 4 J of energy is released.

07.1 Identify whether the reaction is exothermic or endothermic. **[1 mark]**

07.2 Identify **one** way in which the student can measure the energy released. **[1 mark]**

07.3 The reaction is reversible. Complete the sentence. **[1 mark]**

As the forward reaction is _____, the reverse reaction will be _____.

07.4 Determine how much energy the reverse reaction will take in. **[1 mark]**

08 Dinitrogen tetroxide, N₂O₄, can form nitrogen dioxide, NO₂.

08.1 Complete the balanced symbol equation for this process. **[1 mark]**
N₂O₄ ⇌ _____ NO₂

08.2 The forward reaction is endothermic.
Define the term endothermic. **[1 mark]**

08.3 Dinitrogen tetroxide is a colourless gas, whereas nitrogen dioxide is a brown gas. A teacher has a mixture of both gases in a sealed container. When the container is heated, the colour of the mixture starts to look darker brown.
Suggest why. **[1 mark]**

08.4 For an equilibrium to be achieved, the gases must be in a sealed container.
Suggest why. **[1 mark]**

09 Some students want to investigate the reversible reaction:
hydrated copper sulfate ⇌ anhydrous copper sulfate + water
Figure 2 shows the apparatus.

Figure 2

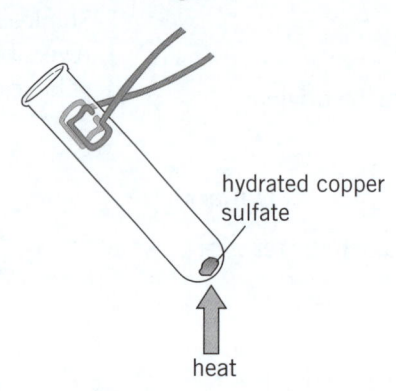

09.1 Explain why equilibrium cannot be reached using the apparatus in **Figure 2**. **[1 mark]**

09.2 Suggest a suitable piece of equipment for heating the hydrated copper sulfate. **[1 mark]**

09.3 Name the substance that leaves the test tube. **[1 mark]**

09.4 Suggest a method to collect the substance that leaves the test tube. **[3 marks]**

> **Exam Tip**
>
> Don't worry if you haven't heard of dinitrogen tetraoxide before. Unfamiliar contexts will be used in an exam to test if you can apply your knowledge to a new situation.

10 The rate of a reaction is affected by several factors.

10.1 Which change would cause an increase in the rate of a reaction? Choose **two** answers. **[2 marks]**

increase in temperature

change in concentration of acid

decrease in mass of reactant

crushing a lump of a reactant into powder

decrease in temperature

10.2 For a reaction to occur, the particles need to collide with sufficient energy.
Give the name of the sufficient energy. **[1 mark]**

10.3 Explain how a decrease in the concentration of acid used in a reaction will affect the rate. **[3 marks]**

> **! Exam Tip**
>
> Do not rewrite the question in your answer to **10.3**. Starting an answer with "A decrease in the concentration of an acid will…." is a waste of time and effort. You won't get any marks for it.

11 Some metals react with water.

11.1 Describe the expected observations in the reaction of potassium and water. **[2 marks]**

11.2 Potassium is in Group 1.
Explain how the reactivity of Group 1 elements with water changes as you go down the group. **[2 marks]**

11.3 Name **one** piece of safety equipment that should be used when carrying out the reaction described in **11.1**. **[1 mark]**

11.4 Name the products of the reaction of lithium with water. **[2 marks]**

11.5 Describe the expected observation when copper is placed in a test tube of water. **[1 mark]**

> **! Exam Tip**
>
> Group 1 elements have a single electron in their outer shell – this is important for explaining their reactivity.

Knowledge

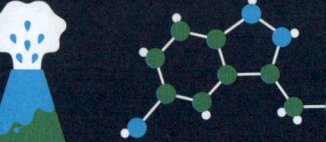

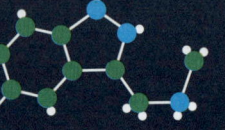

C11 Crude oil and fuels

Crude oil

Crude oil is incredibly important to our society and economy. It is formed from the remains of ancient biomass – living organisms (mostly plankton) that died many millions of years ago.

Raw crude oil is a thick black liquid made of a large number of different compounds mixed together. Most of the compounds are **hydrocarbons** of various sizes. Hydrocarbons are molecules made of carbon and hydrogen only.

Alkanes

One family of hydrocarbon molecules is called **alkanes**. Alkane molecules only have single bonds in them. The first four alkanes are:

methane, ethane, propane, butane

The different alkanes have different numbers of carbon atoms and hydrogen atoms. You can always work out the molecular formula of an alkane by using C_nH_{2n+2}.

> **Revision tip**
>
> **Remember** You can check if you've drawn hydrocarbon compounds correctly since carbon always forms four bonds and hydrogen always forms one bond.

Combustion

Hydrocarbons are used as **fuels**. This is because when they react with oxygen they release a lot of energy. This reaction is called **combustion**. Complete combustion is a type of combustion where the only products are carbon dioxide and water.

Properties

Whether or not a particular hydrocarbon is useful as a fuel depends on its properties. Its properties in turn depend on the length of the molecule.

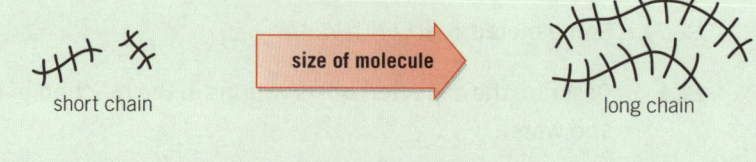

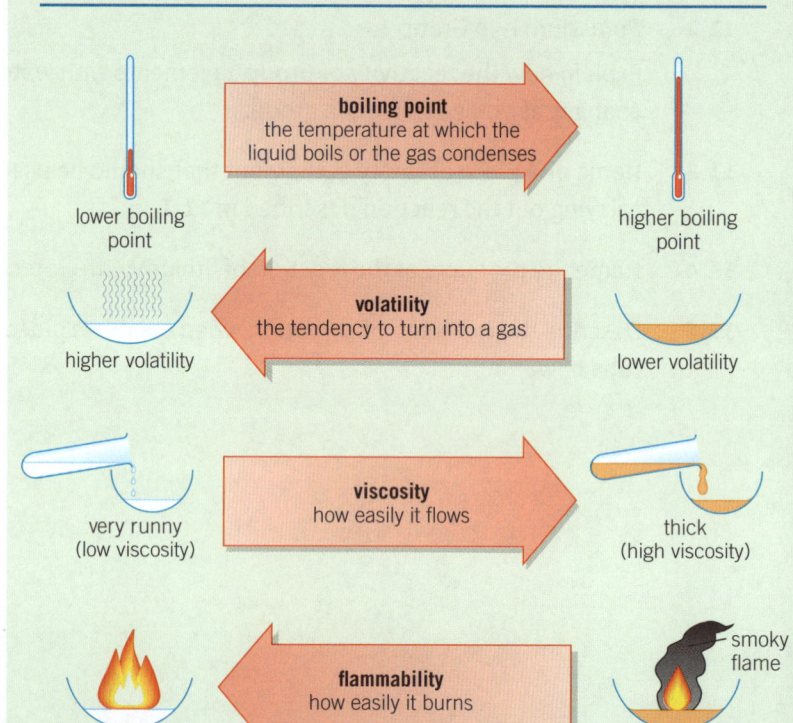

- size of molecule: short chain → long chain
- boiling point: the temperature at which the liquid boils or the gas condenses — lower boiling point ← → higher boiling point
- volatility: the tendency to turn into a gas — higher volatility ← → lower volatility
- viscosity: how easily it flows — very runny (low viscosity) ← → thick (high viscosity)
- flammability: how easily it burns — higher flammability ← → lower flammability (smoky flame)

Key terms

alkane   alkene   boiling point   combustion   cracking   crude oil   feedstock
flammability   fractional distillation   fuel   hydrocarbon   viscosity   volatility

C11

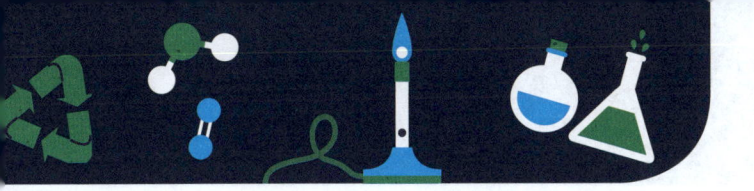

Fractional distillation

The different hydrocarbons in crude oil are separated into fractions based on their boiling points in a process called **fractional distillation**. All the molecules in a fraction have a similar number of carbon atoms, and so a similar boiling point.

The process takes place in a fractionating column, which is hot at the bottom and cooler at the top.

The process works like this:

1. Crude oil is vaporised (turned into a gas by heating).
2. The hydrocarbon gases enter the column.
3. The hydrocarbon gases rise up the column.
4. As hydrocarbon gases rise up the column they cool down.
5. When the different hydrocarbons reach their boiling points in the column they condense.
6. The hydrocarbon fraction is collected.

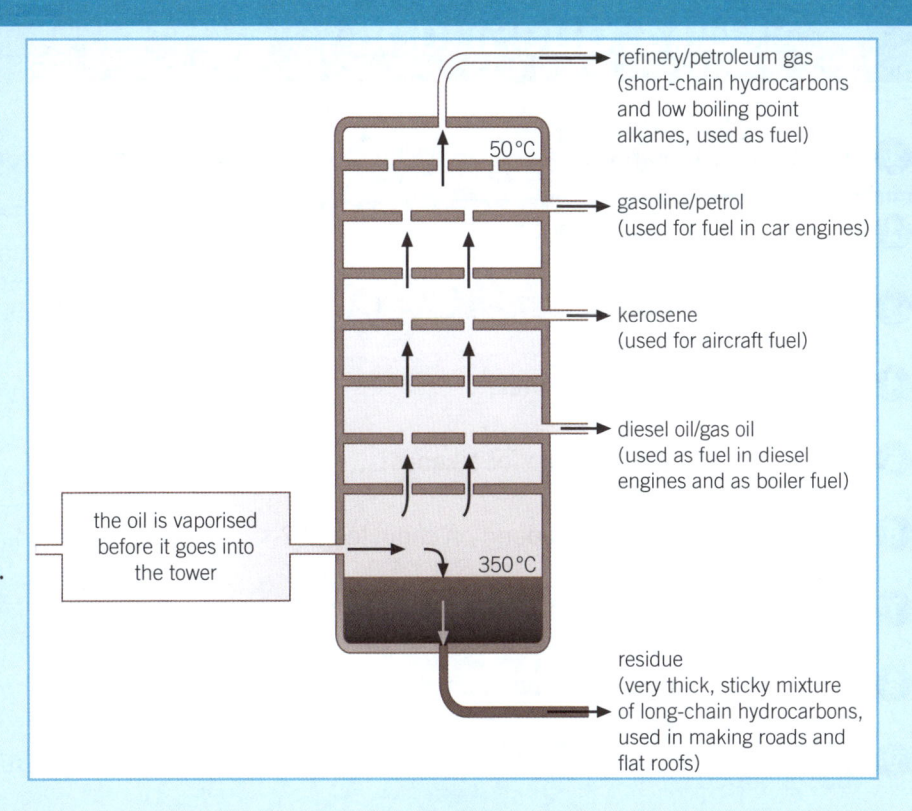

Fractionating column diagram:
- 50 °C → refinery/petroleum gas (short-chain hydrocarbons and low boiling point alkanes, used as fuel)
- gasoline/petrol (used for fuel in car engines)
- kerosene (used for aircraft fuel)
- diesel oil/gas oil (used as fuel in diesel engines and as boiler fuel)
- the oil is vaporised before it goes into the tower
- 350 °C
- residue (very thick, sticky mixture of long-chain hydrocarbons, used in making roads and flat roofs)

Products from fractional distillation

Many useful products come from the separation of crude oil by fractional distillation.

Fuels	Feedstock	Useful materials produced
petrol, diesel oil, kerosene, heavy fuel oil, and liquefied petroleum gases	fractions form the raw material for other processes and the production of other substances	solvents, lubricants, polymers, and detergents

Alkenes

Alkenes are a family of hydrocarbons that contain double bonds between carbon atoms.

Alkenes are also used as fuels, and to produce polymers and many other materials.

They are much more reactive than alkanes. When mixed with bromine water, the bromine water turns from orange to colourless. This can be used to tell the difference between alkanes and alkenes.

Cracking

Not all hydrocarbons are as useful as each other. Longer molecules tend to be less useful than shorter ones. As such, there is a higher demand for shorter-chain hydrocarbons than longer-chain hydrocarbons.

A process called **cracking** is used to break up longer hydrocarbons and turn them into shorter ones.

Cracking produces shorter-chain alkanes and **alkenes**.

Two methods of cracking are:

- catalytic cracking – vaporise the hydrocarbons, then pass them over a hot catalyst
- steam cracking – mix the hydrocarbons with steam at a very high temperature.

C11 Knowledge   277

Retrieval

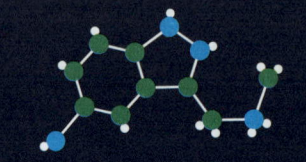

Learn the answers to the questions below, then cover the answers column with a piece of paper and write as many as you can. Check and repeat.

C11 questions | Answers

#	Question	Answer
1	What is a hydrocarbon?	compound containing carbon and hydrogen only
2	How is crude oil formed?	over millions of years from the remains of ancient biomass
3	What are alkanes?	hydrocarbons that only have single bonds
4	What are the first four alkanes?	methane, ethane, propane, butane
5	What is the general formula for alkanes?	C_nH_{2n+2}
6	How does boiling point depend on chain length?	longer the chain, higher the boiling point
7	How does viscosity depend on chain length?	longer the chain, higher the viscosity
8	How does flammability depend on chain length?	longer the chain, lower the flammability
9	How can the different alkanes in crude oil be separated?	fractional distillation
10	What is a fraction?	a group of hydrocarbons with similar chain lengths
11	Name five useful fuels produced from fractional distillation.	petrol, diesel oil, kerosene, heavy fuel oil, and liquefied petroleum gases
12	Name four useful materials produced from crude oil.	solvents, lubricants, polymers, detergents
13	What is cracking?	breaking down a hydrocarbon with a long chain into smaller molecules
14	Name two methods to carry out cracking.	steam cracking and catalytic cracking
15	What are the products of cracking?	short chain alkanes and alkenes
16	What are alkenes?	hydrocarbons with a double bond
17	What are alkenes used for?	formation of polymers
18	Describe the reactivity of alkenes compared to alkanes.	alkenes are much more reactive
19	How can you test for alkenes?	alkenes turn orange bromine water colourless

C11 Crude oil and fuels

C11

Now go back and use the questions below to check your knowledge from previous chapters.

Previous questions — Answers

#	Question	Answer
1	What is a reversible reaction?	when the products of a reaction can react to produce the original reactants
2	What is dynamic equilibrium?	the point in a reversible reaction when the rates of the forward and reverse reactions are the same
3	What are the three reaction conditions that can be changed?	concentration, temperature, pressure
4	What is the rate of a reaction?	how quickly reactants are used up or products are produced
5	What effect does increasing concentration have on the rate of reaction?	increases
6	What effect does increasing surface area have on the rate of reaction?	increases
7	What is the name of the positive electrode?	anode
8	In the electrolysis of aluminium oxide, why is the aluminium oxide mixed with cryolite?	lower the melting point
9	Why do atoms have no overall charge?	equal numbers of positive protons and negative electrons
10	What is an alloy?	mixture of a metal with atoms of another element

(Put paper here)

Maths skills

Practise your maths skills using the worked example and practice questions below.

Finding the mean

Whenever an experiment is conducted, it is important to repeat it to establish how *precise* the values are (how close to each other they are), and how *repeatable* they are (can they be repeated).

Whenever you repeat an experiment and record repeat observations you must calculate a mean to give an average result for that observation.

However, only use values that are close together, and discard any anomalous values.

Worked example

A student burns hexane and uses the heat released to warm up some water. As soon as the water increases by 10 °C, they stop the reaction and measure the mass of hexane used. They repeat this three more times and record the masses: 5.1 g, 6.3 g, 6.5 g, 6.2 g.

Calculate the mean of the values.

Step 1: Establish which values to use – in this case 6.3, 6.5, and 6.2. The first mass (5.1) is ignored because it is not close to the others.

Step 2: Calculate the mean.

$$\text{mean} = \frac{\text{sum of values}}{\text{total number of values}}$$

$$= \frac{(6.3 + 6.5 + 6.2)}{3} = 6.3 \text{ g}$$

Practice

1. A student measures how the mass of a magnesium strip increases when burnt in oxygen. They record the masses: 0.12 g, 0.12 g, 0.14 g, 0.11 g, 0.23 g.

   Calculate the mean increase in mass.

2. The volume of gas produced in three repeats of an experiment is collected, and recorded as: 54 cm^3, 58 cm^3, 55 cm^3.

   Calculate the mean volume of gas produced.

C11 Retrieval 279

Practice

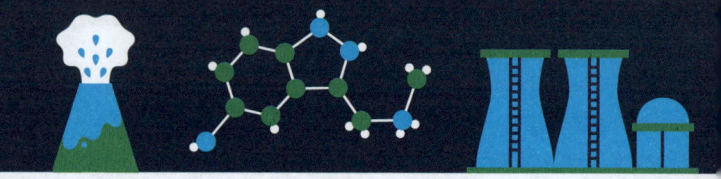

Exam-style questions

01 Fractions of crude oil are separated by fractional distillation.
Figure 1 shows a fractional distillation column.

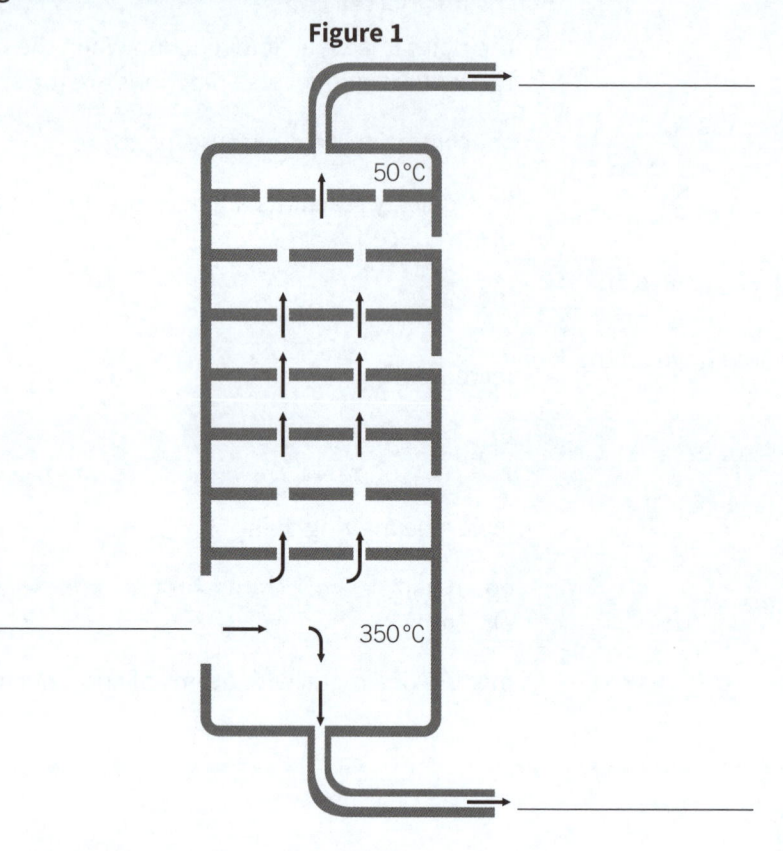

Figure 1

(diagram of fractional distillation column with 50 °C at top and 350 °C at bottom)

01.1 Label **Figure 1** using the phrases given below. **[3 marks]**

long hydrocarbons out

crude oil in

short hydrocarbons out

01.2 Complete the sentences using the correct words from the box. **[2 marks]**

| boiling | higher | lower | melting |

As the fractions pass up the column, they condense at their _____ point. The _____ the boiling point, the further up the column the fraction will pass.

> **Exam Tip**
> Use **Figure 1**, it gives you a lot of information.

01.3 The different fractions of crude oil have different uses.
Draw **one** line from each fraction to its correct use. **[2 marks]**

Fraction	Use
diesel	aircraft fuel
kerosene	car engine fuel
residue	making roads

280 C11 Crude oil and fuels

Paper 4 **C11**

01.4 Name **one** other use of substances obtained from crude oil. **[1 mark]**

_____

02 This question is about alkanes.

02.1 Draw **one** line from each displayed formula of an alkane to its name. **[2 marks]**

Displayed formula   **Name**

H H
| |
H—C—C—H   butane
| |
H H

                                ethane

H H H H
| | | |
H—C—C—C—C—H   methane
| | | |
H H H H

                                propane

02.2 Give the formula of the alkane with 22 carbon atoms. **[1 mark]**
Tick **one** box.

$C_{22}H_{42}$ ☐

$C_{22}H_{46}$ ☐

$C_{22}H_{44}$ ☐

$C_{22}H_{48}$ ☐

Exam Tip

Use the general formula for alkanes to figure out the number of hydrogen atoms that will be in the compound.

02.3 Decane is an alkane with 10 carbon atoms.

How do the properties of decane compare with the properties of ethane? **[1 mark]**

Tick **one** box.

Decane has a higher flammability, lower boiling point, and higher viscosity. ☐

Decane has a higher flammability, higher boiling point, and lower viscosity. ☐

Decane has a lower flammability, higher boiling point, and higher viscosity. ☐

Decane has a lower flammability, lower boiling point, and lower viscosity. ☐

Exam Tip

There are three possible differences within each answer. Go over the properties one at a time (flammability, boiling point, and then viscosity), comparing them to ethane. This should leave you with the correct answer at the end.

For answers and more practice questions visit www.oxfordrevise.com/scienceanswers

Even more practice and interactive revision quizzes are available on kerboodle

C11 Practice 281

03 Alkanes are a group of hydrocarbons.

03.1 Which of the following is an alkane?

Choose **one** answer. [1 mark]

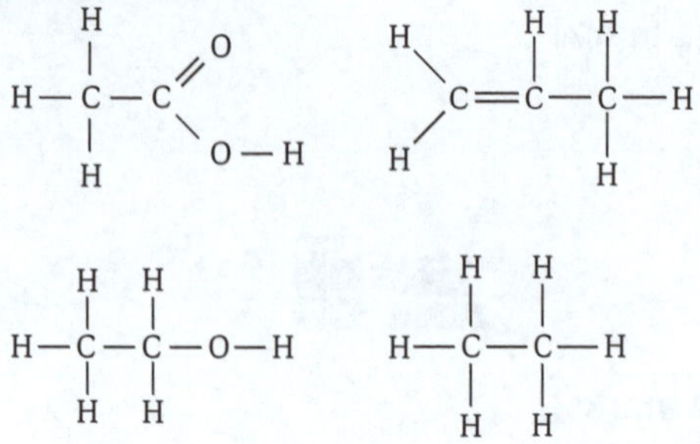

Structure 1: H−C(H)(H)−C(=O)−O−H

Structure 2: H(H)C=C(H)−C(H)(H)−H

Structure 3: H−C(H)(H)−C(H)(H)−O−H

Structure 4: H−C(H)(H)−C(H)(H)−H

> **Exam Tip**
> The number of 'e's in the name can help you remember the difference between alkanes and alkenes. Alkane only has a single e, whereas alkene has two e's.

03.2 The general formula for an alkane is C_nH_{2n+2}.

Use the general formula to complete **Table 1**. [3 marks]

Table 1

Name	Number of carbon atoms	Number of hydrogen atoms	Formula
methane	1	4	CH_4
propane	3	8	
butane	4		C_4H_{10}
icosane	20		

03.3 Name the alkane with the chemical formula C_2H_6. [1 mark]

03.4 Complete the displayed formula of butane. [2 marks]

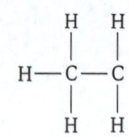

H−C(H)(H)−C(H)(H)

04 This question is about alkenes.

04.1 Describe the difference in structure between alkanes and alkenes. [1 mark]

04.2 Bromine water can be used to test for alkenes.

Give the colour change when there is a positive result. [1 mark]

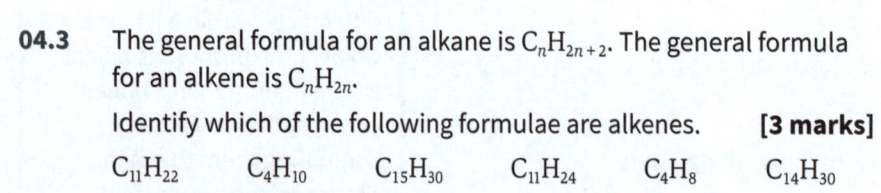

> **Exam Tip**
> Clear is not the answer. Clear just means you can see through it. This does not tell you anything about the *colour*, for example, you can have clear blue solutions.

04.3 The general formula for an alkane is C_nH_{2n+2}. The general formula for an alkene is C_nH_{2n}.

Identify which of the following formulae are alkenes. [3 marks]

$C_{11}H_{22}$ C_4H_{10} $C_{15}H_{30}$ $C_{11}H_{24}$ C_4H_8 $C_{14}H_{30}$

04.4 Name the process by which alkenes can be produced from longer-chain alkanes. [1 mark]

282 C11 Crude oil and fuels

C11

04.5 The chemical formula of ethene is C_2H_4. The chemical formula of pentacontene is $C_{50}H_{100}$.
Describe **two** ways in which the properties of ethene and pentacontene are different. Give a reason for these differences. **[3 marks]**

> **! Exam Tip**
> Don't worry if you've never heard of pentacontene before. Its properties follow the same rules as for other alkenes.

05 Crude oil is a mixture of many different substances. The substances are separated using fractional distillation.

05.1 Describe how crude oil was formed. **[1 mark]**

05.2 Name the **two** processes that occur during fractional distillation. **[2 marks]**

> **! Exam Tip**
> Give the name of each fraction, and what it can be used for.

05.3 Outline the uses of some products obtained from crude oil. **[4 marks]**

06 Crude oil is a finite resource found in rocks.

06.1 What is crude oil made of?
Choose **one** answer. **[1 mark]**

a mixture of atoms

a pure solution of organic compounds

a mixture of different length hydrocarbons

a pure solution of a single length hydrocarbon

06.2 When crude oil is separated by distillation the resulting groups are called fractions. What does each fraction of crude oil contain?
Choose **one** answer. **[1 mark]**

a single hydrocarbon

identical boiling points

similar length hydrocarbon chains

similar number of oxygen atoms

06.3 What property is used to separate the fractions of crude oil?
Choose **one** answer. **[1 mark]**

boiling point   flammability

melting point   viscosity

06.4 Give **three** uses of the products of crude oil. **[3 marks]**

> **! Exam Tip**
> 06.4 does not need lots of writing – a simple list of three things will get the marks.

06.5 Petrol, diesel, and residue are three fractions of crude oil. Describe and explain how petrol, diesel, and residue are separated by fractional distillation. **[6 marks]**

For answers and more practice questions visit www.oxfordrevise.com/scienceanswers

Even more practice and interactive revision quizzes are available on kerboodle

C11 Practice   283

07 This question is about cracking of hydrocarbons.

07.1 Hexadecane, $C_{16}H_{34}$, undergoes cracking to produce two hydrocarbons.

Complete the balanced symbol equation for the cracking of hexadecane, $C_{16}H_{34}$. [1 mark]

$C_{16}H_{34} \rightarrow C_{10}H_{22} + C\_\_\_\_H\_\_\_\_$

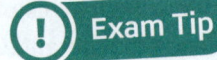

> **Exam Tip**
> You've already been given one of the products, so this becomes a simple subtraction.
> Number of carbon atoms: 16 − 10 = ____
> Number of hydrogen atoms: 34 − 22 = ____

07.2 Identify the product from **07.1** that is an alkane. [1 mark]

07.3 Name the **two** methods that can be used to crack long-chain alkanes. [2 marks]

07.4 Describe why it is useful for longer-chain alkanes to undergo cracking. [2 marks]

07.5 Both substances produced from the cracking of hexadecane are clear colourless liquids. Describe a test that can be used to identify which product is the alkene. In your answer, include the positive result for an alkene. [3 marks]

07.6 Diesel is a long-chain hydrocarbon and petrol is a shorter-chain hydrocarbon. Both are used as fuel in cars. **Figure 2** shows how the consumption of petrol and diesel changed between 1990 and 2017.

Figure 2

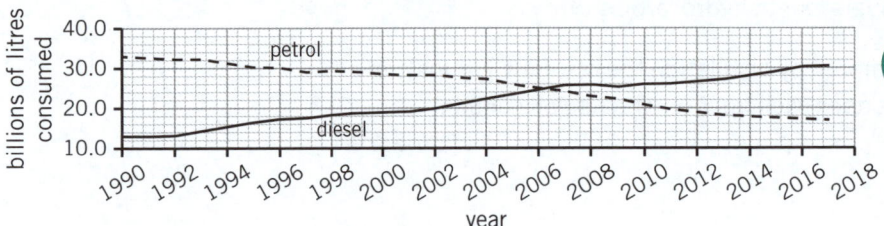

Describe the changes in petrol and diesel use from 1990 to 2017. [2 marks]

> **Exam Tip**
> You need to talk about both lines and use data in your answer to **07.6**. Use the following sentence as an answer template for petrol:
> The amount of petrol consumed has … from … in 1990 to … in 2017.

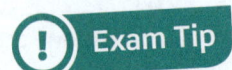

07.7 Suggest **one** effect the data in **Figure 2** may have had on the cracking of crude oil fractions. [1 mark]

08 This question is about cracking.

08.1 Compare the conditions used for steam cracking and for catalytic cracking. [3 marks]

08.2 The equation shows a cracking reaction:

$C_{10}H_{22} \rightarrow C_6H_{14} + \_\_\_\_ C_2H_4$

Balance the equation for the cracking reaction. [1 mark]

> **Exam Tip**
> Start by balancing the carbon atoms.

08.3 Give **two** reasons for carrying out cracking reactions in industry. [2 marks]

C11 Crude oil and fuels

09 Table 2 shows the name and molecular formula of four alkanes.

Table 2

Name	Molecular formula
methane	CH_4
decane	$C_{10}H_{22}$
pentadecane	$C_{15}H_{32}$
icosane	$C_{20}H_{42}$

09.1 Use **Table 2** and the words in the box to complete the sentences. **[5 marks]**

| flammable | highest | length | longest | lowest |
| shortest | viscous |

Some properties of hydrocarbons change depending on the _____ of the hydrocarbon chain.

Methane has the _____ boiling point because it has the _____ hydrocarbon chain.

Icosane is the most _____ because it has the _____ hydrocarbon chain.

Exam Tip

Remember to use the molecular formulae in **Table 2** to help you answer **09.1**.

09.2 Which alkane in **Table 2** is the most flammable?
Choose **one** answer. **[1 mark]**

decane   icosane   methane   pentadecane

09.3 Draw **one** line from each alkane to its correct melting point. **[3 marks]**

Alkane	Melting point
decane	−182 °C
icosane	−30 °C
methane	17 °C
pentadecane	36 °C

09.4 The complete combustion of an alkane gives two products. Complete the word equation for the complete combustion of methane. **[2 marks]**

methane + _____ → _____ + _____

Exam Tip

Unless the question asks for it, don't give the chemical symbols. If you make a mistake writing down a chemical symbol you won't get the marks.

10 Crude oil is a mixture of hydrocarbons.

10.1 Define the term hydrocarbon. **[1 mark]**

10.2 Name the compound in **Figure 3**. **[1 mark]**

Figure 3

```
    H   H   H
    |   |   |
H — C — C — C — H
    |   |   |
    H   H   H
```

10.3 Pentane is a short hydrocarbon with five carbons.
Draw pentane. **[2 marks]**

Exam Tip

Carbon always forms four bonds and hydrogen always forms one bond.

For answers and more practice questions visit www.oxfordrevise.com/scienceanswers

Even more practice and interactive revision quizzes are available on **kerboodle**

C11 Practice 285

Knowledge

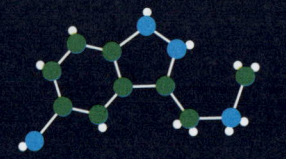

C12 Chemical analysis

Pure and impure

In chemistry, a **pure** substance contains a single element or compound that is not mixed with any other substance.

Pure substances melt and boil at specific temperatures.

An **impure** substance contains more than one type of element or compound in a **mixture**.

Impure substances melt and boil at a range of temperatures.

Jar 1 – oxygen (gas)

Jar 2 – hydrogen (gas)

Jar 3 – Mixture of oxygen and hydrogen (gas). The oxygen and hydrogen are not joined together. The mixture has the same properties as Jar 1 and Jar 2.

Jar 4 – Compound made from oxygen and hydrogen – water (liquid). The atoms of oxygen and hydrogen are joined together. The compound has different properties from the ones in Jars 1, 2, and 3.

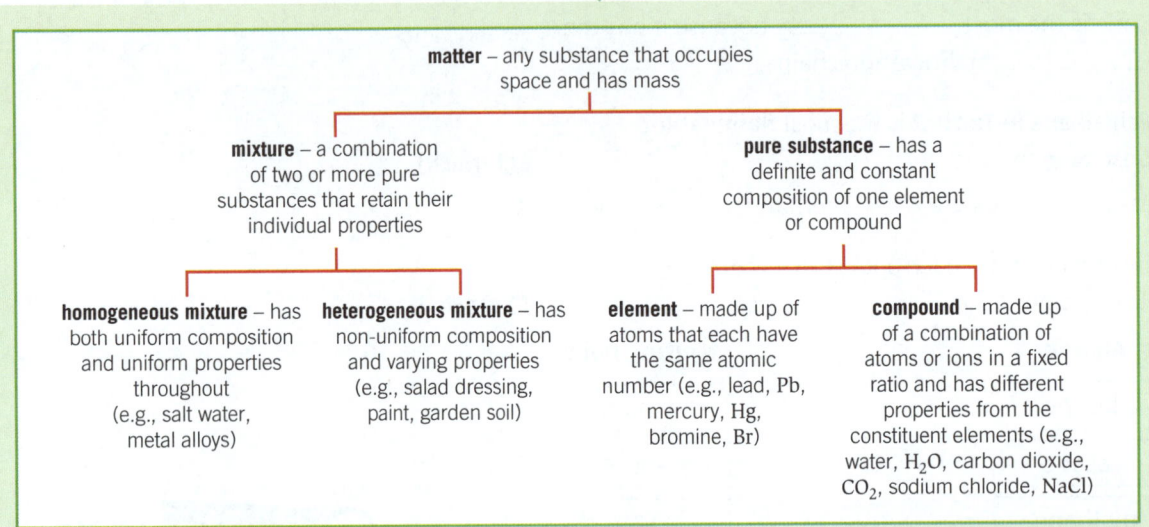

---

matter – any substance that occupies space and has mass

- **mixture** – a combination of two or more pure substances that retain their individual properties
  - **homogeneous mixture** – has both uniform composition and uniform properties throughout (e.g., salt water, metal alloys)
  - **heterogeneous mixture** – has non-uniform composition and varying properties (e.g., salad dressing, paint, garden soil)
- **pure substance** – has a definite and constant composition of one element or compound
  - **element** – made up of atoms that each have the same atomic number (e.g., lead, Pb, mercury, Hg, bromine, Br)
  - **compound** – made up of a combination of atoms or ions in a fixed ratio and has different properties from the constituent elements (e.g., water, H_2O, carbon dioxide, CO_2, sodium chloride, NaCl)

Formulations

Formulations are examples of mixtures. They have many different components (substances that make them up) in very specific proportions (amounts compared to each other).

Scientists spend a lot of time trying to get the right components in the right proportions to make the most useful product.

Formulations include fuels, cleaning agents, paints, alloys, fertilisers, and foods.

Separating mixtures

Mixtures can be separated by

- filtration – separates insoluble solids from a liquid
- crystallisation – evaporates a solvent (liquid) leaving the solute (solid)
- simple distillation – separates solvent from a solution as long as the solvent has a lower boiling point than the solute
- fractional distillation – separates two or more substances from a liquid mixture.

Key terms

Make sure you can write a definition for these key terms.

chromatography   formulation   impure   mixture   mobile phase

C12

Chromatography

Chromatography is a method to separate different components in a mixture. It is set up as shown here, with a piece of paper in a beaker containing a small amount of solvent.

The R_f **value** is a ratio of how far up the paper a certain spot moves compared to how far the **solvent** has travelled.

$$R_f = \frac{\text{distance moved by substance}}{\text{distance moved by solvent}}$$

It will always be a number between 0 and 1.

The R_f value depends on the solvent and the temperature, and different substances will have different R_f values. The R_f values for particular solvents can be used to identify a substance.

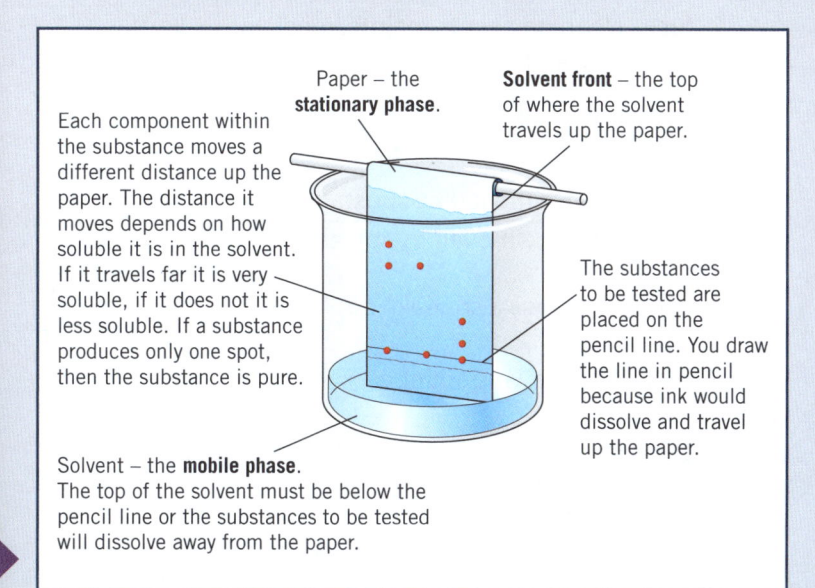

Each component within the substance moves a different distance up the paper. The distance it moves depends on how soluble it is in the solvent. If it travels far it is very soluble, if it does not it is less soluble. If a substance produces only one spot, then the substance is pure.

Paper – the **stationary phase**.

Solvent front – the top of where the solvent travels up the paper.

The substances to be tested are placed on the pencil line. You draw the line in pencil because ink would dissolve and travel up the paper.

Solvent – the **mobile phase**. The top of the solvent must be below the pencil line or the substances to be tested will dissolve away from the paper.

> **Revision tip**
>
> **Practice** Ensure you can describe the function of each piece of equipment used in chromatography – they all have an important role.

> **Revision tip**
>
> **Practice** Use a coloured pencil to help identify which spots appear in more than one sample by drawing horizontal and vertical lines through the spots on the chromatogram.

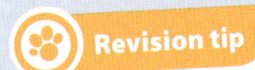

Testing for gases

Common gases can be identified using the following tests:

Gas	What you do	What you observe if gas is present
hydrogen	hold a lighted splint near the gas	hear a squeaky pop
oxygen	hold a glowing splint near the gas	splint re-lights
carbon dioxide	bubble the gas through limewater	the limewater turns milky (cloudy white)
chlorine	hold a piece of damp litmus near the gas	bleaches the litmus white

pure R_f value   solvent   solvent front   stationary phase

C12 Knowledge   287

Retrieval

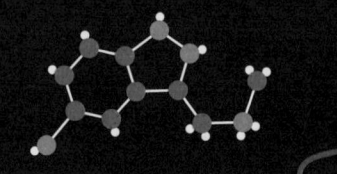

Learn the answers to the questions below, then cover the answers column with a piece of paper and write as many as you can. Check and repeat.

C12 questions | Answers

#	Question	Answer
1	In chemistry, what is a pure substance?	something made of a single element or compound
2	What is the difference between the melting and boiling points of a pure and impure substance?	pure – sharp/one specific temperature impure – broad/occur across a range of temperatures
3	What is a formulation?	a mixture designed for a specific purpose
4	What are some examples of formulations?	fuels, cleaning agents, paints, medicines, alloys, fertilisers, and foods
5	What is chromatography?	a process for separating coloured mixtures, which can help to identify substances
6	How is R_f calculated?	$R_f = \dfrac{\text{distance moved by substance}}{\text{distance moved by solvent}}$
7	What is the test for hydrogen?	a lit splint gives a squeaky pop
8	What is the test for oxygen?	re-lights a glowing splint
9	What is the test for carbon dioxide?	turns limewater milky if bubbled through it
10	What is the test for chlorine?	bleaches damp litmus paper white
11	What are the names of the two phases involved in chromatography?	stationary and mobile
12	How many spots will a pure compound produce on a chromatogram?	one spot

C12

Now go back and use the questions below to check your knowledge from previous chapters.

Previous questions / Answers

#	Question	Answer
1	How is crude oil formed?	over millions of years from the remains of ancient biomass
2	Name four useful materials produced from crude oil.	solvents, lubricants, polymers, detergents
3	What are the products of cracking?	short chain alkanes and alkenes
4	What are the first four alkanes?	methane, ethane, propane, butane
5	What effect does increasing pressure have on the rate of reaction?	increases
6	What is an exothermic energy transfer?	transfer to the surroundings
7	What is a catalyst?	substance that increases the rate of a reaction but is not used up in the reaction
8	In terms of pH, what is an acid?	solution with a pH of less than 7

Required practical skills

Practise answering questions on the required practicals using the example below. You need to be able to apply your skills and knowledge to other practicals too.

Analysing chromatograms

Chromatography can be used to identify unknown substances.

The ratio of the distance moved by a compound (centre of spot from origin) to the distance moved by the solvent can be expressed as its R_f value:

$$R_f = \frac{\text{distance moved by substance}}{\text{distance moved by solvent}}$$

Different compounds have different R_f values in different solvents. Therefore, you can compare your experimental R_f value with a value from a database to identify the substance.

Worked example

A student obtained the following chromatogram.

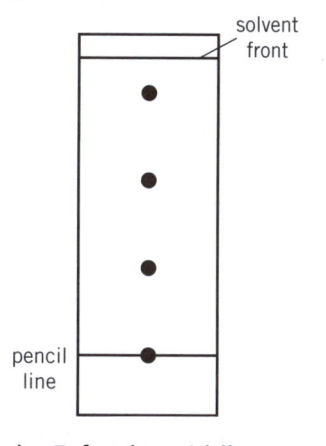

Calculate the R_f for the middle spot.

Measure the distance from the pencil line to the solvent front – 33.5 mm.

Measure the value from the pencil line to the spot – 20 mm.

Put the values into the equation:

$$R_f = \frac{20}{33.5} = 0.59$$

Practice

1. Calculate the R_f value of the bottom spot from the chromatogram.

2. The table shows the R_f values of some dyes. Identify which dye would produce the top spot on a chromatogram.

Dye	R_f
red	0.31
yellow	0.57
blue	0.82

3. A student calculated the R_f value of a spot on a chromatogram as 1.34. Is this value correct? Explain your answer.

C12 Retrieval

Practice

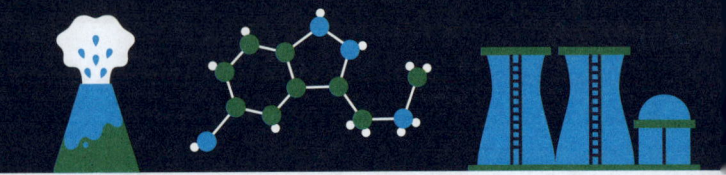

Exam-style questions

01.1 Choose the correct words from the box to complete the sentences. **[3 marks]**

| pure | pressures | temperatures | mixed | bonded |

A pure substance is an element or compound that is not _____ with any other substance.

A pure substance will melt or boil at specific _____.

This can be used to tell the difference between _____ substances and mixtures.

> **Exam Tip**
>
> Make sure you know the definitions of an element, compound, and mixture.

01.2 Name a piece of equipment that can be used to measure when a liquid boils. **[1 mark]**

_____

01.3 Substance **A** boils at 74 °C. Substance **B** melts between 52 °C and 55 °C. Identify which substance is pure. **[1 mark]**
Circle **one** answer.

        substance **A**   substance **B**

01.4 Which substance is pure? **[1 mark]**
Tick **one** box.

air ☐

salty water ☐

carbon dioxide gas ☐

a solution of sodium chloride ☐

01.5 Define the term formulation. **[1 mark]**

_____

_____

01.6 Name **one** example of a formulation. **[1 mark]**

_____

02 Table 1 shows the melting points of five different substances.

Table 1

Substance	Melting point in °C
A	between 88 and 91
B	between 96 and 98
C	98
D	103
E	114

290   C12 Chemical analysis

Paper 4 **C12**

02.1 Identify the temperature at which substance **C** freezes. [1 mark]

> **Exam Tip**
> Freezing is the opposite process to melting, and occurs at the same temperature as the melting point.

02.2 Explain how you can tell that substance **B** is a mixture. [2 marks]

02.3 Suggest what the melting point of a mixture of **C** and **D** would be. [1 mark]

Melting point = _____ °C

> **Exam Tip**
> The substance would be a mixture, so your answer needs to be a range of temperatures.

02.4 Substance **A** is orange juice. The bottle of the orange juice states that it contains pure orange juice.
Explain why the bottle describes it as pure but a scientist would describe it as impure. [3 marks]

03 Petrol is used to fuel cars. **Table 2** shows the different substances that are mixed in a sample of petrol.

Table 2

Substance	Mass of substance in g in 200 g of petrol
alkanes	110
other hydrocarbons	70
ethanol	20

03.1 Petrol is an example of a formulation.
Define the term formulation. [1 mark]

03.2 Use data from **Table 2** to calculate the percentage by mass of ethanol in petrol. [2 marks]

03.3 The molecules of one alkane in petrol have seven carbon atoms.
Give the formula of this alkane. [1 mark]

> **Exam Tip**
> Remember to use the general formula for alkanes: C_nH_{2n+2}.

03.4 Ethanol in petrol is made from plants. The alkanes in petrol are obtained from crude oil.
Suggest **one** advantage of including ethanol in petrol. [1 mark]

C12 Practice 291

04 Table 3 has some information on different methods for separating mixtures.

Table 3

Method	Description
chromatography	Separating liquids based on how far they move through the paper.
filtration	Separating liquids or solutions from solids.
distillation	Separating liquids based on different boiling points.

Identify the best method from **Table 3** to separate each of the following mixtures.

04.1 Insoluble copper oxide from sulfuric acid. **[1 mark]**

04.2 Hexane (boiling point: 68 °C) and water (boiling point: 100 °C). **[1 mark]**

04.3 A mixture of three dyes. **[1 mark]**

04.4 Silicon dioxide (sand) and water. **[1 mark]**

> **Exam Tip**
> Read over the information carefully before you start the question.

05 A student pours dilute hydrochloric acid into a test tube and adds magnesium ribbon. A gas is formed that the student collects.

05.1 Name the **two** products formed in the reaction. **[2 marks]**

05.2 Describe the test the student can carry out to identify the gas collected. Give the expected result. **[2 marks]**

05.3 Another student reacted sulfuric acid with sodium carbonate. A gas was formed that the student collected.
Describe the test the student can carry out to identify the gas collected. Give the expected result. **[2 marks]**

05.4 A scientist had a sample of a pale green gas. They inserted a glowing splint into the gas. The splint went out. The scientist then put some damp litmus paper into the gas. The litmus paper turned white. Identify the gas. **[1 mark]**

> **Exam Tip**
> The introduction to question **05** has given you a clue to one of the products: make sure you've named a gas.

> **Exam Tip**
> Don't worry if you don't know which gas is pale green, it's the result of the test that is important.

06 A new substance called Ocean Friendly Plastic (OFP) is made in a laboratory. OFP is made of three substances. **Table 4** gives the ratio of the three substances.

Table 4

Substance	Ratio
A	6
B	3
C	1

06.1 Which is the best description for OFP
Choose **one** answer. **[1 mark]**

pure substance   compound   formulation

C12 Chemical analysis

06.2 Calculate the percentage of OFP that is substance **C**. **[2 marks]**

06.3 A student wanted to make OFP in the laboratory. Calculate the volume of substance **A** needed to make 250 cm³ of OFP. **[2 marks]**

> **Exam Tip**
> The total for the ratios is 10.

07.1 Draw **one** line from each gas to the correct test for the gas. **[3 marks]**

Gas	Test
hydrogen	relights a glowing splint
oxygen	bleaches damp litmus paper
chlorine	burns with a squeaky pop
	turns bromine water colourless

07.2 When gaseous carbon dioxide is bubbled through limewater, the limewater turns cloudy because solid calcium carbonate is produced.

Complete the balanced symbol equation by adding state symbols. **[1 mark]**

CO_2(____) + $Ca(OH)_2$(____) → $CaCO_3$(____) + H_2O(____)

08 A student has a sample of an ink. The student wants to identify what dyes the ink is made of.

08.1 Describe a method the student can use to separate the dyes in the ink. **[6 marks]**

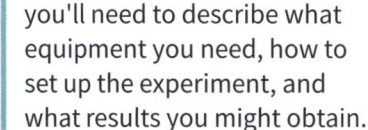

08.2 The student concludes that the ink is made of three dyes. Sketch the chromatogram the student would have obtained. **[1 mark]**

> **Exam Tip**
> This is a 6 mark question, so you'll need to describe what equipment you need, how to set up the experiment, and what results you might obtain.

08.3 The student calculates the R_f value of one of the spots as 1.4. The teacher tells the student that this value is incorrect. Suggest why the teacher knows the value is incorrect. **[1 mark]**

08.4 The student correctly calculates the R_f value as 0.53. **Table 5** shows the R_f values for three dyes.

Table 5

Dye	R_f value
blue	0.90
red	0.53
yellow	0.28

Identify which dye is responsible for the spot. **[1 mark]**

08.5 The label of the ink bottle only gives two substances that the ink is made up of. Suggest a reason why the student obtained three dots on their chromatogram. **[1 mark]**

08.6 Chromatography is often used to test blood samples from athletes for performance-enhancing drugs.

Suggest why the blood samples are sent to an independent laboratory for testing. **[1 mark]**

Exam Tip

Why might someone with no connection to the athletes be the best person to test the samples?

09 A chemist had three unknown gases. The chemist carried out three simple tests to identify the gases. Their observations are shown in **Table 6**.

Table 6

Gas	Burning splint held at open end of tube	Glowing splint inserted into tube	Bubbled through limewater
A	splint goes out	no observation	cloudy
B	burns brighter	splint re-lights	no observation
C	pop sound	no observation	no observation

09.1 Identify the gases **A**, **B**, and **C**. **[3 marks]**

09.2 The chemist has a fourth gas. The chemist thinks the gas is chlorine. Describe how the chemist could confirm that the gas is chlorine. **[2 marks]**

Exam Tip

This is three marks for three short answers. Don't spend time explaining your reasoning because you won't get any extra marks.

10 R_f values can be used to describe how far a spot has moved on the chromatography paper.

$$R_f = \frac{\text{distance moved by substance}}{\text{distance moved by solvent}}$$

Figure 1 shows a chromatogram a student produced.

Figure 1

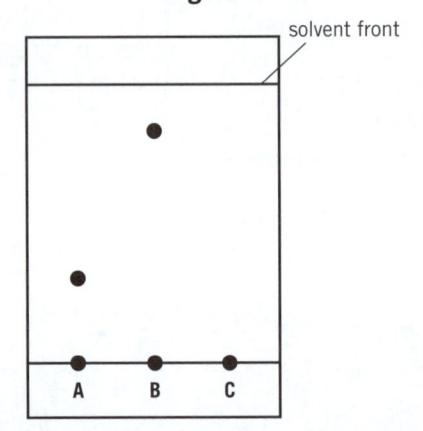

10.1 Calculate the R_f value of **A**. Give your answer to one decimal place. **[2 marks]**

10.2 Is substance **B** pure or impure?
Give a reason for your answer. **[2 marks]**

10.3 The R_f value for **C** is 0.5. Draw the spot for **C** onto **Figure 1**. **[1 mark]**

Exam Tip

Even if you're not sure about the answer to one decimal place you can still get marks by writing down your working.

C12 Chemical analysis

11 A chemist carried out an electrolysis experiment on copper sulfate solution.

11.1 Identify the products that form at the anode and the cathode. **[2 marks]**

11.2 Describe a test the student can use to confirm the identity of the gas produced at the anode. **[2 marks]**

11.3 The chemist then carried out the electrolysis of molten sodium chloride.
Identify the gas produced at the anode. **[1 mark]**

11.4 Describe a test to confirm the identity of the gas produced in the electrolysis of molten sodium chloride. **[2 marks]**

11.5 In the electrolysis of molten sodium chloride, sodium metal is produced at the cathode. The chemist reacts the sodium with water.
Identify the gas produced. **[1 mark]**

11.6 Describe a test to confirm the identity of the gas produced in the reaction between sodium and water. **[2 marks]**

> **Exam Tip**
>
> Remember that the cathode is the negative electrode, and the anode is positive.

12 A student has a selection of mixtures:
- sodium chloride salt dissolved in water
- sand and water
- green ink.

12.1 Name the physical process that can be used to separate the sand and water mixture. **[1 mark]**

12.2 Describe a method that the student could use to obtain a sample of pure, dry sodium chloride from the mixture of sodium chloride dissolved in water. In your method include any equipment you would use. **[6 marks]**

12.3 The student thinks that the green ink is made up of a mixture of two dyes.
Name the physical process the student could use to identify whether they are correct. **[1 mark]**

> **Exam Tip**
>
> This is the same method as for the Required Practical on distillation, just with a different salt.

Knowledge

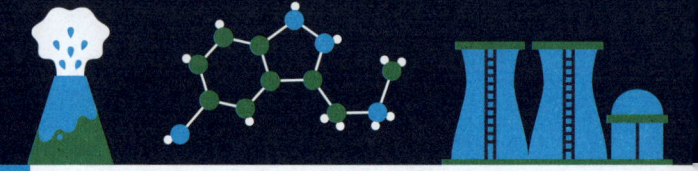

C13 The Earth's atmosphere

The Earth's changing atmosphere

The table below shows how the composition of the atmosphere has changed over the course of the Earth's entire 4.6 billion year history.

Period	Composition of atmosphere	Evidence
about 4.6 billion years to about 2.7 billion years ago	<ul><li>**carbon dioxide, CO_2** Released by volcanoes. Biggest component of the **atmosphere**.</li><li>**oxygen, O_2** Very little oxygen present.</li><li>**nitrogen, N_2** Released by volcanoes.</li><li>**water vapour, H_2O** Released by volcanoes. Existed as vapour as Earth was too hot for it to condense.</li><li>**other gases** Ammonia, NH_3, and methane, CH_4, may also have been present.</li></ul>	Because it was billions of years ago there is very little evidence to draw upon.
about 2.7 billion years ago to about 200 million years ago	<ul><li>**carbon dioxide, CO_2** Amount in atmosphere begins to reduce because:<ul><li>water condenses to form the oceans, in which CO_2 then dissolves</li><li>algae (and later plants) start to photosynthesise</li></ul>carbon dioxide + water $\xrightarrow{light}$ glucose + oxygen $6CO_2 + 6H_2O \longrightarrow C_6H_{12}O_6 + 6O_2$<ul><li>$CO_2$ precipitates in the oceans as solid carbonates (sediments) that form rocks</li><li>CO_2 taken in by plants and animals. When they die, the carbon in them is locked up as fossil fuels.</li></ul></li><li>**oxygen, O_2** Starts to increase as a product of photosynthesis.</li><li>**nitrogen, N_2** Continues to increase. Nitrogen is a very stable molecule so any process that produces it causes the overall amount to build up over time.</li><li>**water vapour, H_2O** Starts to decrease. As the Earth cools, the vapour condenses and forms the oceans.</li></ul>	Still limited as billions of years ago, but can look at processes that happen today (like photosynthesis) and make theories about the past.
about 200 million years ago until the present	<ul><li>**carbon dioxide, CO_2** about 0.04%</li><li>**oxygen, O_2** about 20%</li><li>**nitrogen, N_2** about 80%</li><li>**water vapour, H_2O** Very little overall. Collects in large clouds as part of the water cycle.</li><li>**other gases** Small proportions of other gases such as the noble gases.</li></ul> Pie chart: nitrogen ~80%, oxygen ~20%, small proportions of other gases, such as water vapour, carbon dioxide, and noble gases	Ice core evidence for millions of years ago and lots of global measurements taken recently.

Key terms

Make sure you can write a definition for these key terms.

acid rain   atmosphere   carbon footprint   global climate change

C13

Greenhouse gases

Greenhouse gases, such as carbon dioxide, methane, and water vapour, absorb radiation and maintain temperatures on the Earth to support life.

However, in the last 150 years, more greenhouse gases have been released due to human activities:
- carbon dioxide – combustion of fossil fuels, deforestation
- methane – planting rice fields, cattle farming.

Diagram labels:
① short wave radiation
② the atmosphere absorbs and reflects some radiation
③ energy emitted by the Earth as long wave radiation
④ greenhouse gases in the atmosphere absorb the long waves, trapping the energy and warming the Earth

Global warming

Scientists have gathered peer-reviewed evidence to demonstrate that increasing the amount of greenhouse gases in the atmosphere from the last 150 years will increase the overall average temperature of the Earth. This is called **global warming**.

However, it is difficult to make predictions about the atmosphere as it is so big and complex. This leads some people to doubt what scientists say.

Global climate change

Global warming leads to another process called **global climate change** – how the overall weather patterns over many years and across the entire planet will change.

There are many different effects of climate change, including:
- sea levels rising
- extreme weather events
- changes in the amount and time of rainfall
- changes to ecosystems and habitats
- polar ice caps melting.

Carbon footprints

Increasing the amount of greenhouse gases in the atmosphere increases the global average temperature of the Earth, which results in global climate change.

As such, it is important to reduce the release of greenhouse gases into the atmosphere. The amount of carbon dioxide and methane that is released into the atmosphere by a product, person, or process is called its **carbon footprint**.

Other pollutants released in the combustion of fuels

Pollutant	Origin	Effect
carbon monoxide	incomplete combustion of fuels	colourless and odourless toxic gas
particulates (soot and unburnt hydrocarbons)	incomplete combustion of fuels, especially in diesel engines	**global dimming**, respiratory problems, potential to cause cancer
sulfur dioxide	sulfur impurities in the fuel reacting with oxygen from the air	**acid rain** and respiratory problems
oxides of nitrogen	nitrogen from the air being heated near an engine and reacting with oxygen	acid rain and respiratory problems

global dimming   global warming   greenhouse gas   particulate   pollutant

C13 Knowledge

Retrieval

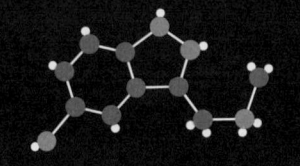

Learn the answers to the questions below, then cover the answers column with a piece of paper and write as many as you can. Check and repeat.

C13 questions / Answers

#	Question	Answer
1	What is the atmosphere?	a layer of gas surrounding the Earth
2	What was the early atmosphere composed of?	mostly carbon dioxide
3	How did the oceans form?	water vapour condensing as the Earth cooled
4	How did the amount of carbon dioxide in the atmosphere decrease to today's levels?	dissolved in the oceans, photosynthesis, converted to fossil fuels, precipitated as insoluble metal carbonates
5	When did life start to appear, and what was the impact of this on oxygen in the atmosphere?	about 2.7 billion years ago; amount of atmospheric oxygen increased as it was released in photosynthesis
6	How has the amount of nitrogen in the atmosphere changed over time?	increased slowly as it is a very stable molecule
7	Why can scientists not be sure about the composition of the Earth's early atmosphere?	it was billions of years ago and evidence is limited
8	What is the current composition of the atmosphere?	approximately 80% nitrogen, 20% oxygen, and trace amounts of other gases such as carbon dioxide, water vapour, and noble gases
9	What is a greenhouse gas?	a gas that traps radiation from the Sun
10	What type of radiation do greenhouse gases absorb?	longer wavelength infrared radiation
11	Name three greenhouse gases.	methane, carbon dioxide, water vapour
12	Give two ways recent human activities have increased the amount of atmospheric carbon dioxide.	burning fossil fuels, deforestation
13	Give two ways recent human activities have increased the amount of atmospheric methane.	rice farming, cattle farming
14	What is global warming?	an increase in the overall global average temperature
15	What is global climate change?	the change in long-term weather patterns across the planet
16	What are some possible effects of climate change?	sea levels rising, extreme weather events, changes in the amount and time of rainfall, changes to ecosystems and habitats, polar ice caps melting
17	What is a carbon footprint?	the amount of carbon a product, process, or person releases into the atmosphere over its lifetime
18	How is carbon monoxide formed, and what is the danger associated with it?	incomplete combustion; can cause death because colourless and odourless toxic gas
19	How are particulates formed, and what are the dangers associated with them?	incomplete combustion; global dimming, respiratory problems, potential to cause cancer
20	How is sulfur dioxide formed, and what are the dangers associated with it?	sulfur impurities in fossil fuels react with oxygen during combustion; acid rain, respiratory problems
21	How are oxides of nitrogen formed, and what are the dangers associated with them?	atmospheric oxygen and nitrogen react in the heat of a combustion engine; acid rain, respiratory problems

C13 The Earth's atmosphere

C13

Now go back and use the questions below to check your knowledge from previous chapters.

Previous questions | Answers

#	Question	Answer
1	In chemistry, what is a pure substance?	something made of only one element or compound
2	What is a compound?	substance made of more than one type of atom chemically joined together
3	What is the test for hydrogen?	a lit splint gives a squeaky pop
4	What is the test for chlorine?	bleaches damp litmus paper white
5	What is the plum pudding model of the atom?	sphere of positive charge with negative electrons embedded in it
6	Describe the structure and bonding of a giant covalent substance.	billions of atoms bonded together by strong covalent bonds
7	What is a fraction?	a group of hydrocarbons with similar chain lengths
8	Name five useful fuels produced from fractional distillation.	petrol, diesel oil, kerosene, heavy fuel oil, liquefied petroleum gases

Maths skills

Practise your maths skills using the worked example and practice questions below.

Lines of best fit

When describing lines of best fit, you need to state:
- its correlation
- if the line is straight or curved
- whether the line plateaus (stops changing, and flattens out)
- whether the line runs through the origin (0,0).

Correlations can be positive or negative and either strong or weak, or there can be no correlation.

If the line of best fit is straight and goes through the origin, the variables are **directly proportional** to each other, meaning as one variable changes the other changes at the same rate.

Worked example

Fully describe the curved line of best fit for the reaction plotted on the graph below.

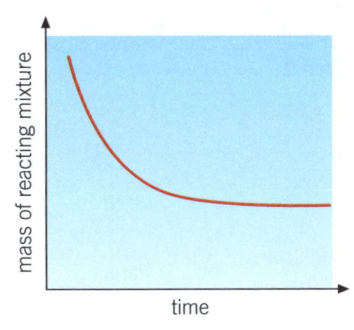

(graph: mass of reacting mixture vs time, curve decreasing and plateauing)

The graph shows a negative correlation.

The curved line of best fit does not pass through the origin.

The mass of the mixture decreases rapidly at first, this decrease then slows down, and finally plateaus as the mass stops decreasing with time.

Practice

The graph below shows how the volume of gas produced changes with time in the reaction between marble chips and hydrochloric acid.

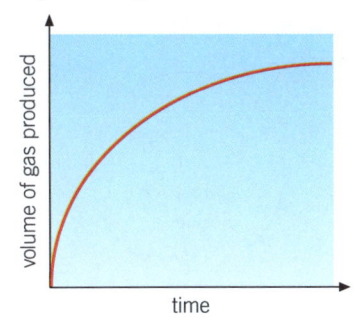

(graph: volume of gas produced vs time, curve increasing and plateauing)

1. Describe the graph.
2. Sketch a graph to show a directly proportional relationship between two variables.

C13 Retrieval 299

Practice

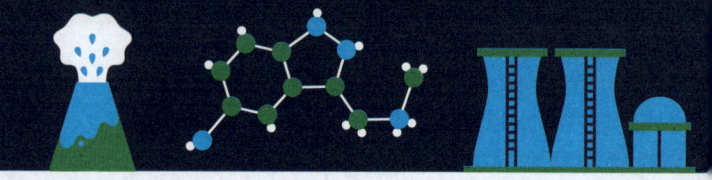

Exam-style questions

01 **Figure 1** shows the composition of the Earth's atmosphere today.

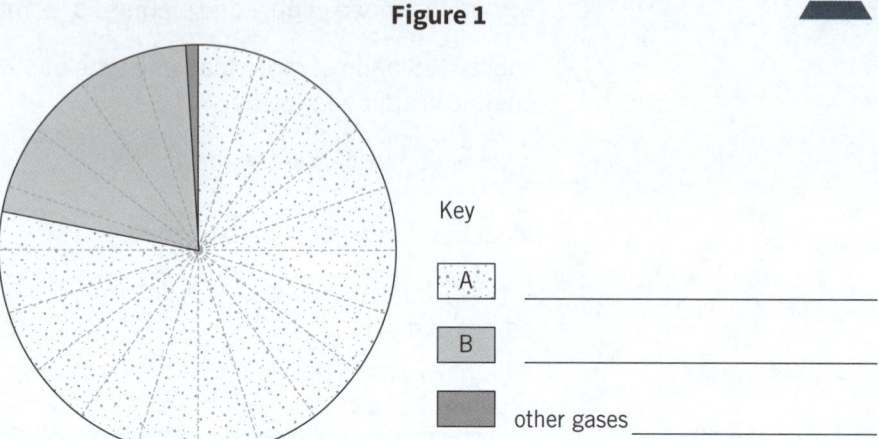

Figure 1

Key
A _____
B _____
other gases _____

01.1 Write the names of gases **A** and **B** on **Figure 1**. [2 marks]

01.2 Determine the percentage of gas **B** in the atmosphere. [2 marks]

Percentage of gas **B**: _____

01.3 Write the name of one of the other gases on **Figure 1**. [1 mark]

01.4 The early atmosphere was very different to the atmosphere today. Which pie chart in **Figure 2** shows the suggested composition of the atmosphere 4.6 billion years ago? [1 mark]

Tick **one** box.

Figure 2

(Pie chart 1: oxygen, carbon dioxide)
(Pie chart 2: nitrogen, oxygen, carbon dioxide)
(Pie chart 3: nitrogen, methane, and ammonia; carbon dioxide)

> **Exam Tip**
>
> **Figure 1** is split into 20 segments. Work out how many are for gas **B**, then work out the percentage using:
>
> $$\frac{\text{number of segments for gas B}}{\text{total number of segments}} \times 100$$

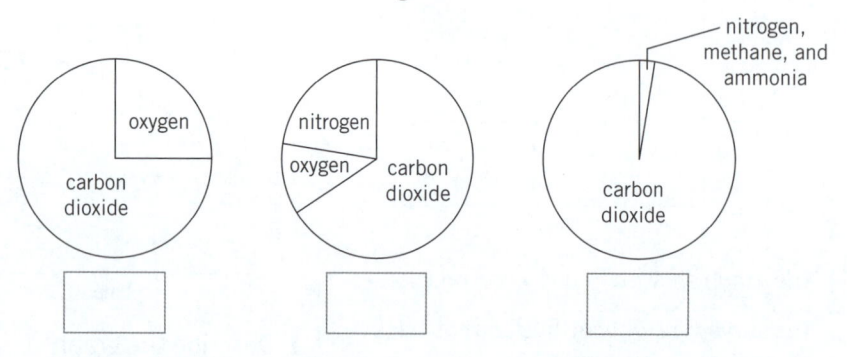

01.5 Describe how the atmosphere changed from **Figure 2** to today (**Figure 1**). [6 marks]

_____
_____
_____
_____

C13 The Earth's atmosphere

Paper 4 — C13

02 This question is about the greenhouse effect.

02.1 Which of the following are greenhouse gases? **[3 marks]**

Circle **three** answers.

| carbon dioxide | chlorine | methane |
| oxygen | water vapour | nitrogen |

02.2 Complete the sentences using the words from the boxes. **[4 marks]**

| short | long | reflected | released |

The Sun releases _____ wave radiation.

Some of this radiation is _____ by the atmosphere and some is absorbed.

| short | long | warms | cools |

Energy that passes through the atmosphere is then emitted by the Earth as _____ wave radiation.

Some of the _____ wave radiation can no longer pass through the atmosphere and _____ the Earth.

02.3 Give **one** human activity that causes an increase in the amounts of greenhouse gases in the atmosphere. **[1 mark]**

_____

03 **Table 1** and **Figure 3** show the average concentration of carbon dioxide in the atmosphere every January from 2010 to 2019.

Table 1

Year	Average concentration of CO_2 in January in parts per million
2010	389
2011	391
2012	393
2013	395
2014	398
2015	400
2016	403
2017	406
2018	408
2019	411

Figure 3

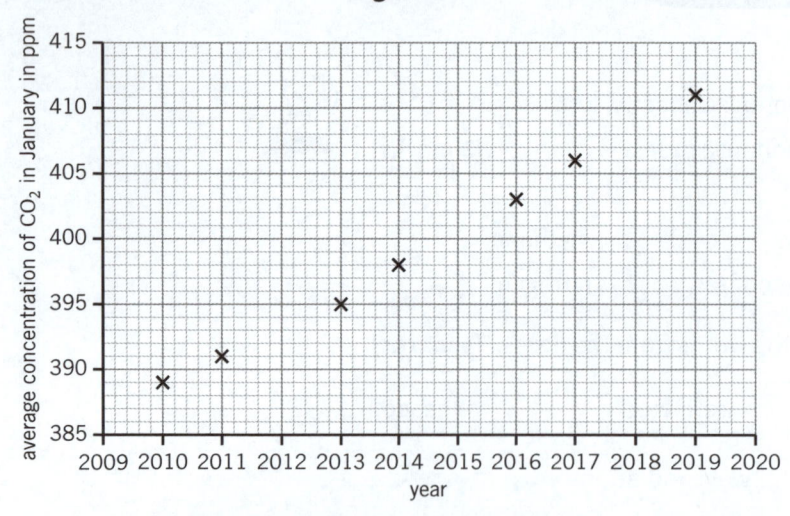

03.1 Complete **Figure 3** by plotting the data points for 2012, 2015, and 2018. Draw a line of best fit. [2 marks]

03.2 Describe the trend shown in **Figure 3**. [1 mark]

03.3 Describe and explain how **two** human activities are responsible for the trend shown in **Figure 3**. [4 marks]

04 This question is about air pollutants.

04.1 Which pollutant is formed in car engines from the reaction between two gases that occur naturally in the atmosphere? Choose **one** answer. [1 mark]

- carbon dioxide
- oxides of nitrogen
- carbon particulates
- sulfur dioxide

04.2 Carbon monoxide is also produced in car engines. Name the process that produces carbon monoxide. [1 mark]

04.3 Balance the symbol equation for the process that produces carbon monoxide from a fuel. [1 mark]

_____ $C_4H_{10}(g)$ + _____ $O_2(g)$ → _____ $CO(g)$ + _____ $H_2O(l)$

04.4 Draw **one** line from each pollutant to an effect of the pollutant. [3 marks]

Pollutant	Effect
oxides of nitrogen	poisoning humans
carbon monoxide	global dimming
particulates	global climate change
	breathing problems

04.5 Name the gas that causes acid rain. [1 mark]

Exam Tips

- Place a clear ruler over the points and see where most of them fit the line with an equal number on either side.
- 03.2 is a one mark question, so a simple description of the shape is all that is needed.
- Think about which gases are found at the highest levels in the atmosphere.
- Start with the carbons, then the hydrogens and leave the oxygens until last.

05.1 Draw **one** line from each pollutant to its correct formula. **[3 marks]**

Pollutant | Formula

carbon particulates

sulfur dioxide

oxides of nitrogen

C

CO

NO$_x$

SO$_2$

Exam Tip

Don't worry if you don't know the exact formula. Use the first letter of the formula to help you work it out, or the Periodic Table.

05.2 Complete the sentences about the pollutants given in **05.1**. **[3 marks]**

_____ are produced when air near an engine is heated.

The _____ in the air reacts with oxygen.

_____ is produced when fossil fuels with _____ impurities are burnt.

_____ are produced in the incomplete combustion of fuels in diesel engines.

05.3 Give the effects caused by these atmospheric pollutants. **[3 marks]**

05.4 When a gas boiler in a house does not receive enough oxygen, the fuel can start to undergo incomplete combustion. This produces carbon monoxide. Carbon monoxide is a toxic gas. The government recommends fitting carbon monoxide alarms in houses to detect the production of carbon monoxide gas.

Explain why a carbon monoxide alarm is needed. **[2 marks]**

Exam Tip

A lot of information is provided in **05.4**, but to answer it you only need to recall what you have learnt about carbon monoxide. Don't let long questions put you off. The information is there to help guide you to the knowledge you already have.

06 Carbon dioxide is a greenhouse gas.

06.1 Define the term greenhouse gas. **[1 mark]**

06.2 Name **one** other greenhouse gas. **[1 mark]**

06.3 Give **two** human activities that increase the amount of carbon dioxide in the atmosphere. **[2 marks]**

06.4 Increasing amounts of greenhouse gases result in an increase in average global temperature. This is a major cause of climate change. Give **one** effect of global climate change and explain the negative impact this could have on humanity. **[2 marks]**

07 This question is about the carbon footprint of a journey by road. **Table 2** shows carbon dioxide emissions data for a car and a bus.

Table 2

Vehicle	Mass of CO$_2$ emitted by the vehicle in g per km
car	100
bus	1050

07.1 Define the term carbon footprint. [1 mark]

07.2 A car travels 120 km. Use data from **Table 2** to calculate the mass of CO_2 emitted by the car on this journey. Give your answer in g and in standard form. [2 marks]

07.3 Two people are travelling in the car during the 120 km journey. Calculate the mass of CO_2 emitted by the car per person for this journey. [1 mark]

07.4 A bus travels on the same 120 km journey as the car. The bus contains 25 people. Calculate the mass of CO_2 emitted per person for the bus journey. [2 marks]

07.5 Identify whether the people travelling on the bus had a greater carbon footprint or a smaller carbon footprint than those travelling in the car. Give a reason for your answer. [2 marks]

07.6 Name **one** other gas that contributes to a carbon footprint. [1 mark]

07.7 Give **one** way in which people can offset their carbon footprint. [1 mark]

08 The atmosphere is made up of different gases.

08.1 Draw **one** line from each atmospheric gas to the correct proportion of the gas that is found in the atmosphere. [2 marks]

Atmospheric gas	Proportion of gas in the atmosphere
carbon dioxide, water, and noble gases	~$\frac{4}{5}$
oxygen	~$\frac{1}{5}$
nitrogen	very small amounts

08.2 Give **two** ways in which the atmosphere of the early Earth is different to today's atmosphere. [2 marks]

08.3 Name the process that algae carry out that produced the oxygen in the atmosphere. Choose **one** answer. [1 mark]

combustion   photosynthesis
oxidation   respiration

08.4 Complete the sentences. [2 marks]

Water vapour in the atmosphere _____ to form the oceans. Carbon dioxide then _____ in the oceans.

08.5 Where did the nitrogen in today's atmosphere come from? [1 mark]

09 The composition of the Earth's atmosphere has changed since the Earth formed about 4.6 billion years ago.

09.1 Why is there little evidence about the early atmosphere? [1 mark]

C13 The Earth's atmosphere

09.2 Describe and explain how the percentages of carbon dioxide and oxygen in the atmosphere have changed over the past 4.6 billion years. **[6 marks]**

09.3 Name **two** greenhouse gases that are added into the atmosphere as a result of human activity. **[2 marks]**

09.4 Name the effect of human activity increasing the greenhouse gases in the atmosphere. **[1 mark]**

10 Scientists believe that the early atmosphere of the Earth contained no oxygen.

10.1 What percentage of the atmosphere today is oxygen?
Choose **one** answer. **[1 mark]**
0.04%   20%   80%

10.2 Describe how plants and algae led to an increase in the percentage of oxygen in the atmosphere. Include a word equation in your answer. **[3 marks]**

10.3 A student wanted to demonstrate that plants produce oxygen. They collected the gas produced by a sample of pondweed. Describe a test that the student can use to confirm that the gas collected is oxygen. **[2 marks]**

10.4 Scientists also believe that the early atmosphere contained a lot more carbon dioxide. Name **one** process by which carbon dioxide was removed from the atmosphere. **[1 mark]**

11 A student wanted to test a sample to see if it was pure. **Figure 4** shows the results they collected.

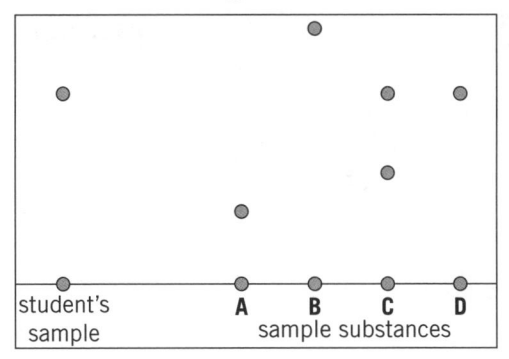

Figure 4

11.1 Name the technique the student used. **[1 mark]**

11.2 Identify which sample substance is a mixture. Give a reason for your answer. **[2 marks]**

11.3 Identify which sample substance is identical to the student's sample. **[1 mark]**

11.4 Another student carried out a similar experiment but the results were a long continuous upwards blur. The only difference in how they set up the experiment was in the drawing of the start line. Suggest the mistake the second student made. **[1 mark]**

Knowledge

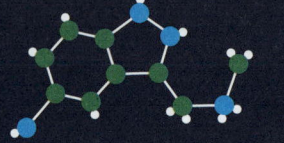

C14 Using the Earth's resources A

Natural and synthetic resources

We use the Earth's resources to provide us with warmth, fuel, shelter, food, and transport.
- Natural resources are used for food, timber, clothing, and fuels.
- Synthetic resources are made by scientists. They can replace or supplement natural resources.

When choosing and synthesising resources, it is important to consider **sustainable development**. This is development that meets the needs of current generations without compromising the ability of future generations to meet their own needs.

Finite and renewable resources

Some resources are **finite**. This means that they will eventually run out.

Fossil fuels are an example of a finite resource. They take so long to form that we use them faster than they are naturally formed.

Resources that will not run out are called **renewable** resources.

Wood is an example of a renewable resource. Trees can be grown to replace any that are cut down for wood.

Potable water

Water is a vital resource for life. **Potable** water is water that is safe to drink. However, most water on Earth is not potable.

Type of water	What it has in it
pure water	just water molecules and nothing else
potable water	water molecules, low levels of salts, safe levels of harmful microbes
salty water (sea water)	water molecules, dangerously high levels of salts, can have high levels of harmful microbes
fresh water (from rivers, lakes, or underground)	water molecules, low levels of salts, often has harmful microbes at high levels

Fresh water

In the UK, potable water is produced from rain water that collects in lakes and rivers. To produce potable water:
1. Choose an appropriate source of fresh water.
2. Pass the water through filters to remove large objects.
3. **Sterilise** the water to kill any microbes using ozone, chlorine, or UV light.

Salty water

Some countries do not have lots of fresh water available. **Desalination** is the process to turn saltwater into potable water. This requires a lot of energy and can be done by:
- distillation
- **reverse osmosis**

Reverse osmosis involves using membranes to separate the salts dissolved in the water. The water needs to be pressurised and the salty water corrodes the pumps. As such, it is an expensive process.

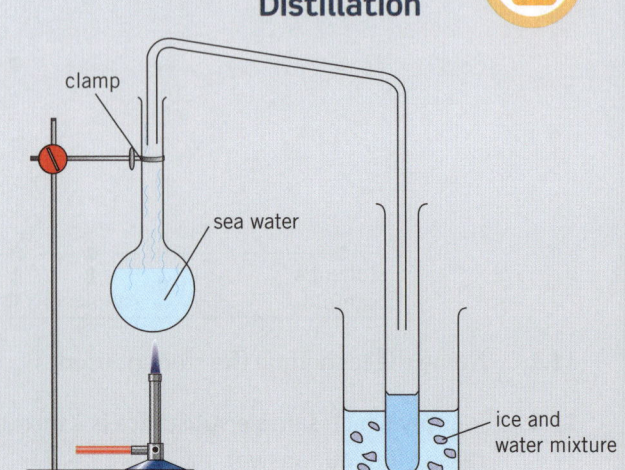

Distillation

Key terms

Make sure you can write a definition for these key terms.

biodegrade · desalination · distillation · effluent · finite resources · life cycle assessment · potable · recycle · renewable resources · reverse osmosis · screening · sedimentation · sewage · sludge · sterilisation · sustainable development

C14

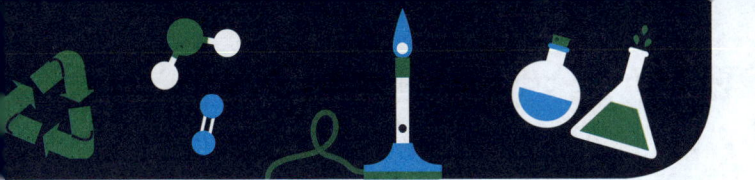

Waste water

Human activities produce lots of waste water as sewage, agricultural waste, and industrial waste.
- **Sewage** and agricultural waste contain organic matter and harmful microbes.
- Industrial waste contains organic matter and harmful chemicals.

These need to be removed before the water can be put back into the environment.

Treating sewage water

screening and grit removal
The sewage passes through a metal grid that filters out large objects.

sedimentation
The sewage is left so that solid sediments settle out of the water. The sediments sink to the bottom of the tank. The liquid sits above the sediment.

Treating sludge

sewage sludge
This sediment is called **sludge**. Sludge contains organic matter, water, dissolved compounds, and small solid particles.

anaerobic treatment
Bacteria are added to digest the organic matter. These bacteria break down the matter anaerobically – with a limited supply of oxygen.

biogas
The anaerobic digestion of sludge produces biogas. Biogas is a mixture of methane, carbon dioxide, and hydrogen sulfide. It can be used as fuel.

remaining sludge used as fuel
The remaining sludge can be dried out and can also be burnt as a fuel.

Treating effluent

effluent
The remaining liquid is called **effluent**. This effluent has no visible solid matter, but still contains some matter and harmful microorganisms.

aerobic treatment
Bacteria are added to the effluent. These bacteria feed on organic matter and the harmful microorganisms in the effluent. The bacteria break down the matter by aerobic respiration – oxygen needs to be present.

bacteria removed
The bacteria are allowed to settle out of the water.

discharged back to rivers
The water is now safe enough to be put back into the environment.

C14 Knowledge   307

Knowledge

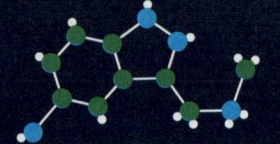

C14 Using the Earth's resources B

Life cycle assessment

A **life cycle assessment (LCA)** is a way of looking at the whole life of a product and assessing its impact on the environment and sustainability. It is broken down into four categories:
- extracting and processing raw materials
- manufacturing and packaging
- use and operation during its lifetime
- disposal at the end of its useful life, including transport and distribution at each stage.

Some parts of an LCA are objective, such as the amount of water used or waste produced in the production of a product.

However, other parts of an LCA require judgements, such as the polluting effect, and so LCAs are not a completely objective process.

Disposal of products

When someone finishes with a product, it can be
- added to a landfill
  This can cause habitat loss and other problems in the local ecosystem. Some items persist in landfills as they do not **biodegrade** and could be there for hundreds of years.
- incinerated
  Some products can be incinerated to produce useful energy. However, the combustion can often be incomplete and result in harmful pollutants being released to the atmosphere.
- reused
  This is when an item is used again for a similar purpose.
- **recycled**
  Recycling requires energy, but conserves the limited resources and often requires less energy than needed to make brand new materials.

The table shows information about the extraction, processing, and disposal of some common materials. This information is used when making an LCA.

Material	Extraction/processing	Disposal
metal	• quarrying and mining cause habitat loss • machinery involved in mining releases greenhouse gases • extraction from metal ores requires lots of energy	• metals can normally be recycled by melting them down and then casting them into new shapes • metals in landfill can persist for a long time
plastic	• normally come from fossil fuels that are non-renewable	• many plastic products can be reused and recycled • plastics often end up in landfills where they persist as they are not biodegradable • incinerating plastics releases lots of harmful pollutants like carbon monoxide and particulates
paper	• produced from trees that require land and lots of water to grow • lots of water also used in the production process	• many paper products can be recycled • paper products can also be incinerated or they can decay naturally in a landfill • incineration and decay release greenhouse gases
glass	• produced from sand, which is a finite resource • sand is heated, which requires a lot of energy	• many glass products can be reused, or crushed and recycled • if glass is added to landfills it persists as it is not biodegradable
ceramics	• come from clay and rocks, which are finite resources • generally require quarrying, which requires energy, releases pollutants from heavy machinery, and causes habitat loss	• most ceramics are not commonly recycled in the UK, and once broken cannot be reused • ceramics tend to persist in landfills

Retrieval

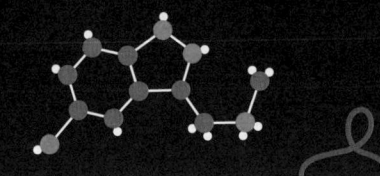

Learn the answers to the questions below, then cover the answers column with a piece of paper and write as many as you can. Check and repeat.

C14 questions / Answers

#	Question	Answer
1	What do we use the Earth's resources for?	warmth, shelter, food, fuel, transport
2	What are some examples of natural resources?	cotton, wool, timber
3	What are some examples of synthetic resources?	plastic, polyester, acrylic
4	What is a finite resource?	a resource that will eventually run out
5	What is sustainable development?	development that meets the needs of current generations without compromising the ability of future generations to meet their own needs
6	What are the four main types of water?	pure water, salt water, fresh water, potable water
7	What is potable water?	water that is safe to drink
8	In the UK, how is potable water extracted from fresh water?	filtration and sterilisation
9	What is sterilisation?	killing microbes
10	What are three examples of sterilising agents?	chlorine gas, UV light, and ozone
11	How can potable water be produced from salt water?	desalination
12	How can desalination be carried out?	distillation or reverse osmosis
13	What are the three main types of waste water?	sewage, agricultural waste, industrial waste
14	What can waste water contain?	organic matter, harmful microbes, harmful chemicals
15	What is the first step in processing waste water?	screening and grit removal
16	What is sedimentation?	separating the waste water into sludge and effluent
17	How is sludge treated?	anaerobic respiration
18	How is effluent treated?	aerobic respiration
19	What is a life cycle assessment?	a way of assessing the energy costs and environmental effect of a product across its lifetime
20	What are the four stages of a life cycle assessment?	• extracting and processing raw materials • manufacturing and packaging • use and operation during its lifetime • disposal at the end of its useful life
21	How can we reduce the amount of new materials manufactured?	by reducing, reusing, or recycling products
22	In what ways can materials that are not recycled be disposed?	landfill or incineration

C14

Now go back and use the questions below to check your knowledge from previous chapters.

Previous questions | Answers

#	Question	Answer
1	What is the atmosphere?	a layer of gas surrounding the Earth
2	Explain why alloys are harder than pure metals.	different sized atoms disturb the layers, preventing them from sliding over each other
3	Give two properties of graphene.	strong, conducts electricity
4	What are alkanes?	hydrocarbons that only have single bonds
5	What is global warming?	an increase in the overall global average temperature
6	What is a carbon footprint?	the amount of carbon a product, process, or organism releases into the atmosphere over its lifetime
7	What is chromatography?	a process for separating coloured mixtures
8	What is the test for carbon dioxide?	turns limewater milky if bubbled through it
9	Name the force that holds oppositely charged ions together.	electrostatic force of attraction

Required practical skills

Practise answering questions on the required practicals using the example below. You need to be able to apply your skills and knowledge to other practicals too.

Water purification

You need to be able to describe how to analyse the purity of a water sample, and how to use distillation to purify the sample.

To do this, you need to know how to test pH, and describe the method of distillation for any solution. In an exam, you may also be asked about the purity and purification of different samples other than water.

You should also learn the different terms describing how water is made safe to drink.

Worked example

A student wanted to determine the identity of a salt dissolved in a sample of water. They evaporated away 100 cm³ of the 1 M solution. The empty evaporating basin weighed 92.78 g, and the basin containing the solids after evaporation weighed 98.63 g. Suggest how you could determine the identity of the salt.

mass of solid salt = 98.63 − 92.78 = 5.85 g

5.85 g salt in 100 cm³ = 58.5 g in 1 dm³

$M_r = \dfrac{mass}{moles}$

$M_r = \dfrac{58.5}{1} = 58.5$

The salt has an M_r of 58.5, so use the relative atomic masses on the Periodic Table to determine a potential identity: 23 (Na) + 35.5 (Cl) = 58.5, so the salt could be NaCl.

This could be confirmed using a flame test and a halide test.

Practice

1. Explain how you could use pH to determine if a sample of water is pure.

2. After carrying out a distillation experiment, a student re-distilled the distillate. Suggest what the student would have observed.

3. Describe the difference between pure and potable water.

C14 Using the Earth's resources

Practice

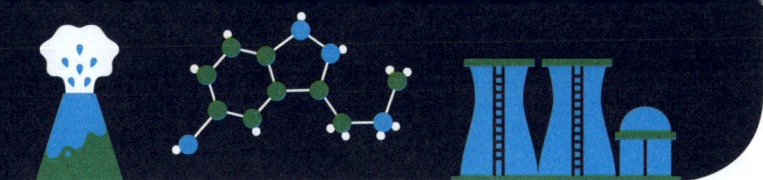

Exam-style questions

01 Some of the resources we use are finite and some are renewable.

01.1 Which resources are finite? **[3 marks]**
Circle **three** answers.

    sunlight   coal   water   oil   natural gas

01.2 Many scientists are trying to reduce the amount of plastic that humanity uses. Describe **one** way in which the amount of plastic we use can be reduced. **[1 mark]**

_____

_____

01.3 More products are being made out of renewable resources to ensure sustainable development.
Define the term sustainable development. **[1 mark]**
Tick **one** box.

Development that meets the needs of current generations without compromising the ability of future generations to meet their own needs.	☐
Development that meets the needs of future generations.	☐
Development that reduces the cost of products and services for future generations.	☐

02 The UK gets most of its potable water from rain, which collects in reservoirs and lakes.

02.1 Define the term potable water. **[1 mark]**
Tick **one** box.

water that contains microbes	☐
water that is pure	☐
water that is safe to drink	☐

Paper 4

02.2 Rain water needs to be treated before it is potable.
Draw **one** line from each treatment of water to the correct purpose of that treatment. **[2 marks]**

Treatment of water	Purpose of treatment
	digest organic matter
filtering	kill harmful microbes
sterilisation	remove objects such as leaves and twigs
	remove salts

02.3 Name **one** sterilising agent. **[1 mark]**

_____

02.4 Potable water has a pH of 7.
What colour would universal indicator turn in potable water? **[1 mark]**
Circle **one** answer.

red   green   purple

02.5 Potable water can be produced from sea water.
Name the process by which sea water is treated to produce potable water. **[1 mark]**

_____

03 A student has an empty glass jar.

03.1 Which is an example of recycling? **[1 mark]**
Choose **one** answer.

washing the jar and using it to store hairclips

crushing and melting the jar to make a bottle

putting the jar in landfill

making an identical jar from raw materials

03.2 **Table 1** lists the raw materials that are used to make glass.

Table 1

Raw material	Chemical formula
silicon dioxide	
calcium carbonate	
	Na_2CO_3

Complete the table. **[3 marks]**

> **Exam Tip**
>
> It is important that you have learnt the key ions from the specification. You can use the charges on the ions to work out the chemical formulae of ionic compounds, such as those in **Table 1**. This is a skill that will come up throughout your chemistry course.

312 C14 Using the Earth's resources

03.3 Outline **three** advantages of making glass objects from recycled glass, rather than from glass that has been newly made from its raw materials. **[3 marks]**

04 This question is about sewage treatment.

04.1 Name **two** types of substance that must be removed from household sewage and agricultural waste water, before the water is released back into the environment. **[2 marks]**

04.2 Give the **four** steps in the treatment of sewage. **[4 marks]**

04.3 Suggest why it is easier to obtain potable water from ground water than from sewage. **[1 mark]**

05 A student was investigating if a water sample was pure enough to drink.

05.1 Describe how the student can test the pH of the sample. **[1 mark]**

05.2 Give the pH the student would expect if the water was pure. **[1 mark]**

05.3 The student heated the sample of water until all of the water had evaporated. There were some white crystals left in the bottom of the evaporating dish.

Identify what the crystals are and where the crystals have come from. **[2 marks]**

05.4 Pure water has a boiling point of 100 °C. The student found their water sample started boiling at 108 °C.
Suggest why the boiling point was not 100 °C. **[1 mark]**

05.5 Calculate the percentage difference between the expected boiling point and the observed boiling point of the water. **[1 mark]**

05.6 The student said:

"*There is no difference between potable water and pure water.*"

Is this statement correct?
Explain your answer. **[3 marks]**

06 Grey water is waste water from all sources within a home except the toilet.

Grey water can be stored in a home and then can be reused within the home for toilet flushing or watering the plants.

Grey water is not treated.

06.1 Suggest why grey water is only used for flushing the toilet and watering plants. **[1 mark]**

> **! Exam Tip**
>
> Don't worry if you've never heard of grey water before. This is just the new context the question is set in.

06.2 Water from the toilet is called sewage water. Sewage water is treated before it is released into the environment.
Describe **two** stages in the treatment of sewage water. **[2 marks]**

06.3 Suggest why using grey water for toilet flushing is considered better for the environment than using potable water. **[3 marks]**

07 Fizzy drinks can be served in glass bottles, plastic bottles, or aluminium cans.

07.1 Identify the raw materials used to produce glass, plastic, and aluminium.
Compare the availability and processing of these raw materials. **[6 marks]**

07.2 Two students are discussing the most environmentally friendly method for disposing of glass bottles, plastic bottles, and aluminium cans at the end of their life cycle.

Student **A** thinks:

"*The bottles and cans should be recycled.*"

Student **B** thinks:

"*We should find another use for them. For example, we could use the aluminium cans as a pen pot.*"

Which student do you think is correct?
Give a reason for your answer. **[1 mark]**

07.3 Give **one** other process in the life cycles of glass bottles, plastic bottles, and aluminium cans that could contribute to their environmental impact. **[1 mark]**

07.4 Life cycle assessments (LCA) are carried out to determine the environmental impact that a product has over the entire course of its life cycle.

LCAs can be sponsored by the manufacturer of a product who wants to demonstrate that their products are more environmentally friendly than a competitor's product.

Suggest why an LCA from the manufacturer of a product may not be trustworthy. **[1 mark]**

08 Many single-use plastic bags are made from crude oil.
Governments around the world are trying to encourage people not to use these plastic bags.

08.1 Suggest why Governments are trying to reduce people's use of single-use plastic bags. **[1 mark]**

> **! Exam Tip**
>
> **06.2** is worth two marks, so you know each description only needs to be brief.

> **! Exam Tip**
>
> **07.1** is the first stage of a life cycle assessment. To gain full marks you need to talk about all three materials. For the comparison, think about the availability of each of the raw materials, and what is involved in turning that raw material into the product.

> **! Exam Tip**
>
> In **07.2** there is no 'correct' answer. You can agree with Student **A** or Student **B**. What you are being asked to do here is *justify* your answer using your scientific knowledge. Think about *why* you agree with the student, and remember to use scientific words.

314 C14 Using the Earth's resources

08.2 In 2015, the UK Government introduced a mandatory 5 pence charge for single-use plastic bags. **Figure 1** shows the sales of single-use plastic bags from 2015 to 2018.

Figure 1

[Bar chart: number of bags sold in billions vs year. 2015: ~7.6; 2016: ~1.3; 2017: ~1.0; 2018: ~0.5]

Describe the trend shown by **Figure 1**. **[2 marks]**

> **Exam Tip**
> 08.2 is a two mark question, so make sure you include data in your description.

08.3 A 'bag for life' canvas bag can cost £1.
Evaluate the use of single-use plastic bags and canvas bags for carrying food shopping home from the supermarket. **[6 marks]**

> **Exam Tip**
> 08.3 is an evaluate question, so you need good things for both plastic bags and canvas bags, bad things for both plastic bags and canvas bags, and to give your opinion on which is best and why.

09 Some students are investigating water from different sources. They want to compare the mass of dissolved solids in three samples of water. They use the following method:

1. Find the mass of an empty evaporating basin.
2. Use a beaker to measure 10.0 cm³ of one of the water samples into the evaporating basin.
3. Heat the evaporating basin and its contents until all the water has evaporated.
4. Find the mass of the evaporating basin again.

09.1 Suggest an improvement to step **2**. Give a reason for this improvement. **[2 marks]**

09.2 Give **two** safety precautions that the students should take. **[2 marks]**

09.3 **Table 2** shows the students' results. The mass of the empty evaporating basin was 95.24 g.

> **Exam Tip**
> Think about how the measurement in step 2 could be made more accurate.

Table 2

Water sample	Mass of solid and evaporation basin after heating in g
A	95.24
B	95.26
C	95.61

Identify the water sample that is pure water. **[1 mark]**

09.4 Identify the water sample that is most likely to be sea water.
Give a reason for your answer. **[2 marks]**

10 This question is about hydrocarbons.

10.1 Draw **one** line from each hydrocarbon to its correct name. **[4 marks]**

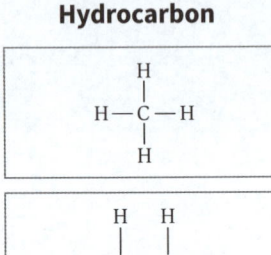

Hydrocarbon		Name
CH₄ structure		butane
C₂H₆ structure		ethane
C₃H₈ structure		methane
C₄H₁₀ structure		propane

10.2 Name the homologous series that the hydrocarbons from **10.1** are part of. **[1 mark]**

10.3 What is the general formula of the homologous series?
Choose **one** answer. **[1 mark]**

C_nH_{2n+2} C_nH_{2n} $C_{2n}H_n$ $C_{2n+2}H_2$

10.4 Describe how the viscosities of the four hydrocarbons shown in **10.1** are different. **[1 mark]**

11 A student carried out three chemical reactions. Each chemical reaction produced a gas.

The student collected the gases and tested them.

Table 3 shows their results.

Table 3

Gas	Does it relight a glowing splint?	Does it burn with a squeaky pop?	Does it bleach damp litmus paper?
A	yes	no	no
B	no	yes	no
C	no	no	yes

> **Exam Tip**
> Highlight each positive result so they stand out and are easier for you to see.

11.1 Identify which gas from **Table 3** was produced from the electrolysis of molten sodium chloride. **[1 mark]**

C14 Using the Earth's resources

11.2 Identify which gas from **Table 3** was produced from the reaction of lithium with water. **[1 mark]**

11.3 A student sets up the apparatus in **Figure 2** to identify the gas released when magnesium reacts with hydrochloric acid.

Figure 2

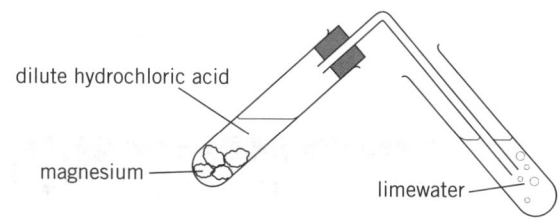

dilute hydrochloric acid
magnesium
limewater

Identify the gas that the student is testing for and explain what the student will observe. **[3 marks]**

12 **Figure 3** shows two reaction profile diagrams.

Figure 3

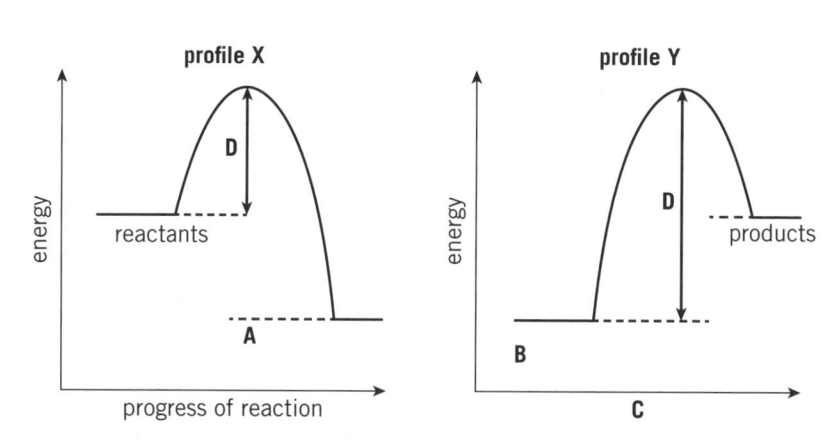

profile X
energy
reactants
D
A
progress of reaction

profile Y
energy
D
products
B
C

12.1 Identify which reaction profile represents an exothermic reaction. **[1 mark]**

12.2 Identify what the arrow labelled **D** represents.
Choose **one** answer. **[1 mark]**

activation energy

energy transferred to surroundings

energy transferred from surroundings

12.3 Complete **Figure 3** by identifying **A**, **B**, and **C**. **[3 marks]**

Knowledge

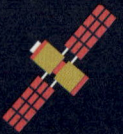

P1 Energy stores and transfers

Systems

A **system** is an object or group of objects.

Whenever anything changes in a system, energy is transferred between its stores or to the surroundings.

A **closed system** is one where no energy can escape to or enter from the surroundings. The total energy in a closed system never changes.

Energy stores

kinetic	energy an object has because it is moving
gravitational potential	energy an object has because of its height above the ground
elastic potential	energy an elastic object has when it is stretched or compressed
thermal (or internal)	energy an object has because of its temperature (the total kinetic and potential energy of the particles in the object)
chemical	energy that can be transferred by chemical reactions involving foods, fuels, and the chemicals in batteries
nuclear	energy stored in the nucleus of an atom
magnetic	energy a magnetic object has when it is near a magnet or in a magnetic field
electrostatic	energy a charged object has when it is near another charged object

Energy transfers

Energy can be transferred to and from different stores by:

Heating
Energy is transferred from one object to another object with a lower temperature.

Waves
Waves (e.g., light and sound waves) transfer energy.

Electricity
When an electric current flows it transfers energy.

Forces (mechanical work)
Energy is transferred when a force moves or changes the shape of an object.

Insulating buildings

Heating bills can be expensive so it is important to reduce the rate of heat loss from buildings.

Some factors that affect the rate of heat loss from a building include:

1. the thickness of its walls and roof
2. the thermal conductivity of its walls and roof.

   lower thermal conductivity = lower rate of heat loss

The thermal conductivity of the walls and roof can be reduced by using thermal **insulators**.

A thermal insulator is a material that has a low thermal conductivity. The rate of energy transfer through an insulator is low.

The energy transfer per second through a material depends on:

1. the material's thermal conductivity
2. the temperature difference between the two sides of the material
3. the thickness of the material.

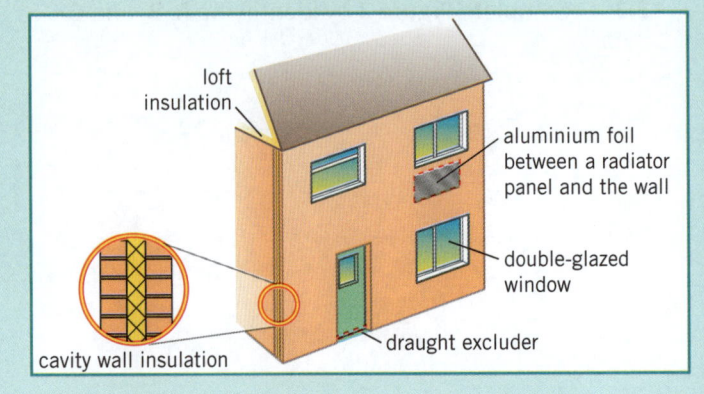

- loft insulation
- aluminium foil between a radiator panel and the wall
- double-glazed window
- draught excluder
- cavity wall insulation

318 P1 Energy stores and transfers

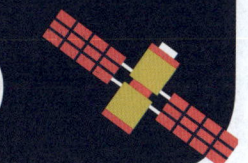

P1

Energy equations

An object's gravitational potential energy store depends on its height above the ground, the gravitational field strength, and its mass.

gravitational potential energy (J) = mass (kg) × field strength (N/kg) × height (m)

(L) $E_p = m\,g\,h$

An object's kinetic energy store depends only on its mass and speed.

(L) kinetic energy (J) = 0.5 × mass (kg) × (speed)² (m/s)

$E_k = \frac{1}{2} m v^2$

Power is how much work is done (or how much energy is transferred) per second. **Work done** means the same thing as energy transferred. The unit of power is the watt (W).

1 watt = 1 joule of energy transferred per second

(L) power (W) = $\frac{\text{energy transferred (J)}}{\text{time (s)}}$

$P = \frac{E}{t}$

or

(L) power (W) = $\frac{\text{work done (J)}}{\text{time (s)}}$

$P = \frac{W}{t}$

The elastic potential energy store of a stretched spring can be calculated using:

elastic potential energy (J) = 0.5 × spring constant (N/m) × (extension)² (m)

$E_e = \frac{1}{2} k e^2$ (assuming the limit of proportionality has not been exceeded)

This equation will be given to you on the *Physics Equations Sheet*, but you need to be able to select and apply it to the correct questions.

Useful and dissipated energy

Energy cannot be created or destroyed – it can only be transferred usefully, stored, or **dissipated** (wasted).

Dissipated energy is often described as being wasted.

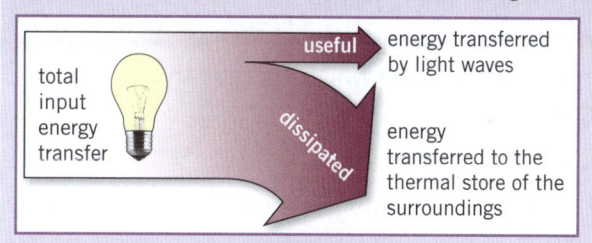

[Diagram: total input energy transfer → useful: energy transferred by light waves; dissipated: energy transferred to the thermal store of the surroundings]

Energy is never entirely transferred usefully – some energy is always dissipated, meaning it is transferred to less useful stores.

All energy eventually ends up transferred to the thermal energy store of the surroundings.

In machines, work done against the force of friction usually causes energy to be wasted because energy is transferred to the thermal store of the machine and its surroundings.

Lubrication is a way of reducing unwanted energy transfer due to friction.

Streamlining is a way of reducing energy wasted due to air resistance or drag in water.

Use of thermal insulation is a way of reducing energy wasted due to heat dissipated to the surroundings.

Efficiency is a measure of how much energy is transferred usefully. You must know the equation to calculate efficiency as a *decimal*:

efficiency = $\frac{\text{useful output energy transfer (J)}}{\text{total input energy transfer (J)}}$

(L) or

efficiency = $\frac{\text{useful power output (W)}}{\text{total power input (W)}}$

To give efficiency as a *percentage*, just multiply the result from the above calculation by 100 and add the % sign to the answer.

Key terms

Make sure you can write a definition for these key terms.

chemical	closed system	dissipated	efficiency	elastic potential	electrostatic
gravitational potential	insulator	kinetic	lubrication	magnetic	nuclear
power	streamlining	system	thermal	work done	

P1 Knowledge 319

Retrieval

Learn the answers to the questions below, then cover the answers column with a piece of paper and write as many as you can. Check and repeat.

P1 questions | Answers

#	Question	Answer
1	Name the eight energy stores.	kinetic, gravitational potential, elastic potential, thermal, chemical, nuclear, magnetic, electrostatic
2	Name the four ways in which energy can be transferred.	heating, waves, electric current, mechanically (by forces)
3	What is a system?	an object or group of objects
4	What is a closed system?	a system where no energy can be transferred to or from the surroundings – the total energy in the system stays the same
5	What is work done?	energy transferred when a force moves an object
6	What is the unit for energy?	joule (J)
7	What is one joule of work?	the work done when a force of 1 N causes an object to move 1 m in the direction of the force
8	Describe the energy transfer when a moving car slows down.	energy is transferred mechanically from the kinetic store of the car to the thermal store of its brakes – some energy is dissipated to the thermal store of the surroundings
9	Describe the energy transfer when an electric kettle is used to heat water.	the electric current in a kettle transfers energy to the heating element's thermal store – energy is then transferred by heating from the heating element's thermal store to the thermal store of the water
10	Describe the energy transfer when a ball is fired using an elastic band.	energy is transferred mechanically from the elastic store of the elastic band to the kinetic store of the band – some energy is dissipated to the thermal store of the surroundings
11	Describe the energy transfer when a falling apple hits the ground.	energy is transferred from the kinetic store of the apple and dissipated to the thermal store of the surroundings by sound waves
12	Name the unit that represents one joule transferred per second.	watt (W)
13	What does a material's thermal conductivity tell you?	how well it conducts heat
14	Which materials have low thermal conductivity?	thermal insulators
15	Give three factors that determine the rate of thermal energy transfer through a material.	thermal conductivity of material, temperature difference, thickness of material

P1 Energy stores and transfers

Required practical skills

P1

Practise answering questions on the required practicals using the example below.
You need to be able to apply your skills and knowledge to other practicals too.

Specific heat capacity

To determine changes in specific heat capacity you need to measure mass, temperature rise, and energy transferred (work done).

To do this, you might use an energy meter, or measure time, current, and potential difference (to calculate power).

In the experiment, you need to:

- insulate the block or beaker, use a heatproof mat, and a lid (for a liquid)
- allow the material to heat up before taking measurements (due to thermal inertia)
- add water to make a good thermal contact between the thermometer and a solid material.

Calculated values for specific heat capacity will usually differ from given values because of energy transferred to the surroundings.

Worked example

A student uses a 12 V, 4 A heater to heat a 1 kg metal block. They measure the temperature of the block every minute for 10 minutes.

1 Calculate the work done.

   power = potential difference × current
   = 12 × 4
   = 48 W

   work done = power × time
   10 min = 600 s
   = 48 × 600 = 28 800 J

2 The temperature rise of the block is 75 °C.

   Calculate the specific heat capacity of the material.

   $$\text{specific heat capacity} = \frac{\text{energy transferred}}{\text{mass} \times \text{temperature rise}}$$

   $$= \frac{28\,800}{1 \times 75}$$

   $$= 384 \text{ J/kg°C}$$

Practice

A student produces a graph of work done against temperature rise of 0.2 kg of a liquid.

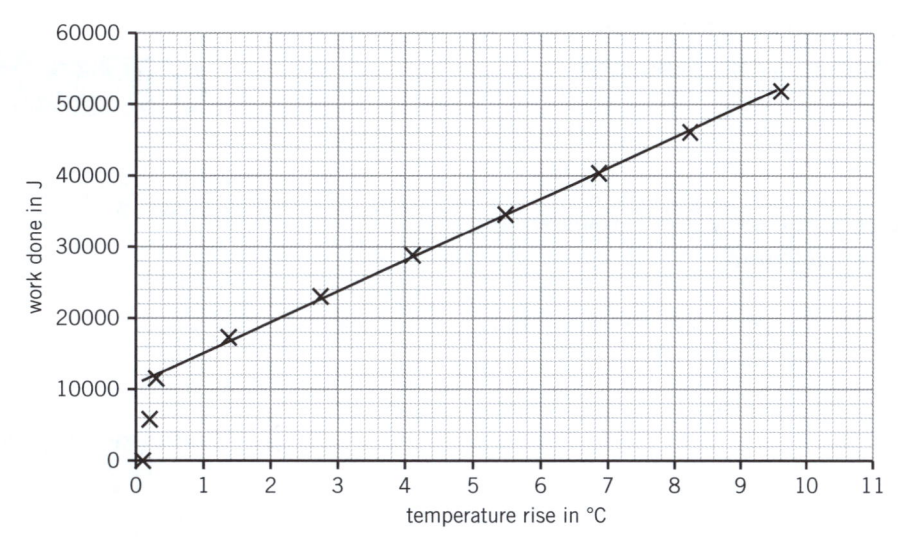

1 Explain why the graph does not go through (0,0).
2 Use the graph to calculate the specific heat capacity. Describe your method.
3 Suggest how you can tell from the graph that the material was well insulated.

P1 Retrieval 321

Practice

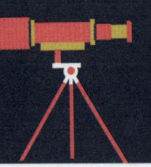

Exam-style questions

01 A child is sitting at the top of a slide.

01.1 As the child moves down the slide, in which energy store will the energy **decrease**? [1 mark]

Tick **one** box.

gravitational potential ☐

kinetic ✓

elastic potential ☐

01.2 Give the unit of energy. [1 mark]

_____W_____

> **Exam Tip**
> All energy is measured in the same unit.

01.3 Name the energy store associated with moving objects. [1 mark]

_____kinetic_____

02 A car is travelling at a steady speed.

02.1 Which statement describes an energy transfer involved to make the car move? [1 mark]

Tick **one** box.

Energy in a gravitational potential energy store is transferred to an elastic energy store. ☐

Energy in a chemical energy store is transferred to a kinetic store. ✓

Energy in an elastic energy store is transferred to a thermal energy store. ☐

Energy in a thermal energy store is transferred to a gravitational potential energy store. ☐

> **Exam Tip**
> Remove any obviously wrong answers first.

02.2 Write the equation that links energy transferred, power, and time. [1 mark]

energy transferred = power / time

02.3 The car transferred 3 120 000 J of energy in 60 seconds. Calculate the power of the car engine.

$$\frac{3\,120\,000}{60} = 52000$$

power = __52000__ [2 marks]

> **Exam Tip**
> Always write down your working as well as your answer. In **02.3** the number you are using is very long. It would be easy to write it incorrectly into your calculator and get the wrong answer, but if you have written down the correct workings you will still get a mark.

P1 Energy stores and transfers

Paper 5 **P1**

02.4 Draw a circle around the correct unit for power. [1 mark]
(J)   N   s   W

03 A student investigated a trolley rolling down a ramp. They calculated the kinetic energy of the trolley at the bottom of the ramp.

03.1 Which is the correct equation to calculate kinetic energy? Choose **one** answer. [1 mark]

kinetic energy = 0.5 × mass × (speed)^2 (kinetic energy = $\frac{mass}{speed^2}$)

kinetic energy = $\frac{0.5 \times mass}{speed^2}$ kinetic energy = mass × (speed)^2

03.2 The mass of the trolley that the student used was 350 g. The student converted the mass reading into kilograms. Give a reason why the student did this. [1 mark]

03.3 The student repeated the experiment with the top of the ramp at 3 different heights: 10 cm, 20 cm, and 30 cm.

Which height would give the highest kinetic energy of the trolley at the bottom of the ramp?

Explain your answer. [2 marks]

Exam Tip

Learning your equations is very important. You will always be asked at least one question that involves you recalling an equation, and they are easy marks to get.

04 A student wants to measure the energy transferred to a gravitational potential energy store when they go upstairs. The height of the stairs is 3 m. Gravitational field strength is 9.8 N/kg.

04.1 Give the other measurement that they need to make. [1 mark]
speed

04.2 The student goes up **two** flights of stairs instead of one. Both flights of stairs have a height of 3 m. Circle the correct bold phrases in the sentences. [3 marks]

The energy transferred to a gravitational potential energy store is **doubled** / **halved** because the height is **doubled** / **halved**.

The energy transferred to a gravitational potential energy store is **is** / **is not** proportional to the height.

04.3 Identify the energy store that has **less** energy when the student reaches the top of the stairs. [1 mark]

Exam Tip

Think about the equation for gravitational potential energy. This is another one of the equations you need to learn. You are not being asked to write it in **04.1** but you are being asked to remember what the other value is needed for it.

05 This question is about conservation of energy.

05.1 Complete the statement of the law of conservation of energy. [1 mark]

Energy cannot be ___created___, or ___destroyed___

only transferred, stored, or dissipated.

P1 Practice

05.2 Define what a closed system is. [1 mark]

no energy can go in or out

05.3 A pendulum swings backwards and forwards. The pendulum gradually stops swinging. Circle the correct bold phrase in the sentence.

A pendulum **is** / **is not** a closed system.

Explain your answer. [3 marks]

06 A teacher drops two balls. Both balls have the same mass. One ball bounces. The other ball hits the floor and stops.

06.1 Complete the sentences. Use the words from the box. Each word can be used once, more than once, or not at all. [3 marks]

| elastic | gravitational potential | kinetic | thermal |

When the teacher lifts the balls up, energy is transferred to a ___*kinetic*___ energy store. The energy in the ___*gravitational potential*___ energy stores of both balls increases as they fall. For the ball that does not bounce, energy is transferred to the ___*elastic*___ energy store of the floor.

06.2 The ball that bounces will stop momentarily before it bounces back up. Which store is energy transferred to at the moment that the ball is stationary? Choose **one** answer. [1 mark]

chemical store   (elastic store)   gravitational store   thermal store

06.3 When the ball bounces, some energy is transferred to the thermal energy store. Describe why this means that the ball does not reach the same height that it was dropped from. [1 mark]

07 A cyclist is at the top of a hill. The combined mass of the cyclist and their bicycle is 80 kg. The hill is 10 m high.

07.1 Write down the equation that links gravitational potential energy, mass, gravitational field strength, and height. [1 mark]

07.2 Calculate the gravitational potential energy of the cyclist at the top of the hill. Show your working. Gravitational field strength is 9.8 N/kg. [2 marks]

07.3 At the bottom of the hill the cyclist is moving with a speed of 12 m/s. Calculate the kinetic energy of the cyclist at the bottom of the hill. Use the equation:

kinetic energy = 0.5 × mass × speed^2 [2 marks]

07.4 Show that the wasted energy is 1040 J. [1 mark]

> **Exam Tip**
> Read the whole paragraph through once before trying to fill in the gaps. Don't just read up to the answer line, the words after the answer lines will also help you to work out the answer. If you can't complete one sentence, move onto the next. Filling out another sentence might help you work out any that you have missed.

> **Exam Tip**
> You will always be given the value for gravitational field strength.

> **Exam Tip**
> BODMAS is still important in science.

324   P1 Energy stores and transfers

08 A tennis player throws a ball upwards. The kinetic energy of the ball when it leaves the tennis player's hand is 1 J. The mass of the ball is 50 g. The ball reaches a height of 1.5 m above the player's hand. Gravitational field strength is 9.8 N/kg.

08.1 Write down the equation that links gravitational potential energy, mass, gravitational field strength, and height. **[1 mark]**

08.2 Give the mass of the ball in kilograms. **[1 mark]**

08.3 Calculate the gravitational potential energy of the ball at its greatest height. **[2 marks]**

08.4 Not all of the kinetic energy is transferred to the gravitational potential energy store when the ball moves upwards. Suggest a reason why this process of energy transfer is not 100% efficient. **[1 mark]**

> **Exam Tip**
> When you convert from kilograms to grams, the number will get bigger – 1 kg = 1000 g.
> When you convert from grams to kilograms, the number will get smaller – 1000 g = 1 kg.
> If you're not sure whether to multiply or divide when converting grams to kilograms, then try both. But remember, if you write both answers down *always* cross out the wrong answer so your examiner knows which one to mark.

09 A student wants to investigate the energy transferred to the surroundings when a pendulum swings. They set up the equipment shown in **Figure 1**.

The student pulls back the metal bob so that it is a certain height above the desk. Then they let go of the bob. The bob swings across the desk and then comes back to its original position. This is one swing.

Figure 1

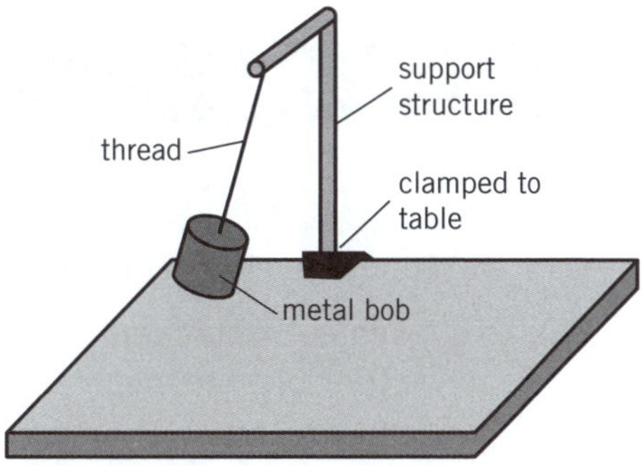

09.1 Describe a method that the student could use to work out the energy lost during 10 swings of the pendulum. Write down the measurements that the student would need to make. Suggest the measuring instruments that they could use. **[4 marks]**

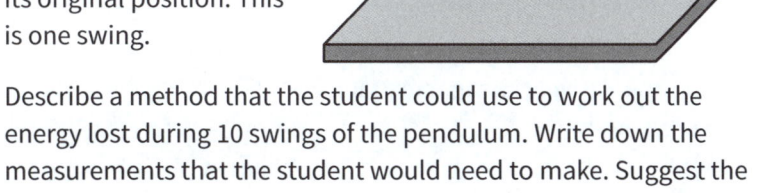

09.2 Identify which measurement would produce the biggest uncertainty. Suggest a way that the uncertainty could be reduced. **[2 marks]**

> **Exam Tip**
> Make sure the method you suggest includes equipment to do the measuring and how to take the readings.

10 A student researches the efficiency of different electric motors used in cars. In electric motors, energy is wasted.

10.1 Describe what is meant by 'wasted energy'. **[1 mark]**

10.2 The student knows that car **A** requires a total energy input of 20 J to move across the floor. It has a useful energy output of 12 J. Write down the equation that links efficiency, total output energy, and total input energy. **[1 mark]**

10.3 Calculate the efficiency of car **A** as a decimal. **[2 marks]**

10.4 The efficiency of car **B** is 50%. Write down which car wastes more energy. Explain your answer. **[2 marks]**

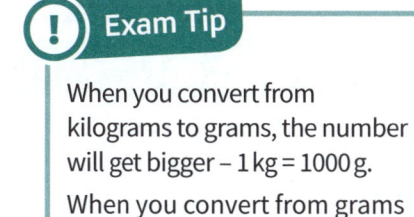

> **Exam Tip**
> Generally you can give efficiency as a percentage or a decimal, but **10.3** specifies how it wants the answer so be sure to give it as a decimal.

Knowledge

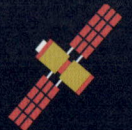

P2 National and global energy resources

Energy resources

The main ways in which we use the Earth's energy resources are:
- generating electricity
- heating
- transport.

Most of our energy currently comes from **fossil fuels** – coal, oil, and natural gas.

Reliability and environmental impact

Some energy resources are more reliable than others. **Reliable** energy resources are ones that are available all the time (or at predictable times) and in sufficient quantities.

Both **renewable** and **non-renewable** energy resources have some kind of **environmental impact** when we use them.

Non-renewable energy resources

- are not replaced as quickly as they are used
- will eventually run out.

For example, fossil fuels and nuclear fuels.

Renewable energy resources

- can be replaced at the same rate as they are used
- will not run out.

For example, solar, tidal, wave, wind, **geothermal**, **biofuel**, and **hydroelectric** energies.

Resource	Main uses	Source	Advantages	Disadvantages
coal	generating electricity	extracted from underground	enough available to meet current energy demands reliable – supply can be controlled to meet demand relatively cheap to extract and use	will eventually run out release carbon dioxide when burned – one of the main causes of climate change release other polluting gases, such as sulfur dioxide (from coal and oil) which causes acid rain oil spills in the oceans kill marine life
oil	generating electricity transport heating			
natural gas	generating electricity heating			
nuclear fission	generating electricity	mining naturally occurring elements, such as uranium and plutonium	no polluting gases or greenhouse gases produced enough available to meet current energy demands large amount of energy transferred from a very small mass of fuel reliable – supply can be controlled to meet demand	produces nuclear waste, which is: • dangerous • difficult and expensive to dispose of • stored for centuries before it is safe to dispose of nuclear power plants are expensive to: • build and run • decommission (shut down)

(Non-renewable energy resources)

> **Revision tip**
>
> **Remember** Nuclear fuel is commonly confused as a renewable energy resource as it doesn't release polluting gases – but it's not!

> **Key terms**
>
> Make sure you can write a definition for these key terms.
>
> biofuel   carbon neutral   environmental impact   fossil fuel   geothermal
>
> hydroelectric   non-renewable   reliability   renewable

P2 National and global energy resources

P2

Resource	Main uses	Source	Advantages	Disadvantages
solar energy	generating electricity	sunlight transfers energy to solar cells	can be used in remote places very cheap to run once installed no pollution/greenhouse gases produced	supply depends on weather and season expensive to buy and install cannot supply large-scale demand
	heating	sunlight transfers energy to solar heating panels		
hydroelectric energy	generating electricity	water flowing downhill turns generators	low running cost no fuel costs reliable and supply can be controlled to meet demand	expensive to build hydroelectric dams flood a large area behind the dam, destroying habitats and resulting in greenhouse gas production from rotting vegetation
tidal energy	generating electricity	turbines on tidal barrages turned by water as the tide comes in and out	predictable supply as there are always tides can produce large amounts of electricity no fuel costs no pollution/greenhouse gases produced	tidal barrages: • change marine habitats and can harm animals • restrict access and can be dangerous for boats • are expensive to build and maintain cannot control supply supply varies depending on time of month
wave energy	generating electricity	floating generators powered by waves moving up and down	low running cost no fuel costs no pollution/greenhouse gases produced	floating generators: • change marine habitats and can harm animals • restrict access and can be dangerous for boats • are expensive to build, install, and maintain dependent on weather cannot supply large-scale demand
wind energy	generating electricity	turbines turned by the wind	low running cost no fuel costs no pollution/greenhouse gases produced	supply depends on weather large amounts of land needed to generate enough electricity for large-scale demand can produce noise pollution for nearby residents
geothermal energy	generating electricity heating	radioactive substances deep within the Earth transfer heat energy to the surface	low running cost no fuel costs no pollution/greenhouse gases produced	expensive to set up only possible in a few suitable locations around the world
biofuels	generating electricity transport	fuel produced from living or recently living organisms, for example, plants and animal waste	can be **carbon neutral** – the amount of carbon dioxide released when the fuel is burnt is equal to the amount of carbon dioxide absorbed when the fuel is grown reliable and supply can be controlled to meet demand	expensive to produce biofuels growing biofuels requires a lot of land and water that could be used for food production can lead to deforestation – forests are cleared for growing biofuel crops

Renewable energy resources

P2 Knowledge

Retrieval

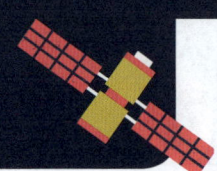

Learn the answers to the questions below, then cover the answers column with a piece of paper and write as many as you can. Check and repeat.

P2 questions | Answers

#	Question	Answer
1	What is a non-renewable energy resource?	an energy resource that will eventually run out, is not replaced at the same rate as it is being used
2	What is a renewable energy resource?	an energy resource that will not run out, it is (or can be) replaced at the same rate as it is used
3	What are the main renewable and non-renewable resources available on Earth?	renewable: solar, tidal, wave, wind, geothermal, biofuel, hydroelectric non-renewable: coal, oil, gas, nuclear
4	What are the main advantages of using coal as an energy resource?	enough available to meet current demand, reliable, can control supply to match demand, cheap to extract and use
5	What are the main disadvantages of using coal as an energy resource?	will eventually run out, releases CO_2 which contributes to climate change, releases sulfur dioxide which causes acid rain
6	What are the main advantages of using nuclear fuel as an energy resource?	lots of energy released from a small mass, reliable, can control supply to match demand, enough fuel available to meet current demand, no polluting gases
7	What are the main disadvantages of using nuclear fuel as an energy resource?	waste is dangerous and difficult and expensive to deal with, expensive initial set up, expensive to shut down and to run
8	What are the main advantages of using solar energy?	can be used in remote places, no polluting gases, no waste products, very low running cost
9	What are the main disadvantages of using solar energy?	only available during hours of daylight, cannot control supply, initial set up expensive, cannot be used on a large scale
10	What are the main advantages of using tidal power?	no polluting gases, no waste products, reliable, can produce large amounts of electricity, low running cost, no fuel costs
11	What are the main disadvantages of using tidal power?	can harm aquatic habitats, initial set up expensive, cannot increase supply when needed, times the energy is available vary each day, hazard for boats
12	What are the main advantages of using wave turbines?	no polluting gases produced, no waste products, low running cost, no fuel costs
13	What are the main disadvantages of using wave turbines?	unreliable, dependent on weather, cannot control supply, initial set up expensive, can harm marine habitats, hazard for boats, cannot be used on a large scale
14	What are the main disadvantages of using wind turbines?	unreliable, dependent on weather, cannot control supply, take up a lot of space, can produce noise pollution
15	What are the advantages and the disadvantages of using geothermal energy?	advantages: no polluting gases, low running cost disadvantages: initial set up expensive, only available in a few locations
16	What are the main advantages and disadvantages of using biofuels?	advantages: can be 'carbon neutral', reliable disadvantages: expensive to produce, use land/water that might be needed to grow food
17	What are the main advantages and disadvantages of using hydroelectric power?	advantages: no polluting gases, no waste products, low running cost, no fuel cost, reliable, can be controlled to meet demand disadvantages: initial set up expensive, dams can harm/destroy aquatic habitats

P2 National and global energy resources

P2

Now go back and use the questions below to check your knowledge from previous chapters.

Previous questions | Answers

#	Question	Answer
1	Name the eight energy stores.	kinetic, gravitational potential, elastic potential, thermal, chemical, nuclear, magnetic, electrostatic
2	What is a system?	an object or group of objects
3	What is work done?	energy transferred when a force moves an object
4	What is infrared radiation?	type of electromagnetic radiation
5	Name three greenhouse gases.	water vapour, carbon dioxide, methane

Put paper here

Required practical skills

Practise answering questions on the required practicals using the example below.
You need to be able to apply your skills and knowledge to other practicals too.

Thermal insulators

You need to be able to measure the temperature change of a material that has been insulated.

Material type and thickness affect the temperature decrease in a given time, which is known as the rate of cooling.

To be accurate you need to:

- take repeated measurements, and ensure that the starting temperatures are the same
- use the same thickness if you are changing the type of insulator
- use a lid and heatproof mat in all experiments
- take measurements over a long period of time.

Worked example

A student uses two different types of foam to insulate a can of water. Here are their data:

- no insulation: starting temperature 85 °C, final 52 °C
- foam 1: starting temperature 86 °C, final 71 °C
- foam 2: starting temperature 87 °C, final 67 °C

1 Calculate the temperature changes.

   85 − 52 = 33 °C
   86 − 71 = 15 °C
   87 − 67 = 20 °C

2 Name the best insulator. Explain your answer.

   Foam 1, as the temperature decrease is the smallest.

3 Suggest why the starting temperature should be the same.

   If the water is hotter for one insulator the rate of cooling may be different.

Practice

A student produces a graph of temperature against time for different thicknesses (**A**, **B**, **C**, and **D**) of an insulator around a beaker of water.

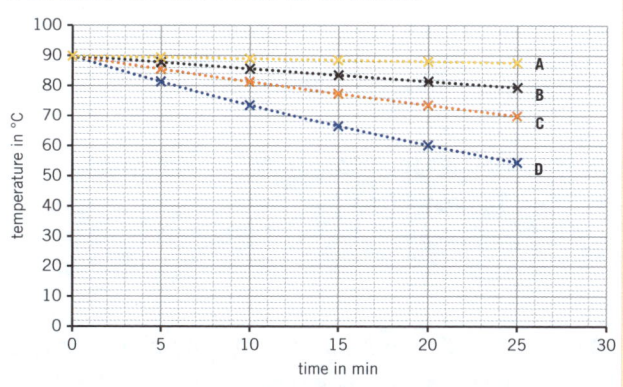

1 Give the letter of the line with the thickest insulator. Explain your answer.

2 Use the graph to calculate the rate of cooling for the thinnest insulator. State the unit.

3 Suggest how the gradients of the graphs would change if the student did not use a lid.

P2 Retrieval 329

Practice

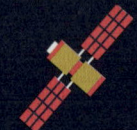

Exam-style questions

01 Some energy resources are renewable. Some are non-renewable.

01.1 Select the renewable energy resources from the list below.
Tick **two** boxes. **[2 marks]**

coal ☐

tides ☐

nuclear ☐

biofuels ☐

> **Exam Tip**
> Be sure to tick the two boxes **01.1** asks for!

01.2 Choose the best definition of a non-renewable resource. **[1 mark]**
Tick **one** box.

a resource that can be used again ☐

a resource that will run out in the near future ☐

a resource made from trees ☐

01.3 Name a renewable resource that you can use directly for heating. **[1 mark]**

_____

> **Exam Tip**
> Read all the questions carefully. **01.3** is asking for a *renewable* resource, but it would be easy when you're rushing in your exam to accidentally read *non-renewable* instead. It happens!

02 A student finds some data about electricity production and how it has changed over time.
They plot the data on the bar chart in **Figure 1**.

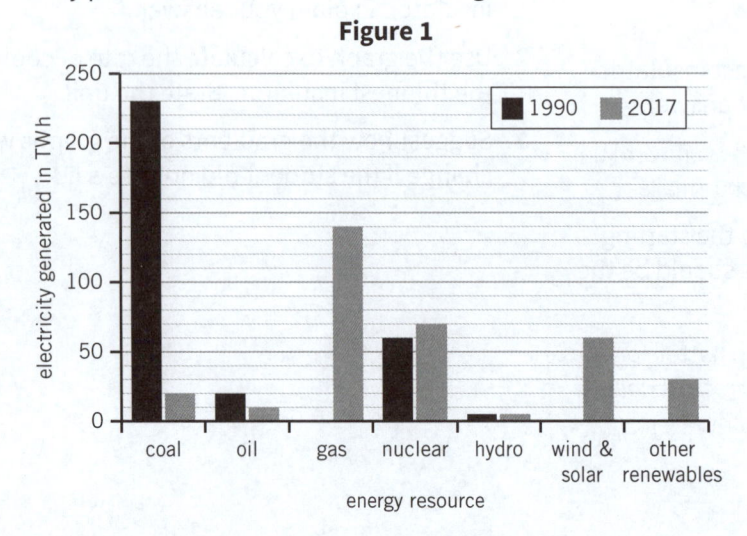

Figure 1

Bar chart showing electricity generated in TWh (y-axis, 0 to 250) against energy resource (x-axis: coal, oil, gas, nuclear, hydro, wind & solar, other renewables). Two bars per resource: 1990 and 2017.

- coal: 1990 ≈ 230, 2017 ≈ 20
- oil: 1990 ≈ 20, 2017 ≈ 10
- gas: 1990 ≈ 0, 2017 ≈ 140
- nuclear: 1990 ≈ 60, 2017 ≈ 70
- hydro: 1990 ≈ 5, 2017 ≈ 5
- wind & solar: 1990 ≈ 0, 2017 ≈ 60
- other renewables: 1990 ≈ 0, 2017 ≈ 30

330 P2 National and global energy resources

Paper 5 P2

02.1 Give a reason why the student plotted the data as a bar chart and not a line graph. **[1 mark]**

_____

_____

02.2 Compare the number of renewable resources used in 1990 with the number used in 2017. **[2 marks]**

_____

_____

_____

> **Exam Tip**
> Use data from **Figure 1**.

02.3 Estimate the change in the use of fossil fuels between the two years in terawatt hours (TWh). **[3 marks]**

> **Exam Tip**
> Don't worry if you've never heard of TWh before. Just use them as the unit for **02.3**, treating them the same as you would any other unit.

change = _____

02.4 There was a large decrease in the use of one non-renewable resource for generating electricity between 1990 and 2017.

Identify this resource.

Suggest why use of this resource in power stations has decreased since 1990. **[2 marks]**

_____

_____

_____

03 Different resources can be used to generate electricity.

03.1 Draw **one** line from each resource to the correct definition. **[3 marks]**

> **Exam Tip**
> Start with the ones you're sure about then try the ones that are left over!

Resource	Definition
wind power	Falling water drives a turbine, which drives a generator.
hydroelectric power	Moving air drives a turbine, which drives a generator.
tidal power	Water moving twice a day drives a turbine, which drives a generator.
solar power	Light from the Sun produces a potential difference directly.

03.2 Suggest **one** environmental consequence of building a tidal power station. **[1 mark]**

03.3 Name **one** other energy resource that produces electricity from moving water. **[1 mark]**

04 Table 1 shows the change in greenhouse gas emissions since 1990.

Table 1

Year	Greenhouse gas emissions in million tonnes CO$_2$
1990	790
2000	700
2010	600
2017	450

04.1 Plot the data from **Table 1** on the bar chart in **Figure 2**. The first bar has been drawn for you. **[2 marks]**

Figure 2

> **Exam Tip**
> Use the first bar as an example and base the bars you draw on that, copy the width of the bar, and make sure you use a ruler.

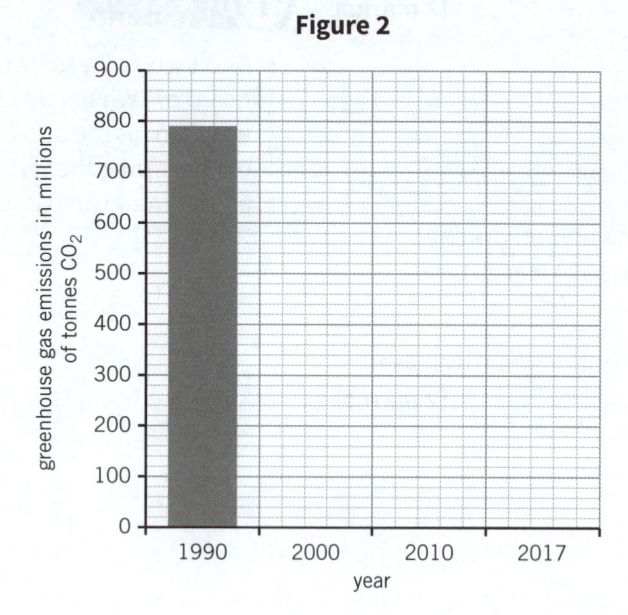

04.2 Describe the change to greenhouse gas emissions between 1990 and 2017. **[1 mark]**

04.3 Which statement about greenhouse gases is correct? **[1 mark]**
Tick **one** box.

Greenhouse gases are a health benefit. ☐

Greenhouse gases generate habitats for wildlife. ☐

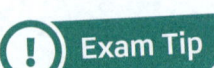

Greenhouse gases contribute to climate change. ☐

> **Exam Tip**
> 04.2 is a one-mark question, so a short answer is all that you need. Just give the general trend.

P2 National and global energy resources

05 Table 2 shows renewable energy resources used in 2017.

Table 2

Type of renewable energy resource	Percentage
solar	5
wind	21
hydroelectricity	3
biofuels	
geothermal	5

05.1 Define the term renewable energy resource. [1 mark]

05.2 Calculate the percentage of energy resources due to biofuels. [1 mark]

05.3 What is one other renewable energy source? Choose **one** answer. [1 mark]

coal   nuclear   tidal

05.4 Give one disadvantage of using a renewable energy resource over a non-renewable energy resource. [1 mark]

> **Exam Tip**
> To work out the percentage of energy left over for biofuels, subtract all the other values from the total of 100%.

06 A homeowner installed a power shower in their home.

06.1 Write down the equation that links energy transferred, power, and time. [1 mark]

06.2 The homeowner takes a shower that lasts 10 minutes (600 seconds). The energy transferred in that time is 4 500 000 J.

Calculate the power of the shower. Give the unit of power. [3 marks]

> **Exam Tip**
> You can give the unit as a word or just the symbol.

06.3 The homeowner's neighbour installs a more powerful shower.

Compare the two showers. Choose **one** answer. [1 mark]

The more powerful shower transfers the same amount of energy in a longer time.

The more powerful shower transfers the same amount of energy in a shorter time.

The less powerful shower transfers the same amount of energy in a shorter time.

07 A government report from 2009 says:

In 2009, 6.7% of the electricity generated in the UK came from renewable sources. By 2020, the UK aims to produce 15% of its energy from renewables.

Table 3 shows sources of energy used to generate electricity in the UK in 2017.

Table 3

Resource	Percentage
gas	40
nuclear	21
wind/solar	18
other renewables	9
coal	7
oil/other non-renewable fuels	3
hydroelectricity	2

07.1 Name the renewable energy resources listed in **Table 3**. [2 marks]

07.2 Calculate the total percentage of electricity generated from renewables. Show your working. Identify whether the government has met its target. [3 marks]

07.3 Give **one** other renewable energy resource that is not listed in **Table 3**. [1 mark]

> **! Exam Tip**
> Highlight the renewables so it's easy to pick the numbers you need from the list when calculating the total percentage.

08 A student is comparing fossil fuels with energy resources that involve water.

08.1 Name **two** fossil fuels. [2 marks]

08.2 The student learns that electricity can be generated using the motion of waves at sea. Name **one** other resource that uses water to generate electricity. [1 mark]

08.3 One benefit of using fossil fuels is that they are a reliable resource. Compare the reliability of the resource you described in **08.2** with that of fossil fuels. [2 marks]

08.4 Fossil fuels produce carbon dioxide when they burn. Explain why this is an environmental issue. [2 marks]

08.5 Describe **one** environmental issue with the resource you described in **08.2**. [1 mark]

> **! Exam Tip**
> There are so many you can pick from for **08.2** – choose the one you know best, not the one you think the examiner wants you to write about.

09 **Table 4** shows the changes in some of the energy resources used for transportation.

Table 4

	Petrol in millions of tonnes	Diesel in millions of tonnes	Biofuels in millions of tonnes
1991	23.75	10.42	0
2017	11.31	24.46	1.22

09.1 Name the fossil fuel that is used to produce petrol. [1 mark]

09.2 A student draws a bar chart (**Figure 3**) to show the changes in energy use.

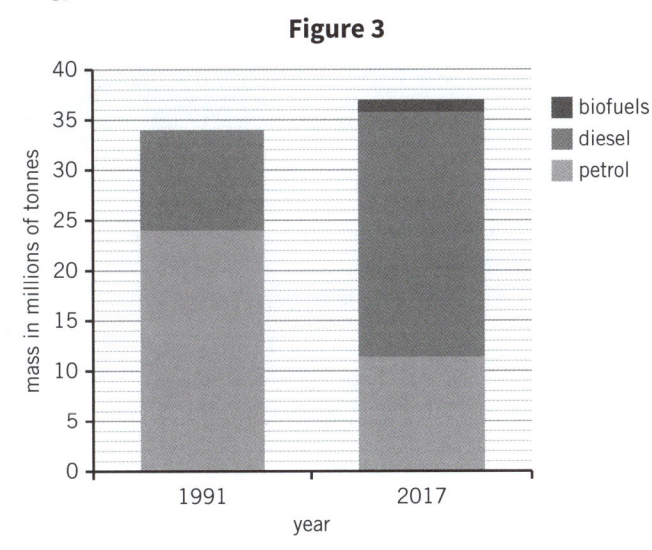

Figure 3

Suggest **one** reason why the student chose a bar chart to display the data. **[1 mark]**

09.3 Suggest why biofuels do not appear in the data for 1991. **[1 mark]**

09.4 A student says:
'*Using biofuels is better than using petrol or diesel because there is very little environmental impact in producing them or using them.*'
Do you agree? Give a reason for your answer. **[1 mark]**

10 A student sets up an experiment to measure the specific heat capacity of water. They use the equipment shown in **Figure 4**.

10.1 The student has not insulated the cup. Suggest why this is not necessary. Explain your answer. **[2 marks]**

10.2 The student stirs the water before they take the temperature. Explain why they do this. **[1 mark]**

10.3 The student makes the following measurements.

Starting temperature	20.0 °C
Final temperature	48.0 °C
Energy supplied	30 000 J
Mass of water	0.25 kg

Calculate the change in temperature. **[1 mark]**

10.4 Use the student's results to calculate the specific heat capacity of water. Use the *Physics Equations Sheet*. Give your answer correct to **three** significant figures. **[3 marks]**

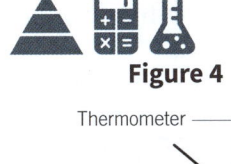

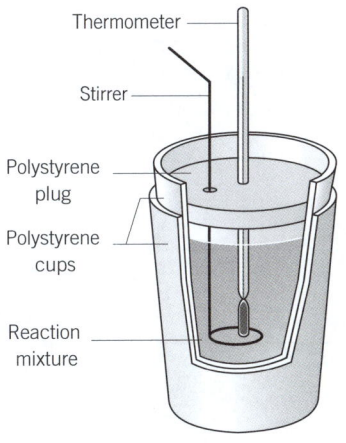

> **Exam Tip**
> Think about the type of data being displayed.

Figure 4

> **Exam Tip**
> If you miss the part about significant figures then you'll be missing out on marks.

Knowledge

P3 Supplying electricity

Mains electricity

A cell or a battery provides a **direct potential difference**. This can produce a **direct current (d.c.)**. A direct current only flows in one direction.

Mains electricity provides an **alternating potential difference**. This can produce an **alternating current (a.c.)**. An alternating current repeatedly reverses direction.

The positive and negative terminals of an alternating power supply swap over with a regular frequency.

The frequency of the mains electricity supply in the UK is 50 Hz and its voltage is 230 V.

Plugs

The earth wire is a safety wire to stop the appliance becoming live. The potential difference of the earth wire is 0 V. It only carries a current if there is a fault.

The neutral wire completes the circuit. It has a potential difference of 0 V.

Plastic is used for the wire coatings and plug case because it is a good electrical insulator.

The **fuse** is connected to the live wire. If the live wire inside an appliance touches the neutral wire a very large current flows. This is called a **short circuit**. When this happens the fuse melts and disconnects the live wire from the mains, keeping the appliance safe.

The live wire is dangerous because it has a high potential difference of 230 V. This would cause a large current to flow through you if you touched it.

Most electrical appliances in the UK are connected to the mains using a three-core cable. Copper is used for the wires because it is a good electrical conductor and it bends easily.

The National Grid

The **National Grid** is a nationwide network of cables and transformers that links power stations to homes, offices, and other consumers of mains electricity.

Transformers are devices that can change the potential difference of an alternating power supply.

Power stations generate electricity at an alternating potential difference of about 25 000 V.

The cables in the National Grid transfer electrical power at a potential difference of up to 400 000 V.

Homes and offices use electrical power supplied at a potential difference of 230 V.

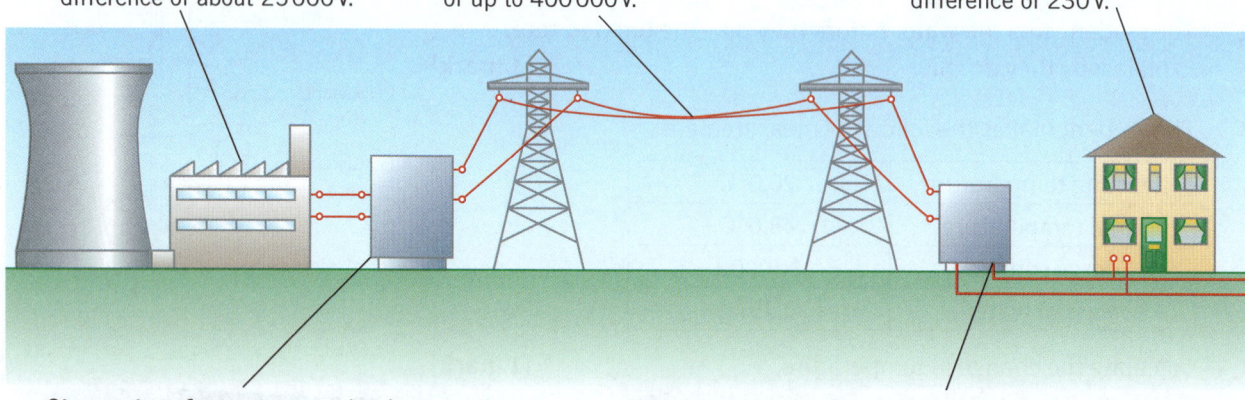

Step-up transformers are used to increase the potential difference from the power station to the transmission cables.

Step-down transformers are used to decrease the potential difference from the transmission cables to the mains supply in homes and offices so that it is safe to use.

Key terms

Make sure you can write a definition for these key terms.

alternating current   alternating potential difference   charge flow
coulombs   direct current

P3

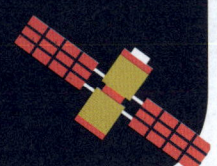

Why do transformers improve efficiency?

A high potential difference across the transmission cables means that a lower current is needed to transfer the same amount of power, since:

(L) power (W) = current (A) × potential difference (V)
$$P = IV$$

A lower current in the cables means less electrical power is wasted due to heating of the cables, since the power lost in heating a cable is:

(L) power (W) = current^2 (A) × resistance (Ω)
$$P = I^2R$$

This makes using transformers in the National Grid a more efficient way to transfer energy.

Energy transfer in electrical appliances

Electrical appliances transfer energy.

For example, a hairdryer transfers energy electrically from a chemical store (e.g. the fuel in a power station) to the kinetic energy store of the fan inside the hairdryer and to the thermal energy store of the heating filaments inside the hairdryer.

When you turn an electrical appliance on, the potential difference of the mains supply causes charge (carried by electrons) to flow through it.

You can calculate the **charge flow** using the equation:

(L) charge flow (C) = current (A) × time (s)
$$Q = It$$

You can find the energy transferred to an electrical appliance when charge flows through it using:

(L) energy transferred (J) = charge flow (C) × potential difference (V)
$$E = QV$$

You can find the energy transferred by an electrical appliance using the equation:

(L) power (W) = $\dfrac{\text{energy transferred (J)}}{\text{time (s)}}$

$$P = \dfrac{E}{t}$$

Revision tip

Remember This topic has the potential for some high level maths questions. If you see a question and you can't decide which equation you need to use to solve it, try looking at combinations of equations.

Revision tip

Practice There are lots of equations in this topic that you need to learn. Find the best way for you to remember them. It could be flashcards, a mnemonic, or writing them out as sides of an equation triangle.

---

direct potential difference   fuse   National Grid   short circuit
step-down transformer   step-up transformer

P3 Knowledge

Retrieval

Learn the answers to the questions below, then cover the answers column with a piece of paper and write as many as you can. Check and repeat.

P3 questions | Answers

#	Question	Answer
1	Why is the current provided by a cell called a direct current (d.c.)?	only flows in one direction
2	What is an alternating current (a.c.)?	current that repeatedly reverses direction
3	What kind of current is supplied by mains electricity?	alternating current
4	What is the frequency and voltage of mains electricity?	50 Hz, 230 V
5	What colours are the live, neutral, and earth wires in a three-core cable?	live = brown, neutral = blue, earth = green and yellow stripes
6	What is the function of the live wire in a three-core cable?	carries the alternating potential difference from the supply
7	What is the function of the neutral wire in a three-core cable?	completes the circuit so a current can flow
8	What is the function of the earth wire in a three-core cable?	safety wire to stop the outer casing of the appliance becoming live
9	When is there a current in the earth wire?	when there is a fault
10	Why is the live wire dangerous?	provides a large p.d. that would cause a large current to flow through a person if they touched it
11	What is the National Grid?	nationwide network of cables and transformers that link power stations to customers
12	What are step-up transformers used for in the National Grid?	increase the p.d. from the power station to the transmission cables
13	What are step-down transformers used for in the National Grid?	decrease the p.d. from the transmission cables to the mains supply in buildings so that it is safe to use
14	How does having a large potential difference in the transmission cables help to make the National Grid an efficient way to transfer energy?	large p.d. means a small current is needed to transfer the same amount of power, small current in the transmission cables means less electrical power is wasted due to heating
15	What two things does energy transfer to an appliance depend on?	power of appliance, time it is switched on for
16	What are the units for power, current, potential difference, and resistance?	watt (W), amp (A), volt (V), ohm (Ω)

P3 Supplying electricity

P3

Now go back and use the questions below to check your knowledge from previous chapters.

Previous questions | Answers

#	Question	Answer
1	What is a black body?	theoretical object that absorbs 100% of the radiation that falls on it, and does not reflect or transmit any radiation
2	Describe the energy transfer when a ball is fired using an elastic band.	Energy is transferred mechanically from the elastic store of the elastic band to the kinetic store of the ball. Some energy is dissipated to the thermal store of the surroundings.
3	What are the main renewable and non-renewable resources available on Earth?	renewable: solar, tidal, wave, wind, geothermal, biofuel, hydroelectric non-renewable: coal, oil, gas, nuclear
4	What are the main advantages and disadvantages of using biofuels?	advantages: can be 'carbon neutral', reliable disadvantages: expensive to produce, use land/water that might be needed to grow food
5	Define specific heat capacity.	amount of energy needed to raise the temperature of 1 kg of a material by 1 °C
6	Name the four ways in which energy can be transferred.	heating, waves, electric current, mechanically (by forces)

🧪 Required practical skills

Practise answering questions on the required practicals using the example below.
You need to be able to apply your skills and knowledge to other practicals too.

Resistance in electrical circuits

You need to be able to measure resistance in an electrical circuit. You can use current and potential difference (p.d.), or an ohmmeter. Length, cross-sectional area, and material all affect the resistance of a wire.
The arrangement of components affects the resistance of a circuit.
When measuring the resistance of a wire, remember to:
- turn off the power supply when not taking readings to stop the wire getting hot
- fix the wire to a ruler so that the wire is straight
- use crocodile clips that make a good contact with the wire.

When measuring the resistance of a circuit experiment, remember to make sure the ammeter measures the total current.

Worked example

A student uses an ammeter and a voltmeter to measure the resistance of a piece of wire.

Length in cm	10	20	30	40	50
p.d. in V	0.47	0.59	0.64	0.69	0.72
Current in A	0.24	0.16	0.14	0.11	0.10
Resistance in Ω	2.0	3.7	4.6	6.3	

1 Calculate the resistance when the length is 50 cm.

$$\text{resistance} = \frac{\text{p.d.}}{\text{current}} = \frac{0.72}{0.10} = 7.2 \, \Omega$$

2 Describe how resistance changes with length of a piece of wire.

As the length of the wire increases, the resistance increases proportionally.

3 Another student finds that resistance does not increase proportionally with the length of wire. Suggest why, and explain your answer.

The wire was heating up, so the resistance was also changing because of the increase in temperature, not just the change in length.

Practice

Describe how to set up an experiment to compare the resistance of a circuit containing three unequal resistors in parallel with the resistance of a circuit containing the same three resistors in series. Include circuit diagrams in your answer.

P3 Retrieval 339

Practice

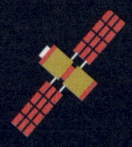

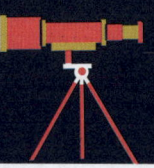

Exam-style questions

01 Electrical appliances have a plug that connects the appliance to the mains.

01.1 Give the potential difference of the mains in the UK. **[1 mark]**

Circle **one** answer from the box below.

6 V	12 V	230 V	1000 V

01.2 Complete the sentence.

Choose the correct word in bold. **[1 mark]**

Mains electricity in the UK produces an **alternating** / **direct** current.

01.3 The sockets in a house can be traced back to a power station.

The power station generates an electrical potential difference that is much higher than the value given in **01.1**. Complete the sentence. Choose the correct word in bold. **[1 mark]**

A **step-down** / **step-up** transformer decreases the potential difference for domestic use.

02.1 Draw **one** line from each wire to the correct function. **[2 marks]**

Wire	Function
live wire	is a safety wire
neutral wire	is attached to an alternating potential difference from the supply
earth wire	completes the circuit

> **Exam Tip**
> You need to practice labelling each part inside a plug, and giving its function.

02.2 Name the two wires in **02.1** that carry the same current when the appliance is working normally. **[1 mark]**

_____

_____

02.3 Complete the sentences.

Choose the correct words from the box. **[3 marks]**

| cannot | case | current | can | neutral | no |

Normally, there is _____ current flowing in the safety wire.

The safety wire is connected to the _____ of an appliance.

This means that the case _____ become live.

340 P3 Supplying electricity

Paper 5 P3

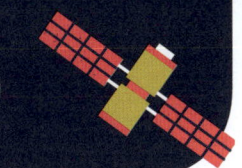

03 A student is heating up soup and notices that the microwave oven has two power settings. The first setting is 700 W and the second setting is 1000 W.

03.1 Complete the sentences. Choose the correct words in bold. **[2 marks]**

The soup will heat faster on the **700 W / 1000 W** setting.

This is because **less / more** energy will be transferred per second.

03.2 The student uses the first setting to heat the soup. They turn the microwave on for 60 s. The equation that links energy, power, and time is:

energy transferred = power × time

Calculate the energy transferred by the microwave oven. Give the unit with your answer. **[3 marks]**

> **Exam Tip**
> Units are worth a separate mark. So, even if you're not sure you have the correct answer, give the units, and you might still get a mark!

Power = _____ Unit = _____

03.3 Complete the sentence. Choose the correct words in bold. **[2 marks]**

The toaster transfers the energy from **batteries / the mains**

to energy in the **kinetic / thermal** store of the soup whilst

it is heating.

04 A student has a small electric motor.

04.1 They connect the motor in a circuit with a 6 V battery. A current of 1.5 A flows in the circuit. Show that the power of the motor is 9 W. **[2 marks]**

> **Exam Tip**
> In a show question, you already know the answer (9 W), so you just need to clearly show the examiner that you can use an equation to get this answer.

Power = _____ W

04.2 The student turns the motor on for 30 seconds. Write down the equation that links energy, power, and time. **[1 mark]**

04.3 Calculate the energy transferred by the motor. **[3 marks]**

Energy transferred = _____ J

04.4 The student finds a lamp with the same power rating as the motor. They connect the lamp to another 6 V battery. They then turn both circuits on for 30 seconds.
Which statement is correct? **[1 mark]**
Tick **one** box.

The motor transfers more energy than the lamp. ☐

Both devices transfer the same amount of energy. ☐

The lamp transfers more energy than the motor. ☐

> **Exam Tip**
> For **04.3** you need to use the answer from **04.1**. This is common in exams – you may have to look back at the question to get all the information you need.

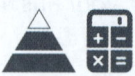

05 A hairdryer is connected to the mains.

05.1 Write down the potential difference that the hairdryer needs to work. **[1 mark]**

_____

05.2 Write down the equation that links the charge, energy transferred, and potential difference. **[1 mark]**

_____

05.3 Calculate the energy transferred by 10 C of charge when the hairdryer is working. **[2 marks]**

Energy transferred = _____ J

05.4 The charge flows in a time of 15 s. The equation for power is

$$\text{power} = \frac{\text{energy transferred}}{\text{time}}$$

Calculate the power of the hairdryer. Give your answer to 2 significant figures. **[3 marks]**

Power = _____ W

> **Exam Tip**
> **05.3** uses numbers from different parts of **05**. It can help to keep notes on the side to prevent confusing the numbers.
> potential difference = (answer to **05.1**)
> charge = 10 C
> energy = (answer to **05.3**)
> time = 1.5s
> power = (answer to **05.4**)

342 P3 Supplying electricity

05.5 Describe the two types of energy stores involved in transfers that happen when the hairdryer is being used. **[2 marks]**

1 _____

_____

2 _____

_____

06 A toaster has a current of 3.5 A flowing in it when it is working. It needs to be connected to a potential difference of 230 V to work.

06.1 Write down the equation that links current, potential difference, and power. **[1 mark]**

_____

06.2 Show that the power of the toaster is about 800 W. **[2 marks]**

> **Exam Tip**
>
> Please spend time learning all your equations. You need them so many times in the exam!

Power = _____ W

06.3 Write down the equation that links current, power, and resistance **[1 mark]**

_____

06.4 Show that the resistance of the toaster is about 66 Ω. **[2 marks]**

Resistance = _____ Ω

06.5 The toaster has a metal casing. Explain why this could cause a problem if the case is not earthed. **[2 marks]**

_____

_____

_____

07 A student compares some household appliances. **Table 1** shows the student's data.

Table 1

Appliance	Power	Potential difference in V
kettle	2.2 kW	230
hairdryer	2000 W	230
vacuum cleaner	1.1 kW	230
microwave	700 W	230

07.1 Identify the appliance that uses the most power. [1 mark]

07.2 Write down the equation that links current, potential difference, and power. [1 mark]

07.3 Identify the appliance that draws the smallest current. [1 mark]

07.4 Calculate the current of the vacuum cleaner. [3 marks]

07.5 The current through the kettle is 9.6 A. Compare the current through the kettle with the current through the vacuum cleaner. [1 mark]

08 A student moves containers of drink from a refrigerator to a cool box.

08.1 Complete the sentences by circling the correct answers. [3 marks]

The air inside the cool box stays cold because the walls of the cool box are made of **a conducting / an insulating** material.

Energy travels very **quickly / slowly** through the material.

The energy travels more slowly through **thicker / thinner** walls.

08.2 The student takes out two containers of drink. The drinks heat up. One container is made of metal. The other container is made of glass. The drink in the metal container heats up more quickly than the drink in the glass container.

Suggest which material, metal or glass, has the lowest thermal conductivity. [1 mark]

09 **Figure 1** shows how electricity is transferred from a power station to a house.

Figure 1

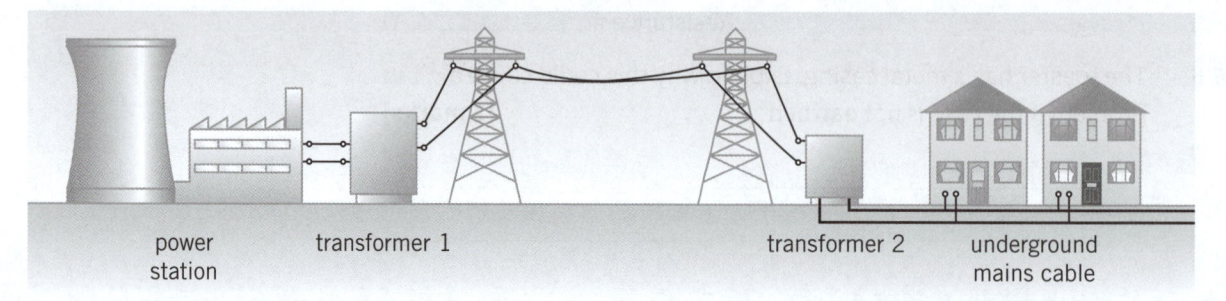

power station   transformer 1   transformer 2   underground mains cable

09.1 Name the system of transformers and power cables that provides electricity to businesses and houses. [1 mark]

09.2 Explain why there are two transformers. [3 marks]

09.3 Give **one** reason why the system is an efficient way of transferring energy. [2 marks]

> **Exam Tip**
>
> **09.3** asks for **one** reason but has **two** marks available. You can assume there is one mark available for your reason and one for why

P3 Supplying electricity

10.1 Draw **one** line from each statement beginning to the correct statement ending. You do not need to use all of the endings. **[3 marks]**

Statement beginning

- The potential difference of the mains electricity in the UK is
- The frequency of mains electricity in the UK is
- The mains supply in the UK produces a current that is

Statement ending

- 50 Hz.
- direct.
- about 230 V.
- 100 Hz.
- alternating.

> **Exam Tip**
> Start **10.1** by looking at the units – once you remember the unit for potential difference the answer should become clear.

10.2 Complete the sentences using the words in the box. You will need to use some of the words more than once. **[5 marks]**

| live | earth | neutral |

The potential difference between the live and _____ wires is 230 V.

The potential difference between the _____ and _____ wires is 0 V.

When an appliance is connected to the mains and turned on a current flows in the _____ and _____ wires.

10.3 Describe why there is an earth wire in a circuit. **[1 mark]**

11 Table 2 shows data about wind turbines and solar cells. **[1 mark]**

Table 2

	Cost in £	Power output in W
wind turbine	200	0.4
solar cells	12 000	10

11.1 Calculate the number of wind turbines you would need to produce the same power as the solar cells. **[2 marks]**

11.2 Calculate the cost to produce a power output of 10 W using wind turbines. **[1 mark]**

11.3 Compare the cost of installing the two systems of electricity generation.

Discuss the environmental issues with the two methods when they are operating. **[3 marks]**

Knowledge

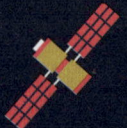

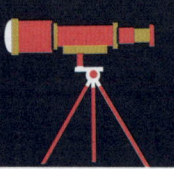

P4 Electric circuits

Charge

An atom has no charge because it has equal numbers of positive protons and negative electrons.

When electrons are removed from an atom it becomes *positively* charged. When electrons are added to an atom it becomes *negatively* charged.

Static charge

Insulating materials can become charged when they are rubbed with another insulating material. This is because electrons are transferred from one material to the other. Materials that gain electrons become negatively charged and those that lose electrons become positively charged.

Positive charges do not usually transfer between materials.

Electric charge is measured in coulombs (C).

Sparks

If two objects have a very strong electric field between them, electrons in the air molecules will be strongly attracted towards the positively charged object. If the electric field is strong enough, electrons will be pulled away from the air molecules and cause a flow of electrons between the two objects – this is a spark.

Electric fields

A charged object creates an **electric field** around itself.

If a charged object is placed in the electric field of another charged object it experiences **electrostatic force**. This means that the two charged objects exert a non-contact force on each other:
- like charges repel each other
- opposite charges attract each other.

The electric field, and the force between two charged objects, gets stronger as the distance between the objects decreases.

Drawing electric fields

Electric fields can be represented using a diagram with field lines. These show the direction of the force that a small positive charge would experience when placed in the electric field.

When drawing electric fields, make sure:
- field lines meet the surface of charged objects at 90°
- arrows always point away from positive charges and towards negative charges.

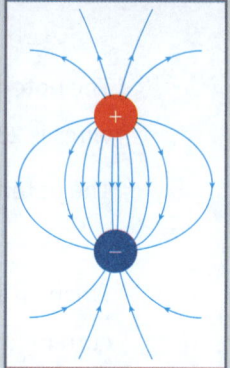

Electric current

Electric current is when charge flows. The charge in an electric circuit is carried by electrons. The unit of current is the **ampere** (amp, A).

1 ampere = 1 *coulomb* of charge flow per second

In circuit diagrams, current flows from the positive terminal of a cell or battery to the negative terminal. This is known as conventional current.

In a single closed loop, the current has the same value at any point in the circuit.

Metals are good conductors of electricity because they contain delocalised electrons, which are free to flow through the structure.

Potential difference

Potential difference (p.d.) is a measure of how much energy is transferred between two points in a circuit. The unit of potential difference is the volt (V).
- The p.d. across a component is the work done on it by each coulomb of charge that passes through it.
- The p.d. across a power supply or battery is the energy transferred to each coulomb of charge that passes through it.

For electrical charge to flow through a circuit there must be a source of potential difference.

Key terms

Make sure you can write a definition for these key terms.

- ampere
- charge
- coulomb
- current
- electric field
- electrostatic force
- parallel
- potential difference
- resistance
- series
- static

P4

Resistance

When electrons move through a circuit, they collide with the ions and atoms of the wires and components in the circuit. This causes **resistance** to the flow of charge.

The unit of resistance is the ohm (Ω).

A long wire has more resistance than a short wire because electrons collide with more ions as they pass through a longer wire.

The resistance of an electrical component can be found by measuring the current and potential difference:

potential difference (V) = current (A) × resistance (Ω)

$$V = IR$$

Circuit components

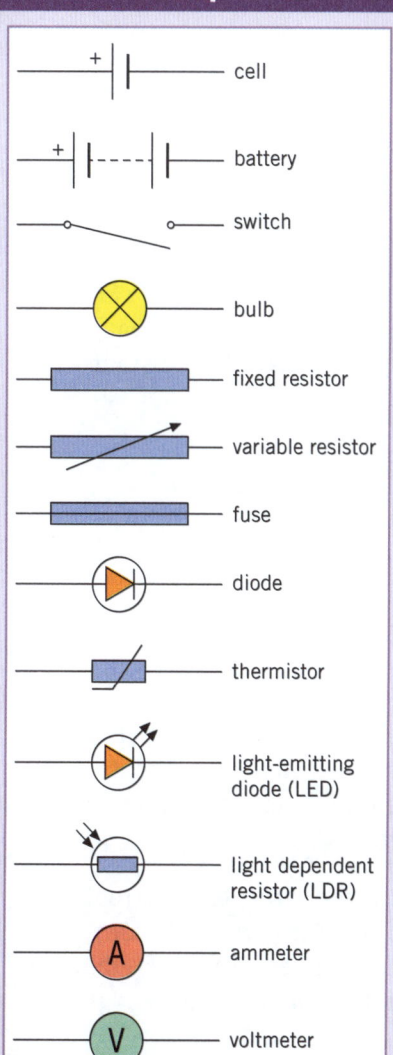

- cell
- battery
- switch
- bulb
- fixed resistor
- variable resistor
- fuse
- diode
- thermistor
- light-emitting diode (LED)
- light dependent resistor (LDR)
- ammeter
- voltmeter

Current–potential difference graphs

A graph of current through a component against the p.d. across it (I–V graph), is known as the component characteristic.

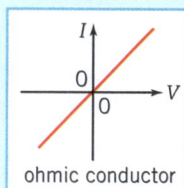

ohmic conductor: Current is directly proportional to the p.d. in an ohmic conductor at a constant temperature. The resistance is constant.

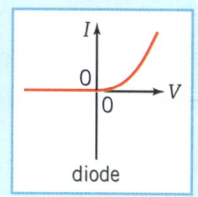

diode: The current through a diode only flows in one direction – called the forward direction. There needs to be a minimum voltage before any current will flow.

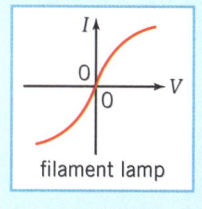

filament lamp: As more current flows through the filament, its temperature increases. The atoms in the wire vibrate more, and collide more often with electrons flowing through it, so resistance increases as temperature increases.

The resistance for an ohmic conductor can be found by calculating:

$$\text{resistance} = \frac{1}{\text{gradient}}$$

Series circuits

In a **series** circuit, the components are connected one after the other in a single loop. If one component in a series circuit stops working the whole circuit will stop working.

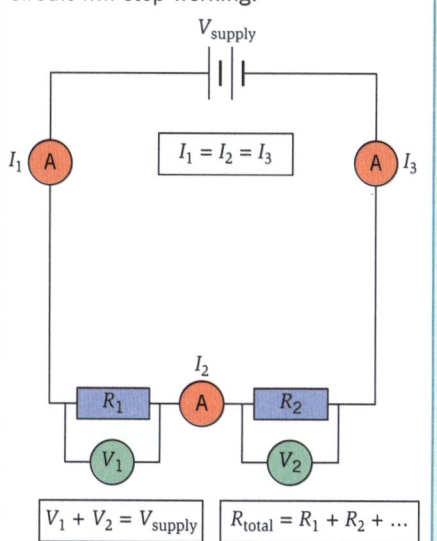

$I_1 = I_2 = I_3$

$V_1 + V_2 = V_{supply}$ $R_{total} = R_1 + R_2 + ...$

Components with a higher resistance will transfer a larger share of the total p.d. because $V = IR$ (and current is the same through all components).

Parallel circuits

A **parallel** circuit is made up of two or more loops through which current can flow. If one branch of a parallel circuit stops working, the other branches will not be affected.

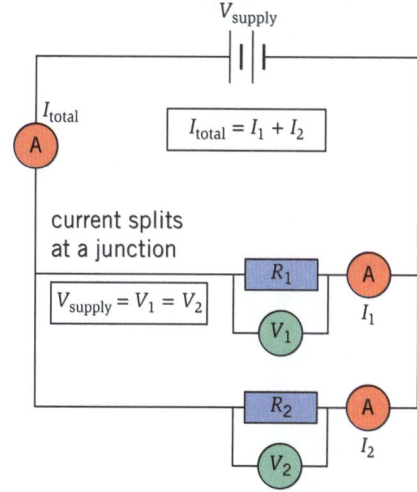

$I_{total} = I_1 + I_2$

current splits at a junction

$V_{supply} = V_1 = V_2$

The total resistance of two or more components in parallel is always less than the smallest resistance of any branch. This is because adding a loop to the circuit provides another route for the current to flow, so more current can flow in total even though the p.d. has not changed. Adding more resistors in parallel decreases the total resistance of a circuit.

P4 Knowledge   347

Retrieval

Learn the answers to the questions below, then cover the answers column with a piece of paper and write as many as you can. Check and repeat.

	P4 questions	Answers
1	How does a material become charged?	becomes negatively charged by gaining electrons and becomes positively charged by losing electrons
2	What will two objects carrying the same type of charge do if they are brought close to each other?	repel each other
3	What is an electric field?	region of space around a charged object in which another charged object will experience an electrostatic force
4	What happens to the strength of an electric field as you get further from the charged object?	it decreases
5	What is electric current?	rate of flow of charge
6	What units are charge, current, and time measured in?	coulomb (C), ampere (A), second (s) respectively
7	What is the same at all points when charge flows in a closed loop?	current
8	What must there be in a closed circuit so that electrical charge can flow?	source of potential difference (p.d.)
9	Which two factors does current depend on and what are their units?	resistance unit: ohm (Ω) p.d. unit: volt (V)
10	What happens to the current if the resistance is increased but the p.d. stays the same?	current decreases
11	What is an ohmic conductor?	conductor where current is directly proportional to the voltage so resistance is constant (at constant temperature)
12	What happens to the resistance of a filament lamp as its temperature increases?	resistance increases
13	What happens to the resistance of a thermistor as its temperature increases?	resistance decreases
14	What happens to the resistance of a light-dependent resistor when light intensity increases?	resistance decreases
15	What are the main features of a series circuit?	same current through each component, total p.d. of power supply is shared between components, total resistance of all components is the sum of the resistance of each component
16	What are the main features of a parallel circuit?	p.d. across each branch is the same, total current through circuit is the sum of the currents in each branch – total resistance of all resistors is less than the resistance of the smallest individual resistor

P4 Electric circuits

P4

Now go back and use the questions below to check your knowledge from previous chapters.

Previous questions | Answers

	Previous questions	Answers
1	What units are charge, current, and time measured in?	coulomb (C), ampere (A), second (s) respectively
2	What is an electric field?	region of space around a charged object in which another charged object will experience an electrostatic force
3	What happens to the resistance of a light-dependent resistor when light intensity increases?	resistance decreases

Required practical skills

Practise answering questions on the required practicals using the example below.
You need to be able to apply your skills and knowledge to other practicals too.

I–V graphs

You need to be able to determine the relationship between current and potential difference (p.d.) for a lamp, resistor, and diode.

You should be able to draw and interpret I–V graphs – the shape of the graph is characteristic of the component. The gradient of the graph is not related to the resistance, but resistance can be calculated from values for p.d. and current.

A variable power supply or resistor should be used to change the current in both directions.

The diode needs to be connected with a protective resistor so it does not get too hot.

Worked example

A student uses a circuit to measure values of current and p.d. for component **X**. They decide to use a variable resistor to change the current.

1 Below are some data for the component. Plot a graph of the data and draw a line of best fit.

p.d. in V	0.0	0.1	0.4	0.6	0.8	1.0
Current in A	0.2	0.38	0.59	0.64	0.69	0.72
p.d. in V	0.0	−0.1	−0.4	−0.6	−0.8	−1.0
Current in A	−0.2	−0.38	−0.59	−0.64	−0.69	−0.72

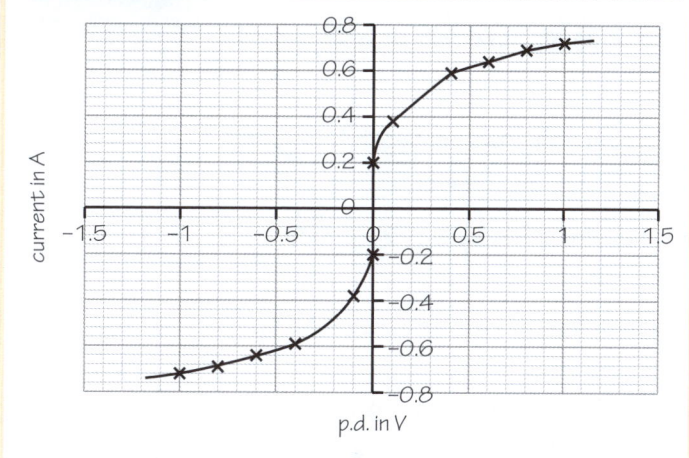

2 Suggest the name of component **X**. Use the graph and data to explain your answer.

X is a lamp as the graph is symmetrical:

$$\text{resistance} = \frac{\text{p.d.}}{\text{current}}$$

$R = \frac{0.1}{0.38} = 0.26\,\Omega$ $R = \frac{1}{0.72} = 1.39\,\Omega$

So as p.d. increases, resistance increases.

Practice

A student has set up an experiment to collect data to plot an I–V graph for a piece of resistance wire.

1 Give two changes the student will need to make to repeat the experiment with a diode.

2 Sketch the I–V graph for a diode. Explain the shape of the graph in terms of resistance.

Practice

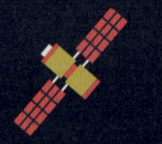

Exam-style questions

01 Circuit components are represented by circuit symbols.

01.1 Draw **one** line from each component to the correct symbol. **[3 marks]**

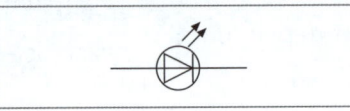

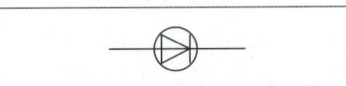

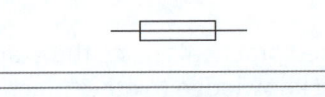

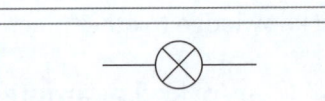

Component	Symbol
lamp	(LED symbol)
LED	(diode symbol)
diode	(fuse symbol)
fuse	(lamp symbol)

> **Exam Tip**
>
> The symbol is closely linked to the function. If you're not sure, think about the function of a fuse, or how we could draw light being emitted from an LED, or the direction for a diode.

01.2 Draw the circuit symbol for a resistor. **[1 mark]**

01.3 There is a reading of 2 A on an ammeter.
What does this mean? **[1 mark]**
Tick **one** box.

An electric charge of 2 coulombs flows per second. ☐

An electric charge of 1 coulomb flows per second. ☐

An electric charge of 1 coulomb flows every 2 seconds. ☐

02 A student finds a box of different resistors. One of the resistors is not marked.

The student wants to find the resistance of the resistor. They place the unknown resistor in the circuit shown in **Figure 1**.

Figure 1

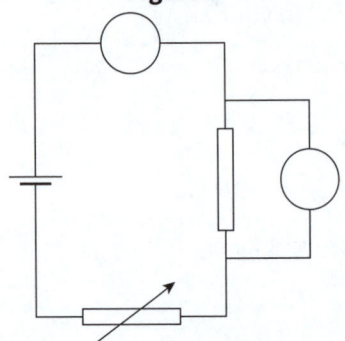

350 **P4 Electric circuits**

Paper 5 P4

02.1 The student has not labelled the diagram.
The ammeter and voltmeter need to be in the correct places.
Write the letters **A** and **V** in the circles in **Figure 1** to show where to put the meters. **[2 marks]**

02.2 Label the resistor in **Figure 1**. **[1 mark]**

02.3 Label the variable resistor in **Figure 1**. **[1 mark]**

02.4 The student measures a current of 0.3 A.
Define current. **[1 mark]**

_____

_____

02.5 Write down the equation that links current, potential difference, and resistance. **[1 mark]**

_____

02.6 The student measures a potential difference of 6 V.
Calculate the resistance of the resistor. **[3 marks]**

Resistance = _____ Ω

> **Exam Tip**
>
> For all maths questions:
> Step 1 – write down the equation you are using (**02.5**)
> Step 2 – put the numbers into the equation
> Step 3 – rearrange the equation
> Step 4 – do the maths
> Step 5 – write down the answer with units.

03 A teacher sets up a data logger to measure the light level in the laboratory over the weekend.

03.1 They use a circuit component that has a resistance that changes with light level.
Name this component. **[1 mark]**

03.2 Draw the circuit symbol for this component. **[1 mark]**

03.3 The teacher finds that at one time of day the resistance of the component is very low.
Complete the sentence by circling the correct word in bold. **[1 mark]**
The resistance is very low when the light level is **high** / **low**.

03.4 Suggest **one** reason why the teacher used a data logger. **[1 mark]**

> **Exam Tip**
>
> What is the advantage of using a data logger instead of manually recording the light levels? How could this help over a long period of time?

P4 Practice 351

04 Figure 2 shows four circuits drawn by a student. The cells and bulbs used in each circuit are identical.

Figure 2

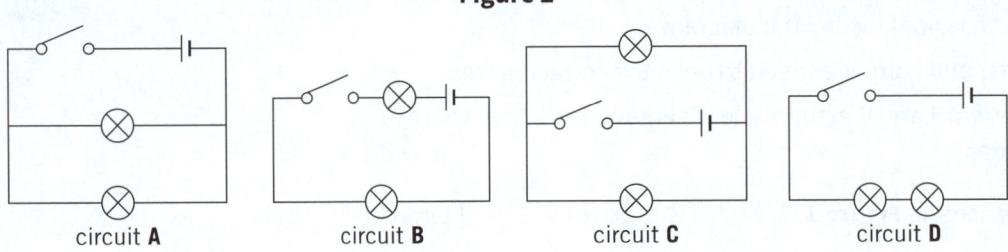

circuit **A**   circuit **B**   circuit **C**   circuit **D**

04.1 Which statement about the circuits in **Figure 2** is correct?
Choose **one** answer. **[1 mark]**

Circuit **A** is a series circuit.

Circuits **A** and **C** are parallel circuits.

Only circuit **A** is a parallel circuit.

Circuits **C** and **D** are series circuits.

04.2 Complete these sentences about the four circuits.
Use the letters **A**, **B**, **C**, or **D**. **[3 marks]**

The bulbs in circuits _____ and _____ are the brightest.

If one of the bulbs in circuit _____ or _____ breaks, the other bulb will go out.

An ammeter placed anywhere in circuit _____ or _____ will measure the same current.

04.3 The student looks at circuit **B** and says:

'I think that when you press the switch, the bulb nearer the battery will be brighter than the bulb that is further away.'

Do you agree? Explain your answer. **[3 marks]**

> **Exam Tip**
>
> Get into the habit of looking at the number of marks available, this will help you work out what the examiners are looking for.
>
> **04.3** is a three-mark question, meaning a 'yes' or 'no' answer won't be enough – you need to explain why as well.

05 A student makes measurements of current and potential difference for a circuit component. They plot the graph shown in **Figure 3**.

Figure 3

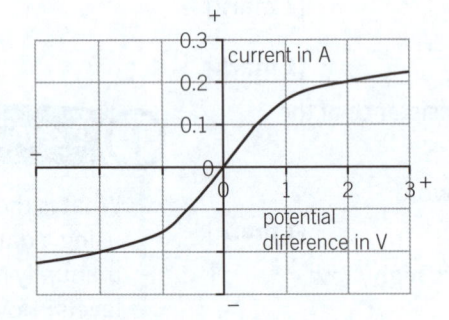

05.1 What is the circuit component? Choose **one** answer **[1 mark]**

lamp   diode

05.2 Complete the sentence. **[1 mark]**

The resistance of the component _____ as the potential difference increases.

> **Exam Tip**
>
> Learning the current – potential difference (I–V) graphs for the different components is really important. You need to be able to recognise them, sketch them, and explain them.

352 P4 Electric circuits

05.3 Complete the sentences below by choosing the correct words in bold. **[3 marks]**

As current flows through the component, the component gets **colder / hotter**. The atoms inside the component vibrate **less / more**. This makes it **easier / harder** for the current to flow.

06 A student connects up a circuit with a single cell, a lamp, a diode, a switch, and an ammeter. The components are connected in series. When the switch is closed, the lamp does not light up. All the components are working.

06.1 Explain why the lamp does not light up. **[2 marks]**

06.2 Write down the equation that links current, potential difference, and resistance. **[1 mark]**

06.3 The student gets the bulb to light and measures a current of 0.12 A. The potential difference of the cell is 1.5 V. Calculate the resistance of the lamp. Give your answer to 2 significant figures. **[4 marks]**

> **Exam Tip**
> Look at the resolution of the other numbers in **06**.

07 A student investigates the power produced by different solar power stations. **Table 1** shows the output of four power stations.

Table 1

Power station	Power output in MW
A	236
B	212
C	200
D	206

07.1 Calculate the mean power output of the four power stations. **[1 mark]**

07.2 Suggest **one** reason why the power outputs of the stations are different. **[1 mark]**

> **Exam Tip**
> The question tells us these are solar powered power stations. Think about the source of the power and if it is constant.

07.3 A hydroelectric power station has an output of 1000 MW. Calculate the number of power stations of the same type and size as power station **C** that would be needed to produce the same output as the hydroelectric power station. **[2 marks]**

07.4 Compare the environmental impact of a solar power station with that of a hydroelectric power station. **[4 marks]**

08 A student is investigating the relationship between length and resistance for a piece of wire.

08.1 Identify the independent variable of the investigation. **[1 mark]**

08.2 Identify the dependent variable of the investigation. **[1 mark]**

08.3 Give one control variable of the investigation. **[1 mark]**

> **Exam Tip**
> There are lots of different controls you could pick but make sure it is relevant to *this* experiment.

08.4 The student expects to finds that resistance is proportional to the length of the wire. Sketch a graph that shows this relationship. Label the axes. **[2 marks]**

08.5 The student does not obtain the graph that they expect. Suggest **one** reason why not. **[1 mark]**

09 A student investigates the I–V characteristic of a resistor. For each voltage, they measure the current three times and calculate the mean. The results are shown in **Table 2**.

Table 2

P.d. in V	Current in ____			
	1	2	3	Mean
0	0	0	0	0
2	0.12	0.13	0.14	
4	0.23	0.25	0.27	0.25
6	0.37	0.38	0.42	0.39
8	0.39	0.52	0.50	0.51
10	0.61	0.61	0.64	0.62
12	0.72	0.73	0.71	0.72

09.1 Give the unit of current. **[1 mark]**

09.2 Identify the outlier in **Table 2**. **[1 mark]**

09.3 Calculate the missing mean. **[1 mark]**

09.4 Complete the graph in **figure 4** of average current against potential difference for the resistor.
Draw a line of best fit. **[2 marks]**

Figure 4

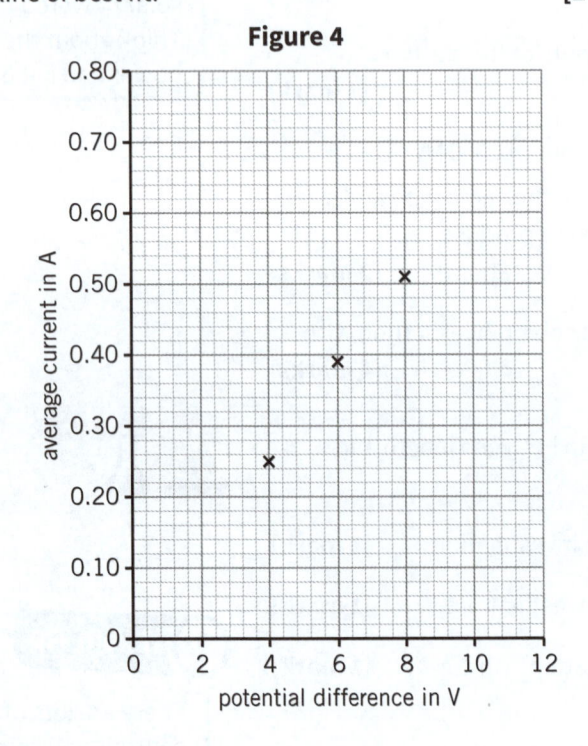

> **Exam Tip**
> Go though the data carefully and see if anything stands out as odd.

> **Exam Tip**
> Use your value from **09.3**, but if you couldn't work that bit out then still attempt this question. In the exam you can get marks for an error carried forward, so you won't lose marks for making the same mistake twice.

P4 Electric circuits

09.5 Draw a line on **Figure 4** to show the results the student would get for a lower resistor. **[1 mark]**

10 A basketball player runs down the court. The player is bouncing the ball up and down.

The speed of the player does not change.

10.1 What happens to the energy in the kinetic energy store of the player?

Choose **one** answer. **[1 mark]**

decreases

increases

stays the same

10.2 The player shoots the ball as shown in **Figure 5**.

At **A**, the player is holding the ball. The ball is not moving.

The ball is moving as it goes through the hoop at **B**. It ends up on the floor.

It is not moving at **C**.

Figure 5

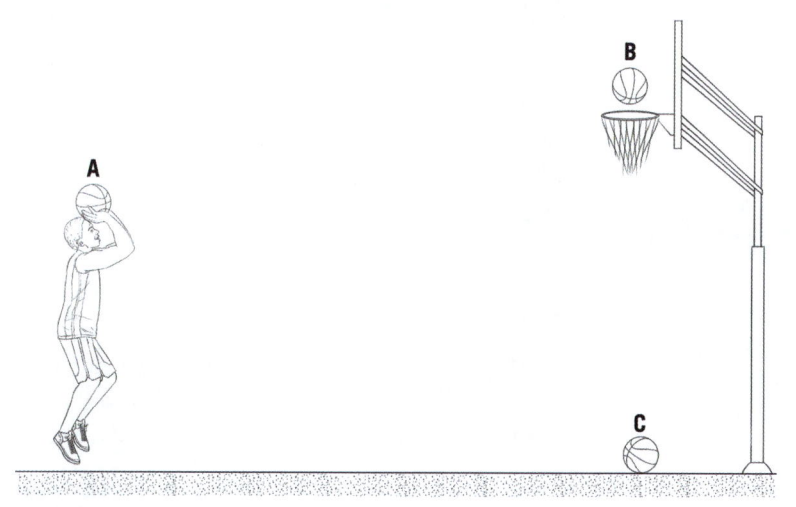

> **Exam Tip**
>
> There is no time pressure in your revision, so annotate each point with the energy stores and changes that are taking place. This is great revision and practice for the exam.

At which point (**A**, **B**, or **C**) does the ball have the largest amount of energy in its gravitational potential energy store? **[1 mark]**

10.3 At which point (**A**, **B**, or **C**) does the ball have energy in its kinetic energy store? **[1 mark]**

Knowledge

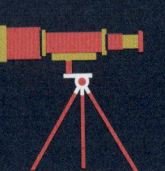

P5 Energy of matter

Changes of state and states of matter

Changes of state and conservation of mass
Changes of state are physical changes because no new substances are produced. The mass always stays the same because the number of particles does not change.

Particles and kinetic energy
When the temperature of a substance is increased, the kinetic energy store of its particles increases and the particles vibrate or move faster.

If the kinetic store of a substance's particles increases or decreases enough, the substance may change state.

Density
You can calculate the density of an object if you know its mass and volume:

(L) density (kg/m³) = mass (kg) / volume (m³)

$$\rho = \frac{m}{V}$$

solid	Arrangement	• particles are in contact with each other and held in fixed positions by strong forces of attraction
	Movement	• vibrate about fixed positions
	Properties	• high density • fixed volume • fixed shape (unless deformed by an external force)
liquid	Arrangement	• particles are in contact with each other • forces of attraction between particles are weaker than in solids
	Movement	• free to move randomly around each other
	Properties	• usually slightly lower density than solids • fixed volume • shape is not fixed so they can flow
gas	Arrangement	• particles are spread out • almost no forces of attraction between particles • large distance between particles on average
	Movement	• move randomly at high speed
	Properties	• low density • no fixed volume or shape • can be compressed and can flow • spread out to fill all available space

Internal energy

Heating a substance increases its **internal energy**.

Internal energy is the sum of the total kinetic energy the particles have due to their motion and the total potential energy the particles have due to their positions relative to each other.

Latent heat

In a graph showing the change in temperature of a substance being heated or cooled, the flat horizontal sections show when the substance is changing state.

The energy transfers taking place during a change in state do not cause a change in temperature, but do change the internal energy of the substance.

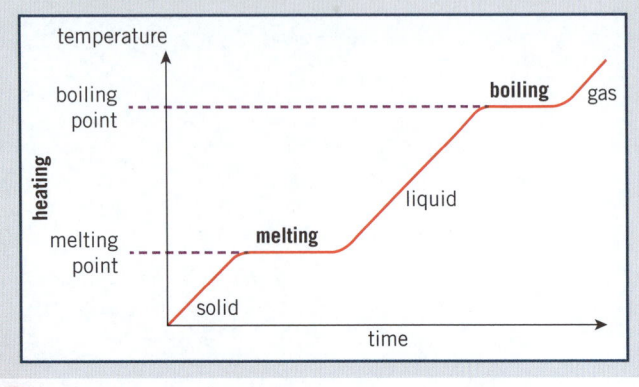

The energy transferred when a substance changes state is called the **latent heat**.

Specific latent heat – the energy required to change the state of 1 kg of a substance with no change in temperature.

Specific latent heat of fusion – the energy required to melt 1 kg of a solid substance with no change in temperature.

Specific latent heat of vaporisation – the energy required to **evaporate** 1 kg of a liquid substance with no change in temperature.

The energy needed to change the state of a substance can be calculated using the equation:

thermal energy for a change in state (J) = mass (kg) × specific latent heat (J/kg)

$$E = ml$$

356   P5 Energy of matter

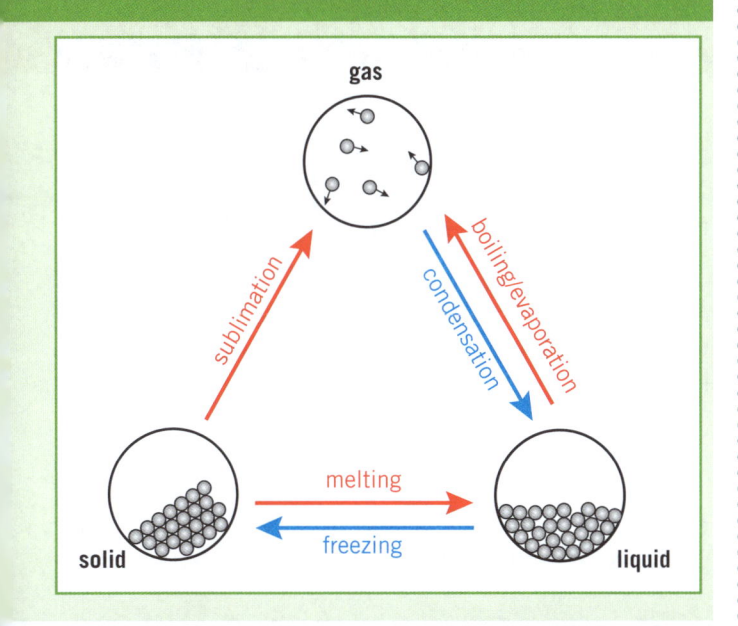

P5

Specific heat capacity

When a substance is heated or cooled the temperature change depends on:
- the substance's mass
- the type of material
- how much energy is transferred to it.

Every type of material has a **specific heat capacity** – the amount of energy needed to raise the temperature of 1 kg of the substance by 1 °C.

The energy transferred to the thermal store of a substance can be calculated from the substance's mass, specific heat capacity, and temperature change:

change in thermal energy (J) = mass (kg) × specific heat capacity (J/kg°C) × temperature change (°C)

$$\Delta E = mc\Delta\theta$$

Key terms

Write a definition for these key terms.

boiling
condensation
conservation of mass
density
evaporation
freezing
internal energy
latent heat
melting
specific heat capacity
specific latent heat
sublimation

The relationship between temperature and pressure in gases

Gas temperature

The particles in a gas are constantly moving in random directions and with random speeds.

The temperature of a gas is related to the average kinetic energy of its particles.

When a gas is heated, the particles gain kinetic energy and move faster, so the temperature of the gas increases.

Gas pressure

The pressure a gas exerts on a surface, such as the walls of a container, is caused by the force of the gas particles hitting the surface.

The pressure of a gas produces a net force at right angles to the walls of a container or any surface.

If the temperature of a gas in a sealed container is increased, the pressure increases because
- the particles move faster so they hit the surfaces with more force
- the number of these impacts per second increases, exerting more force overall.

If a gas is compressed quickly, for example, in a bicycle pump, its temperature can rise. This is because
- compressing the gas requires a force to be applied to the gas – this results in work being done to the gas, since:

    work done = force × distance
- the energy gained by the gas is not transferred quickly enough to its surroundings.

Revision tip

Practice Draw diagrams to show the arrangement of particles in solids, liquids, and gases, with labels to show the movement and forces of attraction. Try writing down the properties of the different states from memory.

Remember The units for specific heat capacity are tricky to remember, so practice writing them as units as well as words!

P5 Knowledge 357

Retrieval

Learn the answers to the questions below, then cover the answers column with a piece of paper and write as many as you can. Check and repeat.

P5 questions | Answers

#	P5 questions	Answers
1	Which two quantities do you need to measure to find the density of a solid or liquid?	mass and volume
2	What happens to the particles in a substance if its temperature is increased?	they move faster and the energy in their kinetic energy store increases
3	Why are changes of state physical changes?	no new substances are produced and the substance will have the same properties as before if the change is reversed
4	Why is the mass of a substance conserved when it changes state?	the number of particles does not change
5	What is the internal energy of a substance?	the total kinetic energy and potential energy of all the particles in the substance
6	Why does a graph showing the change in temperature as a substance cools have a flat section when the substance is changing state?	the energy transferred during a change in state causes a change in the internal energy of the substance
7	What is the name given to the energy transferred when a substance changes state?	latent heat
8	What is the specific latent heat of a substance?	the energy required to change the state of one kilogram of that substance with no change in temperature
9	What is the specific latent heat of fusion of a substance?	the energy required to change one kilogram of the substance from solid to liquid at its melting point, without changing its temperature
10	What is the specific latent heat of vaporisation of a substance?	the energy required to change one kilogram of the substance from liquid to vapour at its boiling point, without changing its temperature
11	On a graph of temperature against time for a substance being heated up or cooled down, what do the flat (horizontal) sections show?	the time when the substance is changing state and the temperature is not changing
12	What property of a gas is related to the average kinetic energy of its particles?	temperature
13	What causes the pressure of a gas on a surface?	the force of the gas particles hitting the surface
14	Give two reasons why the pressure of a gas in a sealed container increases if its temperature is increased.	the molecules move faster so they hit the surfaces with more force and the number of impacts per second increases, so the total force of the impacts increases
15	Give two reasons why the temperature of a gas increases if it is compressed quickly.	the force applied to compress the gas results in work being done to the gas, and the energy gained by the gas is not transferred quickly enough to the surroundings
16	What is specific heat capacity?	amount of energy needed to raise the temperature of 1 kg of a material by 1 °C

P5 Energy of matter

Now go back and use the questions below to check your knowledge from previous chapters.

P5

Previous questions | Answers

	Previous questions	Answers
1	Name the eight energy stores.	kinetic, gravitational potential, elastic potential, thermal, chemical, nuclear, magnetic, electrostatic
2	Name the four ways in which energy can be transferred.	heating, waves, electric current, mechanically (by forces)
3	What is a closed system?	a system where no energy can be transferred to or from the surroundings
4	What is work done?	energy transferred when a force moves an object
5	What is the unit for energy?	joule (J)
6	Give three factors that determine the rate of thermal energy transfer through a material.	thermal conductivity of material, temperature difference, thickness of material
7	What two factors does the rate of heat loss from a building depend on?	thickness of walls and roof, thermal conductivity of walls and roof

🧪 Required practical skills

Practise answering questions on the required practicals using the example below. You need to be able to apply your skills and knowledge to other practicals too.

Density | Worked example | Practice

Density

You need to be able to measure the masses and volumes of regularly and irregularly shaped solid objects, and liquids.

To be accurate and precise in your investigation you need to:
- use dimensions to determine the volume of regularly shaped objects, and displacement for irregularly shaped objects
- use a measuring cylinder to measure the volume of a liquid or displaced water
- choose a measuring cylinder that is just large enough for the object/liquid so that the volume can be read as precisely as possible
- measure from the bottom of the meniscus of a liquid in a measuring cylinder.

Worked example

A student uses a measuring cylinder and digital balance to measure the density of an irregularly shaped lump of putty.

1 Describe how to use the equipment to make the measurements required.

First, measure the putty mass with the digital balance in g. Then place the putty in the cylinder and add water so that the putty is just covered. Record the volume; remove the putty, and record the new volume. Find the difference between these volumes in cm^3.

2 For a putty mass of 65 g, the student recorded three volumes of 54, 56, and 57 cm^3. Calculate the mean volume and the density of the putty.

$$\text{mean volume} = \frac{(54 + 56 + 57)}{3} = 55.67 \, cm^3$$

$$\text{density} = \frac{\text{mass}}{\text{volume}} = \frac{65}{55.67} = 1.17 \, g/cm^3 \text{ to 3 significant figures}$$

Practice

A scientist has two samples of seawater. The volume of each is the same.

Sample **A** has a mass of 235 g and Sample **B** has a mass of 237 g. Calculate the ratio of the densities of Samples **A** and **B**. Show your working and explain your method.

Practice

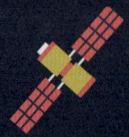

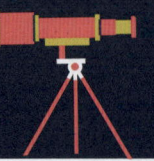

Exam-style questions

01 Water can be in a solid, liquid, or gas state.

01.1 Draw **one** line from each state to the correct particle arrangement. **[2 marks]**

State   Particle arrangement

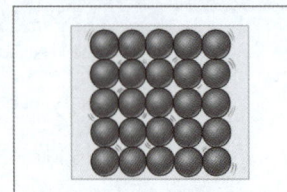

gas state

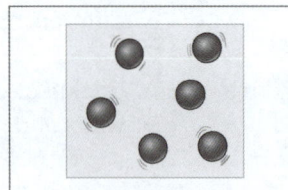

liquid state

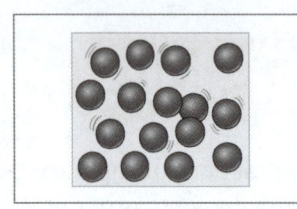

solid state

01.2 Name the state that has the lowest density. **[1 mark]**

> **Exam Tip**
>
> This will be when particles are far apart.

01.3 Complete the sentences to describe what happens to the mass of water when it changes from the liquid to the gas state. **[2 marks]**

The mass of the water **stays the same** / **decreases**. This is because the mass is **conserved** / **destroyed** when there is a change of state.

02 A student carries out an experiment to find the specific latent heat of fusion of ice.

02.1 Write down the **two** measurements the student needs to make to calculate the specific latent heat of fusion of ice.
Use the *Physics Equations sheet*. **[1 mark]**

> **Exam Tip**
>
> You'll be given the equation for specific latent heat in the exam, but you'll still need to recall the units needed.

360   P5 Energy of matter

Paper 5 — P5

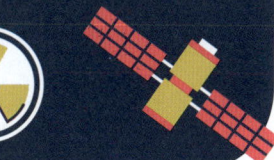

02.2 The student selects the following equipment:
- beaker
- digital balance
- funnel in a stand
- ice
- immersion heater
- joulemeter

Describe how to use the equipment to determine the specific latent heat of fusion of ice. **[6 marks]**

> **Exam Tip**
> In a six-mark question, it is important to organise your answer.

> **Exam Tip**
> This experiment is about latent heat, not specific heat capacity. Make sure that you are clear about the difference.

03 A teacher demonstrates a density tower. They pour liquids of different densities into a large measuring cylinder. The liquids form layers.

03.1 Write down the equation that links density, mass, and volume. **[1 mark]**

03.2 Describe a method to measure the density of a liquid. **[4 marks]**

03.3 **Table 1** shows the density of three of the liquids in the tower.

Table 1

Liquid	Density in g/cm³
oil	0.93
water	1.00
treacle	1.43

The teacher pours equal volumes of each liquid into three beakers. Write down which beaker will contain the largest mass of liquid. **[1 mark]**

03.4 A student measures the mass of 150 cm³ of a liquid. The liquid has a density of 0.80 g/cm³. Show that the mass of the liquid is 120 g. **[2 marks]**

> **Exam Tip**
> This is an equation that you need to recall. The units for density (kg/m³) can help you remember the rest of the equation.

> **Exam Tip**
> If you're given non standard units, check to see if the question wants you to give the answer in them or if you need to convert them to the standard units.

04 A student is learning about internal energy.

They draw two diagrams, **A** and **B**, as shown in **Figure 1**.

Figure 1

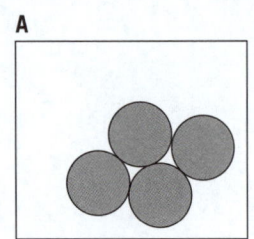

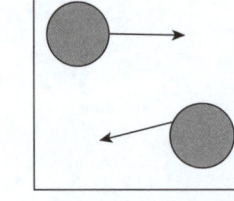

A
The particles in a solid.

B
The particles in a gas.

> **Exam Tip**
>
> In **Figure 1**, they have used arrows to show the speed and direction of movement. Use these to help fill in the gaps.

04.1 Complete the sentences using the words in the box. **[4 marks]**

| gravitational | kinetic | moving fast |
| moving slowly | potential | vibrating |

In diagram **A** the particles are _____. Most of the internal energy is due to the _____ energy of the particles.

In diagram **B** the particles are _____. Most of the internal energy is due to the _____ energy of the particles.

04.2 The sample shown in **Figure 1A** is heated for a long time.

Describe how the internal energy of the sample changes. **[2 marks]**

04.3 The sample shown in **Figure 1B** is heated. The student decides to use the particle model to describe and explain what happens. Which statement is correct? Choose **one** answer. **[1 mark]**

As the gas is heated the average kinetic energy of the molecules decreases.

The average kinetic energy of the molecules is independent of the temperature of the gas.

If the temperature of a gas increases, the pressure that the gas exerts decreases (if the volume stays the same).

The particles in a gas are in random motion.

05 A student wants to find the density of a rectangular wooden block. Here are the dimensions of the block:

length = 20 cm   width = 5 cm   height = 4 cm

05.1 Calculate the volume of the wooden block. **[1 mark]**

05.2 Write down the equation that links density, mass, and volume. **[1 mark]**

05.3 The mass of the block is 300 g. Calculate the density of the wood. Give the unit with your answer. **[3 marks]**

> **Exam Tip**
>
> Units are very important to learn. Here, they are worth a whole separate mark!

362   P5 Energy of matter

05.4 The student finds another block made of metal that has the same volume as the wooden block but a larger mass. Complete the sentence. Choose the correct word in bold. **[1 mark]**

The density of the metal block is **bigger / smaller** than the density of the wooden block.

05.5 An object will float on water if its density is lower than the density of water. Water has a density of 1 g/cm³.
Identify whether the wooden block will float on water. **[1 mark]**

Exam Tip: You can use the equation to help you work this out.

06 A bicycle tyre is made of very stiff rubber that does not expand. The tyre is full of air.

06.1 Complete the sentence.
Choose **one** word from the box. **[1 mark]**

| random | slow | straight |

The air particles in the tyre move around in a _____ motion.

06.2 Draw **one** line from each box to complete the sentences. **[2 marks]**

The temperature of the gas inside the tyre is related to	the pressure of the gas will be bigger.
If the volume of the gas stays the same, then	the average kinetic energy of the gas molecules.
If the molecules are moving faster, then	increasing the temperature will increase the pressure.

Exam Tip: This is only asking about the gas inside the tyre not the tyre itself.

06.3 A student measures the pressure of the air in their bicycle tyre during a hot day. They measure it again in the evening when the air has cooled down.

Complete the sentences. Choose the correct words in bold. **[2 marks]**

The pressure that the student measures during the day is **bigger / smaller** than it is in the evening. This is because the gas molecules are moving more **quickly / slowly**.

07 A student finds the specific heat capacity and melting points of three different metals.
Table 2 shows the student's data.

Table 2

Metal	Specific heat capacity in J/(kg °C)	Melting point in °C	Energy to raise 1 g of metal from room temperature to melting point in J
aluminium	900	660	
copper	385	1084	410
gold	129	1063	135

Exam Tip: First you need to identify the type of data – is it continuous or categoric? This will tell you what type of graph you should draw.

07.1 Name the type of graph the student should plot using these data.
Give a reason for your answer. **[2 marks]**

07.2 Room temperature is 20 °C. Calculate the temperature difference between the melting point of aluminium and room temperature. **[1 mark]**

07.3 Calculate the energy required to raise the temperature of 1 g of aluminium from room temperature to its melting point. Use the *Physics Equations Sheet*. **[2 marks]**

07.4 Since ancient times, people have made jewellery from gold and copper. They would heat the metal until it melted and then pour it into a mould.

Use the data in **Table 2** to suggest one reason why gold was easier to work with than copper. Explain your answer. **[2 marks]**

> **Exam Tip**
>
> You have been specifically asked to use data from **Table 2** in your answer to **07.4**, so make sure you do! Always do what the question asks of you.

08 A student wants to calculate the density of modelling clay. To do this, they take a mass of clay and put it into a measuring cylinder containing water. **Figure 2** shows the water in the measuring cylinder before (**A**) and after (**B**) the clay was added.

08.1 Use **Figure 2** to calculate the volume of the clay. **[2 marks]**

08.2 Give the resolution of the measuring cylinders. **[1 mark]**

08.3 The student measures the mass of the clay. The clay has a mass of 23.41 g. Name the instrument that the student used to find the mass. **[1 mark]**

08.4 Write down the equation that links density, mass, and volume. **[1 mark]**

08.5 Calculate the density of the clay in g/cm³. **[2 marks]**

08.6 Another student makes a cube out of a different piece of clay. Suggest how the student could find the volume of the cube of clay. **[2 marks]**

Figure 2

09 A substance is heated. **Figure 3** shows how the temperature of the substance changes with time. The sections of **Figure 3** are labelled **A**, **B**, **C**, **D**, and **E**.

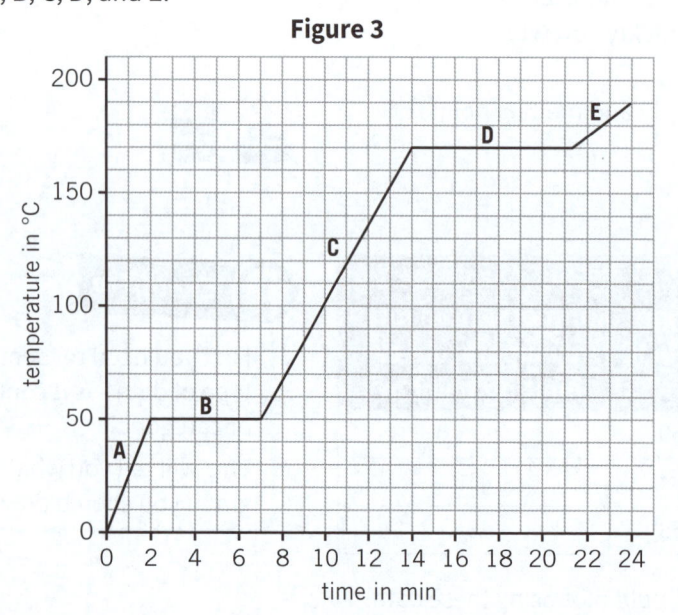

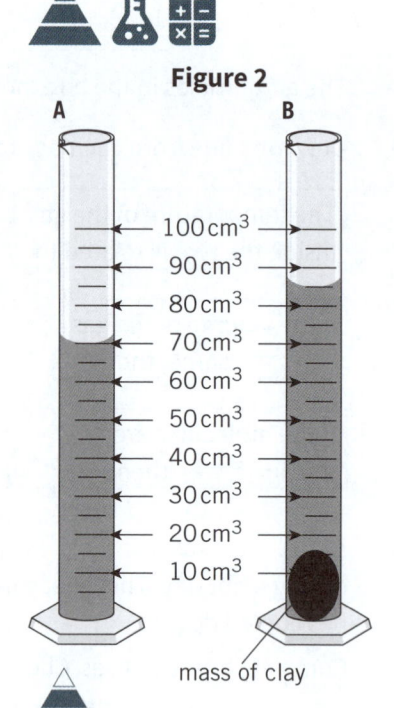

Figure 3

364   P5 Energy of matter

09.1 Identify two sections of **Figure 3** that show a change of state. Give a reason for your answer. **[3 marks]**

09.2 Did the substance start out as a solid or a liquid? Give a reason for your answer. **[2 marks]**

09.3 Write down **one** section of **Figure 3** where the vibration of the particles is increasing. **[1 mark]**

09.4 Write down **two** sections of **Figure 3** where the kinetic energy of the particles is increasing. **[2 marks]**

> **! Exam Tip**
> You might not know what the substance is, but you can still answer **09.2**. Looking at the y-axis will help you work it out.

10 A student is comparing dry ice and water ice. They heat water ice and observe two changes of state. They heat dry ice and observe one change of state. They then reverse the changes of state of the water ice.

10.1 Draw **one** line from each description to the correct change of state. **[3 marks]**

> **! Exam Tip**
> Dry ice is frozen carbon dioxide.

Description	Change of state
The dry ice changes from a solid to a gas.	condensation
Water changes from a liquid to a gas.	evaporation
The water ice changes from a solid to a liquid.	melting
Steam changes from a gas to a liquid.	sublimation

10.2 Why are the changes described in **10.1** physical changes and not chemical reactions? Choose **one** answer. **[1 mark]**

The changes are not reversible.

The matter recovers its original properties if the process is reversed.

The amount of matter decreases during the process.

10.3 The student considers the change of state of dry ice in terms of energy. Choose the **two** correct statements. **[2 marks]**

The energy transferred to the dry ice increases the internal energy of the dry ice.

The energy transferred to the dry ice increases the kinetic energy of the particles.

The energy transferred to the dry ice makes the particles move further apart.

The energy transferred to the dry ice decreases the potential energy of the particles.

Knowledge

P6 Atoms

Development of the model of an atom

The model of the atom we have today was developed over time with the help of evidence from experiments.

Future experiments may change our understanding and lead us to alter or replace this model of the atom.

Dalton's model

John Dalton thought of the atom as a solid sphere that could not be divided into smaller parts. His model did not include protons, neutrons, or electrons.

Plum pudding model

Scientists' experiments resulted in the discovery of charged sub-atomic particles. The first to be discovered were **electrons** – tiny, negatively charged particles.

The discovery of electrons led to the **plum pudding model** of the atom – a cloud of positive charge, with negative electrons embedded in it.

Protons and neutrons had not yet been discovered.

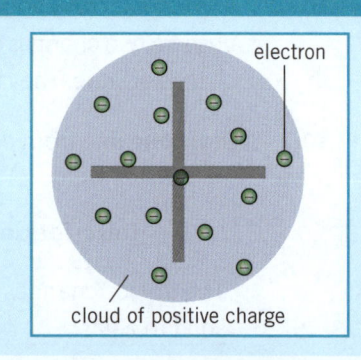

Alpha particle scattering experiment

1. Scientists fired small, positively charged particles (called **alpha particles**) at a piece of gold foil only a few atoms thick.
2. They expected the alpha particles to travel straight through the gold.
3. They were surprised that a small number of the alpha particles bounced back and some were deflected (alpha scattering).
4. To explain why the alpha particles were repelled, the scientists suggested that the positive charge and mass of an atom must be concentrated in a very small space at its centre. They called this space the nucleus.

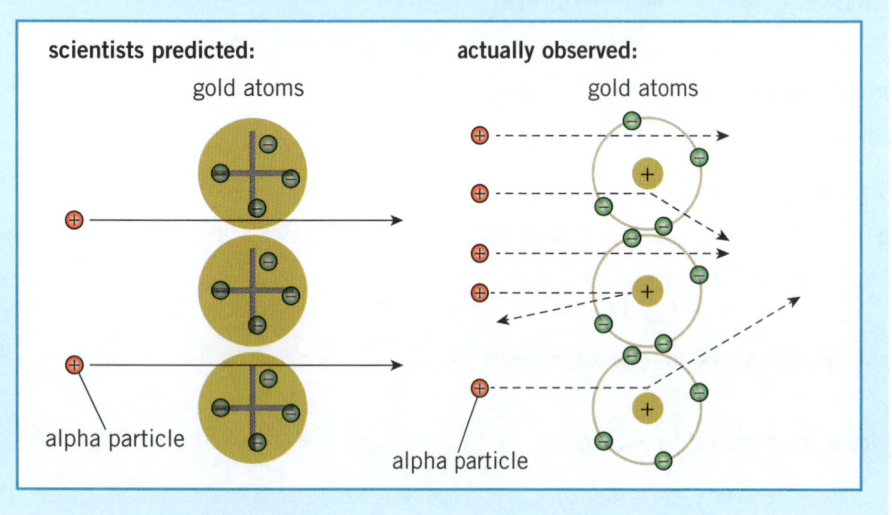

Nuclear model

Scientists replaced the plum pudding model with the **nuclear model**. They suggested that the electrons **orbit** (go around) the nucleus, but not at set distances, and the mass of the atom was concentrated in the charged nucleus.

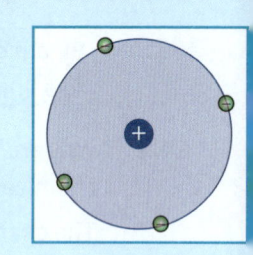

Bohr's model

Niels Bohr improved the nuclear model, and calculated that electrons must orbit the nucleus at fixed distances. These orbits are called shells or energy levels. These calculations agreed with experimental results.

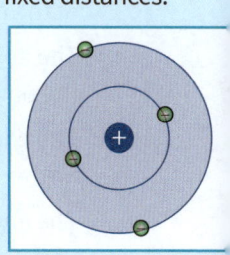

Key terms

Make sure you can write a definition for these key terms.

alpha particle   atom   atomic number   electron   energy level   ionisation

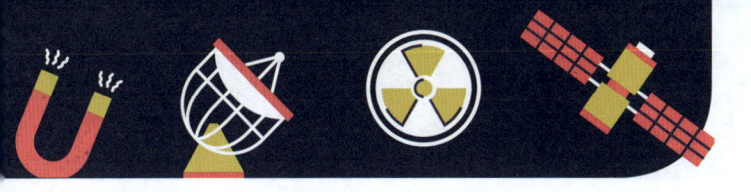

P6

Protons
Later experiments provided evidence that the positive charge of a nucleus could be split into smaller particles, each with an opposite charge to the electron. These positively charged particles were called **protons**.

Neutrons
James Chadwick carried out experiments that provided evidence for a particle with no charge. Scientists called this the **neutron**. They concluded that the protons and neutrons are in the nucleus, and the electrons orbit the nucleus in shells.

Basic structure of an atom
An **atom** has a radius of about 1×10^{-10} metres.

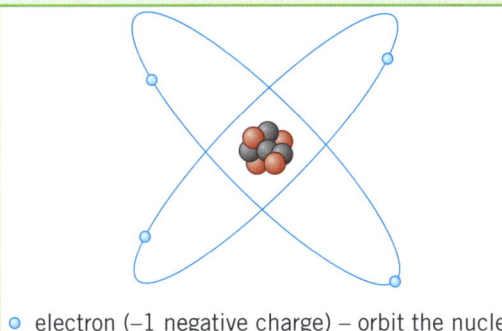

- electron (−1 negative charge) – orbit the nucleus
- proton (+1 positive charge) } in the nucleus
- neutron (no charge)

An atom is uncharged overall, and has equal numbers of protons and electrons.

The nucleus
- has a radius about 10 000 times smaller than the radius of an atom
- contains protons and **neutrons**
- is where most of the mass of an atom is concentrated

Electrons
- Orbit the nucleus at different fixed distances called **energy levels**.
- Can gain energy by absorbing electromagnetic radiation. This causes them to move to a higher energy level.
- Can lose energy by emitting electromagnetic radiation. This causes them to move to a lower energy level.

Element symbols

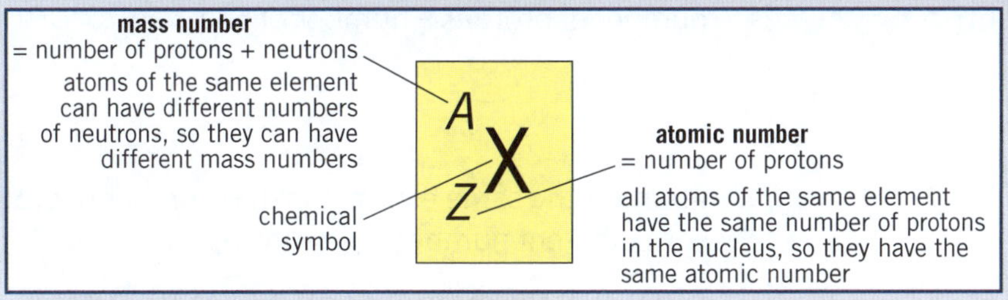

$^{A}_{Z}X$

- mass number = number of protons + neutrons
  - atoms of the same element can have different numbers of neutrons, so they can have different mass numbers
- chemical symbol
- atomic number = number of protons
  - all atoms of the same element have the same number of protons in the nucleus, so they have the same atomic number

Isotopes are atoms of the same element, with the same number of protons but a different number of neutrons.

Electrons
Atoms can become charged when they lose or gain electrons. This process is called **ionisation**.
- A positive ion is formed if an uncharged atom loses one or more electrons.
- A negative ion is formed if an uncharged atom gains one or more electrons.

> **Revision tip**
>
> Remember This content is also in chemistry. If you find some of this confusing when you're revising, you can use your chemistry notes to help you understand this topic.

isotope   mass number   neutron   orbit   plum pudding model   proton

P6 Knowledge 367

Retrieval

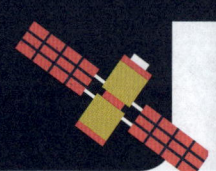

Learn the answers to the questions below, then cover the answers column with a piece of paper and write as many as you can. Check and repeat.

P6 questions | Answers

#	Question	Answer
1	Describe the basic structure of an atom.	nucleus containing protons and neutrons, around which electrons orbit in fixed energy levels/shells
2	Describe the plum pudding model of the atom.	sphere of positive charge with negative electrons embedded in it
3	What charges do protons, neutrons, and electrons carry?	protons = positive, neutrons = no charge, electrons = negative
4	Why do atoms have no overall charge?	equal numbers of positive protons and negative electrons
5	What is the radius of an atom?	around 1×10^{-10} m
6	How small is a nucleus compared to a whole atom?	around 10 000 times smaller
7	How can an electron move up an energy level?	absorb sufficient electromagnetic radiation
8	What is ionisation?	process which adds or removes electrons from an atom
9	What is formed if an atom loses an electron?	positive ion
10	How does an atom become a negative ion?	gains one or more electrons
11	What is the atomic number of an element?	number of protons in one atom of the element
12	What is the mass number of an element?	number of protons + number of neutrons
13	Which particle do atoms of the same element always have the same number of?	protons
14	What are isotopes?	atoms of the same element (same number of protons) with different numbers of neutrons
15	What were the two main conclusions from the alpha particle scattering experiment?	• most of the mass of an atom is concentrated in the nucleus • nucleus is positively charged

Put paper here

P6 Atoms

P6

Now go back and use the questions below to check your knowledge from previous chapters.

Previous questions / Answers

#	Previous question	Answer
1	What are the main advantages of using solar energy?	can be used in remote places, no polluting gases, no waste products, very low running cost
2	How does a material become charged?	becomes negatively charged by gaining electrons and becomes positively charged by losing electrons
3	When is there a current in the earth wire?	when there is a fault
4	What is the specific latent heat of a substance?	the energy required to change the state of one kilogram of that substance with no change in temperature
5	What is specific heat capacity?	amount of energy needed to raise the temperature of 1 kg of a material by 1 °C
6	Why is the live wire dangerous?	provides a large p.d. that would cause a large current to flow through a person if they touched it

Maths skills

Practise your maths skills using the worked examples and practice questions below.

Order of magnitude

Orders of magnitude are useful for comparing the size of numbers.

An order of magnitude is a factor of 10, so it is usually written as 10^n.

For example, if one number is roughly 10 times bigger than another number, it is one order of magnitude bigger.

If a number is 1000 times bigger than another number, it is three orders of magnitude bigger, because: $1000 = 10 \times 10 \times 10 = 10^3$.

Two numbers are of the same order of magnitude if dividing the bigger number by the smaller number gives an answer less than 10. For example, 12 and 45 are the same order of magnitude, but 13 and 670 are not.

If numbers are written in standard form, their orders of magnitude can be compared by dividing the larger power of ten by the smaller power of ten.

Worked example

1. A mouse has a mass of about 40 g, and an elephant has a mass of about 4×10^6 g. How many orders of magnitude heavier is an elephant compared to the mouse?

   Divide the larger power of ten by the smaller power of ten:

   $\frac{10^6}{10^1} = 10^5$, or five orders of magnitude.

2. The mass of the Sun is about 2.0×10^{30} kg. The mass of the Earth is 6.0×10^{24} kg. How many orders of magnitude bigger is the Sun's mass?

   Divide the larger power of ten by the smaller power of ten:

   $\frac{10^{30}}{10^{24}} = 10^6$, or six orders of magnitude.

Practice

1. How many orders of magnitude bigger is the mass of a lorry around 44 000 kg compared to a human body around 70 kg?

2. How many orders of magnitude smaller is the diameter of an atom around 0.1 nm compared to the diameter of a marble of 1 cm?

3. How many orders of magnitude smaller is 70 J compared to 450 MJ?

P6 Retrieval 369

Practice

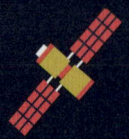

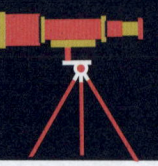

Exam-style questions

01 A student wants to make a model of a hydrogen atom.
They know that the atom is 10 000 times bigger than the nucleus.
The student uses a pea with a diameter of 4 mm to represent the nucleus.

01.1 Convert 4 mm to metres. Give your answer in standard form. **[2 marks]**

_____ metres

> **Exam Tip**
>
> When converting from mm to metres, the value will get *smaller*. As such, do you need to divide 4 mm by 1000 or multiply 4 mm by 1000?

01.2 Calculate the diameter of the student's model atom in metres. **[2 marks]**

Diameter = _____ m

01.3 Suggest where the student should place the electrons in the atom.
Circle **one** answer. **[1 mark]**

2 m from the pea   20 m from the pea   200 m from the pea

> **Exam Tip**
>
> The images you normally see showing an atom, or the diagrams you normally draw are not the correct scale. There is lots of space within an atom that we don't normally draw.

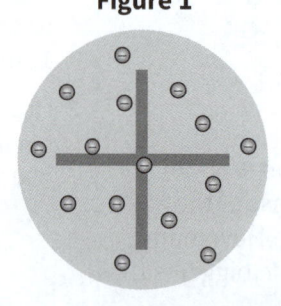

01.4 Write down the radius of an atom.
Choose **one** answer. **[1 mark]**

1×10^{-15} m 1×10^{-6} m 1×10^{-10} m

02 **Figure 1** shows the plum pudding model of an atom.

Figure 1

02.1 Use **Figure 1** to describe the plum pudding model. **[2 marks]**

_____
_____
_____
_____

> **Exam Tip**
>
> All the information you need to answer **02.1** is in **Figure 1**.

> **Exam Tip**
>
> Refer to both the positive and negative parts and their locations.

P6 Atoms

Paper 5 | **P6**

02.2 The plum pudding model replaced the Dalton model of the atom. What is the Dalton model of the atom? **[1 mark]**

Tick **one** box.

Atoms are empty spheres made up of positive and negative charges. ☐

Atoms are tiny spheres that cannot be divided. ☐

Electrons orbit a central nucleus. ☐

02.3 The plum pudding model was disproved by the alpha scattering experiment. In this experiment, a scientist fired alpha particles at a sheet of gold foil.

The scientist made three observations.

Draw **one** line from each observation to the correct conclusion drawn from the observation. **[2 marks]**

Observation

- Most alpha particles passed through the gold foil.
- Some alpha particles passed through the gold foil but changed direction.
- Some alpha particles did not pass through the gold foil.

Conclusion

- Most of the mass of an atom is in a central nucleus.
- The nucleus has a positive charge.
- The mass is spread out evenly across the atom.
- Most of an atom is empty space.
- The nucleus has a negative charge.

> **Exam Tip**
> This is what led to the development of the new model of the atom.

03 Lithium contains three protons and four neutrons.

03.1 Write down the atomic number of lithium. **[1 mark]**

03.2 What is the atomic mass of lithium? Choose **one** answer. **[1 mark]**

3   4   7   12

03.3 How many electrons are there in an atom of lithium? Choose **one** answer. **[1 mark]**

3   4   7   12

> **Exam Tip**
> Electrons have negative charges. If you remove a negative charge from a neutral atom, what charge will you get?

03.4 A lithium atom can become a charged ion.
Complete the sentences. [2 marks]

A lithium atom _____ 1 electron to form a lithium ion

with a _____ charge.

04 Atoms contain different types of particle.

04.1 Put the particles in order of mass, from least massive to most massive. [3 marks]

A	helium nucleus
B	electron
C	proton
D	helium atom

04.2 Complete the sentences. Choose answers from the box.
You can use the words once, more than once or not at all. [5 marks]

| gold | alpha | some | most | all | electron |

The nuclear model was developed after scientists fired

_____ particles at _____ foil.

_____ of the particles went through, but

_____ came back. This was evidence that

_____ of the mass of the atom is concentrated at
the centre.

04.3 Define an energy level. [1 mark]

04.4 **Figure 2** shows the energy levels in an atom. The movement of the electrons are shown by the arrows.

Figure 2

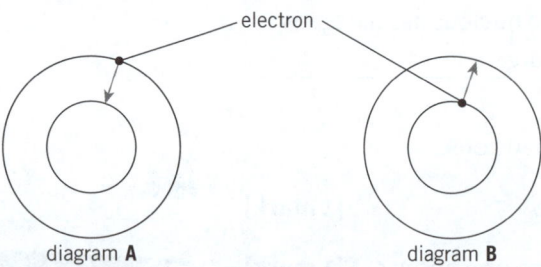

diagram **A**   diagram **B**

Complete the sentences. Choose the correct words in bold. [2 marks]

Electrons can absorb electromagnetic radiation and move from a **higher / lower** energy level to a **higher / lower** energy level. This is shown in diagram **A / B**.

04.5 Describe the model of the atom that scientists used before the discovery of the electron. [1 mark]

> **Exam Tip**
> Lower energy levels are closer to the middle of an atom.

> **Exam Tip**
> **04.5** is asking for the Dalton model of the atom.

05 A student is comparing two atoms. The particles in each atom are shown in **Table 1**.

Table 1

Atom	carbon-12	carbon-14
Number of protons	6	
Number of neutrons	6	
Number of electrons	6	6

05.1 Complete **Table 1** by writing in the number of protons and neutrons in carbon-14. **[2 marks]**

05.2 Complete the sentence. Choose **one** word from the box. **[1 mark]**

isobars   isotopes   isomers

Carbon-12 and carbon-14 are _____ of carbon.

05.3 Complete the sentences by choosing the correct phrases in bold.

An atom has **no charge** / **a positive charge**. This is because an atom has the same number of protons and **electrons** / **neutrons**. **[2 marks]**

05.4 An atom of carbon-12 is represented by the chemical symbol $^{12}_{6}C$. Write the chemical symbol of a carbon-14 atom. **[1 mark]**

> **Exam Tip**
> The mass number is at the top and the atomic number is at the bottom.

06 **Table 2** shows the number of protons and neutrons in the neutral atoms of three elements.

Table 2

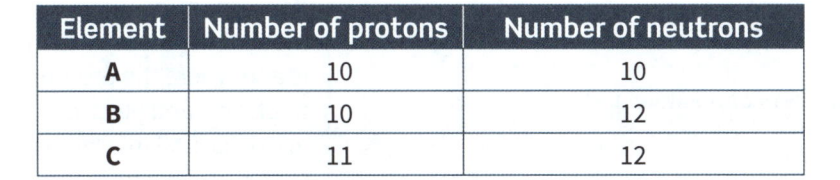

Element	Number of protons	Number of neutrons
A	10	10
B	10	12
C	11	12

06.1 Give the number of electrons in an atom of element **A**. **[1 mark]**

06.2 Give a reason for your answer to **06.1**. **[1 mark]**

06.3 Identify the two elements that are isotopes. **[1 mark]**

06.4 Give a reason for your answer to **06.3**. **[1 mark]**

06.5 Element C loses 1 electron in a chemical reason. The atom is now an ion. Identify the charge on the ion. **[1 mark]**

06.6 Name the part of the atom in which the protons and neutrons are found. **[1 mark]**

> **Exam Tip**
> Remember, the isotopes of an element have the same atomic number.

07 The model of the atom has Model developed over the last 130 years.

07.1 Draw **one** line from each model of the atom to the correct description. **[2 marks]**

Model | Description

plum pudding model

nuclear model

model with energy levels

- mass of an atom is concentrated in the central nucleus
- negative electrons embedded within a ball of positive charge
- electrons orbit nucleus at specific distances

07.2 Complete the sentences. Choose the correct words in bold. **[2 marks]**

The model had to be changed when there was new **experimental / theoretical** evidence or a new discovery. The discovery of the **electron / neutron** led to the development of the plum pudding model.

07.3 Which feature do all the models in **07.1** have in common? Choose one answer. **[1 mark]**

The models all have a nucleus.

The models all have neutrons.

The models have an equal number of positive and negative charges.

The models have different numbers of positive and negative charges.

07.4 Describe how the model of the atom developed from the plum pudding model to the modern model of the atom. **[6 marks]**

> **Exam Tip**
> This a six-mark question, so make sure you write enough to get all those marks.
> You need to describe how all of the different parts of the model of the atom were developed, including where most of the mass of an atom is and where the protons, neutrons, and electrons are. This is all information that is directly from the specification.

08 Mercury is the only metallic element that is liquid at room temperature. Gallium is a metallic element that melts in your hand because it has a very low melting point. The elements are represented in the Periodic Table as shown in **Figure 3**.

Figure 3

200	70
Hg	Ga
mercury	gallium
80	31

08.1 Give the atomic number of gallium. **[1 mark]**

08.2 Give the mass number of mercury. **[1 mark]**

08.3 The atomic radius of a mercury atom is 150 pm. Calculate the radius the nucleus of a mercury atom. **[2 marks]**

08.4 An isotope of gallium has two more neutrons than the atom of gallium shown above. Give the atomic mass and atomic number of the isotope. **[2 marks]**

> **Exam Tip**
> Don't let the unfamiliar unit in **08.3** put you off. This is a very simple calculation. Remember how big the nucleus is compared to an atom.

P6 Atoms

09 A student investigates some electrical appliances used each day in their home. **Table 3** shows their data.

Table 3

Appliance	Power in W	Time in s
shower	5000	900
microwave	1000	600

09.1 Identify the most powerful appliance in **Table 3**. [1 mark]

09.2 Calculate the energy transferred by the shower. Give the unit with your answer.
Use the equation: energy = power × time. [3 marks]

09.3 Complete the sentences. You do not need to do a calculation. Choose the correct words in bold. [3 marks]

The microwave transfers **less / more** energy than the shower. This is because the power is **less / more**, and the time of use is **less / more**.

09.4 Draw **one** line from each wire to the correct colour. [2 marks]

Wire: earth, live, neutral
Colour: blue, brown, green and yellow stripes

> **Exam Tip**
> Make sure you give the unit as a capital letter. A lower case letter is wrong and won't get you the marks.

10 **Table 4** and **Figure 4** show the increase in the use of solar cells to generate electricity for the National Grid since 2010.

Table 4

Year	Percentage of UK energy consumption produced by solar cells
2010	0.01
2011	0.07
2012	0.37
2013	0.64
2014	1.33
2015	2.49
2016	3.1
2017	3.4
2018	3.9

Figure 4 — bar chart: percentage of UK energy consumption vs year (2010–2018)

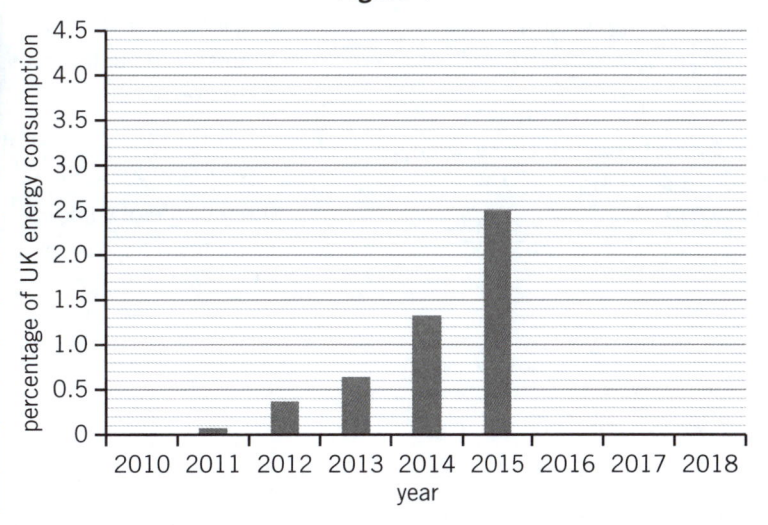

10.1 Plot the remaining three years on the bar chart in **Figure 4**. [3 marks]

10.2 Between which two years did the percentage of UK energy consumption provided by solar energy double? Choose **one** answer from the box. [1 mark]

2011–12   2013–14   2017–18

10.3 Suggest **one** reason why the use of solar cells has increased. [1 mark]

Knowledge

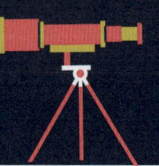

P7 Nuclear radiation

Radioactive decay

Radioactive decay is when nuclear radiation is emitted by unstable atomic nuclei so that they become more stable. It is a *random* process. This radiation can knock electrons out of atoms in a process called **ionisation**.

Type of radiation	Change in the nucleus	Ionising power	Range in air	Stopped by
α **alpha** particle (two protons and two neutrons)	nucleus loses two protons and two neutrons	highest ionising power	travels a few centimetres in air	stopped by a sheet of paper
β **beta** particle (fast-moving electron)	a neutron changes into a proton and an electron	high ionising power	travels ≈ 1 m in air	stopped by a few millimetres of aluminium
γ **gamma** radiation (short-wavelength, high-frequency EM radiation)	some energy is transferred away from the nucleus	low ionising power	virtually unlimited range in air	stopped by several centimetres of thick lead or metres of concrete

Activity and count rate

The **activity** of a radioactive source is the rate of decay of an unstable nucleus, measured in becquerel (Bq).

1 Bq = 1 decay per second

Detectors (e.g., **Geiger-Muller tubes**) record a **count rate** (number of decays detected per second).

$$\frac{\text{count rate after } n \text{ half-lives}}{1} = \frac{\text{initial count rate}}{2^n}$$

Half-life

The **half-life** of a radioactive source is the time
- for half the number of unstable nuclei in a sample to decay
- for the count rate or activity of a source to halve.

The half-life of a source can be found from a graph of its count rate or activity against time.

To find the reduction in activity after a given number of half-lives:
1. calculate the activity after each half-life
2. subtract the final activity from the original activity.

Revision tip

Practice Always work out more than one half life from a graph. The answers should come out the same.

Always draw your construction lines on half-life graphs, it makes it much easier to work out the answers!

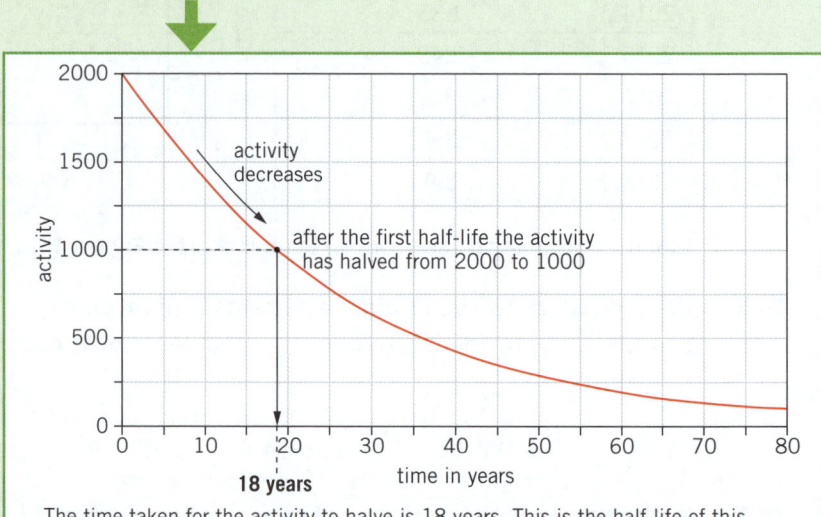

Graph: activity vs time in years, showing activity decreasing from 2000, halving to 1000 at 18 years. After the first half-life the activity has halved from 2000 to 1000. The time taken for the activity to halve is 18 years. This is the half-life of this substance.

Nuclear equations

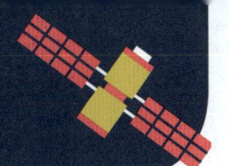

Nuclear equations are used to represent radioactive decay.

Alpha particles

Alpha particles can be represented as $_{2}^{4}\alpha$ or $_{2}^{4}\text{He}$.

Equations are written in the form: $_{Z}^{A}\text{X} \rightarrow \,_{(Z-2)}^{(A-4)}\text{Y} + \,_{2}^{4}\alpha$

This shows us that alpha decay causes both the mass and the charge of the nucleus to change.

Beta particles

Beta particles can be represented as $_{-1}^{0}\beta$ or $_{-1}^{0}\text{e}$.

Equations are written in the form: $_{Z}^{A}\text{X} \rightarrow \,_{(Z+1)}^{A}\text{Y} + \,_{-1}^{0}\beta$

This shows us that beta decay only causes the charge of the nucleus to change.

Ionising radiation

Living cells can be damaged or killed by ionising radiation.

The risk depends on the half-life of the source and the type of radiation.

Alpha radiation is very dangerous inside the body because it affects all the surrounding tissue. Outside the body it only affects the skin and eyes because it cannot penetrate further.

Beta and gamma radiation are dangerous outside and inside the body because they can penetrate into tissues.

> **Revision tip**
>
> **Remember** The maths for nuclear equations can look scary, but just take the sums one line at a time: top row, then bottom row. That way it is much more manageable.

Irradiation versus contamination

irradiation	when an object is exposed to nuclear radiation	cause harm through ionisation	prevented by shielding, removing, or moving away from the source of radiation
contamination	when atoms of a radioactive material are on or in an object		object remains exposed to radiation as long as it is contaminated contamination can be very difficult to remove

Protection against irradiation and contamination

You can protect against irradiation and contamination by:
- maintaining a distance from the radiation source
- limiting time near the source
- shielding from the radiation.

Studies on the effects of radiation should be published, shared with other scientists, and checked by **peer review** as they are important for human health.

Key terms

Make sure you can write a definition for these key terms.

alpha   activity   beta   contamination   count rate   gamma   Geiger-Muller tube
half-life   ionisation   irradiation   peer review   radioactive decay

P7 Knowledge   377

Retrieval

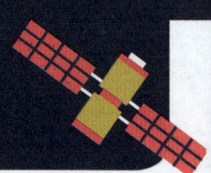

Learn the answers to the questions below, then cover the answers column with a piece of paper and write as many as you can. Check and repeat.

P7 questions / Answers

#	Question	Answer
1	What are the three types of nuclear radiation?	alpha, beta, and gamma
2	What is gamma γ radiation?	electromagnetic radiation from the nucleus
3	Which type of nuclear radiation is the most ionising?	alpha
4	What is the range in air of alpha, beta, and gamma radiation?	a few cm, 1 m, and unlimited, respectively
5	Which materials can stop alpha, beta, and gamma radiation?	sheet of paper, thin aluminium sheet, and thick lead/concrete, respectively
6	Which type of nuclear radiation does not cause a change in the structure of the nucleus when it is emitted?	gamma
7	What are the equation symbols for alpha and beta particles?	$^{4}_{2}\alpha$ and $^{0}_{-1}\beta$
8	What is radioactive activity?	the rate at which a source of unstable nuclei decays
9	What unit is used to measure the activity of a radioactive source?	becquerel (Bq)
10	What is meant by count rate?	number of decays recorded each second (by a detector, e.g., Geiger-Muller tube)
11	What is meant by the half-life of a radioactive source?	time taken for half the unstable nuclei to decay or the time taken for the count rate to halve
12	What is irradiation?	exposing an object to nuclear radiation
13	What is radioactive contamination?	unwanted presence of substances containing radioactive atoms on or in other materials

P7

Now go back and use the questions below to check your knowledge from previous chapters.

Previous questions / Answers

Previous questions	Answers
Describe the plum pudding model of the atom.	sphere of positive charge with negative electrons embedded in it
Give two reasons why the temperature of a gas increases if it is compressed quickly.	the force applied to compress the gas results in work being done to the gas, and the energy gained by the gas is not transferred quickly enough to the surroundings
What is the radius of an atom?	around 1×10^{-10} m
On a graph of temperature against time for a substance being heated up or cooled down, what do the flat (horizontal) sections show?	the time when the substance is changing state and the temperature is not changing
Why is the mass of a substance conserved when it changes state?	the number of particles does not change
What are step-up transformers used for in the National Grid?	increase the p.d. from the power station to the transmission cables
What are the main advantages of using solar energy?	can be used in remote places, no polluting gases, no waste products, very low running cost

Maths skills

Practise your maths skills using the worked example and practice questions below.

Ratios, fractions, percentages

A **ratio** is a way of comparing the size of two quantities.

For example, a ratio of 2:4 of radioactive atoms to non radioactive atoms in a sample means for every 2 radioactive atoms, there are 4 non radioactive atoms.

A ratio can be simplified by dividing both numbers by their highest common factor.

A **fraction** can be a way of expressing part of a whole number, or a way of writing one number divided by another in an equation.

To find fractions from a ratio, each number in the ratio can be a numerator, and the denominator is the sum of both numbers. For example, if the ratio of apples to oranges is 2:3, the fraction of apples is $= \frac{2}{2+3} = \frac{2}{5}$

A **percentage** is a number expressed as a fraction of 100. For example, $45\% = \frac{45}{100}$

To find one number as a percentage of another divide the first number by the second and multiply by 100.

Worked example

1. A sample has a ratio of 8:20 radioactive atoms to non radioactive atoms. Simplify this ratio, and find the fraction that are radioactive atoms.

   Find the greatest common factor for 8 and 12 = 4.

   Divide both sides of the ratio by 4 = 2:5.

   Fraction of radioactive atoms:
   $= \frac{2}{2+5} = \frac{2}{7}$

2. The resistance of a thermistor changes from 250 Ω to 175 ohms when it is heated. Calculate the percentage change in its resistance.

   Calculate the change in resistance: 250 − 175 = 75

   Divide the change by the original value of the resistance:
   $\frac{75}{250} = 0.3 \times 100 = 30\%$

Practice

1. A sample has 40 radioactive atoms for every 120 non radioactive atoms. Write this as a ratio in its simplest form.

2. In the above example, what fraction of atoms are not radioactive?

3. In the above example, what percentage of atoms are radioactive?

P7 Retrieval

Radiation

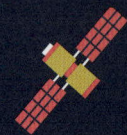

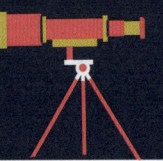

Exam-style questions

01 A student investigates the radioactive decay of iodine-131.

Iodine-131 decays by beta emission.

Figure 1 shows the student's graph of mass of iodine-131 against time.

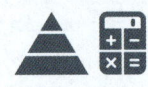

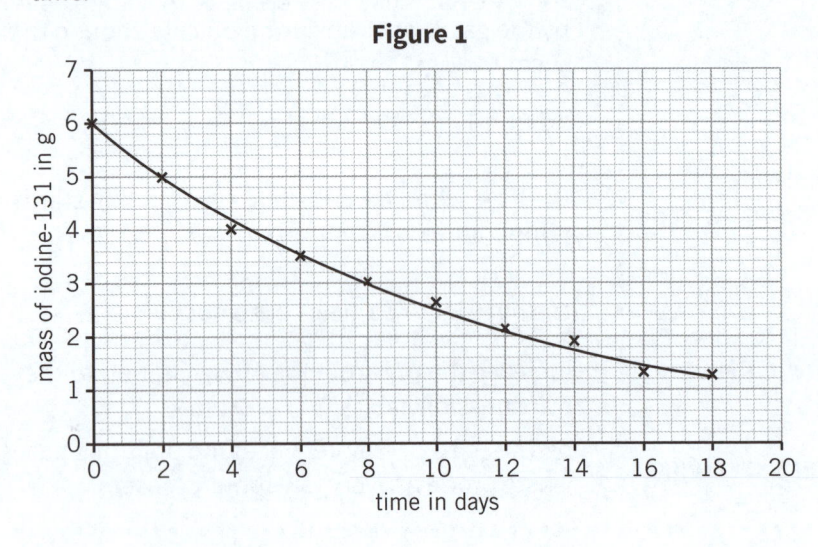

Figure 1

[Graph: mass of iodine-131 in g (y-axis, 0-7) against time in days (x-axis, 0-20), showing exponential decay from about 6 g at day 0 to about 1.3 g at day 18]

> **! Exam Tip**
> When you are given a graph you should immediately look at the quantities on the axes, and pay attention to the units.

01.1 Suggest why the mass of iodine-131 has decreased. **[1 mark]**

_____

_____

01.2 All the points do not lie exactly on the line.

Suggest what this tells you about the nature of radioactive decay. **[1 mark]**

_____

_____

> **! Exam Tip**
> **Figure 1** only records mass of the iodine-131. Think about what is happening to the atoms of iodine-131 during beta decay.

01.3 Use **Figure 1** to work out the half-life of iodine-131. **[2 marks]**

Half-life = _____ days

> **! Exam Tip**
> You must write down how you used the graph in your explanation.

01.4 Calcium-47 has a shorter half-life than iodine-131.

The student plots a graph of the decay of calcium-47 on the same axes.

The initial mass of both substances was the same.

Complete the sentence. Choose the correct word in bold. **[1 mark]**

The line of best fit will be **above / below** the line for iodine.

380 P7 Nuclear radiation

Paper 5 **P7**

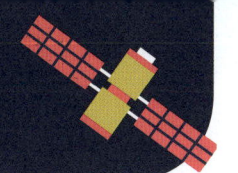

02 A student is investigating radiation.
They write down three descriptions.

A	high-speed electron
B	helium nucleus
C	electromagnetic radiation

02.1 Which describes a beta particle? Choose the correct letter. **[1 mark]**

_____

02.2 Which describes a gamma ray? Choose the correct letter. **[1 mark]**

_____

02.3 What is the symbol for an alpha particle? **[1 mark]**
Circle **one** answer.

α β γ

> **Exam Tip**
> The Greek letters used as symbols for radiation look very similar to the letters we use in our alphabet.

02.4 What is the unit of activity of a radioactive sample? **[1 mark]**
Circle **one** answer.

becquerel days sieverts

02.5 Define the term count-rate. **[1 mark]**

_____

> **Exam Tip**
> Units and definitions are things you can just remember. Use frequent testing to get them in your long term memory.

03 A hospital needs to use a gamma emitter for a medical procedure. The technician is checking the half-life of the material that the doctor is going to use. **Table 1** shows the data they collect.

Table 1

Time in hrs	Activity in Bq
0	1000
3	707
6	500

03.1 Calculate the half-life of the radioactive substance. **[1 mark]**

Half-life = _____ hours

> **Exam Tip**
> How long does it take for the sample to have half of the activity it has at the start?

03.2 Suggest the value of the activity of the substance after 12 hours.
Give a reason for your answer. **[2 marks]**

_____
_____
_____

03.3 The technician measures the activity after 12 hours. The value does not exactly match the expected value. Suggest why. **[1 mark]**

03.4 The substance emits gamma radiation. The doctor injects a patient with the substance. They use the gamma radiation detected outside the body to diagnose a medical problem.
Give **one** reason why a substance that emits alpha radiation would not be suitable for this. **[1 mark]**

> **Exam Tip**
>
> Think about how far each type of radiation can travel, and what it can be stopped by.

04 Different types of radiation can travel different distances through the air.

04.1 Complete **Table 2** with the words alpha, beta, and gamma. **[2 marks]**

Table 2

Type	Range in air
	>3 m
	1 m
	<10 cm

04.2 A student says:

'There is a link between the ionising power of radiation and how far they go in air. If they do not go as far, that means that they are not as ionising.'

Do you agree with the student? Explain your answer. **[3 marks]**

> **Exam Tip**
>
> Notice that there are three marks, so your explanation should include two points.

04.3 A teacher has a source that emits all three types of radiation. The activity of the source is 35 Bq. The teacher puts a sheet of aluminium between the source and the detector. The activity recorded is lower.

Explain why the activity is lower, but radiation can still be detected. **[2 marks]**

> **Exam Tip**
>
> 04.3 tells you that all types of radiation are emitted from this source, so think about each type of radiation individually.

382 P7 Nuclear radiation

04.4 Draw **one** line from each equation to the type of radiation represented. **[2 marks]**

Equation	Type of radiation
$^{12}_{7}$nitrogen → $^{12}_{6}$carbon + $^{0}_{-1}$e	alpha
$^{219}_{86}$radon → $^{215}_{84}$polonium + $^{4}_{2}$He	beta
$^{137}_{56}$barium → $^{137}_{56}$barium + $^{0}_{0}$γ	gamma

Exam Tip

One of the equations in **04.4** you have not met before and you do not need to learn about. However, you should be able to apply what you do know to work out the answer.

05 A student writes an equation for the decay of sodium-24.

$$^{24}_{11}Na \rightarrow\ ^{24}_{12}Mg + \boxed{}X$$

05.1 Determine the missing values for radiation **X**. Choose **one** answer from the box. **[1 mark]**

$$^{4}_{2}X \qquad ^{0}_{-1}X \qquad ^{0}_{0}X$$

Exam Tip

Take the sums one line at a time:
24 = 24 + ?
11 = 12 + ?

05.2 By which type of radiation has sodium-2 decayed? Choose **one** answer. **[1 mark]**

alpha   beta   gamma

05.3 The half-life of sodium-24 is 15 hours. Define the term half-life. **[1 mark]**

05.4 The student measures the count rate from a sample of sodium-24 to be 80 counts per minute. Predict the count rate after 15 hours. **[1 mark]**

Exam Tip

This will be after 1 half life.

05.5 Sodium-24 decays into magnesium-24, which decays very slowly. Suggest how the half-life of sodium-24 compares with the half-life of magnesium-24. **[1 mark]**

06 A student learns about the hazards to the human body associated with radioactive materials.

One of the hazards is due to contamination. Another is irradiation.

06.1 Draw **one** line from each box to match each word to its definition. **[2 marks]**

Key word	Definition
	A material that has atoms that have decayed and become radioactive.
contamination	Making a material radioactive.
irradiation	Process of exposing an object to nuclear radiation.
	The unwanted presence of radioactive atoms on other materials.

06.2 Some people think that being exposed to any type of radiation is dangerous. Choose the correct statement in response to this concern. Choose **one** answer. **[1 mark]**

An irradiated object does not become radioactive.

You cannot place any materials between the source of radiation and the human body to absorb radiation.

All radioactive materials become less radioactive very quickly.

Radioactive material cannot be detected.

06.3 A teacher shows the class some strawberries that have been irradiated. Are the strawberries safe to eat? Explain your answer in terms of radiation. **[2 marks]**

07 Some types of nuclear decay involve a change in the mass of the nucleus.

07.1 Name the type of radiation that involves a change in the mass of the nucleus when it is emitted. **[1 mark]**

07.2 The equation shows the decay of bismouth-214:

$$^{214}_{83}\text{Bi} \rightarrow {}^{214}_{84}\text{Po} + X$$

What is particle **X**? Choose **one** answer.

$^{4}_{2}\text{He}$ $^{0}_{-1}\text{e}$ γ **[1 mark]**

07.3 Explain why the mass of the nucleus does not change, but the identity of the element has changed. **[3 marks]**

07.4 Carbon-14 decays and emits radiation.

$$^{14}_{6}\text{C} \rightarrow \boxed{}\text{N} + {}^{0}_{-1}\text{e}$$

Complete the radiation equation for carbon-14. **[2 marks]**

07.5 Uranium-238 decays by alpha radiation to thorium-234. Write the equation for the decay of uranium-238. The atomic number of uranium is 92. **[2 marks]**

$$\boxed{}\text{U} \rightarrow \boxed{}\text{Th} + \boxed{}$$

08 A nucleus can emit four types of ionising radiation. These are alpha particles, beta particles, gamma rays, and neutrons.

08.1 Put alpha, beta, and gamma radiation in order of increasing ionising power. **[1 mark]**

weakest   strongest

_____   _____   _____

08.2 Complete the sentence. **[1 mark]**

Human body cells can be _____ when exposed to ionising radiation.

> **Exam Tip**
> Read over all of the possible responses and put a cross on the left hand side of any you think are wrong. This should narrow down the ones you can select as the correct answer.

> **Exam Tip**
> Fruit and vegetables are regularly irradiated to kill bacteria on their surfaces.

> **Exam Tip**
> The mass of these atoms is the same so the particle that has been lost has no mass.

> **Exam Tip**
> Ensure you follow the instructions and start with the least ionising.

P7 Nuclear radiation

P7

08.3 A scientist exposes some cells to radiation in a laboratory. They write up the experiment and publish the results. Name the process by which other scientists check the experiment before it is published. **[1 mark]**

08.4 The scientist finds a radioactive source that has not been labelled. Describe how they can use samples of paper, aluminium, and lead to work out which type of radiation is being emitted from the source. **[6 marks]**

> **Exam Tip**
> This is a six-mark question so make sure you write enough to get all those marks.
> How are you going to measure the radiation? What are your predicted results? How will you use the equipment provided?

09 A student is investigating different types of insulation.
Figure 2 shows the equipment they are using. The student boils the water then pours into the can. They then measure how long it takes for the temperature of the water to drop to room temperature.

Figure 2

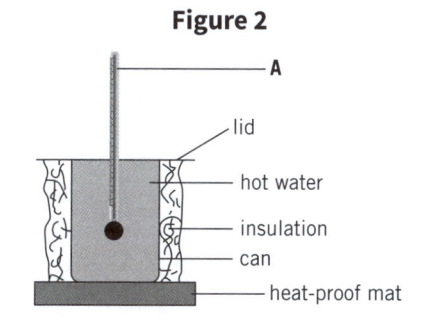

(Diagram showing: A, lid, hot water, insulation, can, heat-proof mat)

09.1 Name the piece of equipment labelled **A**. **[1 mark]**

09.2 Suggest why the student has carried the experiment out on a heatproof mat. **[1 mark]**

09.3 Identify the dependent variable in the investigation. **[1 mark]**

> **Exam Tip**
> Remember, the dependent variable is what you measure.

09.4 The student plots the data from their experiment as a bar chart in **Figure 3**.

Figure 3

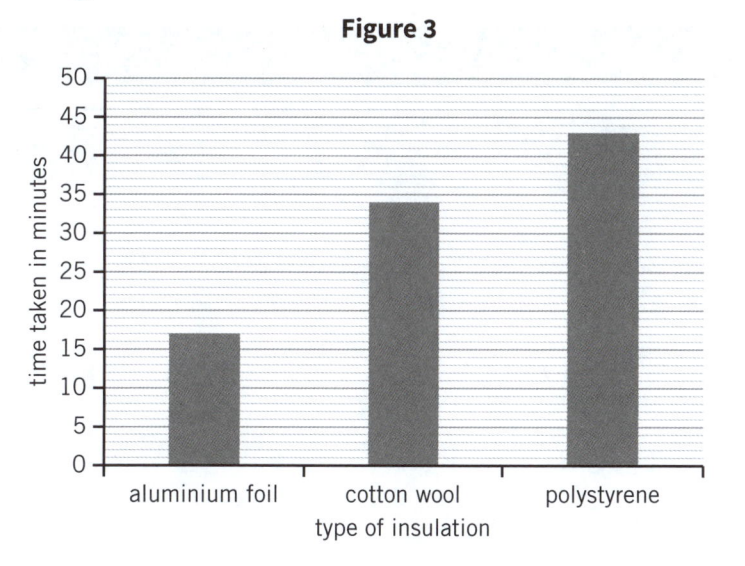

(Bar chart showing time taken in minutes for different types of insulation: aluminium foil ≈ 17, cotton wool ≈ 34, polystyrene ≈ 43)

> **Exam Tip**
> As the water cools, energy is transferred from the thermal energy store of the water to the thermal energy store of the surroundings. An insulator reduces the transfer of energy.

Suggest why the student chose to draw a bar chart. **[1 mark]**

09.5 Use **Figure 3** to identify which material is the best insulator. **[1 mark]**

09.6 Suggest one improvement to the student's method. **[1 mark]**

Knowledge

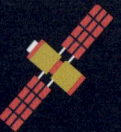

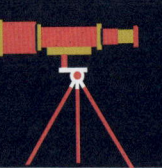

P8 Forces

Scalars and vectors

Scalar quantities only have a magnitude (e.g., distance and speed).

Vector quantities have a magnitude *and* a direction (e.g., velocity and force).

Forces

A **force** can be a push or pull on an object caused by an interaction with another object. Forces are vector quantities.

Contact forces	Non-contact forces
occur when two objects are touching each other	act at a distance (without the two objects touching)
examples: friction, air resistance, tension, normal contact force	examples: gravitational force, electrostatic force, magnetic force

When an object exerts a force on another object, it will experience an *equal and opposite* force.

Gravity

The force of **gravity** close to the Earth is due to the planet's **gravitational field strength**.

Weight is the force acting on an object due to gravity.

The weight of an object
- can be considered to act at the object's **centre of mass**
- can be measured using a calibrated spring-balance (newtonmeter).

(L) weight (N) = mass (kg) × gravitational field strength (N/kg)

$$W = m\,g$$

Weight and mass are directly proportional to each other, which can be written as $W \propto m$, so as the mass of an object doubles, its weight doubles.

Revision tip

Practice To help you work out resultant forces it can help to draw boxes with arrows on. Make sure you add the force on to the arrow and the direction its pointing in. This can help you work out the overall resultant force.

Resultant forces

If two or more forces act on an object along the same line, their effect is the same as if they were replaced with a single **resultant force**. The resultant force is
- the sum of the magnitudes of the forces if they act in the same direction
- the difference between the magnitudes of the forces if they act in opposite directions.

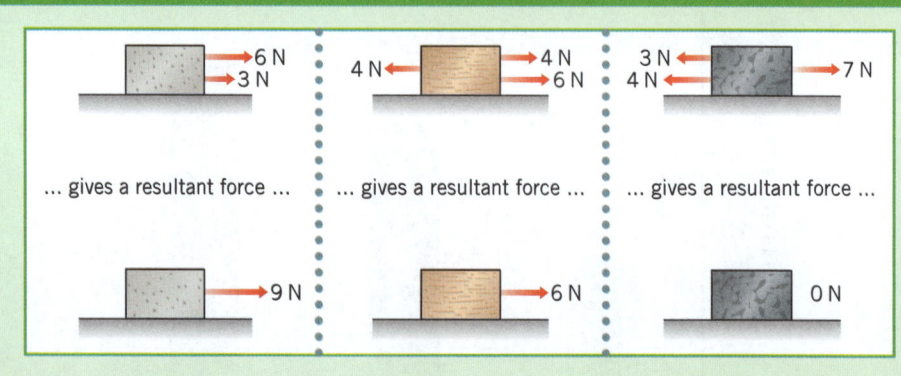

If the resultant force on an object is zero, the forces are said to be balanced.

… gives a resultant force … 9 N

… gives a resultant force … 6 N

… gives a resultant force … 0 N

Key terms

Make sure you can write a definition for these key terms.

| centre of mass | contact force | deformation | elastic | free body diagram |
| limit of proportionality | non-contact force | resultant | | |

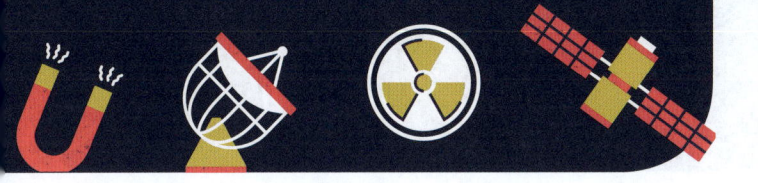

P8

Deformation

Deformation is a change in the shape of an object caused by stretching, squashing (compressing), bending, or twisting.

More than one force has to act on a stationary object to deform it, otherwise the force would make it move.

Elastic deformation – the object can go back to its original shape and size when the forces are removed.

Inelastic deformation – the object does not go back to its original shape or size when the forces are removed.

Graphs of force against extension for elastic objects

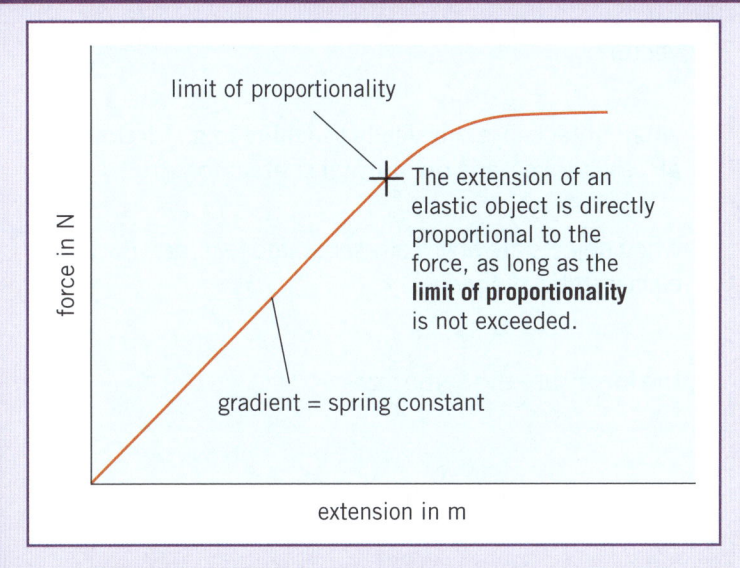

[Graph: force in N vs extension in m, showing a straight line becoming curved. Marked: "limit of proportionality" at the point where the line starts to curve, and "gradient = spring constant" along the straight portion.]

The extension of an elastic object is directly proportional to the force, as long as the **limit of proportionality** is not exceeded.

The spring constant can be calculated using the equation:

(L) force applied (N) = spring constant (N/m) × extension (m)

$$F = k\,e$$

This relationship also applies to compressing an object, where e would be compression instead of extension.

Elastic potential energy

A force that stretches or compresses an object does work on it, causing energy to be transferred to the object's elastic potential store.

The elastic potential energy stored in an elastically stretched or compressed spring can be calculated using:

elastic potential energy (J) = $\frac{1}{2}$ × spring constant (N/m) × (extension)² (m²)

$$E_e = \frac{1}{2} k e^2$$

Revision tip

Remember Your maths skills are important here. It is only the value for extension (e) that is squared in the equation above, not the whole answer.

BIDMAS is a good acronym to help you remember the order you should complete operations in mathematical equations.

Brackets

Indices

Division

Multiplication

Addition

Subtraction

---

force　　gravitational field strength　　gravity　　inelastic

　　scalar　　vector　　weight

P8 Knowledge

Retrieval

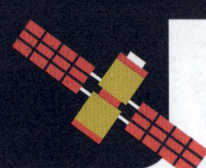

Learn the answers to the questions below, then cover the answers column with a piece of paper and write as many as you can. Check and repeat.

P8 questions / Answers

#	P8 questions	Answers
1	What is a scalar quantity?	only has a size (magnitude)
2	What is a vector quantity?	has both a size and direction
3	What is a force?	a push or pull that acts on an object due to the interaction with another object
4	Is force a vector or scalar quantity?	vector
5	What is a contact force?	when objects are physically touching (e.g., friction, air resistance, tension, normal contact force)
6	What is a non-contact force?	when objects are physically separated (e.g., gravitational, electrostatic, magnetic)
7	What is the same about the interaction pair of forces when two objects interact with each other?	the forces are the same size
8	What is different about the interaction pair of forces when two objects interact with each other?	the forces are in opposite directions
9	What is the size of the resultant force on an object if the forces on it are balanced?	zero
10	What is the name for the force acting on an object due to gravity?	weight
11	What instrument can be used to measure the weight of an object?	calibrated spring-balance (newtonmeter)
12	What is the centre of mass?	the point through which the weight of an object can be considered to act
13	What is elastic deformation?	an object can go back to its original shape and size when deforming forces are removed
14	What is inelastic deformation?	an object does not go back to its original shape and size when deforming forces are removed
15	How do you find the spring constant from a force–extension graph of a spring?	find the gradient of the straight line section

388 P8 Forces

P8

Now go back and use the questions below to check your knowledge from previous chapters.

Previous questions | Answers

1. Describe the basic structure of an atom. | nucleus containing protons and neutrons, around which electrons orbit in fixed energy levels/shells
2. What is the National Grid? | nationwide network of cables and transformers that link power stations to customers
3. What are the equation symbols for alpha and beta particles? | $^{4}_{2}\alpha$ and $^{0}_{-1}\beta$

Put paper here

🧪 Required practical skills

Practise answering questions on the required practicals using the example below. You need to be able to apply your skills and knowledge to other practicals too.

Extension of a spring

In this practical you measure the extension of a spring as different forces are applied to it.

To be accurate and precise you need to:

- measure extension using a pointer directed at the same position on the spring each time
- ensure that the ruler is positioned so that it is parallel to the spring
- make measurements by looking in a direction perpendicular to the ruler
- convert mass to weight (force) if necessary.
- use a measurement of zero force = zero extension
- use the gradient = 1/spring constant for a graph of x against F.

Worked example

A student records the following measurements for a spring.

Force in N						
Mass in kg	0	0.1	0.2	0.3	0.4	0.5
Length in cm	5.0	9.2	13.1	17.4	21	25
Extension in cm						

1 Calculate the spring extensions and forces.

weight (= force) = mass × gravitational field strength (10 N/kg)

extension = length − 5 (original length of spring)

Force in N	0	1	2	3	4	5
Extension in cm	0	4.2	8.1	12.4	16	20

2 Plot a graph of the results. Calculate the spring constant from your graph and give the unit.

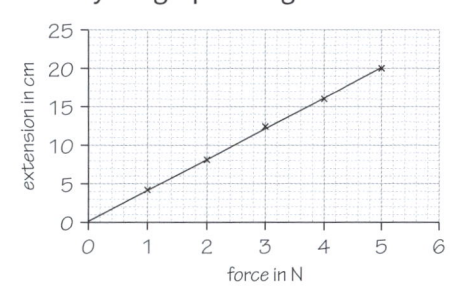

$$\text{gradient} = \frac{20\,\text{cm}}{5\,\text{N}} = 4$$

$$\text{gradient} = \frac{1}{\text{spring constant}}$$

$$\text{spring constant} = \frac{1}{\text{gradient}} = \frac{1}{4} = 0.25\,\text{N/cm or } 25\,\text{N/m}$$

Practice

1. A student measures an extension of 24 mm when they hang a 40 g mass on a spring. Calculate the spring constant in N/m. Show your working.

2. Compare the meaning of the gradient of a graph of force against extension with the meaning of the gradient of a graph of extension against force.

P8 Retrieval

Forces

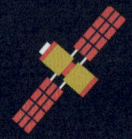

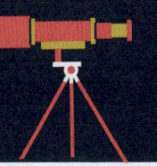

Exam-style questions

01 A student finds a box of springs.
They want to work out the spring constant of one of the springs.

01.1 Write down the equation that links extension, force, and spring constant. **[1 mark]**

_____

_____

> **Exam Tip**
>
> In **01.2** you need to use the equation you wrote in **01.1**. You have probably written the equation in **01.1** as you have learnt it, which means that force will be the subject. As such, you will need to rearrange it to make spring constant the subject. This is an important skill you will need time and time again.

01.2 The student pulls the spring with a force of 2 N. The spring extends by a distance of 0.01 m.
Calculate the spring constant. **[3 marks]**

spring constant = _____ N/m

01.3 Calculate the work done in stretching the spring.
Use the *Physics Equations Sheet*. **[2 marks]**

> **Exam Tip**
>
> Always write down the equation you plan on using first.

work done = _____ J

01.4 Describe a method for finding out whether the relationship between the force and extension is linear for this spring. **[4 marks]**

_____

_____

_____

_____

> **Exam Tip**
>
> In a question like **01.4**, make a clear link between the measurements you make and how you can draw a conclusion, usually with a graph.

02 Force is a vector.

02.1 What is the definition of a vector?
Tick **one** box. **[1 mark]**

A vector has magnitude only. ☐

A vector has direction only. ☐

A vector has magnitude and direction. ☐

> **Exam Tip**
>
> You need to be clear on the difference between vector and scalar.

Paper 6 **P8**

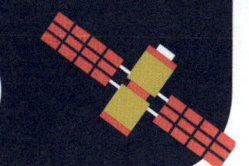

02.2 Some forces are contact forces and some are non-contact forces. Which of these are non-contact forces?

Circle **two** answers. **[2 marks]**

| air resistance | friction | magnetism | weight |

> **! Exam Tip**
> Non-contact forces work without touching the object they are acting on.

02.3 Name a contact force that is not listed in the box in **02.2**. **[1 mark]**

_____

03 A teacher uses a foam sponge to demonstrate the effect of forces.

03.1 **Figure 1** shows how the teacher stretches the sponge.

Figure 1

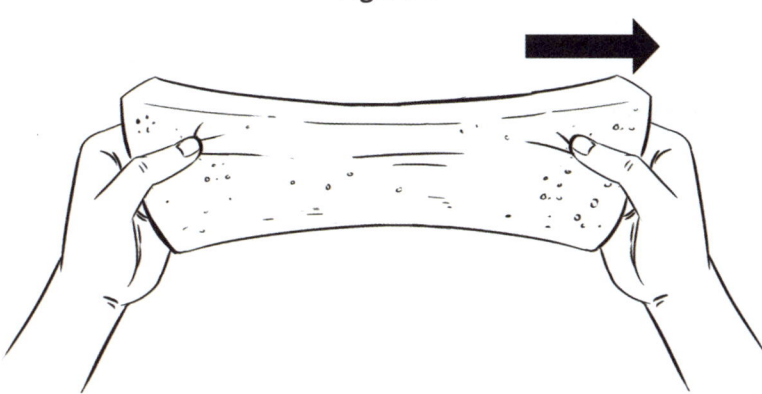

Draw **one** arrow onto **Figure 1** to show the second force involved in stretching the sponge. **[2 marks]**

03.2 The teacher puts the sponge on the table and pushes down. The sponge changes shape. A student says:

'Only one force is acting on the sponge.'

Are they correct? Circle **one** answer.

        yes   no

Give a reason for your answer. **[2 marks]**

_____

_____

03.3 The teacher pushes the side of the sponge. The sponge moves across the bench.

Identify how many forces are acting on the sponge. **[1 mark]**

_____

03.4 The teacher lets go of the sponge and it returns to it's original shape.

Which type of deformation has the sponge undergone? **[1 mark]**

Tick **one** answer.

☐ elastic deformation ☐ inelastic deformation

04 A student measures the mass and weight of a range of objects. The data are shown in **Table 1**.

Table 1

Mass in g	Weight	Weight	Weight	Mean weight
0.3	2.8	3.0	3.3	3.0
1.2	11	12	13	12
1.5	14	15	17	15
2.1	20	21	15	

04.1 Give the unit of weight. **[1 mark]**

_____

04.2 Calculate the missing mean weight. Give your answer to **two** significant figures. **[2 marks]**

_____

04.3 The student plots a graph of mean weight against mass, as shown in **Figure 2**.

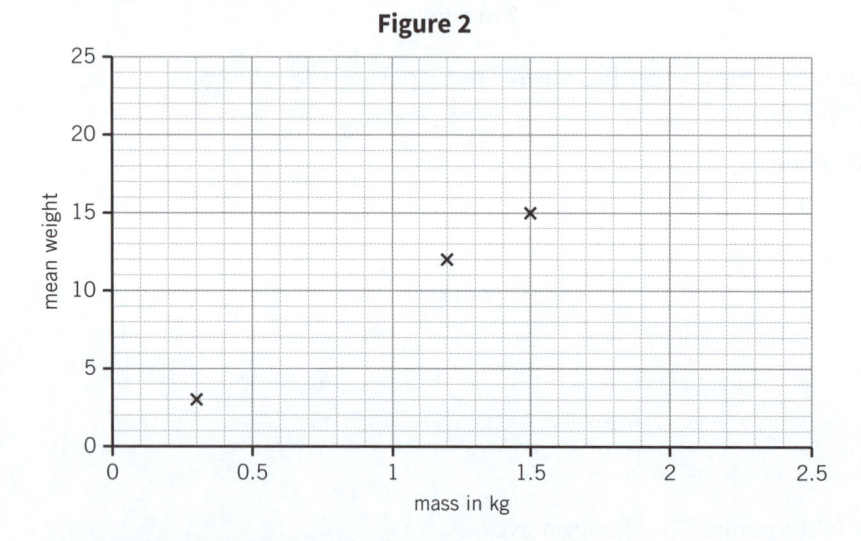

Figure 2

Complete **Figure 2** by plotting the value for mass 2.1 g. Draw a line of best fit. **[2 marks]**

04.4 Describe the relationship between weight and mass shown by the graph. **[1 mark]**

_____

> **Exam Tip**
> When you are asked to calculate a mean, always look for an outlier – if an outlier is present you must make sure you don't include it in your calculation.

> **Exam Tip**
> When rounding:
> • if the number ends in 0 to 4, round down
> • if the number ends in 5 to 9, round up.

> **Exam Tip**
> Practice drawing lines of best fit, and remember the definition of a line of best fit.

> **Exam Tip**
> Lines of best fit can be curved or straight. You can check which one you need to draw by using a clear ruler and seeing if the points line up or not.

P8 Forces

05 A student puts a piece of wood in a tank of water. The wood floats.

05.1 Name the non-contact force acting on the wood. [1 mark]

05.2 Name the contact force acting on the wood. [1 mark]

05.3 The resultant force on the piece of wood is zero. Complete the sentences. [2 marks]

The forces acting on the piece of wood are _____ in magnitude.

The forces are acting in the _____ direction.

05.4 The student places another piece of wood in the water tank. The second piece of wood sinks to the bottom of the tank.

Name **one other** force that is acting on the second piece of wood as it moves through the water.

Identify whether it is a force contact or a non-contact force. [2 marks]

> **Exam Tip**
>
> The force you name must not be one of the forces that have already been identified in the rest of **05**.

06 A student wants to know the difference between weight and mass.

06.1 Draw **one** lines from each key word to the correct definition. [2 marks]

Key word	Definition
mass	A measure of the force of gravity on an object.
weight	A measure of the amount of material in an object.
	A measure of the total amount of force acting on an object.

> **Exam Tip**
>
> Start by working out which measurement goes with each unit, then work out the middle bit!

06.2 What is a gravitational field? Choose **one** answer. [1 mark]

a region where there is no gravity

a region where something has mass

a region where the force of gravity acts

06.3 Complete the sentences. Choose words from the box.
You may need to use the words once, more than once, or not at all. [4 marks]

| mass | weight | kg | N/kg | N |

To calculate the weight of an object you need to know its _____ and the gravitational field strength. Gravitational field strength is measured in _____. The weight of an object can be considered to act at a point called the centre of _____.

You measure _____ with a newtonmeter.

> **Exam Tip**
>
> The equation:
>
> weight = mass × gravitational field strength
>
> can be used to help you work out the units for gravitational field strength. If you rearrange it you'll get:
>
> $$\text{gravitational field strength} = \frac{\text{weight}}{\text{mass}},$$
>
> then you can look at the units for weight and mass.

07 A student is watching two teams competing in a tug-of-war. They draw a diagram to show the forces that the teams are exerting on the rope (**Figure 3**).

Figure 3

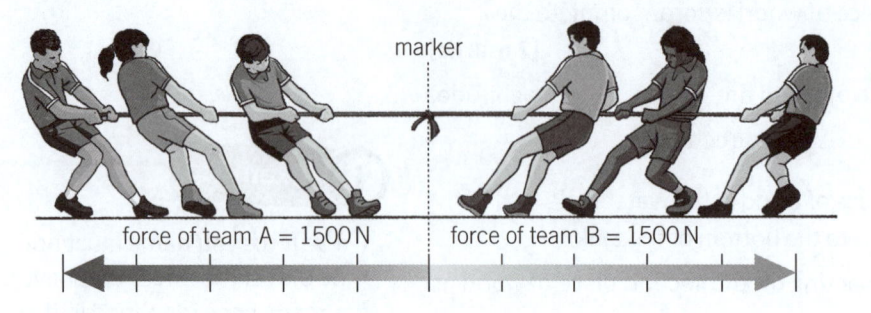

force of team A = 1500 N   force of team B = 1500 N

> **Exam Tip**
>
> When a diagram includes numbers make a note of them so you can use them in your answers.

07.1 What is the definition of resultant force?
Choose **one** answer. **[1 mark]**

The resultant force is what you get when you add the newtons together.

The resultant force is always zero.

The resultant force is the single force that has the same effect as all the forces acting together.

07.2 Determine the resultant force on the rope. **[1 mark]**

07.3 Team **B** add another team member who adds an additional 500 N to the force. Team **A** change their force so that the resultant force remains the same. Calculate the magnitude of the force that Team **A** now produces. Give the direction of the force. **[2 marks]**

08 A student is carrying heavy books in a plastic bag. This has caused the handles of the bag to stretch.

08.1 Changing the shape of an object by stretching requires two forces. One of these forces is the force of the books on the bag. Identify the other force involved in stretching the bag.
Choose **one** answer. **[1 mark]**

the force of the bag on the books

the force of the bag on the hand

the force of the hand on the bag

08.2 When the student takes the book out of the bag there is inelastic deformation of the handles.
Define inelastic deformation. **[1 mark]**

394 P8 Forces

P8

08.3 The student cuts the plastic bag into sections then applies different forces to the plastic sections and measures the extension. The student then repeats the experiment with a spring.
They plot graphs of their data. One of the graphs is a curved line. The other graph is a straight line. Choose **two** answers. **[2 marks]**

The graph for the plastic bag shows a non-linear relationship between force and extension.	
The graph for the plastic bag shows that force is proportional to extension.	
A graph that is a straight line is likely to be for a spring.	
The material that produced a linear graph has been inelastically deformed.	

> **Exam Tip**
> Read the instructions on the question carefully. You'll need to find *two* correct answers, and no more.

09 A student is investigating a spring.
The student does work on the spring, which increases its elastic potential energy store.

09.1 Calculate the elastic potential energy stored in the spring when it is compressed by 2 cm.
Use the *Physics Equations sheet*.
Give the unit with your answer.
spring constant of spring = 2000 N/m **[4 marks]**

09.2 The student compresses a second spring. To compress the second spring 2 cm, the student does more work. Choose the correct word in bold.
The spring constant of the spring in the new toaster is **bigger / smaller** than the spring constant of the spring in the old toaster.
Give a reason for your answer. **[2 marks]**

> **Exam Tip**
> Always write down the equation you choose and every step in your calculation. Even if you make a mistake and get the incorrect answer, you can still get lots of marks.

09.3 The student says:
'I do the same amount of work compressing the spring by 1 cm as I do by extending the spring by 1 cm.'
Are they correct? Give a reason for your answer. **[2 marks]**

10 A person is pushing a shopping trolley. The person exerts a force of 20 N. The total distance travelled by the trolley is 30 m.

10.1 Write down the equation which links distance, force, and work done. **[1 mark]**

10.2 Calculate the work done by the person. **[2 marks]**

10.3 The person is doing work as they push the trolley at a steady speed. Name the force against which they are doing work. **[1 mark]**

10.4 Describe the energy changes when the brother is moving the trolley at a steady speed. **[2 marks]**

> **Exam Tip**
> What force would cause the trolley to slow down?

Knowledge

P9 Speed

Distance and displacement

Distance:
- is how far an object moves
- is a scalar quantity so does not have direction.

Displacement is a vector and includes the *distance* and *direction* of a straight line from an object's starting point to its finish point.

Velocity

The **velocity** of an object is its speed in a given direction.

Velocity is a vector quantity because it has a magnitude and direction.

An object's velocity changes if its direction changes, even if its speed is constant.

Speed

(L) distance travelled (m) = speed (m/s) × time (s)

$$s = vt$$

The symbol for distance is s, and the symbol for speed is v.

In reality, objects rarely move at a constant speed. So it can be useful to calculate average speed:

$$\text{average speed (m/s)} = \frac{\text{total distance travelled (m)}}{\text{total time taken (s)}}$$

Some typical average speeds are:
- walking ≈ 1.5 m/s
- running ≈ 3 m/s
- cycling ≈ 6 m/s

The speed of sound and the speed of the wind also change depending on the conditions.
- speed of sound in air is ≈ 330 m/s

Acceleration

Acceleration is the change in velocity of an object per second. It is a vector quantity.

The unit of acceleration is metres per second squared, m/s^2.

An object is accelerating if its speed or its direction (or both) are changing. A negative acceleration means an object is slowing down, and is called **deceleration**.

Acceleration can be calculated using:

(L) $\text{acceleration (m/s}^2\text{)} = \frac{\text{change in velocity (m/s)}}{\text{time taken (s)}}$

$$a = \frac{\Delta v}{t}$$

Near the Earth's surface any object falling freely under gravity has an acceleration of about 9.8 m/s^2.

Uniform acceleration is when the acceleration of an object is constant.

The following equation applies to objects with uniform acceleration:

(final velocity)^2 − (initial velocity)^2 = 2 × acceleration × distance

$$v^2 - u^2 = 2as$$

> **Revision tip**
>
> **Practice** Try going over all the formulae we use in physics and seeing which quantities are vector and which are scalar.

> **Revision tip**
>
> **Remember** $s = vt$ can be a confusing equation – students frequently get the s for distance travelled confused with speed. Make sure you don't fall into this trap!

Key terms

Make sure you can write a definition for these key terms.

| air resistance | deceleration | displacement | distance |

P9

Distance–time graphs

A distance–time graph shows how the distance travelled by an object travelling in a straight line changes with time.

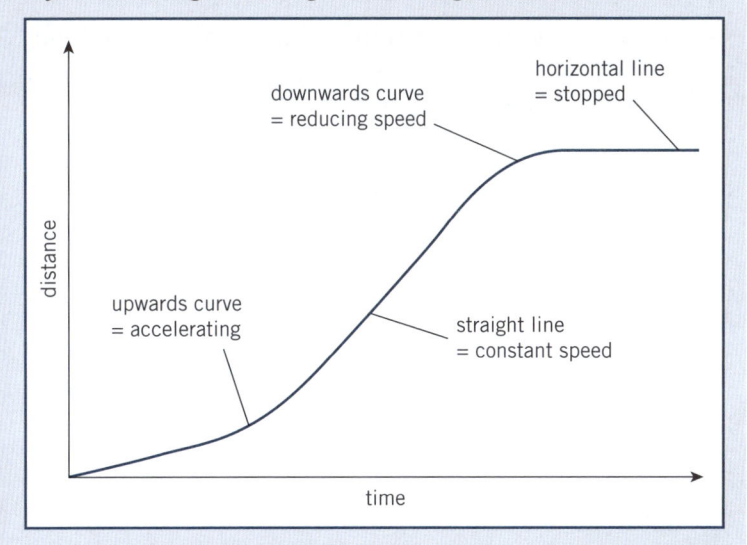

- downwards curve = reducing speed
- horizontal line = stopped
- upwards curve = accelerating
- straight line = constant speed

(axes: distance vs time)

The gradient of the line in a distance–time graph is equal to the object's speed.

Velocity–time graphs

A velocity–time graph shows how the velocity of an object changes with time.

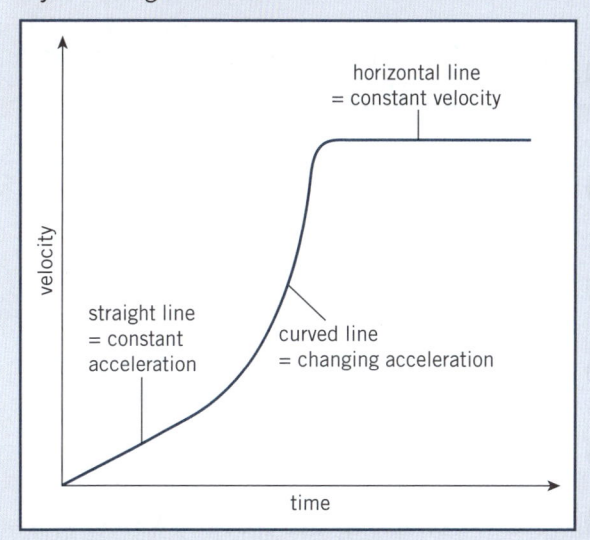

- horizontal line = constant velocity
- straight line = constant acceleration
- curved line = changing acceleration

(axes: velocity vs time)

The gradient of the line in a velocity–time graph is equal to the object's acceleration.

Drag forces

When an object moves through a fluid (liquid or gas) a frictional force drags on it.

These drag forces:
- always act in the opposite direction to an object's movement
- increase with the object's speed – the greater the speed, the greater the frictional force
- depend on the shape and size of the object.

The frictional drag force in air is called **air resistance**.

Streamlining an object reduces the drag it experiences.

Terminal velocity

For an object falling through a fluid:
- there are two forces acting – its weight due to gravity and the drag force
- the weight remains constant
- the drag force is small at the beginning, but gets bigger as it speeds up
- the resultant force will get smaller as the drag force increases
- the acceleration will decrease as it falls
- if it falls for a long enough time, the object will reach a final steady speed.

Terminal velocity is the constant velocity a falling object reaches when the frictional force acting on it is equal to its weight.

streamlining   terminal velocity   uniform acceleration   velocity

P9 Knowledge 397

Retrieval

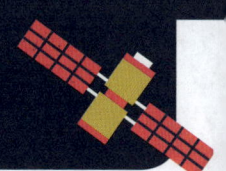

Learn the answers to the questions below, then cover the answers column with a piece of paper and write as many as you can. Check and repeat.

P9 questions | Answers

	P9 questions	Answers
1	What is the difference between distance and displacement?	distance is a scalar quantity and only has a magnitude (size), displacement is a vector quantity and has both magnitude and direction
2	What is the difference between speed and velocity?	speed is a scalar quantity and only has a magnitude (size), velocity is a vector quantity and has both magnitude and direction
3	What factors can affect the speed at which someone walks, runs, or cycles?	age, fitness, terrain, and total distance travelled
4	What are typical speeds for a person walking, running, and cycling?	1.5 m/s, 3.0 m/s, and 6.0 m/s respectively
5	What are typical speeds of a car and a train?	13–30 m/s and 50 m/s respectively
6	What is a typical speed for sound travelling in air?	330 m/s
7	What is acceleration?	change in velocity of an object per second
8	What is the unit of acceleration?	m/s^2
9	How can an object be accelerating even if it is travelling at a steady speed?	if it is changing direction
10	What is happening to an object if it has a negative acceleration?	it is slowing down
11	What information does the gradient of the line in a distance–time graph provide?	speed
12	What information does the gradient of the line in a velocity–time graph provide?	acceleration
13	What is the name for the steady speed a falling object reaches when the resistive force is equal to its weight?	terminal velocity
14	What is the general name for the frictional forces an object experiences when moving through a fluid (liquid or gas)?	drag
15	In which direction does the drag on an object always act?	in the direction opposite to which it is moving
16	What happens to the drag on an object as its speed increases?	the drag increases
17	What can be done to reduce the drag on an object?	streamlining

P9 Speed

Now go back and use the questions below to check your knowledge from previous chapters.

P9

Previous questions | Answers

#	Question	Answer
1	What is a force?	a push or pull that acts on an object due to an interaction with another object
2	What is meant by the half-life of a radioactive source?	the time taken for half the unstable nuclei to decay or the time taken for the count rate to halve
3	How can an electron move up an energy level?	absorb sufficient electromagnetic radiation
4	What does a material's thermal conductivity tell you?	how well it conducts heat
5	Which two quantities do you need to measure to find the density of a solid or liquid?	mass and volume
6	What is the internal energy of a substance?	the total kinetic energy and potential energy of all the particles in the substance
7	What are the three main uses of energy resources?	generating electricity, transportation, heating

Put paper here

Maths skills

Practise your maths skills using the worked example and practice questions below.

Significant figures

We use significant figures (s.f.) to make sure we are not introducing error by giving a false level of accuracy.

When answering questions you use the same number of s.f. as the data with the fewest s.f. in the question. You may also be asked to give your answer to a given number of figures.

For example:

- 4.57 to two significant figures is 4.6 – the 5 after the decimal point is rounded up
- 12 345 to two significant figures is 12 000 – the number is rounded down
- 0.093 to two significant figures is 0.09 – the zero *before* the decimal point is *not* a significant figure, but the zero *after* the decimal point is.

Worked example

A metal ball has a mass of 13.4 kg and a volume of 5.3 m³.

Calculate the density of the metal ball.

Give your answer to an appropriate number of significant figures.

First calculate the density using:

$$\text{density} = \frac{\text{mass}}{\text{volume}}$$

$$\frac{13.4}{5.3} = 2.52830$$

To work out the appropriate number of significant figures, work out which value in the question has the smallest number of significant figures.

- 13.4 = 3 significant figures
- 5.3 = 2 significant figures

So you should give your answer to 2 significant figures.

density = 2.5 kg/m³

Practice

1. Give 67 812 to 3 s.f.

2. Give 0.567 to 2 s.f.

3. A person has a mass of 55.25 kg.

   Calculate the weight of the person. Give your answer to 3 s.f.

   Gravitational field strength = 10 N/kg

4. A plane flies from London to Perth in Australia, a distance of 8977 miles. It takes 17 hours and 45 minutes.

   Calculate the average speed of the plane in metres per second. Give your answer to 4 s.f.

   1 mile = 1609 metres

P9 Retrieval

Radiation

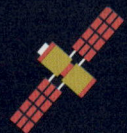

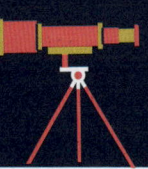

Exam-style questions

01 An object is moving in a straight line.

A student draws a graph of distance against time to describe how the object moves.

01.1 Draw **one** line from each box to complete the sentences. **[2 marks]**

If the distance–time graph is horizontal	the object is moving slowly.
If the line is steep	the object is not moving.
If the line is not very steep	the object is moving quickly.

01.2 **Figure 1** shows some velocity–time graphs.

Figure 1

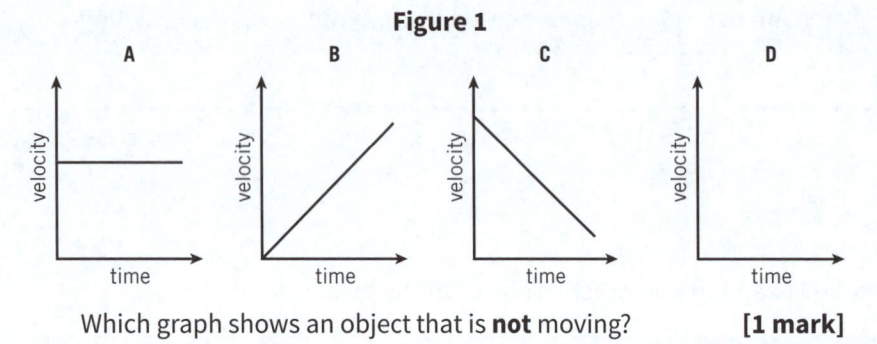

A — horizontal line
B — line increasing from origin
C — line decreasing from y-axis to x-axis
D — (blank axes)

Which graph shows an object that is **not** moving? **[1 mark]**

_____

01.3 Which graph shows an object that is moving at a constant velocity? **[1 mark]**

_____

01.4 Which graph shows an object whose speed is **increasing** at a constant rate? **[1 mark]**

_____

01.5 Complete the sentence. **[1 mark]**

If the speed of an object is increasing, then the object is **accelerating** / **decelerating**.

> **! Exam Tip**
>
> Velocity–time graphs and distance–time graphs look identical. The only way you can tell the difference is by looking at the label on the y-axis. Whenever you see one of these graphs the first thing you should do is to highlight the label on the y-axis to remind you of which type of graph it is.

> **! Exam Tip**
>
> It might help to add some numbers on the graph so you can describe what is happening. Add a 0 to the point where the axes meet, then add a 5 next to both arrow heads. It doesn't matter what numbers you use.

P9 Speed

Paper 6 — P9

02 A student collected data for three car journeys, **A**, **B**, and **C**. The data is shown in **Figure 2**.

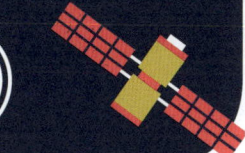

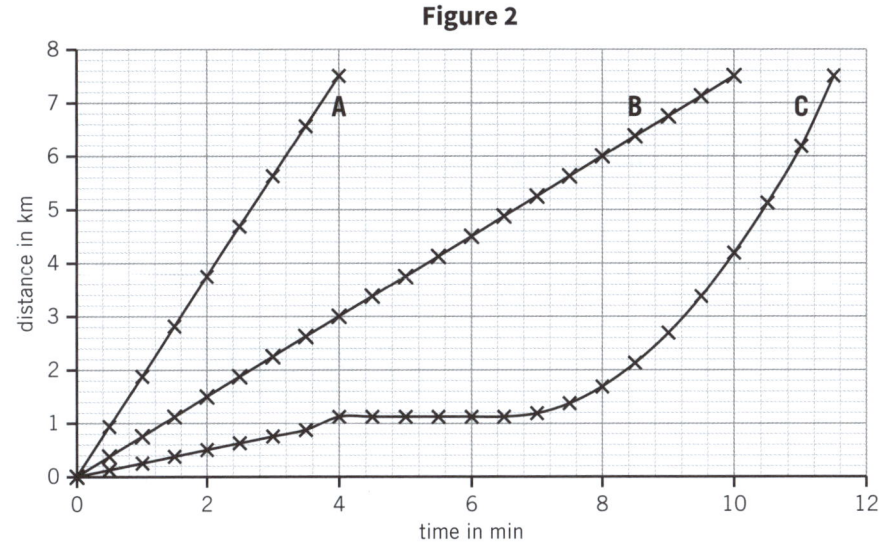

Figure 2

[Graph showing distance in km (y-axis, 0–8) vs time in min (x-axis, 0–12) for three journeys A, B, and C. Journey A is a straight line from origin rising steeply to ~7.5 km at 4 min. Journey B is a straight line from origin rising to ~7.5 km at 10 min. Journey C stays flat at ~1 km from 0 to ~7 min, then curves upward to ~7.5 km at 11.5 min.]

> **Exam Tip**
> Check the units of all graphs in this topic as you will often need to read values from the graph.
> Here the units are *not* SI units.

02.1 Which car travelled at the highest steady speed? Give a reason for your answer. **[2 marks]**

Car: _____

Reason: _____

02.2 Which car stopped at some point during the journey? Give a reason for your answer. **[2 marks]**

Car: _____

Reason: _____

> **Exam Tip**
> **02.1** to **02.4** are all two-mark questions. You'll get one mark for selecting the correct journey from **Figure 2** and the other for saying how you know its the correct journey.

02.3 Which car accelerated? Give a reason for your answer. **[2 marks]**

Car: _____

Reason: _____

02.4 All three cars travelled the same overall distance. Which car has the highest average speed? Give a reason for your answer. **[2 marks]**

Car: _____

Reason: _____

02.5 Write down the equation that links distance, speed, and time. **[1 mark]**

02.6 Calculate the average speed of the car in **02.4**. **[4 marks]**

Average speed = _____ m/s

03 Some quantities are vector quantities, and some are scalar quantities.

03.1 Which of these is a vector quantity? Circle **one** answer. **[1 mark]**

      20 m   20 m to the right

03.2 Complete these sentences. Choose the correct words from the box. You may need to use each word once, more than once, or not at all. **[5 marks]**

direction   displacement   distance   magnitude   metres

_____ is a vector quantity and _____ is a scalar quantity. A vector quantity has _____ and _____. A scalar quantity has _____ only.

03.3 A student walks 10 m to the left and then walks 20 m to the right. Calculate the total distance the student has walked. **[1 mark]**

03.4 Determine the student's final displacement. Show your working. **[2 marks]**

> **Exam Tip**
> There is a difference between the total distance and the final displacement.

04 **Table 1** shows the average speed of three modes of transport.

Table 1

Object	Average speed in m/s
walking	
running	3
cycling	6

04.1 Give the average speed of walking. **[1 mark]**

04.2 Write down the equation that links distance, speed, and time. **[1 mark]**

04.3 A marathon race is 26 miles. The women's world record for the fastest time to complete a marathon is 2 hours and 14 minutes. Calculate the average speed of the world record marathon time in m/s.

1 mile = 1609 metres **[4 marks]**

04.4 Give **one** reason for the difference in the average speed of the world record in **04.3** to the average speed of running given in **Table 1**. **[1 mark]**

04.5 A cyclist travelled 25 000 metres at average speed. Calculate how long the journey took. Give your answer in minutes. **[3 marks]**

> **Exam Tip**
> You'll need to learn the typical speeds for different actions.

> **Exam Tip**
> To make any comparison you need quantities to be in the same unit. It is helpful to convert to SI units first.

P9 Speed

05 A student measures how far two toy cars travel. Their results are shown in **Table 2**.

Table 2

Time in s	Distance in m	
	Car A	Car B
0	0.00	0.00
5	0.05	0.02
10	0.10	0.04
15	0.15	0.08
20	0.20	0.16

The students plotted their results on Figure 3.

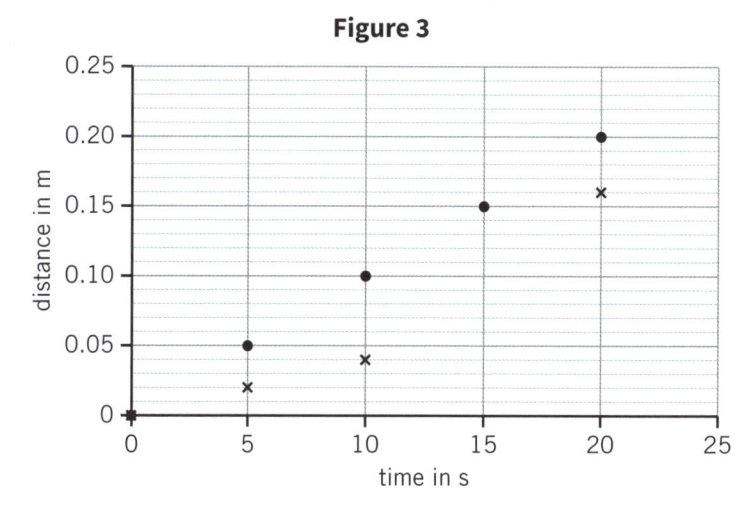

Figure 3

05.1 Draw a line of best fit for student **A**'s data. [1 mark]

05.2 Plot the missing data point from student **B**'s data. Draw a line of best fit. [2 marks]

05.3 Identify which car was moving at a steady speed. [1 mark]

05.4 Identify whether the average speed of car **B** is the same as as the average speed of car **A**. Explain your answer. [2 marks]

> **Exam Tip**
>
> You can carry out a calculation to answer **05.4**, and you would still get the marks, but you don't need to and you haven't been asked to. Look carefully at the data in **Table 2** and think about what the values you need to calculate the average speed of an object.

06 A student is watching other students run a race on sports day.

06.1 What is the typical walking speed of a human? Choose **one** answer. [1 mark]

1.5 m/s   6 m/s   10 m/s   30 m/s

06.2 Write down the equation that links distance, speed, and time. [1 mark]

06.3 Calculate the distance travelled in 10 s by a person running at a speed of 3 m/s. [2 marks]

06.4 Complete the sentences. Choose from the words in bold. [2 marks]

If you use the total distance and total time, then the speed you calculate is the **average / instantaneous** speed. This is because in most situations, the speed **changes / stays the same** throughout the motion.

07 A remote controlled car is travelling at 2 m/s. Its speed changes to 5 m/s. The change in speed takes 6 s.

07.1 Calculate the acceleration of the car. Use the equation:

$$\text{acceleration} = \frac{\text{change in velocity}}{\text{time taken}}$$

Give the unit with your answer. **[3 marks]**

Exam Tip

Make sure that you can list the units of all the quantities in equations that you will be using. Practice often. Flash cards work well for learning definitions and units.

07.2 The car slows down and then stops. Complete the sentences. Choose the correct words from the box. **[2 marks]**

| accelerating | decelerating | decreasing | increasing |

When the car is slowing down it is _____. Its speed is _____.

07.3 A student plots a graph of velocity against time for a different car in **Figure 4**.

Figure 4

[Graph: velocity in m/s (y-axis, 0 to 20) vs time in s (x-axis, 0 to 70). Trapezoidal shape: rises from 0 to 20 m/s between 0 and 10 s, stays at 20 m/s from 10 to 50 s, falls from 20 to 0 m/s between 50 and 60 s.]

Exam Tip

When the car is accelerating, the speed will be increasing.

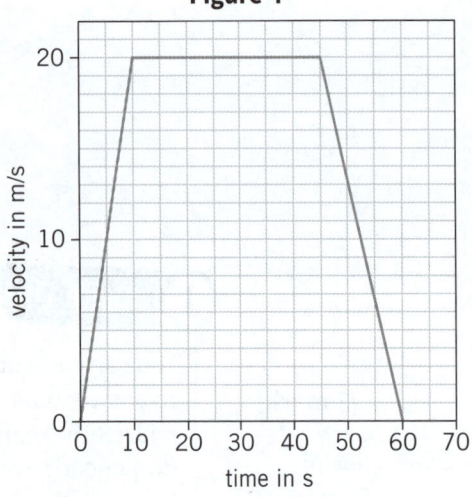

Calculate the acceleration of the car. **[2 marks]**

08 A student stretches a spring and measures the extension. They plot their results in **Figure 5**.

Figure 5

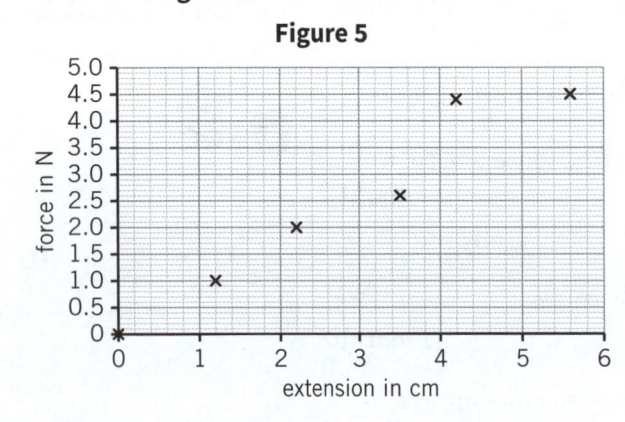

[Graph: force in N (y-axis, 0 to 5.0) vs extension in cm (x-axis, 0 to 6). Points at approximately (1, 1.0), (2, 2.0), (3.5, 2.5), (4, 4.5), (5.5, 4.5).]

08.1 Identify the outlier in **Figure 5**. **[1 mark]**

08.2 Write down the equation that links extension, force, and spring constant. **[1 mark]**

08.3 Use **Figure 5** to find the spring constant of the spring. **[4 marks]**

Exam Tip

You need to use the linear section of **Figure 5**. Remember to ignore the outlier.

404 **P9 Speed**

08.4 The student says:

'The limit of proportionality is somewhere between 4.5 N and 5.5 N.'

Do you agree? Justify your answer. **[2 marks]**

09 **Figure 6** shows the graph of a journey.

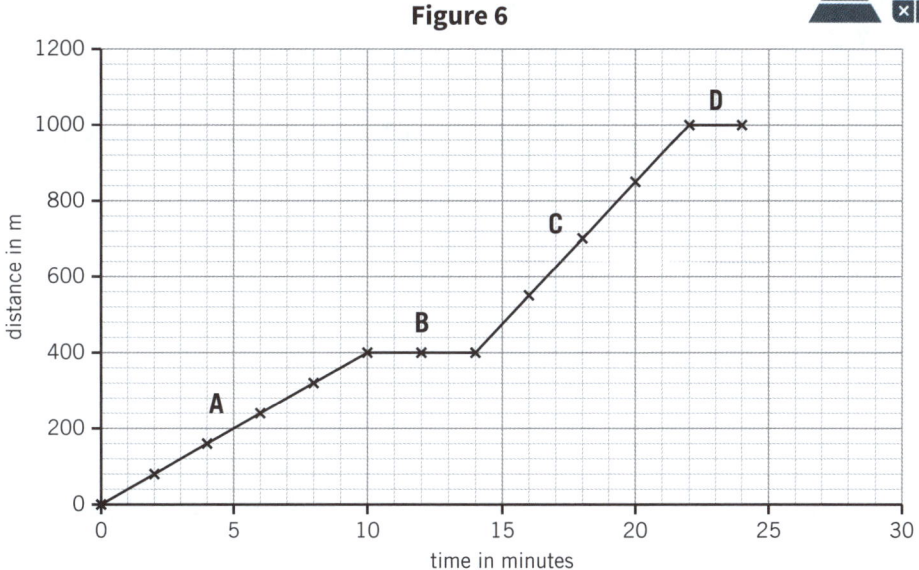

Figure 6

Exam Tip

Label **Figure 6** with when the object was accelerating and when the object was stationary.

09.1 Identify one point, **A**, **B**, **C**, or **D**, when the object was stationary. **[1 mark]**

09.2 Write down the equation that links distance, speed, and time. **[1 mark]**

09.3 Calculate the average speed of the first 10 minutes of the journey. Give your answer in m/s. **[3 marks]**

Exam Tip

Remember, there are 60 seconds in a minute. To convert minutes to seconds, multiple the number of minutes by 60.

09.4 Between which times was the object moving fastest? Give a reason for your answer. **[2 marks]**

09.5 Give the total distance the object travelled in the journey. **[1 mark]**

10 A student has learnt about scalars and vectors.

10.1 Which sentence is correct? Choose **one** answer. **[1 mark]**

Displacement and velocity are scalars.

Distance and speed are scalars.

Distance and speed are vectors.

Speed and velocity are vectors.

10.2 A cyclist travels 10 km north, then 20 km south. Calculate the final displacement of the cyclist. **[2 marks]**

Exam Tip

In **10.2** you need to give the direction of the displacement, as well as the distance.

10.3 Explain why the total distance travelled is not the same as the final displacement. **[2 marks]**

10.4 The cyclist says:

'I travelled at 6 km/h north, then 10 km/h south.'

Is the cyclist describing their speed or velocity? Explain your answer. **[2 marks]**

Knowledge

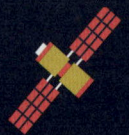

P10 Newton's Laws of Motion

Newton's First Law

Newton's First Law says that the velocity, speed, and/or direction of an object *will only change if a resultant force is acting on it*.

This means that:

- If the resultant force on a stationary object is zero, the object will remain stationary.
- If the resultant force on a moving object is zero, it will continue moving at the same velocity, in a straight line.
- If the resultant force on an object is not zero, its velocity *will* change.

When a car is travelling at a steady speed, the resistive forces (e.g., friction and air resistance) must be balanced with the driving forces.

A change in velocity can mean an object:

- starts to move
- stops moving
- speeds up
- slows down
- changes direction.

There *must* be a resultant force acting on an object if it is doing *any* of the things listed above.

Newton's Second Law

Newton's Second Law says that the acceleration a of an object:

- is proportional to the resultant force on the object

$$a \propto F$$

- is inversely proportional to the mass of the object

$$a \propto \frac{1}{m}$$

Resultant force, mass, and acceleration are linked by the equation:

(L) resultant force (N) = mass (kg) × acceleration (m/s^2)

$$F = ma$$

> **Revision tip**
>
> **Remember** The m means mass, whilst the symbol for momentum is p. Don't get them mixed up!

Newton's Third Law

Newton's Third Law states that whenever two objects interact with each other, they exert *equal and opposite* forces on each other.

This means that forces always occur in pairs.

Each pair of forces:

- act on separate objects
- are the same size as each other
- act in opposite directions along the same line
- are of the same type, for example, two gravitational forces or two electrostatic forces.

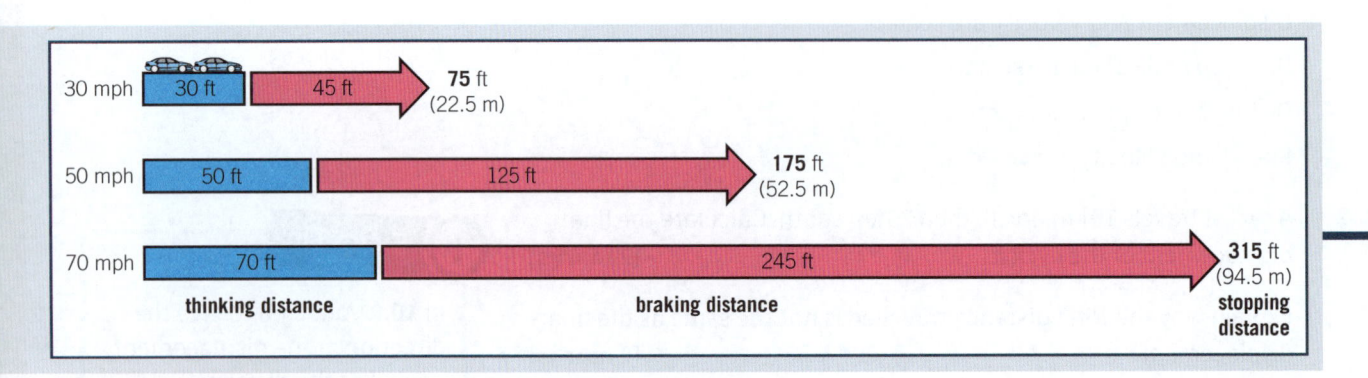

Speed	Thinking distance	Braking distance	Stopping distance
30 mph	30 ft	45 ft	75 ft (22.5 m)
50 mph	50 ft	125 ft	175 ft (52.5 m)
70 mph	70 ft	245 ft	315 ft (94.5 m)

Key terms

Make sure you can write a definition for these key terms.

braking distance   momentum   reaction time

P10

Stopping distance

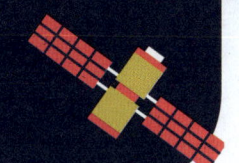

The distance it takes a body, such as a car, to stop is made up of **thinking distance** and **braking distance**.

stopping distance = thinking distance + braking distance

Thinking distance is the distance the vehicle travels during the driver's **reaction time**. Thinking distance is proportional to the speed of the vehicle.

Stopping distance is the distance the vehicle travels once the brakes have been applied. Braking distance is not proportional to speed.

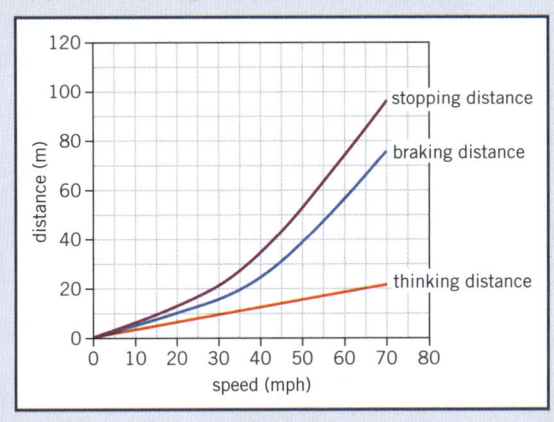

Speed has a bigger effect on braking distance than on thinking distance.

Reaction time

Reaction times vary from person to person, ranging from 0.2 s to 0.9 s.

Reaction time can be affected by:
- tiredness
- drugs
- alcohol
- distractions.

Reaction times can be measured in a number of ways, including:

Computer
A computer is used to time how long someone takes to respond to a sound or image on the screen.

Ruler drop test
The ruler is dropped between someone's fingers and the distance it falls before they catch it is used to calculate their reaction time.

> **Revision tip**
>
> **Remember** The unit for stopping distance, m, is metres not miles.

Factors affecting braking distance

The braking distance of a vehicle can be affected by:
- the speed of the vehicle
- road conditions
- the condition of brakes and tyres.

Any condition that causes less friction between the tyres and the road can lead to skidding, which increases the braking distance.

When the brakes of a vehicle are applied a frictional force is applied to its wheel.

Work done by the frictional force between the brakes and wheel transfers energy from the kinetic energy store of the car to the thermal energy stores of the brakes.

This increases the temperature of the brakes.

The braking force, braking distance, and energy transferred are related by the equation:

$$\text{work done (J)} = \text{braking force (N)} \times \text{distance (m)}$$

$$W = Fs$$

The faster a vehicle moves or the greater its mass:
- the greater the amount of energy in its kinetic energy store
- the more work that has to be done to transfer the energy to slow it down
- the greater the braking force needed to stop it in a certain distance
- the greater the distance needed to stop it with a certain braking force.

---

stopping distance   thinking distance

P10 Knowledge

Retrieval

Learn the answers to the questions below, then cover the answers column with a piece of paper and write as many as you can. Check and repeat.

	P10 questions	Answers
1	What does Newton's First Law say?	the velocity of an object will only change if a resultant force is acting on it
2	What is the resultant force on a stationary object?	zero
3	What is the resultant force on an object moving at a steady speed in a straight line?	zero
4	What will an object experience if the resultant force on it is not zero?	acceleration / change in velocity
5	What forces are balanced when an object travels at a steady speed?	resistive forces = driving force
6	According to Newton's Second Law, what is the acceleration of an object proportional to?	the force acting on it
7	According to Newton's Second Law, what is the acceleration of an object inversely proportional to?	mass
8	What does Newton's Third Law say?	when two objects interact they exert equal and opposite forces on each other
9	What is the name given to the distance a vehicle travels to safely come to a stop after the driver has spotted a hazard?	stopping distance
10	What is thinking distance?	distance vehicle travels during driver's reaction time
11	What is braking distance?	distance vehicle travels once brakes have been applied
12	What is the relationship between stopping distance, thinking distance, and braking distance?	stopping distance = thinking distance + braking distance
13	What are three factors that can affect the braking distance of a vehicle?	speed, road conditions, condition of tyres and brakes
14	What can happen if the braking force used to stop a vehicle is very large?	brakes may overheat / the car may skid

P10

Now go back and use the questions below to check your knowledge from previous chapters.

Previous questions | Answers

#	Question	Answer
1	What is an alternating current (a.c.)?	current that repeatedly reverses direction
2	What is a scalar quantity?	only has a size (magnitude)
3	Which materials have low thermal conductivity?	thermal insulators
4	Which type of nuclear radiation is the most ionising?	alpha
5	What is the centre of mass?	the point through which the weight of an object can be considered to act
6	How do you find the atomic number of an element?	number of protons in one atom of the element

Put paper here

Required practical skills

Practise answering questions on the required practicals using the example below. You need to be able to apply your skills and knowledge to other practicals too.

Force, mass, and acceleration

You need to be able to measure and explain how the acceleration of an object is linked to changes in force and mass.

For this practical, you can use two light gates to measure acceleration, or measure the time to travel a set distance. In the latter case, the acceleration will be inversely proportional to the time.

To produce accurate and precise measurements you should:

- only change either the force or mass at one time
- use a video recording if not using light gates
- take repeat measurements and find the mean.

Worked example

A student sets up a trolley on a track. The trolley is attached to string, which goes over a pulley to a weight stack.

They set up light gates to record the acceleration as the force is changed.

Force in N	0	1	2	3	4	4
Acceleration in m/s²	0	4	8.1	12	16.2	20.2

1. Calculate the mass of the system.

   force = mass × acceleration

   $$\text{mass} = \frac{\text{force}}{\text{acceleration}}$$

   for example, $\frac{1\,\text{N}}{4\,\text{m/s}^2} = 0.25\,\text{kg}$

2. Suggest how the student kept the mass of the system the same even though the number of weights on the stack increased.

   They moved masses from the weight stack to the trolley.

3. What other force could be acting on the trolley, and how would this affect its acceleration?

   Friction, which would cause the trolley's acceleration to be lower than expected.

Practice

A student connects a trolley to a piece of string attached to a weight stack. The weight stays the same, but the student increases the mass of the trolley.

She times how long it takes the trolley to travel 50 cm using a stop clock.

1. Sketch a graph of time against mass. Describe and explain the shape.

2. Describe how the student could ensure that the results are reproducible.

3. Suggest one benefit of using a larger distance.

P10 Retrieval 409

Practice

Exam-style questions

01 A student is learning about Newton's Laws of Motion.

01.1 Draw **one** line from Newton's laws to the correct definition. **[2 marks]**

Newton's law	Definition
Newton's First Law	Forces come in pairs.
Newton's Second Law	Acceleration depends on force and mass.
Newton's Third Law	Motion doesn't change unless a net force acts.

01.2 The student adds up all the forces acting on an object.
Identify which force they have calculated. **[1 mark]**
Cirlce **one** answer.

  residual force   resting force   resultant force

01.3 The student finds that the total force in **01.2** is zero.
How is the object in **01.2** moving? **[1 mark]**
Tick **one** box.

The object is moving at a constant velocity. ☐

The object is moving at a constant velocity in one direction. ☐

The speed of the object is decreasing. ☐

The speed of the object is increasing. ☐

> **Exam Tip**
> Use Newton's First Law to help you answer **01.3**.

02 An ice hockey puck is moving along the ice at a steady speed.
Student **A** says:
'*If the speed is steady, there are no forces acting on the puck.*'

02.1 Do you agree with student **A**? Circle **one** answer.

  yes   no

Give a reason for your answer. **[2 marks]**

_____

_____

_____

> **Exam Tip**
> Use Newton's Law to explain your answer.

410 P10 Newton's laws of motion

Paper 6 **P10**

02.2 Student **B** says:

'The puck will stop only when the force it is carrying runs out.'

Do you agree with student **B**? Circle **one** answer.

yes   no

Give a reason for your answer.   **[2 marks]**

_____
_____
_____

02.3 One of the players hits the puck with a hockey stick and the puck moves away from them.

Student **C** says:

'Whilst the stick is in contact with the puck, the stick exerts a bigger force on the puck than the puck exerts on the stick.'

Do you agree with student **C**? Circle **one** answer.

yes   no

Explain your answer.   **[2 marks]**

_____
_____
_____

02.4 Use the information **02.3** to determine whether the puck experienced an acceleration whilst in contact with the stick.

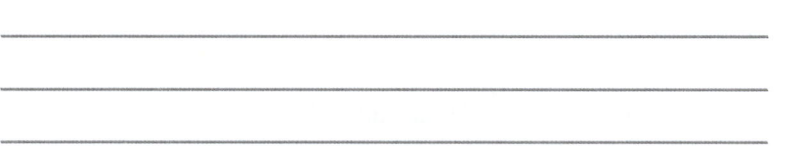

Explain your answer.   **[3 marks]**

_____
_____
_____
_____

> **! Exam Tip**
>
> Sometimes drawing the situation out can help you work out the forces involved, but just draw boxes, not an actual hockey stick.

03 When a driver sees a hazard, they may need to stop their car.

03.1 Draw **one** line from each distance to the correct definition   **[2 marks]**

Distance	Definition
thinking distance	the thinking distance and braking distance added together
braking distance	the distance the car travels whilst the driver reacts
stopping distance	the distance the car travels whilst the driver applies the brakes

> **! Exam Tip**
>
> Start with braking distance – the answer is in the right hand box!

P10 Practice

03.2 What is a typical reaction time for a person?

Choose **one** answer. [1 mark]

    0.05 s   0.5 s   5.0 s   50 s

03.3 What factor affects both braking distance and the thinking distance?

Choose **one** answer. [1 mark]

    reaction time   road conditions   speed

04 **Table 1** lists some factors that affect the thinking distance and braking distance of a car.

Table 1

Factor	Affects thinking distance	Affects braking distance	Affects both braking and thinking distance
road conditions			
distractions in the car			
speed			

04.1 For each row in **Table 2** tick whether the factor affects thinking distance, braking distance, or both. [3 marks]

04.2 Give **one** other factor that affects thinking distance.

Explain the effect of this factor on the thinking distance. [3 marks]

Factor: _____

Explanation: _____

_____

04.3 Give **one** type of road condition that can affect the stopping distance of a car.

Explain why the stopping distance is affected. [3 marks]

Road condition: _____

Explanation: _____

_____

> **Exam Tip**
>
> There are lots of examples to pick from for **04.2** and **04.3**. Have a few examples that you know well so you have good answers ready for the exam.

05 A theme park rollercoaster vehicle travels along a track. The forces acting on the vehicle are shown in **Table 2**.

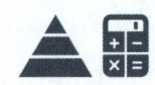

Table 2

Section of straight track	Driving force in N	Resistive force in N
A	3000	2500
B	3000	3500
C	3500	3500

P10 Newton's laws of motion

05.1 Write down the section of track in which the vehicle is decelerating. **[1 mark]**

05.2 Write down the section of track in which the vehicle is travelling at a steady speed. **[1 mark]**

> **! Exam Tip**
> For **05.2** you'll need to find the resultant force.

05.3 At the end of the ride, the only force acting on the vehicle is the resistive force due to the brakes. The mass of the vehicle and passengers is 3500 kg.

Calculate the force required to stop the car with a deceleration of 4 m/s^2.

Use the equation :

resultant force = mass × acceleration **[2 marks]**

05.4 On one section of the track, a resultant force does not produce a change in speed. Suggest why. Choose **one** answer. **[1 mark]**

The resultant force is not large enough.

The resultant force is applied in the wrong direction.

The track is not straight.

The track is straight.

06 Two cars are travelling in a straight line. **Figure 1** shows the forces acting on the cars.

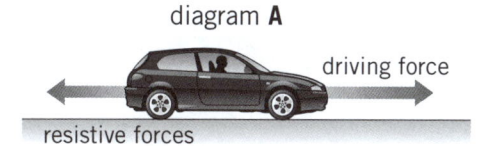

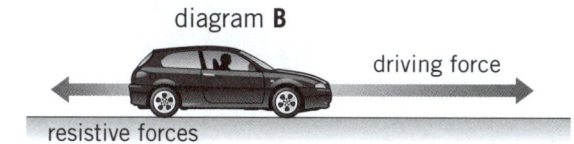

Figure 1

diagram **A**

resistive forces — driving force

diagram **B**

resistive forces — driving force

06.1 Complete the statement about the car in **Figure 1 A**. Choose the correct words in bold. **[2 marks]**

The car is **accelerating / moving at a steady speed** because the driving force is **bigger than / the same size as / smaller than** the resistive force.

06.2 Complete the statement about the car in **Figure 1 B**. Choose the correct words in bold. **[3 marks]**

The motion of the car is **different from / the same as** the motion of the car in **Figure 1A**. This is because the forces acting on the car in **Figure 1B** are **balanced / unbalanced** and the forces acting on the car in **Figure 1A** are **balanced / unbalanced**.

> **! Exam Tip**
> Take each sentence one at a time. If you're not sure about the first sentence then you can still try the next one.

06.3 The driver of the car in **Figure 1B** takes their foot off the accelerator. Describe the motion of the car. **[1 mark]**

07 A company that makes tyres tests them in different road conditions. **Table 3** shows data for braking distance in different road conditions.

Table 3

Road conditions	Mean braking distance in m
dry	45
wet	60
snow	100
ice	120

07.1 Suggest **one** factor that the company should keep the same when doing these tests. **[1 mark]**

> **Exam Tip**
> This is the control variable.

07.2 Plot the data from **Table 3** onto **Figure 2**. **[2 marks]**

> **Exam Tip**
> This is categoric data so you'll need to draw a bar chart.

Figure 2

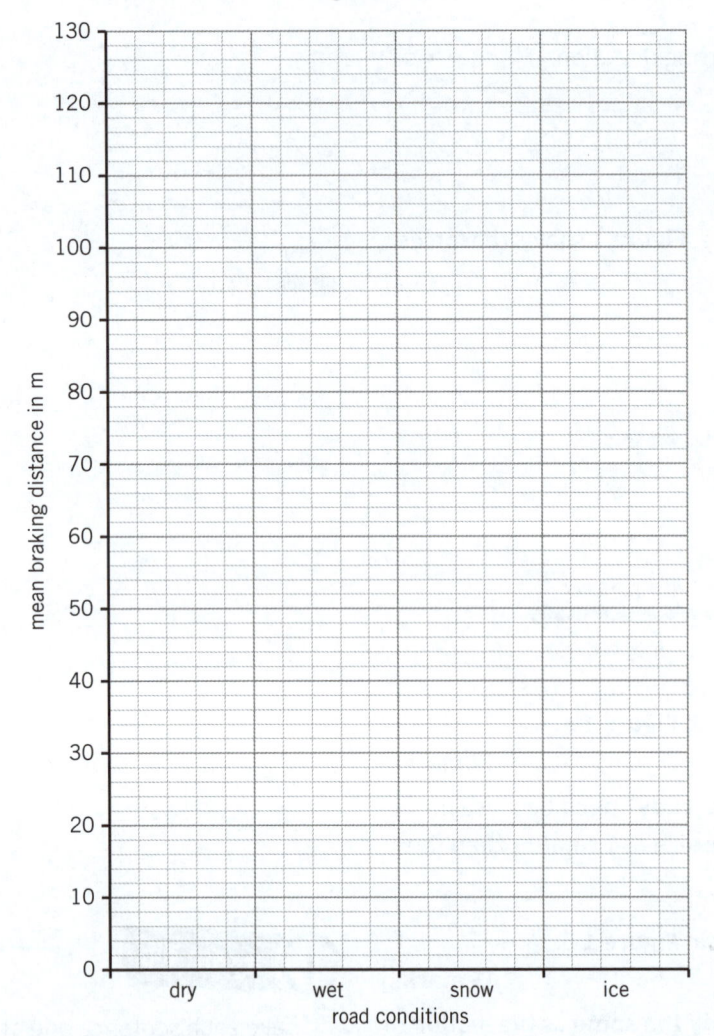

y-axis: mean braking distance in m (0 to 130)
x-axis: road conditions (dry, wet, snow, ice)

07.3 Complete the sentence to describe the relationship between mean braking distance and road conditions shown by **Figure 2**. **[1 mark]**

As the road conditions become more slippery, the braking distance _____

07.4 Suggest a reason for the relationship given in **07.3**. **[1 mark]**

07.5 Suggest the company repeated the tests several times and found the mean braking distance. **[1 mark]**

07.6 Give **one** reason why the company measured braking distance and not thinking distance. **[1 mark]**

08 A student is watching a video of a skateboarder. The skateboarder has a mass of 50 kg.

08.1 Write down the equation that links acceleration, force, and mass. **[1 mark]**

08.2 Calculate the resultant force needed to make the skateboarder accelerate at 2 m/s².
Give the unit in your answer. **[3 marks]**

08.3 The skateboarder uses a force that is double the force calculated in **09.2**.
Describe what will happen to the acceleration of the skateboarder. Explain your answer. **[2 marks]**

> **Exam Tip**
> There is often a whole mark just for the units, so it's worth spending time learning them all really well.

09 A rocket is often used as an example of Newton's Third Law.

09.1 Define Newton's Third Law. **[1 mark]**

09.2 When the rocket engines fire, exhaust gases move downwards out of the rocket. The rocket accelerates upwards.
Explain why there is an upwards force on the rocket. **[2 marks]**

09.3 Before the rocket launches, it is stationary on the launch pad.

A student says:

'*The forces acting on the rocket are equal and opposite. This is an example of Newton's Third Law.*'

Do you agree? Choose **one** answer **[1 mark]**

Yes, because there are two forces acting on the rocket and they are in equilibrium.

No, because Newton's Third Law applies to two different objects interacting, and the student is talking about one object.

> **Exam Tip**
> The different Newton's Laws can be confusing, but try to understand how to apply the laws in different situations and that should help you remember them.

10 A student is floating on the surface of a swimming pool. They get out of the pool and lie on a sunbed. Compare the forces on the student when they are on the sunbed with the forces on the student when they are floating.

Describe the type, relative size, and direction of the forces in each case. **[6 marks]**

> **Exam Tip**
> Question **10** is asking you about two different situations, and for each of these situations the question asks three things. To get all of the six marks you'll need to talk about the type, relative size, and direction of the forces for *both* situations.

Knowledge

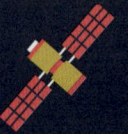

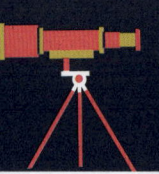

P11 Waves

Waves

Waves transfer energy from one place to another without transferring matter. Waves may be **transverse** or **longitudinal**.

Mechanical waves

Mechanical waves require a substance (a medium) to travel through.

When mechanical waves travel through a substance, the particles in the substance **oscillate** (vibrate) and pass energy on to neighbouring particles.

Transverse waves

The oscillations of a transverse wave are *perpendicular* (at right angles) to the direction in which the waves transfer energy.

Ripples on the surface of water are an example of transverse waves.

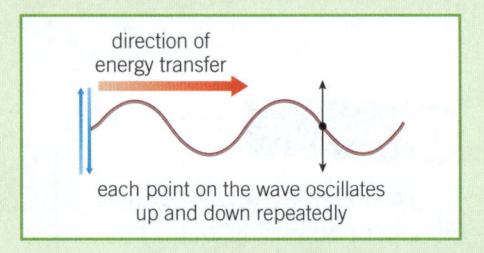

direction of energy transfer

each point on the wave oscillates up and down repeatedly

Longitudinal waves

The oscillations of a longitudinal wave are *parallel* to the direction in which the waves transfer energy.

Longitudinal waves cause particles in a substance to be squashed closer together and pulled further apart, producing areas of **compression** and **rarefaction** in the substance.

Sound waves in air are an example of longitudinal waves.

rarefaction

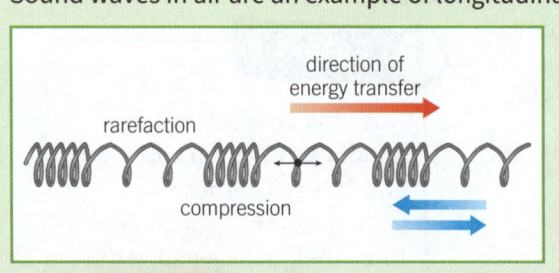

direction of energy transfer

compression

Wave equations

When waves travel from one medium to another, their speed and wavelength may change but the frequency always stays the same.

Frequency and period are related by the equation:

$$\text{period (s)} = \frac{1}{\text{frequency (Hz)}} \qquad T = \frac{1}{f}$$

All waves obey the wave equation:

$$\text{wave speed (m/s)} = \text{frequency (Hz)} \times \text{wavelength (m)}$$
$$v = f\lambda$$

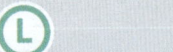

Ⓛ

Wave motion is described by a number of properties.

Property	Description	Unit
amplitude A	maximum displacement of a point on a wave from its undisturbed position	metre (m)
frequency f	number of waves passing a fixed point per second	hertz (Hz)
period T	time taken for one complete wave to pass a fixed point	second (s)
wavelength λ	distance from one point on a wave to the equivalent point on the next wave	metre (m)
wave speed v	distance travelled by each wave per second, and the speed at which energy is transferred by the wave	metres per second (m/s)

Key terms

Make sure you can write a definition for these key terms.

amplitude   compression   electromagnetic wave   frequency
rarefaction   ray diagram   transverse

416 P11 Waves

P11

The electromagnetic spectrum

Electromagnetic (EM) waves are transverse waves that transfer energy from their source to an absorber. For example, infrared waves emitted from a hot object transfer thermal energy.

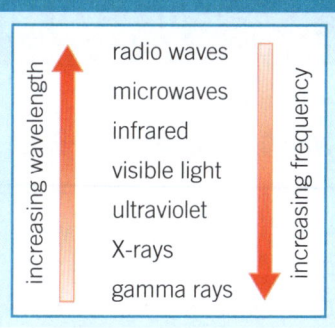

EM waves form a continuous spectrum, and are grouped by their wavelengths and frequencies.

EM waves all travel at the same velocity through air or a vacuum. They all travel at a speed of 3×10^8 m/s through a vacuum.

increasing wavelength ↑ / increasing frequency ↓
- radio waves
- microwaves
- infrared
- visible light
- ultraviolet
- X-rays
- gamma rays

Properties of EM waves

EM waves of a wide range of frequencies can be absorbed or produced by changes inside an atom or nucleus. For example, gamma rays are produced by changes in the nucleus of an atom.

When electrons in an atom move down between energy levels, they emit EM waves.

Uses of EM waves

EM waves have many practical applications, but exposure to some EM waves (such as those that are forms of ionising radiation) can have hazardous effects.

Radiation dose (in sieverts) is the risk of harm from exposure of the body to a particular radiation.

Hazards

- UV can damage skin cells, causing skin to age prematurely and increasing the risk of skin cancer, and can cause blindness.
- X-rays and gamma rays are a form of ionising radiation. They can damage or kill cells, cause mutation of genes, and lead to cancers.

Type of EM wave	Use
radio waves	television and radio signals
microwaves	satellite communications and cooking food

Type of EM wave	Use
infrared (IR)	electrical heaters, cooking food, and infrared cameras
visible light	fibre optic communications

Type of EM wave	Use
ultraviolet (UV)	some energy efficient lights and artificial sun tanning
X-rays	medical imaging and treatments
gamma rays	

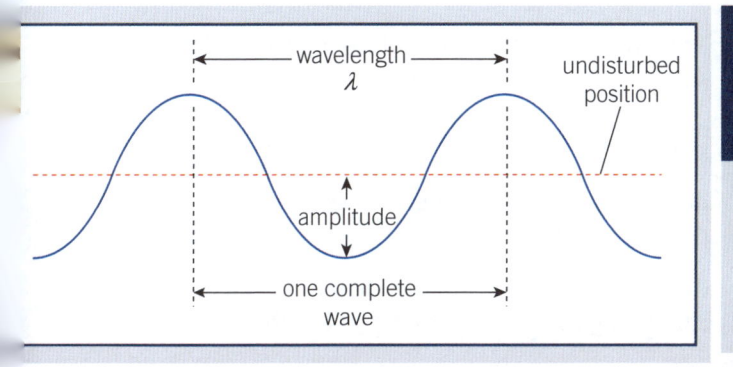

Refraction of electromagnetic waves

Ray diagrams show what happens when a wave is refracted (changes direction) at the boundary between two different substances.

wavelength λ — undisturbed position — amplitude — one complete wave

Revision tip

Remember Longitudinal waves can be drawn as particles, don't get confused if you see it in the exam as a lot of dots!

Practice Draw the diagrams for both waves and add on the wavelength and amplitude.

---

longitudinal   mechanical wave   oscillate   period
        wave speed   wavelength

P11 Knowledge   417

Retrieval

Learn the answers to the questions below, then cover the answers column with a piece of paper and write as many as you can. Check and repeat.

	P11 questions	Answers
1	What is a transverse wave?	oscillations/vibrations are perpendicular (at right angles) to the direction of energy transfer
2	What is a longitudinal wave?	oscillations/vibrations are parallel to the direction of energy transfer
3	Give an example of a transverse wave.	electromagnetic waves
4	Give an example of a longitudinal wave.	sound waves
5	What is a compression?	area in longitudinal waves where the particles are squashed closer together
6	What is a rarefaction?	area in longitudinal waves where the particles are pulled further apart
7	What is the amplitude of a wave?	maximum displacement of a point on the wave from its undisturbed position
8	What is the wavelength of a wave?	distance from a point on one wave to the equivalent point on the adjacent wave
9	What is the frequency of a wave?	number of waves passing a fixed point per second
10	What unit is frequency measured in?	hertz (Hz)
11	What do EM waves transfer from their source to an absorber?	energy
12	List the electromagnetic spectrum in order of decreasing wavelength.	radio, microwave, infrared, visible, ultraviolet, X-rays, gamma
13	Which part of the EM spectrum can humans see?	visible light
14	How can EM waves be produced?	changes inside an atom/atomic nucleus
15	What are radio waves used for?	transmitting television, mobile phone, and Bluetooth signals
16	What are microwaves used for?	satellite communications, cooking food
17	What is infrared radiation used for?	heating, remote controls, infrared cameras, cooking food
18	What are the hazards of being exposed to ultraviolet radiation?	damage skin cells, sunburn, increase risk of skin cancer, age skin prematurely, blindness
19	Why are X-rays used for medical imaging?	they pass through flesh but not bone
20	Why are gamma rays used for treating cancer and sterilising medical equipment?	high doses kill cells and bacteria
21	What is the unit of radiation dose?	sieverts

P11 Waves

P11

Now go back and use the questions below to check your knowledge from previous chapters.

Previous questions | Answers

	Question	Answer
1	What do we mean by inertia?	the tendency of an object to remain in a steady state (at rest or in uniform motion)
2	What is acceleration?	change in velocity of an object per second
3	What is the unit of acceleration?	m/s²
4	What is a non-contact force?	a force between two objects which are physically separated (e.g., gravitational, electrostatic, magnetic)
5	What is inelastic deformation?	an object does not go back to its original shape and size when deforming forces are removed

🧪 Required practical skills

Practise answering questions on the required practicals using the example below. You need to be able to apply your skills and knowledge to other practicals too.

Investigating waves

You need to be able to measure the frequency and wavelength of waves through a liquid and a solid. A ripple tank will be used to make water waves, and a vibration generator to make standing waves on a string.

To be accurate and precise in your investigation you need to:

- count and measure the length of multiple water waves
- measure the length of multiple waves on a string
- repeat your measurements and find the mean.

You should be able to evaluate the suitability of the equipment used to measure wave speeds in liquids and solids.

Worked example

A student sets up a ripple tank.

A lamp above the tank produces this image of the waves on a piece of paper below the tank.

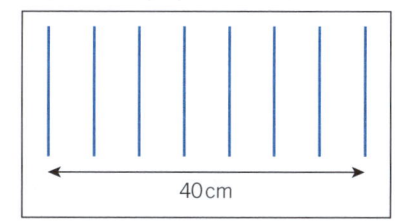

[diagram: 7 vertical lines spanning 40 cm]

1 Calculate the wavelength of the waves.

number of waves = 7

wavelength = $\frac{40}{7}$ = 5.7 cm = 0.057 m

2 The student counts 25 waves reaching the end of the tank in 20 seconds. Calculate the frequency of the waves.

frequency = $\frac{\text{number of waves}}{\text{time}}$

$\frac{25}{20}$ = 1.25 Hz = 1.3 Hz to 2 s.f.

3 Calculate the speed of the waves.

speed = frequency × wavelength

1.25 × 0.057 = 0.0713 m/s = 0.071 m/s to 2 s.f.

4 Suggest one improvement the student could make to improve the accuracy of their speed measurement.

Repeat all measurements of wavelength and frequency and take the average.

Practice

A teacher connects a vibration generator to a piece of elastic.

They change the frequency of the vibration generator and measure the wavelength of the elastic, producing the data below.

Frequency in Hz	Wavelength in m
4	4.86
8	2.51
12	1.25
16	1.29
20	1.02

1 Plot a graph of these data. Identify the outlier.

2 Use the data to calculate the average wave speed in m/s. Show your working.

P11 Retrieval

Practice

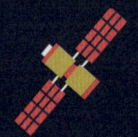

Exam-style questions

01 Here is part of the electromagnetic spectrum.

Two types of wave are missing, indicated by **A** and **B**.

| Radio | A | Infrared | Visible | Ultraviolet | B | Gamma |

Complete the sentences.

Choose words from the box.

You may need to use the words once, more than once, or not at all.

| energy | longitudinal | matter | microwaves |
| transverse | X-rays |

01.1 The waves missing from box **A** are _____ and the waves missing from box **B** are _____. **[2 marks]**

Exam Tip

You need to recall all the waves in order. Use a mnemonic for the first letters.

01.2 All the waves in the electromagnetic spectrum are _____. **[1 mark]**

01.3 Electromagnetic waves spectrum transfer _____. **[1 mark]**

02 A student sets up a ripple tank to measure the speed of water waves.

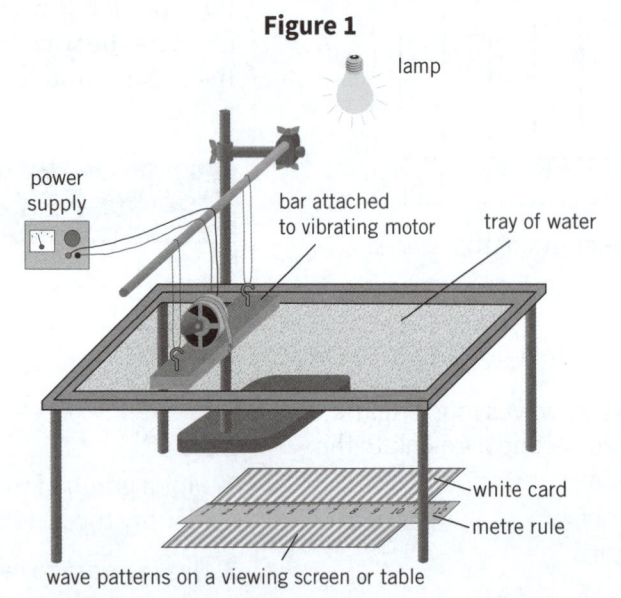

Figure 1

A lamp above the tray of water projects an image of the ripples onto the card below the ripple tank.

420 **P11 Waves**

Paper 6 P11

02.1 The student turns on the motor and sees the image of ripples moving across the card. They count the number of waves passing a point in the ripple tank in 10 s. There are 20 waves. Calculate the frequency of the waves. Use the equation:

$$\text{frequency} = \frac{\text{number of waves}}{\text{time}}$$

Show your working. **[2 marks]**

> **! Exam Tip**
>
> The unit for frequency is Hertz. The H needs to be a capital letter and the z needs to be a lower case letter. Only Hz will get marks in an exam. HZ or hz will not get marks.

_____ Hz

02.2 The student uses the ruler to measure the number of waves in 0.3 m. There are 20 waves. Calculate the wavelength of the waves. Use the equation:

$$\text{wavelength} = \frac{\text{distance}}{\text{number of waves}}$$

[2 marks]

_____ Hz

02.3 Write down the equation that links frequency, speed, and wavelength. **[1 mark]**

_____

02.4 Use the values calculated in parts **02.1** and **02.2** to calculate the speed of the waves in the tank. Give the unit with your answer. **[3 marks]**

Speed = _____ Unit = _____

03 Electromagnetic waves have many uses. For example, visible light is used for communication.

03.1 Draw one line from each electromagnetic wave to the correct use. **[2 marks]**

Electromagnetic wave	Use
	electrical heaters
microwaves	
	mobile phones
radio waves	
	television

> **! Exam Tip**
>
> You need to know the uses of each electromagnetic wave, as listed on the P11 Knowledge organiser.

P11 Practice

03.2 Gamma rays can penetrate the human body. Name **one** other electromagnetic wave that can penetrate the body. Give what the wave is used for. **[2 marks]**

Name: _____

Use: _____

03.3 Ultraviolet waves are used in tanning machines. Give one hazard of using tanning machines. **[1 mark]**

_____

03.4 What is the unit of radiation dose? Choose **one** answer. **[1 mark]**

becquerel   hertz   sievert

04 Compare visible light and X-rays in terms of their use, frequency, wavelength, and dangers. **[6 marks]**

_____
_____
_____
_____
_____
_____
_____
_____

> **Exam Tip**
>
> **04.1** is a compare question, so you'll need to mention things that the waves have in common as well as where the waves are different. Use the following structure for your answer:
> - Both waves are …
> - The frequency of visible light is … whereas the frequency of x-rays is …

05 A student is using a slinky coil to model waves. A wave on the slinky coil has areas where it is compressed and areas where it is rarefacted.

05.1 On **Figure 2**, write the letter **C** above a compression and the letter **R** above a rarefaction. **[2 marks]**

Figure 2

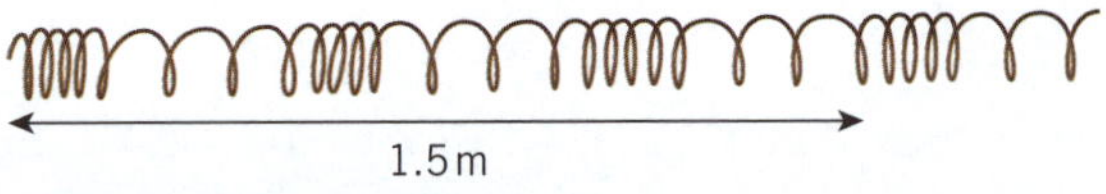

1.5 m

05.2 Show that the wavelength of the wave is 0.5 m. **[2 marks]**

05.3 Write down the equation that links frequency, wavelength, and wave speed. **[1 mark]**

05.4 The wave is travelling at 1.0 m/s. Calculate the frequency of the wave. Give the unit of frequency. **[3 marks]**

05.5 Identify the type of wave the student is modelling in **Figure 2**. **[1 mark]**

> **Exam Tip**
>
> Check that you can recall the similarities and differences between transverse and longitudinal waves.

P11 Waves

06 A student is learning about waves.

06.1 Which statements are correct?
Choose **two** answers. **[2 marks]**

period = the time for one wave in minutes

period = the time for one wave in seconds

period = $\dfrac{1}{\text{frequency}}$

period = $\dfrac{1}{\text{frequency}^2}$

06.2 A wave has a frequency of 500 Hz.
Calculate its period. **[2 marks]**

06.3 The wavelength of the wave is 5 m. Determine the speed of the wave. **[2 marks]**

Use the equation:

wave speed = frequency × wavelength

Choose **one** answer.

 100   450   550   2500

> **Exam Tip**
> The unit of speed should always be consistent with the unit of wavelength.

06.4 Give the unit of wave speed from **06.3**. **[1 mark]**

07 A student draws a ray diagram for a beam of light going from air into a glass block (**Figure 3**).

07.1 Which diagram shows the correct path of the ray?
Choose **one** answer. **[1 mark]**

Figure 3

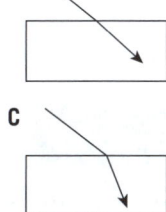

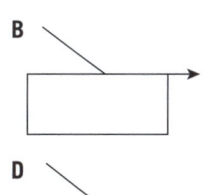

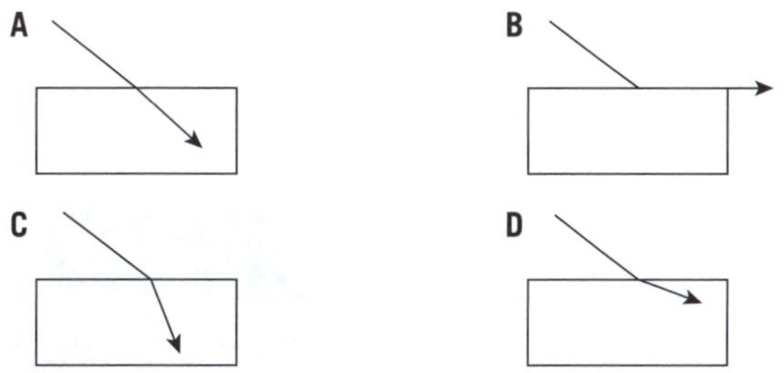

A   B

C   D

07.2 Complete the sentences. Choose the correct words from the box. **[2 marks]**

| direction | mass | reflected | refracted |

When light goes from air into glass it is _____, which means it changes _____.

> **Exam Tip**
> The most common situation is for the light to go into glass, but check the question carefully. Sometimes it is the other way round.

07.3 Describe what happens to the ray in the diagram in **Figure 4**. [1 mark]

Figure 4

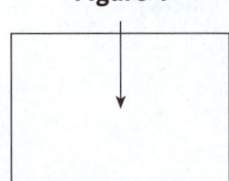

08 A student sets up an experiment to investigate the infrared radiation emitted from different surfaces. They have the following equipment:
- cans with different surfaces: matt black, shiny black, matt white, and shiny white
- kettle
- infrared detector
- thermometer
- heatproof mats
- ruler
- lids

08.1 The student uses this method:
- Put all the cans on heatproof mats.
- Fill the kettle with water and heat the water.
- Fill each can with hot water from the kettle.
- Put the thermometer near each can and write down the temperature after 10 minutes.

Suggest **three** improvements to this experiment.
Write down a reason for each improvement. [6 marks]

> **Exam Tip**
>
> Go over each step and see if it's accurate enough for someone else to repeat this experiment.

08.2 The student labels the cans **A**, **B**, **C**, and **D**. They record the data in **Table 1**.

Table 1

Surface	Temperature after 10 minutes in °C
A	26
B	30
C	24
D	21

Use **Table 1** to suggest which can has a matt black surface. Explain your answer. [2 marks]

> **Exam Tip**
>
> Think about the properties of each type of surface and how this will link to heat.

P11 Waves

09 A lamp emits ultraviolet radiation.

09.1 Which of these statements are true? Choose **two** answers. **[2 marks]**
Visible light has a longer wavelength than ultraviolet radiation.
Visible light has a shorter wavelength than ultraviolet radiation.
Visible light has a higher frequency than ultraviolet radiation.
Visible light has a lower frequency than ultraviolet radiation.

09.2 Describe **one** hazard of gamma radiation. **[1 mark]**

09.3 Complete the sentence. Choose **one** word from the box.

| amplitude | frequency | wavelength |

The risk due to radiation increases with _____.
Explain your answer. **[2 marks]**

> **Exam Tip**
> Use a mnemonic to remember the order of the electromagnetic spectrum. Remember, as frequency *increases* wavelength *decreases*.

10 A man drives to work and then drives home at the end of the day.

10.1 Write down the man's displacement when he has returned home. **[1 mark]**

10.2 Write down the equation that links distance, speed, and time. **[1 mark]**

10.3 The distance from the man's home to his workplace is 4.5 miles. The journey to work takes 20 minutes. There are 1609 m in 1 mile.
Calculate the man's average speed on the way to work. Give your answer in metres per second. **[4 marks]**

10.4 Give **one** reason why the answer to **10.3** is an average speed. **[1 mark]**

10.5 For part of the journey, the car is travelling at a steady speed even though the engine exerts a force on the car.
Explain why the car does not accelerate during this part of the journey, even though the engine exerts a force. Use Newton's Laws of Motion in your answer. **[2 marks]**

> **Exam Tip**
> **10.3** is given in non-standard units, but the question asks for the answer in the standard units for speed (m/s). It is much easier to convert the number to standard units *before* you do the calculation.

> **Exam Tip**
> Even if you can't remember which law comes first, second, or third, it is really important the you know the basics of Newtons Laws as the come up frequently in physics exams.

Knowledge

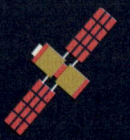

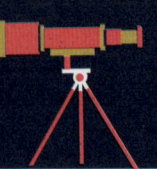

P12 Magnets and electromagnets

Magnets

Magnets have a north (N) and a south (S) pole.

When two magnets are brought close together, they exert a non-contact force on each other.

Repulsion – If the poles are the same (N and N or S and S), they will repel each other.

Attraction – If the poles are different (N and S or S and N), they will attract each other.

The force between a magnet and a magnetic material (iron, steel, cobalt, or nickel) is always attractive.

Induced and permanent magnets

A **permanent** magnet produces its own magnetic field which is always there.

An **induced** magnet is an object that becomes magnetic when it is placed in a magnetic field.

The force between an induced magnet and a permanent magnet is *always attractive* (it doesn't matter which pole of the permanent magnet the induced magnet is near).

If the induced magnet is removed from the magnetic field it will quickly lose most or all of its magnetism.

Magnetic fields

A **magnetic field** is the region around a magnet where another magnet or magnetic material will experience a force due to the magnet.

A magnetic field can be represented by magnetic field lines.

Field lines show the direction of the force that would act on a north pole at that point.

Field lines always point from the north pole of a magnet to its south pole.

A magnetic field's strength is greatest at the poles and decreases as distance from the magnet increases.

The closer together the field lines are, the stronger the field.

Plotting magnetic fields

A magnetic compass contains a small bar magnet that will line up with magnetic field lines pointing from north to south.

A compass can be used to plot the magnetic field around a magnet or an **electromagnet**:

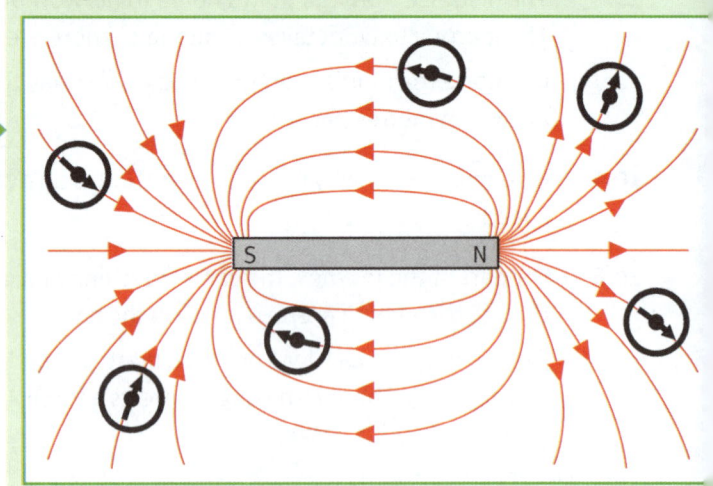

If it is not near a magnet, a compass will line up with the Earth's magnetic field, providing evidence that the Earth's core is magnetic.

As a compass points towards a south pole, the magnetic pole near the Earth's geographic North Pole is actually a south pole.

Key terms

Make sure you can write a definition for these key terms.

| attraction | electromagnet | induced | magnetic field |

P12

Electromagnetism

If an electric current flows through a wire (or other conductor), it will produce a magnetic field around the wire.

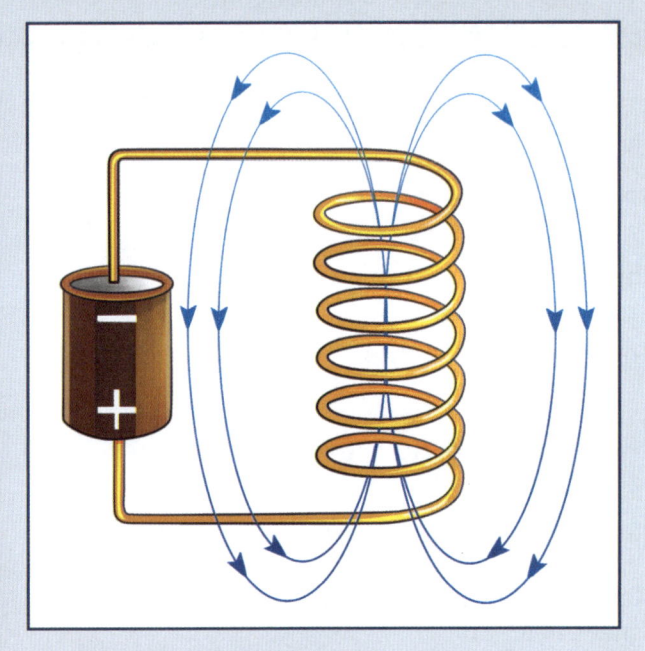

The field strength increases:
- with greater current
- closer to the wire.

The field around a straight wire takes the shape of concentric circles at right angles to the wire.

Reversing the direction of the current reverses the direction of the field.

> **Revision tip**
>
> **Remember** The lines on a diagram that show magnetic field lines will always point from north to south.

Solenoids

A **solenoid** is a cylindrical coil of wire.

Bending a current-carrying wire into a solenoid increases the strength of the magnetic field produced.

The shape of the magnetic field around a solenoid is similar to a magnetic field around a bar magnet.

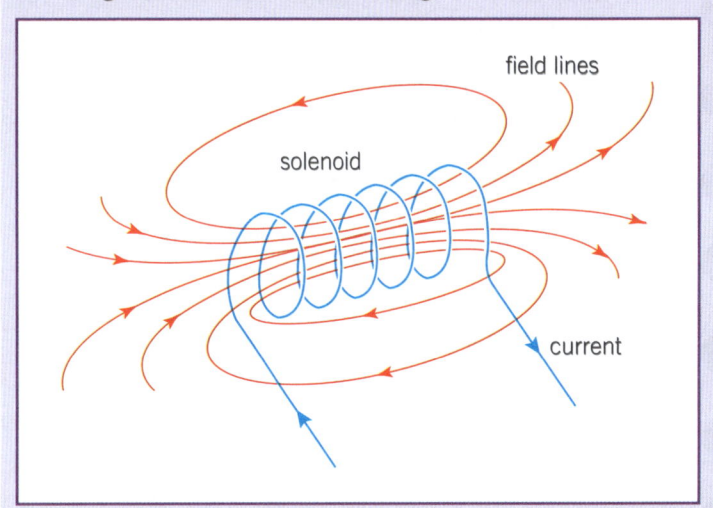

Inside a solenoid the magnetic field is *strong* and *uniform*, which means it has the same strength and direction at all points.

The strength of the magnetic field around a solenoid can be increased by putting an iron core inside it.

If the wire was gripped by someone's right hand so that the fingers curl in the direction of the current in the coil, the thumb will point towards the north pole of the field.

Electromagnets are often solenoids with an iron core.

Advantages of electromagnets

- An electromagnet can be turned on and off.
- The strength of an electromagnet can be increased or decreased by adjusting the current.

---

permanent   repulsion   solenoid

P12 Knowledge   427

Retrieval

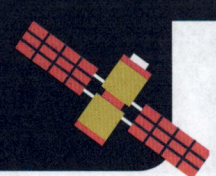

Learn the answers to the questions below, then cover the answers column with a piece of paper and write as many as you can. Check and repeat.

P12 questions | Answers

#	Question	Answer
1	What is a magnetic field?	the region of space around a magnet where a magnetic material will experience a force
2	What happens when like and unlike poles are brought together?	like = repel, unlike = attract
3	What happens to the strength of the magnetic field as you get further away from the magnet?	decreases
4	Where is the magnetic field of a magnet strongest?	at the poles
5	In which direction do magnetic field lines always point?	north to south
6	What does the distance between magnetic field lines indicate?	strength of the field, closer together = stronger field
7	What is a permanent magnet?	material that produces its own magnetic field
8	What is an induced magnet?	material that becomes magnetic when it is put in a magnetic field
9	What does a magnetic compass contain?	small bar magnet
10	What is produced around a wire when an electric current flows through it?	magnetic field
11	What factors does the strength of the magnetic field around a straight wire depend upon?	size of current, distance from wire
12	What effect does shaping the wire into a solenoid have on the magnetic field strength?	increases strength of magnetic field
13	How can the strength of the magnetic field inside a solenoid be increased?	put an iron core inside

P12 Magnets and electromagnets

Now go back and use the questions below to check your knowledge from previous chapters.

P12

Previous questions | Answers

#	Question	Answer
1	What are the main advantages and disadvantages of using biofuels?	advantages: can be 'carbon neutral', reliable / disadvantages: expensive to produce, use land/water that might be needed to grow food
2	What is the frequency and voltage of mains electricity?	50 Hz, 230 V
3	What is a transverse wave?	oscillations/vibrations are perpendicular (at right angles) to the direction of energy transfer
4	What units are charge, current, and time measured in?	coulomb (C), ampere (A), second (s) respectively
5	What does Newton's First Law say?	the velocity of an object will only change if a resultant force is acting on it
6	What are typical speeds for a person walking, running, and cycling?	1.5 m/s, 3.0 m/s, and 6.0 m/s respectively

Required practical skills

Practise answering questions on the required practicals using the example below. You need to be able to apply your skills and knowledge to other practicals too.

Infrared radiation

This practical investigates the rates of absorption and radiation of infrared radiation from different surfaces.

You should be able to plan a method to determine the rate of cooling due to emission of infrared radiation, and evaluate your method.

To be accurate and precise in your investigation you need to:

- use an infrared detector with a suitable meter, where possible
- ensure that you always put the detector the same distance from the surface
- repeat measurements and calculate an average.

Worked example

A student wants to investigate the infrared radiation emitted by a surface coated with different colours of paint.

1. Describe a method to investigate the effect of surface colour on infrared emission rate.

   Paint identical containers with different colours of paint. Fill each container with the same volume of water at the same temperature, and place on a heatproof mat. Place an infrared detector at the same distance and position relative to each container. Record the reading on the detector. Repeat three times.

2. Describe the type of graph the student should plot. Explain your answer.

   A bar chart, because the surface colours are categoric.

Practice

A student paints four jars with shiny and matt black paint, and shiny and matt white paint. They fill the jars with water at room temperature (20 °C), and set the jars outside in the sun. After one hour they record the temperature increase of each jar.

Jar	A	B	C	D
Temperature increase in °C	5.5	8.0	7.0	1.5

1. Suggest the resolution of the instrument used to measure temperature.

2. Write down which jar (**A**, **B**, **C**, or **D**) is covered with matt black paint. Explain your answer.

3. Suggest two improvements the student could make to the experiment. Give an explanation for each improvement.

P12 Retrieval 429

Practice

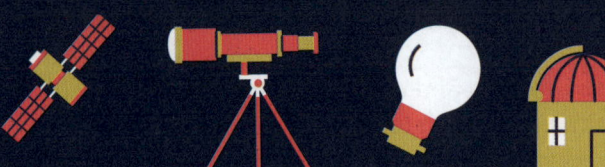

Exam-style questions

01 Figure 1 shows three pairs of magnets.

Figure 1

pair **A** pair **B** pair **C**

[S N][S N]   [S N][N S]   [N S][S N]

01.1 Identify the **two** pairs of magnets that will repel. **[1 mark]**

_____

01.2 Identify the pair of magnets that will attract. **[1 mark]**

_____

> **Exam Tip**
>
> For each pair write 'attract' or 'repel' above the image, then use that to answer **01.1** and **01.2**.

01.3 Complete the sentences. Choose words from the box. You may need to use the words once, more than once, or not at all. **[4 marks]**

| contact   force   magnetic   metal   non-contact   permanent |

The force between the magnets is an example of a

_____ force. The magnets in **Figure 1** are

_____ magnets. There is a region around a magnet

where a _____ acts on a _____ material.

02 A tool set contains a screwdriver.

The screwdriver attracts the screw so that the person using it is less likely to lose it.

02.1 The end of the screwdriver is magnetic. The screw is an induced magnet.

Explain the difference between a permanent magnet and an induced magnet. **[2 marks]**

_____

_____

02.2 There is a magnetic field around the end of the screwdriver.

Identify whether there is a magnetic field around the screw when it is attached to the screwdriver.

Give a reason for your answer. **[2 marks]**

_____

_____

_____

_____

> **Exam Tip**
>
> The idea of a field occurs in three places in physics – gravitational fields, electric fields, and magnetic fields. In all places the idea of a field is linked to a force.

430   P12 Magnets and electromagnets

Paper 6 P12

02.3 On **Figure 2** write N (north) and S (south) in the blank boxes to show the induced poles on the screw. **[1 mark]**

Figure 2

> **Exam Tip**
> Remember opposite poles attract.

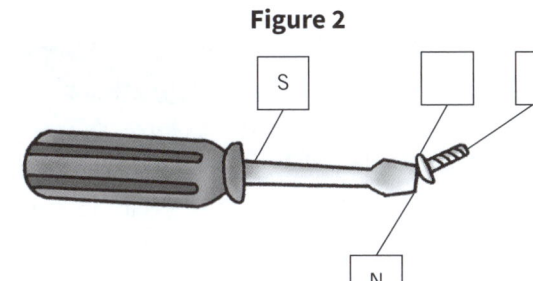

02.4 The screw is put back into a box containing other screws. Predict whether it will attract the other screws in the box. Give a reason your answer. **[2 marks]**

_____

_____

03 A student looks up the magnetic field strength of some permanent magnets. They record their data in **Table 1**.

Table 1

Magnet	Magnetic field strength in tesla
Earth's magnetic field	0.000 004
ferrite (normal bar magnet)	0.3
neodymium	1.2
samarium	0.9

03.1 Identify the strongest magnet. **[1 mark]**

Earth's magnetic field ☐   neodymium ☐

ferrite ☐   samarium ☐

03.2 Name the type of graph the student could plot with these data. Explain your answer. **[2 marks]**

Graph: _____

Explanation: _____

_____

> **Exam Tip**
> Bar charts are used for categoric data and line graphs are used for continuous data.

03.3 Suggest **one** problem they would have when plotting the graph in **03.2**. [1 mark]

_____

_____

03.4 Magnetic resonance imaging (MRI) machines in hospitals need to produce a magnetic field of 2 T. The machine uses an electromagnet and not a permanent magnet.
Suggest **one** reason why an electromagnet is used. [1 mark]

_____

_____

_____

> **Exam Tip**
>
> T is the unit Tesla. It is not a very commonly used unit but it is important to know them all for your exams.

04 **Figure 3** shows a bar magnet.

04.1 Draw magnetic field lines around the magnet. Draw arrows on the lines to show the direction of the magnetic field. [2 marks]

Figure 3

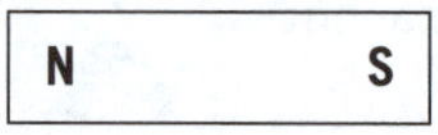

| N | S |

> **Exam Tip**
>
> Field lines should always have arrows because they indicate the direction of the force on an object.

04.2 Name the equipment that the student could use to investigate the field around a magnet. [1 mark]

_____

04.3 A student wants to place a piece of metal in the magnetic field. Choose the metals that will experience a force. [2 marks]
Tick **two** boxes.

aluminium ☐

cobalt ☐

copper ☐

nickel ☐

432 P12 Magnets and electromagnets

05 A student accelerates a toy car. They use a newtonmeter to apply a constant force. They use light gates to measure the speed of the car at two different times.

05.1 Write down the equation that links the change in velocity, time, and acceleration. **[1 mark]**

_____

05.2 The initial velocity is 0.5 m/s. The final velocity is 2.7 m/s. The time between the measurements of velocity is 0.4 s.
Calculate the acceleration of the trolley. **[2 marks]**

Acceleration = _____ m/s^2

05.3 Write down the equation that links acceleration, force, and mass. **[1 mark]**

_____

05.4 The resultant force of the toy car is 2.0 N. The mass of the toy car is 400 g (0.4 kg).
Calculate the acceleration of the toy car. **[3 marks]**

Acceleration = _____ m/s^2

05.5 Suggest one practical reason why the two values of acceleration are not the same. **[1 mark]**

_____

> **Exam Tip**
> It is important that you learn the list of equations that you need to be able to recall in your exam. It will be really hard to answer the maths questions if you don't know what to times or what to divide. Look at the Physics equations section at the back of this book.

> **Exam Tip**
> Remember you will need change in velocity for **05.2**.
> change in velocity = final velocity − initial velocity

> **Exam Tip**
> Don't assume that the parts of the equation appear in the order that is given in the question. Often they are given in alphabetical order.

06 A wire carries a current. There is a region around the wire where there is a magnetic field.

06.1 Complete the sentences. Choose words from the box. You may need to use the words once, more than once, or not at all. **[4 marks]**

| field | force | iron | material | stronger | weaker | wood |

If you put a magnetic _____ such as a piece of

_____ near the wire, a _____ acts on it. As you

move away from the wire, the magnetic field gets _____.

P12 Practice

06.2 The student increases the current.
What effect does this have on the strength of the magnetic field?
Tick **one** box. **[1 mark]**

it gets weaker ☐

it stays the same ☐

it gets stronger ☐

> **Exam Tip**
> There is a close link between the strength of the magnetic field and the current. It is important that you know all the ways that the magnetic field can be changed.

07 Some insects can detect ultraviolet light. Humans can see red light, but some insects cannot.

07.1 Choose the correct words in bold. **[3 marks]**

Ultraviolet light has a **higher / lower** frequency than red light.
Ultraviolet light has a **longer / shorter** wavelength than red light.
Ultraviolet light travels at **a bigger / a smaller / the same** speed as red light.

> **Exam Tip**
> Draw a wave with a wavelength that goes from long to short, and put the first letter of each wave in the right place *before* you answer the question.

07.2 Ultraviolet light is hazardous to the human body.
Describe **one** reason why. **[1 mark]**

07.3 Describe **one** use of ultraviolet light. **[1 mark]**

08 A student winds a length of wire into a coil. They put an iron nail inside the coil. They connect the wire to a battery.

08.1 Complete the sentences. Choose the correct words in bold. **[2 marks]**

The student has made **an electromagnet / a solenoid.** The magnetic field near the end of the nail will be **stronger / weaker** than the field due to the wire alone.

08.2 The student puts a paperclip on the desk. The paper clip is made of steel. They slowly push the electromagnet towards the paperclip. When the paperclip is 5 cm from the electromagnet, it moves towards the electromagnet without being pushed.
Explain why the paperclip moves. **[2 marks]**

08.3 The student reduces the number of coils around the nail and repeats the experiment. Complete the sentence. Choose the correct word in bold.
Explain your answer. **[2 marks]**
To make the paperclip move, the student will need to place it at a **greater / smaller** distance from the electromagnet.

> **Exam Tip**
> You can apply what you have learnt about how the strength of a gravitational field changes as you move away from a planet because all fields behave in the same way.

08.4 The student takes a single piece of wire and lays it straight on the desk. They connect a battery so that a current flows through it.
Suggest whether the paperclip will move when the wire is brought close to it.
Explain your answer. **[2 marks]**

434 **P12 Magnets and electromagnets**

09 A scientist notices that a compass needle is deflected when they turn on a circuit containing a battery and a wire.

09.1 Which direction was the compass pointing before the scientist turned on the circuit?
Explain why the compass points in this direction. **[2 marks]**

09.2 Compare the strength of the Earth's magnetic field with the strength of the magnetic field around the wire.
Give reasons with your answer. **[2 marks]**

09.3 Choose the correct description of a compass needle.
Choose **one** answer. **[1 mark]**
a compass needle always points to the south pole
a compass needle is a magnet
a compass needle can be made from any metal

> **Exam Tip**
> The point of the compass will be attracted to the pole.

10 A student winds some wire around a wooden rod to make a coil and connects the coil to a battery.

10.1 Identify a hazard when doing this experiment.
Suggest a method of reducing the risk of harm. **[2 marks]**

10.2 On solenoid **A** in **Figure 4**, draw lines to show the shape of the magnetic field around the coil.
You do not need to draw arrows on the field lines. **[1 mark]**

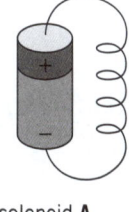

Figure 4

solenoid **A**   solenoid **B**

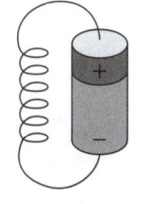

10.3 The student makes another coil, solenoid B, and connects it to a battery.
Write down which solenoid, **A** or **B**, has the strongest magnetic field around it.
Give a reason for your answer. Give **one** assumption that you have made in your answer. **[3 marks]**

10.4 The student takes a compass and places it in the centre of the solenoid. They move it up and down in the middle of the coil.
Will the compass needle move when it is moved in this way in the solenoid?
Justify your answer. **[2 marks]**

> **Exam Tip**
> In **10.1** you need to say *what* could hurt you, *how* it could hurt you, and how you can *prevent* it hurting you. Whatever you mention needs to be specific to *this* experiment.

> **Exam Tip**
> When drawing the lines in **10.2** think about the shape of the lines of a magnetic field for a normal magnet.

P12 Practice

Physics equations

You need to be able to recall the following equations in your exams.

Questions | Answers

#	Question	Answer	Formula
1	What is the equation for weight?	weight = mass × gravitational field strength	$W = mg$
2	What is the equation for work done?	work done = force × distance (along the line of action of the force)	$W = Fs$
3	What is the equation for force on a spring?	force applied to a spring = spring constant × extension	$F = ke$
4	What is the equation for distance?	distance travelled = speed × time	$s = vt$
5	What is the equation of acceleration?	acceleration = change in velocity / time taken	$a = \dfrac{\Delta v}{t}$
6	What is the equation for resultant force?	resultant force = mass × acceleration	$F = ma$
7	What is the equation for kinetic energy?	kinetic energy = 0.5 × mass × (speed)²	$E_k = \dfrac{1}{2}mv^2$
8	What is the equation for gravitational potential energy?	gravitational potential energy = mass × gravitational field strength × height	$E_p = mgh$
9	What equation links power, energy transferred, and time?	power = energy transferred / time	$P = \dfrac{E}{t}$
10	What equation links power, work, and time?	power = work done / time	$P = \dfrac{W}{t}$
11	What are the equations for efficiency?	efficiency = useful output energy transfer / total input energy transfer = useful power output / total power input	
12	What is the equation for wave speed?	wave speed = frequency × wavelength	$v = f\lambda$
13	What is the equation for charge flow?	charge flow = current × time	$Q = It$
14	What is the equation for potential difference?	potential difference = current × resistance	$V = IR$
15	What equation links power, potential difference, and current?	power = potential difference × current	$P = VI$
16	What equation links power, current, and resistance?	power = (current)² × resistance	$P = I^2R$
17	What equation links energy transferred, power, and time	energy transferred = power × time	$E = Pt$
18	What equation links energy transferred, charge flow, and potential difference?	energy transferred = charge flow × potential difference	$E = QV$
19	What is the equation for density?	density = mass / volume	$\rho = \dfrac{m}{V}$

436 Physics equations

You will be provided with a *Physics Equations Sheet* that contains the following equations.
You should be able to select and apply the correct equation to answer the question.

1 (final velocity)² − (initial velocity)² = 2 × acceleration × distance $\quad v^2 - u^2 = 2\,a\,s$

2 elastic potential energy = 0.5 × spring constant × (extension)² $\quad E_e = \frac{1}{2} k\,e^2$

3 change in thermal energy = mass × specific heat capacity × temperature change $\quad \Delta E = m\,c\,\Delta\theta$

4 period = $\dfrac{1}{\text{frequency}}$

5 thermal energy for a change of state = mass × specific latent heat $\quad E = m\,L$

Periodic Table

1	2											3	4	5	6	7	0
							1 **H** hydrogen 1										4 **He** helium 2
7 **Li** lithium 3	9 **Be** beryllium 4											11 **B** boron 5	12 **C** carbon 6	14 **N** nitrogen 7	16 **O** oxygen 8	19 **F** fluorine 9	20 **Ne** neon 10
23 **Na** sodium 11	24 **Mg** magnesium 12											27 **Al** aluminium 13	28 **Si** silicon 14	31 **P** phosphorus 15	32 **S** sulfur 16	35.5 **Cl** chlorine 17	40 **Ar** argon 18
39 **K** potassium 19	40 **Ca** calcium 20	45 **Sc** scandium 21	48 **Ti** titanium 22	51 **V** vanadium 23	52 **Cr** chromium 24	55 **Mn** manganese 25	56 **Fe** iron 26	59 **Co** cobalt 27	59 **Ni** nickel 28	63.5 **Cu** copper 29	65 **Zn** zinc 30	70 **Ga** gallium 31	73 **Ge** germanium 32	75 **As** arsenic 33	79 **Se** selenium 34	80 **Br** bromine 35	84 **Kr** krypton 36
85 **Rb** rubidium 37	88 **Sr** strontium 38	89 **Y** yttrium 39	91 **Zr** zirconium 40	93 **Nb** niobium 41	96 **Mo** molybdenum 42	[98] **Tc** technetium 43	101 **Ru** ruthenium 44	103 **Rh** rhodium 45	106 **Pd** palladium 46	108 **Ag** silver 47	112 **Cd** cadmium 48	115 **In** indium 49	119 **Sn** tin 50	122 **Sb** antimony 51	128 **Te** tellurium 52	127 **I** iodine 53	131 **Xe** xenon 54
133 **Cs** caesium 55	137 **Ba** barium 56	139 **La*** lanthanum 57	178 **Hf** hafnium 72	181 **Ta** tantalum 73	184 **W** tungsten 74	186 **Re** rhenium 75	190 **Os** osmium 76	192 **Ir** iridium 77	195 **Pt** platinum 78	197 **Au** gold 79	201 **Hg** mercury 80	204 **Tl** thallium 81	207 **Pb** lead 82	209 **Bi** bismuth 83	[209] **Po** polonium 84	[210] **At** astatine 85	[222] **Rn** radon 86
[223] **Fr** francium 87	[226] **Ra** radium 88	[227] **Ac*** actinium 89	[261] **Rf** rutherfordium 104	[262] **Db** dubnium 105	[266] **Sg** seaborgium 106	[264] **Bh** bohrium 107	[277] **Hs** hassium 108	[268] **Mt** meitnerium 109	[271] **Ds** darmstadtium 110	[272] **Rg** roentgenium 111	[285] **Cn** copernicium 112	[286] **Nh** nihonium 113	[289] **Fl** flerovium 114	[289] **Mc** moscovium 115	[293] **Lv** livermorium 116	[294] **Ts** tennessine 117	[294] **Og** oganesson 118

key

relative atomic mass
atomic symbol
name
atomic (proton) number

*The lanthanides (atomic numbers 58–71) and the actinides (atomic numbers 90–103) have been omitted.
Relative atomic masses for **Cu** and **Cl** have not been rounded to the nearest whole number.

Notes

Notes

Notes

OXFORD
UNIVERSITY PRESS

Great Clarendon Street, Oxford, OX2 6DP, United Kingdom

Oxford University Press is a department of the University of Oxford.

It furthers the University's objective of excellence in research, scholarship, and education by publishing worldwide. Oxford is a registered trade mark of Oxford University Press in the UK and in certain other countries

© Oxford University Press 2020

The moral rights of the authors have been asserted

First published in 2020

All rights reserved. No part of this publication may be reproduced, stored in a retrieval system, or transmitted, in any form or by any means, without the prior permission in writing of Oxford University Press, or as expressly permitted by law, by licence or under terms agreed with the appropriate reprographics rights organization. Enquiries concerning reproduction outside the scope of the above should be sent to the Rights Department, Oxford University Press, at the address above.

You must not circulate this work in any other form and you must impose this same condition on any acquirer

British Library Cataloguing in Publication Data

Data available

978-1-38-200486-2

10 9 8 7 6 5 4

Paper used in the production of this book is a natural, recyclable product made from wood grown in sustainable forests.

The manufacturing process conforms to the environmental regulations of the country of origin.

Printed in Great Britain by Bell and Bain Ltd, Glasgow

Acknowledgements

Jo Locke would like to thank Dave, Emily and Hermione for their support, as well as providing plenty of tea and cake.

Jessica Walmsley would like to give special thanks to her husband Joe, mum Barbara and Dad Dean for their continued support in everything she does.

Philippa Gardom Hulme would like to thank Mary and Edward Hulme, and Sarah, Catherine and Barney Gardom.

Helen Reynolds would like to thank her editors for their support and feedback, and her wonderful friends Michele, Rob, Lesa, Galla, and Bill for all their support, long walks and coffee. She would also like to thank Oleksiy, her dance instructor, for providing continuing encouragement for her writing and for her foxtrot.

The publisher and authors would like to thank the following for permission to use photographs and other copyright material:

All photos © Shutterstock, except **p8**: JACK BOSTRACK, VISUALS UNLIMITED/SCIENCE PHOTO LIBRARY; **p11, 26**: Shutterstock; **p11**: ERIC GRAVE/SCIENCE PHOTO LIBRARY; **p128, 153**: Shutterstock.

Cover illustration by Andrew Groves

QBS Media Services Inc.

Every effort has been made to contact copyright holders of material reproduced in this book. Any omissions will be rectified in subsequent printings if notice is given to the publisher.